British Royal Weddings

From the Stuarts to the Early Twentieth Century

British Royal Weddings

From the Stuarts to the Early Twentieth Century

Matthias Range

BREPOLS

© 2022, Brepols Publishers n.v., Turnhout, Belgium.

All rights reserved. No part of this publication may be reproduced, stored in a retrieval system, or transmitted, in any form or by any means, electronic, mechanical, photocopying, recording, or otherwise, without the pior permission of the publisher.

Matthias Range asserts his right to be identified as the author of this work in accordance with the Copyright, Designs and Patents Act 1988.

The publishers have no control over, or responsibility for, any third-party website referred to in this book. All internet addresses given in the this book were correct at the time of going to press. The authors and publisher regret any inconvenience caused if addresses have changed or sites have ceased to exist, but can accept no responsibility for any such changes.

ISBN 978-2-503-59696-9
D/2022/0095/107

Designed and typeset in Bembo by
Julia Craig-McFeely, Oxford OX4 4BS
Printed in the EU on acid-free paper.

Cover illustration: Christian Karl Magnussen, *The Marriage of Princess Helena, 5 July 1866,* oil on canvas 1866–69, Royal Collection Trust RCIN 404483 © Her Majesty Queen Elizabeth II 2021.

Contents

Illustrations and Figures	ii
Preface	vii
Acknowledgements	viii
Abbreviations and Conventions	x

—◦◦◦—

1	Setting the Scene	1
2	From Elaborate to Modest: The Seventeenth Century	25
3	The 'Concert' Weddings I: The Children of George II	45
4	The 'Concert' Weddings II: The Later Eighteenth-Century Georgians	77
5	Home Weddings: The Early Nineteenth Century	103
6	'State Marriages': The Early Victorians	113
7	The 'Windsor Castle' Weddings: The Mid-Victorians I	155
8	Routine and Innovation: The Mid-Victorians II	199
9	The Choral Weddings: The Late-Victorians	233
10	The Last 'of the Old Age': The Early Twentieth Century	273
11	The 'Pomp of Old Days': Three Centuries of Royal Weddings	299

Appendices

A	Chronological List of British Royal Weddings	316
B	Texts and Transcriptions	320
C	Royal Weddings and their Music	328

Sources and Bibliography

Printed Orders of Service and Ceremonials	334
Manuscript and Archival Material	337
Published Material (including Dissertations)	341

—◦◦◦—

Index	361

Illustrations and Figures

1.1: 'The Grand Procession from the Drawing Room to the Chapel Royal St. James's', mezzotint with etching and hand-colouring (Haines & Son, 1795), *Royal Collection, RCIN 605192*, Royal Collection Trust / © Her Majesty Queen Elizabeth II 2021. 7

1.2: 'The Marriage of Her Majesty Queen Victoria, with his Royal Highness Prince Albert of Saxe Coburg and Gotha [...]', 'Printed by Leferre, Newman St.' (London: Published by William Spooner, [1840]), *London, British Museum, 1871,0812.5360* © The Trustees of the British Museum. 8

1.3: 'The Signing of the Marriage Attestation Deed, March 10th 1863', chromolithograph by Robert Charles Dudley (1864), Plate 20 in William Howard Russell, *A Memorial of the Marriage of HRH Albert Edward Prince of Wales* [...] (London: Day and Son, [1864]), here from *London, National Portrait Gallery D33999* © National Portrait Gallery, London. 19

2.1: Marriage Procession for the Wedding of Elizabeth Stuart, Daughter of James I, and Frederick V, Elector Palatine, 14 February 1613: Abraham Hogenberg[?], *Eigentliche Abbildung welcher gestalt der Churfurst Pfaltzgraff Friderich der 5. sampt der Princessin in Engelland* [...], etching print 1613, copy in *New York City, The Met [Metropolitan Museum of Art], Accession Number 53.601.152* (Harris Brisbane Dick Fund, 1953). 30

2.2: 'The Marriage of the King 1625', engraving by Nicolas-Gabriel Dupuis after Louis Chéron (1660–1713), (London: Printed and sold by Thomas and John Bowles, Printsellers, [1728]), *Royal Collection, RCIN 601887*, Royal Collection Trust / © Her Majesty Queen Elizabeth II 2021. 35

2.3: Renier Persyn, 'The Betrothal of the Princess Mary to William, Prince of Orange', line engraving, mid-seventeenth century, *National Portrait Gallery, Reference Collection NPG D26430* © National Portrait Gallery, London. 38

2.4: ['Charles II and Catherine of Braganza'], engraving, *c.* 1662–70, *Royal Collection, RCIN 602630*, Royal Collection Trust / © Her Majesty Queen Elizabeth II 2021. 41

3.1: Detail of the ground-floor plan of St James's Palace by Henry Flitcroft, 1729. *Lna WORK 34/121.* With processional route indicated. NB This plan is oriented to have South-East at the top, with North in the bottom-left corner. 49

3.2: 'The Ceremony of the Marriage of the Princess Royal with the Prince of Orange', detail showing the procession to the service, broadsheet print, 1734, *London, British Museum, Mm,3.5* © The Trustees of the British Museum. 51

3.3: 'The Wedding of Princess Anne and William of Orange in the Chapel of St James's, 14 March 1734', etching by Jacques Rigaud after drawings by William Kent, *London, British Museum, Y,5.75* © The Trustees of the British Museum. 57

4.1: Sir Joshua Reynolds, 'The Marriage of George III', sketch in oil on canvas, 1761, *Royal Collection, RCIN 404353*, Royal Collection Trust / © Her Majesty Queen Elizabeth II 2021. 80

4.2: Henry Singleton, 'The Marriage of George IV (1762–1830) when Prince of Wales', oil on canvas, signed and dated 1795, *Royal Collection, RCIN 405845*, Royal Collection Trust / © Her Majesty Queen Elizabeth II 2021. 90

4.3: William Hamilton, 'The Marriage of George, Prince of Wales, and Princess Caroline of Brunswick', sketch in oil on canvas *c.* 1795–97, *Royal Collection, RCIN 404486*, Royal Collection Trust / © Her Majesty Queen Elizabeth II 2021. 93

4.4: 'The Marriage of his Serene Highness the Prince of Wirtemburg, to the Princess Royal of England, in the Chapel at St. James's, on Thursday the 18th of May 1797', mezzotint published by Robert Laurie and James Whittle on 7 August 1797, *London, National Portrait Gallery, Reference Collection NPG D8015* © National Portrait Gallery, London. 99

5.1: 'The Marriage of Frederick, Duke of York and Albany (1763-1827) to Frederica, Princess Royal of Prussia (1767–1820)', anonymous copy after Henry Singleton, oil on canvas *c.* 1791, *Royal Collection, RCIN 402495*, Royal Collection Trust / © Her Majesty Queen Elizabeth II 2021. 105

Illustrations and Figures

5.2: Richard Westall (attr.), 'The Wedding of Princess Charlotte of Wales and Prince Leopold of Saxe-Coburg at Carlton House', pen, oil and watercolour on paper *c.* 1816, *Royal Collection, RCIN 917619*, Royal Collection Trust / © Her Majesty Queen Elizabeth II 2021. 107

5.3: 'Marriage of The Princess Charlotte of Wales to Prince Leopold of Saxe-Coburg, in the Crimson Saloon at Carleton House, May 2, 1816', engraving by Robert Hicks after William Marshall Craig (published by Nuttall, Fisher & Dixon, 1818), *London, National Portrait Gallery, D16053* © National Portrait Gallery, London. 108

6.1: Ceremonial for the Wedding of Queen Victoria and Prince Albert (London: Francis Watts, 1840), 30.5 x 22 x 0.5 cm, printed on silk and bound in blue watered silk, *Royal Collection, RCIN 1053036*, Royal Collection Trust / © Her Majesty Queen Elizabeth II 2021. 117

6.2: 'Drums and Trumpets' during the entrance procession at the wedding of Queen Victoria, as depicted in *Authentic Representation* (1840). Pictures from the private collection of Nigel Pierlejewski, reproduced by kind permission. 119

6.3: Arrival of the procession at the door of the Chapel Royal, from Spooner's Panoramic View of the Queen's Marriage Procession (London: Published by William Spooner, [1840]), lithograph with hand colouring, *Royal Collection, RCIN 813076*, Royal Collection Trust / © Her Majesty Queen Elizabeth II 2021. 120

6.4: Sir George Hayter, 'The Marriage of Queen Victoria, 10 February 1840', oil on canvas 1840–42, *Royal Collection, RCIN 407165*, Royal Collection Trust / © Her Majesty Queen Elizabeth II 2021. 123

6.5: 'Marriage of H.R.H. The Princess Augusta Caroline and the Hereditary Grand Duke of Mecklenburg Strelitz, *ILN*, 1 July 1843, pp. 7–9, here p. 8. Author's collection. 128

6.6: Douglas Morison, 'The Private Chapel at Buckingham Palace', watercolour and bodycolour over pencil 1843–44, *Royal Collection, RCIN 919912*, Royal Collection Trust / © Her Majesty Queen Elizabeth II 2021. 129

6.7: John Phillip, 'The Marriage of Victoria, Princess Royal, 25 January 1858', oil on canvas, signed and dated 1860, *Royal Collection, RCIN 406819*, Royal Collection Trust / © Her Majesty Queen Elizabeth II 2021. 135

6.8: Egron Sellif Lundgren, 'The Wedding of the Princess Royal and Prince Frederick William of Prussia', pencil, watercolour and bodycolour 1858, *Royal Collection, RCIN 919928,* Royal Collection Trust © Her Majesty Queen Elizabeth II 2021. 145

6.9: 'The Galleries of the Chapel Royal, Showing the Queen's Procession Passing up the Aisle', *Illustrated Times*, 30 January 1858. Author's collection. 147

6.10: The procession through the state rooms of St James's Palace to the Chapel Royal at the wedding of Princess Victoria, 1858, centre piece illustration in *Illustrated Times*, 30 January 1858. Author's collection. 149

7.1: George Housman Thomas, 'The Marriage of Princess Alice, 1st July 1862', oil on canvas 1862–63, *Royal Collection, RCIN 404479*, Royal Collection Trust / © Her Majesty Queen Elizabeth II 2021. 156

7.2: W. H. [William Howard] Russell, *A Memorial of the Marriage of HRH Albert Edward Prince of Wales and HRH Alexandra Princess of Denmark […]* (London: Day and Son, [1864]), *Royal Collection, RCIN 1055746*, Royal Collection Trust / © Her Majesty Queen Elizabeth II 2021. 158

7.3: 'Marshalling the Procession of the Bride, Temporary Apartments_ St George's Chapel, March 10th, 1863', chromolithograph by Robert Charles Dudley (1864), *London, National Portrait Gallery, D33995* © National Portrait Gallery, London. 160

7.4: 'The Royal Marriage: The Bride Passing up the Nave of St George's Chapel', *ILN*, 28 March 1863, pp. 348–49. Author's collection. 161

7.5: George Housman Thomas, 'The Marriage of Albert Edward, Prince of Wales, 10 March 1863', oil on canvas before 2 May 1864, *Royal Collection, RCIN 406997*, Royal Collection Trust / © Her Majesty Queen Elizabeth II 2021. 163

7.6: 'The Form of Solemnization of Matrimony: St. George's Chapel, Windsor Castle March 10, 1863' [= OS 1863], with separate printed music text sheet (London: Harrison & Sons, 1863), *Royal Collection, RCIN 1054577*, Royal Collection Trust / © Her Majesty Queen Elizabeth II 2021. 167

British Royal Weddings

7.7: William Powell Frith, 'The Marriage of the Prince of Wales with Princess Alexandra of Denmark, Windsor, 10 March 1863', oil on canvas 1863–65, *Royal Collection, RCIN 404545,* Royal Collection Trust / © Her Majesty Queen Elizabeth II 2021.   175

7.8: 'The Marriage of Princess Mary of Cambridge and Prince Teck Kew Church', from *ILN,* 23 June 1866, pp. 604–05. Author's collection.   179

7.9: Photograph of the Private Chapel at Windsor Castle, reproductive print by Russell & Sons, Windsor, *c.* 1900-18, *Royal Collection, RCIN 705272,* Royal Collection Trust / © Her Majesty Queen Elizabeth II 2021.   181

7.10: Christian Karl Magnussen, 'The Marriage of Princess Helena, 5 July 1866', oil on canvas, signed and dated 1866–69, *Royal Collection, RCIN 404483,* Royal Collection Trust / © Her Majesty Queen Elizabeth II 2021.   183

7.11: 'Marriage of Princess Helena and Prince Christian in the Private Chapel, Windsor Castle', *ILN,* 14 July 1866, p. 32–33. Author's collection.   184

7.12: Detail of the first-floor plan of Windsor Castle, showing the Private Chapel and surrounding rooms – from *The Pictorial Handbook of London* [...] *Together with Some Account of the Principal Suburbs and Most Attractive Localities,* 'Bohn's Illustrated Library' (London: Henry G. Bohn, 1854), p. 865. Author's collection. Location of the private chapel indicated.   185

7.13: Sydney Prior Hall, 'The Marriage of Princess Louise, 21 March 1871', oil on canvas 1878–79, *Royal Collection, RCIN 404485,* Royal Collection Trust / © Her Majesty Queen Elizabeth II 2021.   189

8.1: Nicholas Chevalier, 'Marriage of Alfred, Duke of Edinburgh and the Grand Duchess Marie Alexandrovna of Russia, St Petersburg, 23 January 1874: The Anglican Ceremony', pencil, bodycolour and watercolour painting 1874, *Royal Collection, RCIN 451865,* Royal Collection Trust / © Her Majesty Queen Elizabeth II 2021.   201

8.2: Sydney Prior Hall, 'The Marriage of the Duke of Connaught, 13th March 1879', oil on canvas, signed and dated 1881, *Royal Collection, RCIN 404477,* Royal Collection Trust / © Her Majesty Queen Elizabeth II 2021.   203

8.3: 'Marriage of H.R.H. the Duke of Connaught at Windsor: Trumpeters Announcing the Approach of the Bride', cover picture of *ILN,* 15 March 1879. Author's collection.   207

8.4: 'Arrival of a procession – The Flourish of Trumpets', *Graphic: Royal Wedding Number,* 20 March 1879, p. 18. Author's collection.   208

8.5: Sir James Dromgole Linton, 'The Marriage of the Duke of Albany, 27th April 1882', oil on canvas, signed and dated 1885, *Royal Collection, RCIN 404481,* Royal Collection Trust / © Her Majesty Queen Elizabeth II 2021.   212

8.6: 'Arrival of the Bride', (inside) cover picture [that is, p. 3] of *ILN: Royal Wedding Number,* 2 May 1882. Author's collection.   213

8.7: 'The Wedding March: Sir George Elvey at the Organ', *Graphic: Royal Wedding Number,* 6 May 1882, p. 30. Author's collection.   221

8.8: Richard Caton Woodville, 'The Marriage of Princess Beatrice, 23rd July 1885', oil on canvas, signed and dated 1886, *Royal Collection, RCIN 404480,* Royal Collection Trust / © Her Majesty Queen Elizabeth II 2021.   223

8.9: Jabez Hughes (attr.), 'Whippingham Church, View from Chancel', carbon print *c.* 1873, *Royal Collection, RCIN 2102462,* Royal Collection Trust / © Her Majesty Queen Elizabeth II 2021.   224

8.10: Plan of Whippingham Church at the wedding of Princess Beatrice, 1885, included in Ceremonial 1885; here from the copy in *Wsg XVII.43.3/2.* By permission of the Dean and Canons of Windsor. 225

9.1: 'The Private Chapel, Buckingham Palace. Marriage of Her Royal Highness The Princess Louise of Wales with the Earl of Fife, K.T.', printed seating plan included in Ceremonial 1889a/b; here from the copy in *Wsg XVII.43.4/1.* By permission of the Dean and Canons of Windsor.   236

9.2: Sydney Prior Hall, 'The Marriage of Princess Louise of Wales with the Duke of Fife at Buckingham Palace, 27th July 1889', oil on panel, signed and dated 1890, *Royal Collection, RCIN 404460,* Royal Collection Trust / © Her Majesty Queen Elizabeth II 2021.   237

Illustrations and Figures

9.3: 'The Marriage of Princess Louise of Wales and the Duke of Fife, Buckingham Palace, 27th July 1889', Albumen print by Byrne & Co., Hill Street, Richmond (21.5 x 21.4 cm) contained in 'Portraits of Royal Children Vol. 37: 1888–1889', *Royal Collection, RCIN 2904786*, Royal Collection Trust / © Her Majesty Queen Elizabeth II 2021. 241

9.4: 'The Choir, St George's Chapel, Windsor Castle', platinum print c. 1890, *Royal Collection, RCIN 2101106*, Royal Collection Trust / © Her Majesty Queen Elizabeth II 2021. 243

9.5: T. Walter Wilson, 'The Royal Wedding at Windsor: The Marriage Ceremony in St. George's Chapel', *ILN*, 11 July 1891, pp. 48–49. Author's collection. 244

9.6: 'The Wedding of H.H. The Princess Louise of Schleswig-Holstein to H.H. Prince Aribert of Anhalt', Supplement to *Graphic: Wedding Number*, 11 July 1891, pp. [III-IV]. Author's collection. 245

9.7: Laurits Regner Tuxen, 'The Marriage of George, Duke of York, with Princess Mary of Teck, 6 July 1893', oil on canvas, signed and dated 1894, *Royal Collection, RCIN 402437*, Royal Collection Trust / © Her Majesty Queen Elizabeth II 2021. 251

9.8: Amadée Forestier, 'The marriage of TRH the Duke and Duchess of York, 6 July Illustration 1893', watercolour 1893, *Royal Collection, RCIN 920841*, Royal Collection Trust / © Her Majesty Queen Elizabeth II 2021. 253

9.9: William Creser and S. Flood Jones, 'Royal Marriage Hymn: Father of Life', *ILN: Royal Wedding Number*, 10 July 1893, [supplement between pp 22 and 23]. Author's collection. 257

9.10: Laurits Regner Tuxen, 'The Marriage of Princess Maud of Wales, 22 July 1896', oil on canvas, signed and dated 1896–97, *Royal Collection, RCIN 404464*, Royal Collection Trust / © Her Majesty Queen Elizabeth II 2021. 263

9.11: William Hatherell, 'Marriage of Princess Maud of Wales and Prince Charles of Denmark, 22 July 1896', drawing 1896, *Royal Collection, RCIN 920860*, Royal Collection Trust / © Her Majesty Queen Elizabeth II 2021. 271

10.1: 'The Royal Wedding at Windsor: The Bride and Bridegroom, Prince Alexander of Teck and Princess Alice of Albany, Leaving the Altar', drawing by Samuel Begg, in Supplement to *ILN*, 20 February 1904, pp. IV–V. © Illustrated London News/Mary Evans Picture Library. 275

10.2: Order of service for the 1904 wedding of Princess Alice of Albany and Prince Alexander of Teck, with separate lose hymn sheet. Author's collection. 276

10.3: Sydney Prior Hall, 'Marriage of Princess Margaret of Connaught to Prince Gustavus Adolphus of Sweden', bodycolour and watercolour painting 15 Jun 1905, *Royal Collection, RCIN 451868*, Royal Collection Trust / © Her Majesty Queen Elizabeth II 2021. 281

10.4: Plan of St George's Chapel, Windsor, with seating arrangements. Included in Ceremonial 1905; here from the copy in *Wsg X.33/20*. By permission of the Dean and Canons of Windsor. 282

10.5: 'Drawn by our Special Artist at the Ceremony in the Chapel Royal: The Royal Wedding at St. James's', *ILN*, 18 October 1913, pp. 612–13. © Illustrated London News/Mary Evans Picture Library. 285

10.6: 'The Musical Side of the Wedding: The Organist and Composers' and 'The Religious Aspect of the Wedding: The Clergy and Choristers', in *ILN*, 18 October 1913, pp. 625 and 631. © Illustrated London News/Mary Evans Picture Library. 286

10.7: 'Preparing the Chapel Royal for the Royal Wedding', in Philip Gibbs, 'The Art of Anticipation', *Graphic*, 11 October 1913, p. 658. Author's collection. 289

10.8: Four leaves from Walter Alcock's 'Marche Triomphale' performed at the 1913 wedding of the Duke of Connaught; as reproduced in *Graphic*, 18 October 1913, p. 722. © The Graphic/Mary Evans Picture Library. 291

11.1: 'The Marriage Ceremony of Their Royal Highnesses the Prince & Princess of Wales', mezzotint with etching and hand-colouring (Haines & Son, 1795), *Royal Collection, RCIN 605193*, Royal Collection Trust / © Her Majesty Queen Elizabeth II 2021. 310

11.2: Richard Buckner, 'Portrait of a Boy Chorister of the Chapel Royal', oil painting c. 1873, *London, Victoria and Albert Museum, Accession Number P.30-1962* © Victoria and Albert Museum, London. 311

11.3: Quiver with arrows and bow (as symbols of Cupid) at the bottom of the last page of Ceremonial 1795, here from the copy in *Llp Fulham Papers Porteus 17*, fols 212ʳ–213ᵛ. 313

Figures

1.1: 'Grand Trumpeter March', as reproduced in Jacob Adam Kappey, *Military Music. A History of Wind-Instrumental Bands* (London: Boosey and Co., [1894]), p. 52.   21

6.1: Pelham Humfrey's 'Grant Chant', as used at the coronation of Queen Victoria in 1838: here as reconstructed in Matthias Range, *Music and Ceremonial at British Coronations: From James I to Elizabeth II* (Cambridge: Cambridge University Press, 2012), p. 216.   142

6.2: Plan of 'The Chapel Royal Choir' at the wedding of Princess Victoria, 1858; transcribed from George Smart's handwritten records in *Lbl Add MS 41777*, here fols 322ᵛ–323ʳ.   150

7.1: Prince Albert, *Chorale* (from 1862 Mason edition, here transposed down to D major) with Oliphant's text for the 1863 wedding.   169

8.1: Representation of the sketch of the organ and music gallery at St George's Chapel, Windsor at the 1879 wedding; included in Ponsonby-Fane to A. B. Mitford, 12 December 1878, *Lna WORK 19/138.*   209

Preface

WHEN I FIRST EMBARKED on this project, it could not be foreseen what a colossal enterprise and long journey lay ahead. Eventually, my research into the topic of British royal weddings has ended up covering the weddings of all monarchs, future monarchs, and practically all their children and grandchildren that have taken place in Britain since James VI/I (the *de facto* first monarch of Great Britain). The weddings discussed in this volume stretch from the turn of the sixteenth to the early twentieth century, providing an introduction to, and discussion of over forty royal weddings between 1596 and 1917. As it turned out, each of these weddings had a particular character and some notable features that deserve a closer discussion. The weddings after 1917, when so much had changed for the world at large and for the monarchy in particular, will eventually feature in a separate volume.

The starting point of research had been to write a study on the music at royal weddings, a topic which had not been comprehensively studied. It soon became apparent, however, that there was very little, or indeed no research into these ceremonies as a whole – with most of the literature being of a more general nature, without analysis or in-depth discussion of sources (but with many good pictures). While this study still has a clear emphasis on the role of music at royal weddings, it overall follows a more holistic approach to these occasions, providing informed accounts and contextualizing discussions of the individual ceremonies and their reception. Using a wide range of sources not previously looked at, with much original research in all chapters, this study addresses three main aspects that are very closely interlinked in the staging of these ceremonies: their venue – their ceremonial – and their music. With the encouragement of my publisher I was able to include a considerable number of pictures that greatly illustrate and help to understand the issues discussed in the text. Many of those that are reproduced in smaller size are also available to view in more detail online (for instance those from the Royal Collection).

Each chapter includes several weddings, with the main 'developments' being emphasized in the chapter headings. The straightforward wedding-by-wedding approach allows the reader to obtain a good impression of each individual ceremony while following a clear chronology – which in turn contributes to a better understanding of how the ceremony and its individual parts developed as a whole. Since much of the music from royal weddings is well-known, or studied elsewhere, closer musical discussions are reserved primarily for music that is less well-known or where significant new insights can be provided. In this way, the volume adds also interesting material to studies on specific composers and works, and it is hoped that it will spur further interest in this music.

It may, unfortunately, be inevitable that a study of this scope and length will not be immune to little mistakes and errors, or to inconsistencies creeping in. I have done my utmost to keep these out but am fully aware of the limitations of human perfection. In order to prevent mis-interpretations and enable readers to form their own interpretations more adequately, I have often included direct quotations from the sources – more so than perhaps usual in modern-day academic writing. The accumulation of quotations from different reports and sources will be judged by some readers 'tiring', by others 'fascinating'. I can but hope that I have overall managed to combine an interesting and entertaining read with a thoroughly researched and thought-stimulating study – a resource for more research into what is one of the most captivating ceremonies of the British monarchy.

Acknowledgements

THE AMOUNT OF RESEARCH necessary for this study seemed, at times, simply overwhelming and a truly Herculean task. While I have done all the extensive research for this study, and all the writing of it myself, it would not have become the work it is without the support and help of many individuals and institutions.

First of all, I feel honoured to be able to acknowledge my gratitude and express my humble thanks to HM Queen Elizabeth II for allowing me to consult and use material from the Royal Archives at Windsor Castle and for Her gracious permission to use the beautiful cover picture and other illustrations from the Royal Collection inside the book. Similarly, I thank His Grace, the Archbishop of Canterbury for access to and use of material at Lambeth Palace; and the Dean and Canons of St George's Chapel, Windsor for access to material in the Chapel archives – and both for allowing me to reproduce material from their archives. I am grateful to the Kings, Heralds and Pursuivants of Arms of the College of Arms for allowing me to use the rich material in their collection, and I thank the trustees of the British Museum and the National Portrait Gallery for permission to reproduce some of their images.

I am much indebted to all the librarians and archivists who helped and supported me along my journey: to Laura Hobbs and her colleagues at the Royal Archives who have been of great help with their deep knowledge of the collection; to Kate McQuillian and her predecessor Clare Ryder at the archives of St George's, Windsor for their informative insights and ever-helpful support in finding things in that collection; to the staff at Lambeth Palace who were always most helpful in finding material and in procuring it from their vaults; and to Lynsey Darby, the archivist at the College of Arms for her great help in exploring this little-used archive and locating many of their sources.

In addition, I am very grateful to Martin Holmes (Alfred Brendel Curator of Music at the Bodleian Library at Oxford) for his help in tracking down curious items through the mysterious system of the online catalogue – and similarly to all the staff at the many other research institutions that I visited, in particular at the Bodleian Library, Oxford; the British Library; and the National Archives.

Thanks are also in order to individuals who were of particular help with some more specific issues: Emily Brand for sharing some of her research on royal weddings in general, Lucinda Dean for her valuable help and advice on the Scottish royal weddings, John Plunkett for sharing his notes on the reporting about the Victorian weddings, Peter Mandler for his help in deciphering a newly-found letter by Lord Melbourne, Magnus Williamson for clarifying some details on the earlier wedding music, and Tom Rizzuto for sharing his research on Wagner's wedding march.

I was very lucky to be able to devote much time on this project over the last few years. All the same, I began research for this long ago – as I started finding interesting bits on royal weddings all the way during my work on coronations, and then on royal funerals, beginning over 20 years ago. The comparison with such other royal occasions has proven very helpful and instructive and I thank all those who have been of help during all these years, on this long journey.

Finally, particular thanks are due to my friends near and far: to Michael Lukey for his spontaneous help in tracing important articles across the pond; to Stephen Taylor for always decidedly challenging my ideas; and to Philippa Woodcock for her unfaltering interest, support, and encouragement. Very particular thanks are reserved for Julia Craig-McFeely for her

Acknowledgements

immensely helpful support and encouragement in all kinds of matters and for eventually designing and type-setting this volume so beautifully: it would indeed not look the same without her. Special thanks must go to Thomas Plant and to TeD for their continuous support and confidence in this project, accompanying me on numerous research trips (with some very early starts) and enduring endless discussions and private lectures on all things royal. The last Thank You must go to all those whose name – by my own regrettable neglect – is here missing. The very last and very substantial thanks, however, go to my publisher: I am immensely grateful to Brepols, and in particular to the editor Johan Van der Beke, for showing confidence in this project and encouraging the publication in its current incarnation as such a richly illustrated, beautiful book. I thank them wholeheartedly for embarking with me on this journey and for seeing this study through to publication. May it reach a great many people: inform, enlighten, and educate – but also entertain, and delight them!

Matthias Range
Oxford
January 2022

Abbreviations and Conventions

Bibliographical Abbreviations

The newspapers and magazines used were either from the collection of the British Library or that of the Bodleian Library, Oxford. Most of these can also be consulted in online databases. In titles that include the definite article, this has usually been tacitly omitted for the sake of brevity.

Annual Register	*The Annual Register, or a View of the History, Politics, and Literature, for the Year*
Ceremonial	Ceremonial for wedding in that year – full details in the List of Sources and Bibliography
Gentleman's Magazine	*The Gentleman's Magazine: Or, Monthly Intelligencer*
MLAI	*The Mirror of Literature, Amusement, and Instruction*
New Grove	*The New Grove Dictionary of Music and Musicians*, ed. Stanley Sadie and John Tyrell, 2nd edn, 20 vols (London: Macmillan, 2001). Unless a volume number is given, the (partly updated) online version was used: www.oxfordmusiconline.com
OS	Order of service – full details in the List of Sources and Bibliography
OWC	*Owen's Weekly Chronicle; Or, Universal Journal for the Year*
QVJ	*Queen Victoria's Journals*, available online at www.queenvictoriasjournals.org – as both photographs and transcriptions. The site presents the four different versions of the journal texts next to each other: 'Queen Victoria's handwriting', 'Lord Esher's typescripts', 'Princess Beatrice's copies, and 'Queen Victoria's drafts'. Unless otherwise indicated, the version cited here is from Princess Beatrice's copies; '(LE)' indicates or from Lord Esher's typescripts.
SJC	*St. James's Chronicle or the British Evening Post*
Times	*The* [London] *Times*
Wedding Observer	*The Wedding Observer*: special edition of *The Observer* of 16 and 17 February 1840 (relevant extract in *Lna* WORK 21/19).

Libraries and Archives Sigla

Lbl	London, British Library
Lca	London, College of Arms
Llp	London, Lambeth Palace Library
Lna	London, National Archives
Lwa	London, Westminster Abbey
Ob	Oxford, Bodleian Library
Royal Collection	Windsor, Windsor Castle, Royal Collection Trust (with much of the collection available online at https://www.rct.uk)
Wra	Windsor, Windsor Castle, Royal Archives
Wsg	Windsor, St George's Chapel, Archives

Abbreviations and Conventions

Other Abbreviations

fol./fols	folio/folios: 'r' and 'v' (for 'recto' and 'verso') are included following the number
SATB	soprano, alto, tenor, bass: solo singers
satb	soprano, alto, tenor, bass: choral singers (i.e. choir)
S/s	(for 'soprano') as a technical term is used throughout, even when the top part would in fact have been sung by trebles

General Notes

Quotations and Spelling

Quotations follow the original as much as possible. Any interference with the original text is indicated in square brackets. Unless otherwise stated, all translations from other languages into English are those of the author.

NB The spelling 'quire' has been used throughout when referring to the architectural part of a church building, in order to differentiate it properly from 'choir', which here refers solely to the musical body of singers.

Dates

Up to 1752 the Julian calendar was used in Britain, with the year beginning on 25 March ('Lady Day'). In order to avoid confusion with the primary sources, this present study will follow the established convention of giving both the 'old' and the 'new' style year. It may be worth noting that dates before 1752 differ ten to eleven days from the continental date. A translation of the daily dates, however, would not bring any gain for the present study and merely cause unnecessary complication with the primary sources.

Currency

Up to 15 February 1971, British currency was in pounds, shillings and pennies or pence (abbreviated £ *s. d.*, for instance £5 8*s.* 11*d.* or £5/8/11). A pound consisted of 20 shillings and a shilling of twelve pennies. A guinea was £1 1s.

1

Setting the Scene

ROYAL WEDDINGS ARE AMONG the most notable and significant royal occasions. In distinct contrast to many other royal and state occasions, weddings actually cause a change, they 'create' something new, so to speak. Coronations, thanksgivings, or funerals, for instance, merely celebrate and confirm an existing fact: the monarch is already monarch – the coronation does not change but merely confirms that; and a royal death is not changed by the funeral. In stark contrast to this, weddings cause a clear change by including the actual legal act of uniting two individuals.

This study looks at the British royal weddings from the Stuart accession to the English throne in 1603 up to 1917, after which major changes occurred in the public appearance and perception of the monarchy and the royal family; these affected especially also the way in which royal weddings were celebrated. Almost all British royal weddings since the Reformation have been Anglican ceremonies. Indeed, following the upheavals of the 1688–89 'Glorious Revolution', the 1701 Act of Settlement codified that no member of the royal family was allowed to marry a Roman Catholic without losing the place in the line of succession. The focus of this study is on the wedding service itself, as the main event, and special attention is paid to the venue, the ceremonial and the music at these occasions – three components that are very much interlinked and come together to form the overall ceremony.

With the emphasis on the wedding service, it may be helpful to remember that the term 'wedding' to refer to the ceremony is of relatively recent usage. The Anglican Book of Common Prayer since its first introduction in 1549 uses the expression 'Solemnization of Matrimony', and a term often used up to the nineteenth century was 'nuptials', while the sometimes found term 'espousals' seems to have been used more in reference to the legal act of uniting a couple. The Latin-derived term 'nuptials' was occasionally used, but as a noun it appears to have fallen out of use by the later nineteenth century, surviving more clearly as the adjective 'nuptial'. The term 'marriage', which today more commonly refers to the union of two people and their living together, is also sometimes used to refer to the ceremony – in official titles (such as on the orders of service), 'marriage' is used instead of 'wedding' to the present day.

There is much literature on royal weddings, and especially the weddings since that of Queen Victoria in 1840 have been covered in numerous reports and publications. Whereas these works often include fabulous pictorial records of these events, their texts rarely leave the descriptive frame, and often include various inaccuracies. The earlier royal weddings, up to the accession of the Stuarts to the English throne, in the early seventeenth century, have been considered more seriously by historians, for England and especially also for royal weddings in Scotland.[1] However, the royal weddings from the Stuarts onwards have been widely neglected by historians and by

---

1 For Scotland see Lucinda Hazel Stewart Dean, 'Crowns, Wedding Rings, and Processions: Continuity and Change in the Representation of Scottish Royal Authority in State Ceremony, c. 1214–c. 1603' (unpublished doctoral thesis, University of Stirling, 2013). This study will also be available as *Death and the Royal Succession in Scotland, 1214 to 1543: Ritual, Ceremony and Power* (Boydell, forthcoming).

others alike.[2] For Britain there is as yet nothing comparable to, for instance, Daniel Schönpflug's dedicated study on the marriages of the Hohenzollern dynasty which discusses them in their socio-cultural context.[3]

Moreover, as already mentioned, the present study focuses on three main aspects: the choice of venue, the form of the ceremonial, and the music at royal weddings – aspects that in most other studies are considered only marginally, but not given a more dedicated discussion. Music's function at, and interaction with particular weddings has been especially neglected. Yet, music readily lends itself to exploring such royal ceremonies more closely. At almost all ceremonial occasions, music constitutes an integral part that brings them together and enhances their character. Music breaks the monotony of the spoken words, enhances the gestures and proceedings; it breathes 'life' into them, as it were. Before the wedding of Princess Louise in 1871, an article in the musical journal *The Orchestra* judged that the ceremony 'should have something more to carry in the memory than a mere catalogue of jewels and gold, of silks and satins, of velvet and lace'.[4] Its answer – probably with an expectable bias – was that

> there should be the distinctive presence and operation of that which has more of imagination and the spiritual to mark the affection, reverence, and holiness of the rite. Nothing effects this so thoroughly and so sympathetically as music; and we trust its aid may be secured, and opportunity given for the full expression of its power.

An exemplification of the significance of music for the overall impact at such occasions comes from Queen Victoria herself. On 30 April 1884, she attended the wedding of her granddaughter Princess Victoria of Hesse and by Rhine to Prince Louis of Battenberg in Darmstadt. While the newly-weds were kneeling for their blessing after the exchange of the rings, she noted 'the Organ all the while, being played very softly, which had the most solemn & touching effect'.[5] Overall, because of music's close link with the ceremonial, the discussion of its place and function therein can much contribute to a clearer and more comprehensive understanding of these events.

A Private State Occasion

Regarding the ceremonial nature of royal weddings, there is some unanimity in the literature and in public discussions: the epithet 'state' has been bestowed on many a royal wedding, past and present – as 'state marriage' or 'state occasion', for instance. Many of them are certainly celebrated in a grand manner and are hence occasions of great state; and even though they have nothing to do with the actual workings of *the* state, with their dynastic implications they are, of course, of direct relevance to the state. However, technically royal weddings are not 'state occasions' such as coronations, or state funerals, or the state opening of parliament. Their proceedings do not need to be approved by the Privy Council or any other official, governmental body, and they are not fully paid for by the state. In addition to the distinction between 'state' and 'not state' occasion, another important differentiation is that between 'public' and 'private', which is of relevance for the organization of royal weddings: while public and state occasions are under

---

[2] A very useful table (in form of a family tree) of all royal weddings from Henry VII up to 1986 is included in Nigel Arch and Joanna Marschner, *The Royal Wedding Dresses* (London: Sidgwick & Jackson, 1990), [pp. 138–39]. For a chronological list of all the royal weddings in this book, see Appendix A.

[3] Daniel Schönpflug, *Die Heiraten der Hohenzollern: Verwandtschaft, Politik und Ritual in Europa 1640–1918*, 'Kritische Studien zur Geschichtswissenschaft', 207 (Göttingen: Vandenhoek & Ruprecht, 2013).

[4] 'Royal Wedding Music', *The Orchestra*, 388 (3 March 1871), pp. 361–62, here p. 362.

[5] *QVJ*, 30 April 1884.

1—Setting the Scene

the direction of the Earl Marshal assisted by the heralds of the College of Arms, private royal occasions are under the auspices of the Lord Chamberlain, the most senior official of the royal household. Anthony Richard Wagner, himself one-time Garter King of Arms, with reference to a dispute at the christening of Prince William in 1717 summarized that since then 'there has been a constant tendency to turn into *private* functions Royal christenings, marriages, funerals, thanksgivings and the like, which formerly were *public ceremonies*, thus removing them out of the Earl Marshal's and into the Lord Chamberlain's jurisdiction'.[6] However, this trend towards private ceremonies had started even earlier, with royal funerals having been mostly 'private' occasions from the early seventeenth century onwards.[7] Indeed, before that, all six of Henry VIII's weddings had been private, if not reclusive occasions and Alison Weir has highlighted that the wedding of his elder brother Prince Arthur to Catherine of Aragon at Old St Paul's Cathedral in 1501 had been the last public royal wedding for over 50 years.[8] After this, she notes, the wedding of Mary I in Winchester Cathedral in 1554 was the last public royal wedding for another 300 years.[9]

The distinction between 'private' and 'public' has not always been clear in the following centuries. In 1764, Sir Stephen Cottrell, Assistant Master of the Ceremonies, noted that the 1734 wedding of George II's daughter Princess Anne and the Prince of Orange in the palace chapel had been 'publick', but that the 1764 wedding of Princess Augusta, sister of George III, to the Prince of Brunswick 'in the Great Drawing room' was 'private'.[10] Nevertheless, the 1734 wedding had notably been a nocturnal ceremony – like otherwise 'private' ones (see below). One report in 1858 circumvented the difficulty of exact nomenclature very elegantly by describing that the wedding of Queen Victoria's oldest daughter, the Princess Royal in that year had been 'solemnized with all the dignity of a state ceremonial'.[11] In 1871, on the occasion of the wedding of Princess Louise at St George's Chapel, Windsor, one writer regretted that it was 'to be *private*' and explained

> We like not this prevailing fashion of privacy touching great public events; royal weddings are not of every day occurrence, and they hold their proper place and significance.[12]

Royal weddings in the following decades opened somewhat more to the public, before eventually becoming grand public occasions from 1919 onwards. Yet, they have remained technically 'private' events in so far as they have remained in the Lord Chamberlain's domain.

---

[6] Anthony Richard Wagner, *Heralds of England: A History of the Office and College of Arms* (London: Her Majesty's Stationery Office, 1967), p. 340 (emphases original). See also his *John Anstis: Garter King of Arms* (London: HMSO, 1992), p. 44.

[7] See Matthias Range, *British Royal and State Funerals: Music and Ceremonial since Elizabeth I* (Woodbridge: Boydell Press, 2016) [hereinafter *BRSF*], pp. 9–15 and Chapter 1.

[8] Alison Weir, '"Princely Marriage": Royal Weddings from 1066 to 1714', in: Alison Weir, Kate Williams, Sarah Gristwood, and Tracy Borman, *The Ring and the Crown: A History of Royal Weddings 1066–2011* (London: Hutchinson, 2011), pp. 9–51, here p. 38. For this wedding see lately also Arlene Naylor Okerlund, *Elizabeth of York*, 'Queenship and Power' (New York: Palgrave Macmillan, 2009), Chapter 15 (pp. 165–80).

[9] Weir, "Princely Marriage", p. 42. For this wedding see Alexander Samson, 'Changing Places: The Marriage and Royal Entry of Philip, Prince of Austria, and Mary Tudor, July–August 1554', *Sixteenth Century Journal*, 36 (2005), pp. 761–84; and more recently by the same author, *Mary and Philip: The Marriage of Tudor England and Habsburg Spain*, 'Studies in Early Modern European History' (Manchester: Manchester University Press, 2020), esp. Chapter 4: 'A Marriage Made in Heaven?' For the Tudor weddings in general see also Sarah Duncan, *Mary I: Gender, Power, and Ceremony in the Reign of England's First Queen* (Basingstoke: Macmillan, 2012); and some unpublished material in *Llp MS 285*.

[10] *Lna LC 5/4*, pp. 42–43. For the room see the account in *LC 5/7*, p. 44.

[11] *Annual Register … 1858* (1859), pp. 355–58, here p. 355.

[12] 'Royal Wedding Music', *Orchestra*, p. 362 (emphasis original).

British Royal Weddings

The Time of the Ceremony

In relation to the public/private distinction at royal weddings, an important aspect was the time of day at which these ceremonies took place. In the earlier seventeenth century, the two grand royal weddings in London of 1613 and 1641 took place during daytime, around noon or in the early afternoon; while the wedding of Charles I in Paris in 1625 took place in the evening. The rather low-key, unceremonious royal weddings after the Restoration, beginning with Charles II's own wedding in 1662, also took place in the evening. During the eighteenth century, and in the first half of the nineteenth century, royal weddings continued to be evening ceremonies, with a singular exception in the 1797 wedding of Princess Charlotte, daughter of George III, to Prince Frederick-William of Württemberg. This coincided with a general preference for nocturnal royal ceremonies of this kind.[13] Late evening weddings were also *en vogue* for the aristocracy and others with aspirations and in the late seventeenth century, one writer had noted the secretive character of English weddings:

> One of the Reasons that they have for marrying secretly, as they generally do in *England*, is, that thereby they avoid a great deal of Expense and Trouble. [...] Persons of Quality, and many others who imitate them, have lately taken up the Custom of being marry'd very late at Night in their Chamber, and very often at some Country House.[14]

However, aristocratic evening weddings also took place in churches. For instance, on 14 February 1734 John Spencer, youngest son of the 3rd Earl of Sunderland and grandson of the famous Duke of Marlborough, as well as brother of the 3rd Duke, married Georgiana Caroline Carteret, 'between eight and nine o' the clock at night' at St George's, Hanover Square, as Mary Delany recorded.[15] One reason for this fashion of evening weddings was the desire to demote these occasions, as it were, from elaborate public day-time ceremonies to more 'private', nocturnal events, with a less elaborate and less strict ceremonial – as seen in the above quotation, in order to 'avoid a great deal of Expense and Trouble'.[16]

Incidentally, evening weddings became an exception to the law, which between 1753 and 1886 stipulated that weddings in England had to take place between 8am and noon, later extended to 3pm.[17] In 1879, for the wedding of Queen Victoria's son Prince Arthur, Duke of Connaught, one commentator pointed out that 'the present marriage was solemnised after the usual hour of twelve' – but this followed the explanation that the wedding had the usual 'special license' which permits 'the parties to be married at any time, in any church or chapel, or other meet and convenient place'.[18] In successive laws the time was gradually extended to 6pm; and the time restriction was fully repealed by the Protection of Freedoms Act in 2012.[19]

---

[13] For funerals see Range, *BRSF*. For a royal christening in the evening see, for instance, Donald Burrows and Rosemary Dunhill, *Music and Theatre in Handel's World: The Family Papers of James Harris, 1732–1780* (Oxford: Oxford University Press, 2002), p. 1020 (referring to the christening of Prince Octavius on 23 March 1779).

[14] Henri Misson de Valbourg, *M. Misson's Memoirs and Observations in his Travels over England. With Some Account of Scotland and Ireland*, transl. from the French by 'Mr. Ozell' (London: Printed for D. Browne et al., 1719), p. 349. This work may have been written by Henri's brother, the writer François Maximilien Mission. I am very grateful to Emily Brand for pointing me to this source.

[15] Mary Delany, *The Autobiography and Correspondence of Mary Granville, Mrs. Delany*, ed. by Lady Llanover, first series, 3 vols (London: Richard Bentley, 1861), I, p. 427.

[16] For the same reasons at funerals see Range, *BRSF*, pp. 12–13.

[17] See Roderick Floud and Pat Thane, 'The Incidence of Civil Marriage in Victorian England and Wales', *Past & Present*, 84 (1979), pp. 146–54, here pp. 150–51.

[18] 'The Marriage of H.R.H. The Duke of Connaught, K.G., and H.R.H. Princess Louise Margaret of Prussia', *The London Reader of Literature, Science, Art and General Information*, 29 March 1879, pp. 524–26, here p. 526.

1—Setting the Scene

Heralds and Weddings

Notwithstanding the fine distinctions between the categories of 'public', 'state', and 'private' ceremony, and their implications, one very 'visible' aspect of ceremonial elaboration at the grander royal weddings was the participation of heralds. For medieval England, Maurice Keen has observed that the heralds 'were the common accompaniment of such events as royal marriages' and other occasions.[20] Wagner summarized that before 1400 the evidence 'is scanty, merely establishing the presence of heralds on great occasions', but he observed that in about 1440 Nicholas Upton stated that 'heralds wear their coats of their masters' arms at their feasts and weddings'.[21] In Scotland, heralds had taken part in royal weddings since the reign of Malcolm IV (r. 1153–65) and received special payment for their participation at these ceremonies.[22]

There are at least two instances of heralds having had a particularly prominent role at weddings. For the wedding of Mary I and Philip of Spain in Winchester Cathedral in 1554, one account noted that 'after the holy Communion' four heralds stood at the steps of the altar and 'published', that is proclaimed, the titles of the king and queen in Latin, French and English.[23] This proclamation may have been due to the particularities of this event: through this marriage Prince Philip also became king of England.[24] There was a similar proclamation at the 1613 wedding of James I's daughter to the Count Palatine.[25] This wedding, too, had a strong political context. Finally, such a proclamation was still scheduled in a draft ceremonial for the wedding of Princess Anne and the Prince of Orange in 1734, but it was eventually not included.[26] While it was not heard at any royal wedding since 1613, such a proclamation has been – and still is – part of royal funerals.[27]

In 1765, Antoine Pyron du Martre, a French Master at Eton College, under the pseudonym of Mark Anthony Porny published his *Elements of Heraldry*, in which he explained that 'the business of Heralds' included 'To marshal and order all Royal Cavalcades, Ceremonies at Coronations, Installations, Creations, &c. […] under the authority of the Earl-Marshal.'[28] While this did not explicitly refer to weddings, in 1776, Nathan Bailey detailed in his *New Universal English Dictionary* that the 'office' of the heralds included their assistance 'at the ceremonies of

---

[19] https://www.gov.uk/government/news/new-measures-allow-couples-to-tie-the-knot-at-any-time (accessed on 5 July 2021). I am grateful to Catherine Robinson for drawing my attention to this legal regulation.

[20] Maurice Keen, 'Introduction', in *Heraldry, Pageantry and Social Display in Medieval England*, ed. by Peter Coss and Maurice Keen (Woodbridge: The Boydell Press, 2002), pp. 1–16, here p. 12. The heralds at weddings are mentioned in several of the chapters in this collection.

[21] Anthony Richard Wagner, *Heralds and Ancestors* (London: British Museum Publications, 1978), p. 68.

[22] See George Seton, *The Law and Practice of Heraldry in Scotland* (Edinburgh: Edmonston and Douglas 1863), p. 164.

[23] See C.V. Malfatti (ed.), *The Accession, Coronation and Marriage of Mary Tudor as Related by Four Manuscripts of the Escorial* (Barcelona: Sociedad Alianza de Artes Gráficas and Ricardo Fontá, 1956), pp. 3–61: 'Events of the Kingdom of England […] as related by Monsignor G.F. Commendone', with the account of the wedding on pp. 51–60, here p. 60. For Mary I's wedding see also Duncan, passim and *Llp MS 285*, fols 39ᵛ–40ʳ.

[24] For wider considerations of this wedding see Judith M. Richards, 'Mary Tudor as "Sole Quene"?: Gendering Tudor Monarchy', *The Historical Journal,* 40:4 (December 1997), pp. 895–934.

[25] Details below, in Chapter 2.

[26] Fragmentary draft ceremonial for the 1734 wedding, in *Lca Miscell: Coll: By Anstis*, in about the middle of the unfoliated volume, p. [2] of this (transcr. in Appendix B 3.1).

[27] See Range, *BRSF*, esp. pp. 32–33.

[28] Mark Anthony Porny, *The Elements of Heraldry: Containing a Clear Definition, and Concise Historical Account of that Ancient, Useful, and Entertaining Science* […] (London: Printed for J. Newbery, 1765), entry for 'Herald' [the volume does not have page numbers].

coronations, christenings, weddings and funerals of princes'.[29] This was taken on in the 1795 revised and extended edition of Porny's *Elements of Heraldry*, where the entry for 'Herald' listed that 'the business of heralds with us is, to marshal, order, and conduct all royal cavalcades, ceremonies at coronations, royal marriages, installations, creations of dukes [...] under the authority of the Earl-Marshal, to whom they are subservient'.[30] Similarly, the entry for 'Earl Marshal', in this edition explained that 'at present, his office consists chiefly in marshalling the ceremony at the proclamation, and coronation of kings, their marriages, funerals festivals, &c.' At least the reference to the Earl Marshal's and the heralds' responsibility at 'marriages', however, needs to be read in a more limited way. The organization of the ceremonies at royal weddings clearly fell into the Lord Chamberlain's area. For the 1734 wedding, Stephen Martin Leake, at the time Norroy King of Arms and later Garter King of Arms, had distinctly pointed out:

> N.B. the Officers of Arms [that is, the heralds] had no directions to place any person in the Chapel, & therefore they left them to be placed by the Lo Chamberlain's Officers.[31]

While the heralds were not directly responsible for anything 'in the Chapel', throughout the eighteenth century, the heralds' main task at royal weddings appears to have been the marshalling, and even arranging of the processions to and from the venue. For the 1797 wedding of Princess Charlotte, Sir Stephen Cottrell, Assistant Master of the Ceremonies, noted that 'The scheme of the Procession was made out as usual, I believe, by Garter King at Arms'.[32] Two years previously, at the wedding of the Prince of Wales in 1795, the bride's procession to the Chapel Royal had been led by the Lord Chamberlain with his wand of office and two heralds, as depicted in a contemporary print (Illustration 1.1). Cottrell then recorded that, after the bride's procession to the Chapel Royal,

> The Lord Chamberlain and Vice Chamberlain, with a Herald, returned to attend the Bridegroom; the Senior Herald remaining in the Chapel, to conduct the several Persons to their respective Places.[33]

Thus, the heralds' task at royal weddings encompassed not only the planning, marshalling, and leading of the (outdoor) processions. Rather, they also functioned more generally as ushers in the chapel where the wedding took place – and this is perhaps what had been expected of them at the 1734 wedding, leading to Leake's above-cited remark.

Heralds were understood as literally heralding royalty: for Queen Victoria's wedding in 1840, one report observed in a picturesque way that near the beginning of the entrance processions 'some of the heralds, in their gorgeous tabards, gave evidence of the coming presence of royalty'.[34] Several such heralds wearing tabards can be seen in one of the many contemporary prints depicting the scene in the Chapel Royal – in this case also showing Garter King of Arms wearing his coronet and carrying his sceptre (Illustration 1.2). Referring to the overall splendour of the occasion, one account commented on the heralds' presence at this wedding with a rather cutting undertone:

---

[29] N[athan] Bailey, *The New Universal English Dictionary* [...], 7th edn (London: Printed for William Cavell, 1776), p. 15.

[30] This and the following M[arc]A[nthony] Porny, *The Elements of Heraldry* [...], 5th edn, 'with considerable alterations and additions' (London: Printed for G. G. and J. Robinson [...], 1795), no page numbers.

[31] 'The Ceremonial of the Marriage of William Prince of Orange, with the Princess Royal of Great Britain, Anne, Eldest daughter of his Majesty King George the 2.d At St James's, on thursday the 14th March 1733/4', in *Lca S.M.L. 30* (Leake, 'Ceremonials', vol. 3), pp. 37–42, here p. 41.

[32] *Lna LC 5/5*, p. 67.

[33] *Lna LC 5/6*. This volume also includes a manuscript ceremonial of the 1795 wedding; here p. 2 of this. For the individual processions see the following chapters.

[34] 'Marriage of Her Majesty with Prince Albert of Saxe Coburg and Gotha, on Monday', *Niles' National Register*, 5th series, vol. 8, no. 3 (21 March 1840), pp. 1 and 34–37, here p. 35.

1—Setting the Scene

Illustration 1.1: 'The Grand Procession from the Drawing Room to the Chapel Royal St. James's', mezzotint with etching and hand-colouring (Haines & Son, 1795), *Royal Collection, RCIN 605192*, Royal Collection Trust / © Her Majesty Queen Elizabeth II 2021.

Garter King-of-Arms, with all his heraldic pomp and pride, and the head of his college, the Earl Marshal, the Duke of Norfolk, passed unnoticed in the throng.[35]

In an undated memorandum preserved in the College of Arms, Charles George Young, Garter King of Arms from 1842 until 1869, pointed out that heralds had no responsibility at weddings – based on the aforementioned fact that weddings were under the direction of the Lord Chamberlain, and not the Earl Marshal.[36] Nevertheless, the reference to heralds' duties at royal weddings was included in heraldic writings up to at least the 1860s.[37] In fact, a copy of the printed ceremonial for the 1858 wedding of Princess Victoria preserved in the College of Arms includes many manuscript corrections, possibly indicating the heralds' involvement in the organization of the event.[38]

One report of this wedding, in a poetical but probably not completely unjustified way, referred to 'the ceremonial, as arranged by chamberlains and heralds', as though they had been

---

[35] 'The Queen's Marriage', *The Examiner*, 16 February 1840, p. 105.

[36] *Lca Marriages & Baptisms of the Royal Family* (C.G.Y. 893). For a full transcription see Appendix B 1.1.

[37] See, for instance, *The Art of Heraldry; Explaining the Origin and Use of Arms and Armorial Bearings* […] (Harding & King, 1834), p. 66; and Thomas Wright, *The Royal Dictionary-Cyclopædia, for Universal Reference* […], 5 vols (London: The London Printing and Publishing Company, [1862–67]), vol. 3: H to M, p. 77: entry for 'Herald'.

[38] *Lca Ceremonials (printed), Loose Papers*, no 12. This looks like a draft of the text eventually published in the *London Gazette*, with corrections. For printed ceremonials in general see below.

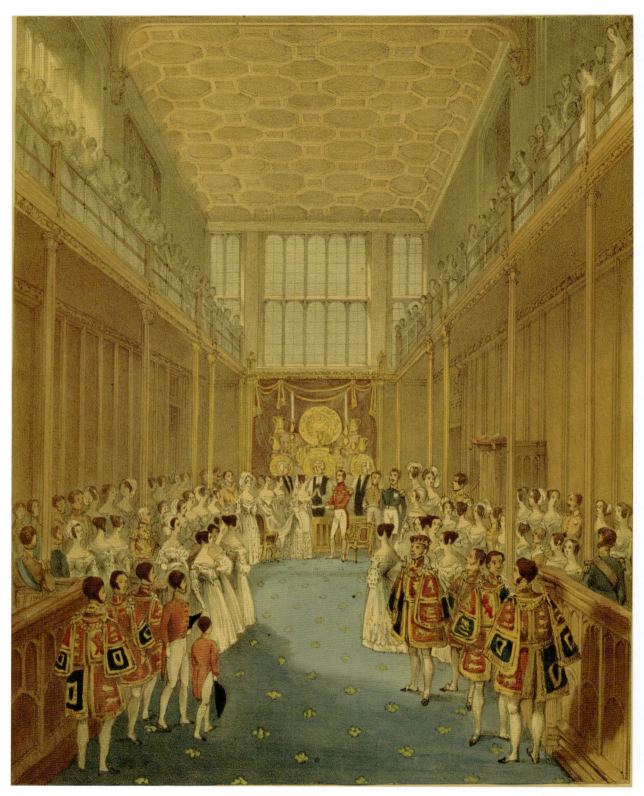

Illustration 1.2: 'The Marriage of Her Majesty Queen Victoria, with his Royal Highness Prince Albert of Saxe Coburg and Gotha […]', 'Printed by Leferre, Newman St.' (London: Published by William Spooner, [1840]), *British Museum, 1871,0812.5360* © The Trustees of the British Museum.

1—Setting the Scene

responsible in equal parts.[39] The prominent role of the heralds at this and the following weddings remained clearly apparent, as the bride was still 'preceded by Norroy and Clarenceux Kings of Arms'.[40] The ceremonials for Victorian royal weddings (and also christenings, for instance) regularly mention heralds.[41]

It is noteworthy that the aforementioned examples from heraldic tracts refer merely to 'royal' weddings ('of princes'), but not to weddings of the aristocracy. For earlier centuries, Robert Tittler has observed that heralds generally 'presided at the weddings and funerals of armigerous families [that is, families who bear arms], so as to keep straight the implications of those generational comings and goings for family pedigrees'.[42] More straightforwardly, Ruth A. Johnston has pointed out that heralds

> needed to witness and register aristocratic weddings because, when the bride and groom both inherited coats of arms, their children would inherit a combination coat of arms with both designs quartered.[43]

However, heralds are not known to have taken part at any aristocratic wedding since the early-modern period.

Regarding, the participation of the heralds at British royal weddings it is striking that only the *English* heralds were involved. It is important to note that England and Scotland have retained entirely independent systems of heraldry and heralds (with the English College of Arms also looking after Wales and Ireland, now Northern Ireland respectively). At the wedding of Princess Anne in 1734, the head of the Scottish heralds took part: the aforementioned Stephen Martin Leake, then Norroy King of Arms, noted 'The Officers who attended', adding 'And Lyon King of Arms of Scotland who was not in the Ceremonials.'[44] This appears to have been the only instance of a Scottish herald taking part in a London royal wedding. Indeed, in another account of this ceremony, Leake commented:

> Lyon King of Arms proceeding with Garter as one Officer was a great absurdity and ought not to have been tamely Submitted to [added above, in same hand: 'not being either in the written or Printed Ceremonial in the Gazette'] It was indeed allowed at the Coronation But this Establisht it To the Dishonour of his Office and the English Nation. A point of honour gaind by the Scotch w[hich] the Articles of Union never intended.[45]

The last royal weddings at which the heralds are reported to have taken part were those of Prince George, Duke of York and Princess Victoria Mary of Teck – the later George V and Queen Mary – and of his sister Princess Maud with Prince Christian of Denmark – later King Haakon VII and Queen Maud of Norway – in 1893 and 1896, respectively.

---

[39] 'The Marriage of The Princess Royal', *Times*, 26 January 1858, pp. 7–9, here p. 8. This was reproduced, without title, in *Gentleman's Magazine*, 204/v. 4 new series (1858), pp. 203–04, here p. 204.

[40] 'Marriage of The Princess Royal', in *Lca Funerals, Ceremonials, 1843–1861*, pp. 85–101, here pp. 97–99. See also 'The Ceremony and Dresses at the Royal Nuptials', *The London Journal, and Weekly Record of Literature, Science, and Art*, 6 March 1858, pp. 5–6, here p. 6.

[41] See, for instance, those collected in *Lbl Add MS 41777*.

[42] Robert Tittler, *Portraits, Painters, and Publics in Provincial England, 1540–1640* (Oxford: Oxford University Press, 2012), p. 104.

[43] Ruth A. Johnston, *All Things Medieval: An Encyclopedia of the Medieval World*, vol. 1: A–I (Santa Barbara, CA: ABC-CLIO, 2011), p. 335.

[44] *Lca S.M.L. 30*, p. 42.

[45] *Lca S.M.L. 44* (Leake, 'Heraldic Annals', vol. 1), pp. 135–40, here p. 140. See also the account in another of Leake's manuscripts: *Lca S.M.L. 65* (Leake, 'Heraldo Memoriale', vol. 2), pp. 78–80.

British Royal Weddings

The Venue

There is no fixed venue for royal weddings – such as there is Westminster Abbey for coronations. In the later seventeenth and then in the early nineteenth century, the rather low-key, unceremonious royal weddings of the time took place in bedchambers and drawing rooms, respectively – not in a religious building. Yet, these aside, from the early seventeenth to the mid-nineteenth century, most royal weddings took place in one of the royal chapels: first at Whitehall Palace and then at St James's Palace, as the monarch's official London residences. From 1863, this was joined by other venues, especially St George's Chapel, Windsor, but also the private chapels at Buckingham Palace and Windsor Castle, and occasionally other, more unusual venues for some particular weddings.

The individual arguments for the choice of venue at each wedding will be discussed in some detail in the following chapters. Overall, this choice seems to have been motivated by tradition as much as by personal preferences, as approved by the monarch. There is one intriguing general fact to note: as in other monarchies, British royal bridegrooms have very rarely followed a custom that is followed by many other couples – not many royal bridegrooms have married where the bride is from. The most notable exceptions were probably James VI/I, who travelled to Oslo in 1596 to marry his Danish bride in person, then Charles I who married the French Princess Henrietta Maria in Paris in 1625, and finally Prince Alfred who married the Russian Grand Duchess Maria Alexandrovna in St Petersburg in 1874.

The Ceremonial

Codified Ceremonial

The details of the service apart, the ceremonial proceedings of royal weddings were stipulated in a specially prepared ceremonial. For the earlier weddings, these survive – if at all – merely in manuscript form. In the earlier eighteenth century, the ceremonial for royal weddings was usually reproduced in the *London Gazette*; but it does not appear to have been printed separately before 1795.[46] Once these ceremonials were printed separately, they were probably intended mainly for those involved in arranging and regulating the events – such as the heralds – as much as for spectators. This is indicatd by their decoration with printed ornaments and later also with lavish bindings. For the wedding of Princess Victoria in 1858, it is documented that guests attending the service were sent their ticket together with a copy of the ceremonial.[47] It was from the wedding of Queen Victoria's cousin, Princess Augusta of Cambridge in 1843 onwards that there were two versions of the printed ceremonial: a 'Ceremonial to Be Observed', written in the future tense as those before – and also a 'Ceremonial Observed', written in the past tense.

The copies in the past tense, which are often bound more elaborately, may have served as memorabilia: for the wedding of Princess Louise of Wales in 1889, for instance, the surviving records include a list of 'Distribution of Past Ceremonials'.[48] This commemorative use of ceremonials seems to have been similar at other royal events: a printed copy of the ceremonial for the 1872 thanksgiving service at St Paul's on the Prince of Wales's recovery from illness survives with the

---

[46] For a listing of all the printed ceremonials and their sources see the List of Sources below, Section 1.

[47] See the 'specimen' of admission tickets with a sample accompanying letter by the Lord Chamberlain and a copy of the printed ceremonial in *Wra RA F&V/WED/1858*.

[48] Included in *Lna LC 2/120*.

1—Setting the Scene

manuscript annotation that it was 'prepared after the Event' and was the 'same as Gazetted'.[49] There seems to have been a curious gap in the production of these double ceremonials in present and in future tense: for the three weddings between 1871 and 1889 all the known ceremonials are written in the past tense. From 1889 onwards, however, again two versions of the ceremonial survive. The production of these did not end until the early twentieth century.

In 1913, after the wedding of Prince Arthur of Connaught and the Duchess of Fife, the correspondent of the *Illustrated London News* referred to the specially produced ceremonial and in the next sentence pointed out 'The official arrangements were, of course, followed.'[50] While it is not certain that the ceremonials were always followed as a matter 'of course' in all the details, due to their official nature they are overall a reliable guide – even if their accuracy in recording what actually happened at the ceremonies may certainly vary to some degrees.

Processions

In pre-mass-media times, especially in the pre-television age, the processions to (and from) weddings were the one component of the event that the largest number of people could enjoy. Coronations up to 1661 were preceded by lavish processions through London and up to 1821 they also featured foot processions from Westminster Hall to the Abbey and back; similarly, big public funerals also included processions to Westminster Abbey or St Paul's Cathedral. Weddings, however, were rather unspectacular in this respect: there were no fully public processions until the wedding of Queen Victoria in 1840, since when there usually have been distinct carriage processions to and from the wedding venue. Nonetheless, especially in the eighteenth century, the elaborate walking processions to the venue of the wedding were witnessed by a reatively large number of invited guests and were one of the most noted ceremonies of royal weddings. It was here that participants' and spectators' status became most apparent, with the minutely regulated proceedings highlighting important hierarchies.

Notably, there was not just one long continuous procession – rather there were three distinct processions, or 'three Divisions', as Leake worded it in an account of the 1734 wedding of Princess Anne.[51] There were separate processions for the bridegroom, for the bride, and finally for the king (with his queen). These processions also included the peers of the realm, walking before the king, and the peeresses in the bride's procession.[52] Once the first procession, of the bridegroom, had arrived in the chapel, the Lord Chamberlain and Vice-Chamberlain returned back to accompany the bride's procession and then did the same for the king and queen (who came in one procession, one walking behind the other). A change in the order of the processions came only after the wedding of Queen Victoria in 1840, who was both bride and monarch and therefore entered last. In the following weddings she forfeited her right of precedence and since then the bride has been the last to enter. Generally, it was since the Victorian era that the entrance processions inside the building received more attention, at least in the reports and records.

In common perception, if not in fact, all the other entrance processions have received far less attention than the entrance of the bride. In 1863, at the wedding of the future Edward VII and Queen Alexandra, the bridal procession was perceived as one of the core moments of

---

[49] *Ceremonial: Thanksgiving at St. Paul's Cathedral, 27th February, 1872*, copy in *Lna LC 2/81*.

[50] 'From Sketches by our Special Artist at the Ceremony: The Royal Wedding at St. James's Palace. Drawn by A. C. Michael from Sketches by Frédéric de Haenen, our Special Artist at the Wedding Ceremony in the Chapel Royal', *ILN*, 18 October 1913, pp. 616–17, picture caption.

[51] *Lca S.M.L. 65*, pp. 78–80, here p. 80.

[52] See, for instance, the respective accounts in the *London Gazette*.

British Royal Weddings

the ceremony, with one account summarizing that the bride's entrance 'of course, was the leading point of interest in the ceremonial of the day'.[53] Similarly, in 1871, an account of the wedding
of Queen Victoria's daughter Princess Louise referred to the entrance of 'the fair central group
of all this grandeur and state, the bride and bridesmaids'.[54] For the 1896 wedding of Princess
Maud, the *Times* implied that royal weddings and non-royal weddings were no different in this
respect by explaining that 'here, as elsewhere, the bride's procession was the feature to which
every one attached the most importance'.[55]

While the entrance of the bride gained ever more attention, that of the bridegroom became less and less distinct. The processions when leaving the chapel have also seen some change.
Although it appears that the bridal couple has always been the first to leave, before the rest of
their families, the newly-weds did not always walk together, next to each other. This, incidentally,
may have matched with English folk traditions.[56] In 1761, Queen Charlotte still walked behind
her new husband, George III, when they left the Chapel Royal, as Leake recorded.[57] At the
great, ceremonial occasions of state, royal couples did generally not walk together. Indeed, at
coronations, they have walked separately up to the most recent one in 1953. From a twenty-
first century point of view, however, it seems striking to observe such a detail at a wedding,
which is precisely the celebration and formal sanction of a couple's union. The detail of walking
together was still discussed for Queen Victoria and Prince Albert's wedding in 1840: in the end,
they did walk together, and the issue was apparently not discussed thereafter.

The Wedding Service: The Clergy

Similar to the variability of the venue, it is not 'fixed' which cleric is to marry royalty. The
Archbishop of Canterbury holds the right to crown the monarch, but this does not mean an
automatic right to officiate at other royal occasions. During the eighteenth century, royal funerals, for instance, were the prerogative of the Dean of Westminster Abbey, where they took
place; and the first two major royal weddings of the eighteenth century, in 1734 and 1736, were
conducted by the Bishop of London, as Dean of the Chapel Royal, where these took place.
However, after the Prince of Wales's wedding in 1795, Beilby Porteus, Bishop of London and
Dean of the Chapel Royal wrote a 'Memorandum' on the issue of who was to officiate at
royal weddings.[58] Porteus considered historical precedents back to the early seventeenth century, and while he noted that the 1734 and 1736 weddings had been conducted by Edmund
Gibson, Bishop of London and Dean of the Chapel Royal, he also pointed out that 'In both
these instances, ABp Wake was infirm & incapable of doing any Duty.'[59] By the time of the
next royal wedding, that of Princess Mary in 1740, William Wake, the Archbishop of Canterbury,
was dead and a dispute arose between his successor John Potter and Gibson, who was still in

---

[53] *A Chapter from the History of England in the Twenty-sixth Year of the Reign of our Blessed Sovereign Lady Queen Victoria, March 1863* (London: Emily Faithfull, 1863), p. 88.

[54] Anonymous, quoted in 'Lady Elvey', *Life and Reminiscences of George J. Elvey* […] *Late Organist to H. M. Queen Vic-toria, and Forty-seven Years Organist of St. George's Chapel, Windsor* (London: Sampson Low, Marston & Company, Ltd, 1894), p. 206.

[55] 'The Royal Wedding', *Times*, 23 July 1896, pp. 5–6, here p. 5.

[56] See Ann Monsarrat, *And the Bride Wore …: The Story of the White Wedding* (London: Gentry Books, 1973), p. 34.

[57] *Lca S.M.L. 65*, p. 295 (quoted in Chapter 4, with fn. 58).

[58] 'Memorandum / Concerning the Marriage of the Prince of Wales / To the Princess of Brunswick / In his Maj-esty's Chapel Royal / att St James's / April. 8. 1795.', in *Llp Fulham Papers Porteus 17*, fols. 214ʳ–217ʳ.

[59] *Llp Fulham Papers Porteus 17*, f. 215ᵛ.

1—Setting the Scene

office.[60] Lord Hervey, in 1740 Vice-Chamberlain of the Household and then Lord Privy Seal, in his *Memoirs* noted sarcastically:

> Both these prelates claimed the honour of officiating, and had produced a great deal of Churchlearned rubbish to support their pretensions.[61]

Archbishop Potter's actual arguments are well documented in a small hand-written volume, preserved at Lambeth Palace.[62] On over thirty pages, the archbishop shows and discusses several historical precedents that support his claim to lead the ceremony but he also concedes that, after all, the king may chose whatever cleric he wishes to officiate at such royal occasions. In the end, Archbishop Potter was appointed and Gibson did not even attend: 'The Bishop of London was absent', as Hervey recorded.[63] Porteus later suggested: 'It is imagined that He was offended He did not perform the Ceremony'.[64] This is also indicated in an account of the three weddings of the children of George II that is included among Archbishop Secker's papers, compiled in preparation of the 1761 wedding of George III:

> The name of the Bishop of London, Dean of the Chapel, is not amongst the witnesses. And he was not present; probably staying away because the Archbishop was appointed to perform the Service.[65]

Hervey's records apart, the 'elevation', with a higher-ranking cleric at the 1740 wedding does not seem to have been more widely remarked upon. The reason could be that this particular wedding was merely a ceremony by proxy, with the actual wedding vows to follow in a service in the princess's future home-town. As Hervey explained, it was 'said in the Cabinet' that this

> avoided a decision in the dispute between the Archbishop and the Bishop of London, since a Secretary of State, and not an ecclesiastic, would be to officiate at the ceremony of these espousals in the Chapel.[66]

All the same, Hervey emphasized:

> […] but as the Archbishop, at the end of the ceremony, was to pronounce the benediction and to bless the nuptials, after making a Latin speech, I think it did manifestly decide the episcopal dispute, and in favour of the Archbishop.

Nonetheless, the 'episcopal dispute' was not permanently decided. At the wedding of George III in September 1761, the issue arose again. The Bishop of London and Dean of the Chapel Royal, Thomas Sherlock had died only a few weeks previously, on 18 July 1761. With regarding to the wedding, *Owen's Weekly Chronicle* reported:

> We hear for certain there will be no Bishop of London appointed until after the marriage of our most gracious Sovereign; for this reason, the present Archbishop of Canterbury [who] had the honour of baptizing his Majesty, is also intended of having the high honour of marrying him to his intended royal Consort; which honour would be claimed as a matter of right by the prelate who should otherwise happen to be Bishop of London.[67]

---

[60] See Donald Burrows, *Handel and the English Chapel Royal* (Oxford: Oxford University Press, 2005) [hereinafter *HECR*], p. 355, fn. 51, who refers to Lord Hervey (see the following fn.).

[61] John Lord Hervey, *Some Materials towards Memoirs of the Reign of King George II*, ed. by Romney Sedgwick, 3 vols, continuously paginated (London: Eyre and Spottiswoode, 1931; reprint New York: AMS Press, 1970), III, p. 930.

[62] *Llp MS 887*: Precedence in the Chapel Royal (1740).

[63] Hervey, *Some Materials*, III, p. 932.

[64] *Llp Fulham Papers Porteus 17*, fol. 215ᵛ.

[65] *Llp MS 1130*, I, no. 46 (fols 92ʳ–92ᵛ), here fol. 92ᵛ.

[66] This and the following Hervey, *Some Materials*, III, p. 932.

[67] *OWC,* 22–26 August 1761, p. 279.

British Royal Weddings

The 'present Archbishop of Canterbury' was Thomas Secker, and he recorded the details of his appointment for the wedding:

> The King said to the Duke of Devonshire, Lord Chamberlain, that as the Bp of London, Dean of the Chapel, was dead, & his place vacant, he had Thoughts of being married by the Bishop of Winchester, his Preceptor. The Duke told his majesty, that he believed the performance of that Office belonged to the Archbishop of Canterbury and soon after he acquainted me with what had passed. I put into his Hands the little Book in the MS Library, which contains the Dispute between ABp Potter & Bishop Gibson on a similar Occasion: and he shewed it to the King, or told him the Contents of it; with which he was satisfied.[68]

Yet, the uncertainty continued. In relation to the 1795 wedding of the Prince of Wales, Bishop Porteus observed in his aforementioned 'Memorandum':

> It was thought at the time by most people that as this marriage was celebrated in the Chapel Royal St James's (of which I was Dean) the ceremony was to be performed by me, especially as it was known that the Kings Father, when Prince of Wales [in 1736] was married by Bishop Gibson the Dean of the Chapels Royal. But I knew on the contrary that the King himself [George III] was married by Archbishop Secker, that it was at least doubtful which way the Precedent went upon the whole & that after all the King himself might undoubtedly appoint whomever he pleaset [sic] for this Office.[69]

Nevertheless, referring to Secker' officiating at George III's wedding, Porteus concluded:

> This instance therefore seems to decide the weight of Precedents in favour of the Archbishop, & it is now strengthend by his having married the Prince of Wales in 1795. Still however there being Precedents both ways, The King will notably always chuse either[:] the Bp or the Dean, just as he happens to be disposed at the moment. For there seems to be no absolute claim on either Side; though the Abp's pretensions appear to be best-founded.[70]

At least in public perception, however, the Archbishop of Canterbury seems to have established his right to perform royal wedding services. In relation to the wedding of Princess Charlotte in 1797, this was particularly emphasized, for instance, in the reporting of the *True Briton*:

> The ceremony will, of course, be performed by the ARCHBISHOP of CANTERBURY, assisted by the BISHOP of LONDON.[71]

Overall, since 1740 almost all major royal weddings have been conducted by the Archbishop of Canterbury – and there seem not to have been any notable discussions on the issue since the late eighteenth century. All the same, as will be seen, the overall responsibility for the preparation of the services seems usually to have rested with the cleric of the host venue.

The Wedding Service: The Liturgy

For the wedding of Henry VIII and Anne of Cleves in 1540, Retha Warnicke suggested that Archbishop Cranmer had then

> probably used the Sarum Rite for the service, since it was the one on which he later based the liturgy for the Edwardian Prayer Books; he also used it for Katherine Parr's wedding in 1543.[72]

---

[68] *Llp MS 1130*, I, no. 48 (fol. 96). This 'little Book' may have been *Llp MS 887* (mentioned in fn. 62, above).

[69] *Llp Fulham Papers Porteus 17*, fol. 215ʳ.

[70] *Llp Fulham Papers Porteus 17*, fol. 217ʳ.

[71] 'Royal Nuptials', *True Briton* 18 May 1797, p. [2].

[72] Retha M. Warnicke, *The Marrying of Anne of Cleves: Royal Protocol in Early Modern England* (Cambridge: Cambridge University Press, 2000), p. 157.

1—Setting the Scene

The 'Sarum Rite', or 'Use', refers to a medieval English variant of the Roman (Catholic) rite, which had originated at Salisbury.[73] The 'Edwardian Prayer Books' refers to the first and second Book of Common Prayer from 1549 and 1552. The Prayer Book included a rather short and straightforward service of 'Solemnization of Matrimony' and this service did not change much throughout the different Prayer Book versions, from 1549 up to 1662 (the most recent one to date).[74] On the occasion of the wedding of Princess Louise in 1871, one account aptly summarized that 'Nothing could be plainer than the form of the service', explaining that there is 'not a vestige of Ritualism in it all'.[75] Indeed, the Prayer Book rite is not that much of a service but predominantly an administrative, effectively legal act – rather compact and short. For the 1896 wedding of Princess Maud of Wales and Prince Charles of Denmark, one report summarized befittingly: 'Brief as it is impressive, it seemed quickly over.'[76] Very broadly speaking, the Prayer Book wedding rite consists of two main portions:

- Administration of the wedding vows
- Prayers for and blessing of the newly-weds

At the beginning, the priest explains the purpose of Christian marriage, which is followed by his confirming that there is no legal impediment against the suggested union, leading into the administration of the couple's declarations and the marriage vows – in the church, but not yet at the altar. After a blessing for the couple, and during the psalm, the minister and the couple move to the altar. While the 1549 Prayer Book ambiguously stipulates that an undefined 'they' shall go into the quire, the fact that the newly-wed couple is also to go to the altar is implied by the instruction that the couple are to be kneeling there once the psalm has ended. The minister begins the so-called 'Lesser Litany' (the 'Kyrie', as responsorial) and Lord's Prayer as in morning prayer and evensong, followed by a set of special Wedding Responses and then more prayers and another blessing for the newly-weds.[77] Finally, at the end of the ceremony, there is meant to be a sermon 'declaring the duties of Man and Wife' – or alternatively a prescribed text to the same effect, often called 'the exhortation'. The order of service in the 1662 Book of Common Prayer, the only authoritative one up to the earlier twentieth century, can be summarized in the following scheme:

- Entrance into the church (no particular order mentioned: eventually the bride and bridegroom stand together)
- Opening, with explanation of purpose of Christian marriage
- Wedding vows, prayers and blessing of the newly-weds (in the church, but not yet at the altar)
- Minister and newly-weds go to the altar; during this: Psalm
- Couple kneeling at the altar, minister begins the Lesser Litany, Lord's Prayer, Responses
- Prayers for and blessing of the newly-weds
- Sermon or reading of a prescribed text detailing the duties of husband and wife

---

[73] See Philip Baxter, *Sarum Use: The Ancient Customs of Salisbury* (Reading: Spire Books, 2008).

[74] For the different versions see Brian Cummings (ed.), *The Book of Common Prayer: The Texts of 1549, 1559, and 1662* (Oxford: Oxford University Press, 2011); and Joseph Ketley (ed.), *The Two Liturgies A.D. 1549 and A.D. 1552: With Other Documents Set Forth by Authority in the Reign of King Edward VI* (Cambridge: Cambridge University Press, 1844). All the different texts are also reproduced on the website of the Church of England, http://justus.anglican.org/resources/bcp/england.htm (accessed on 31 August 2021).

[75] [3rd correspondent], 'Marriage of The Princess Louise and Marquis of Lorn', *Scotsman*, 22 March 1871, p. 2.

[76] 'The Marriage of Princess Maud of Wales and Prince Charles of Denmark at Buckingham Palace', *ILN: Royal Wedding Number*, 29 July 1896, pp. 2–8, here p. 4.

[77] For the Lesser Litany see still Evan Daniel, *The Prayer-Book: Its History, Language, and Contents* (London: William Wells Gardner, 1877), p. 145.

British Royal Weddings

None of the versions of the Prayer Book stipulates a final blessing for the whole congregation. Nevertheless, this appears to have been included customarily for a long time. Notably, many accounts of weddings use the terms 'blessing' and 'benediction' indifferently, with either term referring to the blessings of the couple alone and/or the blessing of the whole of the congregation at the end. All the same, some accounts use 'first' and 'second' blessing for these, even though there are already two blessings just for the couple.

Phillip Tovey has pointed out that Archbishop Cranmer for the marriage service 'assumed a eucharistic setting and so had no ministry of the word'.[78] Indeed, the 1549 first Edwardine Prayer Book stipulated that 'The newe maried persones (the same daye of their mariage) must receive the holy communion.' This requirement was kept in the following revised versions of the Prayer Book, but it was somewhat 'softened down' in the 1662 version to suggest more liberally that 'the new-married persons should receive holy Communion at the time of their Marriage, or at the first opportunity after their Marriage'. The celebration of Holy Communion does not seem to have been included at any royal wedding since that of Mary I and Philip of Spain in 1554.[79] Although scheduled for the 1641 wedding of Princess Mary, daughter of Charles I, and Prince William of Orange, it was eventually omitted.

At the same time, there was an intriguing, similar ceremony. Ivan Day has summarized that the sharing of specially brought wine and bread, or cake was an ancient custom at weddings, dating from pre-Reformation times.[80] This custom has been mostly neglected by modern scholars.[81] However, it was included by the late-Georgian writers John Brand and Henry Ellis in their comprehensive *Observations on Popular Antiquities* that received several editions and revisions throughout the nineteenth century.[82] They still provide the best overview:

> This custom is enjoined in the Hereford Missal. By the Sarum Missal it is directed that the Sops immersed in this Wine, as well as the liquor itself, and the cup that contained it, should be blessed by the Priest. / The beverage used on this occasion was to be drunk by the Bride and Bridegroom and the rest of the company. [...] The pieces of Cake, or Wafers, that appear to have been immersed in the Wine on this occasion, were properly called Sops, and doubtless gave name to the Flower named 'Sops in Wine.'

Some decades later, Edward Wood – who otherwise referred heavily to Brand and Ellis – added that this custom of taking wine and bread had been 'derived by the English from their Gothic ancestors'.[83] Brand and Ellis, and then Wood, referred in particular to the royal weddings of Mary I and Philip of Spain in 1554 and that of Princess Elizabeth, daughter of James VI/I, and the Count Palatine in 1613. Indeed, a perhaps contemporary account of the 1554 wedding recorded very clearly that the couple after the wedding vows withdrew into

---

[78] Phillip Tovey, 'Emerging Models of Blessing, Marriage Theology and Inculturation in Anglican Weddings', in *Anglican Marriage Rites: A Symposium*, ed. by Kenneth W. Stevenson, Thomas Cooper, and Phillip Tovey, 'Joint Liturgical Studies', 71 (Norwich: Hymns Ancient and Modern, 2011), pp. 49–65, here p. 51.

[79] See fn. 23 above.

[80] Ivan Day, 'Bridecup and Cake: The Ceremonial Food and Drink of the Bridal Procession', in *Food and the Rites of Passage*, ed. by Laura Mason (Totnes: Prospect Books, 2002), pp. 33–61, here esp. 37 and 45.

[81] For 'the ceremonial drinking in the church that sometimes followed' a wedding, see Paul Jennings, *A History of Drink and the English, 1500-2000* (Routledge/Taylor & Francis, 2016), p. 103. Unfortunately, Jennings does not elaborate on this.

[82] John Brand and Henry Ellis, *Observations on Popular Antiquities: Chiefly Illustrating the Origin of our Vulgar Customs, Ceremonies and Superstitions*, 2 vols, first published in 1813, reprinted in 'Cambridge Library Collection' (Cambridge: Cambridge University Press, 2011), II, pp. 63–64: 'Drinking Wine in the Church at Marriages'.

[83] Edward J. Wood, *The Wedding Day in All Ages and Countries* (London: Richard Bentley, 1869), here p. 181.

1—Setting the Scene

a 'Traverse in the Quier' and did not return 'tyll Maße was done at wch tyme, Wyne & Sopps were hallowed and delyuered to them bothe', immediately followed by the heralds' proclamation of their 'Styles in Latyne Frenche & Englishe'.[84] The 1613 wedding was the last to include this sharing of wine and wafers.

A sermon was included at the grander royal weddings up to the seventeenth century: notably at those in 1589, 1613, and 1641. After that, however, a sermon does not appear to have been included at royal weddings before the later nineteenth century. For the wedding of Princess Frederica of Hanover at Windsor in 1880, Queen Victoria recorded: 'The Bishop, gave a short & pretty address.'[85] Since then, such an 'address' has been included at most royal weddings.

For the earlier weddings, it would appear that simply copies of the Prayer Book were used at the ceremony. This seems to match with other such occasions: for royal and state funerals the 'Order for the Burial of the Dead' is also fixed in the Prayer Book and there was no need for it to be printed specially; the earliest instance for a printed order of service stems from as late as the funeral of Queen Victoria in 1902.[86] By contrast, for coronations, a special order of service had been printed since 1727.[87] However, it is worth remembering that the order of service for coronations is not codified in the Prayer Book and was, in fact, prepared for each coronation anew.

No specially produced order of service for a royal wedding is known before the 1797 wedding of Princess Charlotte and Prince Frederick-William of Württemberg, when it was also printed. The production of such orders of service, however, became a regular feature of royal weddings only from the 1858 wedding of the Princess Royal onwards. Yet, these specially produced orders of service were merely extracts from the Prayer Book, with their actual text not including details referring to a particular wedding (1797 had at least included the names). All the same, like the printed ceremonials, the printed orders of service may have had the dual function of being both practical and commemorative objects. In 1885, at the wedding of Princess Beatrice, an additional version of the order of service was produced with some elaborate initials and also personalized by including the full names of the couple; a copy of this, now in the archives of St George's, Windsor, has a note appended that 'This book was specially printed by command of The Queen as a Memento of the Marriage Service. ordered by RTD [Randall T. Davidson, Dean of Windsor] / from Rivingtons [the printers] / & p^d for by Privy / Purse'.[88] This confirms that the orders of service in general, like the ceremonials observed earlier, were clearly not mere purpose objects but decidedly souvenirs of the occasion.

The Signing of the Register

The signing of the register by the two wedding parties, the minister, and the witnesses is today an integral part of wedding proceedings. However, it was not included in wedding ceremonies until the 1753 Clandestine Marriages Act, also known as 'Lord Hardwicke's Marriage Act': up to

---

[84] 'The Mariadge of Queen Marie vnto / Phillip Prynce of Spayne Sonne of / Charles the .5. Emperour, in the Cathedrall / Churche of Wynchester vpon Wenesdaye / the 25th [corr. from '29?] of July 1554.', in *Llp MS 285*, fols 39^v–40^r, here fol. 40^r.

[85] *QVJ*, 24 April 1880.

[86] Range, *BRSF*, p. 26.

[87] See Matthias Range, *Music and Ceremonial at British Coronations: From James I to Elizabeth II* (Cambridge: Cambridge University Press, 2012) [hereinafter *MCBC*], p. 130.

[88] *The Form of Solemnisation of Matrimony. Whippingham Church, Thursday, July 23, 1885* ([London]: Printed for Rivingtons, Waterloo Place, [1885]). Copy in *Wsg XVII.43.3/1*.

then a simple 'verbal contract' had been the 'essense of a valid marriage'.[89] At those royal weddings after 1753 that took place in a chapel, the signing of the register was clearly separated and removed from the church ceremonies. At the wedding of Queen Victoria in 1840, the Bishop of London, as Dean of the Chapel Royal where the wedding took place, sent a note to the 'Commissioner of Woods & Forests' and this has an intriguing pencil annotation at the top:

> The Bishop mentioned also that an Inkstand & small table would be required for signing the Register which should be though[t] of.

Thus it appears that the signing of the register may at some point have been meant to be included in the ceremony in the Chapel. Yet, by the end of January, a 'very large Table for the Register covered with crimson cloth' was stipulated to be put up in the 'Throne Room'.[90] At this and all subsequent weddings, the signing took place not in the chapel or church, but back in the royal residence. In Victorian times, this signing was also called the 'Attestation', alluding to its mere confirmatory character (Illustration 1.3).[91]

For the 1885 wedding of Princess Beatrice in Whippingham Church, near Osborne House on the Isle of Wight, the *Times* noted

> The marriage register, instead of being, as usual, signed in the vestry of the church, was subsequently signed in the drawing-room of Osborne House.[92]

However, 'usual' here must refer to other weddings: at royal weddings at the time – and up to 1919 – the signing of the register was clearly independent and distinctly separate from the service, and took place back in the palace or royal residence. One notable, singular exception was the wedding of Princess Mary at the Chapel Royal in 1740, which did include a signing right within the service, before the final blessing. However, this was due to the special nature of this wedding: for, what was signed was not actually the register but a document attesting that the wedding had taken place by proxy.

Interestingly, in this respect tradition at the London court seems to have differed from continental customs, notably from that in France. An account of the wedding of Louis XV and Marie Leszczyńska in September 1725 – published in English in 1726 – had detailed that the signing of the register took place in the chapel, right in the middle of the ceremony: it occurred between the celebration of the mass with the 'Nuptial Benediction' and the singing of the Te Deum, still followed by a further blessing of the newly-weds and the archbishop's address.[93] In Britain, the signing of the register was never that closely incorporated into the religious service, and it does not seem to be known why it did not happen in the actual space where the service took place.

---

[89] For a more detailed discussion see David Lemmings, 'Marriage and the Law in the Eighteenth Century: Hardwicke's Marriage Act of 1753', *The Historical Journal*, vol. 39, no. 2 (1996), pp. 339–60, here p. 344. NB The act did not come into force until 25 March 1754 (as 26 Geo. II. c. 33).

[90] Note by the Bishop of London, 13 January 1840, and a list with 'Preparations for the Marriage of Her Majesty Queen Victoria', both in *Lna WORK 21/12/1*, fols 38 and 41.

[91] See also, for instance, the respective illustration 'The Attestation', in *The Authentic Representation of the Magnificent Marriage Procession and Ceremony of Her Most Gracious Majesty Queen Victoria with His Royal Highness Prince Albert of Saxe Coburg, Celebrated at the Chapel Royal, St. James's, February 10, 1840* (London: Published solely by Messrs. Fores [1840?]).

[92] 'Royal Wedding', *Times* (1885), p. 5, 2nd column. Same in 'The Marriage of Princess Beatrice', *ILN: Royal Wedding Number*, 27 July 1885, pp. 2–6, here p. 6.

[93] *An Exact Account of the Ceremonies Observed at the Marriage of His Most Christian Majesty Lewis XV. with the Princess Mary, Daughter of Stanislaus, Late King of Poland* [...] (London: Printed for Tho. Worrall, 1726), p. 55–56.

1—Setting the Scene

Music at Royal Weddings

For the sixteenth century, Ann Monsarrat suggests that music was generally a particularly prominent ingredient of weddings:

> From the time a Tudor bride left her house till the end of the boisterous bedding, a constant 'noyse of musicians' was the order of the day – and next morning she was awoken with a musical *reveille* beneath her window.[94]

There is, however, little detailed information on music at royal weddings, or indeed any weddings, before the eighteenth century.

The Prayer Book does not stipulate much music for the wedding service – the only music mentioned is the psalm after the wedding vows and blessing of the couple. This lack of specific music may be the explanation why the marriage service was not included in Merbecke's 1550 *Book of Common Prayer Noted*.[95] Nevertheless, the grander royal wedding services always seem

Illustration 1.3: 'The Signing of the Marriage Attestation Deed, March 10th 1863', chromolithograph by Robert Charles Dudley (1864), Plate 20 in William Howard Russell, *A Memorial of the Marriage of HRH Albert Edward Prince of Wales* [...] (London: Day and Son, [1864]), here from London, National Portrait Gallery D33999 © National Portrait Gallery, London.

---

[94] Ann Monsarrat, *And the Bride Wore*, p. 29. For the music at early-modern weddings in general see also Christopher Marsh, *Music and Society in Early Modern England* (Cambridge: Cambridge University Press, 2010), passim. Marsh mentions the music at wedding feasts only – but nothing on the church music.

[95] See John Eric Hunt, *Cranmer's First Litany, 1544, and Merbecke's Book of Common Prayer Noted, 1550* (London: Society for Promoting Christian Knowledge, 1939), which includes a facsimile.

to have included elaborate music, consisting of both instrumental music – on the organ or by a band – and choral music. The royal wedding music was usually organized by the musicians of the venue where the wedding took place. In addition to the actual service music, there was much music before and after the service proper.

Music at the Outdoor Processions

At the earlier weddings, the walking processions to the wedding service were prominently accompanied by music. The processions were headed by trumpets and drums, playing separately for each of the aforementioned 'three Divisions', or individual processions of the bridegroom, the bride, and the monarch. The music they played is not known and it is doubtful that this was anything specially composed; otherwise at least some music could be expected to have survived or been mentioned in reports or accounts. It was probably more fanfare-like music; for the eighteenth century possibly akin to the anonymous 'Grand Trumpeter March' from 'around 1725' (Figure 1.1).[96]

The general importance for royalty of being accompanied by trumpets and drums – these 'musical insignia', as one might call them – is well documented. In relation to the wedding of George III in 1761, the considerable sum of over £425 was spent on the 'Serg:ᵗ Trumpetter and Six other Trumpetters and a Kettle Drummer' who were to attend the future queen, Charlotte of Mecklenburg-Strelitz on her journey 'from Stade', that is half way of her journey from Germany to London: in comparison, William Boyce was paid just over £351 for composing the anthem for the wedding service, for hiring additional musicians to perform it and for smaller 'other Disbursements'.[97]

Music at the Indoor Processions

Until the Victorian weddings, the details of the music accompanying the various entrance processions are not known, let alone credited with any significance. From then onward, it is known that the entrance processions were accompanied by instrumental marches. The use of actual, distinct 'marches' – as opposed to other free-style music – drew attention to the processional aspect. In fact, music appears to have sounded only during the actual processions, and there is no evidence for music before the various entrance marches until 1879. All the same, these marches seem not to have had any direct associations or specific connotations as to whom they accompanied and were used interchangeably.

The procession of the bride saw significant changes in this respect. As early as 1866, Princess Mary Adelaide of Cambridge entered the church for her wedding to the singing of a hymn and later in the century this became a tradition followed by all royal brides up to the later twentieth century. The use of a hymn for the bride's entrance was not a royal peculiarity but seems to have been (or become) a more common practice. For instance, a hymn sheet for the wedding of Alfred Richard Clemens and Editha Mary Wray Flood-Jones on 27 July 1886, in Henry VII's Chapel at Westminster Abbey stipulates the hymn 'Jesus Calls Us' to be sung 'Before the Service'.[98] More distinctly, for the wedding of 'E. V. Arnold & Miss Osborne' on 12 July 1894, also in Henry VII's

---

[96] Jacob Adam Kappey, *Military Music. A History of Wind-Instrumental Bands* (London: Boosey and Co., [1894]), p. 52, describes it as a 'fanfare in the ancient style'. For the date see Caldwell Titcomb, 'Baroque Court and Military Trumpets and Kettledrums: Technique and Music', *Galpin Society Journal*, 9 (1956), pp. 56–81, here p. 79.

[97] *Lna LC 5/168*, pp. 248 and 246.

[98] *Lwa WAM Service Papers*, 27 July 1886.

1—Setting the Scene

Grand Trumpeter March

Anonymous

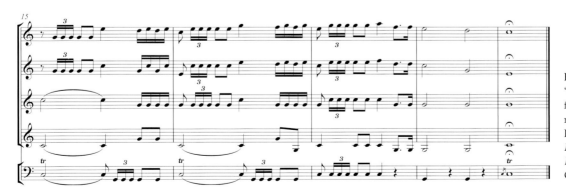

Figure 1.1: 'Grand Trumpeter March', for four trumpets and timpani, as reproduced in Jacob Adam Kappey, *Military Music. A History of Wind-Instrumental Bands* (London: Boosey and Co., [1894]), p. 52.

Chapel, the service paper stipulates the hymn 'O God, our Help in Ages Past', to be sung 'As the Bride enters the Chapel.'[99] After all, an 1891 publication of music for the wedding service included two alternatives for a processional hymn on the bride's entrance.[100]

Regarding the performance of the bride's processional hymn at royal weddings, there was an important innovation in that year: at the wedding of Princess Marie Louise of Schleswig-Holstein at St George's Windsor, the hymn was sung by the choir walking in front of the bride in her procession. This custom was followed at royal weddings up to the later twentieh century. Yet, this was again not a royal peculiarity. For instance, in late January 1892 – that is about half a year after Princess Marie Louise's Windsor wedding, which had taken place in July 1891 – Lady Olivia Taylour, daughter of the Earl and Countess of Bective, married Lord Henry Bentinck, brother of the Duke of Portland, at St Margaret's Church, Westminster; and it was reported that 'As the bridal party advanced up the centre aisle to the chancel steps they were preceded by the choir, who sang the nuptial hymn – The King of love my Shepherd is [...]'.[101]

Apart from the bride's entrance, another important procession was of course that at the end, of the newly-wed couple leaving the church. At least since the mid-nineteenth century this was accompanied by what is usually referred to as the 'wedding march'. For this, one particularly popular choice at royal weddings has been one of the most recognizable pieces of all wedding music: the Wedding March by Felix Mendelssohn Bartholdy, widely known simply as *The* Wedding March. Little needs to be commented on Mendelssohn's well-known music: with its catchy fanfare at the beginning, its majestic gravitas sections and rich harmonies, this march lends itself perfectly to being used as a recessional piece at a grand occasion. Originally part of Mendelssohn's *Ein Sommernachtstraum* from 1842–43, the incidental music to Shakespeare's *A Midsummer Night's Dream*, the Wedding March became a well-known piece in its own right from early on. It was first performed at a royal wedding, as the recessional music, at the wedding of the Princess Royal in 1858.[102] From the wedding of her brother Prince Arthur in 1879 onwards, Mendelssohn's march was used at more or less every elaborate royal wedding, not to mention countless others. While in its original context the march is scored for full orchestra, at most weddings – royal and otherwise – it has been played in an arrangement for organ only. The appropriateness of its use in church was questioned in the early decades, although it seems never in relation to royal weddings. Mendelssohn's march became an indispensable part of wedding celebrations and in the early twentieth century was a firmly established choice.

Psalm and Responses

The 1549 Prayer Book stipulates that after the marriage vows and couple's blessing, 'Then shal they goe into the quier, and the ministers or clerkes shal saye or syng, this psalme folowyng.' This direction was kept in all the following versions of the Prayer Book and for the text of 'this psalme' all versions include the full English text of Ps. 128 (*Beati omnes* = 'Blessed are all they that fear the Lord'). As an alternative, all versions of the Prayer Book give the text of Ps. 67

---

[99] *Lwa WAM Service Papers*, 12 July 1894. This must be the unnamed wedding in Westminster Abbey to which Jessica M. Kerr dates the beginning of the hymn tradition. See her 'English Wedding Music', *Musical Times*, 106 (January 1965), pp. 53–55, here p. 54.

[100] See fn. 105 below, here pp. 6–7 of this.

[101] 'Marriage of Lady Olivia Taylour with Lord H. Bentinck, MP', *The Lancaster Gazette*, 30 January 1892, p. 8.

[102] For the march's origins and early performance history see the author's article 'Mendelssohn's Wedding March and Weddings: The Early Decades', *Musical Times*, 160 (Summer 2019), pp. 97–112.

1—Setting the Scene

(*Deus misereatur* = 'God be merciful unto us'), with either psalm to be followed by the doxology. While there is only sketchy evidence for the singing of the psalm in its liturgical place at royal weddings before the late eighteenth century, this is well documented from them on, and the psalm was indiscriminately chanted to various chant tunes.

For the following Lesser Litany, the Lord's Prayer, and the Wedding Responses the Prayer Book merely stipulates that the priest shall say his versicles – implying that the responses to these are also to be said. While there is evidence that these were sung at royal weddings in the first half of the seventeenth century, after that they were probably just read. One of the earliest known musical settings of the Wedding Responses dates from 1858: Paul Jerrard's *The Order for the Solemnization of Holy Matrimony* provides music for all the liturgical parts of the service: recital tones for the priest's texts and prayers, a four-part chant tune for the psalm, and a four-part setting of the Responses.[103] This was followed, for instance, some decades later by the very similar *The Service for the Solemnization of Holy Matrimony as Used in Westminster Abbey. With a Special Anthem Composed by J. Frederick Bridge.*[104] In 1891, F. A. J. Hervey published his *Musical Setting of Such Portions of the Solemnization of Holy Matrimony as May Be Chorally Rendered.*[105] However, none of these was used at any royal wedding – although, intriguingly, Percy Scholes has stated that the edition with the Bridge anthem had been published in 1893 on the occasion of the wedding of Prince George, Duke of York, and Princess May of Teck, for a 'simultaneous ceremony' that 'took place in Westminster Abbey'.[106] This, however, could not be verified.

For the wedding of the Prince of Wales in 1863, one report still noted explicitly that the service was 'conducted with commendable simplicity, everything being read by the Archbishop of Canterbury, and no chanting being interpolated'.[107] The early-seventeenth century examples aside, the singing of the Responses at royal weddings is not confirmed before 1889, after which they were, however, still not regularly sung.

Wedding Anthems

None of the different versions of the Prayer Book stipulates the inclusion of an anthem at weddings. However, weddings may nonetheless have included special anthems from early on. The psalm scheduled for weddings in the Prayer Book, Ps. 128 (127 in the Vulgate counting), had already featured in the wedding mass in the Sarum rite, and Joseph Kerman has suggested that John Sheppard's setting of *Beati omnes* may have been written for the wedding of Mary I and Philip of Spain in Winchester in 1554.[108]

---

[103] Paul Jerrard, *The Order for the Solemnization of Holy Matrimony, Set to Music, Op. 10* (London: Paul Gerrard and Son, [1858]).

[104] (London: Novello, Ewer and Co [1890]). This was re-issued in 1926.

[105] F. A. J. Hervey, *A Musical Setting of Such Portions of the Solemnization of Holy Matrimony as May Be Chorally Rendered*, words of the litany and hymns by S. C. Clarke, with two 'Short Addresses on Holy Marriage from the Bishop of Wakefield's "Pastor in Parochia"' (London: Skeffington and Son, [1891]).

[106] Percy Scholes, *The Mirror of Music, 1844–1944: A Century of Musical Life in Britain as Reflected in the Pages of the Musical Times*, 2 vols (London: Novello, 1947), II, p. 873.

[107] 'Marriage of the Prince of Wales and Princess Alexandra of Denmark', Supplement to *ILN*, 14 March 1863, pp. 278–87, here p. 279.

[108] Joseph Kerman, *The Masses and Motets of William Byrd* (Berkeley: University of California Press, 1981), p. 25. See also his 'The Elizabethan Motet: A Study of Texts for Music', *Studies in the Renaissance*, 9 (1962), pp. 273–308, here p. 279. I am very grateful to Magnus Williamson for drawing my attention to this.

British Royal Weddings

For royal weddings, special anthems on a freely-chosen sacred text are known at least since the wedding of Princess Elizabeth in 1613.[109] The next royal weddings that were celebrated with more elaborate ceremonies were those of three of George II's children in the eighteenth century, to each of which Handel contributed a grand anthem. Importantly, these anthems on specially-chosen texts came at the very end of the ceremony, outside the actual service, and were listened to like topical concerts. An anthem actually within the service was not included until the wedding of the Princess Royal in 1858.

Hymns

'Chorales', or hymns, have been included in royal weddings since the 1858 wedding of the Princes Royal. They were first used as introits at the beginning of the service, following the entrance of the bride, and sung by the choir alone. The inclusion of hymns at major royal weddings paused after 1866. At the 1880 wedding of Princess Frederica of Hanover, one account had noted 'two hymns being introduced', sung by the choirs.[110] F. A. J. Hervey in his 1891 publication scheduled a second hymn at the very end, even suggesting it for the recess.[111] Indeed, the aforementioned wedding of Princess Marie Louise of Schleswig-Holstein in that year included a hymn for the bride's entrance and also a second hymn towards the end of the service.

The text sheet for the aforementioned Westminster Abbey wedding in July 1894 reads at the top 'Hymns and Psalm (*in which the Company are requested to join*).'[112] This appears to be one of the earliest known invitations to the congregation to join in the singing. However, notwithstanding that joining in the psalm would have been somewhat difficult, at royal weddings the congregation's singing in the hymns seems not to have been, or to have become a regular feature for a while. Whereas some members of the congregation reportedly joined in a hymn at the 1889 wedding of Princess Louise of Wales and the Duke of Fife, the 1904 wedding of Princess Alice of Albany and Prince Alexander of Teck appears to be the earliest royal wedding at which the congregation was explicitly invited to join in the singing of the entrance hymn.

One very particular 'hymn' at royal weddings is the National Anthem. At least since Victorian times this was performed at various moments in the overall proceedings, especially outdoors at the arrival of processions. However, the National Anthem was not included and sung in the actual, indoors wedding ceremony before 1922.[113]

——✦✦✦——

Overall, music was an important component of most royal weddings since the sixteenth century. Music helped structure and accentuate the proceedings, and enhanced both the religious and the ceremonial aspect of royal weddings. The following chapters provide an introduction to and discussions of all the British royal weddings from the Stuarts to the early twentieth century. Chronologically grouped together, each group highlights a particularly notable characteristic of those weddings. Yet, the overall guiding parameters will be the three topics that are the focus of this study: the weddings' venue, ceremonial, and music.

---

[109] See Kerr, 'English Wedding Music', p. 54.

[110] 'Royal Marriage at Windsor', *Weekly Irish Times*, 1 May 1880, p. 1.

[111] F. A. J. Hervey, *Musical Setting*, p. 21.

[112] *Lwa WAM Service Papers*, 12 July 1894. Emphasis in the original.

[113] For the royal weddings from 1919 onwards see the author's *British Royal Weddings: The House of Windsor* (Turnhout: Brepols, forthcoming).

2

From Elaborate to Modest: The Seventeenth Century

IN THE YEAR 1603 THE Scottish Stuarts acceded to the English throne. The new 'British' dynasty staged its ceremonies with appropriate pomp: the first royal wedding of the century was celebrated with much grandeur and ceremonial elaboration, including a rich musical programme. There was at least one more such occasion before the Civil War. Yet, the remaining royal weddings of the seventeenth century did not have much elaboration and were celebrated in rather modest ways – indeed, after the Restoration, royal weddings appear to have been literally 'quiet' in not including any music. Furthermore, in a different sense, most of the weddings in the century were 'quiet' in so far as the sources are rather 'quiet'. These weddings were not much publicized and there is altogether not much material on the royal weddings before the eighteenth century.

James VI and Princess Anne of Denmark, 1589

The first Stuart king of England, James I, had married when he was still king of Scotland alone, as James VI, in 1589. His wedding to Princess Anne, daughter of Frederick II of Denmark, has received some closer attention, especially in a dedicated study by David Stevenson.[1] Furthermore, Lucinda Dean has provided much research on the earlier Scottish weddings, including a discussion of the circumstances of this wedding, which she has placed into its longer historical context.[2]

The wedding was split into two separate ceremonies: a civil ceremony by proxy took place on 20 August at Kronborg Castle in Northern Denmark (which ten years later was to be the home of Shakespeare's Hamlet); the church wedding was planned to follow later, in Edinburgh, and Stevenson summarized that it had been agreed 'the Scots would look after the religious side of things'.[3] The bride's Lutheranism would thus have been subsumed in the Scots' Calvinism. As the bride's crossing the North Sea was much delayed by bad weather, James VI eventually braved the storms and travelled himself to Norway (then in a union with Denmark) to meet his bride there; and in the end the religious wedding took place on 23 November 1589 in Christianstadt, today's Oslo.[4] The wedding was described in an anonymous Danish manuscript

---

[1] David Stevenson, *Scotland's Last Royal Wedding: The Marriage of James VI and Anne of Denmark* (Edinburgh: John Donald Publishers, 1997). For the shortcomings of this study see Maureen M. Meikle's review in *Scottish Historical Review*, 78 (October 1999), pp. 263–65. For more literature on this wedding see also J. Leeds Barroll, *Anna of Denmark, Queen of England: A Cultural Biography* (Philadelphia: University of Pensylvania Press, 2003), p. 176, n. 6; and Steve Murdoch, *Britain, Denmark-Norway and the House of Stuart 1603–1660* (East Linton, Tuckwell Press, 2003), esp. Chapter 1.

[2] Lucinda Hazel Stewart Dean, 'Crowns, Wedding Rings, and Processions: Continuity and Change in the Representation of Scottish Royal Authority in State Ceremony, *c.* 1214 – *c.* 1603' (unpublished doctoral thesis, University of Stirling, 2013), esp. pp. 304–16: 'Section VI: Scotland's Last Consort Coronation and Royal Wedding, James VI and Anne' This is currently being revised for a monograph: *Death and the Royal Succession in Scotland, 1214 to 1543: Ritual, Ceremony and Power* (Boydell, forthcoming). I am very grateful to Lucinda Dean for her advice regarding the 1589 wedding.

[3] Stevenson, *Scotland's Last Royal Wedding*, p. 22.

account that survives in an eighteenth-century copy.[5] As Stevenson suggests, this account's particular observation that the ceremony took place 'with all the splendour possible at that time and place' may imply that it 'had not been as magnificent as it should have been'.[6] The ceremony was celebrated by James VI's Scottish court preacher David Lindsay, who had accompanied him to Norway, and it would thus have been a Calvinist service.[7] It took place in the afternoon, 'in the great hall in Christen Mule's house', that is the Old Bishop's Palace. The Danish manuscript account records that 'trumpeters [...] stood at Christen Mule's gate and blew' – probably referring to their playing fanfares on the arrival of the royal participants. The trumpeters may have included at least one Scottish trumpeter. Dean has shown that James VI spent £124 on 'the clothing, wage, and trumpet of the king's trumpeter'.[8] Furthermore, she notes that the accounts of the Scottish Lord Chancellor, John Maitland, 1st Lord Maitland of Thirlestane, include some 'small payments to trumpeters, bell ringers, [and] an organist'.[9]

The ceremony itself 'began with oral music – but only for a very short time'.[10] No further details about this short 'oral music' are known. If nothing else, the payment to an organist confirms that there was at least organ music – and as no payment for a choir is recorded, the 'oral music' referred to may have been a congregational hymn, befitting a Calvinist as much as a Lutheran service. This was followed by Lindsay's sermon, delivered in French, the administration of the marriage vows, blessings, and an 'oration' in Danish, before 'everything ended with music'.[11] This may have been more organ music, while the couple left. Notably, in the recess the royal couple did not walk together but the bride and her retinue went before her husband – thus following strict court hierarchy rather than emphasizing nuptial union.

It is not known where the musicians at the Oslo ceremony came from: they may have been provided by the Danish court or could have been local Oslo musicians. On occasion of this marriage, Abraham Praetorius, cantor in Copenhagen, had composed and published his *Harmonia Gratulatoria*, in a set of partbooks.[12] It has been suggested that some of Praetorius's music was performed at the proxy ceremony at Kronborg Castle.[13] If that was the case, the civil ceremony would possibly have outdone the Oslo church wedding, at least in terms of musical elaboration.

The accession of the Scottish Stuarts to the throne of England in 1603 saw momentous changes in the whole character and public presentation of the monarchy. This affected not the

---

[4] Stevenson, *Scotland's Last Royal Wedding*, p. 36.

[5] 'The Danish Account of the Marriage of James VI and Anne of Denmark', transl. by Peter Graves, in Stevenson, *Scotland's Last Royal Wedding*, pp. 79–122, with details on p. ix.

[6] Stevenson, *Scotland's Last Royal Wedding*, p. 36.

[7] This and the following Stevenson, *Scotland's Last Royal Wedding*, p. 92.

[8] Dean, 'Crowns', p. 307.

[9] Dean, 'Crowns', p. 308, with fn. 517, referring to the accounts in *Lbl Add MS 22958*.

[10] Stevenson, *Scotland's Last Royal Wedding*, p. 92.

[11] Stevenson, *Scotland's Last Royal Wedding*, p. 94.

[12] Abraham Praetorius, *Harmonia gratulatoria nuptiis et honori [...] Iacobi VI. Scotorum regis: et [...] Friderici II. Daniæ, Norvegiæ etc. Regis Filiæ Annæ [...] Scotiæ Reginæs, Sex vocibus composita etc. dedicata, ab Abrahamo Prӕterio* (Copenhagen: Laurentius Benedictus [i.e. Lorentz Benedicht], 1590). Stevenson, *Scotland's Last Royal Wedding*, p. 23, explains that 'The only complete copy of Praetorius's music is at BL, K.3.f.2.' For this publication see also Mara R. Wade, *Triumphus nuptialis danicus. German Court Culture and Denmark: the "Great Wedding" of 1634* (Wiesbaden: Harrossowitz 1996), p. 35.

[13] Stevenson, *Scotland's Last Royal Wedding*, p. 23; who refers to 'O Kongsted, H Ilsøe, etc. (eds), *Festmusik fra Renaissancen* (Copenhagen, 1990), 47.'

2—From Elaborate to Modest: The Seventeenth Century

least the marriage culture and weddings. Barbara Ravelhofer has summarized that James I 'began to sponsor high-profile nuptials at Whitehall' in 'Aristocratic marriages under royal auspices' which 'reflected current political issues and formalized monarchical (self-)representation'.[14] In the following decades, royal marriages themselves revealed how much they were imbued with political weight and significance, as shown in a recent volume on *Stuart Marriage Diplomacy*.[15] In two notable instances, this was underlined by ceremonial elaboration at the wedding ceremonies, including a sumptuous musical programme.

The 'Palatine Wedding': Princess Elizabeth and Prince Frederick V, Elector Palatine, 14 February 1613

In England, indeed the whole of Britain, the first grand royal wedding in decades took place ten years after the Stuarts had come to the throne. It was on St Valentine's Day, 14 February 1613 that the Princess Elizabeth, daughter of James VI/I, was married to Prince Frederick V, the Elector Palatine: this wedding is therefore usually known as the 'Palatine Wedding' – notably being the only royal wedding with such a distinct epithet. Incidentally, it may be interesting to note that St Valentine's Day does not yet seem to have had any romantic connotations, and nothing seems to have been mentioned in that respect at the time.

This wedding displayed unprecedented grandeur for such an event and Kevin Curran has pointed out that 'such magnificence had not been witnessed for a nuptial event' since 1501, since the wedding of Prince Arthur and Catharine of Aragon.[16] Similarly, R. Malcom Smuts has summarized that this wedding 'provided the occasion for the single most spectacular series of festivals in London during the whole of the early modern period'.[17] One of the reasons for the elaboration and attention was the wedding's huge political significance. Much has been written about this 'Court Festival' in relation to the 'Protestant Alliance'.[18] Notably, the wedding occurred not long after the death of Prince Henry Frederick, Prince of Wales, and Curran has observed that with his demise 'the ideology of militant Protestantism became more sharply focused on Princess Elizabeth's marriage'.[19] Similarly, Steve Murdoch has summarized that the wedding 'was greeted with enthusiasm in Britain' because it was understood as 'a positive move for European Protestantism' – but he also notes that the match was planned to be counterbalanced by the heir to the throne marrying a Catholic princess, either Spanish or French.[20] Despite much scholarly interest in the Palatine wedding, the actual wedding service itself has received but little attention.

---

[14] Barbara Ravelhofer, Review of *Marriage, Performance, and Politics at the Jacobean Court* by Kevin Curran, *Renaissance Quarterly* 63 (2010), pp. 689–91, here p. 690.

[15] Valentina Caldari and Sara J. Wolfson (eds), *Stuart Marriage Diplomacy* (Woodbridge: Boydell Press, 2018).

[16] Kevin Curran, *Marriage, Performance, and Politics at the Jacobean Court* (Aldershot: Ashgate, 2013), p. 90.

[17] R. Malcom Smuts, 'Introduction. Festivals, Dynastic Alliances, and Political History: Notes on the History and Historiography of Royal Weddings', in *The Wedding of Charles I and Henrietta Maria, 1625: Celebrations and Controversy*, ed. by Marie-Claude Canova-Green and Sara J. Wolfson, 'European Festival Studies: 1450–1700' (Turnhout: Brepols, 2021), pp. 21–40, here p. 22.

[18] See esp. the chapters in Sara Smart and Mara R. Wade (eds), *The Palatine Wedding of 1613: Protestant Alliance and Court Festival*, 'Wolfenbütteler Abhandlungen zur Renaissanceforschung', 29 (Wiesbaden: Harrassowitz, 2013).

[19] Kevin Curran, 'James I and Fictional Authority at the Palatine Wedding Celebrations', *Renaissance Studies*, 20:1 (February 2006), pp. 51–67, here p. 52.

[20] Murdoch, *Britain, Denmark-Norway and the House of Stuart*, p. 45.

British Royal Weddings

The elaborate wedding celebrations were only slightly affected by the death of the bride's brother, Prince Henry Frederick, Prince of Wales: court mourning lasted only a month, and the ceremony was merely slightly postponed.[21] The festivities were recorded in at least three notable published accounts, the first two of which are written in French and English, respectively. The French account was published in Heidelberg, the home of the bridegroom, and has been ascribed to David Jocquet; the second, anonymous account was published in London:

> D[avid] Jocquet, *Les Triomphes, Entrées, Cartels, Tournois, Céremonies, et aultres Magnificences, faites en Angleterre, & au Palatinat, pour le Mariage & Reception, de Monseigneur le Prince Frideric V Comte Palatin du Rhin* [...]. *Et de Madame Elisabeth, Fille vnique et Princesse de la Grande Bretagne* [...] (Heidelberg: 'Chez Gotard Vogvelein' [Gotthardt Vögelin], 1613).

> *The Marriage of the Tvvo Great Princes, Fredericke Count Palatine, &c: and the Lady Elizabeth, Daughter to the Imperial Maiesties of King Iames and Queene Anne: Vpon Shroue-Sonday Last. With the Showes and Fire-Workes vpon the Water: As also the Masks & Reuells, in his Highnes Court of White-Hall* ('Printed at London: By T[homas] C[reede] for William Barley', 1613).

While these two accounts provide much information on the surrounding ceremonies of this wedding, they do not include many details on the wedding service itself. Details on this are found in the third account, written in German and ascribed to Tobias Hübner – and also published in Heidelberg, by the same publisher as the French account:

> [Tobias Hübner], *Beschreibung der Reiß: Empfahung deß Ritterlichen Ordens: Vollbringung des Heyraths: und gliicklicher Heimführung* [...] *Des* [...] *Herrn Friederichen deß Fünften* [...] *Mit* [...] *Princessin Elisabethen* [...] *Mit schönen Kupfferstücken gezieret* ([Heidelberg]: In Gotthardt Vögelins Verlag, 1613).[22]

As Thurstan Dart has pointed out, this 'rare, elaborately illustrated book' is 'the best description of all the festivities connected with the marriage' and Andrew Ashbee similarly summarized that it is 'the most detailed account of all'.[23] Yet, another detailed account of the service alone was entered into the Old Cheque Book of the Chapel Royal:

> The order & manner of the solemne celebracōn of the marriage of the two great Princes, Frederick Prince ellector, Counte Palatine of Rhenie & Ladie Elizabeth the only daughter of the Right highe & mightie Prince the Kinge of great Brittaine [...].[24]

This account in the Chapel Royal Cheque Book and Hübner's *Beschreibung* agree in most points. The wedding took place 'vpon Shrove-Sunday' (the Sunday before Lent).[25] The service was celebrated in the chapel at Whitehall Palace, and according to the Cheque Book, the proceedings commenced 'betweene xj & xij', before midday.[26] The procession took a long-winded

---

[21] Graham Parry, 'The Wedding of Princess Elizabeth', *The Golden Age Restor'd: The Culture of the Stuart Court, 1603–42* (Manchester: Manchester University Press, 1981), pp. 95–107, here p. 95.

[22] For the published accounts of this wedding, and for Hübner's authorship of the *Beschreibung*, see Paulette Choné, 'Firework Displays in Paris, London and Heidelberg (1612–1615)', in *Dynastic Marriages 1612/1615: A Celebration of the Habsburg and Bourbon Unions*, ed. by Margaret M. McGowan, first publ. by Ashgate in 2013 (London and New York: Routledge, 2016), pp. 201–14, here pp. 209–10.

[23] Thurston Dart, 'Two English Musicians at Heidelberg in 1613', *Musical Times*, 111 (1970), pp. 29 and 31–32, here p. 29; Andrew Ashbee (ed.), *Records of English Court Music*, 9 vols (Aldershot: Scolar Press, 1991), IV, p. 208.

[24] Transcr. in Andrew Ashbee and John Harley (eds), *The Cheque Books of the Chapel Royal*, 2 vols (Aldershot: Ashgate, 2000), I, pp. 172–75.

[25] *Marriage of the Tvvo Great Princes*, title.

[26] This and the following Ashbee and Harley, *Cheque Books*, I, pp. 173 and 175. See also 'The manner of the Marriage vpon Shrove-Sunday [...]', in *Marriage of the Tvvo Great Princes*, [pp. 1 and 3 of this].

2—From Elaborate to Modest: The Seventeenth Century

route, which included passing 'throughe a new bankettinge house erected of purpose for to solemnenize this feast in'. The newlyweds returned to the Banqueting House after the ceremony to dine in state. This new Banqueting House stood on the same site as Inigo Jones's famous successor built between 1619 and 1622, with Rubens's famous ceiling paintings, which is the only remaining part of Whitehall Palace that was spared by the great fire of 1698.[27]

The Cheque Book account describes that there was a raised platform 'in the middest of the Chappell' with a 'stately Throne or seate' on which the bride and groom were to sit.[28] The account also explains:

> Upon the sides of the Chappell from the stales up to the Comunion table weare a duble rowe of seates made for the Gent: of the Chappell arayed withe tapstery very comely.

Thus it seems that the choir was split into two, on either side of the chapel. They were not high up in galleries, but simply on ground level with the congregation, as was – and is – common practice in most Anglican cathedrals and chapels. It is worth considering that the term 'Gent: of the Chapell' probably refers to the whole choir, including the boys; the account, like many others, uses this term throughout. Hübner's *Beschreibung* in the corresponding passage uses the description 'nobiles cantores Capellæ', the 'noble singers of the Chapel'.[29]

This appears to be the earliest royal wedding for which a detailed account survives and the order in which the main participants entered the chapel is noteworthy: first came the bridegroom, then the bride, and after her the king and queen. This corresponded with other royal occasions where the monarch had the privilege to be the last to arrive. The entrance procession was depicted in a contemporary engraving, probably by Abraham Hogenberg (see Illustration 2.1)[30] Hogenberg's engraving shows '6 Teutsche Trommeter', or 'six German trumpeters' at the head of the procession. This corresponds with the account in *The Marriage of the Tvvo Great Princes* which recorded that, in the return procession from the chapel, the bridegroom was preceded by

> sixe of his owne Country gallants, clad in crimson Veluet, laide excædingly thicke with gold lace, bearing in their hands sixe siluer Trumpets, who no sooner comming into the Banquetting house, but they presented him with a melodious sound of the same, flourishing so delightfully, that it greatly reioyced the whole Court.[31]

For the processions inside, entering the chapel, there is no information as to whether these were accompanied by any music. However, the Cheque Book records that once the 'Royall assemblie' had been 'settled in y^er places', when all the processions had fully arrived, 'then began the Gent: of the Chapell to singe a full Anthem'.[32] Interestingly, Hübner's *Beschreibung* records for this point that 'so wol vf der Orgel als sonst figurirt worden' – that 'music was played as well on the organ as otherwise'.[33] The term 'figurirt' was usually used for polyphonic music, which

---

[27] For part of a plan of Whitehall Palace from *c.* 1670, showing also the position of the chapel, see Ashbee and Harley, *Cheque Books*, I, p. xxvii. The Banqueting House/Hall is to the north of the 'COURT' at the top.

[28] This and the following, Ashbee and Harley, *Cheque Books*, I, pp. 172–73.

[29] Hüber, *Beschreibung*, p. 46.

[30] *Eigentliche Abbildung welcher gestalt der Churfurst Pfaltzgraff Friderich der 5. sampt der Princessin in Engelland* […]. The collection of the British Museum holds two slightly different versions of this: *Lbm 1856,0308.178* and *Lbm 1880,0612.215* (both available online via www.britishmuseum.org, accessed 16 March 2021). Illustration 2.1 is the same as the first of these (1856,0308.178).

[31] *Marriage of the Tvvo Great Princes*, p. [3].

[32] Ashbee and Harley, *Cheque Books*, I, p. 174.

[33] Hübner, *Beschreibung*, p. 48.

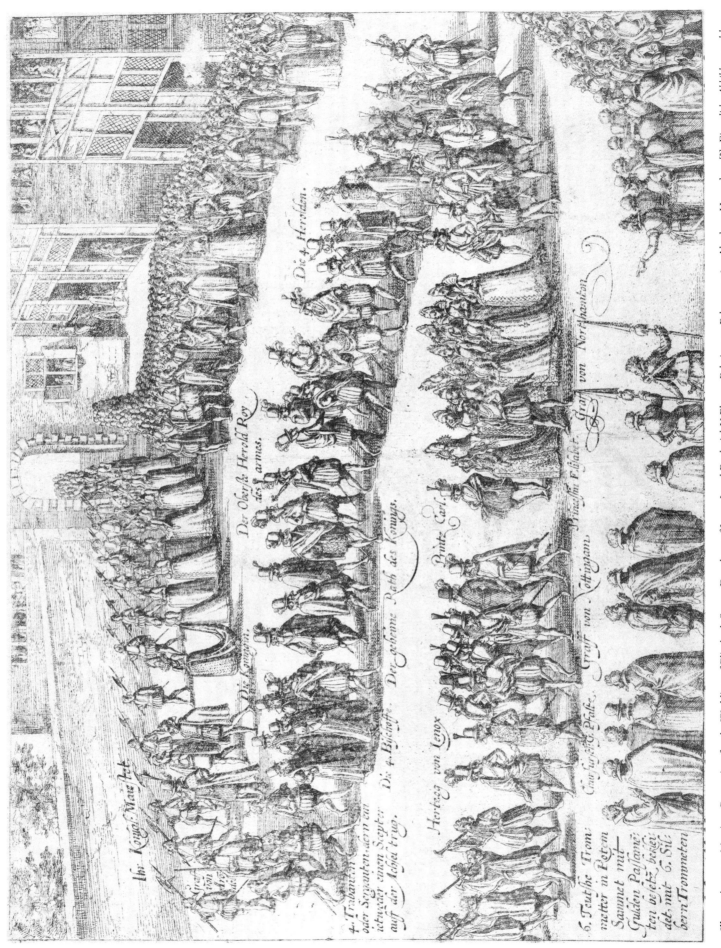

Illustration 2.1: Marriage Procession for the Wedding of Elizabeth Stuart, Daughter of James I, and Frederick V, Elector Palatine, 14 February 1613: Abraham Hogenberg[?], *Eigentliche Abbildung welcher gestalt der Churfürst Pfaltzgraff Friderich der 5. sampt der Princessin in Engelland [...]*, etching print 1613, copy in *New York City, The Met* [Metropolitan Museum of Art], Accession Number 53.601.152 (Harris Brisbane Dick Fund, 1953).

2—From Elaborate to Modest: The Seventeenth Century

means that the mentioned 'full Anthem' may have been an anthem for the full choir but not necessarily a homophonic setting.

Without mentioning any liturgy, the Cheque Book account explains that, once the anthem had ended, the Bishop of Bath and Wells, as Dean of the Chapel, went to the pulpit to preach his sermon which lasted 'not much above halfe an hower'.[34] Thus the service did not simply follow the Prayer Book – which does not stipulate an introit anthem, and has the sermon at best at the end. This sermon was followed by another anthem, 'wch was the psalme: Blessed art thou that fearest god &c.' – thus psalm 128, as prescribed in the Prayer Book. Similarly, Hübner's *Beschreibung* records that the sermon was followed by another prayer that was finished with 'einer stattlichen Music', or 'imposing music', but erroneously counting it as Psalm 123.[35] The identity of this anthem is not clear. The text had been set by, for instance, John Mundy in a composition for three voices published in his *Songs and Psalmes* (1594) and there are other sixteenth-century settings by Philip van Wilder (or Peter Philips) and Christopher Tye.[36] Orlando Gibbons, one of the organists of the Chapel Royal at the time, also set this text (in slightly different wording) in *Blessed Are All They that Fear the Lord*.[37] However, this is clearly inscribed as 'A Weddinge Anthem first made for my lord of Summersett' in one source, and the Earl of Somerset did not marry until later in the year.[38]

The Cheque Book account is explicit in detailing that during this anthem after the sermon the Archbishop of Canterbury and the Dean of the Chapel Royal both went into the vestry to put on their rich copes, from where they returned to stand at the altar 'till the Anthem was ended'.[39] Then they approached the royal couple who were sitting on their 'Throne', or raised platform, and the archbishop performed the marriage rites. The account continues with some more information on the music:

> When the ArchBisshopp had ended the Benediccōn, God the ffather, god ye sonne &c the Quier sange the same benediccōn in an Anthem made new for y^t purpose by Doctor Bull[.]

John Bull was another organist of the Chapel Royal and, as Dart has noted, he had also been Princess Elizabeth's keyboard teacher.[40] Notably, this is the only one of the anthems in this service for which the Cheque Book gives the title and the composer's name. Bull's anthem on the text of the benediction, *God the Father, God the Son*, does not seem to have survived.[41] Hüber's *Beschreibung* does not mention this anthem, or in fact any music at this place, but the Cheque Book might be the more reliable source in this respect. If this anthem was indeed included, it would be notable for having the very same words as the preceding blessing. Such a doubling of texts – first spoken and then sung – is rather unusual but was perhaps intended to strengthen the blessing of the newly-weds.

---

[34] This and the following Ashbee and Harley, *Cheque Books*, I, p. 174.

[35] Hübner, *Beschreibung*, p. 48.

[36] For the setting by Wilder see Peter Le Huray, *Music and the Reformation in England, 1549–1660*, first publ. in 1967, corr. repr. (Cambridge: Cambridge University Press, 1978), p. 185. For that by Tye see *Lbl Add MS 15166*, fol. 85^r and *Cambridge, Queens' College, Old Library G.4.17*, fol. 78^v.

[37] For the Chapel organists at the time see David Baldwin, *The Chapel Royal – Ancient and Modern* (London: Duckworth, 1990), p. 284.

[38] *Oxford, Christ Church, MS Mus. 21*, p. 262; and see John Harley, *Orlando Gibbons and the Gibbons Family of Musicians* (Aldershot: Ashgate, 1999), p. 41, fn. 63.

[39] This and the following Ashbee and Harley, *Cheque Books*, I, pp. 174–75.

[40] See O. W. Neighbour and Susi Jeans, 'Bull [Boul, Bul, Bol], John [Jan] [Bouville, Bonville, Jean]', *NG*; and Dart, 'Two English Musicians', p. 31.

[41] See Neighbour and Jeans, 'Bull', under 'Anthems'.

The anthem would have received due attention: according to the Cheque Book account, it was only once the anthem had ended that the archbishop and the dean, followed by the royal couple went to the altar.[42] There they knelt 'while the versickles and prayers were sunge by yᵉ ArchBisshopp & answered by yᵉ Quier', probably referring to the Lesser Litany, Lord's Prayer, Responses and prayers stipulated in the Prayer Book. While this is probably the earliest evidence for these liturgical parts of the wedding service to have been sung, no setting of the Wedding Versicles and Responses from this time seems to have survived. With the sermon already earlier in the service, the prayers were followed by yet 'an other Anthem', as the Cheque Book laconically recorded. Hübner's *Beschreibung* noted more generally that the archbishop prayed and that 'After that they made music again.' ('Darauff man abermals Musicirt.').[43] There is no more information on what this anthem was, but the *Beschreibung* explains that the couple – possible during the anthem or music – returned again to the platform where they received the king's congratulations.

The Cheque Book account does not mention such congratulations but records that after the anthem Garter King of Arms 'published the stile of the Prince & Princes' – that is, that he proclaimed the couple's full titles and invoked upon them 'All health happines & honoʳ'.[44] The *Beschreibung* details that Garter was accompanied by 'four of his assistants in the usual habits' ('Vier seiner Gesellen, in gewöhnlichem Habit'), most probably referring to four heralds in their tabards.[45] None of the reports indicates that this proclamation was followed by a fanfare – as its counterpart at royal funerals was, and is.[46] Instead, there was another intriguing, ceremonial 'answer' to this proclamation.

The Cheque Book records that, after the heralds' proclamation, 'ther was brought out of the vestery by divʳse of the Lord[es], wine & wafers, wᶜʰ when they had eaten they dep[ar]ted'.[47] This might at first seem like the preparations for the celebration of Holy Communion. However, the *Beschreibung* detailed that after the king's congratulation, and during ('Inmittelst') the heralds' proclamation 'several gentlemen dished up *Confect* and a cup with wine', which they served first to the king and queen, and then to the newly-weds ('Vnd ist also bald von etlichen Herren daß Confect vnd ein Becher mit Wein vffgetragen vnd erstlich dem König vnd Königin hernach Ihrer Churfl. Gn. vnd der Princessin vorgesetzt worden.').[48] The use of the word 'Confect', akin to 'biscuits' – instead of 'Brot', or 'bread' which would usually be used for communion – is notable. Equally notable is the Cheque Book's wording 'when they had eaten', which seems not to fit a description of the taking of Holy Communion, and also the fact that the reports neither mention the clerics partaking, nor refer to any communion liturgy.

Indeed, that the consuming of the 'wine & wafers' was not the celebration of communion becomes clear from a draft ceremonial for the royal wedding in 1734 that was based on the ceremonial for 1613. This explicitly refers to 'the former Customs, of bringing Wafers & Wine' and notably explains that 'after tasting the Wafers, an health is to be begun to the Prosperity of the marriage out of a Gold Bowl' by the bridegroom and 'pledged' by the bride, her parents, other

---

[42] This and the following Ashbee and Harley, *Cheque Books*, I, p. 175.

[43] Hübner, *Beschreibung*, p. 50.

[44] Ashbee and Harley, *Cheque Books*, I, p. 175.

[45] Hübner, *Beschreibung*, p. 51.

[46] For royal funerals see Matthias Range, *British Royal and State Funerals: Music and Ceremonial since Elizabeth I* (Woodbridge: Boydell Press, 2016) [hereinafter *BRSF*], esp. pp. 32–33.

[47] Ashbee and Harley, *Cheque Books*, I, p. 175.

[48] Hübner, *Beschreibung*, p. 50.

2—From Elaborate to Modest: The Seventeenth Century

relatives and by 'the Lords in their Order'.[49] This means that the 1613 wedding included the ceremony of drinking (and eating) to the newly-weds' health, as discussed in Chapter 1 above.[50] Interestingly, while the communion part seems to have been simply omitted from the service without any comment, this non-religious custom at the end of the ceremony was retained. In contrast, however, to the 1554 wedding of Mary I and Philip of Spain – the last elaborate royal wedding at which this ceremony had been performed – it now came not before the heralds' proclamation, but after it. All in all, with the consuming of wafers and wine, this ceremony appears almost like secular celebration of communion. This was well introduced by, and at the same time itself enhanced the immediately preceding herald's proclamation with its plea for 'All health happines & honoᵣ'.

For the return procession, the Cheque Book account merely notes that 'they dep[ar]ted after the same mannᵣ as they came in'.[51] Hübner's *Beschreibung* is more explicit and records that the Elector, the bridegroom, left first, then the princess his bride with her attendants, and then the king, queen and the prince their son (Prince Charles).[52] The *Marriage of the Tvvo Great Princes* furthermore details that the bride 'was led backe, not by two Batchellors as before, but by the Duke of *Lineux* [Lenox], and the Earl of *Notthingham*, in a most reuerend manner'.[53] Thus, as in 1589, the newly-wed couple did again clearly not walk together in the return procession. It may be assumed that the return procession in the chapel was accompanied by some organ music, although the accounts are curiously silent on this. As already seen, the bridegroom in this procession was preceded by his own trumpeters with 'sixe siluer Trumpets', but they are distinctly reported not to have played in the procession until they reached the Banqueting House.[54]

Overall, with three anthems (introit, benediction, final anthem) plus the Responses and presumably some instrumental pieces, the wedding service included an impressive amount of music, accustically enhancing the grandeur of the event. Given the involvement of such high-profile musicians as Gibbons and Bull among the personnel of the Chapel Royal, the music would presumably have been of a high standard. Rapin de Thoyras, later summarized that 'Nothing was spared to render the entertainments on these occasions as magnificent as possible.'[55] He explained that the king raised the traditional aid money to pay for the wedding of his oldest daughter. With all the elaborate festivities, this was truly, as Dart called it, 'a state marriage'.[56] The unprecedented elaboration matches with the fact that, in the wider historical context, the 1613 marriage of Princess Elizabeth and the Elector Palatine has become of special importance in British history. Not only would the princess later become known as the 'Winter Queen', following her husband's short period on the throne of Bohemia in 1619; but more importantly, this marriage was the first notable link of the British monarchy with Germany. It has very much proven to be crucial, as it is from this branch of the family that the Hanoverians stem: in 1714,

---

[49] Draft ceremonial in *Lea Miscell: Coll: By Anstis*, here p. [2] of this, fully transcr. in Appendix B 3.1. For details on this draft see also Chapter 3.

[50] For this and the following see Chapter 1, with fns 80–84.

[51] Ashbee and Harley, *Cheque Books*, I, p. 175.

[52] Hübner, *Beschreibung*, p. 50f.

[53] *Marriage of the Tvvo Great Princes*, p. [3].

[54] *Marriage of the Tvvo Great Princes*, p. [3]. Fully quoted above, with fn. 31. Hübner, *Beschreibung*, p. 52, similarly details that the trumpets played before dinner.

[55] This and the following [Paul] Rapin de Thoyras, *The History of England*, transl. with 'Additional NOTES' by N. Tindal, 2nd edn, 2 vols (London: Printed for James, John, and Paul Knapton, 1732), II, p. 182.

[56] Dart, 'Two English Musicians', p. 31.

Princess Elizabeth's grandson, the Elector of Hanover, succeeded the last Stuart monarch, Queen Anne, as the closest Protestant heir to the throne and became George I.

The grand 1613 'Palatine' wedding was soon followed by a similarly noteworthy wedding: ten months later, on 26 December, the Earl of Somerset married Lady Frances Howard, also in the chapel of Whitehall Palace, and with the king and queen present.[57] The Chapel Royal Cheque Book records the attendance of 'the gent: of the Chappell', presumably referring to the whole choir.[58] As already mentioned, it was for this wedding that Orlando Gibbons reportedly wrote his anthem *Blessed Are All They that Fear the Lord*.[59] Four years later, in September 1617, Sir John Villiers married Francis Cooke in the chapel at Hampton Court Palace and the 'gent:' of the Chapel Royal were again present and received a fee.[60] The participation of the Chapel Royal at such aristocratic weddings gave these ceremonies much added elaboration while providing a possibility of further income for the singers. It also rings with Ravelhofer's aforementioned observation regarding 'Aristocratic marriages under royal auspices'.[61] 'From a ceremonial point of view, this meant that, at least musically, royal weddings did not stand out quite that much from aristocratic weddings of the time.

Charles I and Princess Henrietta Maria of France, May 1625

When Charles I acceded to the throne in March 1625, he was still unmarried. A match with a Spanish Habsburg princess had been envisaged for several years but eventually came to nothing.[62] In the end, he married another Catholic princess: Henrietta Maria of France, sister of Louis XIII. This wedding has recently received much attention in various essays within a dedicated volume that discusses especially also the political background and the confessional context.[63]

As for the king's parents, there were two ceremonies: this time a Roman Catholic wedding by proxy in France, and then a civil ceremony in person once the new queen had arrived in London. The wedding festivities in Paris were described in a published French account that was also published in London in English translation:

> *A Relation of the Gloriovs Trivmphs and Order of the Ceremonies, Obserued in the Marriage of the High and Mighty Charles, King of Great Brittaine, and the Ladie Henretta [sic] Maria, Sister to the Most Christian King of France. [...] Whereunto the Originall French Copie Is Added* (London: 'Printed by T[homas] S[nodham and others] for Nathaniel Butter, and are to be sold at the Signe of the Pyde-Bull, neere S. Austens Gate', 1625).[64]

---

[57] Harley, *Gibbons*, p. 50. See also Thoyras, *History of England*, p. 184.

[58] Ashbee and Harley, *Cheque Books*, I, p. 175.

[59] See above, fn. 38.

[60] Ashbee and Harley, *Cheque Books*, I, pp. 175–76.

[61] See above, fn. 14.

[62] See Glyn Redworth, *The Prince and the Infanta: The Cultural Politics of the Spanish Match* (New Haven: Yale University Press, 2003). See also the essays in Caldari and Wolfson (eds), *Stuart Marriage Diplomacy*.

[63] Marie-Claude Canova-Green and Sara Wolfson (eds), *The Wedding of Charles I and Henrietta Maria, 1625: Celebrations and Controversy*, 'European Festival Studies: 1450–1700' (Turnhout: Brepols, 2021). For more good sources on this wedding see Katie Whitaker, *A Royal Passion: The Turbulent Marriage of King Charles I and Henrietta Maria* (London: Phoenix, 2011), p. 42, fns 79 and 80.

[64] For this see lately Margaret Shewring, 'Appendix 2. *A Relation of the Glorious Triumphs and Order of the Ceremonies*: An English-Language Version of the French Festival Book', in Canova-Green and Wolfson, *Wedding of Charles I and Henrietta Maria*, pp. 343–51. Shewring transcribes the full English text from the copy in the *Lbl 605.B.17*.

2—From Elaborate to Modest: The Seventeenth Century

The proxy ceremony took place in Paris on 1/11 May 1625 (the first date being that in the Julian calendar used in Britain at the time, the second that in the Gregorian calendar used on the continent). The published account highlights the calibre of the match and the resulting need for an appropriate venue: 'as such an vnion as this could not be performed without great pompe, and infinite ioy and contentment: So our *Ladies Church* was chosen', the cathedral of Notre Dame.[65] Francis Sandford some fifty years later recorded that the ceremony 'was solemnly performed in the Church of *Nostredame*' and 'by Cardinal *Richlieu*'.[66]

There appear to be no contemporary illustrations of this wedding. However, some decades later, Louis Chéron depicted the scene in a highly stylized way that emphasized the Catholic nature of the ceremony and this image was more widely disseminated through reproduction in print (Illustration 2.2).

Illustration 2.2: 'The Marriage of the King 1625', engraving by Nicolas-Gabriel Dupuis after Louis Chéron (1660–1713), (London: Printed and sold by Thomas and John Bowles, Printsellers, [1728]), *Royal Collection*, RCIN 601887, Royal Collection Trust / © Her Majesty Queen Elizabeth II 2021.

[65] *Relation*, p. [3].

[66] Francis Sandford, *A Genealogical History of the Kings of England, and Monarchs of Great Britain, &c. From the Conquest, Anno 1066. to the Year, 1677* ([London:] Printed by Tho. Newcomb, 1677), p. 540.

The *Relation* detailed that the exchange of the vows took place 'at the entry of the great Portall of the said Church' and that the remainder of the ceremony, for which it refers merely to 'Prayers', took place inside.[67] A little more detail is found in an informative French manuscript account of the wedding:

> Relation de / ce qui s'est fait tant / aux fiançailles de Madame / Henriette Marie de France / Soeur [*sic*] du Roy, avec Charles / premier Roy de la grande / Bretagne, Lesquelles furent / faites au L'Ouvre [*sic*], en La / Chambre du Roy, le jeudy / huitiéme Jour de May / Jour de L'assention, / Qu'au Mariage de La d[ite] / Dame qui fut fait en / L'Eglise de N'ótre Dame / Le Dimanche x.e du d[ite] mois / et an 1625[68]

For the wedding at Notre Dame, this refers distinctly to the celebration of the mass, which began 'after seven o'clock in the evening'.[69]

In addition to the published *Relation* there was another, similar English pamphlet that described both the French proxy wedding and the ceremonies in England once the couple had arrived there:

> *A Trve Discovrse of all the Royai [sic] Passages, Tryvmphs and Ceremonies, Obserued at the Contract and Mariage of the High and Mighty Charles, King of Great Britaine, and the Most Excellentest of Ladies, the Lady Henrietta Maria of Burbon, Sister to the Most Christian King of France: Together with her Iourney from Paris to Bulloigne, and Thence vnto Douer in England, Where the King Met Her, and the Manner of their Enterview. As also the Tryumphant Solemnities which Passed in their Iournies from Douer to the Citie of London, and so to Whitehall, &c.* (London: Printed by Iohn Haviland for Hanna Barret, 1625).[70]

Whereas little seems to be known about the ceremonial particulars of the wedding ceremony at Notre Dame, the *Relation* describes the music of the procession to the cathedral in at least some detail. Near the beginning, the procession included the Swiss guards, 'their Drumbe beating and their Ensigne displayed'.[71] These were followed by '12. *Hautbois* […] which rauished the hearts of the hearers. Then eight Drumbes […] which were so lustily beaten vp, that the most coward courages were animated with the noyse thereof.' Then came 'Ten Trumpets' which 'sounded so merrily that it rejoyced all the hearers', and finally followed the long procession. While it cannot be known what music all these played, it is interesting that the account for each of the three groups after the first drums points out how their music caused the spectators to react in a joyous way. This emphasized the role of the music in enhancing the festive atmosphere, in anticipation of the following ceremony.

The description of the procession in *A Trve Discourse* shows only minor differences to that in the *Relation*: for the head of the procession, it lists several 'Drummes beating' and 'the Fifes whistling'; and for the final group of trumpets 'at least a dozen'.[72] The French

---

[67] *Relation*, pp. [5–6].

[68] *Lbl King's MS 136*, fols 463ʳ–499ᵛ.

[69] *Lbl King's MS 136*, fol. 494ᵛ ('on commança la Messe' qu'il estoit plus de sept heures du soir').

[70] For this see lately Ella Hawkins, 'Appendix 1. *A True Discourse of All the Royal Passages, Tryumphs and Ceremonies, Observed at the Contract and Mariage of the High and Mighty Charles, King of Britain*: The Principal English Festival Book of the 1625 Wedding, Including Two Addresses at Canterbury by John Finch', in Canova-Green and Wolfson (eds), *Wedding of Charles I and Henrietta Maria*, pp. 321–42. Hawkins transcribes the full text from the copy in the British Library, presumably *Lbl G.6189*. For the chronology of the published accounts see Anna-Marie Linnell, 'Becoming a Stuart Queen Consort: Nuptial Texts for Henrietta Maria of France and Catherine or Braganza, Queens of Britain', *Queens Consort, Cultural Transfer and European Politics, c.1500–1800*, ed. by Helen Watanabe-O'Kelly and Adam Morton (Abingdon: Routledge, 2017), pp. 153–71, here p. 158.

[71] This and the following *Relation*, pp. [3–4].

[72] *Trve Discourse*, pp. 8 and 9–10.

2—From Elaborate to Modest: The Seventeenth Century

manuscript account plainly lists 'Les Tambours, Les Trompettes, et les hautbois du Roy, Jouants chacun de leurs jnstruments', but unlike the *Relation* does not mention any reactions of the spectators.[73]

Following on from the ceremonies in France, Sandford recorded that the queen arrived at Dover where the king met her, and that they then went to Canterbury where 'the Royal Nuptials were most gloriously accomplished' before they proceeded to London.[74] This accomplishment, however, did not include an actual wedding ceremony. The pre-marriage treaty had stipulated that the contract should be publicly read in England but 'without the intervention of any Church-Ceremony', as Paul Rapin de Thoyras emphasized.[75] Moreover, it is well-known that the reason for the curtailed, low-key celebrations of the king's wedding in Britain was a combination of the recent and sudden death of James I and an outbreak of the plague.[76]

The *Trve Discourse* describes that once the couple arrived in London, a ceremony took place in 'the great Banquetting-house of Whitehall', that is the one still standing today, and that 'the Articles of the Marriage were read there in publique assembly, and approued by the King and the French Embassadors'.[77] Even though there does not appear to have been an actual wedding service, this ceremony yet ended with the 'blessing being giuen by a Bishop' – thus, strictly speaking, breaking the terms of the contract. No music is reported for this ceremony itself, but the banquet afterwards was accompanied by 'musicke playing all the while'.

Princess Mary and Prince William of Orange, 2 May 1641

The last important royal wedding before the Civil War was that of Princes Mary, eldest daughter of Charles I, to the Dutch Prince William of Orange on 2 May 1641. The bride and groom were a mere nine and fifteen years old, respectively. After the Catholic match of Charles I himself, with its well-known difficulties in the challenging behaviour of Queen Henrietta Maria, this wedding was another affirmation of the Protestant nature of the British monarchy.[78] Indeed, John Finet, at the time Master of the Ceremonies, noted that Charles I had declared three reasons for this marriage in 'the higher house' of parliament, the first of which had been 'the cause of religion, which their[s] being one with ours there should be no dispensation'.[79] With the confessional congruence, this marriage bore considerable political and symbolical weight, which was appropriately illustraded, for instance, in an allegorical engraving by Renier Persyn's that emphasizes the bridal couple's youth and the difference in rank of their parents as much as the religious connotations (Illustration 2.3). Eventually, Princess Mary was to become the mother

---

[73] *Lbl King's MS 136*, fol. 490ᵛ.

[74] Sandford, *Genealogical History* […] *Great Britain*, p. 540.

[75] Thoyras, *History of England*, p. 233. For the stop-over in Canterbury see also Margaret Toynbee, 'The Wedding Journey of King Charles I', *Archeologia Cantiana*, 69 (1955), pp. 75–89, here p. 87.

[76] See the various essays in Canova-Green and Wolfson (eds), *Wedding of Charles I and Henrietta Maria*, especially the chapter by Karen Britland ('A Ring of Roses: Henrietta Maria, Pierre de Bérulle, and the Plague of 1625–1626', pp. 85–104).

[77] This and the following *Trve Discourse*, pp. 34–36.

[78] For the wider political implications of this match see, for instance, Wouter Troost, *William III the Stadholder-King: A Political Biography*, transl. by J. C. Graysons (Aldershot: Ashgate, 2005), pp. 12–13; and Pieter Geyl, *Orange and Stuart 1641–1672*, first publ. in Great Britain by Weidenfeld & Nicolson in 1969, paperback edn (London: Phoenix Press, 2001), Chapter 1.

[79] John Finet, *Ceremonies of Charles I: The Notebooks of John Finet, 1628–1641*, ed. by Albert J. Loomie (New York: Fordham University Press, 1987), p. 302.

Illustration 2.3: Renier Persyn, 'The Betrothal of the Princess Mary to William, Prince of Orange', line engraving, mid-seventeenth century, *National Portrait Gallery, Reference Collection NPG D26430* © National Portrait Gallery, London.

of William III, of 'Glorious Revolution' fame, thus eventually fulfilling the Protestant hopes with which the union had been imbued.

Finet also recorded details of the wedding ceremony.[80] In addition, a very informative, hitherto seemingly unknown account of the wedding is preserved in one of the Harleian manuscripts in the British Library. The writing indicates an eighteenth-century hand, but an annotation at the end explains that the text comes 'From the Bip: of Ely [Bp: Wrenn's] Copy.' (square brackets original).[81] This refers to Matthew Wren, Bishop of Ely since 1638 and also Dean of the Chapel Royal and Clerk of the Closet to the King – thus seemingly giving this account prime credibility, since it was he who married the couple.

The wedding took place on 'Low Sunday' (the Sunday after Easter) in the chapel in Whitehall Palace, as in 1613, and Bishop Wren's account describes its interior in detail. The account also provides some details on the ceremony: the music included organ music and choral singing and 'The Gentlemen of ye Chapel set beneath.' This probably refers to the whole of the choir sitting on the ground-level with the congregation, rather than up in a gallery, again as in 1613.

---

[80] Finet, *Ceremonies*, pp. 310–12.
[81] 'The Marriage of the Princess Mary May 2: 1641.', *Lbl Harley MS 7034*, no. 7 (pp. 422–23).

2—From Elaborate to Modest: The Seventeenth Century

When the first procession arrived, 'the organ play'd a Voluntary, & so continued playing till all were come in'. The first procession was that of the bridegroom with his retinue, followed by that of the bride, and then that of the king, after which 'The organ ceased, & a full Anthem began wch being ended before the Queen was come unto the window of her Closet, the organ played again for a while.' It is not clear what this 'Anthem' was, but with it being described as a 'full Anthem' it may have been a short introit, and with the organ 'ceased' it was seemingly sung unaccompanied. The last remark, that the organ 'played again for a while', seems to refer to organ improvisation until the queen's arrival: with her being Catholic she witnessed the service merely from her closet, not the main part of the chapel like the king. As Finet noted, 'the queen and queen mother [Maria de Medici] entred last into her closet above and there were beholders during the ceremony'.[82]

After the exchange of vows and their blessing, the couple knelt 'just without the Rail [of the altar]'; at the same time the king together with his sons Princes Charles and James went to 'his Travers' and the ambassadors to 'the other Travers', seemingly in silence. The account continues in detail (square brackets original):

> Then was sung by ye Quier [Blessed are all they that fear the Lord &c:] That Anthem being ended, the Clerk of ye Closet kneeled down, but the Bp: standing, & turning towards ye: married Couple (who still remained kneeling) he began with a loude voice [Lord have mercy upon us] & the Quier answered, & so they sang the Lord's prayer, with ye versicles, Answeres & prayers following in the liturgy, for matrimony.[83]

Again, it is not known what the music of the liturgical parts was. Similarly, it is not clear what the mentioned anthem 'Blessed are all they that fear the Lord &c:', on the text from Ps. 128, was. It could have been the setting by Orlando Gibbons mentioned earlier. He had died in 1625 and none of the musicians of the Chapel Royal at the time is known to have set this text.[84] Finet described that 'a hymn (purposely framed for the work in hand) was sung, others following'.[85] The 'hymn' may be the anthem and with the 'others following' Finet seems to refer to the Lesser Litany, Lord's Prayer, and the Responses, which he does not otherwise mention.

Bishop Wren's account records that after the blessing beginning 'Almighty God, which at the beginning' – that is, at the end of the proscribed liturgy – 'the organ began again to play a voluntary, while the King went up to his Closet, & with him the married Couple &c.'.[86] This organ music may again have been (at least partially) improvised so as to cover the time of the procession precisely. Notably, it appears that the service was meant to include the celebration of Holy Communion, which would have made it the first royal wedding since that of Mary I and Philip of Spain in 1554 to include this. The account continues that the clerics 'began ye Communion Service, howbeit because the time was so far spent, the Commandments & ye nicene Creed (by the Dean's appointment from the King) were omitted'. Furthermore, it records that after the reading of the Gospel and the Bishop of Rochester's sermon 'all the other Service (excepting only the prayer for the King & the Queen) were omitted, & ye Blessing was given, & so away they went to dinner'. Thus, it appears that not only the celebration of Holy Communion was omitted but that the sharing of wafers and wine with the toast to the newly-weds, as seen in 1613, was also left out.

---

[82] Finet, *Ceremonies*, p. 310.

[83] *Lbl Harley MS 7034*, p. 423.

[84] For these musicians see Baldwin, *Chapel Royal*, esp. p. 284.

[85] Finet, *Ceremonies*, p. 310.

[86] This and the following *Lbl Harley MS 7034*, p. 423.

As at the 1613 wedding, the bride and bridegroom returned separately, with her going before him. Finet gave as the reason for this that the princess was 'going first out of the chappell, as now a married woman'.[87] Unfortunately, his reasoning is not further explained. No music is reported for the return procession, and as in 1613 it could be that there was none.

According to Wren's account it was 'twelve of the Clock ere they came to the Chappel' and when they left it was 'past two of ye Clock'.[88] The whole of the ceremony would thus have taken over two hours and Finet referred to 'the ceremony of the church having taken up an hour or more'.[89] With the exchange of the vows and the proscribed liturgy being rather short, much of this time would have been taken up by the two anthems and (probably most of it) by the sermon. Notwithstanding all this ceremonial elaboration, it is noteworthy that according to Finet 'the day before' the wedding, the king had 'signified his pleasure *viz.*, that […] he would have it pass with the greatest privacy that might be and would not therefore have so much as a show of a publick feast at it […].'[90]

Charles II and Princess Catherine of Braganza, 21 May 1662

Like his father, Charles I, King Charles II was still unmarried when he came to the throne with the Restoration of the monarchy in 1660. Once again, the chosen bride was a Roman Catholic princess: Catherine of Braganza, daughter of John IV of Portugal and sister of Alfonso VI. This was once again a royal wedding that came with weighty political implications.[91] However, notwithstanding some lavish celebrations in Portugal, in contrast to Charles I's wedding, this time the union was solemnized in only one ceremony – or at least only one confirmed, public one – and that an Anglican one.[92] A marriage treaty had been signed on 22 June 1661, in England, by the Portuguese ambassador.[93]

Referring to the memoirs of the king's brother, at the time Duke of York and later James II, James Macpherson a hundred years later pointed out that Catherine of Braganza was 'the first princess ever permitted to leave her native country without being married by proxy; a ceremony to which the Portuguese would by no means agree, as the [English] ambassador was a Protestant'.[94] In contrast to this, the Scottish philosopher and historian, and later Bishop of Salisbury, Gilbert Burnet in his posthumously published memoirs recorded that there had indeed been a proxy wedding in the bride's home country, with the Earl of Sandwich representing Charles II.[95] As will be seen, there was reportedly also a secret Roman Catholic ceremony in person at some later point.

---

[87] Finet, *Ceremonies*, p. 310. Compare also the following Chapter 3, fn. 109.

[88] *Lbl Harley MS 7034*, pp. 422–23.

[89] Finet, *Ceremonies*, p. 310.

[90] Finet, *Ceremonies*, p. 311.

[91] For a succinct study of the celebrations and implications of this wedding see Lorraine Madway, 'Rites of Deliverance and Disenchantment: The Marriage Celebrations for Charles II and Catherine of Braganza, 1661–62', *The Seventeenth Century*, 27:1 (2012), pp. 79–103.

[92] The Portuguese celebrations are discussed in Madway, 'Rites of Deliverance and Disenchantment'.

[93] Sarah-Beth Watkins, *Catherine of Braganza: Charles II's Restoration Queen* (Alresford: Chronos, 2017), p. 11.

[94] James Macpherson, *The History of Great Britain, from the Restoration, to the Accession of the House of Hanover*, 2 vols, vol. 1 (Dublin: Printed for J. Exshaw […], 1775), p. 41.

[95] [Gilbert] Burnet, *Bishop Burnet's History of his Own Time*, vol. I: *From the Restoration of King Charles II. to the Settlement of King William and Queen Mary at the Revolution* (London: Printed for Thomas Ward, 1724), p. 174.

2—From Elaborate to Modest: The Seventeenth Century

In any case, the main ceremony was an Anglican one, celebrated in person. There is a striking dearth of sources on this wedding. The most informative published one, of the time, is a passage in Sandford's *Genealogical History of the Kings of Portugal*.[96] Sandford recorded that the wedding took place on British soil, in Portsmouth, where the princess had landed.[97] Based on contemporary letters and diary entries, Anna Keay has provided a brief description of the ceremony.[98] She explains that the best venue to house the king and his bride that could be found in Portsmouth was the governor's house, which had been built out of the remains of the 'Domus Dei', a medieval pilgrim's hospital. The ceremony on 21 May took place in the king's (improvised) presence chamber and Keay summarizes that 'The use of secular space for the wedding ceremony was a long-standing convention of royal weddings.' Yet, while this matches with Henry VIII's exceptional weddings and the Oslo ceremony of James VI and Anna of Denmark, this celebration of a royal wedding in a secular space stood in striking contrast to the earlier grand chapel weddings of 1613 and 1641. The time of the ceremony seems not to be known.

The Anglican service followed the Prayer Book. It appears that, as at the 1641 wedding of his sister, the king was not married by the Archbishop of Canterbury but the ceremony was performed by Gilbert Sheldon, Bishop of London and Dean of the Chapel Royal.[99] It is not known that there was any music during the service. As for the wedding of the king's father, Charles I, there does not appear to be a contemporary depiction of the actual wedding, but there is again a rather stylized representation of the scene (Illustration 2.4). This is contemporary, and with the distinct representation of the Anglican cleric it clearly highlights the Protestant nature of the wedding ceremony.

Referring to testimony by the king's brother, the Duke of York, Burnet recorded that the king and queen were also married 'by the Lord *Aubigny* according to the *Roman* ritual'.[100] Also refering to the duke's memoirs, Macpherson explained that prior to the Anglican wedding the king was 'privately married to Catharine by the Lord Aubigny, a secular priest, and almoner to

Illustration 2.4: ['Charles II and Catherine of Braganza'], engraving, c. 1662–70, *Royal Collection, RCIN 602630*, Royal Collection Trust / © Her Majesty Queen Elizabeth II 2021.

---

[96] Francis Sandford, *A Genealogical History of the Kings of Portugal* [...], written in French by Scévole and Lovis de Saincte-Marthe up to 1623, transl. and extended to 1662 by Francis Sandford (London: Printed by E. M. for the author, 1662), pp. 133–34.

[97] Sandford, *Genealogical History* [...] *Portugal*, p. 134.

[98] This and the following Anna Keay, *The Magnificent Monarch: Charles II and the Ceremonies of Power* (London: Continuum, 2008), p. 123.

[99] Sandford, *Genealogical History* [...] *Portugal*, p. 134. Burnet, *History*, p. 174, states that they were married by the 'Archbishop of *Canterbury*'.

[100] Burnet, *History*, p. 174.

the Queen-dowager, according to the rites of the Romisch church' and he observed that 'None but some of her [the new queen's] Portuguese attendants were privy to the first marriage.'[101] All the same, Macpherson also notes that the Duke of York was not present, as he had gone to Plymouth, where the princess had been expected to land. Whether this ceremony took place or not, it would not have included any elaborate ceremonial or music.

Overall, Lorraine Madway has summarized that the lack of ceremonial elaboration and impact at the king's wedding was simply due to his not being that interested in the whole affair.[102] In contrast to the subdued wedding ceremonies themselves, there was an impressive river pageant on 23 August 1662 to celebrate the grand official entry of the king and his new queen – yet, this was organized not by the court, but by the City of London.[103] At least for this event, it is reported that it included 'loud Musick'.

James II and his Daughters

With Charles II not having any legitimate offspring, his heir and successor was his brother James, Duke of York, who eventually came to the throne as James II in 1685. He had been married twice before he became king: in September 1660, he had married Anne Hyde rather secretly, and it took a while until the marriage was publicly recognized.[104] Soon after her death, he married the Italian Roman Catholic Princess Mary of Modena in 1673. This match was so unpopular that parliament protested against it.[105] Almost no details seem to be known about these two weddings. Out of his first marriage, James II had two daughters who were brought up as Protestants and who in turn succeeded him as Mary II and Queen Anne.

Princess Mary and William III of Orange, 4 November 1677

Like her aunt and namesake in 1641, Princess Mary, the daughter of the then Duke of York and future James II, in 1677 married a Prince of Orange: William III, who was in fact the offspring of the 1641 union and thus her cousin. Again, like with her aunt, this match emphasized and strengthened the Protestant nature of the restored Stuart monarchy, which at the time was much weakened by the Duke of York's open adherence of Roman Catholicism. As Odai Johnson has summarized, 'the Protestant populace looked with great hope' on this wedding.[106] Indeed, the *London Gazette* recorded that there were numerous public rejoicings with bonfires and bell ringing all over the country, as well as in Edinburgh and Dublin.[107]

---

[101] This and the following Macpherson, *History*, p. 2. See also Madway, 'Rites of Deliverance', p. 91.

[102] Madway, 'Rites of Deliverance', esp. p. 91.

[103] For this river pageant see Madway, 'Rites of Deliverance', pp. 93–96; and also Margaret Shewring, 'The Iconography of Populism: Waterborne Entries to London for Anne Boleyn (1533), Catherine of Braganza (1662) and Elizabeth II (2012)', *Ceremonial Entries in Early Modern Europe: The Iconography of Power*, ed. by J. R. Mulryne (Farnham: Ashgate, 2015), pp. 221–44, esp. pp. 228–36.

[104] See John Miller, *James II*, first publ. in 1978 by Wayland Ltd, re-issue of 2nd edn by Methuen from 1989 (New Haven: Yale University Press, 2000), pp. 44–45.

[105] See W[illiam] A[rthur] Speck, *James II*, first publ. in 2002 by Pearson Education Ltd (London: Routledge, 2016).

[106] Odai Johnson, *Rehearsing the Revolution: Radical Performance, Radical Politics in the English Restoration* (Newark: University of Delaware Press, 2000), p. 67. For the political significance of the match see also, for instance, Troost, *William III*, p. 138.

[107] See *London Gazette*, 5–8 November 1677; and *LG*, 3–6 December 1677.

2—From Elaborate to Modest: The Seventeenth Century

The couple eventually came to the throne as joint monarchs after the 'Glorious Revolution' of 1688–89.

However, notwithstaning the reported public rejoicings through the country, the wedding itself seems to have been a very low-key, simple ceremony. Once again, the most informative account of the wedding appears to be that by Francis Sandford in his *Genealogical History of the Kings of England*, which was published in the same year.[108] Sandford had been Lancaster Herald since November 1676 and was a supporter of James II. It is not clear whether Sandford himself attended the ceremony. He recorded that the couple was married on 4 November 1677 by Henry Compton, Bishop of London and Dean of the Chapel Royal. The ceremony was 'privately celebrated' in the princess's own 'Bed-chamber at *St. James's*' at 'about Eight of the Clock in the Evening'. It was the king himself who gave away the bride, his niece, not her father, who was not in favour of the match.

Notwithstanding that there must obviously have been only very limitated space in the princess's chamber, Sandford recorded for the ceremony that 'some of the most eminent Nobility of this Kingdom and of the *United Provinces*', that is the Netherlands, were 'present thereat'. Nevertheless, despite the presence of such a noble assemblage, there is no evidence of any ceremonial elaboration of the rite, let alone any music. It would appear that Compton merely read the service in the Prayer Book.

Princess Anne and Prince George of Denmark, 28 July 1683

Princess Anne, the younger daughter of the Duke of York and herself later Queen Anne was married to Prince George, brother of Christian V of Denmark, in 1683. This union with a Lutheran prince further strengthened the Protestant bonds of the Stuart monarchy in the later years of Charless II's reign – although it has been shown that the future William III, for instance, was against this marriage, as Denmark was an ally of Catholic France.[109]

For 28 July, the *London Gazette* reported that the wedding was to be solemnized 'this Evening at St. James's by the Bishop of London, in the Presence of their Majesties, their Royal Highnesses, and the cheifest [*sic*] of the Nobility'.[110] This did not state where exactly the ceremony was celebrated. The earliest reference for the exact venue of the wedding appears to be Samuel Stebbing's continuation of Sandford's *Genealogical History of the Kings of England*, where Stebbing noted that the wedding took place 'in the Chapel Royal in St. *James's*'.[111] If this is correct, this would have been the earliest royal wedding in this chapel.

As for the 1677 wedding of Princess Mary, it is not known whether there was any ceremonial elaboration at this wedding. Similarly, the records again do not mention any music for the service, and it is possible that it was again have read.[112] All the same, the wedding celebrations at least at some point featured a bit of specially composed, commemorative music. It was on this occasion that Henry Purcell, who was at the time organist of Westminster Abbey as well as one of the organists of the Chapel Royal, wrote *From Hardy Climes*, 'A song y^t was

---

[108] This and the following Sandford, *Genealogical History* […] *Great Britain*, p. 567.

[109] See Troost, *William III*, p. 174.

[110] *London Gazette*, 26–30 July 1683.

[111] Francis Sandford and Samuel Stebbing, *A Genealogical History of the Kings of England, and Monarchs of Great Britain, &c. From the Conquest, Anno 1066. to the Year, 1707*, continued from 1677 by Samuel Stebbing (London: Printed by M. Jenour, for John Nicholson, 1707), p. 758.

[112] See esp. Ashbee and Harley, *Cheque Books*, II, p. 293 (from Marmaduke Alford's Notes).

British Royal Weddings

perform'd to Prince George upon his Marriage with ye Lady Ann'.[113] Purcell's musical offering, with its quasi dedication to the bridegroom, was presented at the reception on the morning after the wedding.[114] If there was a ceremony with music in the Chapel Royal, Purcell would *qua office* probably have contributed to this too.

⁓

British royal weddings in the seventeenth century saw a considerable change from grand elaborate court occasions to far more modest, almost secret ceremonies, matching with David Cressy's more general observation that 'By the late seventeenth century the English were said to be famous for cheap weddings and lavish funerals.'[115] The spectacular ceremonial and the rich musical programme of the two elaborate pre-Civil War royal weddings greatly emphasizes that the weddings after the Restoration were rather low-key, plain and straightforward ceremonies. By the 1670s, weddings had become one of the most inconspicuous royal ceremonies and in terms of their music were literally 'quiet'. Yet, the ceremonial character of royal weddings was again to change very much in the next century; and the musical contributions to these events were to become much more prominent.

---

[113] Robert Thompson, 'Purcell's Great Autographs', in *Purcell Studies*, ed. by Curtis Price (Cambridge: Cambridge University Press, 1995), pp. 6–34, here p. 23, referring to *Lbl R.M. MS 20.h.8*. See also Ian Spink, 'Purcell's Odes: Propaganda and Panegyric', in *Purcell Studies*, ed. Price, pp. 145–71, here pp. 166–68.

[114] See esp. James Anderson Winn, *Queen Anne: Patroness of Arts* (Oxford: Oxford University Press, 2014), 43–49; and his, 'Praise the Patroness of Arts', in *Queen Anne and the Arts*, ed. by Cedric D. Reverand II (Lanham: Bucknell University Press, 2015), pp. 7–39, here pp. 16–18.

[115] David Cressy, *Birth, Marriage, and Death: Ritual, Religion, and the Life-Cycle in Tudor and Stuart England* (Oxford: Oxford University Press, 1997), p. 454. For the funerals see Range, *BRSF*, chapters 1 and 2.

3

The 'Concert Weddings' I: The Children of George II

MARY II AND WILLIAM III did not have any survivig offspring and none of the children of Queen Anne survived into adulthood. When George I came to the throne in 1714, both of his children were already married and his grandchildren were still very young. Therefore it was not until the second quarter of the eighteenth century that the London court saw again the celebration of a royal wedding. The London weddings of three of the children of George II and Queen Caroline, between 1734 and 1740, were rather splendid affairs and turned out to be very influential on those that followed – both in terms of their ceremonial and especially also in respect to their music.

During the eighteenth century, royal and state occasions were often also grand musical occasions, containing much elaborate music. For coronations and royal funerals in the period, the additional denominator of 'concerts' has been suggested.[1] While weddings seem generally to have contained somewhat less music than other royal occasions, the Georgian royal weddings stand out for having included elaborate, large-scale and lengthy anthems that were appended to the liturgical ceremony almost like a topical concert.

The Children of George II and Queen Caroline

Three of the eight children of George II and Queen Caroline married in London. At least from a music perspective, their weddings are among the best researched and best known of all royal weddings, because for all three it was George Frideric Handel who was called upon to provide the music. Donald Burrows has provided accounts of the negotiations, problems and issues that occurred leading up to these weddings as well as of the arrangements for the ceremonies themselves, including detailed discussions of the music and its performance.[2] Matthew Gardner has added some more informative details on Handel's pieces.[3] Nevertheless, the overall ceremonial of these occasions and in particular the place of the music within them have not been discussed in detail. A fresh approach, together with some newly discovered sources provides the opportunity for further exploration.

---

[1] See Matthias Range, *Music and Ceremonial at British Coronations: From James I to Elizabeth II* (Cambridge: Cambridge University Press, 2012) [hereinafter *MCBC*], Chapters 5 and 6, and Matthias Range, *British Royal and State Funerals: Music and Ceremonial since Elizabeth I* (Woodbridge: Boydell Press, 2016) [hereinafter *BRSF*], Chapter 4. The terminology refers to a suggestion by Sabine Henze-Döhring in relation to the 1727 coronation; see her 'Händels Coronation Anthems', *Händel-Jahrbuch*, 49 (2003), pp. 105–13, here p. 110.

[2] Donald Burrows, *Handel and the English Chapel Royal* (Oxford: Oxford University Press, 2005) [hereinafter *HECR*], Chapters 12 and 13. For the historical background and context of these weddings see Veronica P. M. Baker-Smith, 'The Daughters of George II: Marriage and Dynastic Politics', in *Queenship in Britain 1660–1837: Royal Patronage, Court Culture and Dynastic Politics*, ed. Clarissa Campbell Orr (Manchester: Manchester University Press, 2002), pp. 193–206.

[3] Matthew Gardner, 'Preface' to Georg Friedrich Händel, *Wedding Anthems (HWV 262 and HWV 263)*, ed. by Matthew Gardner, *Hallische Händel-Ausgabe*, series III, vol. 11 (Kassel: Bärenreiter, 2013), pp. xvii–xxv.

British Royal Weddings

Princess Anne and William IV, Prince of Orange, 14 March 1734

Princess Anne was the eldest daughter of George II and Queen Caroline, with the honorary title 'Princess Royal'. In March 1734 she married William IV, Prince of Orange-Nassau and later *stadtholder* of the Netherlands from 1747. The wedding had originally been planned to take place in the autumn of 1733, but it had to be postponed to the spring of 1734: first because of the prince's late arrival in Britain and then due to his ill health.[4] As Gardner has pointed out, it was only one week before the actual wedding that the date of 14 March was officially announced by the Lord Chamberlain.[5]

This marriage was important due to its strengthening the ties with the House of Orange, thus endorsing the *status quo* after the 'Glorious Revolution' and emphasizing the Protestant character of the monarchy.[6] It was probably in consequence of this that the wedding was a rather grand court affair. As one journal at the time pointed out there had been 'no such thing in *England*, since the Marriage of the Princess *Elizabeth*, Daughter of *James* I. and Great Grand-Mother to his present Majesty [George II], with the Elector *Palatine*'.[7] There was furthermore an additional reason for the elaboration at this wedding: as Hannah Smith has argued, 'international rivalry' stimulated the king to spend considerable amounts on the weddings of his children – and she referred particularly to the 1734 wedding of Princess Anne, which competed with the recent 'splendid' wedding celebrations of the children of Frederick William I at the Prussian court.[8]

Ceremonial Character and Venue

As this was the first royal wedding for a long time, the College of Arms was asked about precedents for English princesses marrying 'Foreign Princes', and the records of the House of Lords were also checked.[9] It is interesting that the heralds were consulted, when – strictly speaking – the organization of royal weddings no longer fell into their domain.[10] They were apparently still involved in such ceremonial matters and were esteemed as reliable record keepers.

Burrows has pointed out that a 'relevant and accessible' precedent for the wedding was that of Princess Elizabeth, eldest daughter of James VI/I, in 1613: the ceremonial for this wedding had handily been entered in the Chapel Royal's Old Cheque Book.[11] Indeed, a newly found source in the College of Arms confirms that the 1734 ceremonial was modelled directly on that of 1613: a collection of miscellania by John Anstis, at the time Garter King of Arms, includes an untitled fragmentary draft for the 1734 ceremony with many corrections and additions that heavily refer back to 1613, in particular mentioning John Finet's account of that wedding.[12]

---

[4] For details see Veronica P. M. Baker-Smith, *A Life of Anne of Hanover, Princess Royal* (Leiden: Brill, 1995), Chapter 5.

[5] Gardner, 'Preface', p. xviii, who refers to *St James's Evening Post* of 7–9 March 1734.

[6] See Hannah Smith, *Georgian Monarchy: Politics and Culture, 1714–1760* (Cambridge: Cambridge University Press, 2006), p. 46.

[7] Untitled account (under 'Thursday, 14'), in *London Magazine*, March 1734, pp. 151–53 here p. 151.

[8] Hannah Smith, *Georgian Monarchy*, p. 102.

[9] See Burrows, *HECR*, p. 314, fn. 23.

[10] See the discussion in Chapter 1, above.

[11] Burrows, *HECR*, p. 314, and Andrew Ashbee and John Harley (eds), *The Cheque Books of the Chapel Royal*, 2 vols (Aldershot: Ashgate, 2000), I, pp. 172–75. See also the previous chapter, fn. 24.

[12] *Lea Miscell: Coll: By Anstis*: in about the middle of the unfoliated volume. For the transcription of a longer passage from this see Appendix B 3.1.

3—The 'Concert Weddings' I: The Children of George II

This draft very much accords with the 1734 ceremonial and accounts of the ceremony as published in newspapers and journals before and after the event.

The overall ceremonial character of the princess's wedding was not at all a foregone conclusion. John Perceval, 1st Earl of Egmont, noted in his diary:

> I was also told that when the Queen and the Princess Royal desired to the King some time ago to suffer the wedding to be private, on account of the Prince's late indisposition, his Majesty answered, it should be public or not at all.[13]

In the end, the wedding was what was heraldically styled 'private' and took place 'in the evening', as the *London Gazette* reported.[14] A very detailed account of the wedding is included in a letter from Edward Godfrey (former Privy Purse to Queen Anne) to his daughter Mary, wife of the clergyman and antiquarian Cox Macro.[15] This has not previously been used in discussions of this wedding; yet, – except for the service itself – it provides a beautifully intriguing, personal impression by an eye-witness. Godfrey recorded that the procession began 'about a Quarter before 8', concurring with other sources which state that it began 'About Eight'.[16] According to Godfrey, the procession 'Closed' at 'a little before 9', when the ceremony in the chapel began.[17] The whole of the procession would thus have taken about an hour. The service itself 'was concluded about a Quarter before Ten', and thus took about 45 mins.[18] The published accounts do not mention exact times for the end of the ceremony, with the *Gazette* merely noting that 'About Eleven the Royal Family supp'd in Publick in the great State Ball-Room'.[19] As mentioned in Chapter 1, a late-evening, nocturnal ceremony was in accordance with other royal ceremonies of the period. However, it could be that Queen Caroline and the Princess Royal, with their aforementioned request to the king, had meant 'private' more in the modern sense, of a low-scale ceremony: Stephen Martin Leake, at the time Norroy King of Arms, afterwards recorded: 'It is thought the Court wisht the Wedding had been more private.'[20] In the end, the overall more public character of the event as a whole could probably not be mistaken. According to one record there were clear public markers of the day:

> In the cities of *London* and *Westminster*, the morning was ushered in by ringing of bells and firing of guns. All the ships in the river were adorned with flags and streamers, and fired their guns.[21]

Details of the ceremony, especially the order of the processions, were reported in the *London Gazette*, as well as many other newspapers.[22] The more public character of the ceremony

---

[13] John Perceval, *Manuscripts of the Earl of Egmont. Diary of Viscount Percival afterwards First Earl of Egmont* (Viscount Percival), 3 vols (London: His Majesty's Stationery Office, 1923), II, p. 59.

[14] *London Gazette*, 12–16 March 1733/4.

[15] Edward Godfrey to 'M.ʳ [Cox] Macro' [but actually to Macro's wife, Godfrey's daughter], 16 March 1733/4, *Lbl Add MS 32556*, fols 156ʳ–57ʳ (no. 90). See transcr. in Appendix B 3.2.

[16] *Lbl Add MS 32556*, fol. 156ʳ; and, for instance, 'Nuptials Solemnized at St. James's', *The Political State of Great Britain*, 47 (1734), pp. 321–26, here p. 321.

[17] *Lbl Add MS 32556*, fol. 156ᵛ.

[18] *Lbl Add MS 32556*, fol. 156ᵛ.

[19] *London Gazette*, 12–16 March 1733/4. Burrows (*HECR*, p. 319) concludes that the 'service itself took place about 10 o'clock at night', and the ball at midnight.

[20] *Lea S.M.L. 44*, p. 140.

[21] Report reprinted in *The British Chronologist*, 2 (1775), pp. 187–89, here p. 187.

[22] *London Gazette*, 12–16 March 1733/4. For the other sources see below. A manuscript order of the procession survives in the Royal Archives: 'Procession on / the Princess Royalls / Marriage. / March 14.ᵗʰ 1733/4', *Wra GEO/MAIN/52790-52794*; available online via https://gpp.royalcollection.org.uk (accessed 4 September 2021).

was also emphasized by the choice of venue. It appears that from early on, it was decided that the wedding should take place in the French Chapel at St James's Palace: the newspapers had reported this in late October.[23] This was before the prince arrived in London in November, and before the wedding was postponed several times. The 'French' Chapel is the chapel named after the French Protestants in the service of William III, today known as 'the Queen's Chapel'. It is a curious coincidence that this chapel owes its sheer existence to a royal wedding, so to speak: the building was begun in 1623, in order to provide a place of Catholic worship for the future Charles I's expected bride-to-be, the Infanta Maria of Spain — and it was eventually used by his actual bride, Henrietta Maria of France.[24]

There is good evidence for the reasons why the wedding was celebrated in this chapel, and not in the 'regular' Chapel Royal within the palace — or even in the chapel at Hampton Court Palace, as reported by *The Daily Courant* on 16 October 1733.[25] The choice was motivated, as Leake recorded, by 'the Chapel Royal being too small and not admitting of a Procession'.[26] Yet, in another record Leake commented that eventually the chosen chapel was still 'much too little for the Company'.[27] The desire to have a longer processional route was better rewarded.

The Procession

The long procession to the service was one of the main features of this wedding. Another newly found contemporary account from the heralds' collection recorded some details of the processional route:

> A Covered Gallery was erected from the Garden Door of St James's house cross the Garden & over the wall thereof into the Parke, & from thence continued to yᵉ Great Door of yᵉ French Chappel of the Friary opening towards yᵉ Park, in which Gallery on each side were seats made for yᵉ Spectators, who were admitted with Ticketts.[28]

This was a rather long processional route, and the procession was more or less entirely outdoors. The account's description that the route went over the garden wall and 'into the Parke' indicates that it crossed, or at least came close to what is today the Mall, before turning back towards the chapel, at the other end of the palace. Leake also recorded a description of this route, neatly summarizing that it formed 'a half H':

> About 7 a Clock the Procession began from the drawing room thrō a boarded Gallery of Great length making a half H. oneside going into the Garden the other crossing from thence into the passage into the Park & the third / parrallel to the first leading to the Door of the Lutheran Chapel[.][29]

---

[23] See Burrows, *HECR*, p. 313.

[24] For the history of this chapel see David Baldwin, *The Chapel Royal – Ancient and Modern* (London: Duckworth, 1990), Chapter 6, here p. 129. For a succinct historical overview see also Simon Bradley, 'The Queen's Chapel in the Twentieth Century', *Architectural History*, 44: 'Essays in Architectural History Presented to John Newman' (2001), pp. 293–302. Burrows, *HECR*, pp. 515–18, provides further literature on the history of the chapel in fn. 43.

[25] See Burrows, *HECR*, p. 313.

[26] 'The Ceremonial of the Marriage of William Prince of Orange, with the Princess Royal of Great Britain […]', in *Lca S.M.L. 30*, pp. 37–42, here p. 37.

[27] *Lca S.M.L. 44*, p. 138.

[28] 'Concerning yᵉ marriage of yᵉ Princess Royall / with yᵉ Prince of Orange.', in *Lca Briscoe I*, p. 282.

[29] *Lca S.M.L. 44*, p. 135. NB This account also gives a detailed description of the covered gallery; it calls the chapel the 'Lutheran Chapel'.

3—The 'Concert Weddings' I: The Children of George II

The 'Door of the Lutheran Chapel' in Leake's account – which is the 'Great Door' at the 'Friary opening towards ye Park' in the heralds' account – must refer to the porch at the chapel's south side that faced a broad passage leading to the park: this can be seen in an engraving from 1690.[30] The modern main entrance of the chapel, at the west end, facing the palace, was not easily accessible from the park. The garden front of the palace, with the chapel in the background, is depicted in an engraving showing the arrival of George I in 1714 – and the garden/park situation can also be compared with a 'bird's-eye' view by Johannes Kip from 1705.[31] Even more clearly, Henry Flitcroft's plan of the palace from 1729 does not show a direct passage from the park to the chapel's west end. The possible route of the procession, forming 'a half H', is superimposed onto Flitcrof's plan in Illustration 3.1.[32]

The 'boarded Gallery', or raised gangway, had been built so that the procession could be seen better. It had a cover in bright orange, the prince-bridegroom's colour, that caused the Duchess of Marlborough, who lived next door, to complain.[33] Godfrey recorded that the gallery for the procession was lit by 'Candles' that were 'replenished Three times before the Procession ended[;] the Wind coming through the Crevices made them burn away so fast the Place was neither too hot nor too cold'.[34] The gallery did probably not miss the desired effect. One account judged enthusiastically that the wedding as a whole was 'solemnized in a most magnificent and grand Manner', mentioning especially that 'The Procession from St. *James*'s-*House*, thro' the Gallery that was built for the Purpose, to the Chapel, was exceeding splendid.'[35] Referring to the bride's part in the procession, Godfrey emphasized that

> The agreeableness of which Sight was beyond expression[:] I don't think the most Splended part of a Coronation comparable to it.[36]

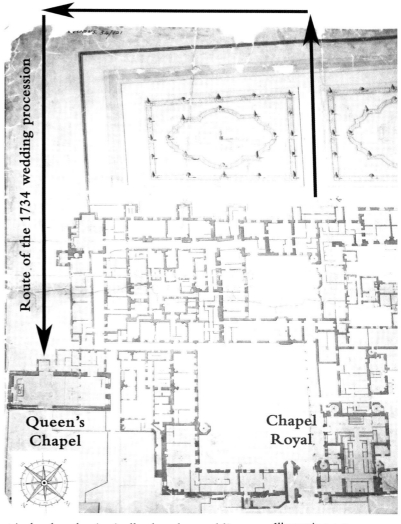

Illustration 3.1: Detail of the ground-floor plan of St James's Palace by Henry Flitcroft, 1729. *Lna WORK 34/121*. The processional route reported for 1734 is indicated (and compass added).

---

[30] Reproduced in Kenneth Scott, *St James's Palace: A History* (London: Scala, 2010), p. 58.

[31] Both are reproduced in Scott, *St James's Palace*, pp. 69 and 56.

[32] NB In Flintcroft's plan, the rooms are shown with coloration, contrasting clearly with the blank courtyards and passages. See also the corresponding first-floor plan in *Lna WORK 34/122* and Scott, *St James's Palace*, p. 72.

[33] See Scott, *St James's Palace*, p. 77.

[34] *Lbl Add MS 32556*, fol. 156^r. See also Leake's description in *Lca S.M.L. 44*, p. 135.

[35] *London Magazine*, March 1734, p. 151, under 'THURSDAY, 14.'.

[36] *Lbl Add MS 32556*, fol. 156^v.

British Royal Weddings

The special provisions for the spectators of the procession are noteworthy. Hannah Smith observes that the seats along the processional way were 'to hold four thousand people', while Burrows calculates only 2000 people in the scaffolding.[37] Godfrey estimated that the gallery 'contained about 5 Thousand Spectators'.[38] At any rate, this procession was a major aspect of the proceedings. Admission to see it was by ticket only and the *London Magazine* recorded for the day before the wedding:

> This Morning early the Tickets were distributed for seeing the Ceremony and Procession of the Royal Marriage of his Highness the Prince of *Orange* with the Princess Royal, when 6 Tickets were deliver'd to every Nobleman and Foreign Ambassador, 4 to each of the Foreign Ministers, and 2 to every Member of Parliament, Officer of State, &c.[39]

This would mean that the spectators of the procession were more or less all from the élite, or at least clearly not from the general public. Godfrey enthusiastically recalled, the 'Spectators, all richly drest which Sight alone was worth Seeing'.[40] However, while it was not possible simply to buy a ticket, the procession was yet a much more public part of the event than the ensuing service. Not only was there much reporting about it; moreover, an image of the procession, together with a description of the ceremony in both English and French, was sold after the event, in an early form of merchandising at such royal events (Illustration 3.2).[41]

According to Godfrey, the king made good use of the spectacle of this procession to present himself to those lining the route:

> His Majesty was so complaisant as to Walk athwart the Gallery not strait forwards[,] turning himself continually half round as he went [so] that People might have a full View of him[.][42]

The procession was accompanied by instrumental music, increasing the impression of splendour and the extraordinary statyus of its participants. The accounts and the aforementioned illustration agree that the procession was headed by a fife, four drums (only two in the illustration), a kettle-drum and twice four trumpeters, together with the drum-major and the serjeant-trumpeter (the latter not shown).[43] In slight contrast to these, Godfrey recorded:

> First a Man Playing on a Pipe with 5 Drums Beating followed by the Drum Major[,] then 12 Trumpets & Kettle Drums in the Middle the Serjeant Trumpeter with his Mace[.] The Pipe & Drums, & Trumpets & Kettle Drums Playing alternately to the Chapel [...].[44]

Godfrey's observation that the two musical groups played in alternation is particularly noteworthy. One of Leake's accounts also lists the drums and trumpets at the head of the procession, and he confirms their actually playing with the annotation 'The Drums beating & Trumpets Sounding'.[45]

---

[37] Hannah Smith, *Georgian Monarchy*, p. 104; Burrows, *HECR*, p. 313.

[38] *Lbl Add MS 32556*, fol. 156ʳ.

[39] *London Magazine*, March 1734, p. 151, under 'WEDNESDAY, 13.'

[40] *Lbl Add MS 32556*, fol. 156ʳ.

[41] *The Ceremony of the Marriage of the Princess Royal with the Prince of Orange* (1734). This was printed in at least two different versions, which differ in the length of the accompanying text but not the image of the procession: See *London, British Museum Mm,3.5* ('Printed for Bispham Dickinson') and *London, British Museum Mm,2.149* ('Printed for Sold by Eliz: Foster').

[42] *Lbl Add MS 32556*, fol. 156ᵛ.

[43] *London Magazine*, March 1734, p. 151. The accounts in the *Gentleman's Magazine*, 4 (1734), pp. 160–61, here p. 160, and 'Nuptials Solemnized', p. 321, list twice 'Eight Trumpets'.

[44] *Lbl Add MS 32556*, fol. 156ʳ.

[45] *Lca S.M.L. 30*, p. 37.

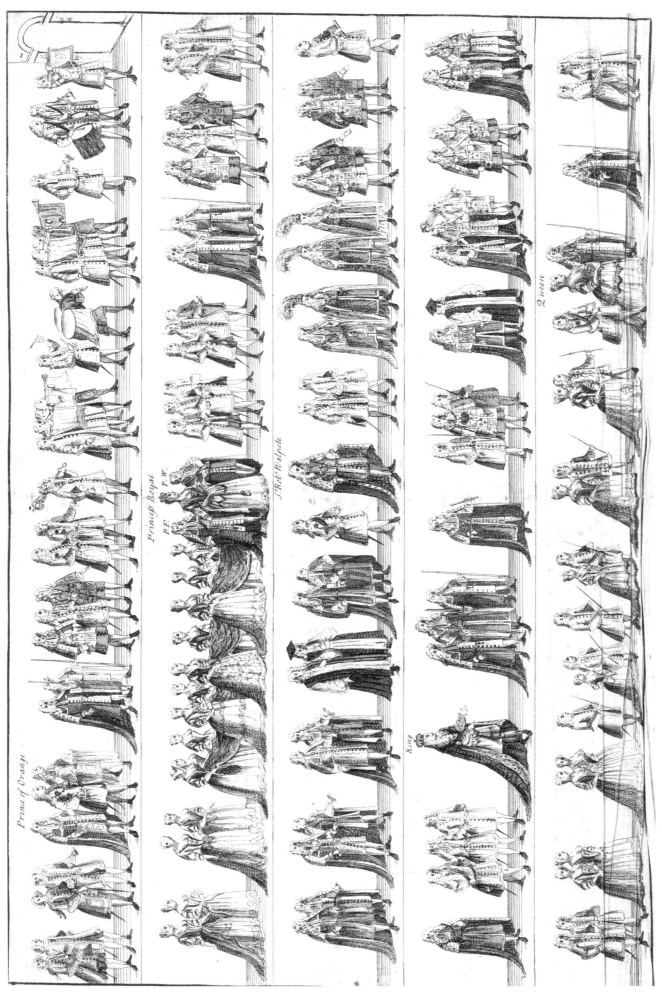

Illustration 3.2: 'The Ceremony of the Marriage of the Princess Royal with the Prince of Orange', detail showing the procession to the service, broadsheet print, 1734, here from *London, British Museum, Mm,3.5* © The Trustees of the British Museum.

British Royal Weddings

In fact, each of the three sections of the procession – those of the bridegroom, the bride, and the monarch – was accompanied by separate music. One account detailed that, after the bridegroom's procession had reached the chapel,

> The Drums and Trumpets likewise returned back to their first Station without playing, and then play'd in like manner before the Procession of the Bride; and did the same in the Procession of his and her Majesty.[46]

Similarly, Godfrey distinctly records the musicians as returning for the king's procession.[47] Given the length of the processional route, and unless they took a shortcut, their walking back – whether in silence or not – would have created notable gaps in the proceedings.

Burrows suggests 'Hanoverian practice' as precedent for the incorporation of these instruments in the procession.[48] All the same, it is worth remembering that they were also a traditional component of British royal processions at coronations and funerals, for instance.[49] Furthermore, another possible precedent was of course French practice, already seen at the proxy wedding of Charles I in Paris. Indeed, there was a more recent example: as mentioned in Chapter 1, in September 1725, Louis XV had married Marie Leszczyńska in the chapel of the Château de Fontainebleau, recorded in an English account of the ceremony published in the following year. This account detailed that the procession 'went out [...] at the Sound of Trumpets, Fifes and Tabors [=Tambours?]'.[50] It continued to explain that 'the Musick' of the procession did not enter the chapel but 'staid without', and this too corresponds with what is reported for the 1734 wedding: the accounts make it clear that the instrumentalists did not enter the chapel but 'filed off, standing upon each side'.[51]

The Service

Inside the chapel, Princess Anne was led to the altar by her brothers, 'the Prince of Wales and the Duke [of Cumberland]'.[52] As for the previous royal weddings, the king and queen entered the Chapel Royal only after the bride. Leake and other sources recorded that the organ played during these entrance processions:

> From the first appearance of the Procession, the Organ played; and all persons being seated, the Organ ceased, and Divine Service began.[53]

The couple was married by 'Dr Edmund Gibson (Lord Bishop of London)', as Dean of the Chapel Royal.[54] As already mentioned in Chapter 1, a later memorandum on the matter pointed out that he officiated because the Archbishop of Canterbury, William Wake, was not able to attend this and the following wedding; indeed, Leake recorded that the ceremonial had

---

[46] This and the following 'Nuptials Solemnized', p. 322. The same in the account in *Gentleman's Magazine*, 4 (1734), here on p. 161.

[47] *Lbl Add MS 32556*, fol. 156ᵛ.

[48] Burrows, *HECR*, p. 314.

[49] See Range, *MCBC* and Range, *BRSF*, passim.

[50] *An Exact Account of the Ceremonies Observed at the Marriage of His Most Christian Majesty Lewis XV. with the Princess Mary, Daughter of Stanislaus, Late King of Poland* [...] (London: Printed for Tho. Worrall, 1726), p. 51.

[51] 'Nuptials Solemnized', p. 321.

[52] See the report in the *Gentleman's Magazine*, 4 (1734), here at p. 160.

[53] *Lca S.M.L. 30*, p. 41. This also in *Gentleman's Magazine*, 4 (1734), p. 160; and 'Nuptials Solemnized', p. 325.

[54] *Llp Moore 6*, fol. 46ʳ 'Register of the Chapel Royal / Nᵒ 1 / Marriage of Princess Royal and Prince of Orange March 14:ᵗʰ 1733¾' (copy from 1791 by the Windsor Herald).

3—The 'Concert Weddings' I: The Children of George II

scheduled the two archbishops for the procession but then explained in a marginal note 'Neither of yᵉ Archbisᵖˢ present'.[55] In the end, the *London Magazine* recorded for the service:

> The Lord Bishop of *London*, Dean of the Chapel, and the Lord Bishop of *Winchester*, Clerk of the Closet, stood before the Communion-Table with Prayer-Books in their Hands; [...].[56]

Thus, it seems that the participants used the usual copies of the Prayer Book. Specially produced orders of service had been prepared for earlier thanksgiving services; they were not, however, standard for such royal occasions: for coronations, they had been introduced only at the most recent one, in 1727, and then only for those actually officiating at the event – and for funerals they were not produced until 1902.[57]

With the service following the Prayer Book, the music would have included the psalm and possibly the Responses and Lord's Prayer. Indeed, the draft for 1734 based on the 1613 wedding scheduled the choir to sing 'Blessed are they that fear the Lord &c', that is the appointed psalm, and it also lists that 'Lord have mercy upon [later: 'us'] which the Choir answers, & then the Lords Prayers [*sic*], the Versicles, Answers &t are sung'.[58] It is, however, not known that these were eventually performed. Yet, apart from organ music at the beginning, the known accounts for 1734 also refer to one other item that was, without doubt, the most outstanding musical feature. At the end of the ceremony came a grand anthem: Handel's *This Is the Day which the Lord Has Made* (HWV 262).[59]

The Anthem

The choice of Handel as composer of the anthem for the wedding has been interpreted as a personal preference of the royal family. With reference to Maurice Greene, the regular organist of the Chapel Royal, Victor Schoelcher suggested that Princess Anne, 'who always showed a great partiality for Handel, preferred to have anything by him rather than the work of Greene'.[60] Anthony Hicks also put Handel's appointment down to the princess's influence, pointing out that she was Handel's pupil, and Burrows concluded that 'we must assume that Handel was given priority at the Princess's request'.[61] More recently, Burrows has proposed that the request for Handel could also have come from the king or the queen.[62]

In this context, it has been suggested that the anthem's text had been 'written by Anne herself', or that the princess 'had paraphrased the text of Psalm 45 herself', respectively.[63] However, the evidence for such suggestions is not clear. Burrows interestingly proposes that the text was

---

[55] *Lca S.M.L. 30*, p. 40. For the later memorandum see Chapter 1, fn. 59.

[56] *London Magazine*, March 1734, pp. 151–53, here p. 152.

[57] See Range, *MCBC*, p. 130, and Range, *BRSF*, pp. 26 and 91.

[58] See above, fn. 12, and the transcription in Appendix B 3.1.

[59] For an edition of Handel's wedding anthems see Georg Friedrich Händel, *Wedding Anthems (HWV 262 and HWV 263)*, ed. by Matthew Gardner, *Hallische Händel-Ausgabe*, series III, vol. 11 (Kassel: Bärenreiter, 2013).

[60] Victor Schoelcher, *The Life of Handel* (London: Trübner and Co., 1857), p. 166.

[61] Anthony Hicks, 'Handel and "Il Parnasso in festa"', *Musical Times*, 112 (1971), pp. 339–40, here p. 339; and Donald Burrows, *Handel*, 'The Master Musicians', ed. by Stanley Sadie (Oxford: Oxford University Press, 1994, paperback edn 1996), p. 235.

[62] Burrows, *HECR*, p. 316.

[63] Baker-Smith, *Life of Anne of Hanover*, p. 47; and Andrew C. Thompson, *George II: King and Elector* (New Haven: Yale University Press, 2011), p. 110. See also John van der Kiste, *King George II and Queen Caroline* (Thrupp: Sutton Publishing, 1997), p. 133 ('written by the bride').

British Royal Weddings

chosen to suit the pre-existing music – for, as will be seen, Handel re-used much of his earlier music.[64] If this was the case, it would at least somewhat seem to undermine the importance, if not relevance of the text. In this context, it is worth remembering that the text would not have been available to anyone at the service, even though it had been published in a newspaper prior to the occasion.[65]

Notwithstanding a possible royal commission of the wedding anthem, Handel seems to have been 'determined not to write anything afresh', as Burrows has put it.[66] Apart from some smaller borrowings from two other, earlier works, most of the music in his wedding anthem *This Is the Day* is adapted from the oratorio *Athalia* (HWV 52) that Handel had written for and performed at his recent visit to Oxford in 1733.[67] These 'borrowings' may have been very deliberate and calculated: as Gardner suggests, considering that Princess Anne had at another time specifically requested performances of Handel's oratorio *Esther*, she could have asked for the borrowings from *Athalia* because she wanted to hear the music before leaving the country.[68] Altogether, only one accompanied recitative and possibly a portion of the penultimate chorus of the anthem were newly written music.[69] All this, however, does of course not change the fact that the anthem is a sumptuous and impressive piece: it is scored for full choir and orchestra, including trumpets; the grand opening chorus, which incorporates a central solo section for alto, is followed by five solo movements before a grand finale consisting of a chorus followed by an extended 'Alleluja-Amen' chorus. Burrows has highlighted some of the unusual features of the anthem – such as 'the inclusion of two full da capo arias' and the fact that it does not in-clude a central chorus.[70] Handel's *This Is the Day* is one of his grandest such occasional anthems and Burrows aptly describes it as an 'oratorio-type anthem'.

A Second Anthem?

Handel's anthem was not the only one written for this wedding. It is well-known that early on, in October, the newspapers had announced that the anthem for the wedding was to be composed by Maurice Greene.[71] Greene was Organist and Master of the Children of the Chapel Royal and such a commission would naturally have fallen to him. Greene's anthem *Blessed Are All They that Fear the Lord* survives in an autograph score that does not mention any details, but a copy supposed to be by his pupil William Boyce includes the following ascription:

> The / ANTHEM / Composed for the Nuptials of the Princess Royal / ANNE / Eldest Daughter of George II / KING of Great Britain / with / The Prince of Orange &c. / Composed by the Master of the Band / by D. Maurice Greene.[72]

---

[64] Burrows, *HECR*, p. 321. On the search for precedence regarding the texts of wedding anthems, see Burrows, *HECR*, p. 320–21.

[65] For this text publication see Burrows, *HECR*, p. 316–17.

[66] On the anthem and its performance in general, see Burrows, *HECR*, pp. 320–38, here p. 329.

[67] For these borrowings see Bernd Baselt, *Händel-Handbuch* [*HHB*], 3 vols (Kassel: Bärenreiter, 1978–86), II, pp. 727–28. See also Gardner, 'Preface', and for a more detailed discussion Gardner's 'Handel's Wedding Anthems', *Händel-Jahrbuch*, 59 (2013), pp. 217–28, here esp. pp. 220–23 and 227.

[68] Gardner, 'Preface', p. xix; and Gardner, 'Preference', p. 177.

[69] See Burrows, *HECR*, p. 324, Table 12.2.

[70] This and the following Burrows, *HECR*, pp. 321 and 329.

[71] See Burrows, *HECR*, p. 314–15.

[72] *Lbl Add MS 17859*, front page. The autograph score is *Ob MS Mus. d. 46*.

3—The 'Concert Weddings' I: The Children of George II

Greene's anthem is somewhat more modest than Handel's. The instrumental scoring does not include trumpets, as Handel's does, but merely strings and two oboes; and, despite being an elaborate work, it is a little shorter than Handel's anthem.[73] Greene's anthem was announced to be rehearsed on 27 October:

> This day will be a Rehearsal of the Anthem composed by Mr. Green, on Account of the Princess Royal's Nuptials, and the Gentlemen of the Chappel Royal and several others are ordered to perform the same in the Royal Chappel at Whitehall.[74]

It does not seem to be known whether this rehearsal ever took place. Only a few days later, Handel was reported to be the composer of the anthem for the wedding.[75] Gardner has referred to the interesting parallel between the neglect of Greene at the 1734 wedding and his rejection in favour of Handel at the 1727 coronation, where Greene also ought to have contributed music *qua* office.[76] The reason for the change of composer at the wedding is not known. It is plausible that initially the usual procedures for such a royal occasion were set in motion and that Greene, as the official leading musician of the Chapel Royal, was asked to contribute music – or that he simply assumed he would be asked by right of his office. It is notable that Green was yet paid for writing his anthem.[77] This payment raises doubts about Greene's having been simply rejected and may indicate that he had indeed been asked to write the anthem.

Intriguingly, Greene's anthem somewhat matches with the aforementioned draft ceremonial from the heralds' records. This basically appears to schedule two anthems: after the vows and the blessing of the couple, it lists the text of 'Blessed are they that fear the Lord &c', and then it schedules for 'another anthem' at the very end, after the liturgy, for which it does not give a text.[78] It is not clear whether the first, 'Blessed', is meant to be an anthem, or whether it merely refers to Ps. 128 as scheduled in the Prayer Book. It is possible that at some early part of the planning two anthems were thought to be needed – and Greene therefore wrote one beginning with the text 'Blessed are all they that fear the Lord'. In his anthem, only the first verse is from this psalm, but the remainder of the text is taken from Ps. 45. Burrows points out that Handel's anthem is also based on Ps. 45 and that it is 'noticeable that Handel avoided most of Greene's text, with only two verses appearing in both anthems, those beginning 'The king's daughter is all glorious within' and 'I/We will remember thy name'.[79]

It is possible that the wedding initially had been planned to include several anthems – like those in the earlier seventeenth century. It could be that it was decided only at a later stage to have merely one anthem at the wedding – and Handel was lucky to have been given the 'another anthem' at the end that was retained. After all, if only one anthem had been scheduled from the beginning and Handel had 'replaced' Greene as composer for this anthem, then Handel would not have had much time to compose his anthem. As seen above, Handel was first announced as composer in the newspapers in late October, incidentally at the same time that one of these papers also published the full text of Greene's anthem with details of the setting

---

[73] See Matthew Gardner, 'The Preference of the Hanoverians for Handel, 1727–1821', *Händel-Jahrbuch*, 61 (2015), pp. 167–85, here p. 177.

[74] *The Daily Post Boy*, 27 October 1733.

[75] See the references given in Burrows, *HECR*, p. 315, fn. 30.

[76] Gardner, 'Preface', p. xviii.

[77] Burrows, *HECR*, p. 316.

[78] Draft ceremonial in *Lca Miscell: Coll: By Anstis*, here p. [2], fully transcr. in Appendix B 3.1.

[79] Burrows, *HECR*, pp. 316 and 320. For a comparison of the texts of Greene's and Handel's anthems, as printed in London newspaper at the time, see Burrows, *HECR*, p. 317.

(whether chorus or solo); but already on 5 November, Handel's anthem was rehearsed in the 'Chapel Royal' before the royal family.[80] It was the *St. James's Evening Post* of 27–30 October that had included both the announcement of Handel as composer and the full text of Greene's anthem. The publication of the text and details of Greene's setting could have come from someone interested in securing this piece a performance at the wedding – possibly even Green himself. Regarding the timing, of course, Handel would certainly have started work before he was mentioned in the newspapers; and the pressure of time could explain the heavy re-use of earlier music. Yet, one may wonder whether he may not have started much earlier – at the same time as Greene. In any case, from this wedding onwards, royal weddings were to contain only one anthem, with this number not being increased until later in the twentieth century.

In this context it may also be interesting to note that John Weldon, who had been one of the organists and additional composer of the Chapel Royal for more than two decades, seems not to have been involved in the wedding music at all.[81] In fact, his compositional output seems to have tapered off in the 1720s (he died in 1736).

Performance

The performance conditions at the wedding were appropriately impressive. An important source is a contemporary engraving depicting the ceremony in the chapel (Illustration 3.3). This shows the performers placed in specially built galleries behind – and over – the altar. Burrows has already suggested the possibility that these musicians' galleries included the space of the removed windows.[82] This is very possible: a newly discovered source confirms that the same was done at the wedding of George III in 1761 in the Chapel Royal: the window over the altar was taken out and a gallery for the music put in its place.[83] After all, with these weddings taking place at night time, the blocking of windows did not matter. Burrows calculates that the performing body consisted of about 75 musicians: the full Chapel Royal choir and an orchestra including strings, oboes, bassoons and two trumpets – but, in contrast to *Athalia* (the source for much of the music) no horn players and possibly no timpani.[84] The inclusion of timpani is a moot point: a timpani part was copied in the opening movement, but not for the remainder of the anthem.[85] Because of this, Burrows argues that timpani were not included in the performance of the anthem, adding that they are also not visible in the engraving of the ceremony.[86] The omission of timpani, however, would seem to be in contrast to the otherwise rather generous arrangements for the music, including a new organ, specially built by John Knoppell.[87] As Gardner has observed there is the possibility that Handel meant timpani to be used only in the first movement.[88] Indeed, the situation is the same for Handel's newly-written wedding anthem *Sing unto God* from 1736, which also has timpani only in the opening movement (see below). This may seem to be too peculiar to be a mere coincidence. For the 1736 anthem, Burrows suggests that timpani

---

[80] See Burrows, *HECR*, p. 316–17.

[81] Margaret Laurie, 'Weldon, John', in *New Grove*, 27, pp. 265–66.

[82] Burrows, *HECR*, p. 332.

[83] *Lea Briscoe I*, p. 415. See also the longer quotation from this in the following Chapter 4, with fn. 19.

[84] Burrows, *HECR*, p. 333 (for the overall number) and p. 325 (for horns and timpani).

[85] For details see Gardner, 'Preface', p. xxiv.

[86] Burrows, *HECR*, pp. 325 and 333.

[87] Burrows, *HECR*, p. 517.

[88] Gardner, 'Preface', p. xxiv.

3—The 'Concert Weddings' I: The Children of George II

Illustration 3.3: 'The Wedding of Princess Anne and William of Orange in the Chapel of St James's, 14 March 1734', etching by Jacques Rigaud after drawings by William Kent, *London, British Museum*, Y,5.75 © The Trustees of the British Museum.

were not used in the last movement because the player had to walk in the return procession straight after the anthem.[89] This could also have been the reason in 1734. Incidentally, however, the same circumstance should then also have applied to the trumpets players, and it seems unlikely that the London court had only one capable timpani player.

Notwithstanding the impressive number of performers, the conditions of the venue are noteworthy. Burrows calculates that 500 people were in the temporary galleries that had been built for spectators and musicians, and in addition there were lavish decorations with tapestries and other hangings.[90] The large number of people and the extra fittings in the chapel would, as Burrows put it, have 'deadened most of the building's normal reverberation'.[91] At the same time, however, Burrows appreciates that 'the likely dryness of the acoustics' may have counterbalanced the employment of the large number of musicians in the 'more intimate' space of the chapel.[92] With the musicians' placement in different galleries high up above the altar, the performing conditions may have been rather challenging, and the arrangements could have caused 'considerable communications problems'.[93] Yet, at least no bigger mishaps in the music are reported – in contrast to the 1727 coronation, for instance.[94]

It is noteworthy that the aforementioned rehearsal of Handel's anthem on 5 November appears to have taken place in the actual 'Chapel Royal', not in the 'French Chapel' where the wedding was to take place.[95] While no further rehearsal is documented, Burrows suggests that there was 'presumably at least one' more and Gardner also concludes that 'there must also have been another rehearsal sometime in early March 1734'.[96] This rehearsal could possibly have taken place in the actual wedding venue of the French Chapel, giving the performers a chance to acquaint themselves with the special conditions.

Position of the Anthem

Last but not least, it is instructive to consider the exact position of Handel's anthem in the ceremony. The accounts, in various wording, all make clear that the anthem was performed at the very end, after the service proper, outside the liturgy:

> [...] the Lord Bishop of *London* perform'd the Service, after which the Bride and Bridegroom arose, and retir'd to their Places, whilst a fine Anthem compos'd by Mr. *Handell*, was perform'd by a great Number of Voices and Instruments.[97]

> When the Dean had finish'd the Service in the Liturgy, the married Couple rose, and retired to their Stools where they remained while the Anthem was sung.[98]

---

[89] Burrows, *HECR*, p. 353. The same in Gardner, 'Preface', p. xxv.

[90] Burrows, *HECR*, pp. 313 and 315.

[91] Burrows, *HECR*, p. 332.

[92] Burrows, *HECR*, p. 517.

[93] Burrows, *HECR*, p. 333

[94] See Range, *MCBC*, Chapter 5, esp. p. 139.

[95] See Burrows, *HECR*, p. 316.

[96] Burrows, *HECR*, p. 318–19; and Gardner, 'Preface', p. xix.

[97] *London Magazine*, March 1734, pp. 151–53, here p. 152.

[98] *Lca MS Ceremonials L. 19*, pp. 189–95: 'The Ceremonial of the Marriage of William Prince / of Orange; with the Princess Royal of Great Britain / Anne eldest daughter of his Majesty King George the / second [...]', here p. 193. See also the following fn.

3—The 'Concert Weddings' I: The Children of George II

The latter is from an account in the records of the College of Arms and nearly identical with the reports in some magazines. It could be that the heralds simply copied one of the published accounts or that both, journalists and heralds, drew on the same source. In any case, the heralds' using this account for their records gives it additional credibility.

The anthem coming at the very end would very much have followed the custom of the time for such occasional services: at grand funerals, for instance, the anthem was also appended to the end of the service. Such an addition, outside the actual liturgy, meant that the anthem itself received a special status. It is worth considering this in the context of the ceremonial details for the end of the wedding:

> After the Bishop of London as Dean of the Chapel had given the Blessing, their Majesties removed to the Traverse erected at one Side of the Altar. The Prince of Orange then leading the Princess, they went up to the Rails of the Altar, and kneeled there. / When the Dean had finished the Service in the Liturgy, the married Couple rose and retired back to their Stools upon the Hautpas; where they remained while the Anthem was sung.[99]

The 'Hautpas', also 'haut-pas', refers to a large dais or raised platform that was built in the altar area for many weddings through to the late nineteenth century. The mentioned 'Traverse' could have been a partly curtained-off area, or closet, so that the king and queen were more or less out of sight: there was also a 'travers' in the Chapel Royal, in which they received communion.[100] However, in the aforementioned contemporary engraving of the wedding (Illustration 3.3), this 'Traverse' is merely a grand canopy on the left-hand side, its top in the shape of a big crown.

The king and queen's 'removing' to the 'Traverse' is notable, as this was the first time that they came together during the ceremony: before that, throughout the service, they had sat separately on either side of the altar:

> His Majesty was seated in his Chair of State in the Upper Angle of the Haut-pas, on the Right Side. Her Majesty was seated in her Chair of State, on the other Side of the Hautpas [...].[101]

In this way, the king was on the side of the groom (who stood on the right in front of the altar) and the queen on that of the bride (who stood on the left). The 'joining' of the king and queen at the end of the ceremony was well calculated: the newly-weds had become a couple and this was heightened by the king and queen's displaying their marital union. This appears to have coincided with that point in the proceedings when the officiating minister had pronounced his blessing over the couple and was reading out the 'duties of Man and Wife', while they kneeled in from of him. The authenticity of this admonition was probably heightened when the congregation could see that the king and queen – man and wife – had moved to sit together.

After the final blessing, the newly-weds rose and also sat together, on 'their Stools upon the *Haut-pas*'.[102] As Burrows has pointed out, this appears to have been the only time of the ceremony that they took seat on the elevated area in front of the altar.[103] It was at this point that the musicians performed the anthem. The newly-wed royal couple was visible to the congregation for the whole time of the anthem – almost like in a *tableau vivant*; and with nothing

---

[99] *London Gazette*, 12–16 March 1733/4. See also *Gentleman's Magazine*, 4 (1734), p. 161; and 'Nuptials Solemnized', p. 325. The same is also recorded by Leake in *Lca S.M.L. 30*, p. 41.

[100] See John Adamson, 'The Tudor and Stuart Courts 1509–1714', in *The Princely Courts of Europe. Ritual, Politics and Culture under the Ancien Régime 1500–1750*, ed. by John Adamson, first publ. by Weidenfeld & Nicolson in 1999, paperback edn (London: Seven Dials, 2000), pp. 95–117, here p. 104.

[101] *London Gazette*, 12–16 March 1733/4.

[102] *Gentleman's Magazine*, 4 (1734), p. 161; and 'Nuptials Solemnized', p. 325.

[103] This and the following Burrows, *HECR*, p. 320.

else going on, Burrows concludes: 'the implication is that everyone's full attention was given to the music'. Yet, there may have been another effect: the ceremonial re-seating of both royal couples, just for the end of the service, was akin to an 'inthronization' and the music interacted with the ceremonial to great effect.[104] The festive strains of Handel's anthem enhanced the sight of the enthroned king and queen, and the newly-weds in their chairs. The royal family's solemnly listening to the anthem was a ceremony in itself.

The draft ceremonial had scheduled that, after the anthem, 'if the styles are to be proclaimed, this is the time'.[105] This refers to the proclamation of the newly-weds' styles and titles by the heralds, as seen in the previous chapter. There is no evidence that this proclamation was eventually included. Therefore, Handel's anthem would have been the final feature of the ceremony.

Immediately after the anthem, the return procession to the palace began. Godfrey recorded that 'all returned in One entire Procession in the same Order as before[,] the Drums & Trumpets Playing'.[106] Thus the procession went along the same extended route as it came and was again accompanied by music. Notably, however, the procession now was not split up, but 'entire', meaning just one continuous procession. It took much less time, presumably also because the instrumentalists did not have to walk back: according to Godfrey, it began 'before Ten' and 'ended a Quarter past Ten'.[107] Once again, as in the weddings in the previous century, the newly-weds, did not walk together; this time, the Prince went first with his entourage, followed by the Princess with hers.[108] Interestingly, an annotation in the draft ceremonial pointed out that Finet's observation about the bride's returning first at the 1613 was 'a mistake & contrary to Precedents'.[109] Accordingly, in 1734, Princess Anne went after her husband.

Overall, while Burrows explains that the 1613 arrangements 'were not followed exactly', he also notes that the precedent of that ceremony 'gave licence for considerable extravagance'.[110] The 1613 plans were most notably not followed in so far as the ceremony of eating wafers and drinking wine to the couple's health at the end of the ceremony was not included. The 'considerable extravagance', on the other hand, became clear in the lengthy outdoor processions and especially also in Handel's lavish anthem at the end of the ceremony.

Given the wide dismay at the popular princess's leaving the country, Lord Hervey, the Vice Chamberlain, reported harshly that the wedding resembled more 'the mournful pomp of a sacrifice than the joyful celebration of marriage'.[111] However, this may refer more to the overall context of the marriage than to the wedding itself. It does certainly not apply to Handel's anthem: this would have been the grand climax of the ceremony, very much expressing the 'joyful celebration of marriage'. With the inclusion, or rather addition, of an elaborate anthem after the service, this wedding had set a precedent that was followed at royal weddings up to the end of the century.

---

[104] For the term and details on the ceremony, see Range, *MCBC*, esp. p. 11–12.

[105] Draft ceremonial in *Lca Miscell: Coll: By Anstis*, here p. [2], fully transcr. in Appendix B 3.1.

[106] *Lbl Add MS 32556*, fol. 156ᵛ. See also *Gentleman's Magazine*, 4 (1734), p. 161: 'The Drums and Trumpets as before.'

[107] *Lbl Add MS 32556*, fols 156ᵛ and 157ʳ.

[108] *Gentleman's Magazine*, 4 (1734), p. 161; *London Magazine*, March 1734, p. 152.

[109] Draft ceremonial in *Lca Miscell: Coll: By Anstis*, here p. [2], fully transcr. in Appendix B 3.1. For Finet see Chapter 2, fn. 87.

[110] Burrows, *HECR*, p. 314.

[111] John Hervey (2nd Baron Hervey), *Some Materials towards Memoirs of the Reign of King George II*, ed. by Romney Sedgwick, 3 vols, continuously paginated (London: Eyre and Spottiswoode, 1931; repr. New York: AMS Press, 1970), I, p. 271. See also Andrew Thompson, *George II*, p. 110.

3—The 'Concert Weddings' I: The Children of George II

Prince Frederick, Prince of Wales, and Princess Augusta of Saxe-Gotha-Altenburg, 27 April 1736

Two years after Princess Anne's wedding, on 27 April 1736, her brother Prince Frederick, Prince of Wales, married Princess Augusta of Saxe-Gotha-Altenburg.[112] The wedding of the heir apparent was of supreme dynastic importance, and therefore this could have been expected to be a grander occasion than the 1734 wedding. In March, one newspaper reported that the wedding was to take place at St Paul's Cathedral, preceded by a procession from St James's Palace 'with the utmost State and Magnificence'.[113] Burrows argues that it would have been 'unprecedented' to have a royal wedding anywhere else than in a royal chapel.[114] However, as seen above, Mary I had married in Winchester, and Henry VIII's elder brother, Prince Arthur, had married in Old St Paul's in 1501. Nevertheless, eventually, the 1736 wedding took place 'in the Royal Chapel at St. James's, with the greatest Magnificence and Splendour', as the *London Gazette* dutifully recorded.[115] This refers to the 'Chapel Royal' within St James's Palace (see Illustration 3.1, above).

The short accounts of the wedding in the newspapers were mostly concerned with the processions.[116] An important source for the service itself is a diary entry by John Perceval, Earl of Egmont, who attended the ceremony. Furthermore, there is a hitherto neglected, detailed account among the 'Walpole Papers' in the British Library; written in French and hereinafter referred to as 'French account'.[117] According to the catalogue entry, it is 'in Sansom's hand', which may refer to the French-born Peter Augustus Samson (1674–1748) who was part of the circle of Horace Walpole and his brother Robert.[118] Due to its meticulous descriptions, one may assume that this account has some degree of credibility, and it provides some intriguing, hitherto unknown details. In fact, in some ways it appears to be more reliable than other accounts. For instance, the *Gentleman's Magazine* reported that 'the joining of Hands was proclaim'd to the People by firing of Guns'.[119] The French account, however, contradicts this and points out that the guns were not fired on this occasion, credibly arguing that it was 'pretended' that the whole wedding should pass 'without the slightest ceremony'.[120] It could be that some of the published reports merely drew on the 1734 coverage and other sources, without reflecting what was actually done.

It appears that the date of the wedding was not announced publicly until rather late. In a letter written only five days before the wedding, the Earl of Shaftesbury explained that 'the Town is very busy in preparing for the grand wedding which will be certainly very soon, & ingrosses

---

[112] For a detailed discussion of this wedding, with relevant newspaper sources, see also Burrows, *HECR*, pp. 339–54.

[113] *The London Evening-Post*, 13–16 March 1736; quoted in Burrows, *HECR*, p. 340.

[114] Burrows, *HECR*, p. 340.

[115] *London Gazette*, 27 April–1 May 1736.

[116] See, for instance, that in *London Evening-Post*, 27–29 April 1736.

[117] 'Relation de la Solennite des noces du Prince de Galles avec la Princesse de Saxe-Gotha', *Lbl Add MS 73773* (Walpole Papers, vol. IV: 1716–1747), no. 8/fols 149ʳ–168ʳ. This title is from the catalogue, but the piece itself is untitled and at the beginning, on fol. 149ʳ, merely has a pencil note in square brackets: '[aft 9 May 1736].' All translations from this source are my own.

[118] See Rachel Hammersley, *The English Republican Tradition and Eighteenth-Century France: Between the Ancients and the Moderns* (Manchester: Manchester University Press: 2010), passim.

[119] *Gentleman's Magazine*, 6 (1736), p. 230.

[120] *Lbl Add MS 73773*, fol. 161ᵛ: 'Il est à remarquer qu'on ne tira point le canon à l'occasion de ce marriage, par la raison qu'on pretendoit que le tout devoit se faire sans la moindre ceremonie.'

all the conversation in it'.[121] Burrows has shown that the wedding may have been intended for the very evening of the princess's arrival – in the end, it did not take place until the following day.[122] This sequence was, nonetheless, still much more compact than the proceedings in 1734, when the bridegroom had been around for many weeks.

The exact times of the proceedings are unclear. Burrows summarized that the procession formed at 8.30 and the service itself began at about 9pm.[123] In contrast, the Earl of Egmont recorded that he 'was present at the wedding, which ended about nine at night'.[124] However, it appears that Egmont somehow confused the times. The French account also reports that the procession began at 8.30.[125] While it does not give the times for the actual service, it does report that after the service the procession went back to the palace where the newly-weds received the king and queen's blessing and that after more than half an hour of conversation, supper was announced 'shortly after ten o'clock.[126] Thus, the 'conversation' would have started at around half past nine. From this, one still has to subtract the time for the procession from the chapel – so that the service itself, if it had begun about 9pm, would have been rather short. The *Gentleman's Magazine* reported that the Procession began 'At Eight' and that it was 'half an Hour after Ten' that 'their Majesties sat down to Supper'.[127] These times would leave more room for the actual ceremony. In any case, notwithstanding the exact timing, the wedding clearly took place in the late evening and would, heraldically speaking, not have been a 'public' state occasion. Indeed, Leake noted in his accounts that the wedding 'was said to be private', and that the prince 'was privately married'.[128]

The Procession

According to the Earl of Egmont's account, there was no actual procession to the service:

> There was a prodigious crowd, for the King's pleasure was that there should be no procession, but lords, gentlemen, and ladies might fill the chapel as they came, without order of distinction.[129]

Similarly, Lord Hervey recorded that 'no gallery' had been built, which meant that 'there could be no procession in form' – and Burrows explains that this 'gallery' refers to the walkway for an elaborate outdoor procession as in 1734.[130] In contrast, the French account describes the procession to the service in detail.[131] According to this, the procession began in the king's apartment,

---

[121] 4th Earl of Shaftesbury to James Harris, in Salisbury, on 22 April 1736; transcr. in Donald Burrows and Rosemary Dunhill, *Music and Theatre in Handel's World: The Family Papers of James Harris, 1732–1780* (Oxford: Oxford University Press, 2002), p. 15.

[122] Burrows, *HECR*, p. 341, fn. 11. He refers to the *DA* of 9 April 1736. A wedding on the very same day of the bride's arrival was eventually, done at the wedding of George III in 1761; see below.

[123] Burrows, *HECR*, p. 341.

[124] Perceval, *Manuscripts*, II, p. 264: entry of 27 April 1736. This is noted by Burrows, *HECR*, p. 343, fn. 23, but the contradiction to his suggested timeframe is not discussed.

[125] *Lbl Add MS 73773*, fol. 157ʳ: 'A huit heures et demie la Procession commença […].'

[126] *Lbl Add MS 73773*, fol. 162ʳ: 'La Conversation ayant duré plus d'une bonne demie heure, on vint annocer au Roy [162ᵛ] un peu après dix heures sonnées, que le souper étoit servi […].'

[127] *Gentleman's Magazine*, 6 (1736), p. 230–31.

[128] *Lca S.M.L. 44*, p. 159, marginal note; and *Lca S.M.L. 65*, p. 86.

[129] Perceval, *Manuscripts*, II, p. 264.

[130] Hervey, *Some Materials*, II, p. 552; Burrows, *HECR*, p. 342.

[131] *Lbl Add MS 73773*, fol. 157ᵛ–159ʳ.

3—The 'Concert Weddings' I: The Children of George II

down the grand staircase, and so to the Chapel, through guards forming a passage. It consisted of the procession of the bride – who was led by the Duke of Cumberland – then the procession of the bridegroom, and finally that of the king and queen, each followed by attendants and court officials. This description matches with other reports.[132] What the accounts do not mention, are peers and peeresses walking in the procession; and this may explain both Hervey's observation that they just filled the Chapel as they arrived, not 'in form', and also Egmont's summary that there was 'no procession'. Overall, the procession to the Chapel Royal was distinctly shorter than that to the French Chapel in 1734 had been. Nonetheless, it was still accompanied by music: the account in the *Daily Journal* mentions trumpets and timpani.[133] The French account includes a more detailed description of the instruments at the head of the procession, and these instruments are also mentioned in other accounts:

> Douze Tambours et quatre Fiffres, – precedes par le Tambour Major du premier Regiment des Gardes, ouvrirent la marche avec bien du bruit. Ils furent suivis – par huit Trompettes en deux rangs, et un Timbalier; un Portefaix en haillons – portant les Timbales sur son Dos, ce qui ne fit pas un fort bon effet dans une auguste ceremonie.

> Twelve drummers and four fifes – preceded by the drum major of the first regiment of guards – opened/began the procession with a lot of noise. They were followed by eight trumpets in two ranks, and a timpanist, a *Portefaix* carrying the timpani on his back – which did not make a very good effect in [such] an august ceremony.[134]

The latter remark in the French account is particularly intriguing. The report that the timpani were carried by the 'Portefaix' on his back matches with the aforementioned engraving of the 1734 procession (see Illustration 3.2, above). This reminds of such processions at other, earlier royal occasions: for instance, for the coronation of James II in 1685, the same can clearly be seen in one of the engravings in Francis Sandford's lavish account.[135] It is noteworthy that this somewhat archaic-looking practice was still used at these weddings in the 1730s – obviously provoking a sharp remark for not producing 'a very good effect'.

The Ceremony

The French account details that the music inside the chapel began the moment that the king entered and that it played until all the family was in their places.[136] This would mean that the earlier processions of the bridegroom and of the bride towards the altar had not been accompanied by any music; and this must have further made the monarch's entrance seem ceremonially more weighty and significant, more important. The French account specifies that the music on the king's entrance was 'un Prelude sur les orgues éxécuté par le Sʳ Handel' – an organ prelude, played by Handel.[137] Moreover, the same account had earlier explained that the musicians were 'dirigée [*sic*] par le fameux Hendel', or 'directed by the famous Handel' – which indicates that

---

[132] For instance, *London Evening-Post*, 27–29 April 1736. According to the *Daily Journal*, 28 April 1736, the bridegroom came before the bride.

[133] *Daily Journal*, 28 April 1736.

[134] *Lbl Add MS 73773*, fol. 157ᵛ. For the other accounts; see, for instance, *Daily Journal*, 28 April 1736.

[135] Francis Sandford, *The History of the Coronation of the Most High, Most Mighty, and Most Excellent Monarch, James II.* […] *1685* (London: Printed by Thomas New Comb, 1687): the second engraving, from the head of the procession.

[136] *Lbl Add MS 73773*, fol. 160ᵛ: 'Au moment que le Roi entra dans la chapelle, la musique commença par un Prelude sur les Orgues éxécuté par le Sʳ Handel, et continué jusqu'à ce que toute la famille Royale fût placée.'

[137] *Lbl Add MS 73773*, fol. 160ᵛ.

British Royal Weddings

he was also responsible for the performance of the music throughout the service.[138] He may, once again, have been overall in charge of the music.

Burrows has suggested that the choice of Handel for the wedding music was a favour by the king and queen, not by the Prince of Wales, who supported the composer's competitor opera company.[139] In contrast to the 1734 wedding, this time Greene, who was still in his position as Master of the Chapel Royal, is not referred to in any of the sources relating to the service. Greene, however, had also been Master of the King's Musick since 1735 and he was paid for providing ten extra performers for the ball celebrating the royal wedding – although this payment does not imply that he also contributed any music.[140]

The Anthem

From a musical point of view the 1736 wedding was somewhat more noteworthy than that in 1734. While there is again no information on the psalm and Responses, Handel provided another anthem: *Sing unto God* (HWV 263). Although this is altogether shorter than *This Is the Day* from 1734, it has the distinction of being an original composition – a new, specially written piece. The music of Handel's anthem has been well-covered in the literature, notably by Burrows's research.[141] The scoring of *Sing unto God* is as grand as in the 1734 wedding anthem: several soloists and choir are accompanied by an orchestra including full strings, oboes and two trumpets – and possibly timpani (see below).

Again, it is not known who compiled the text for the anthem. Following the 1734 precedent, the service was conducted by the Bishop of London as Dean of the Chapel Royal, still Edmund Gibson.[142] However, it is not known that he was in any way involved in the anthem. As for Handel's anthem in 1734, the full text was published by at least one newspaper, but this time only after the event.[143] Gardner has pointed out that one line of the text is missing in this and also that 'the composer was not named'.[144] Nevertheless, such publicizing of the anthem text, even after the event, may perhaps show a greater interest in the music of the ceremony: it stands in marked contrast to the overall rather superficial reporting of the wedding.

The anthem consists of six movements: an opening and final chorus framing two solo numbers, another chorus and a short recitative. The text of the second to fourth movements is particularly noteworthy: the soprano aria 'Blessed Are All They that Fear the Lord', the bass aria 'Thy Wife Shall Be as the Fruitful Vine' and the chorus 'Lo, Thus Shall the Man Be Blessed'. These texts are based on verses 1–4 of Ps. 128, and thus the 'traditional' wedding psalm scheduled in the Prayer Book forms the core of the anthem. It is possible that the texts of the outer movements (Psalms 68:32 and 106:48, respectively) were simply chosen because they have a more triumphantly joyful character than anything in Ps. 128.

It has been suggested that the solo violoncello in 'Thy Wife Shall Be as the Fruitful Vine' could have been intended as a compliment to the Prince of Wales, who was a good cello player

---

[138] *Lbl Add MS 73773*, fol. 160ʳ.

[139] Burrows, *HECR*, p. 344. See also Gardiner, 'Preface', p. xx.

[140] *Lna LC 5/20*: 'Warrants of Several Sorts, 1735–38', p. 131.

[141] See Burrows, *HECR*, esp. Chapter 13.

[142] *Lbl Add MS 73773*, fol. 161ʳ: 'Ce fut l'Evêque de Londres qui y officia.'

[143] *London Daily Post and General Advertiser*, 30 April 1736. For the 1734 text see fn. 79 above.

[144] Gardner, 'Preface', p. xx.

3—The 'Concert Weddings' I: The Children of George II

himself.[145] This is certainly a possibility. Specific references to one of the wedding parties in Handel's wedding anthems have also been observed by Schoelcher. He summarized that the 1734 anthem *This Is the Day*

> is truly an anthem for a wedding, where everything tends to the honour of the bride. The words of the *Wedding Anthem* of 1736, on the contrary, are chosen more in honour of the husband: – "Thy wife shall be;" "Lo, thus shall the man be blessed:" &c.[146]

All the same, Handel's 1734 wedding had also included one aria with a prominent solo cello part (no. 2, 'Blessed is the Man') – and Greene too had included a movement with a prominent solo cello in his anthem intended for the 1734 wedding: the tenor solo 'Hearken, O Daughter' in the second half. Therefore, it could be that the violoncello in the 1736 anthem had no particular meaning but that Handel in those years simply had a proficient cello player at hand and made good use of him.

It is well-known that the whole of the chorus 'Lo, Thus Shall the Man Be Blessed' is an adaptation 'with very little alteration' from the first chorus 'Lasset uns aufsehen' in Carl Heinrich Graun's so-called 'Große Passion', or 'Great Passion' (also 'Brunswick Passion') *Kommt her und schaut*, which probably dates from the 1720s.[147] Intriguingly, the English text that Handel put under the music arguably works much better with it than the original German text: the accents in the German text do not correlate with the rhythmic accents of the fugue theme at all, whereas the English ones do.[148] Handel's reason or motivation for this elaborate reference to Graun's music – in fact amounting to plagiarism – is not known. It seems somewhat curious that Handel used a movement from a passion setting for a wedding anthem. At the same time, it is tempting to suggest that the Prince of Wales may have already known Graun's music: whereas his parents moved to Britain upon the Hanoverian accession to the throne in 1714, their little son stayed behind in Hanover and did not join them in London until 1728.[149] In the 1720s, Graun was in Brunswick and it seems possible that the young prince heard this passion music there.

The final chorus of the anthem is another borrowing, although this time from Handel's own music: from his serenata *Il Parnasso in festa* (HWV 73) written for the 1734 wedding of Princess Anne. It cannot be known, however, whether this borrowing, providing a link between the weddings of the prince and his sister, was more than just topical.[150]

The accounts agree unequivocally that Handel's anthem came again only 'after' the service, outside the actual liturgical frame. The *Gentleman's Magazine* reported distinctly that it was only 'after' the service 'was over', that 'a fine Anthem was perform'd by a great Number

---

[145] Hans-Georg Hofmann, '"Sing unto God" – Bemerkungen zu Händels Festmusik anlässlich der Hochzeit des Prinzen Frederick of Wales mit Prinzessin Augusta von Sachsen-Gotha (1736)', *Händel-Jahrbuch*, 49 (2003), pp. 147–62, here p. 151.

[146] Schoelcher, *Life of Handel*, p. 165. In contrast, Burrows (*HECR*, p. 345) interprets that 'The texts of neither of Handel's wedding anthems give any prominence to the husband.'

[147] Burrows, *HECR*, p. 349. The origin of the music in Graun's work had been discovered by Ebenezer Prout, 'Graun's *Passion Oratorio*, and Handel's Knowledge of It', *Monthly Musical Record*, 24, no. 281 (May 1894), pp. [97]–99; and no. 282 (June 1894), pp. [121]–123.

[148] See the comparative examples of the beginning of Graun's movement vis-à-vis Handel's adaptation in Burrows, *HECR*, p. 350.

[149] For biographical details see Michael De-la-Noy, *The King Who Never Was: The Story of Frederick, Prince of Wales* (London: Peter Owen, 1996).

[150] Compare Hofmann, 'Sing unto God', p. 150. For the borrowings in this anthem see also Gardner, 'Handel's Wedding Anthems', esp. pp. 224–25.

of Voices and Instruments'.[151] The *Daily Journal* recorded the whole scene at the end of the ceremony in some detail:

> After the Bishop of London and Dean of the Chapel had given the Blessing, their Majesties removed to the Throne, erected on the Right Hand of the Altar, of Crimson Velvet richly l[a]ced with Gold. / Then the Prince of Wales, leading the Princess Augusta, went up to the Altar, and kneeled there. / When the Dean had finished the Divine Service, the married Pair rose and retired back to their Stools upon the Hauptpas; where they remained while an Anthem composed by Mr. Handel was sung by his Majesty's Band of Musick, which was placed in a Gallery over the Communion Table.[152]

This overall concurs with the description in the French account; but according to this, the royal couple changed their seats only once the anthem had started:

> Dès que l'antienne commença Leurs Majestes allérent Se placer du côté gauche dans les Fauteils sous le Dais, et les nouveaux marries occuperent les deux chaises, qui leur étoient destinées près du reste de la famille Royale du côté Droit dè la Chapelle, un peu au dessous des Fauteuils où avoient été assis auparavant le Roy et la Reine.

> As soon as the anthem began, their majesties went to place themselves on the left side, in the armchairs on the dais, and the newly-weds took the chairs that were assigned to them, near the rest of the royal family, on the right-hand side of the chapel, a little beneath the armchairs where, on the opposite side, the king and queen had been sitting.[153]

The music would thus have accompanied the couple's movements. It is noteworthy that, as in 1734, this was the first time in the service that the king and queen sat together: for the beginning of the ceremony, the king had again sat to the right of the altar, and the queen to the left.[154] For the end of the service, however, they were together, on full display, sitting in their armchairs, or 'the Throne'. Once again, the effect of this scene was heightened by Handel's grand music. The difference of the king and queen eventually sitting together on the 'Right Hand of the Altar' in the *Daily Journal* account and 'on the left side' in the French account appears stem from the accounts' different perspective – with the right-hand side of the altar being the left side when looking at it.

The French account records that the return procession back to the state appartments went along the same way, and roughly in the same order, that the procession to the service had gone; moreover it confirms that the procession was again accompanied by music, 'the noise of the drums, the fifes, the trumpets, and of the timpani bringing the procession back to the Hall of Guards'.[155] There was, nevertheless, a notable and significant ceremonial difference in the return procession. The published accounts in their descriptions seem to have merely followed the reports of the previous wedding in 1734. For instance, the *Daily Journal* reported that the Prince of Wales went before the Princess, and that each of them was 'supported' by dukes and maids respectively.[156] According to the French account, however, the newly-weds this time walked together in the return procession– quite obviously, in fact – and given the

---

[151] *Gentleman's Magazine*, 6 (1736), pp. 230–31, here p. 231.

[152] *Daily Journal*, 28 April 1736. Same or similar in other accounts. See the also the similar wording in 1734 (see above, fn. 99).

[153] *Lbl Add MS 73773*, fol. 161ʳ–161ᵛ.

[154] See, for instance, *Daily Journal*, 28 April 1736.

[155] *Lbl Add MS 73773*, fol. 161ᵛ:'[…] par le même chemin, et à peu près dans le même ordre qu'on étoit venu, le bruit des Tambours, des Fiffres, des Trompettes, et des Timbales ramenant la Procession jusqu'à la Sale des Halebardiers.'

[156] *Daily Journal*, 28 April 1736.

3—The 'Concert Weddings' I: The Children of George II

clear emphasis on this detail, this account's description is perhaps the more reliable one. With reference to the arrangements in the procession to the ceremony, the French account emphasized that in the return the prince went hand in hand with his new wife:

> Tout ce qu'il y avoit de changé au retour, c'est que le Prince de Galles donna la main à la Princesse sa nouvelle marriée, et que le Duc de Cumberland conduisit la Reine.[157]

> All that was different in the return was that the Prince of Wales gave his hand to the princess, his new wife, and that the Duke of Cumberland led the queen.

Interestingly, such a display of marital union by the newly-weds would have stood in contrast to the account's notion that the queen was led by her son, the Duke of Cumberland but not by her husband, the king.

Performance

The Earl of Egmont judged that Handel's anthem 'was wretchedly sung by Abbot, Gates, Lee, Bird and a boy', referring mainly to the soloists.[158] Andrew Thompson has concluded that 'its first performance was not, as often happened with Handel's royal compositions, as good as he might have hoped'.[159] However, it is not exactly clear what Egmont meant in his description and there does not appear to be any other source on the performance of Handel's anthem. Notably, only one rehearsal of the music is known – on Easter Monday, the very day before the wedding. As Burrows has shown, this probably took place at the house of Bernard Gates, the Master of the Children of the Chapel Royal.[160] Thus, there was probably no audience and the rehearsal was merely for the performers to practise the music, but the locality of the Chapel Royal and the musicians placement therein could not be tried out.

The performing conditions appear to have been similar to those in 1734 in the French Chapel. Egmont detailed that the Chapel Royal

> was finely adorned with tapestry, velvet, and gold lace, all the pews taken down, and benches raised one above another for the conveniency and to make more room for spectators.[161]

There were again special provisions for the musicians, who were 'placed in a Gallery over the Communion Table'.[162] This gallery was most probably built by removing the big window over the altar and the musicians sat basically inside the window, in an extension, as described in the aforementioned newly-found source of the 1761 wedding of George III, also in the Chapel Royal.[163] The Earl of Egmont's 1736 account furthermore refers to an organ in this gallery.[164] Other sources confirm that there was, as in 1734, again a new organ – this time built by Christopher Shrider.[165] As Burrows explains, this may have been done to have 'an instrument that

---

[157] *Lbl Add MS 73773*, fol. 161ᵛ.

[158] Perceval, *Manuscripts*, II, p. 264.

[159] Andrew Thompson, *George II*, p. 116.

[160] Burrows, *HECR*, p. 342.

[161] Perceval, *Manuscripts*, II, p. 264. See also *Lbl Add MS 73773*, fol. 159ᵛ: 'La Chapelle Royal […] étoit tendüe des deux côter de deux Grandes Pieces de Tapisserie bordées de larges bandes de velours cramoisi galonnées d'or.'

[162] See above, fn. 152, for a longer quotation. See also Burrows, *HECR*, 351–52; and *Lbl Add MS 73773*, fol. 160ʳ: 'Au dessus de l'Autel il y avoit une Tribune pour la musique de la Chapelle du Roy […].'

[163] *Lca Briscoe I*, p. 415, quoted in the following Chapter 4, with fn. 19.

[164] Perceval, *Manuscripts*, II, p. 264.

[165] See Burrows, *HECR*, p. 612–13.

matched orchestral pitch'.[166] A list of 'Necessaries for the Chapel' for the 1736 wedding stipulates the coverage 'with new Crimson Baze' of, among other things, 'the Musick Gallerys'.[167] It is not clear whether the plural, 'Gallerys', here has any significance, but it is possible that, as in 1734, there were several galleries for the music, maybe above each other. After all, Burrows estimates that there were about forty to fifty performers in total.[168]

The inclusion of timpani in the band is again uncertain, with Handel's score, as in 1734, again including them only in the first movement.[169] If they were used in *Sing unto God*, Burrows concludes that this 'might have been the first occasion that timpani were heard in the Chapel Royal'.[170] At the same time, however, he observes generally that there is 'some doubt' about the inclusion of timpani 'in Handel's performances' of the wedding anthems and points out that for Handel's Chapel Royal music of the next decade, the 1740s, 'it is possible that practical difficulties in the Chapel (concerning both performing space and acoustics) may have eventually prevented their participation'.[171] Yet, it is noteworthy that when Handel's *Dettingen Te Deum* (HWV 283) was performed in the Chapel Royal in 1743, the score included timpani very prominently. Even though this piece had most probably been intended for performance in St Paul's Cathedral, it is not known that the Chapel performance omitted the timpani.[172] After all, from a musical performance point of view, timpani would not have been too much out of place at the royal weddings, or the 1743 thanksgiving service for that matter: with all the extra seating and decorations mentioned above, the acoustics of the small Chapel Royal, which are not grand anyway, would have been rather subdued.

Decreased Ceremony

Burrows has already discussed the impression that the 1736 wedding of the Prince of Wales was 'not on the lavish scale of that of his elder sister' in 1734.[173] As seen above, the French account observed that this wedding was pretended to be executed 'without the slightest ceremony'.[174] Notably, the chosen venue of the Chapel Royal is somewhat smaller than the 'Queen's Chapel' (formerly 'French Chapel') across the road (see Illustration 3.1, above).[175] Whereas there had presumably been about 500 people at the 1734 wedding, the French account pointed out that the Chapel Royal was 'so small' that it could not accommodate more than 400 people.[176] Moreover, there was no elaborate, lengthy outdoor procession with the participation of the aristocracy and the possibility of more spectators before the service.

---

[166] Burrows, *HECR*, p. 352.

[167] Bound in as the last item in *Lna LC 2/29*.

[168] Burrows, *HECR*, p. 352.

[169] See Burrows, *HECR*, p. 353; and Gardner, 'Preface', p. xxv. Matters are complicated by the fact that Handel's original score of this anthem does not seem to have survived (see Gardner, 'Handel's Wedding Anthems', p. 224, fn. 15).

[170] Burrows, *HECR*, p. 486, fn, 92.

[171] Burrows, *HECR*, p. 487.

[172] For the *Dettingen Te Deum* see Burrows, *HECR*, Chapter 14, here esp. pp. 386–87.

[173] Burrows, *HECR*, p. 342–43. See also Andrew Thompson, *George II*, p. 116.

[174] See above, fn. 120.

[175] See also the comparative ground-plots in *HECR*, p. 500.

[176] *Add MS 73773*, fol. 160ᵛ: 'Comme la Chapelle Royale est for petite, tout ce qu'elle pouvoit contenir de monde en cette occasion ne passoit pas le nombre de 400. Personnes à tout prendre.'

3—The 'Concert Weddings' I: The Children of George II

Regarding the ceremony's overall less lavish character, Thompson offers the practical explanation that there had been 'little time to prepare the Chapel Royal between Easter communion on 25 April and the wedding on 27 April'.[177] The argument of lack of time is of course an undeniably valid one, and this was also mentioned in the French account:

> La Chapelle Royal étoit ornée autant que l'avoit pû permettre le peu de tems qu'on avoit eu pour cela, Leurs Majestes et la Famille Royal y ayant communié le même Dimanche que la Princesse étoit arrivée à Greenwich, ce jour là étant le Dimanche de Pâques selon le vieux Stile; de Sort qu'on n'avait eu que deux jours en tout pour accommoder la Chapelle pour la ceremonie du Marriage.[178]

> The Chapel Royal was decorated as much as the shortness of time allowed for [doing] that, their majesties and the royal family there having taken communion on the same Sunday that the princess arrived at Greenwich, that day being Easter Sunday in the Old Style [calendar]. Thus one had no more than two days in total to arrange the Chapel for the marriage ceremony.

The reason for this rushing of affairs between the bride's arrival and the wedding could have been the king's desire to go to Hanover. At the beginning of February, Egmont recorded some court gossip that the king was going to 'hasten the Prince's wedding with the Princess of Saxe Gotha', since he wanted to go to Hanover in that year; but that the queen was rather in favour of delaying the wedding, so that the king could not go to Hanover, which she and Robert Walpole opposed anyway.[179] Curiously, none of the known source explains why the wedding was not simply held in the French Chapel, as the wedding in 1734, which would have prevented any clash with the Easter celebrations in the Chapel Royal and would have provided much time for the preparation of the chapel. It must appear that such an elevation to a larger venue, with a resulting longer procession, was particularly not desired.

Leake in one of his accounts noted another intriguing detail, on the ceremonial arrangements at the wedding:

> Memo[d] there was no Ceremonial deliverd to the Officers of Arms nor was it setled by the Vice Chamblñ and M[r] Anstis till just before the procession began[.][180]

Thus, it seems as though the exact ceremonial details had been rather neglected and not prepared properly in advance, and that they were – quite literally – debated until the last minute.

In the wider context, the reason for the overall scaled-down proceedings at this wedding could have been the famously bad relationship of the king and his oldest son.[181] The 1736 wedding celebrations as a whole appear to have been somewhat contested – even within in the royal family, as seen above in the king's wanting to 'hasten the Prince's wedding' in order to go to Hanover and the queen's opposition to this.[182] After the event, the Earl of Egmont summarized cynically that 'the Court has put itself to small expense on occasion of this marriage'.[183] Nonetheless, at least musically this wedding was very much a noteworthy occasion: Handel's grand, new anthem was an appropriate tribute to this music-loving prince.

---

[177] Andrew Thompson, *George II*, p. 116. See also Burrow, *HECR*, p. 341–42.

[178] *Lbl Add MS 73773*, fol. 159[v].

[179] Perceval, *Manuscripts*, II, p. 229.

[180] *Lca S.M.L. 44*, p. 159.

[181] See Burrows, *HECR*, p. 342–43.

[182] See above, fn. 179.

[183] Perceval, *Manuscripts*, II, p. 264.

British Royal Weddings

Princess Mary and Prince Frederick of Hesse,
8 May (and 28 June) 1740

Four years after the Prince of Wales's wedding, his sister Princess Mary married Prince Frederick (later Frederick II) of Hesse. This wedding was noteworthy and important from a political and especially from a dynastic point of view. Not only was Prince Frederick the heir to his uncle the Landgrave of Hesse, a wealthy Protestant principality in central Germany, but this uncle also happened to be the king of Sweden: Frederick I of Hesse had married Ulrika Eleonora of Sweden in 1715; she became queen in 1718 but in 1720 relinquished the throne in his favour. Since the couple had no children, there was a realistic possibility that Prince Frederick might one day succeed his uncle as king, and his wife Princess Mary would thus become queen of Sweden. The eventual successor to the Swedish throne, Adolf Frederick of Holstein-Gottorp was not elected until 1743, succeeding in 1751. Therefore, as Thomas Rahn has summarized, the 1740 wedding was seen as a 'union of the powers of England and Sweden via the linker Hesse-Kassel'.[184]

With such international significance behind it, it is little surprise that this wedding caused much excitement. Even though the wedding eventually did not to take place until May, as early as in December, Frances Countess of Hartford reported:

> We talk a great deal of the princess Mary's wedding; but I think it is still uncertain whether the prince of Hesse is to come over, or whether the duke is to marry her by proxy.[185]

In the end, the bridegroom-to-be did not 'come over' and the wedding was split into two parts: first there was a wedding by proxy in London; and once the princess had travelled to Hesse, there was a second ceremony in Kassel, with the actual husband. Andrew Thompson has explained that George II initially 'welcomed the idea that the wedding would be celebrated in Kassel', but that he then had some scruples whether it was proper to send 'his unmarried daughter out into the world'.[186] With that Thompson can refer to Lord Hervey who recorded that the king had long determined that the princess should be married by proxy, so as not to leave unmarried.[187] Weddings by proxy were not unusual for royalty on the continent and as seen in the previous chapter, both James VI and Charles I (and possibly Charles II) had first been married by proxy. This time, however, Britain was on the side of the bride, not of the bridegroom and Thompson interprets that 'Unfortunately, there were few post-Reformation precedents for such a procedure and neither the clergy nor the lawyers who were consulted seemed happy about this way of proceeding'.[188] According to Lord Hervey, the Privy Council concluded that the only precedent was the marriage of Princess Mary, only daughter of Henry VII, to Louis XII of France – when the proxy espousals in England had been followed by the wedding in France; and Hervey noted that George II 'consented that this precedent should be followed'.[189] With the bridegroom not present at the London ceremony in 1740, the princess's brother, the Duke of Cumberland, stood in for him.

---

[184] Thomas Rahn, *Festbeschreibung: Funktion und Topik einer Textsorte am Beispiel der Beschreibung höfischer Hochzeiten* (Berlin: De Gruyter, 2009, repr. 2011), p. 61.

[185] 'F. Hartford' to 'The Countess of Pomfret', 13/24 December 1739, in *Correspondence between Frances, Countess of Hartford, (afterwards Duchess of Somerset,) and Henrietta Louisa, Countess of Pomfret: between the Years 1738 and 1741*, 3 vols, vol. 1, 2nd edn (London: Printed for Richard Phillips, 1806), pp. 204–08, here p. 208.

[186] Andrew Thompson, *George II*, p. 133.

[187] Hervey, *Some Materials*, III, p. 931.

[188] Andrew Thompson, *George II*, p. 133.

[189] Hervey, *Some Materials*, III, p. 932.

3—The 'Concert Weddings' I: The Children of George II

The London Ceremony

Notwithstanding that the London ceremony was a proxy-wedding, it was quite similar to the weddings of the princess's siblings in 1734 and 1736. The service took place in the Chapel Royal at St James's Palace, again late in the evening. As already discussed in Chapter 1, in contrast to the two previous weddings, the service was conducted not by the Dean of the Chapel Royal – still Edmund Gibson – but by the Archbishop of Canterbury, John Potter. The wedding vows *per procurationem*, however, were administered not by a cleric, but by the Duke of Newcastle, as principal secretary of state.[190] This arrangement caused Leake to comment that it 'seemed to be Usurping the Office of the Bishop and certainly was a great Impropriety'.[191]

The ceremony 'began at Seven a-Clock' with the procession through the state rooms to the Chapel Royal.[192] However, as the bridegroom was not present in person, the procession consisted of only two sections: that of the princess and her attendants, and that of the king (Queen Caroline had died in 1737). There was no representative for the groom to walk in a separate procession. In fact, the Duke of Cumberland who stood proxy for him during the service, during the procession was the one who led his sister, the bride. Both processions were, as previously, headed by a fife, drums, kettledrums, and trumpets.

Egmont relates how the heralds called out the participants in the procession.[193] This is notable in so far as it confirms the heralds' defined role at weddings. For the end of the ceremony, Egmont similarly recorded that 'the heralds called on the unmarried ladies, baronesses, viscountesses and duchesses to march, and then on the privy councillors not peers, &c., to go, who accordingly left their places and returned back to the palace, but not in exact order by reason of the crowd, and negligence of the peers'.[194]

As at the previous two weddings, the anthem was performed after the service proper. The report in the *London Gazette* reported in detail about the exchange of wedding rings and a speech by the archbishop, which was given in Latin – perhaps in the hope that the German attendants could thus follow it.[195] After this, the archbishop pronounced the 'Benediction' over the couple:

> After which an Anthem was sung. And a proper Instrument, attesting that the Ceremony was perform'd in the Matter above mention'd, was sign'd by the following Persons, in the Presence of Dr. Paul and Mr. Greenly, Notaries Publick, who attested the same.

The same wording is used in a contemporary account preserved at the College of Arms.[196] This account furthermore explains that the proxy-bridegroom and the bride themselves had signed the 'Instrument' already earlier in the ceremony, immediately following the administration of

---

[190] *London Gazette*, 6–10 May 1740. See also the entry in *Lea Briscoe I*, pp. 174–81, here p. 176: 'Then his Grace the Duke of Newcastle, his Majesty's Principal Secretary of state, publickly read ye Procuration signed by ye most serene Prince William of Hesse [father of the bridegroom], & ye most serene Prince Frederick of Hesse, which is as followes, [text in Latin].'

[191] *Lea S.M.L. 44*, p. 197–98.

[192] This and the following *London Gazette*, 6–10 May 1740. See also *Lea Briscoe I*, p. 174–75.

[193] Perceval, *Manuscripts*, III, p. 137.

[194] Perceval, *Manuscripts*, III, p. 138.

[195] This and the following *London Gazette*, 6–10 May 1740. See also the mostly identical accounts 'Ceremonial of the Espousals or Contract / of Marriage between Prince Frederick of / Hesse Cassel and the Princess Mary, perform'd in the / Royal Chapel at St James Thursday May / the 8.th 1740.', in *Lea MS Ceremonials L. 19*, pp. 196–99; and *Lea S.M.L. 44*, pp. 197–98.

[196] *Lea Briscoe I*, p. 180. Similar wording also in *Lea MS Ceremonials L. 19*, pp. 198–99.

the wedding vows.[197] Egmont's diary entry concurs with the account in the *London Gazette* and notes that the witnesses signed the document only after the archbishop's blessing. He records the scene in more detail:

> Then an anthem was sung, during which time the peers present went up to the table placed beside the altar and signed their names to the contract, but without rank or order. As they went up, they made their bows to the King, Princesses and the Duke, who were seated, the King on the right hand, and the others before the altar, and the same at their return.[198]

The signing of a register was not part of weddings prior to the 1753 Marriage Act, and from the Victorian royal weddings onwards this took place distinctly after the service, back in the palace.[199] By including the signing of the 'Instrument', a certificate confirming that the wedding had been performed, the 1740 ceremony was therefore the first and only pre-twentieth-century wedding to include any signing, all the more highlighting the legal aspect within the religious rite, if not the political significance of the union.

The above-cited accounts also confirm that the anthem was again an extra-liturgical piece, after the service proper. The music was once again provided by Handel. Two days before the wedding, one newspaper reported of the rehearsal of 'a fine new Anthem compos'd by Mr. Handel' for the ceremony.[200] However, in the end, the anthem that Handel provided for the ceremony may have been fine but was not 'new', not an original composition; rather it was made up of his two previous wedding anthems, as Handel's friend, the lawyer Thomas Harris explained in a letter two days after the wedding.[201] The full text of the anthem, beginning 'Sing unto God', was published in some newspapers on the day of the wedding.[202] This text, as Burrows has pointed out, is the only source for the content of Handel's anthem, as no musical source 'survives for an anthem in this form'.[203]

Regarding the performance at the service, Burrows has highlighted that there is no evidence for a specially erected gallery for the musicians over the altar or for a new organ, as at the previous weddings.[204] This might imply that there were, overall, fewer musicians. In any case, the possibly simpler conditions and Handel's economical re-use of the earlier anthems did not diminish the grandeur of the event. With the inclusion of an elaborate orchestral anthem, this proxy-wedding was yet a notable and impressive court ceremony. In fact, as Burrows has pointed out, it is curious that, through the 'assembly process', this wedding anthem turned out to be 'more extensive' than that for the Prince of Wales in 1736 had been.[205]

Egmont described the anthem as 'concluding the ceremony'.[206] It is notable that none of the accounts mentions a ceremonial re-seating of the king or the proxy-newly-weds, as at the

---

[197] *London Gazette*, 6–10 May 1740; *Lea Briscoe I*, p. 177.

[198] Perceval, *Manuscripts*, III, p. 138.

[199] See Chapter 1, fns 90–92.

[200] See Burrows, *HECR*, p. 358, who quotes from *DA* of 6 May 1740.

[201] See Burrows, *HECR*, p. 356–57. For a transcription of the letter see Burrows and Dunhill, *Music and Theatre*, p. 97. The anthem's pasticcio character is the reason why it does not have its own HWV-number in the Handel work catalogue (*HHB*).

[202] *DA*, 8 May 1740, reproduced in Burrows, *HECR*, p. 356, who states that it was also included in the *Daily Gazetteer* of the same day.

[203] Burrows, *HECR*, p. 356. See also, p. 357, where Burrows provides an overview of the borrowings in Table 13.1.

[204] Burrows, *HECR*, p. 359.

[205] Burrows, *HECR*, p. 357.

[206] Perceval, *Manuscripts*, III, p. 138.

3—The 'Concert Weddings' I: The Children of George II

previous two weddings. It is possible that the king's now being a widower and the bridegroom's being represented by a proxy made this public display of marital union obsolete.

The return procession included, as at the previous weddings, the 'Fife, Drums, and Trumpets' that had also accompanied the procession to the Chapel Royal.[207] Their music was further heightened by the noise of canons, as one of the accounts in the College of Arms recorded:

> The Guns in St James's Parke were fired when y^e Procession ended [= 'entered'?] to y^e Chappel, wch was answered by y^e Tower Guns, & also when return'd.

Thus, in contrast to 1736, there was now again an aspect of public rejoicing, marked by the firing of guns; and this mixed with the music and other sounds of the ceremony, providing an audible collage of joy for those present.

The Kassel Ceremony

The ensuing wedding celebrations in Kassel were captured for posterity in a dedicated publication that described the festivities between 26 June and 1 July, focusing especially on the Princess's *Heimführung* – literally her 'home-leading', or entry to Kassel – and on the wedding on 28 June itself:

> *Beschreibung aller Solennitäten Bey dem Hohen Vermählungs-Feste, Ihro Hoch-Fürstl. Durchläucht Printz Friedrichs Mit Ihro Hoheit Der Königl. Groß-Brittannischen Princessin Maria Welches Ende Junii und Anfangs Julii des Jahrs 1740. An Ihro Königl. Majestät in Schweden Hoch-Fürstlich Hessischen Hoffe zu Cassel, vollzogen worden* (Kassel: Hampesche Erben, [1740]).[208]

Notably, the full title of this publication explained that the wedding was celebrated at 'his royal majesty in Sweden's high and princely Hesse court in Kassel', followed by a depiction of the Swedish king's royal coat of arms. Thus, this was at least officially a Swedish royal wedding, emphasizing the afore-mentioned international dimension of the match.

Once the princess had travelled to Kassel, the wedding was confirmed in a second, Calvinist service. Similar to the London wedding, this Calvinist wedding service in Kassel also took place late in the day: in the evening of 28 June, beginning at 8 o'clock.[209] It was performed by the main court chaplain ('Ober-Hoff-Prediger') but took place merely in a hall of the town palace. The published account does not mention any music, apart from the timpani and drums during the entrance procession of the bridegroom and during the firing of cannons once the couple was married. Given that this was a Calvinist service this is not surprising and there was most probably no elaborate music, if any.

Another Royal Wedding and the Afterlife of the Music

Apart from the London weddings of Princess Anne, Prince Fredrick, and Princess Mary, there was also the wedding of their youngest sister, Princess Louisa, to Prince Frederick of Denmark, later Frederick V, in 1743. Again, there was a proxy ceremony – and again with the Duke of Cumberland standing in for the groom – but this time not in London: it took place in Hanover on 11 November (30 October in Britain/OS). King George II was in Hanover at the time, participating in the military campaign on the continent; he had just famously led his troops

---

[207] This and the following *Lea Briscoe I*, p. 180.

[208] For this publication see also Rahn, *Festbeschreibung*.

[209] See *Beschreibung aller Solennitäten*, pp. 27–30.

to victory at the battle of Dettingen.[210] The *London Gazette* reported that the ceremony in Hanover was 'performed in the Chapel of the Castle, with the greatest Magnificence and Solemnity'.[211] It is not known, however, whether this included any music. A later Georgian list of Handel's anthems in the possession of George III curiously referred to an anthem 'on the Marriage of Princess Louisa to the late King of Denmark' but explained that, together with the other three wedding anthems, this was 'still wanting to render this Collection of Anthems compleat'.[212] There does not seem to be any other evidence that such an anthem by Handel for Princess Louisa's wedding ever existed.

The Hanover proxy ceremony was followed by a second ceremony with the actual groom at Christiansborg Palace in Copenhagen on 11 December. This took place in the king's antechamber, and the *London Gazette* reported that there was 'Musick'.[213] However, no further details are known. At least, one can probably safely assume that this music would not have been anything in English, but most probably a contribution of the Danish court composers and musicians.

The remaining children of George II and Queen Caroline did not marry and there was no major royal wedding in Britain for the next almost twenty years. Moreover, there appears not to have been any other notable, elaborate society wedding that could vie with these occasions.

Handel's Anthems after the Royal Weddings

It does not seem to be documented that Handel himself ever repeated any of his wedding anthems in other performances. However, Burrows has pointed out that the text of Handel's 1734 anthem was included in the 1741 wordbook of the Philharmonic Society in Dublin.[214] In fact, the wordbook contains both of Handel's wedding anthems and according to the title page, all the pieces in this book were 'performed':

> *The Te Deum, Jubilate, Anthems, Odes, Oratorios and Serenatas, as They Are Performed by The Philharmonic Society in Dublin, for the Improvement of Church Musick and the Further Support of the Mercer's Hospital* ([Dublin:] 'Printed in the Year MDCCXLI' [1741]).[215]

No details about these possible Dublin performances seem to be known. Intriguingly, the publication date of this wordbook may coincide with Handel's own visit to Dublin in the winter of 1741–42, when he famously premiered his *Messiah*. Winton Dean has remarked that the Mercer's Hospital in Stephen Street, the one mentioned on the title page, 'was one of the charities to benefit from the first performance of *Messiah*'.[216] It is tempting to speculate that Handel may have wanted to 'cash in' on his occasional royal music and himself provided copies of the mentioned pieces to be included in the concerts of the Philharmonic Society prior to, around the time of his visit.[217]

---

[210] See *HECR*, p. 386.

[211] *London Gazette*, 12–15 November 1743.

[212] 'Some Anecdotes of a Collection of Anthems, by the late G. F. Handel; in His Majesty's Possession', [fragment, 1760–1805], *Wra GEO/ADD/32/2430-2434*, here fol. 2434; available online via https://gpp.royalcollection.org.uk (accessed 4 September 2021).

[213] *London Gazette*, 13–17 December 1743.

[214] Burrows, *HECR*, p. 338. For details of this word-book see Winton Dean, *Handel's Dramatic Oratorios* (London: Oxford University Press 1959), p. 186–87.

[215] The '1st WEDDING ANTHEM.' and 'II. WEDDING ANTHEM.' are on pp. 4–7. The beginning of the second anthem is wrongly given as 'O Sing unto God'.

[216] Winton Dean, *Handel's Dramatic Oratorios*, p. 186–87.

[217] Compare Winton Dean, *Handel's Dramatic Oratorios*, p. 187, where Dean concludes that 'the works were given in Dublin before Handel's visit'; yet, his reference for this is not clear.

3—The 'Concert Weddings' I: The Children of George II

In addition to these possible Dublin performances, also in the 1740s, James Harris had wanted to perform Handel's anthem *Sing unto God* at Salisbury, and he was in contact with John Snow in Oxford who had a copy.[218] While it is not clear what came of that, *Sing unto God* was performed 'most usually' in the concerts of the Academy of Ancient Music in the 1760s.[219] Thus, Handel's royal wedding anthems clearly had an 'after-life' beyond the occasions for which they had been written; and particularly the music of his second anthem, from 1736, seems to have found some wider circulation and performances. As will be seen, it was also included at two notable royal weddings towards the end of the century.

Overall, from 1734 onwards, the inclusion of an elaborate anthem became an integral part of major royal weddings at the London court. While not much is known about the other music at these ceremonies, Handel's grand anthems turned these weddings into notable musical events. With the lengthy music listened to distinctly after the service, and forming a substantial part of the overall ceremony, these occasions may be aptly described as 'concert weddings'.

---

[218] See Burrows and Dunhill, *Music and Theatre*, p. 131–32.

[219] *The Words of Such Pieces, as Are Most Usually Performed by the Academy of Ancient Music* (London: s.n., 1768), p. 60: headed 'Composed for the Prince of Wales's Wedding'.

4

The 'Concert Weddings' II:
The Late Eighteenth-Century Georgians

THE WEDDINGS OF GEORGE III and of his elder offspring continued the precedents set earlier in the century. They were grand nocturnal court ceremonies that prominently included lengthy elaborate anthems at the end, thus combining the nuptial rites with a sort of commemorative 'concert'. Handel's music, in particular, looked set to achieving a special status at these occasions.

George III and Princess Charlotte of Mecklenburg-Strelitz, 8 September 1761

The highest-ranking royal wedding of the eighteenth century, so to speak, occurred in 1761: King George III married the German Princess Charlotte Sophia of Mecklenburg-Strelitz. Weddings of a reigning monarch are relatively rare in most monarchies – and for Britain this was the first such ceremony since the wedding of Charles II to Catherine of Braganza nearly one hundred years earlier. George III's wedding stood out also for another reason: the king had succeeded to the throne less than a year before, in October 1760, and his coronation was scheduled for 22 September 1761. The new king's wedding was to take place before the coronation, at which the royal couple was then to be crowned together.

The 'Treaty of Marriage' was signed on 15 August 1761 at Strelitz, by 'ye Earl of Harcourt (his Maj^tys Ambassador Extraordinary and Plenipotentiary, so appointed for the purpose)'.[1] Due to the bride's having to cross the sea, her exact arrival date remained uncertain. She had been expected since 20 August at least, when one writer commented with a critical undertone:

> Mean while half the Nation are at Greenwich were they have been looking out of their Windows ever since Monday. If this poor Princess is not sick with her tedious Voyage & the strange transition into such a near tumultuous World, she is to be brought up to Town & married the same Evening she arrives.[2]

Over a week later, on 5 September, another correspondent, whose attendance at the wedding had been required by the Board of Trade, reported that

> I was in hopes her Majesty wou'd have been in England above a Week ago. but Winds are as unattentive to the desires of the highests as well as the lowest of Mankind.[3]

---

[1] *Lea Briscoe I*, pp. 414–19: entry on the wedding of George III (in margin of p. 414: 'Contract of / marriage / between K. / Geo. 3^d, & his / Queen.'), here p. 414.

[2] 'C: Talbot' [presumably Sir Charles Henry Talbot, 1st Baronet] to 'Mrs George Berkeley', 20 August 1761, in *Lbl Add MS 39311*, fols 102^r–03^r, here fols 102^v–103^r.

[3] C.[?] Bacon to 'Mr [Frank] Bacon' [at Trinity Hall, Cambridge], Petersham, 5 September 1761, *Sheffield City Archives, BFM/1313/32*, [here p. 1 of the letter].

British Royal Weddings

In the end, Horace Walpole observed with pleasure that: 'When we least expected the Queen, she came, after being ten days at sea'.[4] She arrived in London on 8 September, just a fortnight before the coronation, and after having spent only one night in Britain on her way to the capital.[5] The wedding took place on the very day of her arrival in London.

The Ceremony

There had been no royal wedding for the last twenty years and Jeremy Black has shown that the forthcoming coronation and wedding were the talk of the town.[6] However, what exactly the town talked about seems not to be known. The relative modesty of the wedding is noteworthy. Even though this time it was the sovereign who married, the overall scale was the same as for the weddings of George II's children. The venue was again the Chapel Royal at St James's Palace. At one point, *Owen's Weekly Chronicle* had reported that 'The Royal wedding, we are informed, is to be public, and the door of the Chapel-Royal left open.'[7] However, in the next issue, this journal pointed out:

> 'None will be admitted into the chapel, at the time of the wedding, but Foreign Ministers, some of the principal nobility, and the necessary attendants upon the ceremony.'[8]

During the preparations, Sir Robert Wilmot, Secretary to the Lord Chamberlain, was in contact with Stephen Martin Leake, Garter King of Arms since 1754. Wilmot explained:

> It will certainly be Necessary that you should be at S:[t] James's on the Evening of the Wedding at Seven o'Clock, for the Procession, as I hear, will begin at Eight or soon after – ~~You have to~~ but I presume you will have exact Information of Every thing from the Earl Marshall [...].[9]

This shows that the heralds were again involved in arranging the ceremony. However, a reply letter by Leake makes it clear that they merely followed the orders of the Lord Chamberlain. Referring to royal weddings earlier in the century, Leake wrote:

> The Heralds Officiated at all these Weddings, and will be glad to receive his Graces Commands in relation to his Majestys, if they are to attend at it.[10]

Apart from the fact that the service, like at the previous royal weddings, took place in the evening, the reports are contradictory as to the actual time-frame of the ceremony. One account stated that it was 'About eight o'clock in the evening' before 'the procession to the chapel began', thus matching with Wilmot's note.[11] According to another account, however, the 'Marriage Ceremony' itself began only at 9pm.[12] These two accounts together would then mean

---

[4] Walpole to Horace Mann, 17 August and 10 September 1761, in Horace Walpole, *Letters of Horace Walpole to Horace Mann* [...] *From 1760 to 1785*, 'Concluding Series', 4 vols (London: Richard Bentley, 1843–44), vol. 1 (1843), pp. 38–39 and 39–44, quotation on p. 39.

[5] For details of her journey see *London Gazette*, 5–8 September 1761.

[6] Jeremy Black, *George III: America's Last King* (New Haven: Yale University Press, 2008), p. 48.

[7] *OWC*, 15–22 August 1761, p. 270.

[8] *OWC*, 22–26 August 1761, p. 278.

[9] 'Sir Rob.[t] Wilmot to M:[r] [Stephen Martin] Leake / Garter. 1st September 1761 / About the procession at His / Majesty's Wedding.', in *Lna LC 2/29*: 'Court Proceedings / 1761 / George 3.rd Wedding'.

[10] 'Garter to Sir Rob.[t] Wilmot / 23.[d] Aug.[st] 1761 / rec.[d] 24.th', in *Lna LC 2/29*.

[11] *Annual Register* [...] *1761*, 6th edn (London: Printed for J. Donsley, 1796), p. 211. *London Gazette*, 8–12 September 1761, stated merely 'This evening', without giving concrete times.

[12] *Ipswich Journal*, 12 September 1761.

4—The 'Concert Weddings' II: The Late Eighteenth-Century Georgians

that the procession took the best part of an hour. The *London Chronicle* reported that the ceremony was over by half past ten, 'which was announced by the firing of the guns at the Park and the Tower'.[13] In stark contrast to all these, Walpole, who was present at some part of the ceremony, reported 'About ten the procession began to move towards the chapel, and at eleven they all came up into the drawing-room.'[14] This would leave a mere hour for the processions to and from the chapel and for the service. The entry relating to the wedding in William Lovegrove's Manuscript associated with the Chapel Royal more broadly records that the ceremony took place 'between the Hours of 9 and 12, o.'Clock at Evening', which probably includes the entertainments after the service.[15] Whatever the exact times, it is clear that the wedding service took place rather late in the evening.

Again, the small Chapel Royal was heavily rearranged and refurbished. A surviving document indicates that seats were prepared for '283 persons', which does probably not yet include the royal family on their chairs and the clergy.[16] Preparations began about a month before the wedding, as recorded by William Lovegrove in a 'Memorandum':

> The 12th: Day of August 1761. The Royal Chapel at S.t James's was Shut up, and the Seats, Altar, Pulpit, and Organ taken down, and a Gallery and Temporary Organ erected over the Altar; and the whole Chapel properly prepared for the Royal Wedding.[17]

One of Leake's various accounts of this wedding also detailed that 'Over the Altar' were placed 'the Organ and Gallery for the Musick & Choir'.[18] At least some surpliced singers in this gallery can be seen in a sketch by Sir Joshua Reynolds (Illustration 4.1). A newly discovered account from the heralds' collection provides a detailed description of the special arrangements in the Chapel:

> The King resolving to be married in yᵉ Chappel Royal at Sᵗ James's, it was decorated in a most magnificent manner, it was hung with 2 Cartoons of Tapistry, which covered yᵉ sides thereof, & above and below was a rich hanging of Crimson Velvet with a festoon of Gold Fringe & Lace: & all yᵉ rest of yᵉ Chappel was hung with Tapestry[.] The Musick was placed behind yᵉ Altar, but so as to be visible. The King & Queen were under Canopies of state, & yᵉ Kings & other Closetts were fitted up for Spectators: The Partitions below stairs were taken down, wᶜʰ lengthned yᵉ Chappell greatly, the Pews were taken away, & 3 Rows of Seats placed on each side; at yᵉ Altar was erected on a kind of stage, an organ, & on yᵉ outside of yᵉ window was a Gallery in which was yᵉ Band of Musick, & new altar was made which projected about 6 feet, and the flooring of yᵉ Chappel was covered with Silver Tissue in the same manner that it was at yᵉ marriage of the Princess Dowager of Wales [that is, in 1736].[19]

---

[13] *London Chronicle*, 8–10 September 1761, p. 242.

[14] Walpole to H. S. Conway, 9 September 1761, in Horace Walpole, *The Letters of Horace Walpole*, ed. by J. Wright, 4 vols, vol. 3: 1759–1769 (Philadelphia: Lea and Blanchard, 1842), pp. 144–45, here p. 144.

[15] Andrew Ashbee and John Harley (eds), *The Cheque Books of the Chapel Royal*, 2 vols (Aldershot: Ashgate, 2000), II, pp. 107–08, here p. 107.

[16] 'Seats in the Chapel at S.t James's / against H.M.s Wedding / 30th. Aug.t 1761', in *Lna LC 2/29*. Donald Burrows offers a partial transcription of this list in his *Handel and the English Chapel Royal* (Oxford: Oxford University Press, 2005) [hereinafter *HECR*], p. 506.

[17] Ashbee and Harley, *Cheque Books*, II, pp. 104–05, here p. 104. Payment to William Boyce, the Chapel organist, for putting up the organ for the wedding is recorded in *Lna LC 5/168*, p. 246.

[18] *Lca S.M.L. 45* ('Heraldic Annals', vol. 2), p. 131.

[19] *Lca Briscoe I*, pp. 414–19 (see fn. 1), here p. 415. See also the similarly detailed account in *Lca S.M.L. 65*, pp. 293–96. For the hangings see also the anonymous, untitled report in *The Royal Magazine: Or Gentleman's Monthly Companion*, 5 (August 1761), pp. 104–05, here p. 104.

Illustration 4.1:
Sir Joshua Reynolds, 'The Marriage of George III', sketch in oil on canvas, 1761, *Royal Collection, RCIN 404353*, Royal Collection Trust / © Her Majesty Queen Elizabeth II 2021.

From this, it seems that the specially built organ stood in its own little gallery ('on a kind of stage', near the usual altar) but was not in the same gallery as the band – which was placed in the chapel window, in a bay or extension projecting out of the building.

Overall, this wedding seems to have been quite well prepared. A few days before the ceremony, one paper reported that the effect of putting lights into the Chapel for the evening ceremony had been tried out:

> On Tuesday night at eight o'clock, his Majesty, attended by the duke of Devonshire, Lord Chamberlain of the houshold, and several other Officers of the court, were in the Chapel Royal, which was illuminated before-hand by order of his Majesty, to see the noble appearance it would have when lighted up, and the effect was beyond expectation [...].[20]

Following the established pattern, the service was preceded by processions to the Chapel. With the king himself being the bridegroom, however, there were this time only two sections or divisions in the procession – with the king entering the Chapel after the bride.[21] The accounts

---

[20] *OWC*, 29 August–5 September 1761, p. 286.

[21] See the ceremonial in *London Gazette*, 8–12 September 1761.

4—The 'Concert Weddings' II: The Late Eighteenth-Century Georgians

agree that the processions were again accompanied by trumpets and drums. Indeed, the account from the heralds' collection notes distinctly 'yᵉ Trumpetts sounding a march yᵉ whole time', and 'Drums & Trumpetts' are mentioned for both the procession of the princess and that of the king.[22] Even though the somewhat archaic 'fife', which had been present at the previous wedding processions, is not mentioned as part of the ensemble, Fiona Smith has shown that a fife player was paid to attend both the wedding and the ensuing coronation.[23]

As in 1740, the service was conducted by the Archbishop of Canterbury, now Thomas Secker. He left many notes regarding the ceremony and its preparations, and also a detailed account of it.[24] It appears that Secker had done some research into previous royal weddings: his records include a chronological account of 'Marriages of the Royal family since Hen. 8ᵗʰ', beginning with that of Mary I to Philip of Spain in 1554.[25]

The order of service was again followed simply via copies of the Prayer Book. An entry in William Lovegrove's Manuscript records that 'Two Quarto Prayer Books was [sic] provided by Mʳ: Hart the Closet Keeper, and placed by the Serjeant before their Majesty's.'[26] Such copies were given only to the king and queen but not even, it seems, to the bridal couple.

In contrast to the previous weddings, the sources do not mention organ music accompanying the entrance processions. However, another intriguing detail of the music during the service is known: Secker's account records 'Ps. 128 was chanted.'[27] This is notable in so far as there is no evidence for the inclusion of the psalm at the royal weddings earlier in the century. It is not quite clear whether Secker meant that the psalm was sung to a simple chant tune, or in a simple, straightforward setting – throughout the eighteenth and nineteenth century, the verb 'to chant' was also used to apply to the latter.[28] There is no chant tune that is particularly associated with weddings, in the way that there is a specific 'burial chant' by Thomas Purcell.[29] Overall, Secker's reference to the psalm raises the question of whether it was not also included at the three previous royal weddings. Indeed, all these weddings also ought to have included the Wedding Responses and the Lord's Prayer, as scheduled in the Prayer Book, but there is no evidence that these were sung, and they were probably just read.

Boyce's Wedding Anthem

The 1761 wedding followed the precedent of the royal weddings earlier in the century in that it included a grand, elaborate anthem. This anthem was now unmistakably understood to be outside the liturgy of the service. Archbishop Secker himself made the particular point that the anthem 'being no appointed part of the Service, was performed after the Conclusion of it'.[30]

---

[22] *Lca Briscoe I*, pp. 414–19, here p. 417.

[23] Fiona Eila Joyce Smith, 'Original Performing Material for Concerted Music in England, *c.*1660–1800' (unpublished doctoral thesis, University of Leeds, 2014), p. 315–16. She refers to a warrant in *Lna LC 5/168*, p. 248.

[24] 'An Account of what passed / in relation to the Kings / marriage, so far as I was / concerned in it', in *Llp MS 1130*, I, no. 48 (fols 96ʳ–97ʳ).

[25] *Llp MS 1130*, I, no. 45, at the top dated 'Dⁿ Commons July 23 1761'.

[26] Ashbee and Harley, *Cheque Books*, II, p. 107.

[27] *Llp MS 1130*, I, no. 48 (fol. 96ᵛ).

[28] For the meaning of 'chanting' see Matthias Range, *Music and Ceremonial at British Coronations: From James I to Elizabeth II* (Cambridge: Cambridge University Press, 2012) [hereinafter *MCBC*], p. 150–51, esp. fn. 95, and p. 191.

[29] See Matthias Range, *British Royal and State Funerals: Music and Ceremonial since Elizabeth I* (Woodbridge: Boydell Press, 2016) [hereinafter *BRSF*], p. 28.

[30] *Llp MS 1130*, I, no. 48 (fol. 96ᵛ).

Similarly, Leak noted 'The Ceremony of the Marriage was according to the Rubrik [...] And afterwards there was an Anthem'.[31]

The anthem was *The King Shall Rejoice* by William Boyce, the organist and composer of the Chapel Royal. It is an elaborate composition for choir and orchestra. Notwithstanding the general excitement about the forthcoming coronation, the planning for the wedding, and in particular the anthem, aroused much public interest. Details of the 'Anthem, composed by Dr. Boyce, for the Royal Wedding', together with the full text, were published in advance in several London magazines:[32]

A GRAND FESTAL SYMPHONY.

Chorus.
The King shall rejoice in thy strength, O Lord: exceedingly glad shall he be of thy salvation.

Duet by Mr. Savage and Mr. Cooper. [the 'duet' is part of the opening chorus]
Thou hast given him his heart's desire, and has not denied him the request of his lips.
Chorus repeated.

Solo by a Boy, accompanied by Mr. Vincent on the Hautboy.
Blessed is the man that hath a virtuous wife, for the number of his days shall be doubled.

Solo by Mr. Mence, accompanied by Mr. Weidemann on the German Flute.
A virtuous woman is a crown to her husband, her price is far above rubies.
Strength and honour are her cloathing [*sic*], and she shall rejoice in time to come.

Solo by Mr. Beard.
Hearken, O daughter, consider and incline thine ear, forget thine own people and thy father's house.
So shall the King have pleasure in thy beauty.
Instead of thy fathers thou shalt have children, whom thou mayest make Princes in all lands.

Chorus.
Children are an heritage of the Lord, and the fruit of the whomb is his reward[.]
Lo! thus shall they be blessed that fear the Lord.

As will be seen below, the anthem text may have been compiled by Archbishop Secker. It appears to have a well-calculated structure: the first two movements form a unit in addressing the king as the husband; the following two address the queen as the wife; and the beginning of the final chorus refers to the main purpose of their union: producing children, which are not only a 'heritage of the Lord' but in the royal couple's case also successors to the throne – while the very end of the anthem is a general statement addressing everybody with the reminder to fear the Lord. Donald Burrows has argued that 'the texts of neither of Handel's wedding anthems give any prominence to the husband'.[33] As seen in the previous Chapter, this may not quite be the case; nevertheless, the apparently calculated structure in Boyce's 1761 anthem is certainly notable.

---

[31] *Lca S.M.L. 45*, p. 132. See also Leake's account in *Lca S.M.L. 65*, pp. 293–96, here p. 293 ('after which there was an Anthem').

[32] *The Royal Magazine: Or Gentleman's Monthly Companion*, 5 (August 1761), pp. 104–05, here p. 104. See also the report in *The London Magazine: Or, Gentleman's Monthly Intelligencer*, 30 (August 1761), p. 446; and *OWC*, 22–26 August 1761, p. 278. The same is included, with only slight differences, in the account of the wedding in *Lca Briscoe I*, pp. 414–19, here p. 416.

[33] Burrows, *HECR*, p. 345. See also the discussion in the previous Chapter, before fn. 146.

4—The 'Concert Weddings' II: The Late Eighteenth-Century Georgians

It is possible that at least some people could follow the anthem text on paper. A copy of a sheet with the printed anthem text has survived among Archbishop Secker's records.[34] In contrast to the newspaper versions, this does not include any details on the music, not even indicating the separate movements. The printing of the anthem text seems to have been a first for a royal wedding. In relation to this, an entry in William Lovegrove's Manuscript is noteworthy:

> When the Anthem was going to be Sung, the Bishop of Winchester came from within the Rails, and presented to the King, Queen, and the Rest of the Royal Family, the Anthem […].[35]

Secker similarly recorded that the Bishop of Winchester at some undefined point during the ceremony 'deliver'd the Anthems to the King, Queen & Royal Family'.[36] In these reports, the words 'presented' and 'deliver'd' may quite plausibly refer to copies of the anthem text being given to the royal family. If that was the case, it would then be noteworthy that these were handed out almost ritually during the ceremony, and not simply put on people's seats beforehand. This would have drawn more attention to these text sheets, heightening their – and the following music's – importance. As Secker's account indicates, the king and queen sat on their chairs during the anthem.[37]

The music of Boyce's anthem is exceptionally well preserved, even including the very parts used at the ceremony.[38] Based on the surviving material, and taking into account the sharing of some parts, Fiona Smith calculates that 'around 18 adult singers, 8 to 10 boys and around 52 players took part', making a total of about seventy-eight to eighty performers.[39] Burrows observes that the surviving performing parts would be 'adequate for about seventy performers' but concludes that 'the set must be seriously depleted'.[40] As he points out, judging by the payments, there were 'about three times as many additional performers' as there had been for Handel's anthem at the grand 1734 wedding, when the total number of musicians was seventy-five.[41] Boyce was paid £351 4s. 6d. 'for Musicians Hired for the Performance of the Anthem on account of Their Majesties Wedding, and other Disbursements, and also for the Doctor's own Composition and extraordinary Trouble'.[42] This sum was remarkably lower than the £425 spent on the trumpeters and drummers that had been sent over to accompany the princess on her journey to London.[43] With all the other costs that the payment to Boyce covered, it would seem that there cannot have been that many hired musicians.

Boyce probably started the composition of his wedding anthem at the latest in the first half of August, that is several weeks before the ceremony. In a letter of 14 August, Archbishop Secker wrote to Boyce:

---

[34] *Llp MS 1130*, I, no. 44. The previous item is a manuscript copy of the text.

[35] Ashbee and Harley, *Cheque Books*, II, p. 107.

[36] *Lbl MS 1130*, I, no. 48 (fol. 96ᵛ).

[37] *Lbl MS 1130*, I, no. 48 (fols 96ᵛ–97ʳ).

[38] *Ob MS Mus. Sch. c. 117a–c* (score, vocal and instrumental parts, mostly autograph). For a detailed study of these parts see Fiona Eila Joyce Smith, 'Original Performing Material for Concerted Music in England, c.1660–1800' (unpublished doctoral thesis, University of Leeds, 2014), esp. pp. 312–16.

[39] Fiona Smith, 'Original Performing Material', p. 315.

[40] This and the following Burrows, *HECR*, p. 336. For the payments he refers to *Lna LC 5/168*, p. 246.

[41] For 1734 see also the previous chapter.

[42] *Lna LC 5/168*, p. 246.

[43] *Lna LC 5/168*, pp. 248. See also Chapter 1, fn 96.

> These things [the suggestions regarding the coronation anthems], it is hoped, will not increase Dʳ Boyces Difficulties. As he hath represented, that the proposed Alterations in the Wedding Anthem would, they are withdrawn & laid aside by His sincere Friend [Thomas Secker][44]

The 'Alterations in the Wedding Anthem' that the archbishop had demanded most plausibly refers to changes in the text – which, in turn, implies that he was at least involved in choosing it. The fact that Boyce had claimed that such alterations would 'increase' his 'Difficulties' indicates that he had by then finished at least a substantial part of the composition. Indeed, Archbishop Secker later recalled that Boyce had pleaded that there would 'not be Time for making the Alterations in the Anthem'.[45] The excuse of want of time may at first seem somewhat surprising, given that there were still more than three weeks until the ceremony: from 14 August, when Secker wrote his letter – if not earlier – until 8 September when the wedding took place. However, as seen above, the princess had been expected to arrive at least since 20 August, and the wedding would then have taken place much earlier. Furthermore, Boyce would have been under time pressure from his simultaneously preparing the music for the coronation service. In addition, as already mentioned, Boyce also received payment for hiring extra performers for a ball on 9 September on occasion of the wedding.[46] Since all this was added to his regular duties at the Chapel Royal, he must overall have faced a considerable workload.

Boyce's wedding anthem is a grand composition: three vocal soloists and a five-part chorus (ssatb, although the two sopranos are mostly in unison) are joined by two instrumental soloists and a full orchestra of two trumpets, timpani, two oboes, two bassoons, four-part strings and basso continuo.[47] The published anthem texts mention 'A GRAND FESTAL SYMPHONY' before the opening chorus.[48] While no symphony is indicated in Boyce's score or parts, it is perfectly plausible that Boyce opened the anthem with such a symphony – as he did in his court odes. In this context it is interesting to note that John Alcock's elaborate orchestral Wedding Anthem *We Will Rejoice*, written in the same year for the wedding of Arthur Chichester, 5th Earl of Donegal (First Marquess from 1791) to Lady Anne Hamilton also has a symphony of several movements at the beginning.[49] The comparison with Alcock's anthem is particularly intriguing as Donegal's wedding took place on 11 September 1761 – just three days after the royal wedding, at which Donegal had walked in the procession.[50]

Whether Boyce's anthem had a symphony or not, the first chorus itself makes for an appropriately grand opening, employing all the forces available. The chorus is based on Ps 21: 'The King Shall Rejoice', a text traditionally sung at coronations. This choice seems to highlight the fact that this was the wedding of a reigning king, not a mere prince. Indeed, for his Coronation Anthem *The King Shall Rejoice* – which would have been written at about the same time, if not earlier – Boyce used much the same music as for the opening chorus of his wedding anthem:

---

[44] *Llp MS 1130*, I, no. 38.

[45] *Llp MS 1130*, I, no. 48 (fol. 96ᵛ).

[46] See *Lna LC 5/168*: p. 246. See also Fiona Smith, 'Original Performing Material', p. 296. For Boyce's coronation music see Range, *MCBC*, Chapter 6.

[47] For a more detailed discussion of the music see Matthias Range, 'William Boyce's Anthem for the Wedding of King George III', *Musical Times*, 147 (Summer 2006), pp. 59–66. For a modern edition see William Boyce, *Two Anthems for the Georgian Court*; Part ii: *The King Shall Rejoice*, ed. by John R. van Nice, 'Recent Researches in the Music of the Baroque Era', 8 (Madison: A-R Editions, 1970).

[48] See the sources in fn. 32. Some sources render this as 'FESTIVAL'.

[49] For this anthem see Edward James Michael Chaddock, 'Two Orchestral Anthems by John Alcock (1715–1806): A Critical Edition with Commentary' (unpubl. M.Phil thesis: University of Birmingham, 2010).

[50] For the Irish peers walking in the 1761 wedding procession see the account in *LM* 30 (1761), p. 558.

4—The 'Concert Weddings' II: The Late Eighteenth-Century Georgians

the first 82 bars of the coronation movement (with 122 bars in total) are the same as in the wedding anthem, the only difference being the inclusion of three trumpets in the coronation version instead of two in the wedding setting. Since the two events followed each other so closely, this 'self-borrowing' could have been intended. Those present at both occasions – most of those at the wedding would also have attended the coronation – may still have had the wedding music in their ears when hearing it again at the coronation. This musical link created a neat parallel to the well-known interpretation of the coronation as 'the marriage of the monarch to the people'.[51] After all, this idea could have been the reason why this traditional coronation text was chosen for the wedding anthem in the first place. Referring to the close succession of wedding and coronation, Jane Roberts referred to these as 'events that symbolised the fusion of public and private responsibilities in a marital partnership.[52]

The other movements of the coronation anthem, however, have texts that are clearly different from those in the wedding anthem. Boyce therefore composed these anew, with their own independent material, continuing in the style of a full anthem with orchestral accompaniment.[53] It is possible that Boyce decidedly intended his anthem for the wedding to be somewhat less grand than the anthems he wrote for the coronation, with the verses creating a more intimate tone that was better suited to the smaller scale of the ceremony and also to the much smaller space of the Chapel Royal compared to Westminster Abbey.

After the imposing opening chorus, the following movement, 'Blessed is the Man that has a Virtuous Wife', with its overall much more intimate tone, is particularly noteworthy. Boyce scored it for a solo treble and an oboe, and it is tempting to interpret that these two soloists might somehow be meant to represent the 'blessed man' and the 'virtuous wife' – although it does not seem obvious which would be which.

Similarly, in the following 'A Virtuous Woman is a Crown' Boyce has, willingly or not, included a little irony: in this movement that may refer to the bride, to the German Princes Charlotte, the male solo singer is accompanied by a 'German Flute', as Boyce notes in the score.[54] This term for the flute was widely used at the time, and the idea that this could have been an intended allusion to the bride is supported by the fact there was probably yet another reference in this scoring. Incidentally, George III, who was of course also of German descent, was a competent flute player himself and this fact was emphasized just at the time of the wedding: when some newspapers referred to the musical skills of the new queen they also added that the king 'is a good Proficient on the German Flute'.[55] After all, the '*Mr.* Weidemann' who was reported to be the flautist in this movement at the wedding service was none other than Carl Friedrich Weideman, the king's own flute teacher.[56]

---

[51] For this see, for instance, William Le Hardy, *The Coronation Book. The History and Meaning of the Ceremonies at the Crowning*, first publ. in 1937 for the coronation of George VI and Queen Elizabeth, rev. edn for the coronation of Queen Elizabeth II (London: Staples Press, 1953), p. 35.

[52] Jane Roberts (ed.), *George III and Queen Charlotte; Patronage, Collecting and Court Taste*, catalogue to the exhibition in the Queen's Gallery Buckingham Palace (London: Royal Collections Publications, 2004), p. 15.

[53] See Range, *MCBC*, p. 165–66.

[54] See *Ob MS Mus. Sch. c. 117a*, fol. 21a^r.

[55] See Roberts, *George III and Queen Charlotte*, p. 312; and *Ipswich Journal*, 12 September 1761, under 'London, &c. Tuesday, Sept. 8'. The latter referred to a report in the *Whitehall Evening Post*.

[56] See Philip H. Highfill Jr, Kalman A. Burnim, and Edward A. Langhans, *A Biographical Dictionary of Actors, Actresses, Musicians, Dancers, Managers & Other Stage Personnel in London, 1660–1800*, 16 vols (Carbondale: Southern Illinois University Press, 1973–1993), vol. 15: 'Tibbett to M. West' (1993), p. 335. For Weidemann's playing in the wedding anthem see above, the quotation with fn. 32.

British Royal Weddings

Return Procession

After the wedding service, the procession back to the state appartments in the palace was presumably also accompanied by music of the trumpets and drums. There was, however, a significant change in the ceremonial order. Initially, mirroring proceeding going to the Chapel, there had been meant to be two separate processions. The newly-found account from the heralds' records lists 'The Queen's Returne / Drums & Trumpetts, as before' and later notes that 'The King's Returne, was in ye same manner he came.'[57] This indicates two separate sections in the return procession: one for the queen and one for the king. However, the account is not accurate in this detail. The order of the return procession was eventually changed, very much at the last minute. One of Leake's accounts, in which he referred to himself as 'Garter' and in the third person, explains:

> Accord.^g to the Ceremonial, the Queen was first Conducted to the Chapel with her procession, and then the King with his; And the same Order was to have been Observed in the Return; but while the Marriage Ceremony was performing in the Chapel, the Lord Chamberlain signified to Garter there was to be but one procession back, and he must Order it accordingly. This made a Considerable alteration in the Ceremonial, which he was obliged to adjust as well as the short time would permit; And all returned in one procession: The Peeresses and Peers going before the King, and the Queen with her attendants following.[58]

In another account, Leake detailed that

> after their Majestys were in the Chapel the Lord Chambln signified to me they must go back in one procession, which I was therefore obliged to draw up with my pencil as follows [...][59]

In this new arrangement, Leake did curiously not list the king; and for the queen he detailed that she was to go 'betw: the D. of York & P. William', who had also led her to the Chapel – instead of between her Vice Chamberlain and Lord Chamberlain who had been scheduled to lead her back.[60] In contrast to this, at one point, there seem to have been some 'Notes' evidencing that the king and queen actually walked together. In 1839, during the preparations for her own wedding, Queen Victoria and Lord Melbourne had looked at historic precedents, including the 1761 wedding, and she recorded:

> I had observed that George III didn't lead the Queen out; well, it was settled they should go separate, but by these Notes it says the King insisted on leading her out and did so.[61]

Unfortunately, it does not seem to be known in which 'Notes' this had been found. It is interesting that this gives the king himself as initiating this change. It is then noteworthy that, with such a change, this procession would have matched with what had probably been done at the wedding of the king's parents in 1736: as seen in the previous chapter, they had reportedly walked hand in hand in the return procession.

Public Dissemination

When the magazines published the full anthem text and details, they also announced that the anthem had been rehearsed in Hickford's Music Room:

---

[57] *Lea Briscoe I*, pp. 418 and 419.

[58] *Lea S.M.L.* 65, p. 295.

[59] *Lea S.M.L.* 45, p. 131–32.

[60] *Lea S.M.L.* 45, p. 132.

[61] *QVJ*, 28 November 1839 (LE). For the following compare Chapter 3, fn. 156.

86

4—The 'Concert Weddings' II: The Late Eighteenth-Century Georgians

> On the 24th [of August], the following Anthem, composed by Dr. Boyce, for the Royal Wedding, was rehearsed at Mr. Hickford's Room.[62]

This was quite possibly a public rehearsal: after all, Hickford's Room was a popular London Concert Room.[63] The date of 24 August was still two weeks before the eventual wedding, but again the uncertainty about the exact date of Princess Charlotte's arrival probably meant that the planning had to be much more generous. There was another rehearsal on the day before the ceremony. Under the heading 'London, &c. *Tuesday, Sept.* 8' one newspaper reported:

> Yesterday the Anthem for his Majesty's Wedding was rehearsed in the Chapel Royal before many Persons of Distinction.[64]

The 'many Persons of Distinction' may refer to a specially invited group of people. They are not mentioned in a note by the Lord Chamberlain that refers to this rehearsal and specifies it to be in the 'Morning at Twelve o'Clock'.[65] Originally, the wedding had been supposed to be in the evening of the same day:

> The Royal Nuptials were expected to have been solemnized on Monday evening, for which purpose the Bishops and all the Officers attended till near nine o'clock, when an express arriving with the advice that the Princess had not been landed [*sic*] so soon as expected, it was put off till last night.[66]

This second rehearsal would have given the performers some opportunity to acquaint themselves with the special conditions in the Chapel Royal. For, as seen above, the Chapel was decorated with lavish hangings and there were other ephemeral arrangements, including the floor covering. Apart from the great number of people, especially all the hangings and carpet would have affected the acoustics of the rather small Chapel Royal considerably.[67]

Overall, the reporting on the king and queen's wedding was at least as intense as that on the forthcoming coronation. On the one hand, the king's wedding was confined to the relative privacy of the Chapel Royal – but on the other hand, the detailed reports in the newspapers indicate the growing interest in these royal occasions. These reports' detailed reference to the music is as remarkable as obvious. After all, the music was the only part of the ceremony that could at least somehow be experienced by the public, as it could be heard in public rehearsals and at least one public concert: Fiona Smith has shown that Boyce presented the anthem 'performed at their Majesties Nuptials' at a charity concert for the Westminster Infirmary, at St Margaret's Church, Westminster on 29 April 1762 – with a public rehearsal on 27 April.[68] With these performances, a much greater number of people, and from outside the court circle, had a chance to hear their king and queen's wedding anthem and thus 'participate' at least to some extent in the ceremony.

---

[62] *The London Magazine: Or, Gentleman's Monthly Intelligencer*, 30 (1761), p. 446. See also the report in *The Royal Magazine: Or Gentleman's Monthly Companion*, 5 (August 1761), pp. 104–05; and *OWC*, 22–26 August 1761, p. 278.

[63] Simon McVeigh, 'London (i), § V, 2: Musical Life, 1660–1800: Concert Life', *NG* 15, pp. 119–25, here p. 122. McVeigh points out that the room had 'lost its predominance after the death of the leader Festing in 1752'.

[64] *The Ipswich Journal*, 12 September 1761.

[65] From an unnumbered, loose document in *Lna LC 2/29*, quoted in Fiona Smith, 'Original Performing Material', p. 316.

[66] *Lloyds's Evening Post*, 7–9 September 1761, p. 245.

[67] Compare Burrows's remarks on the 1734 performance in the Queen's Chapel; see Chapter 3, with fns 90–93.

[68] Fiona Smith, 'Original Performing Material', p. 313, with references in fn. 84. The quotation is from *London Chronicle*, 22–24 April 1762.

British Royal Weddings

George III's Siblings and Children

George III was the first of his siblings to marry. More than two years later, on 16 January 1764, his elder sister Princess Augusta married Charles William Ferdinand, Duke of Brunswick-Wolfenbüttel at St James's Palace. However, this ceremony was very different to the previous royal weddings of the century. Horace Walpole recorded: 'On Monday evening they were married by the archbishop in the great drawing-room, with little ceremony'.[69] The reports were rather meagre too, with that in the *London Gazette* consisting of only a few lines.[70] This was the earliest Georgian wedding that did not to take place in a chapel.

Two years later, in 1766, Princess Caroline Matilda, younger sister of George III, was married by proxy to Christian VII of Denmark (of later Struensee fame). Similar to the 1740 wedding of Princess Mary with a proxy for Prince Frederick of Hesse, the 1766 wedding consisted of two ceremonies: a London ceremony by proxy and then a ceremony with the bridegroom in Copenhagen, once the princess had arrived in Denmark. Although the 1740 scheme provided a good precedent for a full proxy-wedding in chapel, in 1766 the London ceremony was overall very similar to that in 1764: a simple ceremony in the council chamber at St James's Palace between seven and eight o'clock in the evening of 1 October.[71] The princess's brother, the Duke of York and Albany, acted as proxy for the bridegroom, and the Archbishop of Canterbury 'read a few prayers', as Sir Stephen Cottrell, Assistant Master of the Ceremonies, noted.[72] There does not seem to have been any music at this ceremony and the simplicity emphasized the mere contract-like character of the proceedings. For the Copenhagen ceremony, an interesting detail is that the Archbishop of Canterbury was sent a draft of the ceremonial that was to be used, in order to see whether it was 'comfortable to Precedent'.[73]

Also in 1766, Prince William Henry, Duke of Gloucester and Edinburgh, younger brother of George III, married Maria Countess Waldegrave, in a secret ceremony at Cumberland House, the Duke's London home. Similarly, in 1771, Prince Henry, Duke of Cumberland and Strathearn, another younger brother of George III, secretly married Anne Horton. This marriage did not meet with the king's approval and ultimately led to the introduction of the famous Royal Marriages Act in 1772.[74]

Twenty years later, in 1791, the children of George III began to marry: Prince Frederick, Duke of York and Albany, his second child, married Princess Frederica of Prussia; and in 1793 the king's ninth child, Prince Augustus Frederick, Duke of Sussex, married Lady Augusta Murray. These weddings in their scope followed those of George III's sisters and were of a rather un-ceremonious nature. They will be discussed in more detail in the next chapter.

---

[69] Walpole to Horace Mann, 18 January 1764, in Walpole, *Letters [...] to Horace Mann*, pp. 181–84, here p. 183.

[70] *London Gazette*, 14–17 January 1764. NB this has 'Great Council Chamber'. The same in the entry in the New Cheque Book of the Chapel Royal; see Ashbee and Harley, *Cheque Books*, II, p. 135. See also the accounts in *Lna LC 5/4*, pp. 40–43 and *Lna LC 5/7*, pp. 43–44.

[71] For details on the London ceremony and the wedding in Copenhagen (also an evening ceremony) see William Henry Wilkins, *A Queen of Tears: Caroline Matilda, Queen of Denmark and Norway and Princess of Great Britain and Ireland*, 2 vols (London: Longmans, Green and Company, 1904), I, Chapter 6.

[72] *Lna LC 5/4*, p. 52.

[73] *Llp MS 1130*, II, no. 133.

[74] For both marriages see Jeremy Black, *The Hanoverians: The History of a Dynasty* (London: Hambledon and London, 2004), p. 184. On the legal aspect see still C. d'O. Farran, 'The Royal Marriages Act, 1772', *Modern Law Review*, 14 (1951), pp. 53–63.

4—The 'Concert Weddings' II: The Late Eighteenth-Century Georgians

Prince George, Prince of Wales, and Princess Caroline of Brunswick, 8 April 1795

The first royal wedding after that of George III and Queen Charlotte that was marked by a more elaborate ceremony was the wedding of their eldest son, the heir to the throne. Prince George, Prince of Wales, married Princess Caroline of Brunswick on 8 April 1795. There had been public rumours at least since 1788 that Prince George had secretly married Mrs Fitzherbert.[75] However, such a marriage would have been against the stipulations of the Royal Marriage Act and not legally valid. The news of the Prince of Wales's forthcoming actual wedding had similarly been around for a while – but it was not until 20 March 1795 that the Lord Chamberlain's Office announced that the wedding was to take place in the Chapel Royal at St James's Palace.[76]

The wedding was again a nocturnal ceremony in the Chapel Royal, the ceremonial following the precedents of the previous weddings there. Notably, while the ceremonial had been published in newspapers for the weddings since 1734, this appears to be the first royal wedding for which it was also printed separately.[77] This printed ceremonial, however, is mainly concerned with details of the procession and contains only very little about the actual service. It is possible that it was intended mainly for those organizing the procession: a copy of the ceremonial in the British Library, which apparently belonged to someone actively involved in the proceedings, has at the back the ominous manuscript note 'Begin at the Altar or not?'.[78] This may have been written, for instance by one of the heralds wondering whether the return procession was to begin at the altar. Yet, the printed ceremonial may also have been intended for spectators: at the bottom of last page, it features the picture of a quiver with arrows and a bow – the symbol of Cupid, the Roman God of Love (see Illustration 11.3). This ornamental feature is as decorative as it is unnecessary and would not make sense if the ceremonial had been intended only as a practical guide for the use of the officials.

There is no evidence for a specially produced order of service. At the ceremony, the participants probably again simply used copies of the Prayer Book: Henry Singleton's well-known painting of the wedding service shows both the officiating clergy, George III, and one of the ladies standing behind the queen's chair all holding a book in their hands (Illustration 4.2).

The Processions

The main participants arrived again in three distinct processions: first the bride, then the bridegroom, and finally the king and queen.[79] The Lord Chamberlain had announced that nobody was to walk in the processions but the royal family with their attendants.[80] Beilby Porteus, Dean of the Chapel Royal, in his notebook recorded that they 'came to the Chapel from the Drawing

---

[75] For these rumours see, for instance, *The New Annual Register, or General Repository of History* [...] *for the Year 1787* (London, 1788), p. 114. For a more detailed study on this issue see James Munson, *Maria Fitzherbert: The Secret Wife of George IV* (London: Robinson 2002).

[76] See *The True Briton*, 7 April 1795.

[77] *Ceremonial for the Nuptials of His Royal Highness The Prince of Wales, with the Princess Caroline of Brunswick, at St. James's* [1795]. See under Ceremonial 1795.

[78] *Lbl Add MS 34453*, fols 231ʳ–232ᵛ.

[79] Ceremonial 1795. For a detailed listing of the processions to the Chapel see also John H. Adolphus, *The Royal Exile: Or, Memoirs of the Public and Private Life of Her Majesty, Caroline, Queen Consort of Great Britain* [...], vol. 1, 18th edn (London: Published by Jones and Co., 1821), up to p. 28.

[80] See *True Briton*, 7 April 1795.

Illustration 4.2: Henry Singleton, 'The Marriage of George IV (1762–1830) when Prince of Wales', oil on canvas, signed and dated 1795, Royal Collection, RCIN 405845, Royal Collection Trust / © Her Majesty Queen Elizabeth II 2021.

Room in their different Processions about 9 at night', and were then 'ranged in the Chapel by the Heralds according to antient forms'.[81] The processions to the Chapel were headed by the usual musicians. The ceremonial listed 'Drums and Trumpets', 'Kettle Drums' and the 'Serjeant Trumpeter', all of which were

> To file off at the Door of the Chapel. Not to play but in the several Processions to the Chapel, except on the last return.[82]

The instructions when the instruments were to play are interesting: only on their way 'to' the Chapel, and thus not when they go back to fetch the next procession, and then again 'on the last return'. The latter most likely refers to the return after the service, when they walked ahead

---

[81] *Llp MS 2103*, fols 69ʳ–70ʳ: entry for 8 April 1795, here fol. 69ʳ. The same in *Llp MS 2100*, fols 81ʳ–84ʳ: entry for 8 April 1795, here fol. 82ʳ.

[82] Ceremonial 1795, at beginning. See also the accounts of the wedding: for instance, 'The Prince's Wedding', *Gentleman's Magazine*, 45 (1795), pp. 429–31, here p. 431.

4—The 'Concert Weddings' II: The Late Eighteenth-Century Georgians

of the newly-weds. The status of the last, the monarchs' entrance procession was pointed out by its special music: one source refers to 'the Household Trumpets and Kettle Drums in their State Coats, 16 in number, playing "*God save the King*," &c.'[83]

At previous weddings, the music that accompanied the entering of the individual processions into the Chapel Royal had been organ music. However, for this wedding, the accounts noted for the bride's entrance:

> The King's Band, in an orchestra erected for the occasion, opposite the King's Gallery, and over the Altar, played part of Handel's Overture to *Esther* which was discontinued as soon as she was seated.[84]

This appears to be the earliest known detail of what was effectively to become known as the 'Bridal March'. Notably, the bride's entrance was musically linked with the bridegroom's entrance, as the latter was accompanied by 'the Band again playing another part of the same Overture'.[85]

The Ceremony and Music

The service was again performed by the Archbishop of Canterbury, now John Moore, assisted by the aforementioned Beilby Porteus, Bishop of London, as Dean of the Chapel Royal.[86] It would appear that the archbishop had by now established his prerogative to officiate at royal weddings. Like his predecessor Secker, Archbishop Moore had done some research into previous royal weddings.[87] However, the same applied to Bishop Porteus.[88] It is not clear whether this indicates competition or cooperation between the two.

Regarding the music of the service, there does not seem to be any information on the psalm or the Responses, but there is some vague indication from the next wedding (in 1797) that Ps. 67 could have been included in some way.[89] There is clear evidence that the anthem came again at the very end, outside the actual liturgy – 'after the Ceremony', as the *True Briton* reported.[90] The anthem's coming at the very end is highlighted by the wording in the report in the *Gentleman's Magazine*: 'THE RETURN OF THE PROCESSION / Commenced as soon as the anthem was finished [...].'[91]

No details are known for the music of the return procession. One other notable detail for this is recorded, however: as in 1736, but in contrast to 1761, the ceremonial now scheduled that the newly-wed royal couple walk next to each other and it is indeed reported that 'the Prince of Wales [was] leading the Princess', followed by the king and queen walking separately with their respective entourages.[92]

---

[83] Untitled report of the Prince of Wales's wedding, *The Oracle and Public Advertiser*, 9 April 1795, no page number.

[84] Untitled report in *The Oracle* (as in previous fn.). See also *True Briton*, 9 April 1795; *SJC*, 7–9 April 1795; and 'Ceremonial of the Nuptials of His Royal Highness the Prince of Wales with the Princess Caroline of Brunswick', *The Sun*, 9 April 1795, p. [2].

[85] Untitled report in *The Oracle* (as in fn. 83).

[86] The printed ceremonial mentions merely the Archbishop of Canterbury. Ffor the dean's participation see 'The Prince's Wedding', *Gentleman's Magazine*, p. 431.

[87] See *Llp Moore 6*, fols 66ʳ–69ʳ.

[88] *Llp Fulham Papers Porteus 17*, fols 197ʳ–200ᵛ. For Beilby's discourse on clerical precedence at royal weddings see also Chapter 1, fn. 58.

[89] See below, fn. 137–39.

[90] *True Briton*, 9 April 1795.

[91] 'The Prince's Wedding', *Gentleman's Magazine*, p. 431.

[92] Last page of Ceremonial 1795; and 'The Prince's Wedding', p. 431.

British Royal Weddings

The Anthem

The printed ceremonial stipulated that 'at the Conclusion' of the service 'the bridegroom and bride [were] to retire to their seats while the Anthem is performing'.[93] This does not mention what the king and queen were to do at this point in the ceremony, but this is detailed in a manuscript ceremonial from the heralds' records:

> At the conclusion of the Marriage Service their Majesties retired to their Chairs of State under the Canopy while the Anthem was performing.[94]

As at the earlier weddings, the anthem accompanied a sort of 'inthronization' of the king and queen, and the *Gentleman's Magazine* described graphically that 'their Majesties ascended an elegant Throne erected for the occasion on the right hand of the altar'.[95] These 'Chairs of State under the Canopy', this 'Throne' for the king and queen, can be clearly seen in William Hamilton's contemporary sketch for a painting of the ceremony, on the far right (Illustration 4.3).

The changing of seats by the royal couple was all the more significant as it seems that this time generally only the royal family was seated during the service. In 1734, the ceremonial had stipulated that the retinue of the royal personages was to go 'to the Seats allotted to them', implying their sitting down.[96] In 1761, it had still been reported that, apart from the royal family in their chairs of state and 'stools', 'the peers, peeresses, bishops, and foreign ministers' all sat 'on benches'.[97] For 1795, Bishop Porteus observed that 'The Royal Family were seated on Chairs placed in a Semicircle on the haut Pas facing the Altar.'[98] However, no general seating of the congregation seems to be reported and the pictures of the ceremony show only the king and queen seated (see Illustrations 4.2 and 4.3). Indeed, the account in the *Gentleman's Magazine* detailed:

> The persons in the procession occupied the several places appointed for them, **all of whom were standing**.[99]

If the congregation in 1795 remained standing throughout the ceremony, this would have turned the performance of the anthem, with the re-seating of the royal couple, even more into an 'occasion', in to a sort of ceremony in itself.

The anthem was Handel's *Sing unto God*, the anthem that had been written for the wedding of a previous Prince of Wales, in 1736. Bishop Porteus recorded:

> After the Marriage there was an Anthem composed by M[r] Handel, which had been performed at the Marriage of The Kings Father, Frederick Prince of Wales, & was therefore chosen by him for the present Occasion.[100]

According to this, the anthem had been chosen by George III himself, explicitly because it had been performed at this parents' wedding. Yet, Handel's anthem was not performed in its original

---

[93] *Lbl Add MS 34453*, fol. 232[r]. This also in the report in *Morning Chronicle*, 9 April 1795.

[94] 'Ceremonial of the Marriage of His Royal Highness / the PRINCE of WALES with her Highness the / Princess Caroline of Brunswick on Wednesday / the 8:[th] day of April 1795.', *Lca MS Ceremonials L. 19*, pp. 227–29, here p. 229.

[95] 'The Prince's Wedding', *Gentleman's Magazine*, p. 431.

[96] *London Gazette*, 12–16 March 1733/4. The corresponding engraving of the wedding is not quite clear in this respect (see Illustration 3.2).

[97] 'An Account of the Royal Marriage', *The Scots Magazine*, 23 (September 1761), pp. 493–94, here p. 494.

[98] *Llp MS 2100*, fol. 82[r].

[99] 'The Prince's Wedding', *Gentleman's Magazine*, p. 431 (my emphasis).

[100] *Llp MS 2103*, fol. 69[r]. Same in *Llp MS 2100*, fol. 82[r].

4—The 'Concert Weddings' II: The Late Eighteenth-Century Georgians

version of 1736, but in an extended version by Samuel Arnold, who was one of the organists of the Chapel Royal and played the organ at the wedding.[101] Arnold's version from the 1795 wedding is found in two editions of the anthem. Gardner has explained that these were 'issued as nos. 153–154' of Arnold's 'edition of Handel's collected works'; the two are identical, from the same printing plates, just with different title pages: the first referring to 1736, the second to the 1795 wedding.[102] Arnold's editions appeared in January and February, a couple of months before the April wedding, and before the official announcement of the wedding location on 20 March (see above). Nevertheless, the advertisements for both described the music specifically as the anthem 'to be performed in the Chapel Royal' at the forthcoming wedding.[103] This may indicate how established, and expectable, the choice of the Chapel Royal had become.

Illustration 4.3: William Hamilton, 'The Marriage of George, Prince of Wales, and Princess Caroline of Brunswick', sketch in oil on canvas *c.* 1795–97, *Royal Collection, RCIN 404486,* Royal Collection Trust / © Her Majesty Queen Elizabeth II 2021.

---

[101] For Arnold's playing the organ see below, fns 118–19.

[102] Gardner, 'Preface', p. xxiii. He refers to the copies in *Lbl I 5* and *Lbl R.M. 6.d.1*. The copy *Ob Deneke 27 (6)* is a conflated version of both editions: it has 'Nº 153' printed in the bottom right corner of the pages, changing to '154' on p. 43.

[103] See the advertisements in *TB* on 1 January and 28 February 1795.

As in 1761, the text of the anthem was printed separately: at least one copy of a text sheet survives in the British Library.[104] Overall, this printed text matches with Arnold's edition, merely with the addition of 'O' before 'ye kingdoms' in the opening chorus and the omission of the second line of the chorus 'Lo, Thus Shall the Man Be Blessed' (that is, the words 'Blessed shall he be; he shall be blessed'). In contrast to 1761, the printed anthem text gives not merely the words, but also musical details on soloists and chorus – although notably not the composer's name.

Anthony Hicks has pointed out that Arnold's score of Handel's anthem is 'a heavily re-orchestrated arrangement with additional items from operas and a cantata'.[105] Gardner explains that Arnold's edition broadened the scoring with the addition of horns and occasionally an additional viola part.[106] More importantly, Gardner details that this edition includes three additional movements. First of all, there is an overture 'made up of inflated movements taken from the overture to *Il pastor fido*, HWV 8a [from 1712]'. Then there are two numbers added between the chorus 'Lo, Thus Shall the Man Be Blessed' and the recitative preceding the final chorus:

> – the solo aria 'Instead of thy Father Thou Shalt Have Children', which is 'an arrangement of the aria no. 34, "Vivi, tiranno", from Handel's opera *Rodelinda*, HWV 19 (1725)'
> – and the duet 'Lo Children Are an Heritage', which is 'based on "Tra amplessi innocenti", from the cantata *Cecilia, volgi un sguardo*, HWV 89 (1736)'.

These additions extended Handel's anthem considerably. The inclusion of an overture – not listed in the printed text sheet – intriguingly correlates with the reports of the 1761 wedding, that Boyce's anthem then had an overture. Regarding the vocal additions to Handel's anthem, they do not lack a certain irony. The source for 'Instead of thy Father Thou Shalt Have Children' – the aria from *Rodelinda* that sarcastically exclaims that the 'tyrant', or ruler, shall live – does not immediately seem to offer itself to the new context and new text, which sits somewhat uncomfortably with such a bravura aria. Moreover, in the opera, the aria refers to Grimoaldo whose life has been spared from assassination: he gives up his claim to the throne that he had usurped and returns to his home region. This could have been a very subtle reference to the Prince of Wales, who had a notoriously bad relationship with his father George III (the 'tyrant') and had *de facto* attempted to usurp the throne through a regency back in 1788–89. In this context it maybe meaningful, and not a mere misprint, that the opening text from Ps. 45:16 in the printed score reads 'Father', in the singular, instead of the usual translation 'Fathers', in the plural. The arranged aria clearly points to the 'children', the purpose of the prince's marriage: appropriately, the solo singer is noted in treble clef, intended to be a boy.

The following duet 'Lo Children Are an Heritage' is similarly scored for two boys (Canto Primo and Secondo, in treble clef) – again musically pointing to the theme of 'children'. The source of this movement, the final and joyful number of the cantata, seems well-chosen with its direct reference to the 'innocent embraces' and the joy of the heart.

---

[104] *Lbl Add MS 6332*, fol. 159ʳ; on the back with the manuscript annotation 'Peformd In the Chapel Royal Sᵗ James's at the Marriage of The Prince & Princess of Wales April 8.ᵗʰ 1795.'

[105] Anthony Hicks, 'Ravishing Semele' [review article], *Musical Times*, 114 (March 1973), pp. 275 and 278–280, here p. 279. See also Burrows, *HECR*, p. 354.

[106] For details of this and the following see Gardner, 'Preference', p. 184, and Gardner, 'Preface', pp. xxiii–xxiv.

4—The 'Concert Weddings' II: The Late Eighteenth-Century Georgians

The *Morning Chronicle* described the anthem that was performed at the wedding as

the same piece of music, as that performed on the Marriage of his present Majesty's father, with some few alterations. It was composed by Handel, but it is not in his best manner.[107]

This reference to 'some few alterations' strengthens the possibility that Arnold's altered version was performed at the wedding – and may perhaps be the reason for the judgment that the anthem was not in Handel's 'best manner'. As seen above, the advertisements of Arnold's edition proclaimed that this was the piece to be performed at the ceremony. Gardner suggests that the arrangement of, and the additions to Handel's anthem were made by Arnold himself.[108] It is not clear, however, why he extended the anthem in the first place.

Another Anthem?

There can be no doubt that Handel's anthem was performed at the service. Nevertheless, as in 1734, there is again another anthem associated with the wedding: *Blessed Are All They that Fear the Lord* by Thomas Sanders Dupuis. In the composer's autograph score this is headed 'Anthem / compos'd for the Ceremony / of the Marriage / of / His R. H. the Prince of Wales. / 1795'.[109] Dupuis was at the time the senior organist of the Chapel Royal, and it would thus have been part of his duties to contribute something to the wedding music. At least the beginning of the anthem's text is taken from Ps. 128, the psalm scheduled for a wedding in the Prayer Book. The anthem is an elaborate composition of considerable length, employing a full orchestra including four-part strings, two oboes (changing to flutes in one movement), two trumpets and timpani. After a French-style overture, the opening chorus is of lavish dimensions, with obvious references to Handel's Hallelujah Chorus, and the anthem continues in a similarly grand manner.

The ascription that Dupuis's anthem was 'compos'd for the Ceremony of the Marriage' indicates that it was not merely a topical work written on the occasion of the wedding but actually a piece intended for the service. The score at the end is dated to January 1795, about three months before the wedding. While it is not implausible that this anthem could have been intended to be performed *in lieu* of the psalm, which is not otherwise mentioned for the service, it seems altogether more likely that Dupuis, as Chapel Royal organist, expected to contribute the anthem to such an occasion and hence wrote this piece. At some point, however, it was decided that the anthem should be Handel's *Sing unto God* – at the latest by January, when Arnold advertised his edition of the anthem with the statement that it will be performed at the forthcoming wedding. As already mentioned, Bishop Porteust recorded that it had been the king himself who had chosen Handel's anthem for the ceremony.[110] It is not implausible that Arnold could have furthered this choice: the wedding neatly coincided with the publication of his edition of the piece, and the one could have stimulated the other. After all, his announcing Handel's anthem as to be performed at the wedding – at about the time that Dupuis finished his anthem – could have been premature anticipation.

Although it was not performed at the ceremony, Dupuis's anthem was by no means forgotten like Greene's anthem for the 1734 wedding had been. After the 1795 royal wedding, Dupuis's anthem was performed at a concert, as the composer John Marsh recorded, describing

---

[107] *Morning Chronicle*, 9 April 1795.

[108] Gardner, 'Preface', p. xxiv.

[109] *Lbl Add MS 27757*: this inscription in the composer's hand is on a leaf at the beginning.

[110] See above, fn. 100.

British Royal Weddings

it as 'an anthem or epithalamium' – a song or poem celebrating a wedding.[111] Indeed, Dupuis's piece seems to have gained some popularity: it was listed in different anthem word-books up to the mid-nineteenth century at least, which may possibly indicate that it was also performed – although if it was performed, then almost certainly not with its lavish scoring, but in an arranged, now lost version with organ accompaniment only.[112]

The Performance

The performance conditions for the music were probably similar to those at the earlier weddings. A 'Memorandum' on the wedding listed some details and explained that

> on this ocasion the Chapel was fitted up – by gutting the whole of it & making it like a large Room – The floor & Altar was covered with Carpet – the Window over the Altar taken out & an Orchestra put in its place – a Galary on the South Side uniform with the Organ Galary & hung with Crimson Velvet fringed with Gold[,] the Stands & Seats in the Orchestra Covered with Crimson Baize [...].[113]

The *Morning Chronicle* reported that the performers 'were ranged in the two galleries on each side of the Altar, and in a circular gallery behind it.'[114] William Hamilton's painting of the ceremony shows a row of surpliced singers in a gallery to the right above the altar (Illustration 4.3, above).[115] With the altar of the Chapel Royal pointing to the North-West (see Illustration 3.1), this gallery would have been on the North-East side, not the 'South Side' as mentioned in the 'Memorandum'. Yet, it could be that the latter referred to the altar as the so-called 'liturgical East' (as altars were traditionally pointing to the East); and in this sense the gallery would have been on the 'South Side'. The musicians in the galley over and behind the altar were obviously a prominent part of the scene and were also depicted in a very much stylized contemporary print that accords with the above description of the gallery and even shows the conductor (Illustration 11.1).

Incidentally, Joseph Haydn happened to be in London at the time of the royal wedding and recorded an interesting anecdote in relation to the performance of the wedding music.[116] Haydn recalled that he had dinner at the home of William Parsons, the 'master of the king's band', during which there was an argument between Parsons, Dupuis and Arnold, the latter two the senior and the junior organist of the Chapel Royal, respectively: the issue was who of the three should conduct Handel's anthem at the forthcoming wedding, and they asked Haydn for his opinion. Haydn replied that the senior organist of the Chapel should conduct the singers, while the younger one should play the organ, and Parsons (not being organist) should conduct

---

[111] John Marsh, *The John Marsh Journals: The Life and Times of a Gentleman Composer (1752–1828)*, ed., introduced and annotated by Brian Robins (Stuyvesant, NY: Pendragon Press, 1998), p. 571.

[112] See, for instance, William Marshall, *A Collection of Anthems Used in the Cathedral and Collegiate Churches of England and Wales* (Oxford: John Henry Parker, 1840), no. 64; William Mulready Terrott, *Anthem Book: Containing the Words of All the Anthems Commonly Sung in the Cathedrals and Collegiate Churches of England and Ireland* (London: Joseph Masters, 1856), no. 187; and John Calvert, *A Collection of Anthems Used in Her Majesty's Chapel Royal, the Temple Church, and the Collegiate Churches and Chapels in England and Ireland* (London: George Bell, 1844), p. 41.

[113] 'Memorandum.', dated 18 April 1795, transcr. in Ashbee and Harley, *Cheque Books*, II, pp. 253–54.

[114] *Morning Chronicle*, 9 April 1795.

[115] See also the admittedly rather stylized depiction in a contemporary print (Illustration 11.1 below) that shows the organ and music gallery above and behind the altar.

[116] See Karl Geiringer, *Haydn: A Creative Life in Music*, in collaboration with Irene Geiringer, first publ. in 1946, 3rd rev. and enlarged edn (Berkely: University of California Press, 1982), p. 148, who quotes a long passage from Haydn's fourth (reconstructed) diary.

4—The 'Concert Weddings' II: The Late Eighteenth-Century Georgians

the band. Haydn observed that 'This did not suit them'. After the wedding, the report in the *Whitehall Evening Post* detailed that the anthem had been

> performed by Messrs. Gore, Knyvett, Hudson, and Bellamy, and the rest of the choir belonging to the chapel. The band was conducted by Dr. Wm. Parsons. Dr Arnold was at the organ.[117]

A separate conductor for the singers is not mentioned, but otherwise this agrees with Haydn's suggestion. However, the reports in other newspapers differed more clearly from Haydn's suggestion, stating that 'CRAMER led the band, and Dr. ARNOLD was at the Organ.'[118] This 'Cramer' is yet to be identified. In any case, Haydn's anecdote provides an interesting insight regarding such royal occasions: while everything *appears* to be strictly regulated and following precedent, there was in fact still a lot of room for subtle variations.

The total number of musicians does not seem to be known. However, the performing group was probably of considerable size. Arnold's edition indicates at the very least that the orchestra now also included horns. Overall, the performance of the music at the 1795 wedding service was impressive: even though the *Morning Chronicle* had judged that the anthem was not in Handel's 'best manner', both the *True Briton* and the *St. James's Chronicle* reported that Handel's anthem had been performed 'in a very perfect and admirable style'.[119]

The *St. James's Chronicle* recorded that 'The ceremony commenced at half an hour after nine, and concluded at a quarter before eleven.'[120] This matches with the report in the *Whitehall Evening Post* which observed that it was 'past nine o'clock before the procession began to move.'[121] Leake similarly detailed in one account that 'The Ceremony of the Marriage', the service including the anthem, lasted 'from ½ past 9 to ½ past Ten'.[122] In another version, however, Leake noted 'the whole Ceremony being over in about three Quarters of an hour.'[123] Notwithstanding the exact times, Handel's lengthy anthem took up a big portion of the ceremony, especially with its additions, which made it substantially longer than Handel's original. Such lengthening of the musical contribution after the service all the more underlined its significance – especially considering that the congregation had to remain standing all the time, while the royal family were sitting in state.

Arnold's edition of Handel's anthem probably has the distinction of being the earliest publication of any British royal wedding music. Both its inclusion in the ceremony and its publication helped give Handel's anthem a boost in popularity. It was performed in various concerts and services, months before and after the wedding. One concert was on 27 February at the Theatre Royal, Covent Garden, coinciding with the second publication of the anthem.[124] After the wedding, the anthem was performed on two succeeding Sundays at the Foundling Hospital, on the second Sunday 'both Morning and Evening'.[125] Overall, it seemed as though Handel's anthem, albeit in an altered version, was on the way to becoming a repertoire piece.

---

[117] *Whitehall Evening Post*, 7–9 April 1795.

[118] *True Briton*, 9 April 1795; the same in *SJC*, 7–9 April 1795; and 'Ceremonial of the Nuptials'.

[119] *True Briton*, 9 April 1795; *SJC*, 7–9 April 1795. For the *Morning Chronicle* see fn. 107 above.

[120] *SJC*, 7–9 April 1795.

[121] *Whitehall Evening Post*, 7–9 April 1795. The report in *True Briton*, 9 April 1795, stated that the princess entered the Chapel 'about a quarter before nine', but the 'before' could be a misprint for 'past', which would then match with the other reports.

[122] *Lca S.M.L.* 45, p. 132.

[123] *Lca S.M.L.* 65, p. 293.

[124] *True Briton*, 24 February 1795; and see above, fns 102–03.

[125] *True Briton*, 5 June 1795, which refers to the previous and the following Sunday.

Princess Charlotte, Princess Royal, and Prince Frederick-William of Württemberg, 18 May 1797

Two years after the Prince of Wales's wedding, his sister, Princess Charlotte-Augusta-Matilda, Princess Royal, married Prince Frederick-William, Hereditary Prince of Württemberg. The ceremony took place in the Chapel Royal on 18 May. There do not seem to have been any discussions on the bride possibly going over to the continent or an having a proxy-wedding, and the bridegroom was present in person.

The ceremony was commemorated in a stylized contemporary print, which is one of the earliest depictions of a royal wedding to show the bride kneeling, thus presenting an actual scene from the service (Illustration 4.4). The bridegroom is curiously standing upright and, in contrast to the 1795 pictures, so are George III and Queen Charlotte.

Following the precedent of 1795, the ceremonial for the wedding was again printed – and again it included, in a simplified form, the Cupid symbol of quiver and bow, possibly indicating that the ceremonial was intended to be given to spectators.[126] In addition, this appears to be the earliest royal wedding for which the order of service was specially produced, with at least one printed copy, bound in crimson velvet, preserved in the British Library.[127] This is a simple extract from the Prayer Book, without a title page – yet, the text of the wedding promises includes the full names of the bride and bridegroom, thus identifying this volume and perhaps implying that it was prepared for and used at the service. Much information on this wedding, especially on the prince's stay in the country, is contained in the extensive notes and memoranda of Sir Stephen Cottrell, by then Master of the Ceremonies.[128] In addition, the published reports and accounts of the *True Briton* are especially informative.

The Ceremony

Most of all, it is noteworthy that this wedding took place in the afternoon, not in the evening as the previous royal weddings. The published accounts give 'one o'clock' as the time for the beginning of the proceedings.[129] A note sent to the foreign ministers also specified that the wedding was to be celebrated 'at one o'Clock in the Afternoon'.[130] In slight contrast, William Lovegrove's Manuscript recorded that the wedding 'took place this day about two o'clock'.[131] The discrepancy may stem from a different perspective: the one referring to the beginning of the proceedings, the other perhaps to the beginning of the service as the main point of interest

---

[126] Ceremonial 1797. Compare also Illustration 11.3.

[127] *Lbl C.136.f.29*. NB Both the ceremonial and the printed order of service give the princess's name as 'Charlotta-Augusta-Matilda'; however, she is usually known as 'Princess Charlotte'.

[128] See his long account in *Lna LC 5/5*, pp. 27–98, here p. 67. Some of this is transcribed in Edgar Sheppard, *Memorials of St James's Palace*, 2 vols (London: Longmans, Green, and Co., 1894), II, pp. 92–95.

[129] See the account in *European Magazine*, 31 (1797), pp. 363–64, and 'The Royal Wedding', unidentified newspaper cutting (1797), in *Lbl 871.f.3*, no. 32. See also 'Account of Ceremonial of the Marriage of the Princess Royal with the Hereditary Prince of Wirtemberg [*sic*]', *The Lady's Magazine*, 23 (1797), pp. 195–98, here p. 195. This records that the participants gathered 'soon after eleven o'clock' in the great council-chamber and that 'about twelve' the king and queen arrived with six princesses. For a meticulous record of the times of all the ceremonies see the account in *True Briton*, 19 May 1797. The account in *London Gazette*, 16–20 May 1797, pp. 443–45, did curiously not give any time for the wedding.

[130] For this see *Lna LC 5/7*, p. 47 and p. 50–51.

[131] Ashbee and Harley, *Cheque Books*, II, p. 254.

4—The 'Concert Weddings' II: The Late Eighteenth-Century Georgians

for its writer. In any case, the change to a daytime ceremony was a notable breech of precedent, and the *True Briton* pointed out that the wedding

> will be performed in the Chapel Royal, in the same manner, and with the same ceremonies, as on the Marriage of the Prince and Princess of Wales. On this occasion, however, the Nuptials are to be consecrated by day-light.[132]

It does not seem to be known what caused the change of time. It was reported that 'Soon after the ceremony was over, all the Royal Family set off for Windsor.'[133] Thus, the change to an earlier time could have been stimulated by the plan to go away after the ceremony.

For the procession to the Chapel Royal, Cottrell noted that he 'found it to be the same exactly as on the Marriage of the Prince of Wales', in 1795, and the accounts confirm that it saw the usual split into three distinct divisions, all three accompanied by 'music, heralds, drums'.[134] As before, the musicians played in the three processions to the Chapel and 'on the last return', the return procession after the service, as the *True Briton* observed.[135] This account furthermore noted that:

> A Piece of Music preceded the Ceremony. – The BRIDE and BRIDEGROOM advanced to the Altar, to which the KING also came forward, for the purpose of bestowing his Daughter in marriage.

Illustration 4.4: 'The Marriage of his Serene Highness the Prince of Wirtemburg, to the Princess Royal of England, in the Chapel at St. James's, on Thursday the 18th of May 1797', mezzotint published by Robert Laurie and James Whittle on 7 August 1797, *National Portrait Gallery, Reference Collection NPG D8015* © National Portrait Gallery, London.

From the wording it appears that this unidentified 'Piece of Music' was performed while the individuals entered the Chapel, as in 1795. For the service itself, the *True Briton* recorded: 'After the Service was over, but before the Prayers, was chaunted *Deus Misereatur* [...].'[136] 'Service' must here refer to the wedding vows (before the prayers). *Deus misereatur* is, of course, Ps. 67 – one of the two psalms scheduled in the Prayer Book. Incidentally, a volume with material on late seventeenth to early nineteenth-century royal weddings in the British Library contains a leaf with the printed text of 'DEUS MISEREATUR / PSALM LXVII', 'God be merciful unto us'.[137] This is found amidst other material on the 1795 and 1797 weddings and may thus belong to these ceremonies. The sheet gives merely the full text, under the heading 'ANTHEM.', but

---

[132] *True Briton*, 18 May 1797.

[133] *European Magazine*, 31 (1797), p. 364.

[134] *Lna LC 5/5*, p. 67, and 'Account of the Ceremonial', p. 195. See also *London Gazette*, 16–20 May 1797, p. 443; and *European Magazine*, 31 (1797), p. 363.

[135] This and the following *True Briton*, 19 May 1797.

[136] *True Briton*, 19 May 1797.

[137] *Lbl Add MS 6332*, fol. 158ʳ, on back, added by hand 'Miss Banks' (probably the collector Sarah Sophia Banks, 1744–1818).

no other details. Since the full text of this psalm is also included in the order of service in the Prayer Book, it is not immediately clear why it was printed separately: maybe not everyone at the servicehad a copy of the Prayer Book.

Notably, the report that *Deus misereatur* was 'chaunted' could refer either to a simple, chanted psalm as in the modern usage of the word, or it could more generally refer to any singing.[138] The fact that the text sheet has the heading 'Anthem' very much indicates that this was sung as a proper composition. This rather specific term would in all likelihood not have been used if the text was simply sung to a mere chant tune. There does, however, not seem to be a setting of the *Deus misereatur* text by Arnold, Parsons, Knyvett, or Cramer, all of whom were involved in the music. All the same, this appears to be the earliest reference for the inclusion of Ps. 67 at a royal wedding. Yet, it is noteworthy that this inclusion could refer to either the 1795 or the 1797 wedding, since the *True Briton* in one of its reports in 1797 emphasized that 'The same music will be performed' as had been in 1795 – although it is of course not sure how well-informed and meticulous the paper was in such details.[139]

The Anthem

The actual 'Anthem' came again at the end of the ceremony. Following the precedent of the previous royal weddings, the printed ceremonial stipulated that 'at the Conclusion', the bride and bridegroom were 'to retire to their Seats while the Anthem is performing'.[140] Similarly, the accounts and the ceremonial recorded by the heralds include the customary formulation:

> At the conclusion of the Marriage Service their Majestys retired to their Chairs of State under the Canopy, where they remained while the Anthem was performing.[141]

The account in the *True Briton* reported that

> after the wedding, HANDEL'S *Wedding Anthem* was performed by the Band, directed by Sir WILLIAM PARSONS, and the Gentlemen Choristers of his Majesty's Chapels, conducted by Dr. ARNOLD.[142]

'Handel's *Wedding Anthem*' refers to his *Sing unto God*, in Arnold's extended version. As in 1795, the full anthem text was printed separately.[143] Furthermore, the full text of the anthem was afterwards published by at least one paper.[144]

The return procession was somewhat more formal than in 1795 in so far as the newly-weds did probably not walk next to each other. In contrast to then, the ceremonial now stipulated distinctly that the bridegroom was to go first, 'Attended by two Dukes, as before', then the bride 'Supported by their Royal Highnesses the DUKE OF CLARENCE and PRINCE ERNEST AUGUSTUS', then the king, and then the queen.[145]

---

[138] See above, fn. 28.

[139] *True Briton*, 18 May 1797. For a longer quotation see below, fn. 146.

[140] Ceremonial 1795, last page.

[141] 'Ceremonial of the Marriage [...]', in *Lca MS Ceremonials L. 19*, pp. 231–35, here p. 234. The same wording in the manuscript ceremonial in *Wra RA GEO/MAIN/73943-73944* and published in *London Gazette*, 16–20 May 1797, p. 445. See also 'Account of the Ceremonial', p. 197; and *European Magazine*, 31 (1797), p. 364.

[142] *True Briton*, 19 May 1797.

[143] *Lbl Add MS 6332*, fol. 160ʳ (the only known copy).

[144] Unidentified newspaper cutting in *Lbl Add MS 6332*, fol. 153ᵛ, all written in the past tense (and hence a report published after the wedding).

[145] Ceremonial 1797.

4—The 'Concert Weddings' II: The Late Eighteenth-Century Georgians

The Performance

On the day of the wedding, the *True Briton* had provided valuable details on the arrangements for the music in the Chapel:

> The same music will be performed as on the former occasion [the 1795 wedding]. The temporary Gallery for the Vocal Performers will be formed as on the Nuptials alluded to; but the Instrumental Band will not be placed in the same situation. The latter will be arranged in the Organ Gallery, for which purpose the Chapel Organ has been removed, and one of smaller size is placed before the window. The Vocal Performers will be conducted by Dr. ARNOLD; the Instrumental by Sir WILLIAM PARSONS. Mr. KNYVETT will sit at the Organ, and Mr. CRAMER will lead the Band.[146]

The 'former occasion' must refer to the 1795 wedding. As seen above, there had then already been three galleries for the musicians, two on the side and one 'in a circular' behind the altar.[147] The above description indicates that the choir and orchestra at the 1797 wedding were more separated, and that again a temporary organ was built.

The anthem was to be rehearsed only in the morning of the day before the wedding.[148] This does not appear to have been a public rehearsal and there is no evidence of any earlier rehearsals. Altogether, in contrast to 1795, there do not seem to have been any public performances of the anthem.

⟠

The performance of an elaborate anthem had been part of the major royal weddings since 1734. All the same, these anthems appear to have been clearly dominated by one composer: Handel. Especially with his 1736 anthem *Sing unto God*, repeated at two weddings and at various public rehearsals and concerts towards the end of the century, Handel had left a clear mark on these events – just as he did on coronations and funerals. The 'elaboration' of this anthem, with additional movements, all the more enhanced the prominent role of lengthy music at these ceremonies. Boyce's anthem from 1761 was a notable composition, but it was never repeated at a royal wedding.

Following the pattern established in the 1730s, at the major royal weddings from 1761 to 1797, the grand, lengthy anthems were invariably performed only after the actual service and were listened to by the king (and queen) and the newly-weds sitting in state. They were thus not merely part of the liturgy, not a mere elaboration and adornment of the service. Rather the elaborate and lengthy anthems helped enhance the splendour of the ceremony and the grandeur of the monarchy in what effectively became topical state concerts.

---

[146] *True Briton*, 18 May 1797.

[147] See fn. 114.

[148] *True Briton*, 17 May 1797.

5

The 'Home' Weddings: The Early Nineteenth Century

THE TURN FROM THE EIGHTEENTH to the nineteenth century saw a notable accumulation of royal weddings. However, these were very much scaled-down ceremonies. They did not take place in a church or chapel but 'at home', as it were, in a room of a royal residence. This choice of venue alone heightened the plain administrative component of the weddings.

In addition, these weddings contained not much ceremonial elaboration and, by all accounts, they included no music. It is not known what had caused the simpler character of these weddings. Notwithstanding the very modest weddings towards the end of the seventeenth century, this approach of reducing wedding ceremonies to their bare minimum had been employed at the modest royal weddings of the king's sister and brother in 1764 and 1766, which have already been mentioned in the previous chapter; yet, it became especially prominent in the later years of George III's reign.

Prince Frederick, Duke of York and Albany, and Princess Frederica of Prussia, 29 September and 23 November 1791

In 1791, Prince Frederick, Duke of York and Albany, second son of George III and Queen Charlotte, married Princess Friederike (Frederica) of Prussia. He was the first of the king's many children to marry legally, that is with the consent of the king – two of his brothers had contracted unsuitable, and un-approved marriages marriages, as seen in the previous chapter, and his older brother, the Prince of Wales, did not marry until 1795. As for the weddings in 1740 and 1766, there were two ceremonies; but this time – with the bridegroom and not the bride being the British party – they were the other way round: the first ceremony took place in Berlin on 29 September, and the second in London on 23 November.[1]

Daniel Schönpflug has explained that the official reason for the two ceremonies was the difference in religion, or rather in denomination: the bride was Reformed (Calvinist) while the bridegroom was, of course, Anglican.[2] John Watkins, in his biography of the Duke, had further explained: 'The ceremony of a re-marriage, according to the ritual of the established church of this kingdom, was rendered indispensable by the Royal Marriage Act'.[3] The terms 'remarrying' and 'remarriage'/'re-marriage' for the second, London ceremony were also used

---

[1] For an account of the two weddings see 'Ceremonial of the Duke of York's Marriage', *Gentleman's Magazine*, 61, part 2 (1791), pp. 1057–58. This account was used in John Watkins, *A Biographical Memoir of His Late Royal Highness Frederick, Duke of York and Albany* (London: Printed for Henry Fisher, 1827), pp. 176–77. See also W. H. Pyne, *The History of the Royal Residences of Windsor Castle, St. James's Palace, Carlton House, Kensington Palace, Hampton Court, Buckingham House, and Frogmore. Illustrated by One Hundred Highly Finished and Coloured Engravings*, 3 vols, vol. 2 (London: Printed for A. Dry, 1819), section on Buckingham House, p. 23.

[2] This and the following Daniel Schönpflug, *Die Heiraten der Hohenzollern: Verwandtschaft, Politik und Ritual in Europa 1640–1918*, 'Kritische Studien zur Geschichtswissenschaft', 207 (Göttingen: Vandenhoek & Ruprecht, 2013), p. 141.

[3] John Watkins, *Biographical Memoir* (as in fn. 1), p. 175.

by John More, the Archbishop of Canterbury, and by Beilby Porteus, Dean of the Chapel Royal, as well as in several publications.[4] These two terms express the fact that the initial 'marriage' ceremony, in Berlin, was not sufficient.

The earlier Berlin wedding had been a 'double-wedding': the couple married in the same ceremony in which the bride's sister, Princess Wilhelmine, married Prince William of Orange, later William V.[5] Both the Berlin and the London ceremonies took place in the evening, and like the Berlin ceremony, that in London was not in a chapel.[6]

The London wedding took place at 'Buckingham House', at the time also called the 'Queen's house'.[7] It was the earliest royal wedding in this then relatively new royal residence – now known as Buckingham Palace. The wedding followed the precedent of the weddings at St James's Palace in the 1760s and took place in the 'Grand Saloon', or 'Her Majesty's Drawing Room', as Porteus called it in his detailed account.[8] It is noteworthy that there appears not to have been a chapel that could have been used. None is mentioned in the description of Buckingham House in W. H. Pyne's *History of the Royal Residences* from 1819.[9] It was not until 1829 that it was proposed to convert the Octagonal Library into a chapel, for the display of the famous Raphael Cartoons in the Royal Collection.[10]

The reports detailed that 'Books of the marriage ceremony were delivered to all the Royal Family by the Archbishop of Canterbury.'[11] Porteus similarly recorded that 'Every one had Books of the Marriage Service sent them by the AB.ᴾ'.[12] This may just refer to copies of the Prayer Book, as no specially produced order of service is known. Some of the participants holding books in their hands can be seen in a contemporary painting of the ceremony (Illustration 5.1). The one surviving copy of the printed order of service for the later 1797 wedding, mentioned in the previous chapter, has a curious pencil inscription inside the front cover: 'Used in the Chapel Royal at the Marriage / of the Duke of York, son of George 3. P. S.'[13] However, apart from the fact the personalized text would not match, this re-use is of course chronologically impossible.

George III and Queen Charlotte had not travelled to Berlin for the wedding, but they were both present at the London ceremony. In the same way as for the earlier weddings in the

---

[4] Moore to George III, 23 November 1791, in *Llp Moore 6*, fols 64ʳ–65ʳ; Porteus's account in *Llp MS 2100*, fols 43ʳ–46ʳ; 'Ceremonial of the Duke of York's Marriage', *Gentleman's Magazine*, p. 1057; also in Pyne, *History*: 'Buckingham House', p. 23.

[5] See Schönpflug, *Die Heiraten der Hohenzollern*, pp. 136–37, 140–41, 186 and 214–15. ('Doppelhochzeit').

[6] For details on the Berlin wedding see 'Ceremonial of the Duke of York's Marriage', *Gentleman's Magazine*, p. 1057–58. and *Llp MS 2100*, fol. 45ʳ.

[7] This and the following details of the London wedding from Andrew Ashbee and John Harley (eds), *The Cheque Books of the Chapel Royal*, 2 vols (Aldershot: Ashgate, 2000), II, p. 126 (entry from William Lovegrove's Manuscript); and 'Ceremonial of the Duke of York's Marriage', *Gentleman's Magazine*, p. 1057. See also Bishop Porteus's account in *Llp MS 2100*, fols 43ʳ–46ʳ.

[8] *Llp MS 2100*, fol. 44ʳ.

[9] Pyne, *History*: 'Buckingham House', p. 23.

[10] See John K. G. Shearman, *Raphael's Cartoons in the Collection of Her Majesty the Queen, and the Tapestries for the Sistine Chapel* (London: Phaidon, 1972), p. 156. For the location of the Octagon Chapel see also the ground plans in John Harris, 'The Architecture', in: John Harris, Geoffrey de Bellaigue, and Oliver Millar, *Buckingham Palace*, with an introduction by John Russell (London: Thomas Nelson and Sons, 1968), pp. 19–100, here pp. 41–42.

[11] 'Ceremonial of the Duke of York's Marriage', *Gentleman's Magazine*, 61, p. 1057; see also John Watkins, *Biographical Memoir*, p. 176.

[12] *Llp MS 2100*, fol. 45ʳ.

[13] *Lbl C.136.f.29.*

5—The 'Home' Weddings: The Early Nineteenth Century

Chapel Royal, they were placed on opposite sides during the ceremony: 'his Majesty standing at one end of the altar, and her Majesty at the other extremity', as the reports detailed and as shown in the aforemmentioned painting (see Illustration 5.1). In contrast to those chapel ceremonies, however, there does not seem to have been a symbolical uniting of the couple at the end. Moreover, neither of the two wedding ceremonies appears to have included any music. In fact, for the London ceremony, Porteus stressed that 'His Grace read the whole Service.'[14]

Schönpflug has very much emphasized the political character of this union, the fact that it was 'suited to cement' the friendship and alliance between Prussia and Britain, as the Prussian king himself summarized aptly in French.[15] Yet, especially in this context one may wonder why the Duke of York's wedding – after all the first wedding of a child of George III – was not a grander occasion. One possible explanation could be that any more lavish celebration would have drawn attention to the fact that he married before his elder brother, the Prince of Wales.

Illustration 5.1: 'The Marriage of Frederick, Duke of York and Albany (1763–1827) to Frederica, Princess Royal of Prussia (1767–1820)', anonymous copy after Henry Singleton, oil on canvas c. 1791, *Royal Collection, RCIN 402495*, Royal Collection Trust © Her Majesty Queen Elizabeth II 2021.

[14] *Llp MS 2100*, fol. 45ʳ.

[15] Schönpflug, *Die Heiraten der Hohenzollern*, p. 186–87 ('propre à cimenter les liens d'amitié et d'alliance').

British Royal Weddings

Prince Augustus Frederick, Duke of Sussex, and Lady Augusta Murray, 5 December 1793

Two years after the Duke of York, on 5 December 1793, his brother Prince Augustus Frederick, Duke of Sussex, ninth child of George III, married Lady Augusta Murray. This wedding was even less lavish: the marriage did not meet with the king's approval and was a more or less secretive occasion.[16] A secretive ceremony in Rome in April was followed by an equally secretive one in London in December. The latter took place in a church building – but one with no royal connections: at St George's, Hanover Square.

The wedding of the Prince of Wales finally occurred two years later, in 1795. As seen in the previous chapter, this was a much grander ceremony, in the Chapel Royal. So was the wedding of his sister, the Princess Royal, in 1797. These grand occasions, in the Chapel Royal and with elaborate music, stand out against the other weddings of the era. Their grander scope may have been due mainly to the higher status of the prince and his sister, as the most senior son and daughter of the sovereign. After these, here was no notable royal wedding for the next almost two decades.

Prince Ernest Augustus, Duke of Cumberland, and Princess Frederica of Mecklenburg-Strelitz, 29 May and 29 August 1815

In 1815, Prince Ernest Augustus, the fifth son of George III, Duke of Cumberland and later king of Hanover, married Frederica of Mecklenburg-Strelitz. A church wedding in Germany, rather publicly in the Strelitz city church on 29 May, was followed by a wedding ceremony at Carlton House, the Prince Regent's London residence, on 29 August.[17] The London wedding seems not to have been widely reported at the time.[18] However, a far more notable wedding, at least in its meaning if not in elaboration, occurred in the following year.

Princess Charlotte of Wales and Prince Leopold of Saxe-Coburg-Saalfeld, 2 May 1816

The most important wedding in the later reign of George III was certainly that of Princess Charlotte-Augusta, daughter of the Prince Regent and second in line to the throne (and usually known just as 'Princess Charlotte'). On 2 May 1816, she married Prince Leopold of Saxe-Coburg-Saalfeld. Despite the huge dynastical importance, this wedding was a modest, short ceremony. First of all, the king was not present: by this time, George III was suffering from illness and was confined to Windsor Castle. Queen Charlotte attended alone.[19] The ceremony took place at Carlton House, the Prince Regent's London residence.[20] There it was

---

[16] For this wedding see Roger Fulford, *Royal Dukes: The Father and Uncles of Queen Victoria*, first publ. by William Collins & Co. 1933; repr. of the new and rev. edn 1973 (London: Penguin Books, 2000), pp. 254–56.

[17] For the German wedding see the 'Extract of a letter from New Strelitz, June 4', under 'Abstract of Foreign Occurrences', *Gentleman's Magazine*, 85, part 1 (January–June 1815), pp. 636–39, here p. 637.

[18] For the date and place of the London wedding see the obituary of the King of Hanover in *Gentleman's Magazine*, 37n.s. (January–June 1852), pp. 85–88, here p. 87.

[19] See the short account in 'Principal Occurrences', *The New Annual Register [...] for the Year 1816* (1817), p. 19.

[20] See the entries in the New Cheque Book of the Chapel Royal and in William Lovegrove's Manuscript, in Ashbee

5—The 'Home' Weddings: The Early Nineteenth Century

celebrated in the 'great crimson room [...] which had been previously fitted up for the occasion with a temporary altar'.[21] It was performed by the Archbishop of Canterbury and the Bishop of London. As in 1791, this set-up resulted in a curious mixture of palace room and chapel, as can be seen very clearly in a contemporary sketch for a painting of the ceremony (Illustration 5.2).

The most recent more elaborate royal wedding, that of the Princess Royal at the Chapel Royal in 1797, had seen a notable change in the ceremonial in so far as it took place not in the

Illustration 5.2: Richard Westall (attr.), 'The Wedding of Princess Charlotte of Wales and Prince Leopold of Saxe-Coburg at Carlton House', pen, oil and watercolour on paper, c. 1816, *Royal Collection, RCIN 917619*, Royal Collection Trust / © Her Majesty Queen Elizabeth II 2021.

---

and Harley, *Cheque Books*, I, p. 216 and II, p. 254–55, respectively. For the arrangements and a list of people invited to the ceremony see also *Lna LC 5/204*, fols 302ʳ–05ʳ.

[21] 'Wedding of the Princess Charlotte of Wales with Prince Leopold of Saxe Coburg', *La Belle Assemblée: Or Court and Fashionable Magazine* (May 1816), pp. 237–39, here p. 238. For a more detailed description see 'The Nuptials of the Princess Charlotte of Wales and the Prince of Saxe-Cobourg', *Annual Register [...] 1816* (1817), pp. 57–60. See also 'The Royal Nuptials', *Times*, 6 May 1816, p. 3; and *Lna LC 5/204*, fol. 303ʳ, which refers to 'The Altar and arrangements in the Great / Crimson Room'.

Illustration 5.3: 'Marriage of The Princess Charlotte of Wales to Prince Leopold of Saxe-Coburg, in the Crimson Saloon at Carleton House, May 2, 1816', engraving by Robert Hicks after William Marshall Craig (published by Nuttall, Fisher & Dixon, 1818), *National Portrait Gallery, D16053* © National Portrait Gallery, London.

evening but in daytime.[22] The 1816 wedding, however, reverted to the previous custom and took place late in the evening:

> The illustrious personages had all taken their stations by a little after nine o'clock, when the service began. […] It concluded at half-past nine, when the happy event was announced to the public by the Park and Tower guns.[23]

As for the previous non-chapel weddings, it is not known that an order of the proceedings was produced. In fact, an entry in the Cheque Book of the Chapel Royal recorded specifically that 'Two Folio Prayer Books and Two Quarto prayer Books' were used at the ceremony.[24]

There was no music at the ceremony itself and the whole would have been a straightforward administrative act, highlighted by the secular surroundings as was shown in the aforementioned sketch and also more widely circulated in a contemporary print depicting the ceremony (Illustration 5.3). The fact that the ceremony was yet half an hour in length is probably explained by the circumstance that 'At the conclusion of the marriage service, the registry of the marriage was attested with the usual formalities'.[25] The only music that the reports mentioned for the whole occasion is that by the outside band: it played 'God Save the King' as each of the main participants arrived at Carlton House.[26]

---

[22] See the previous chapter.

[23] 'Wedding of the Princess Charlotte of Wales', p. 239.

[24] See Ashbee and Harley, *Cheque Books*, I, p. 216.

[25] 'Principal Occurrences', p. 19.

[26] 'Wedding of the Princess Charlotte of Wales', p. 238.

5—The 'Home' Weddings: The Early Nineteenth Century

Despite the fact that this wedding was a comparatively inconspicuous, modest ceremony, the total expenses for it amounted to over £8,000.[27] It is not quite clear on what all this money was spent. In any case, such expenditure reflected the overall joyous mood on the occasion: one account emphasized that, apart from the firing of the 'Park and Tower guns', 'the evening concluded with other public demonstrations of joy throughout the metropolis'.[28]

Princess Mary and Prince William Frederick, Duke of Gloucester and Edinburgh, 1816

Only a couple of months after Princess Charlotte, her aunt Princess Mary, eleventh child of George III, married her cousin Prince William Frederick, Duke of Gloucester and Edinburgh, himself a nephew of the king. As the Chapel Royal Cheque Book recorded, the wedding took place on 22 July 'at the Queen's House' (today's Buckingham Palace), 'at Nine oClock in the Evening [...] in the grand Saloon'.[29] The room for the wedding was lavishly set up with 'a costly display of massy communion plate'.[30] Yet, again the ceremony was straightforward and simple and there was no music. The queen was present, and the bride was given away by her brother, the Prince Regent. Despite the simple character of the ceremony, the expenses were again quite high – this time amounting to £5,000.[31]

The Urgent Weddings: Leading to a Royal Double, 1818

Princess Charlotte of Wales died in childbirth on 6 November 1817, with a stillborn son. This meant that there was no (legitimate) heir to the throne in the generation after George III's children. With no further children to be expected from her father, the Prince of Wales or his next brother, the Duke of York, the remaining unmarried brothers rushed (or were rushed) to the altar – notwithstanding their previous relationships and numerous illegitimate children. The first was Prince Adolphus, Duke of Cambridge, seventh son of George III, and among his brothers 'the most eligible suitor'.[32] On 7 May 1818, he married Princess Augusta of Hesse-Kassel in a simple ceremony in Kassel.[33] On 1 June, a second ceremony took place 'at the Queens House', with the *Times* reporting that 'the indisposition of the Queen' had 'prevented an earlier solemnization of this necessary ceremony'.[34] As in 1791, the London wedding was referred to as a 're-marriage' and had been necessitated by the legal requirement for an Anglican ceremony.[35]

---

[27] *Lbl Add MS 27543*, fols 23ʳ–25ᵛ: 'The Earl of Effingham's / Account of the Expenses incurred / by Order of Her Majesty on the / Marriage of the Princess / Charlotte of Wales.', dated 25 June 1816: £8,195-9-11¾. Unfortunately, this lists only the names of the recipients, but not the purpose of the payments.

[28] 'Principal Occurrences', p. 19.

[29] Ashbee and Harley, *Cheque Books*, I, p. 216–17. See also Pyne, *History*: 'Buckingham House', p. 25.

[30] See the account in 'Principal Occurrences', *The New Annual Register* [...] *for the Year 1816* (1817), pp. 32–33. The same in 'Domestic Occurrences', *Gentleman's Magazine*, 86 (1816), Part 2, p. 78–79.

[31] *Lbl Add MS 27543*, fols 19ʳ–21ʳ: 'The Earl of Effingham's / Account of the Expenses incurred / by Order of Her Majesty on the / Marriage of Her Royal / Highness the Princess Mary.', dated 23 October 1816. For the arrangements and list of people invited to the ceremony see also *Lna LC 5/204*, fols 308ʳ–310ʳ.

[32] Fulford, *Royal Dukes*, p. 291.

[33] See the short note in the *Times*, 13 May 1818, p. 2.

[34] 'Marriage of the Duke and Duchess of Cambridge', *Times*, 2 June 1818, p. 3.

The ceremony was originally scheduled for 5 o'clock, but at the last minute brought forward to 2 o'clock; however, as this change could not be realized it was again postponed to the original 5 o'clock.[36] The *Times* noted that the 'great Officers of State, and others, who are frequently invited for the purpose of giving additional splendour to the proceedings, were not summoned'.[37] It explained that Queen Charlotte had wished 'that the marriage should be as private as possible, in order to spare Her Majesty all unnecessary fatigue'. The Chapel Royal Cheque Book also noted that the ceremony 'was private', pointing out that 'none of the Furniture or Plate from the Chapel Royal where had on this occasion'.[38] At other similar weddings in secular rooms, paraphernalia such as altar plate and kneelers had been brought from the Chapel Royal – for instance, only a couple of months previously, at the wedding of Princess Elizabeth, seventh child of George III, to Prince Frederick of Hesse-Homburg on 7 April 1818 'at the Queens House [now Buckingham Palace] in the Saloon in the Evening'.[39]

The Double Wedding of 1818

One of the probably most unusual royal weddings in British history occurred in 1818, for the two remaining sons of George III: Prince William, Duke of Clarence and St Andrews (later William IV), and Prince Edward, Duke of Kent and Strathearn (father of Queen Victoria). As Jeremy Black summarized bluntly:

> To save bother and presumably expense, William and his brother Edward were married at the same time in a double wedding at Kew Palace on 11 July 1818.[40]

A double-wedding of two brothers was, and still is, a rather unusual event – but especially so for British royalty. Some precedent could have been the aforementioned double-wedding in Prussia in 1791 in which a British prince had taken part. The Cheque Book of the Chapel Royal has two separate entries, one for each wedding; and although it lists the provisions for the ceremony only once, it refers to 'these occasions', as though there had been two ceremonies.[41] Yet, the provisions included 'Four Kneeling Stools' and 'Four Quarto Prayer Books', indicating that the two couples were indeed married in the same ceremony.

Prince Edward, Duke of Kent and Strathearn, had already married Princess Victoria of Saxe-Coburg-Saalfeld in a ceremony in Coburg in May 1818. The Kew wedding was thus again a re-marriage. Emily Brand has pointed out that, overall, three sons of George III married first in Germany and then again in Britain.[42] In contrast, his brother Prince William, Duke of Clarence and St Andrews, married Adelaide of Saxe-Meiningen only in the London double-wedding. Accordingly, the *Gentleman's Magazine* wrote distinctly of the 'marriage' of the Clarences and the 're-marriage' of the Kents, referring to the whole as a 'double ceremonial'.[43]

---

[35] Pyne, *History*: 'Buckingham House', p. 26.

[36] See 'Marriage of the Duke and Duchess of Cambridge', *Times* (1818).

[37] 'Marriage of the Duke and Duchess of Cambridge', *Times* (1818).

[38] Ashbee and Harley, *Cheque Books*, I, p. 217.

[39] Ashbee and Harley, *Cheque Books*, I, p. 217; see also Pyne, *History*: 'Buckingham House', p. 25.

[40] Jeremy Black, *The Hanoverians: The History of a Dynasty* (London: Hambledon and London, 2004), p. 184. For the date see also fn. 43, below.

[41] Ashbee and Harley, *Cheque Books*, I, p. 218.

[42] Emily Brand, *Royal Weddings*, 'Shire Library', 665 (Oxford: Shire Publications, 2011), p. 28.

[43] 'Occurrences in London and its Vicinity', *Gentleman's Magazine*, 88, part 2 (July–December 1818), p. 79. NB This gives 13 July as date for the wedding.

5—The 'Home' Weddings: The Early Nineteenth Century

Kew Palace was the residence of Queen Charlotte and the wedding took place in the 'Queen's drawing-room', which was fitted up with an altar and the necessary paraphernalia brought from the Chapel Royal.[44] The choice of Kew Palace for the 1818 wedding may have been very pragmatic: it has been suggested that the double-wedding took place there for the simple reason that 'Queen Charlotte was too ill to travel'.[45] The separate entries for both weddings in the Chapel Royal Cheque Book noted that 'the ceremony was Privately performed'.[46] Notably, the ceremony did not take place late in the evening, but rather in the afternoon, with the queen taking her seat at 'four o'clock', as the *Gentleman's Magazine* noted.[47]

———⁂———

In analogy to the modest and 'quiet' weddings of the seventeenth century, the late eighteenth-century and early nineteenth-century 'home' weddings could be described as 'silent' weddings. They still followed the service as prescribed in the Prayer Book, but they included merely the spoken words and there was no music. The low-key, 'home' weddings around the turn to the nineteenth century, and in its second decade, stood in some contrast to the 'invented traditions' at the time: big, large-scale, public events such as thanksgivings, investitures and state funerals.[48] Despite their importance for the dynasty and the continuation of the monarchy as a whole, these weddings were relatively simple administrative acts, rather than lavish court occasions – in some cases emphasizing the pure necessity and urgency that had led to these weddings in the first place.

---

[44] 'Occurrences in London', p. 79.

[45] Susanne Groom and Lee Prosser, *Kew Palace: The Official Illustrated History* (London: Historic Royal Palaces in association with Merrell, 2006), p. 100.

[46] Ashbee and Harley, *Cheque Books*, I, p. 218.

[47] 'Occurrences in London', p. 79.

[48] For these see David Cannadine, 'The Context, Performance and Meaning of Ritual: The British Monarchy and the "Invention of Tradition", *c.* 1820–1977', in *The Invention of Tradition*, ed. by Eric Hobsbawm and Terence Ranger (Cambridge: Cambridge University Press, 1983; repr. 2002), pp. 101–64.

6

'State Marriages': The Early Victorians

THE REASON FOR THE ROYAL double-wedding in 1818 had been the lack of (legitimate) offspring from the children of George III. Accordingly, there were no young princes or princesses old enough to marry in the reigns of George IV (1820–30) or William IV (1830–37). and the first royal wedding, after over twenty years, was that of Queen Victoria in 1840. After decades of barely any notable royal marriage ceremonial – since 1797 – the wedding of the queen, followed by that of her cousin, and then especially that of her eldest daughter in 1858 were relatively grand occasions, at the time aptly described with the term 'state marriage'.[1]

Queen Victoria and Prince Albert of Saxe-Coburg and Gotha, 10 February 1840

Queen Victoria had come to the throne in 1837, at eighteen, and married Prince Albert of Saxe-Coburg and Gotha on 10 February 1840. The sources for this wedding are much better than for any previous royal wedding: newspapers and magazines reported widely about the ceremony, some very elaborately.[2] In addition, the queen herself recorded many details in her journal.

This wedding was a notable 'first' in several respects: it was the first royal wedding for many years and the first grander royal church wedding since 1797; it was the first wedding of a sovereign for almost 80 years, since 1761; and it was the first wedding of a queen regnant since that of Mary I to Philip of Spain in 1554. Indeed, this latter fact was at the time explicitly pointed out by at least one commentator:

> Long as the English monarchy has endured, the marriage of Queen VICTORIA with Prince ALBERT is the first marriage of a QUEEN REGNANT, with one exception, which the English people ever witnessed. That one exception was, in every respect, an unhappy one. This second instance of a *reigning* QUEEN will, we trust, be in every respect its auspicious contrast.[3]

With the long distance to a previous comparable ceremony, there were few precedents that could be easily reverted to, as John Plunkett has aptly summarized:

> If the coronation [in 1838] could not but be heavily orchestrated by precedent, Victoria's marriage to Prince Albert, the first wedding of a Queen Regnant in historical memory, was not so hindered by the weight of the past.[4]

---

[1] 'Marriage of The Princess Royal', *Gentleman's Magazine*, 204/v. 4 new series (1858), pp. 322–23, here p. 322. For a longer quotation see below, with fn. 238.

[2] For an extensive collection of newspaper cuttings on this wedding see *Lca Marriage of Queen Victoria 1840 (red volume – 'W.C. 107' on spine)*. For one particularly detailed account see 'Marriage of Victoria the First [...] with Prince Albert [...]', *MLAI*, 35:992, Supplementary Number ([1840]), pp. 113–22. Much information is also found in *The Wedding Observer*, a special edition of *The Observer* of 16 and 17 February 1840 [hereinafter *Wedding Observer*].

[3] 'Marriage of Victoria the First', p. 119.

[4] John Plunkett, *Queen Victoria: First Media Monarch* (Oxford: Oxford University Press, 2003), p. 29.

Indeed, that much was indicated by Queen Victoria herself. One the earliest references in her journal to the discussion of the actual wedding ceremony was on 6 November 1839.[5] She recorded that she returned to Lord Melbourne, her Prime Minister, 'the Annual Register', which must refer to a copy of this publication with the account of an earlier royal wedding – most likely that in 1761, as the most recent wedding of a sovereign. She noted that the ceremony of her own wedding was 'to be formed upon that, but adapted to the present time'.

The Venue

Queen Victoria's journal entries provide a good inside to the discussions on the choice of venue for the wedding, which was closely linked with the question of the appropriate ceremonial. For 28 November she recorded that she discussed the wedding with Lord Melbourne and noted that they 'Talked of the Chapel Royal being such a shocking locale' and that her uncle Leopold (and Princess Charlotte, in 1816), had been 'married at Carlton House in private'.[6] She also recorded that Sir William Woods, Garter King of Arms, had shown Lord Melbourne 'some very curious precedents of former Royal Marriages' and that Woods was 'intending to draw up a Programme' for her forthcoming wedding. On the next day, 29 November, their discussion of the venue continued. She specified that they talked 'of the Chapel Royal; of the possibility of perhaps having the ceremony at Buckingham Palace; _not_ at Westminster Abbey, as that would be like a 2nd Coronation, and the expense would be too great'.[7] It is not clear who had brought Westminster Abbey into the discussion but with the suggestion of Buckingham Palace, the queen and Melbourne may have been thinking of the royal weddings of the last few decades that had taken place in rooms of the royal residences – such as the wedding of her uncle Leopold in 1816 that she had mentioned the previous day.

A few days later, the queen recorded that she and Melbourne had talked of Lord Uxbridge, the Lord Chamberlain, going away and of his 'having to settle the Ceremonial of the Marriage, with Sir William Woods'.[8] Yet, they agreed that the ceremonial

> could not be settled until we knew <u>where</u> the Ceremony was to take place, and Lord M. said he would write to the Archbishop to know "if he sees any objection to having it in Buckingham Palace; you think he certainly will." I said I did [write to the archbishop?]; that I should like it so much better, as it would be so much less trouble, and so much less trouble about the procession which would then only be from one room to another. &c.[9]

Thus, Queen Victoria was obviously in favour of a more subdued event, simply at Buckingham Palace and without a long and distinct procession. Lord Melbourne's reference to the archbishop's assumed opposition is notable in so far as no clerical comments about the non-church weddings in the previous decades and centuries are known.

It may be worth pointing out that, regarding the arrangements of the wedding, neither Lord Melbourne nor Queen Victoria seem to have referred to Prince Albert. It would appear that the queen's wedding was a matter of state that was confidentially talked over by the monarch and her Prime Minister. Like previous royal consorts, the future Prince Consort – who was to become so influential later on – apparently had no say in these matters.

---

[5] _QVJ_, 6 November 1839 (LE).

[6] _QVJ_, 28 November 1839 (LE).

[7] _QVJ_, 29 November 1839 (LE), emphasis original.

[8] _QVJ_, 2 December 1839 (LE).

[9] _QVJ_, 2 December 1839 (LE), emphasis original.

6—'State Marriages': The Early Victorians

In the end, Queen Victoria and Lord Melbourne agreed on the Chapel Royal as the venue for the wedding. Woods was slow in coming up with a programme, as is indicated in a newly discovered letter, preserved among the records of the College of Arms, dated two weeks later, 16 December 1839. In this, Lord Melbourne urged Woods that he should 'c[on]sider immediately the Manner in which the Queens Marriage May be solemnized & the attendance thereat so limited & regulated as to be consistentt with the limits of the Chapel Royal'.[10] Wood's reply to this is not known, but it may have led to Lord Melbourne's realization that there was going to be a large attendance and that the Chapel Royal was too small for the occasion. For, on 27 December, Queen Victoria again recorded about the wedding that she talked with Lord Melbourne 'of having it at Westminster, which I said [I] never would do; of the attendance which Lord M. said would be large'.[11] From this, it seems that it was Lord Melbourne who had returned to the idea of having the wedding at the Abbey, possibly for the reason of the 'large' attendance. As Sir Robert Chester, Assistant Master of the Ceremonies, had emphasized in relation to the 1797 wedding – the most recent one in the Chapel Royal – 'the Chapel itself is very small and inconvenient for an affair of Ceremony'.[12]

David Duff has interpreted that Queen Victoria was happy to take the limited space of the Chapel Royal as an excuse for not having to invite more members of the Tory party that she disliked; and he points out that she 'made an exception in the case of Lord Liverpool, of whom she was very fond, and the Duke of Wellington'.[13] Similarly, Richard Williams has argued that the queen 'was inclined to view the wedding as a private rather than a state event' and shows that she refused Lord Melbourne's suggestion to invite more members of the opposition.[14]

Eventually, as the *Musical World* explained, the Chapel Royal was 'judiciously fitted up so as to afford increased accommodation to the many distinguished individuals who were invited'.[15] The details were meticulously recorded in a 'Memo / Preparations made by the Office of Woods & Works at the Chapel Royal St James, for the Marriage of HM. Queen Victoria, to HRH Prince Albert […].'[16] Significant temporary fittings were installed:

> Galleries to afford two Seats in the width to be placed on each side of the Chapel the whole length and to be continued over the Altar. The organ to remain in its present situation provision being made in that part of the proposed Gallery immediately in front of it for the Choir.[17]

The *Examiner* also reported of a much more radical way of making more room in the Chapel for all the guests that had to be invited to the queen's wedding:

> Below the choir, on the right, and in the galleries opposite, usually appropriated as Royal closets, the walls of the building were thrown out, and six benches on each side fitted up for the accommodation of peers, peeresses, and other distinguished spectators.[18]

---

[10] *Lca Marriage of Queen Victoria. 1840 (green volume, 'CA' on spine)*, letter bound in near the beginning of the volume; transcr. in Appendix B 6.1. I am very grateful to Peter Mandler for his help with deciphering the writing.

[11] *QVJ*, 27 December 1839 (LE).

[12] *Lna LC 5/7*, p. 57.

[13] David Duff, *Victoria and Albert* (London: Frederick Muller Ltd, 1972), p. 158.

[14] Richard Williams, *The Contentious Crown: Public Discussion of the British Monarchy in the Reign of Queen Victoria* (Aldershot: Ashgate, 1997), p. 235.

[15] [Editorial], *The Musical World*, 13 (February 1840), p. 89. Detailed descriptions of the Chapel Royal at this wedding are included in 'Marriage of Victoria the First'; and in *Wedding Observer*.

[16] *Lna WORK 21/19*, unfoliated.

[17] 'Office of Woods &c / 21 December 1839 / Draft Minute', in *Lna WORK 21/12/1*, fol. 6[v].

[18] 'The Queen's Marriage', *Examiner*, 16 February 1840, p. 105.

The *Mirror of Literature, Amusement, and Instruction* intriguingly concluded that

> the area of the chapel, though confined, presented a *coup d'œil* of exquisite grandeur and effect. Many tasteful judges thought the spectacle here was more interesting than at the coronation; for the eye, without being fatigued in surveying an almost interminable succession of splendid figures, could, within a small compass, view a selection of colours and objects best calculated to please and impress the senses.[19]

From this point of view, the rather limited space of the Chapel Royal was actually an advantage and the crowded conditions, if anything, enhanced the impression of 'exquisite grandeur'.

The venue of the Chapel was not the only significant difference to the weddings earlier in the century. Another notable difference – not only to those earlier weddings, but also the similar weddings in chapel in the previous century – was the time of the ceremony. The exact time was decided only a couple of weeks before the wedding. On 25 January, Queen Victoria still recorded that she had talked with Lord Melbourne 'of the hour for the ceremony' and noted that they thought it 'should be 12'.[20] Surely, the most recent royal wedding in the Chapel Royal, in 1797, had also taken place in day-time. Nonetheless, with most royal weddings in the preceding more than a century having taken place in the evening, the change to a day-time ceremony for the sovereign's wedding was a noteworthy breach with precedent. Interestingly, this circumstance seems not to have been remarked upon in the public reports – which, however, may not have been quite aware of the history of nocturnal weddings. After all, this change of time of the ceremony brought royal weddings on a par with 'normal' weddings throughout the country, and into accordance with the law that weddings had to take place before the afternoon.[21]

The Processions

The ceremonial proceedings of the day took off at Buckingham Palace, Queen Victoria's newly chosen principal residence. Two separate carriage processions, consisting of three and seven carriages respectively, conveyed the queen's husband-to-be and then the queen herself over to St James's Palace.[22] As Paula Bartley has observed, these processions were a public spectacle, with thousands of people watching.[23] Indeed, the press reported how the populace attended with much enthusiasm.[24] After all, the wedding day 'was celebrated as a universal holiday throughout the metropolis'.[25] The Scottish novelist Henrietta Keddie, thirteen at the time and who later wrote under the pseudonym Sarah Tytler, pointed out that the aforementioned change to a day-time wedding 'was a great boon to the London public' and explained:

> It was said that never since the allied sovereigns visited London in 1814 had such a concourse of human beings made the parks alive, as on this wet February morning, when a dismal solitude was changed to an animated scene, full of life and motion.[26]

---

[19] *MLAI*, 35 (1840), p. 114.

[20] *QVJ*, 25 January 1840.

[21] See above, Chapter 1, fn. 17.

[22] For details see the account in *London Gazette*, 13 February 1840, pp. 291–95, here pp. 291–92.

[23] Paula Bartley, *Queen Victoria* (Abingdon: Routledge, 2016), p. 74.

[24] See, for instance, 'The Queen's Marriage', *Morning Chronicle*, 11 February 1840, pp. 1–2.

[25] 'Marriage of Her Majesty with Prince Albert of Saxe Coburg and Gotha, on Monday', *Niles' National Register*, 5th series, vol. 8, no. 3 (21 March 1840), pp. 1 and 34–37, here p. 1. This Washington, DC journal produced a compilation of several different accounts, thus providing many details.

[26] Sarah Tytler, *Life of Her Most Gracious Majesty the Queen*, ed. and with an introduction by Lord Ronald Gower, 3 vols (London: J. S. Virtue & Co., [1897?]), I, pp. 114 and 115.

6—'State Marriages': The Early Victorians

Illustration 6.1: Ceremonial for the Wedding of Queen Victoria and Prince Albert (London: Francis Watts, 1840), 30.5 x 22 x 0.5 cm, printed on silk and bound in blue watered silk (front cover and first page), *Royal Collection, RCIN 1053036*, Royal Collection Trust / © Her Majesty Queen Elizabeth II 2021.

For the arrivals of the distinguished guests at the Chapel Royal some accounts noted an interesting musical detail:

> As the band which mounted guard at the palace approached the chapel, we could hear them play the very appropriate air of "Haste to the Wedding," the aptitude of which made most persons smile.[27]

As at the eighteenth-century weddings, the main participants walked in distinct processions through the state apartments and courtyard of the palace to the Chapel Royal, giving the higher echelons of society (but who were yet not high enough to be invited inside the Chapel) a chance to see the royal couple and get at least a glimpse of the ceremony.[28]

Again, the ceremonial for these processions was printed, but now also in an imminently more lavish manner: several copies, printed with black ink on white silk pages, with smart mint-green silk covers, survive in the National Archives; moreover, there are some even more extravagant copies, printed with blue ink on white silk pages, bound in dark blue watered silk covers and embossed with the royal coat of arms in gold (Illustration 6.1).[29]

---

[27] 'Marriage of Her Majesty with Prince Albert', p. 35. Similar in 'Queen's Marriage', *Morning Chronicle*, p. 2.

[28] For the processions see the queen's own account in *QVJ*, 10 February 1840.

[29] See the sources listed for Ceremonial 1840. For a wide collection of printed ceremonials (on paper), tickets, and newspaper cuttings relating to this wedding see *Lca Marriage of Queen Victoria 1840 (red volume – 'W.C. 107' on spine)*. Another copy with blue silk covers is in *Wra RA F&V/Weddings/1840/QV*.

117

Due to the lavish production of these copies, it may be presumed that they were made for the more prominent participants, either to use at the ceremony or to take home – with the simpler paper copies for less important attendants and spectators.

The processions to the service are well documented in a lavish contemporary publication: *The Authentic Representation of the Magnificent Marriage Procession and Ceremony*.[30] This spectacular, twenty-feet-long, hand-coloured sequence of pictures explained to be

> Displaying the correct Costumes, Dresses, &c., worn by the Nobility and Gentry in attendance, whose names and official appointments are given, and showing the State Apartments through which the Procession passed

First came the procession of the bridegroom and then that of the bride. Prince Albert's procession is reported to have commenced at 'twenty-five minutes past twelve o'clock', announced by a 'flourish', or fanfare, 'of trumpets and drums' who walked at the head of his procession; and as in the past, these went back after the prince's procession to accompany that of the queen.[31] These musicians are well illustrated in the *Authentic Representation*, which shows distinctly how the drums were carried on the back of a uniformed carrier (Illustration 6.2). It is remarkable that this archaic practice, already criticized in 1734, was still employed over a hundred years later.[32]

The *Authentic Representation* shows that the processions were accompanied by several heralds and these then also attended the ceremony in the Chapel Royal. Their attendance is depicted in several contemporary prints (for instance Illustration 1.2 above).[33] Once the trumpet and drums arrived at the door of the Chapel, they stayed outside, in the Ante Chapel, where they may have continued playing while the procession approached and entered (Illustration 6.3).

It is not known whether Queen Victoria and Lord Melbourne discussed the musical programme of the ceremony, but it is known that they spoke about details such as the performance of the music. The queen recorded that they had talked 'of the singing at the Chapel Royal, being shockingly bad, & who had the management of it?'[34] The 'management' lay with Sir George Smart, senior organist of the Chapel Royal since April 1822, and he was also in charge of the music of the wedding service. In his journal, Smart recorded merely that he 'presided at the organ', and for more details he referred to a 'separate bound book', which seems to be lost.[35] Smart was assisted by William Hawes, Master of the Children of the Chapel Royal, and these two together may have chosen the music for the ceremony.[36]

---

[30] *The Authentic Representation of the Magnificent Marriage Procession and Ceremony of Her Most Gracious Majesty Queen Victoria with His Royal Highness Prince Albert of Saxe Coburg, Celebrated at the Chapel Royal, St. James's, February 10, 1840* (London: Published solely by Messrs. Fores [1840?]). Seen as *Lna EXT 11/82*. For a similar such publication see Illustration 6.3.

[31] 'Marriage of Victoria the First', pp. 116–17. See also 'Queen's Marriage', *Examiner*.

[32] Compare Chapter 3, with fn. 134.

[33] For another such print see 'The Marriage of Her Majesty Queen Victoria […]', (London: Published by William Spooner, [1840]), in *Lna Work 21/19*, just before the cuttings from *Wedding Observer*.

[34] *QVJ*, 20 January 1840.

[35] See George Smart, *Leaves from the Journals of Sir George Smart*, ed. by H. Bertram Cox and C. L. E. Cox, first publ. 1907, repr. in the 'Cambridge Library Collection' (Cambridge: Cambridge University Press, 2014), p. 293, and fn. 1, explaining that this book could not be found. Smart refers to this book also in *Lbl Add MS 41772*, fol. 101ᵛ.

[36] 'Marriage of Her Majesty with Prince Albert', p. 36. For biographical details on Hawes see W. H. Husk, Bernarr Rainbow and Leanne Langley, 'Hawes, William (i)', *New Grove* (accessed 29 October 2021). For Hawes' assistance at royal funerals in the period see Matthias Range, *British Royal and State Funerals: Music and Ceremonial since Elizabeth I* (Woodbridge: Boydell Press, 2016) [hereafter *BRSF*], Chapter 5.

6—'State Marriages': The Early Victorians

Illustration 6.2: 'Drums and Trumpets' during the entrance procession at the wedding of Queen Victoria, as depicted in *Authentic Representation* (1840). Pictures from the private collection of Nigel Pierlejewski, reproduced by kind permission.

Illustration 6.3:
Arrival of the procession at the door of the Chapel Royal, from *Spooner's Panoramic View of the Queen's Marriage Procession* (London: Published by William Spooner, [1840]), lithograph with hand colouring, *Royal Collection, RCIN 813076*, Royal Collection Trust / © Her Majesty Queen Elizabeth II 2021.

For Prince Albert's procession within the Chapel, the accounts recorded that 'Immediately on his entrance, a voluntary was performed by Sir George Smart on the organ.'[37] Returning to the aforementioned 'aptitude' of some of the music, it is intriguing that what Smart played has been suggested to have been an arrangement of Handel's chorus 'See the Conquering Hero Comes' from *Judas Maccabaeus*.[38] However, the evidence for this idea is not clear. It appears to have been first mentioned in George Barnett Smith's biography of Queen Victoria from 1887:

> At twenty minutes past twelve a flourish of trumpets and drums gave notice of the approach of the royal bridegroom, and shortly afterwards the band played the triumphant strains of 'See the conquering hero comes!'[39]

While Smith's source is not mentioned, it has to be noted that he describes the 'triumphant strains' as being played by 'the band' – which indicates that this refers not to the (organ) music during Prince Albert's entrance procession inside the Chapel but to the music accompanying his procession to the Chapel. In either case, if this striking piece was indeed played, this could have been expected to be remarked upon at the time: for the well-known tune alone would

---

[37] 'Marriage of Victoria the First', p. 116. See also 'Queen's Marriage', *Examiner*; and [Editorial], *Musical World*.

[38] See Christopher Warwick, *Two Centuries of Royal Weddings*, with a foreword by Elizabeth Longford (London: A. Barker, 1980), p. 18; and Michael Joe Budds, 'Music at the Court of Queen Victoria: A Study of Music in the Life of the Queen and her Participation in the Musical Life of her Time', 3 vols (unpublished doctoral dissertation, University of Iowa, 1987), II, p. 695.

[39] George Barnett Smith, *Life of Her Majesty Queen Victoria* (London: G. Routledge & Sons, 1887), p. 128.

6—'State Marriages': The Early Victorians

probably have evoked the chorus's familiar original words.[40] Assuming that the march was played, Duff bluntly described it as 'surely one of the silliest musical selections in English ceremonial history'.[41] In a more subtly sarcastic way, Michael Joe Budds pointed out that this march for the bridegroom would have been 'a somewhat prophetic choice in terms of later developments'.[42] Indeed, Prince Albert had conquered not only the queen's heart but was eventually also to conquer the respect of the British public and be of huge influence and importance for Victorian cultural life. Nevertheless, without more evidence, the idea that 'See the Conquering Hero Comes' was played during Prince Albert's procession could simply be indebted to fanciful, late Victorian imagination.

Due to the special circumstance at this wedding that the monarch was at the same time the bride, this was the first modern royal wedding at which the bride was the last to enter. Notably, this was a mere coincidence caused by the fact that she was the sovereign and nobody was to enter after her. For the queen's procession, it was reported that 'As her Majesty approached the chapel, the national anthem was performed by the instrumental band.'[43] Like the prince's procession, the queen's entrance into the Chapel was 'announced by a flourish of trumpets and drums'.[44] Queen Victoria recalled: 'The Flourish of Trumpets ceased, as I entered the Chapel, when the organ began to play.'[45] This was again an unidentified voluntary played by Smart.[46] It reportedly included some more musical 'aptitude': the correspondent of one paper referred to Smart playing 'a voluntary',

> in which we remarked his introduction of the subject of Handel's chorus: – 'A virtuous wife shall soften fortune's frowns.'[47]

This is the final chorus of the oratorio *Susanna* (HWV 66). Such a musical quotation would be particularly notable, as a few years earlier Queen Victoria had expressed her aversion to 'tiresome old Handel's dull music'.[48] Indeed, in 1835, after a performance of Handel's *Messiah*, of which she liked only two choruses and one aria, she had recorded that she was 'not at all fond of Handel's music'.[49]

If the accompanying music alluded to the queen as a wife, the ceremonial details yet highlighted her exalted position as monarch. She was not led into the Chapel by a male relative but walked alone, preceded by the sword of state and followed by her maids of honour.[50] This stressed her independent status, emphasizing that she was the sovereign. Lady Wilhelmina Stanhope, later

---

[40] For the tune's being associated with these words in the 1830s see I. D. McCalman, 'Popular Irreligion in Early Victorian England: Infidel Preachers and Radical Theatricality in 1830s London', in *Religion and Irreligion in Victorian Society: Essays in Honor of R. K. Webb*, ed. by R. W. Davis and R. J. Helmstadter (Abingdon: Routledge, 1992; digital repr. 2006), pp. 51–67, here p. 60.

[41] Duff, *Victoria and Albert*, p. 159.

[42] Budds, 'Music', II, p. 695. For the tune's having been 'appropriately' chosen, see also Jules Stewart, *Albert: A Life* (London: I. B. Tauris, 2011), p. 45.

[43] 'Marriage of Victoria the First', p. 118. The same in 'Queen's Marriage', *Examiner*. See also the account in *Wedding Observer*; and 'Marriage of Her Majesty with Prince Albert', p. 36.

[44] 'Queen's Marriage', *Examiner*.

[45] *QVJ*, 10 February 1840. In Lord Esher's transcript (LE), there is an additional clause: 'which had a beautiful effect.'

[46] Budds, 'Music', II, p. 695; and [Editorial], *Musical World*.

[47] 'Queen's Marriage', *Morning Chronicle*, p. 2.

[48] *QVJ*, 16 March 1837 (LE). See also *QVJ*, 15 April 1836 ('such a deal of old, tiresome, Handel's music').

[49] *QVJ*, 9 September 1835 (QV's handwriting and LE).

[50] Ceremonial 1840, p. 2.

Duchess of Cleveland, was one of Queen Victoria's bridesmaids and recorded the ceremony in her diary.[51] Stanhope noted that, when the queen had entered the Chapel Royal, 'She took her place on the left side of the altar, and knelt down in prayer for a few minutes and Prince Albert followed her example.' Other accounts recorded the same, but furthermore noted that after these private devotions the queen went to sit down in her 'chair of state', and only then joined Prince Albert at the altar rails.[52] A surviving sketch of the area around the altar shows the position of all the seats, with the queen's chair to the left of the altar.[53] Even though the queen sat in her chair for 'a few seconds' only, as one account emphasized, this was in effect a kind of inthronization before the marriage ceremony began.[54] It highlighted the fact that the queen was present as sovereign and underlined her exalted status *vis-à-vis* her future husband. Another account curiously detailed more romantically, although probably less accurately:

> On her majesty reaching the altar, she shook hands with the queen dowager and the other members of the royal family; immediately after which, prince Albert conducted her majesty to the part of the communion table [...].[55]

When it came to the actual wedding part of the service, the queen was 'given away' by her uncle, Prince Augustus Frederick, Duke of Sussex.[56] Thus, even though she was the sovereign, in the context of the ecclesiastical marriage rites she was a normal woman – 'given away' by a senior (that is older) male relative. Indeed, notwithstanding that she was the sovereign, the queen promised to 'obey' and to 'serve' her husband.[57] This scene is captured in Sir George Hayter's famous painting of the wedding which gives a good impression of the overall grandeur of the ceremony - which, in turn, was to some extent also conveyed to the public in the numerous coloured and un-coloured prints depicting the occasion (Illustration 6.4 and, for instance, Illustration 1.2).

The Service

The order of service was in a way specially produced, at least for the officiating clergy. In a note of 13 January 1840, the Bishop of London, Dean of the Chapel Royal, asked the 'Commissioner of Woods & Forests' for the provision of 'two new Service Books, covered with crimson & purple velvet'.[58] These were dutifully provided: the aforementioned 'Memo' from the Office of Woods & Works lists that 'New Service Books bound in purple velvet were provided for the Altar'.[59] These velvet-covered 'New' but not 'Special' service books, however, were probably simply new copies of the Prayer Book – nothing like those produced for later weddings (see Illustration 7.6).

---

[51] See Wilhelmina Stanhope, 'The Diary of a Royal Bridesmaid', *Picture Post*, 29 November 1947, p. 15.

[52] 'Marriage of Victoria the First', p. 118. See also 'Queen's Marriage', *Examiner*, and the account in *Wedding Observer*.

[53] See *Lna WORK 21/19* (unfoliated). On the preceding folios there is also a 'Sketch of Chair approved by Her Majesty / for the Marriage' – possibly the mentioned chair of state. A list of 'Furniture prepared for the Altar, on the Ceremony of Her Majestys Marriage. 10th Feb*y*. 1840' includes also a 'State Chair' for Prince Albert (as well as for the Duchess of Kent, the queen's mother, and for the Dowager Queen Adelaide).

[54] 'Marriage of Victoria the First', p. 118.

[55] 'Marriage of Her Majesty with Prince Albert', p. 37.

[56] See *QVJ*, 30 January 1840. See also 'Marriage of Victoria the First', p. 118.

[57] Account in 'Marriage of Victoria the First', p. 118.

[58] *Lna WORK 21/12/1*, fol. 38.

[59] *Lna WORK 21/19*, unfoliated.

6—'State Marriages': The Early Victorians

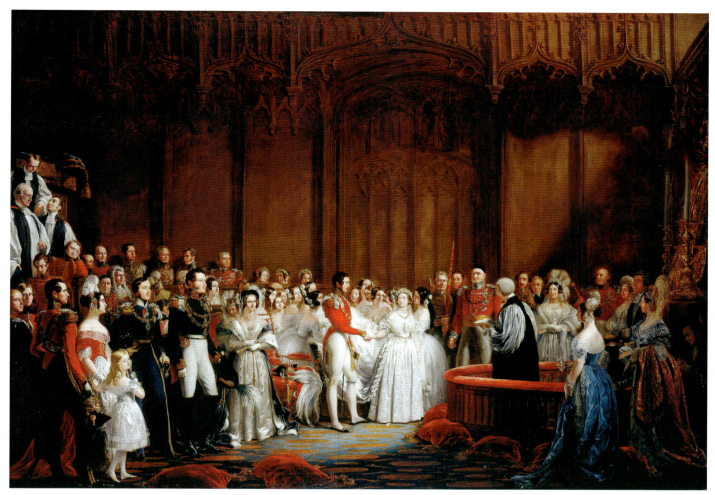

Illustration 6.4:
Sir George Hayter, 'The Marriage of Queen Victoria, 10 February 1840', oil on canvas 1840–42, *Royal Collection, RCIN 407165*, Royal Collection Trust / © Her Majesty Queen Elizabeth II 2021.

The wedding vows were followed by Ps. 67 – the alternative psalm at wedding services, already included at the 1795 and/or 1797 wedding. There is clear evidence that this was sung in a proper by Charles King, from his service in B-flat.[60] It is noteworthy that Ps. 67, or *Deus misereatur* is at the same time one of the canticles scheduled in the Prayer Book for the service of evensong, as alternative to the *Nunc dimittis*. King had been Master of the Choristers at St Paul's Cathedral in the first half of the eighteenth century and his service settings were a prominent part of English cathedral repertoire, not the least because most of them had been included in Arnold's edition of *Cathedral Music* in 1790.[61] The music of King's *Deus misereatur* is relatively straightforward and mostly homophonic in four parts, but nicely varying between sections in the full choir and verses.

Next came the Lord's Prayer and Responses, with one account noting that the Bishop of London was 'making the responses', but another that 'The Archbishop of Canterbury then

---

[60] See, for instance, [Editorial], *Musical World*; 'Marriage of Victoria the First', p. 119; and 'Queen's Marriage', *Morning Chronicle*, p. 2.

[61] See Watkins Shaw and H. Diack Johnstone, 'King, Charles', *New Grove* (accessed 29 October 2021). King's B-flat service was published in *Cathedral Music: Being a Collection in Score, of the Most Valuable & Useful Compositions for that Service*, ed. by Samuel Arnold, 4 vols (London: Printed for the Editor, [1790]), I, pp. 106–50, with the *Deus misereatur* on pp. 144–50. An accompanying organ part by Arnold is in vol. 4: *Cathedral Music: Organ Part, Selected and Revised by Dr. Samuel Arnold*, pp. 51–52.

British Royal Weddings

proceeded [...]'.[62] In any case, as no singing is mentioned, the responses were probably just said, with the choir or congregation making the responses. There was no address and the *Morning Chronicle* reported:

> After the blessing, which was pronounced by the Archbishop of Canterbury, Kent's celebrated anthem, 'Blessed be thou, Lord God,' was beautifully sung.[63]

At the time, even a satirical publication noted the inclusion of music by the composers King and Kent as 'a curious fact', although without further explanation.[64] Yet, the wording obviously implied some criticism of this choice. One American periodical later observed that this wedding had taken place 'at a time which can hardly be considered the brightest period of English music' and that, while 'no special work seems to have been written' for the wedding, Kent's 'not too meritorious anthem [...] was revived' instead.[65] In a similar vein, another late-Victorian commentator opined:

> But, truly, the selection of music did not invite a minute account, though possibly it called for a question as to the preference repeatedly shown on State occasions to the works of worthy Mr. Kent, of Winchester. That composer was certainly popular, and 'Kent's Blessed' held first place in the esteem of village choirs all the land over; but this could hardly have recommended the anthem to the authorities at St. James's.[66]

Kent's mentioned popularity matches with the choice of his anthem *Hear my Prayer* for several royal funerals earlier in the century.[67] Moreover, the anthem from the wedding, Kent's *Blessed Be Thou*, had been a favourite of the queen's uncle, George IV, and had been sung at his coronation in 1821.[68] The anthem had been included in Kent's popular collection *Twelve Anthems*, which had seen at least two more editions since its first publication in 1773.[69] Notably, this anthem on its own was reissued in a new edition in about 1840, the year of the wedding, by A. T. Corfe.[70] Musically, Kent's anthem is similar to King's psalm setting: mostly homophonic with only short polyphonic sections. Two outer sections for the full four-part choir frame a verse for four voices and one for two trebles.

The anthem followed only after the final blessing, as at the eighteenth-century weddings. It was listened to by the royal couple, presumably sitting in state: in contrast to earlier centuries, the reports in 1840 were curiously silent about what happened during the anthem.

For the newly-weds' leaving the Chapel, the printed ceremonial stipulated that 'his Royal Highness will conduct Her Majesty in the Return', and it was reported that Prince Albert

---

[62] 'Marriage of Her Majesty with Prince Albert', p. 35; 'Marriage of Victoria the First', p. 119 (giving the full texts).

[63] 'Queen's Marriage', *Morning Chronicle*, p. 2. See also [Editorial], *Musical World*, which wrongly gives the anthem's title as 'Blessed be the Lord God'.

[64] Rigdum Funnidos (coll. and arr.), *The Royal Wedding Jester; or, Nuptial Interlude: A Collection of the Wedding Faceciæ Displayed on this Joyful Event: [...] together with Numerous Comic Songs, and other Amusing Matters, Forming a Rich Banquet of Wit and Humour [...]* (London: Printed and published by J. Duncombe & Co, [1840?]), p. 35.

[65] 'Royal Wedding Music', *The Musical Visitor: A Magazine of Musical Literature and Music,* 18:9 (September 1889), p. 227.

[66] 'X.', 'From my Study', *Musical Times*, 38 (1897), pp. 374–76, here p. 375.

[67] See Range, *BRSF*, Chapter 5.

[68] See Range, *MCBC*, p. 191.

[69] James Kent, *Twelve Anthems Composed by James Kent [...]* (London: Printed for the Author [...] Published by William Randall, 1773). There were also editions in *c.* 1775 and 1811, 'Printed & sold by Preston and Son'.

[70] James Kent, *Kent's Twelve Anthems, (vol. 1.) A New Edition. Arranged with a Separate Accompaniment for the Organ or Piano Forte by A. T. Corfe. No. 10* [number entered by hand] (London: Published by Coventry & Hollier. [*c.* 1840, according to the catalogue of the Bodleian Library]). Seen as *Ob Tenbury Mus. c. 480 (19)*.

6—'State Marriages': The Early Victorians

took Queen Victoria by the hand.[71] This ceremonial detail had been decided early on: when Queen Victoria in early November had recorded that aspects of the ceremony were to be 'adapted to the present time', she noted immediately afterwards 'Albert is to lead me out of the Chapel'.[72] With the prince leading his sovereign-wife in the procession, the separated exits of a newly-wed couple had most clearly become a mere curiosity of the past. All the same, it appears that the queen's concentration was not fully set on walking with her new husband. One account recorded:

> While the procession was proceeding down the aisle, her Majesty spoke frequently to the Earl of Uxbridge [the Lord Chamberlain], who was on her right hand, apparently giving directions as to the order of the procession.[73]

However, it is not clear how the arrangement of the procession was affected by these 'directions'.

None of the known sources mentions the music that accompanied the recess procession, but it may be presumed that this was again an organ voluntary. Indeed, the report in *The Wedding Observer*, after having mentioned the procession leaving the Chapel Royal, included a rather intriguing phrase:

> The demeanour of the 'happy, happy pair,' was firm, self-possessed, and dignified throughout.[74]

It is not implausible that the quotation marks indicate a reference to Handel's well-known chorus 'Happy, Happy, Happy Pair' from *Alexander's Feast* (HWV 75): if that was the case, and if that was meant to indicate that the music quoted the tune of Handel's chorus, the recessional music would have corresponded to the aforementioned quotation of Handel's music in the organ voluntary during the queen's entrance procession.

Practical Arrangements

The account of the wedding in the *Morning Chronicle* described the practical arrangements of the music in much detail:

> On the level of the West Gallery, or that at the right hand of the altar [looking from the altar], and forming about one-third (in the centre) of the entire length thereof, were the organ and the seats appropriated to the choristers. [...] There was no other instrument but the organ, to which a very ingenious *long movement* was added by Mr. Gray; for, in consequence of the temporary gallery erected before the organ, it could not have been used had the keys remained in the usual position. In the centre of this temporary gallery, the choir were placed thus: – On the 'Decani' side (nearest the altar), five boys, Messrs. W. Knyvett, Wylde, Hawkins, Nield, Vaughan, Willing (for Mr. Hobbs), J. B. Sale, and Bradbury. On the 'Cantores' [*sic*] side, five boys, Messrs. Salmon, Evans, Hawes, Roberts, Horncastle, Welsh, Clark, and Chapman. The organist was placed in the centre.[75]

The observation that there was 'no other instrument but the organ' is noteworthy: thus, the accompaniment of the music was relatively simple and modest. Regarding the choir, the same account highlighted that the *Deus misereatur* psalm was

---

[71] Ceremonial 1840, p. 3; and 'Marriage of Victoria the First', p. 119. See also 'Marriage of Her Majesty with Prince Albert', p. 37.

[72] *QVJ*, 6 November 1839.

[73] *Wedding Observer*. This is also referred to by Tytler, *Life*, I, p. 122.

[74] *Wedding Observer*.

[75] 'Queen's Marriage', *Morning Chronicle*, pp. 1 and 2. These singers' names were also included in the reports in [Editorial], *Musical World*; 'Marriage of Victoria the First', p. 119; and *Wedding Observer*.

sung, in verse and chorus, by the ten boys and sixteen gentlemen of the Chapel Royal, and (the whole strength of the choir being employed on this occasion) produced a very striking and impressive effect.[76]

The accounts were generally full of praise, such as that in the *Observer*:

It is but justice to the gentlemen of the chapel royal to state that this service was executed in the most effective and spirit-stirring manner.[77]

While the choir consisted of the Chapel Royal only, there is at least a slight possibility that it also included female singers, just as at the queen's coronation two years previously: at least one report noted that, when 'the choir boys and the senior singers entered' and went to their places, 'in this nook were two females not in dress; but who they were nobody seemed to know'.[78]

Emily Brand has pointed out that the service took only about fifteen minutes in length.[79] Indeed, it would have begun at about twenty minutes to one, when all the processions had entered; and regarding its end, the report in *The Mirror of Literature* explained that 'at a few minutes past one the procession began to re-marshal itself for its return'.[80] Of these fifteen to twenty minutes, the music with King's *Deus misereatur* and Kent's anthem took a significant portion; moreover, there was also the music that accompanied the processions at the beginning and (presumably) the end. Nonetheless, overall the music at the queen's wedding was somewhat moderate – both in choice and performance. The afore-cited late-Victorian commentator interpreted that 'No special interest appears to have been taken in the music prepared for the marriage service.'[81] As Budds has summarized, the wedding 'was not especially elaborate from a musical point of view and reflected the conservative nature of Anglican church music of the day'.[82] Indeed, notably both choral pieces at the service came from the standard repertoire – and could, in theory, be heard in any Anglican cathedral or larger parish church in the country, performed in the same way by singers and organ. Such straightforward choices could have been due to the state of the Chapel Royal observed by Queen Victoria and Lord Melbourne, seen above. At the time, however, the lack of elaboration at the wedding was also seen as positive. The account in *The Mirror of Literature* emphasized that 'The whole of the impressive ceremony was conducted with the utmost dignity and simplicity.'[83] The queen herself, in fact, recorded:

The Ceremony was very impressive & fine, yet simple, & I think ought to make an imperishable impression, on every one who promises at the altar to keep the vows he or she have have [*sic*] made.[84]

Whether the ceremony as such made an 'imperishable impression' or not, some of its details – famously especially the bride's simple white dress, but also her entering last – were to become staples of wedding traditions, eventually on a world-wide scale.

---

[76] 'Queen's Marriage', *Morning Chronicle*, p. 2. See also 'Marriage of Her Majesty with Prince Albert', p. 36.

[77] *Wedding Observer*.

[78] 'Marriage of Her Majesty with Prince Albert', p. 35. For the coronation see Range, *MCBC*, p. 222.

[79] Emily Brand, *Royal Weddings*, 'Shire Library', 665 (Oxford: Shire Publications, 2011), p. 32.

[80] 'Marriage of Victoria the First', p. 120.

[81] 'X.', 'From My Study', p. 374.

[82] Budds, 'Music', II, p. 695.

[83] 'Marriage of Victoria the First', p. 119.

[84] *QVJ*, 10 February 1840. See also the discussion on 'Simplicity' in the final chapter.

6—'State Marriages': The Early Victorians

Princess Augusta of Cambridge and Frederick William, Hereditary Prince of Mecklenburg-Strelitz, 28 June 1843

On 28 June, 1843, Princess Augusta-Caroline-Charlotte of Cambridge, daughter of Prince Adolphus, Duke of Cambridge (seventh son of George III), and thus cousin of Queen Victoria, married Frederick William, Hereditary Prince (later Grand Duke) of Mecklenburg-Strelitz, grand-nephew of Queen Charlotte (his grandfather was her brother). There does not seem to be a painting of the ceremony, but the *Illustrated London News*, for instance, commemorated the wedding with a full-page picture (Illustration 6.5). Replete with putti carrying a medallion of the bridal couple into heaven, this is a highly stylized depiction. Yet, with the cleric prominently in the centre, and the Chapel Royal communion plate in the back, it clearly underlines the Anglican nature of the ceremony; furthermore, Prince Albert and Queen Victoria are distinctly visible standing next to the bridegroom in the foreground.

This wedding is notable not the least because its ceremonial and musical arrangements are very well documented. As in 1840, the music was provided by the Chapel Royal, again under George Smart, although he may not have conducted it at the ceremony (see below). This time Smart's detailed hand-written account of the ceremony has survived.[85] In addition, he left some more notes, and especially also an annotated copy of the printed ceremonial.[86] The press-reporting was – unsurprisingly – not as extensive as for the queen's wedding three years previously; however, again even such details as the names of the singers were published.[87] As noted in Chapter 1, this was seemingly the first wedding for which the ceremonial was produced in two versions: one in the future tense and the other in the past tense, as an official record of the proceedings.[88]

Time and Venue

Notwithstanding the 1840 change to a day-time ceremony, this wedding took place in the evening. Smart recorded that the 'Marriage Ceremony' had been 'ordered at 9', with performers having to be in their places by 8pm, and he detailed that 'The Archbishop of Canterbury Began to read the Marriage Ceremony at 20 Minutes past 9'.[89] For the end, he noted that, following the bridal couple, 'Her Majesty & H.R.H. The Prince Albert left the Chapel at 13 Minutes to 10'.[90] Thus, the service itself took just over twenty-five minutes (from 9:20pm until about 9:47pm). It is not clear what had caused the recurrence to a nocturnal ceremony: it could perhaps have been an attempt to distinguish the ceremony from the queen's day-time wedding three years previously.

---

[85] *Lbl Add MS 41777*, fols 249ʳ–251ʳ: 'Royal Marriage Ceremony / in / The Chapel Royal / Buckingham Palace / Wednesday Evng: June 28.ᵗʰ 1843'. In the top left corner of fol. 249ʳ (in the same ink as the account): 'Private. / George Smart'. More material on this wedding is in *Lca Marriages & Baptisms of the Royal Family (C.G.Y. 893)*.

[86] *Lbl Add MS 41777*, fols 247ʳ–248ᵛ, which at the top has the annotation: 'Given me by The Lord Chamberlain in the Chapel Royal just before the Ceremony commenced[:] His Lordship said this was a correct Copy.'

[87] The names of the adult singers of the Chapel Royal were included in 'From the Court Circular', *Times*, 29 June 1843, pp. 4–5, here p. 5; transcr. in Appendix B 6.2.

[88] Ceremonial 1843a/b and Chapter 1, following fn. 47.

[89] *Lbl Add MS 41777*, fols 250ʳ and 250ᵛ. For the latter, Smart had originally written 'past 10, but then erased the '10' and corrected it in pencil to '9'. For these times see also Smart's annotation on fol. 248ᵛ (there without correction).

[90] *Lbl Add MS 41777*, fol. 251ʳ.

Illustration 6.5: 'Marriage of H.R.H. The Princess Augusta Caroline and the Hereditary Grand Duke of Mecklenburg Strelitz, *ILN*, 1 July 1843, pp. 7–9, here p. 8. Author's collection.

6—'State Marriages': The Early Victorians

Illustration 6.6: Douglas Morison, 'The Private Chapel at Buckingham Palace', watercolour and bodycolour over pencil 1843–44, *Royal Collection, RCIN 919912*, Royal Collection Trust / © Her Majesty Queen Elizabeth II 2021.

It was only two days before the wedding, on 26 June, that the *Times* reported that the ceremony would take place at Buckingham Palace, 'and not at the Chapel Royal, St. James's, as was originally intended'.[91] The wedding took place in the Private Chapel at Buckingham Palace, and this appears to have been the first royal wedding that was celebrated there. In fact, this chapel was still rather new: it had been consecrated only about three months earlier, on 25 March 1843.[92] It replaced the Octagonal Chapel in the south wing, which had been demolished to make space for the new ballroom and supper room.[93] The new chapel was built in the space of one of the palace conservatories projecting out of the façade on the garden side of the palace, and according to Arthur Beaven it had been Prince Albert himself who decided that the former conservatory 'would be suitable for a chapel' and had 'designed' the 'original plan'.[94] The decoration of the new chapel was not completed until March 1844.[95] Its appearance was captured in a watercolour

---

[91] 'The Approaching Royal Marriage', *Times*, 26 June 1843, p. 5.

[92] For a report of the 'ceremony of consecrating the new Chapel Royal, Buckingham Palace' and a detailed description of the chapel see 'Court Circular', *Times*, 27 March 1843, p. 6. See also 'The New Royal Chapel, Buckingham Palace', *ILN*, 8 April 1843, p. [235].

[93] See Harold Clifford Smith, *Buckingham Palace: Its Furniture, Decoration & History* (London: Country Life Limited, 1931), pp. 14 and 18.

[94] Arthur H[enry] Beaven, *Popular Royalty* (London: Sampson Low, Marson and Company: 1897), pp. 65–66.

[95] See Jonathan Marsden (ed.), *Victoria & Albert: Art & Love,* ed. and with an introduction by Jonathan Marsden (London: Royal Collection Enterprises, 2010), p. 187, which also refers to *QVJ*, 3 March 1844.

painting by Douglas Morison (Illustration 6.6). Following heavy damage in the bombings of 1940, the remains of the chapel were demolished after the war.

Similar to the change of time, the move away from the Chapel Royal at St James's Palace to the new Private Chapel could have been a means of differentiating this occasion from the 1840 wedding. At the same time, it was probably just as much a confirmation of the status of the relatively new royal residence of Buckingham Palace. Only a couple of weeks earlier, on 3 June, the queen's second daughter Princess Alice had been baptized in the Private Chapel.[96]

With the effective reclusion in the 'private' chapel instead of the more official Chapel Royal, and thus without notable outside processions, the wedding could be described as more 'private'. Indeed, the ceremonial was not published in the papers, nor was there an account in the *London Gazette*. Nonetheless, from a ceremonial – and especially from a musical – point of view, the wedding was rather elaborate. For instance, the music was now accompanied by an orchestra, not merely by the organ: the *Times* described that 'the gallery at the lower end of the chapel [near the altar] was set apart for the gentlemen choristers of the Chapel Royal and the queen's private band'.[97] Similarly, the Court Circular explained that 'Her Majesty's private band' was 'stationed in the Royal closet, under the direction of Mr. Anderson', that is George Frederick Anderson.[98] With the participation of an orchestra, the ceremony stood in clear contrast to the royal weddings in the previous six decades and especially to the queen's own wedding three years previously. It seems that Smart merely played the organ but did not conduct.

Entrance Processions

The bride had been the last to enter the chapel in 1840, due to the coincidence that she had then been the monarch. This order was adopted and further extended in 1843: the printed ceremonial stipulated that the bridegroom too was to enter only after 'Her Majesty the Queen, the Prince Albert, the Queen Dowager, and other Royal Illustrious Personages, having taken their seats'.[99] Altogether, all the guests were in their places before the bridegroom entered, with only the bride to come after him. The queen had thus demonstratively given up her prerogative to be the last to enter in favour of the bridal couple. Furthermore, in the ceremonial, the bridegroom and bride were printed in bigger letters than the queen and the prince – giving them a distinct prominence on this occasion.[100]

Smart's notes are not concerned with the processions from the state apartments to the chapel before the service. These initial processions again included heralds, but they did not include the traditional accompaniment of trumpets and drums and thus no music.[101] For the procession of the royal guests within the chapel, Smart recorded that he 'began the voluntary upon a Signal from M.ʳ Sanders (when the Procession was entring) <u>a few Minutes after 9</u>', but it is not known what this 'voluntary' was and it may just have been some improvisation.[102] Smart also noted that

---

[96] See *London Gazette*, 6 June 1843.

[97] 'Marriage of Her Royal Highness The Princess Augusta', *Times*, 29 June 1843, pp. 4–5, here p. 4.

[98] 'From the Court Circular', *Times*, 29 June 1843, p. 5. Anderson does not have an entry in the latest edition of *NG*. For his position, see for instance *The Musical World*, 17:4 (1842), p. 25.

[99] Ceremonial 1843a/b, p. 3. The Dowager Queen (Adelaide) was in the end prevented from attending 'in consequence of indisposition'; see 'Marriage of Her Royal Highness', p. 5.

[100] See Ceremonial 1843a/b.

[101] See 'Marriage of Her Royal Highness', pp. 4–5.

[102] This and the following *Lbl Add MS 41777*, fol. 250ᵛ. Smart's writing looks more like 'Samders', but he might refer to 'Mr. Sanders, the Inspector of Palaces', mentioned in 'Marriage of Her Royal Highness', p. 4.

6—'State Marriages': The Early Victorians

he stopped the voluntary again when the queen and Prince Albert entered the chapel. This moment saw (or better heard) an additional musical feature, stipulated in the printed ceremonial:

> Upon the entrance of the Queen into the Chapel, the Coronation Anthem will be performed previous to the commencement of the Service (being the Anniversary of Her Majesty's Coronation), the Queen's Private Band assisting.[103]

This refers to Handel's *Zadok the Priest*, which was commonly known simply as 'the Coronation Anthem'. However, not the whole of the anthem was performed. In his manuscript account, Smart detailed that one of the pieces rehearsed was the 'last Movement of Coronation Anthem, Handel'.[104] This refers to the third section of the anthem, beginning 'God save the King', and Smart pointed out that the text was amended to 'God save the Queen' for the wedding performance.[105] This was in accordance with the contemporary fashion of amending Biblical texts to suit a female monarch. For instance, one of the anthems at Queen Victoria's coronation in 1838 had been *The Queen Shall Rejoice*, an adaptation of Handel's *The King Shall Rejoice*.[106] As it was only the third section of Handel's anthem that was given at the wedding, the performance took a mere '3 Minutes', as Smart noted meticulously.[107]

The performance of Handel's 'God save the King/Queen' may have been included solely as a reference to the queen's coronation anniversary, as indicated by Smart. However, especially with the changed text – which had of course not been changed at the coronation, when it would not have made sense in the context of the whole anthem – the performance of this chorus also echoed the singing of the National Anthem. The Court Circular noted that the actual National Anthem had been played earlier, but as in 1840 not in the chapel:

> The band of the Grenadier Guards attended in the Grand Hall, and a Guard of Honour of the Goldstream Guards was on duty on the Palace lawn with the band of the Regiment, both bands receiving the Royal Family on their arrival with the national anthem.[108]

The inclusion of Handel's chorus strongly emphasized the monarch's presence. This chorus was even more noteworthy since the following processions of the bridegroom and of the bride were not accompanied by any music. In one of his accounts, Smart noted that the bridegroom's procession 'came first into the Chapel' and then 'there was a long pause in silent expectation of the arrival of the Bride's procession'.[109] In another account, Smart recorded that, after the bridegroom's procession, 'there was a delay with the Bride's Procession' and he emphasized that there was 'No Music for these 2 Processions – a solemn silence!'[110] However, even though Smart here described the silence as 'solemn', in his memorandum on the ceremony he criticized that

> Music would have been better than the awful silence when waiting for the entrance of the Processions of the Bride & Bridegroom.[111]

With the lack of music for these two processions, the impression incidentally must have been that the queen had been the last to arrive in a fully ceremonial way.

---

[103] Ceremonial 1843a.

[104] *Lbl Add MS 41777*, fol. 249ᵛ.

[105] *Lbl Add MS 41777*, fol. 250ᵛ.

[106] See Range, *MCBC*, pp. 216 and 279.

[107] *Lbl Add MS 41777*, fol. 250ᵛ.

[108] 'From the Court Circular'. For 1840, see above, fn. 43.

[109] *Lbl Add MS 41772*, fol. 106ʳ.

[110] *Lbl Add MS 41777*, fol. 250ᵛ.

[111] *Lbl Add MS 41777,* fol. 251ᵛ.

British Royal Weddings

Service and Music

It is not known who chose the music of the service. Smart noted merely that Prince Albert was in the Chapel before the second rehearsal, but then left, as he felt unwell, and did not hear the music rehearsed.[112] Yet, the fact that the prince was there in the first place indicates his interest in the arrangements. His general interest in music would certainly have been in favour of including the band, for instance, and this could have been his idea.

The first music of the service proper was the psalm after the vows, again Ps. 67.[113] There were two rehearsals of the wedding music, on 26 and 28 June, both at about one o'clock. In his list of the 'Pieces Rehearsed' at the first, Smart specified that the psalm was done in the setting by 'C. King, M.B. [= Music Batchelor]'.[114] This most probably referred to King's *Deus misereatur* from his service in B-flat, the one used at the queen's wedding in 1840. However, Smart noted:

> Mr. Anderson had Instrumental Parts added to King's Service which were well adopted and effective / But The Lord Chamberlain and others thought the Service dull in comparison with the other Music.

For the second rehearsal, on the day of the wedding, Smart recorded that he had rehearsed the same pieces as in the first and that 'in addition, "God be merciful unto us." was Chanted to the Earl of Morningtons Chant N° 21 in Mr. Hawes's Book' – presumably in response to the criticism of King's setting. In the evening previous evening, the Bishop of London had sent Smart a note specifying which gentlemen of the choir were to sing in the verses in King's setting, if it were used. Smart thought that it 'went much more effectively at this 2.ᵈ than at the 1.ˢᵗ Rehearsal'.[115] However, he furthermore detailed:

> Lord E. Bruce [the Vice Chamberlain] and others thought the Chant would be more effective than King's Service, which takes 6 Minuts [*sic*] the Chant 3 M, but as I understood it was left for Mr. Anderson to decide which was to be performed.

'Mr. Anderson' obviously agreed with the Lord Chamberlain, Vice Chamberlain and the 'others': after the wedding, Smart recorded that the psalm had indeed been 'Chanted to the Earl of Mornington's Chant in E-♭, No. 21 in Mr. Hawes's Chant Book'.[116] He also noted:

> Mr Anderson was highly indignent [*sic*] that the Lord Chamberlain gave the order thro Mr. Hawes that "God be merciful" was to be chanted instead of being sung to King's Music. The Bishop of London & Lord E. Brue [*sic*] the Vice Chamberlain, settled this affair with Mr. Anderson.[117]

Interestingly, regarding the actual performance of the psalm, Smart wrote down the detail that he gave 'only a Chord before commencing – no giving out'.[118] Thus he did not give each voice-part their note separately, possibly so as to make it sound more dignified for the occasion, and it is noteworthy that he thought this difference worth recording. A remark in the printed ceremonial, but not confirmed by Smart, curiously reads that the psalm 'will be sung by the Gentlemen Choristers of the Chapel Royal', that is by the adult male voices only.[119] Nevertheless, there is no reason why it should not have been sung by the whole choir.

---

[112] *Lbl Add MS 41777,* fol. 249ᵛ.

[113] *Lbl Add MS 41777,* fol. 250ᵛ.

[114] This and the following *Lbl Add MS 41777,* fol. 249ᵛ.

[115] This and the following *Lbl Add MS 41777,* fol. 250ʳ.

[116] *Lbl Add MS 41777,* fol. 250ᵛ.

[117] *Lbl Add MS 41777,* fol. 251ᵛ.

[118] *Lbl Add MS 41777,* fol. 250ᵛ.

[119] Ceremonial 1843a, p. 4.

6—'State Marriages': The Early Victorians

In his copy of the printed ceremonial, Smart recorded that 'upon the conclusion of the Service the Hallelujah Chorus will be sung'.[120] The *Times*, for instance, reported simply that 'the Hallelujah Chorus was given in splendid style'.[121] This, however, was not the Hallelujah Chorus from Handel's *Messiah*. Rather, as Smart noted in his account of the wedding, it was 'The last Chorus in "Judas Macc: Handel. "Hallelujah Amen"'.[122] Notably, the chorus now came clearly within the service; for Smart noted that 'After this Chorus, The Archbishop of Canterbury gave the Blessing.'[123] The festive atmosphere created by the triumphant strains of Handel's music would thus have been counterbalanced by the calm and reflective words of the blessing. Smart did not record that this was answered by a choral 'Amen'.

During the recess, the bride was, as in 1840, again 'led by the Bridegroom'.[124] There is no evidence that this ceremonial arrangement had been questioned. The procession, however, was markedly characterized by another circumstance. Smart recorded that there was 'No Music during the Processions leaving the Chapel'; and he detailed that

> Before the Service commenced, The Lord Chamberlain said, that he thought a last Voluntary would be desirable, but; I had not receivd any directions through Mr. Anderson to play one.[125]

It is noteworthy that Smart ignored the Lord Chamberlain's suggestion and referred strictly to the 'directions through Mr. Anderson'. According to Smart's wording, in the end, there was no music at all as the newly-wed couple left the Chapel. This is interesting in so far as it indicates that the issue of music for the recessional procession seems not to have been thought about beforehand – notably not at the two rehearsals, where details such as the performance of the psalm were fixed. Indeed, despite the two rehearsals, the arrangements of the performance seem to have been somewhat disorganized. Smart afterwards complained:

> The Duchess of Buchleugh, 3 other Ladies and a Page were behind me when I played; the latter I just stopped in time from walking over the Pedals. owing to these unexpected personages, I had scarcely room to play.[126]

It is not known how the bridal couple would have begun their procession out of the Chapel without any music having started, without being given a signal to begin their walk, as it were. All the same, the silence during the recess created a curious parallel to the silence during the bridegroom's and the bride's entrance processions at the beginning of the ceremony. Even though the bridal couple had ceremonially received more prominence by not only being the first to leave but also the last to enter – even after the queen – their processions were marked by a rather unceremonious silence. At the same time, this meant that the ceremony had been neatly framed by Handel's grand choral music– by his *Zadok the Priest* on the queen's entrance and the Hallelujah Chorus from *Judas Maccabaeus* as the last piece of all music.

The *Times* summarized that 'The whole ceremony lasted little more than half an hour.'[127] Smart recorded with more detail that 'The whole of the Ceremony' from the organ voluntary

---

[120] *Lbl Add MS 41777*, fol. 248v.

[121] 'Marriage of Her Royal Highness', p. 5.

[122] *Lbl Add MS 41777*, fol. 251r. See also the account in 'From the Court Circular'. For the rehearsal of 'Hallelujah_Amen (Judas Mac:) Handel', see *Lbl Add MS 41777*, fol. 249v.

[123] *Lbl Add MS 41777*, fol. 251r.

[124] 'Marriage of Her Royal Highness', p. 5; and Ceremonial 1843a/b, p. 4.

[125] *Lbl Add MS 41777*, fol. 251r.

[126] *Lbl Add MS 41777*, fol. 251v.

[127] 'Marriage of Her Royal Highness', p. 5.

that he played as the first procession entered, before the queen arrived, to Queen and Prince Albert's leaving, 'took about 40 Minutes'.[128] Notwithstanding the omitted ceremonial processions to the Chapel, the ceremony would thus would have been distinctly longer than the queen's own wedding in 1840 had been. All in all, the 1843 wedding was a rather elaborate court occasion; and music – or indeed also its absence – had a distinct part in it.

Princess Victoria, The Princess Royal and Prince Frederick William of Prussia, 25 January 1858

The first of Queen Victoria's children to marry was her first-born, Princess Victoria, The Princess Royal, who married Prince Frederick William of Prussia on 25 January 1858. According to the then order of succession, she was only sixth in line to the throne, coming only after her five brothers. Nevertheless, as suggested for the 1734 wedding of Princess Anne, there was a special appreciation of the marriage of the sovereign's eldest daughter. The *Annual Register* opened its report of the 1858 wedding with a historical explanation:

> THE Princess Royal of England is by our ancient feudal law regarded with peculiar honour, inasmuch as, besides rules which invest her with especial respect, the Sovereign is entitled to levy an aid for marrying her, and her only of his daughters.[129]

With such a special status the wedding took place in London – not in Berlin, as had been demanded by the Prussian husband's family. In a letter to the Earl of Clarendon, Secretary of State for Foreign and Commonwealth Affairs, Queen Victoria famously quipped:

> Whatever may be the usual practice of Prussian princes, it is not every day that one marries the eldest daughter of a Queen of England.[130]

Overall, both the ceremonial and the music of this wedding are probably better documented than for any other pre-twentieth-century wedding. The *London Gazette* published an informative account of the wedding in a special supplement, while George Smart was again involved in the music and again left meticulous records and notes.[131] The ceremonial was again printed, but it was now also prepared in another, extended and more detailed version that also mentions some more details of the music.[132] In addition, a separately printed sheet with the list of the music and its full texts was produced.[133] Finally, the actual music of the ceremony was preserved with the means of the time: an as yet unidentified 'C.' (probably 'Christian') Cramer published a collection of the 'Wedding Music', that is the music of the wedding service, in an arrangement for the piano.[134] All these sources combined leave relatively little doubt about the details of the ceremony and the music, including its actual performance.

---

[128] *Lbl Add MS 41777*, fol. 251ʳ. For the following compare fn. 79 above.

[129] 'Marriage of The Princess Royal, Jan. 25', *Annual Register* [...] *1858* (1859), pp. 355–58, here p. 355.

[130] Queen Victoria to Earl of Clarendon, 25 October 1857, in Queen Victoria, *The Letters of Queen Victoria: A Selection from Her Majesty's Correspondence between the Years 1837 and 1861*, ed. by Arthur Christopher Benson and Viscount Esher, 3 vols (London: John Murray, 1907), III, p. 321.

[131] Supplement to *London Gazette*, 2 February 1858. For Smart's records see *Lbl Add MS 41772* and *Lbl Add MS 41772*.

[132] Several copies in *Wra RA F&V/WED/1858*.

[133] For this sheet see *Lbl Add MS 41777*, fol. 319ʳ. Another copy in *Lna LC 2/79*, near the beginning. See also fn. 167.

[134] C. Cramer, *The Royal Wedding Music Arranged for the Piano Forte* (London: Charles H. Purday, [1858]), seen as *Lbl Music Collections h.725.b*, no. 14.

6—'State Marriages': The Early Victorians

Ceremony and Venue

Heightening the importance of the event, the wedding was, as in 1840, a day-time occasion. The printed ceremonial gave the beginning of the ceremonies as 'half past Twelve o'Clock', and the *Times* recorded that the service proper 'commenced at exactly 10 minutes to 1'.[135] Smart noted that, after the service, 'the Procession left the Chapel, at 10 M. past one', summarizing that 'The whole Ceremony from the Entrance of the 1st. Procession to the departure of the last Procession took 50 Minutes.'[136] These timings would mean that the first procession had entered at 12:20pm, and that the actual service took a mere twenty minutes, from 12:50pm to 1:10pm.

The ceremony returned to the Chapel Royal at St James's Palace but it seems that at some point it had been thought to take place at Buckingham Palace, as in 1843. In early December the Lord Chamberlain, John Campbell, 2nd Marquess of Breadalbane, wrote to the Office of Works:

> With reference to my Letter of the 21d. Ultimo, I have the honor to inform you, that the Marriage of Her Royal Highness The Princess Royal will take place at the Chapel Royal St. James's Palace, not at Buckingham Palace as therein stated.[137]

Richard Williams has shown that the choice of the Chapel Royal – instead of a grander and also more public venue, especially with a longer processional route – was 'widely criticized'.[138]

Illustration 6.7: John Phillip, 'The Marriage of Victoria, Princess Royal, 25 January 1858', oil on canvas, signed and dated 1860, *Royal Collection, RCIN 406819,* Royal Collection Trust / © Her Majesty Queen Elizabeth II 2021.

---

[135] Ceremonial 1858a/b, p. 1; and 'The Marriage of The Princess Royal', *Times*, 26 January 1858, pp. 7–9, here p. 7. See also the entry in William Lovegrove's Manuscript (transcr. Ashbee and Harley, *Cheque Books*, II, p. 271): 'was commenced at 10 minutes to one o'Clock'.

[136] *Lbl Add MS 41777*, fol. 311v.

[137] Lord Chamberlain to Office of Works, dated 'St. James's Palace / 3 December 1857', *Lna WORK 21/12/2*, no. 27. For copies of this letter and also the mentioned letter of 21 November see *Lna LC 2/81*, p. 25.

[138] Richard Williams, *Contentious Crown*, p. 239, fn. 65.

He refers to reports in the *Times* and the *Morning Herald*, observing that the latter 'declared that the wedding should have taken place at Westminster Abbey'. Indeed, the *Times* highlighted that 'The old edifice of St James's' was 'still the palace of diplomacy and ceremonial'; but after lamenting the small size of the Chapel Royal, it noted sarcastically: 'St. James's is not so much a residence as a tradition.'[139] The ceremony itself is captured in John Phillip's well-known painting that conveys the stately grandeur of the occasion as much as it highlights the limitation of space in the crowded Chapel Royal (Illustration 6.7).

In an article expressing the general disappointment about the (comparative) lack of 'splendour' at the wedding, *The Saturday Review* concluded that 'there never was an opportunity of which so little use was made' – and it referred particularly to 'regrets that use was not made of Westminster Abbey'.[140] On the other hand, Charles Maybury Archer explained that the Chapel Royal had been chosen because of 'its furnishing more accommodation than was to be found in Buckingham Palace, and from its being distinguished by many royal historic associations'.[141] Similarly, a comment in the *Illustrated London News* decidedly defended the choice of the Chapel Royal.[142] At first, it pointed out that 'the only regret which seems to be felt in the matter is that the ceremonial will be comparatively private', and it explained:

> The country would perhaps have been better pleased with a public celebration in our great cathedral church, and with a procession through the streets of the metropolis.

This seems to be suggesting a service in St Paul's Cathedral in London. Nevertheless, in the following, the comment offered a broad defence of the actual plans for the wedding:

> If that be so, we may venture to remind those who hold that opinion that, in the first place, the ceremony as now proposed is more in accordance with our habits as connected with the marriage of a very young woman, which usually partakes as much as possible of the character of a family celebration; in the next place, the season of the year is not particularly well adapted for a public demonstration; and, lastly, it should be remembered that any social pageant as has been hinted at could only be got up with the sanction of Parliament.

Yet, a little closer to the wedding, the same magazine seemed to take up the other's complaints:

> Perhaps, in the whole of this matter, the only drawback which is felt and expressed is, that so little is to be done to give popular éclat to an event in which the people generally evince so deep an interest. If the popular voice was followed, the ceremonial would have been next only to a coronation in splendour and extent.[143]

Any possible criticism, however, was countered by the pragmatically practical explanation that 'an out-door pageant in the depth of winter' would be too dangerous. Therefore, by way of self-advertisement the paper concluded

> that really the general public must be content with the pleasures of imagination, enlarged and abundantly ministered to by the copious descriptions which will flood the columns of the daily papers, and the truthful and elaborate Illustrations which will cover the pages of this Journal.

---

[139] 'The Marriage of The Princess Royal', *Times*, p. 7.

[140] 'Æsthetics of the Wedding', *The Saturday Review of Politics, Literature, Science and Art*, 5:119, 6 February 1858, pp. 135–36, here p. 135.

[141] Charles Maybury Archer, *A Guide and Descriptive Account of the Marriage of The Princess Royal with Prince Frederick William of Prussia* (London: H. Elliot, 1858), pp. 11 and 12.

[142] This and the following 'The Princess Royal', *ILN*, 9 January 1858, pp. 25–26, here p. 26. I am very grateful to John Plunkett for drawing my attention to the reports and comments on this wedding in *ILN*.

[143] This and the following 'The Royal Marriage', *ILN*, 23 January 1858, pp. 73–74.

6—'State Marriages': The Early Victorians

In the end, the public aspect of the wedding was in fact widened, although possibly unintendedly. As in 1840, a carriage procession conveyed the main participants from Buckingham Palace to St James's Palace. Whereas this procession then had included altogether only ten carriages, it was now significantly longer – as bride and queen went separately: the *Observer* reported that it consisted of 'sixteen of the royal carriages, [...] escorted by the Life Guards', while according to the *Times* it 'consisted of upwards of 20 carriages' and the *Annual Register* counted 'more than twenty carriages'.[144] There was a nicely printed programme of the carriage processions, listing all the participants, possibly for the spectators, and the procession's attraction was captured in a contemporary, published broadsheet that also shows the queen riding in her golden state coach.[145] This latter detail made the procession even more spectacular: in 1840, going to her own wedding, Queen Victoria had used a normal coach.[146]

Processions

The service in the Chapel Royal was preceded by the traditional processions through the state apartments of St James's Palace that were accompanied by the music of trumpets and drums, and as at the eighteenth-century weddings these musicians returned after each procession to accompany the next one.[147] As in 1843, Anderson was again very much involved in the music at this wedding. He had become Master of the Queen's Musick in 1848, in succession of Franz Cramer, and was informed 'That the Arrangements of the Household Trumpeters & Kettle Drummers at the Marriage are to be placed under his Superintendence.'[148] Moreover, the *London Gazette* eventually recorded that 'Mr. Anderson conducted the Performance of Music in the Chapel', whereas Smart 'presided at the Organ'.[149]

The ceremonial stipulated: 'As each Procession enters the Chapel a March will be played.'[150] Queen Victoria again forfeited her right of precedence in favour of the bridal couple and arrived before both the bridegroom and the bride.[151] Their processions entered over the next fifteen minutes, as Smart recorded meticulously:

> A <u>short</u> Tuning at a ¼ before 12, as the Princess of Prussia arrived in the Chapel about that time. {At 20 M. past 12, The Queen's Procession entered the Chapel, the Band [entered above: 'only'] playing the March in the "Occasional Oratorio". {At ½ past 12, the Bridegroom's Procession entered the Chapel, the Band playing the March in "Joseph". {At 25 M. to 1, the Bride's Procession entered the Chapel, the Band playing the March in "Judas Macc:", with the Side Drums.[152]

---

[144] 'Marriage of The Princess Royal: Ceremony of the Marriage', *Observer*, 25 January 1858, p. 1; 'Marriage of The Princess Royal', *Times*, p. 7; 'Marriage of The Princess Royal', *Annual Register* [...] *1858* (1859), pp. 355-58, here p. 355.

[145] 'Procession from the Palace to the Chapel Royal of the Wedding of Princess Royal to Prince Frederick of Prussia' [London, 1858], seen as *Lbl 1881.c.6.(18A)*. For the two sheets of printed programme, here with many manuscript corrections, and also for other details on this carriage procession see *Lna LC 2/79*.

[146] See the report and illustration in *Wedding Observer*.

[147] Ceremonial 1858a/b, pp. 2–5.

[148] Copy of a note to Anderson of 21 December 1857, *Lna LC 2/81*, p. 35.

[149] Supplement to *London Gazette*, 2 February 1858, p. 482. Same in the extended ceremonial in *Wra RA F&V/WED/1858*, p. 15 of this. In a copy among the heralds' records, this whole passage is crossed out without explanation. See *Lca Ceremonials (printed), Loose papers*, no. 12.

[150] Ceremonial 1858a, p. 5.

[151] See Ceremonial 1858a/b.

[152] *Lbl Add MS 41777*, fol. 311ᵛ. See also *Lca Funerals, Ceremonials: 1843–1861*, pp. 85–101, here pp. 97–99; and 'The Ceremony and Dresses at the Royal Nuptials', *The London Journal, and Weekly Record of Literature, Science, and Art*, 6 March 1858, pp. 5–6.

These three marches are also named in the aforementioned printed list of the music of the ceremony.[153] While the queen's march from the *Occasional Oratorio* (HWV 62) is from its overture and the bridegroom's march from *Joseph and his Brethren* (HWV 59) is from part 1 of that oratorio (scene 5, no. 3), it might not be quite clear what the bride's march from *Judas Maccabaeus* (HWV 63) was: in part 3 of the oratorio, there is a march (no. 59) which follows directly after the famous chorus 'See the Conquering Hero Comes'. Yet, in Victorian reports this chorus itself was also occasionally referred to as a march. Notwithstanding that the chorus clearly refers to a male hero, with their blatantly martial character either piece (the march or the chorus/march) would have been a rather interesting choice for the bridal procession, curiously foreboding her future life at the strongly militaristic Prussian court.

Elizabeth Pleck has stated that, as Princess Victoria 'walked to the altar, the organist played the Bridal Chorus from Richard Wagner's opera *Lohengrin*'.[154] The use of Wagner's piece at this wedding has been widely cited and perpetrated in several publications. However, this is clearly contradicted by Smart's reliable account; the confusion may stem from the fact that Wagner's piece was heard at a concert at Buckingham Palace on the wedding day.[155]

The queen herself, in her journal, left an intriguing account of the entrance processions:

> The drums & trumpets played Marches, the organ playing others, as the Processions approached & entered. There was of course a slight pause between each, & the effect was thrilling & striking as one heard the music coming nearer & nearer.[156]

Her notion that the marches were played by the organ is very curious, because the *Observer* pointed out that the marches during the entrance processions were 'performed by the whole orchestra'.[157] Moreover, in his aforementioned account, Smart noted distinctly that there was 'No Organ in the 4 Marches', that is the three before and the one after the service.[158]

Returning to Smart's list of the entrance marches, his addition of 'only' to the instruction that 'the Band' was to play the march from the *Occasional Oratorio* could refer to the exclusion of the organ. However, another possibility is that Smart added 'only' because he had suggested that the band should also play the National Anthem upon the queen's entrance. For 22 January 1858, Smart recorded that he 'told his Lordship [= Lord Ernest Bruce, the Vice Chamberlain] what music was to be performed, and named the marches: recommended the one in "Scipio" and that "God save" should be played when the Queen entered'.[159] In the end, however, his suggestion was apparently not followed, and 'God Save the Queen' was not played, and his additional 'only' may refer to the band playing 'only the march'. Although Smart's recommendation of the march from Handel's *Scipio* was ignored, it is noteworthy that all three entrance marches were yet by Handel, resulting in a stylistically coherent group. As seen above, Queen Victoria was not fond of Handel, but then – as will be seen – the music for this wedding had been chosen not by her but by Prince Albert.

---

[153] *Lbl Add MS 41777*, fol. 319ʳ.

[154] Elizabeth H. Pleck, *Celebrating the Family: Ethnicity, Consumer Culture, and Family Rituals* (Cambridge, MA: Harvard University Press, 2000), p. 212.

[155] 'Ceremony and Dresses', p. 6. For this concert see also 'Concert at Buckingham Palace', *The Musical World*, 36 (January 1858), pp. 75–76. For copies of the programme see *Wra RA F&V/WED/1858*. For the history of Wagner's Bridal March at weddings see also Matthias Range, 'Wagner's "Brautchor" from *Lohengrin* and its Use as a Wedding March', *Journal of the Royal Musical Association* (forthcoming).

[156] *QVJ*, 25 January 1858.

[157] 'Marriage of The Princess Royal', *Observer*, p. 1.

[158] *Lbl Add MS 41777*, fol. 311ᵛ. See also the longer quotation above, with fn. 152.

[159] *Lbl Add MS 41772*, fol. 149ʳ.

6—'State Marriages': The Early Victorians

The bride's entrance had now become a moment of particular interest and dramatic impact. The *Gentleman's Magazine* recorded in an enthusiastic way the moment after the bridegroom had arrived at the altar:

> Here a pause ensued. The whole assembly grew perfectly still with expectation; the movement of plumed and jewelled heads ceased, and all eyes were bent upon the entrance. The strains of the trumpets were once more heard; and soon – her father the Prince Consort on one side, her grand-uncle King Leopold on the other – entered the bride, followed by her youthful bridesmaids.[160]

The *Times* also emphasized the 'heavy silence of suspense' during the wait for the bride, which 'deepens as the moments pass'; and regarding the bride's two male supporters, it noted that they were identifiable through the 'Court list of the ceremonial', stressing:

> Without these aids to recognition, even these Royal personages would pass to the altar unnoticed and unknown, so deep, so all-absorbing is the interest excited by the appearance of the Bride herself.[161]

The ceremonial stipulated that

> On arriving at the Chapel The Bride will be conducted to Her Seat in the Chapel, on the left side of the Haut Pas leading to the Altar, near Her Majesty's Chair of State.[162]

Thus, it appears as though she was meant to sit down on her arrival, before joining the bridegroom at the altar – possibly as her mother had done in 1840. However, her sitting down seems eventually to have been omitted, as a surviving seating plan for the Chapel Royal as set up for this wedding does not indicate a chair for the bride near the queen.[163]

The Service

A letter sent to the Office of Works after the wedding referred to 'the Books of the Form of Prayer used at the Chapel Royal on the Marriage of H.R.H. the Princess of Prussia'.[164] This may refer to the specially produced order of service: several copies of this survive, some lavishly bound in red velvet others in white silk, both with cold imprints.[165] Incidentally, in Phillip's aforementioned painting of the ceremony (Illustration 6.7, above), one can clearly see the bridegroom's mother, Princess Augusta of Prussia (the third from the left), holding one such order of service bound in red velvet in her hand. She is the only member of the congregation to hold one visibly in the picture, but the officiating clergy also holds such a copy in his right hand.

A note in the records of the Lord Chamberlain reads 'Programme of Ceremony given to all having Tickets In "Ticket Book"'.[166] This follows not long after the aforementioned printed sheets with the programme of music and the full texts, and this note might plausible refer to these sheets rather than to a copy of the actual order of service.

---

[160] 'Marriage of The Princess Royal', *Gentleman's Magazine*, p. 323.

[161] 'Marriage of The Princess Royal', *Times*, p. 7. The same in 'Marriage of The Princess Royal', *Annual Register*, p. 357, which applies this observation to the whole of the procession.

[162] Ceremonial 1858a, p. 5.

[163] The (partly printed) seating plan is included in *Lna LC 2/81*.

[164] 'Thomas Gordfrey' to 'G. Russel Esq.', undated, but Office of Works stamp that it was received on 'JULY 16 / 1858', *Lna WORK 21/12/2*, no. 70.

[165] See the sources listed for OS 1858. For their appearance compare Illustration 7.6.

[166] This note is in *Lna LC 2/79*, just before a letter to 'Mon cher Monsieur Ponsonby', which is dated 2 January 1858. For the programmes of music see fn. 133 above.

Similar to the specially-produced order of service for the wedding in 1797, the 1858 version is merely a verbatim copy of the text from the Prayer Book – but this time it does not give any specific details pointing to this particular wedding in the text, and the only concrete reference is the date imprinted on the front cover. While the order of service does not include the programme of the music, this is found in the aforementioned printed list of music, which also includes the full texts of all the vocal pieces.[167] Moreover, in addition, to this there is also another, similar sheet with lavish floral decorations and the texts of the vocal music, presumably intended for the higher-ranking members of the congregation.[168]

Smart's records confirm that Prince Albert was heavily involved in the musical preparations and that it was the prince who chose the music for the service himself. For 29 December, Smart recorded that he had been presented by 'D.ʳ Wesley' to the Bishop of London and that he (Smart) 'communicated M.ʳ Anderson's <u>verbal</u> account of the music to be performed at the Royal Marriage'.[169] Dr Charles Wesley was the Subdean of the Chapel Royal, and the Bishop of London was, following custom, the Dean of the Chapel Royal.[170] However, it was only a couple of weeks later, on 11 January, two weeks before the wedding, that Anderson informed Smart of the final details, and in written form:

> I am Commanded to inform you that the vocal Music to be performed at the Marriage of H.R.H. The Princess Royal by the Choir of the Chapel Royal is to be as follows[:] The service to commence with a Choral of which [verso] I send you the vocal Parts. The 67ᵗʰ Psalm is to be Chanted. The Service to conclude with the Hallelujah from the Messiah [space] Handel. You will have the goodness to make this communication to the Lord Bishop of London.[171]

It is notable that neither Smart nor the Dean of the Chapel seem to have been as much as consulted about these details – the latter only being informed through Smart. The dean could do no more than confirm to Smart that he wished the music 'to be in accordance with the Prince Consort's express desire as intimated to Mr. Anderson'.[172]

Furthermore, it is noteworthy that Smart was sent details of the 'vocal Music' only, as this was what he had to practise with the choir and accompany on the organ. He was not, however, informed about the instrumental marches. He was clearly considered to be, and treated as a mere performer, but not like the leading musician of the Chapel Royal.

This appears to have been the earliest royal wedding to include a chorale/hymn and at least one publication noted that this had been 'selected by the Prince Consort'.[173] It is not implausible that Prince Albert had also suggested its inclusion in the first place. There was a precedent of adding chorales to such services: Budds observed that at four christenings of the children of Queen Victoria 'the performance of a chorale preceded the ritual'.[174]

The printed ceremonial scheduled that, once the bridal procession had fully arrived at the altar, 'a Hymn will be sung and the Service will commence'.[175] The printed sheets with the

---

[167] See above, fn. 133.

[168] Several copies of this sheet are in *Lna LC 2/80*.

[169] *Lbl Add MS 41772*, fol. 144ʳ.

[170] For Wesley see 'The Chapel Royal', *Musical Times*, 43 (1902), pp. 88–92, here p. 89.

[171] Anderson to Smart, 'Windsor Castle / Janʸ 11ᵗʰ 1858', *Lbl Add MS 41777*, fol. 306ʳ⁻ᵛ.

[172] Bishop of London to Smart, 13 June 1858, *Lbl Add MS 41777*, fol. 309ʳ.

[173] 'The Marriage of The Princess Royal, with Prince Frederick William of Prussia', *The Primitive Church (Or Baptist) Magazine*, 15 new series (London: Arthur Hall & Co., 1858), p. 51.

[174] Budds, 'Music', II, p. 698; see also I, pp. 375–76.

[175] Ceremonial 1858a, p. 5.

6—'State Marriages': The Early Victorians

programme and texts of the music detailed that this was 'CHORALE. (1599)', followed by the full text, which was also included in some newspaper reports:[176]

> This day, with gladsome voice and heart,
> We praise Thy name, O Lord, who art
> Of all good things the giver!
> For England's first-born Hope we pray!
> From hour to hour, from day to day,
> Be near her now, and ever!
> King of Kings—Lord of Lords—
> Father, Son, and Holy Spirit—
> We adore Thee!
> Hear us, while we kneel before Thee!

Smart noted that 'Mr Oliphant' – Thomas Oliphant, one of the directors of the Philharmonic Society – had 'adapted the words' of the chorale.[177] In almost astonishing directness, the text refers specifically to 'England's first-born', the bride. Smart furthermore recorded that Anderson had shown him 'the Corale by [empty gap] in the Prince Consort's Book which is to be performed at the <u>beginning</u> of the Service'. The 'Prince Consort's Book' may well have been some German hymn book: for the hymn or 'chorale', with the new words, was published not long after the wedding, and the tune was that of the German chorale 'Wie schön leuchtet der Morgenstern'.[178] The setting of the 'Choral Hymn', without text, was also included in Cramer's aforementioned edition of the wedding music, and this also details that the music came 'From a German Chorale, 1599'.[179]

The account in the *Times* recalled the scene at the beginning of the wedding ceremony in some detail, observing that

> the service commences with the chorale, which peals through the little building with the most solemn effect. The words are particularly appropriate, full of feeling and piety, and the audience follow them in a whispered cadence as the choir sing—[…].[180]

This confirms that the hymn/chorale was sung by the choir only, without the congregation who were the mere 'audience' – but who could, however, at least follow the text, either by hear or on one of the printed sheets. The *Illustrated London News* also noted explicitly that the chorale was 'sung by the choir', implying that the congregation did not join in; and according to Anderson's note sent to Smart, the choir would have sung the chorale in parts, that is in harmony.[181] After all, the distinct title 'chorale' could have been chosen explicitly to indicate that this was not a congregational 'hymn'.

---

[176] Text here as in the printed text sheet in *Lna LC 2/80* (also in *Lbl Add MS 41777*, fol. 319^r; and in *Lna LC 2/79*). The text was published, for instance, in 'Marriage of The Princess Royal', *Observer*, and 'Marriage of The Princess Royal', *Times*, p. 7.

[177] This and the following *Lbl Add MS 41772*, fol. 144^v.

[178] *Choral Hymn for Four Voices, Sung at the Marriage of The Princess Royal […] the Words Written for the Occasion by Thos Oliphant Esqr* (London: Addison, Hollier & Lucas, [1859]).

[179] Cramer, *Royal Wedding Music*, p. 5. NB In this version, the repeat sign in the top line is wrongly placed and in the second line two bars are missing.

[180] 'Marriage of The Princess Royal', *Times*, p. 7.

[181] 'The Marriage of The Princess Royal', Supplement to *ILN*, 30 January 1858, pp. 117–28, here p. 122. Anderson's note is cited above, with fn. 171.

For the service proper, Smart after the event recorded a list of the 'Music, Performed.' This list matches with the music that Anderson had informed him to include and also tallies with the printed ceremonial and with the printed music list. Yet, Smart in his list included precise details of when exactly the music had been performed at the service, obviously trying to be as precise as possible:

> Immediately after the Bride & Bridegroom got to the Altar, "The Chorale" commenced. After the last words by the Archbishop of [scribbled out –Cbe?] Prayer, ending "Ye man have life everlasting", The Rev.d D.r Wesley, gave out the 67.th Psalm with these words only: "God be merciful to us and bless us"; (As G.F.S. [= George Frederick Smart] was conducting "The Grand Chant" in the Choir & Band Gally) Mr. Cooper played the Chord of D. only; then all the Voices commenced, the Band joining in the ["]Gloria Patri" only. After the Prayer, read by The Bishop of London, ending, "with any amazements", "The Hallelujah Chorus" (Messiah) Handel. The Arch. of Canterbury gave the usual "Blessing" immediately after the Chorus.[182]

As in 1843, there had been some doubt about how to perform the psalm, and Smart's records again present interesting insights. At some early stage in the preparations, he had recorded that 'It is not yet decided by the Prince if the 67th Psalm is to be Chanted, or to be King's in Bb'.[183] However, Smart later noted that he had been informed 'that The Prince Consort had decided that the 67th Psalm was to be Chanted, but H.R.H. did not fix upon any particular Chant'.[184] Based on this, Smart had sent his own suggestion to Subdean Wesley:

> As there is no command for any particular Chant, I beg to name for your approbation, the Grand Chant instead of Lord Mornington's, the Band can be introduced in the "Gloria Patri" only, of the former Chant, which will render it effective.[185]

The 'Grand Chant' refers almost certainly to that by Pelham Humfrey, which Smart had previously used, for instance, at Queen Victoria's coronation in 1838 (Figure 6.1).[186]

Figure 6.1: Pelham Humfrey's 'Grant Chant', as used at the coronation of Queen Victoria in 1838: here as reconstructed in Matthias Range, *Music and Ceremonial at British Coronations: From James I to Elizabeth II* (Cambridge: Cambridge University Press, 2012), p. 216.

The chant that Smart had suggested was apparently approved to be used at the wedding service. However, Smart later recorded in his notes that he had found that this chant 'did not go well at the Rehearsal'.[187] He had therefore amended the music slightly:

---

[182] *Lbl Add MS 41777*, fol. 311v.

[183] *Lbl Add MS 41777*, fol. 144v.

[184] *Lbl Add MS 41777*, fol. 145r. See also fn. 171 above.

[185] Smart to 'the Rev.d D.r Wesley' on '11 Jan. 1858', *Lbl Add MS 41777*, fol. 308r.

[186] Range, *MCBC*, p. 215–16 (with Example 7.2).

[187] This and the following *Lbl Add MS 41777*, fol. 312r: headed 'Remarks.'

142

6—'State Marriages': The Early Victorians

> I requested M[r]. Anderson to send me all the Inst. Parts of it. He did so, and I wrote the words of the "Gloria Patri" in e[ach] Part, and made Semibreves of the two Minims and put Bindes [ties?], in most of their Parts.

It does not seem immediately clear which notes Smart may have changed. However, he recorded that, after another rehearsal, he had 'tried with the Queens P. Band "The Grand Chant", and left all the Parts of it with M[r]. William Hardy'.[188] In the end, Smart's suggestion was followed and only the *Gloria Patri* at the end of the psalm was accompanied by the 'full Orchestra'.[189] Thus Smart was able to contribute at least some, albeit small details to the wedding music.

An account of the wedding from the heralds' collection explains that, after the psalm,

> the Archbishop continued the Service to the end of the Second Blessing. The Bishop of London then read the Exhortation which was followed by Handel's Hallelujah Choras [*sic*] from 'The Messiah" and the Ceremony was concluded by the Archbishop of Canterbury with the Blessing which terminates the Communion Service[.][190]

The 'Second Blessing' refers to the blessing of the couple after the prayers. Regarding the following 'Exhortation', at least one account emphasized that the bishop 'read that portion of the service which [in the Prayer Book] is appointed to be read on occasions when "there is no sermon, declaring the duties of man and wife," […].'[191]

The well-known, rousing Hallelujah Chorus from *Messiah*, performed by the full forces, must have made for a grand and impressive ending of the ceremony. Regarding its position, the printed ceremonial detailed that 'At the conclusion of the Service Handel's Hallelujah Chorus will be sung'.[192] The *Times* account emphasized the position of the chorus at the ending of the service by describing that 'At the concluding words the Hallelujah Chorus [giving the full text] rose clear and loud, with thrilling effect.'[193] It is noteworthy, however, that the Hallelujah Chorus was still followed by what Smart called 'the usual "Blessing"' and what the heralds described as 'the Blessing which terminates the Communion Service'.[194] This clarifies that, as in 1843, a final blessing was added to the service and that the Hallelujah Chorus was clearly included within the liturgical frame.

Cramer's aforementioned piano arrangement of the wedding music includes a setting of 'God Save the Queen' before the Hallelujah Chorus.[195] Yet, the singing, or just playing of the National Anthem in the service is not confirmed by any other source. Cramer's edition most probably does not reflect what was actually performed at the ceremony, but was more of a topical collection. Indeed, it also includes – after the Hallelujah Chorus – the chorus 'Per te d'immenso giubilo' from Donizetti's opera *Lucia di Lammermoor* – a piece highly unlikely to have been performed during the service in the Chapel Royal.[196]

---

[188] *Lbl Add MS 41772*, fol. 149[v]. For the rehearsals see below.

[189] See *Lbl Add MS 41777*, fol. 311[v]; extended ceremonial in *Wra RA F&V/WED/1858*, p. 12 of this; and *Lca Funerals Ceremonials, 1843–1861*, p. 99. See also, for instance, 'Ceremony and Dresses', p. 6.

[190] *Lca Funerals Ceremonials, 1843–1861*, p. 99. The same wording is found in the extended ceremonial in *Wra RA F&V/WED/1858*, p. 12 of this.

[191] 'Marriage of The Princess Royal', *Observer*, p. 1.

[192] Ceremonial 1858a, p. 6.

[193] 'Marriage of The Princess Royal', *Times*, p. 8.

[194] *Lbl Add MS 41777*, fol. 311[v]; and *Lca Funerals Ceremonials, 1843–1861*, p. 99.

[195] Cramer, *Royal Wedding Music*, p. 6.

[196] Cramer, *Royal Wedding Music*, p. 10–11.

British Royal Weddings

Mendelssohn's Wedding March

In the wider historical context, the most notable piece of music at the 1858 wedding was certainly the one that accompanied the newly-weds' leaving the Chapel Royal. The printed ceremonial stipulated that 'Mendelssohn's Wedding March will be played as the Procession is leaving the Chapel' and the more detailed version of the ceremonial explained furthermore that the march was 'from Mendelssohn's "Midsummer Night Dream," [sic]'.[197] Smart recorded that 'Mendelssohn's Wedding March (with the Jingling Inst.ˢ) was played by the Band as the Procession left the Chapel'.[198] While it is not clear to what instruments Smart referred, the addition of such 'jingling instruments' as perhaps a triangle, tambourine, or little bells may have contributed to the joyfully festive character of the music.

Colin Timothy Eatock proposed that it was Princess Victoria herself who chose Mendelssohn's march for her wedding.[199] However, the evidence for that idea is not clear, and given that Prince Albert had chosen all the other music of the ceremony, this march could quite plausibly also have been his choice.[200] After all, Prince Albert and Queen Victoria had been well acquainted with Mendelssohn and were enthusiastic patrons of his music.[201]

From a ceremonial point of view, it is interesting that there was a short interval before the Wedding March in which the royal couple received the congratulations of the queen and relatives.[202] This was rather unceremonious, with the Times noting that 'the bride, giving vent to her evidently long pent-up feelings, turned and flung herself upon her mother's bosom with a suddenness and depth of feeling that thrilled through every heart'.[203] The resulting clear separation of the procession from the preceding service, and its following such a sentimentally loaded scene, would have given the procession more impetus. It was not merely the ending of the service, not merely the necessary physical act of leaving the chapel; rather, it was a distinct ceremony in its own right – appropriately elevated by Mendelssohn's magnificent march. After all, up to this point, Handel's music had dominated the ceremony – with three marches during the initial processions and the Hallelujah Chorus at the end – and Mendelssohn's Wedding March for the recess was an effective use of more recent, more modern music.

Practical Arrangements

Archer noted that the Chapel Royal had been 'thoroughly altered and refitted for the ceremony' and the various accounts detailed that the pews had been removed and instead 'raised benches placed along each side of the chapel'.[204] As for the 1840 wedding of the queen, temporary galleries

---

[197] Ceremonial 1858a, p. 6; extended ceremonial in Wra RA F&V/WED/1858, p. 12 of this. See also the discussion of Mendelssohn's march in Chapter 1, above, with fn. 102.

[198] Lbl Add MS 41777, fol. 311ᵛ.

[199] Colin Timothy Eatock, Mendelssohn and Victorian England (London: Routledge, 2009), p. 123.

[200] This had already been suggested by F. G. Edwards, 'Mendelssohn's "Wedding March"', Musical News, 6:170 (June 1894), p. 517.

[201] See Eatock, Mendelssohn, passim; and also W[illia]m. A. Little, Mendelssohn and the Organ (Oxford: Oxford University Press, 2010), p. 66. For Queen Victoria singing Mendelssohn's songs, see Tytler, Life, I, pp. 170–72.

[202] 'Ceremony and Dresses', p. 6.

[203] Marriage of The Princess Royal', Times, p. 8. A more detailed discussion of the royal family's public display of affection on such occasions will have to be the topic of a later study.

[204] Archer, Guide and Descriptive Account, pp. 11 and 12. For detailed descriptions of the Chapel see also 'Marriage of The Princess Royal: The Completed Preparations', Observer, 25 January 1858, pp. 5–6; 'Marriage of The Princess Royal', Observer, p. 1; and 'Marriage of The Princess Royal', Times, p. 7.

6—'State Marriages': The Early Victorians

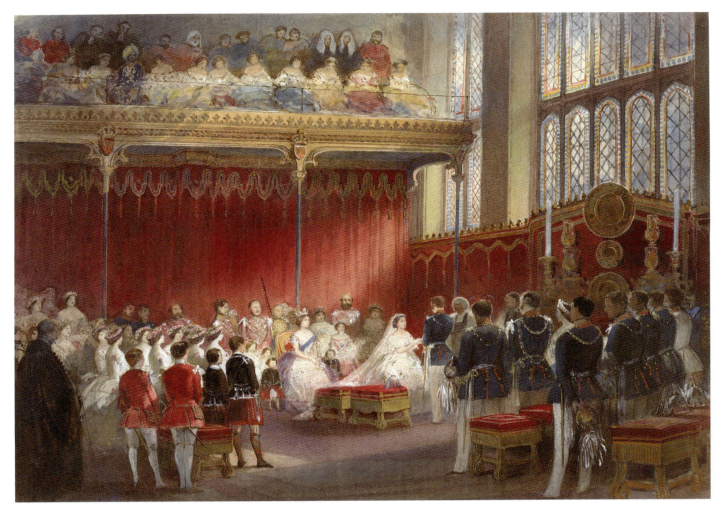

Illustration 6.8:
Egron Sellif Lundgren, 'The Wedding of the Princess Royal and Prince Frederick William of Prussia', pencil, watercolour and bodycolour 1858, *Royal Collection, RCIN 919928*, Royal Collection Trust © Her Majesty Queen Elizabeth II 2021.

were built on both sides.[205] Moreover, there were also some more drastic changes to the fabric of the building. The window above the altar 'had been greatly increased in size, by being lowered to a short distance above the communion-table, and was filled with neat stained glass'.[206] The resulting appearance is well represented in the many images depicting the ceremony, such as the watercolour by Egron Sellif Lundgren that shows both the enlarged window and one of the temporary galleries (Illustration 6.8). The latter are also shown very clearly in one of the many pictures of the wedding included in the *Illustrated Times* (Illustration 6.9).

Another major change to the fabric was occasionsed by the special provisions to accommodate the musicians. As for the eighteenth-century weddings, a whole window was taken out – this time in one of the side walls of the Chapel. A letter to the Office of Works explained that 'more space may be obtained at the window in the Gallery Pew opposite the Organ loft. Musicians or Singers will be placed here', and a surviving plan of the Chapel Royal in its arrangement

---

[205] See the picture of the Chapel Royal as prepared for the 1858 wedding, in Ashbee and Harley, *Cheque Books*, II, p. [x]. The picture is meant to be from *ILN* of 23 January 1858 but is not in there. However, on pp. 104–05, this issue includes another good illustration of the wedding scene, as seen from the altar, showing the two galleries.

[206] 'Marriage of The Princess Royal', Supplement to *ILN* (1858), p. 119. The account in 'Marriage of The Princess Royal', *Times*, p. 7, described this as 'the extra window which has been added to that end of the chapel'.

British Royal Weddings

as set up for the 1858 wedding clearly shows the built extension, the extra bay in the gallery.[207] The resulting 'more space' was yet rather limited, as Smart detailed:

> The Choir 32 Boys & Man with M.ʳ Oliphant (in a Surplice) and Mʳ. Bowley (without a Surplis) also the Band were all <u>much crouded</u> in their Gally, built over the Piaza in the Court Yard, with <u>large thick Glass</u> forming the <u>Roof</u> of the orchestra [...].[208]

Despite its limitation in size (see also Figure 6.2, below), this extension or bay, projecting out into the courtyard, was a notable feature, and its glass roof was an especially intriguing detail. It literally highlighted that this was a day-time wedding: at the eighteenth-century weddings, such extensions had not needed windows, as the ceremonies took place after dark anyway. The afore-mentioned picture in the *Illustrated Times* shows the side of the Chapel where the musicians' gallery was: the musicians as such are not shown, but the bay were they were placed, the 'Gallery Pew opposite the Organ loft', can be seen on the left, where the taken-out window for the extension is indicated by the missing wall and the bright light shining in from behind the people (Illustration 6.9).

In contrast to the other evidence (see especially Figure 6.2 below, p.150), the account in the *Times* curiously recorded that the choir was placed in the organ gallery and only the band in the gallery on the opposite side:

> The old recess of the organ loft and that facing it have been much enlarged, the former for the accommodation of the members of the choir, the latter for Her Majesty's private band.[209]

Yet, this may have been based on an earlier plan, rather than being an accurate account of the scene at the service. Indeed, the Court Circular's description, cited in the same *Times* article, tallied with Smart's details: 'The musical performers were placed behind the company in the gallery opposite the organ.'[210] The placement of spectators in front of the musicians did certainly not make coordination with the ceremony, let alone with the organ on the other side, any easier. Nevertheless, no mishaps in the performance appear to have been reported. All the same, as in 1840, the erection of the long galleries along the side of the Chapel affected at least the very working of the organ and necessitated a special solution, as the Court Circular noted:

> A movement was added to the organ to elevate the keys of it, in consequence of the temporary gallery erected in front of the organ.[211]

There is usually not much information on the organs that were used at royal weddings. This time, however, there is some more information, through an illustrated sketch of the 'Section thr° Organ Gallery'.[212] From this it appears that the organ was a three-manuals instrument, and thus of substantial size. It does not seem to be known, however, whether the instruments itself was specially modified for the wedding.

With all the extra fittings and alterations in the Chapel, the costs for this wedding were significantly higher than those at the queen's own wedding in 1840. The Office of Works prepared

---

[207] 'Breadalbane' (then 'Lord Chamberlain') to Office of Works, undated, *Lna WORK 21/12/2*, no. 29. The plan is in *Lna WORK 34/880* (available to view online via https://images.nationalarchives.gov.uk).

[208] *Lbl Add MS 41777*, fol. 312ʳ: headed '<u>Remarks</u>.' For this extension see also the description in Archer, *Guide and Descriptive Account*, p. 14.

[209] 'Marriage of The Princess Royal', *Times*, p. 7.

[210] 'Marriage of The Princess Royal', *Times*, p. 8 (quoting from the 'Court Circular').

[211] Quoted in 'Marriage of The Princess Royal', *Times*, p. 8. Compare also fns 75 and 207, above.

[212] *Lbl Add MS 41777*, fol. 321ʳ. The organ, in a niche in the wall and with a Gothic façade, appears to be depicted in the newspaper cuttings in *Lna LC 2/81*, p. 104.

6—'State Marriages': The Early Victorians

Illustration 6.9: 'The Galleries of the Chapel Royal, Showing the Queen's Procession Passing up the Aisle', *Illustrated Times*, 30 January 1858. Author's collection.

an estimate for the Treasury and first of all recorded that the 'Cost of the preparations for Her Majesty's Marriage in the Year 1840' had been '£2713..6..10.' It took this as a starting point for its calculation for the 1858 wedding and in addition to this sum stipulated £1,600 of 'Probable costs', for 'Additional Works' such as the musicians' gallery and the enlarging of the windows – altogether coming to '£4.313..6..10'.[213] The final total expenditure for the 1858 wedding does not seem to be known, but given the amount of work done it was probably not far off the above estimate. Despite the cost, the commentator in *The Saturday Review*, for one, overall found that 'there never was an opportunity of which so little use was made' and judged that the arrangements in the Chapel Royal showed 'the absence of a controlling artistic mind' and were overall highly ungratifying.[214] This comment came with a repeated reference to the criticism of choosing the Chapel Royal in the first place.

---

[213] 'Preparations for the Marriage of / Her Royal Highness The Princess Royal', in *Lna WORK 21/12/2*, no. 43; this is partially transcr. in Appendix B 6.3.

[214] 'Æsthetics of the Wedding', pp. 135–36 (quotations from p. 135).

Smart's meticulous notes confirm that Prince Albert was involved not only in the choice of the music but also very directly in the practical arrangements of its performance:

> I left a Paper of <u>Memos</u> dated Decr 30 (See Copy) with The Bishop for him to talk with Prince Albert as to <u>where</u> the Choir is to be placed &c.[215]

It seems that Prince Albert took the issue very much to heart and was very active in forming his opinion on where to place the choir. Smart later recorded the details of the musicians' originally intended disposition, which was based on the precedent at the queen's wedding in 1840, and then pointed out the prince's interference with that plan:

> At Her Majesty's Marriage the whole Choir (No Band) was placed in the <u>2 Rows</u> of the Gally adjoining [that is, in front of] the Organ Loft, the Organ Keys being then elevated into the same height as on the present occasion, but the Prince would not permit the Choir being so placed. He measured the Organ Loft himself, said it would <u>hold the Choir</u>.[216]

There is no indication why Prince Albert did not allow the choir sit in the gallery in front of the organ. In any case, Smart did obviously not agree with the prince's suggestion. Consequently, he asked the Bishop of London, in his capacity as Dean of the Chapel Royal, to explain to Prince Albert

> that the Choir could <u>not</u> be placed [above: 'in the Organ Loft'] but that they might be <u>with the Band</u> in the <u>opposite newly made Recess</u>, opposite the O. Loft.

As already seen, the choir was eventually placed in this position. It is not known how Prince Albert's seemingly very decided opinion on this matter was changed.

All the same, the surviving sources show that the prince's involvement in, and occupation with the preparations of the overall ceremony stretched to the smallest minutiae. For instance, the 'Master of Household' had been asked

> if the Household Trumpeters may be allowed to wear Trowsers at the Marriage instead of Breeches & Stockings as heretofore there being none in store & it being thought that Trowsers may give a more Military appearance.[217]

To this he replied a couple of days later that 'The Prince Consort thinks that the Trumpeters might wear Trowsers with a gold stripe.'[218] Incidentally, the whole of the procession was depicted in the *Illustrated Times* after the wedding.[219] One of the pictures shows the trumpeters and drummers walking at the head of the procession to the Chapel (Illustration 6.10). They are wearing high riding boots, which obscure breeches as much as trousers with gold stripes.

As in 1843, there were two rehearsals of the music. Of the first rehearsal, at the Chapel Royal on 19 January, Smart left two detailed accounts.[220] In these he noted that the boys of the Chapel Royal were 'weak and out of tune', and 'too weak' in the Hallelujah Chorus – and

> consequently for the Performance on the 25 Inst. Two Boys from S:[t] Paul's Cathedral and two from Westminster Abbey were invited making a total of ['X' in pencil] Boys.[221]

---

[215] *Lbl Add MS 41772*, fol. 144[v]. In between the lines he noted: 'which he has <u>not</u> returned'.

[216] This and the following *Lbl Add MS 41777*, fol. 312[r].

[217] *Lna LC 2/81*, p. 35 (copy of a note of 22 December 1857).

[218] Note from 'Master of the Household', 23 December, copied in *Lna LC 2/81*, p. 36.

[219] *Illustrated Times*, 30 January 1858. These pictures are also included in *Lna LC 2/81*, beginning at p. 85.

[220] *Lbl Add MS 41772*, fol. 147[r] and *Add MS 41777*, fol. 311[r]; partially transcr. in Appendices B 6.4 and 6.5.

[221] *Lbl Add MS 41772*, fols 147[v]–148[r] and *Lbl Add MS 41777*, fol. 311[r].

Illustration 6.10: The procession through the state apartments at St James's Palace to the Chapel Royal at the wedding of Princess Victoria, 1858, centre piece illustration in *Illustrated Times*, 30 January 1858. Author's collection.

Put up in the Gallery for the Choir & Band.

Front Seat in the Gallery.

Back Seat in the Gallery.

The Chapel Royal Choir.

25th January 1858.

Cantoris. | Decani.

Third Bench.

| F.C. Large_M: Hepworth, G.A. Broone, A.J. Wilmore, T. Allen, Boys. {2 From Westminster Abbey Henry A. Dykes_Edward Loyd.} | + Conductor. | G.W. Seoirle, J.D. Carmichael, A. Cellier, T.C. Hepworth, T.C.E.*Helmore, Boys. 2 {From St Paul's Cathedral. _ Morgan, _ Orton.} ★ Deputy for T.F. Mitchell. |

The 2 West. Abbey Boys and were not at the the 2 St Paul's Boys, Rehearsal.

Second Bench.

Cantoris:

Cont'ralto N.º 18.	Cont'ralto N.º 17.	Tenor N.º 16.	Tenor N.º 15.	Tenor N.º 14.
M.r Goss. Composer.	M.r Foster.	M.r M: Smith. Deputy for M.r Roberts.	M.r Benson.	M.r Lockey.

Decani:

Cont'ralto N.º 13.	Cont'ralto N.º 12.	Tenor N.º 11.	Tenor N.º 10.	Tenor N.º 9.
M.r Barnby.	M.r Francis.	M.r Bennett.	M.r Hobbs.	The Rev.d T. Helmore. Master of the Boys.

First Bench.

Cantoris:

Cont'ralto N.º 8.	Bass N.º 7	Bass N.º 6.	Bass N.º 5.
M.r Baxter. Deputy for M.r Salmon.	M.r Winn Deputy for M.r Chapman.	M.r Thomas.	M.r Lawler.

Decani:

Cont'ralto N.º 4.	Bass N.º 3.	Bass N.º 2.	Bass N.º 1.
M.r Martin. Deputy for M.r Wylde.	M.r Whitehouse.	M.r Machin.	M.r Bradbury.

{All the above Gents were at the Rehearsal} on Tuesday, January 19.th 1858.

The Band

{The SubDean appointed the 4 Deputies.}

The Sub-Dean procured Tickets of admission from The Lord Chamberlain's Office, (as per George Smart's list) for all the above Boys and Gents_
and in addition, for,
Sir George T. Smart,
G. Cooper Esqr
M.r Hill_ Organ Tuner,
M.r Hill's Assistant,
Howard Bellows Blower

C. Wesley D.D. Sub Dean.

Door.

Figure 6.2: Plan of 'The Chapel Royal Choir' at the wedding of Princess Victoria, 1858; transcribed from George Smart's handwritten records in *Lbl Add MS 41777*, here fols 322v–323r.

6—'State Marriages': The Early Victorians

Smart's records include a detailed plan of 'The Chapel Royal Choir', providing all the names of the singers and their positions (Figure 6.2).[222] The additional boys among the trebles are not named, with Smart's plan merely noting 'The 2 West. Abbey Boys and the 2 S.ᵗ Paul's Boys'. The Court Circular recorded that Smart together 'with Mr. George Cooper, presided at the organ' and that 'Mr. Goss assisted in the choir'.[223] Cooper had been assistant organist at St Paul's Cathedral since 1838 and is also mentioned in Smart's detailed notes; Goss is listed by Smart as no. 18 of the choir singers, and described as 'Composer'.[224] Some published reports included also the singers' names, and among these is listed a 'J. Goss'.[225] This, then, could plausibly have been the well-known John Goss who was at the time organist of St Paul's Cathedral (knighted after his retirement in 1872).

Smart's plan shows that the orchestra was placed behind the three benches with the choir. While the exact composition of the band does not seem to be known, there were clearly instruments such as trombones and even a tuba. For the first rehearsal, Smart recorded that

> The Alto & Tenor Boni were placed (at one Desk) on the <u>left</u> (Bass) side of the Organ, the Bass Boni & Tuba (at one Desk) on the Right (Treble) side of the organ.[226]

Yet, Smart 'complained [...] of the loudness of the Boni' and suggested 'to place them in the orchestra instead of near the organ'.[227] As the trombones would not have been much less loud when being placed in the opposite gallery, he probably meant that their proximity to the organ, where he was sitting, made them too loud for him to hear the rest of the music.

The second rehearsal took place at Buckingham Palace on 23 January. Smart does not seem to have been present for all of it. He recorded that this rehearsal was to be from '½ past 9 to 3' but that he 'Got to B. Palace Rehearsal about ¼ to 11 left it about 4.'[228] This rehearsal had possibly begun with the processional, purely instrumental music, for which Smart was not needed, and it then took longer than initially scheduled.

The coordination of the music was also well-prepared. Anderson sent a list requesting 'The Signals to be given by The Lord Chamberlain for the Orchestra':[229]

1. Her Majesty enters the Chapel Door
2. The Bridegroom – Dᵒ·–
3. The Bride – Dᵒ·–
4. Her Majesty, & Bride & Bridegroom are seated
5 At the conclusion of the Service

Overall, Smart's meticulous record-keeping at this wedding is noteworthy. He generally left good accounts of the royal occasions in which he was involved, but his records of the 1858 wedding

---

[222] *Lbl Add MS 41777*, fols 322ʳ–323ʳ.

[223] Quoted in 'Marriage of The Princess Royal', *Times*, 8. Cooper is also mentioned in 'The Marriage of The Princess Royal', *ILN*, 23 January 1858, p. 79.

[224] For Cooper see, for instance, *Lbl Add MS 41777*, fol. 311ʳ; transcr. in Appendix B 6.5. For Goss see *Lbl Add MS 41777*, fols 322ʳ–323ʳ (see Figure 6.1).

[225] For instance, 'Marriage of The Princess Royal', *Times*, p. 8 (quoting the 'Court Circular'); 'Marriage of The Princess Royal', *ILN*, 23 January 1858, p. 79; and 'Marriage of The Princess Royal: The Completed Preparations', p. 5; the latter trascr. in Appendix B 6.6.

[226] *Lbl Add MS 41777*, fol. 311ʳ.

[227] *Lbl Add MS 41772*, fol. 149ʳ (under 22 January 1858).

[228] *Lbl Add MS 41772*, fols 149ʳ and 149ᵛ.

[229] *Lna LC 2/81*, p. 36 (summary extract of a letter from Anderson to Lord Chamberlain's Office, 1 February 1858).

seem especially detailed. It would be difficult to determine whether this is just by chance, simply because more material has survived — after all, his 'separate bound book' on the 1840 wedding is lost — or whether he had indeed produced more material to start with. It is feasable that Smart considered this wedding to be particularly significant and made a special effort to record all the details relevant to him. After all, it is notable that his records contain many repeats and revisions: they may have served as drafts for a final account that never materialized or is lost.

All the detailed work on the wedding service, and all the detailed preparations apparently paid off. Prince Albert afterwards wrote to Baron Stockmar, his confidant and advisor:

> Die Ceremonie ist vorüber & sehr feierlich gewesen, alles ging sehr gut. / The Ceremony is over. It was very solemn — all went well.[230]

Possibly only few, if any, previous weddings had been so well prepared and executed.

Significant Innovations

As already alluded to earlier, with its carriage processions from Buckingham Palace to St James's Palace, the 1858 wedding featured a distinct widening of the public aspect. Before the event, the *Observer* had reported that 'additional consideration' had been shown for the press and that 'instead of there being accommodation for only ten persons accorded to it, seats are now provided for twenty'.[231] David Reed has shown that eventually twelve publications received passes for their representatives in the Chapel Royal, and three of these 'were also accorded a second pass for their illustrators, who were only to be allowed into the lesser privilege of the Colonnade'.[232] There were two galleries 'Reserved for the Press!' in the Chapel.[233] The press interest extended decidedly also to the music. Smart recorded that he 'left "The Morning Chronicle" with the account of the Queen's Marriage' and furthermore 'talked in the Chapel with a <u>Reporter</u> of "The Times"'.[234] This was probably the first time that that the press took such a direct interest in the music, even talking to one of the musicians.

The public aspect of the wedding was widened even further. Four weeks before the wedding, the 'Master of Household' was informed:

> The Prince [Albert] thinks that the Chapel sh.d be shewn to the Public after the Marriage and the State apartmets [*sic*] after the Drawing Room on the 30. Inst.[235]

In the end, the public was admitted by tickets to see the Chapel Royal in its wedding setting between 27 and 29 January and to see both 'the Chapel and State Apartments in the following week'.[236] Altogether, one publication emphasized:

---

[230] Prince Albert to Stockmar, 25 January 1858, *Wra RA VIC/MAIN/Y/189*, no. 88; English transl. in *Wra RA VIC/MAIN/Y/187*, no. 38. Also transcr. in *Letters of the Prince Consort, 1831–1861*, selected and ed. by Kurt Jagow, and transl. by E. T. S. [Edgar Trevelyan Stratford] Dugdale (London: John Murray, 1938), pp. 287–88.

[231] 'Marriage of The Princess Royal: The Completed Preparations', p. 5.

[232] David Reed, '"What a Lovely Frock": Royal Weddings and the Illustrated Press in the Pre-Television Age', *Court Historian*, 8:1 (July 2003), pp. 41–50, here p. 43–44.

[233] See the plan of the Chapel Royal at the 1858 wedding in *Lbl Add MS 41777*, fol. 320r. For a great amount of correspondence with the press regarding this wedding see *Lna LC 2/79*.

[234] *Lbl Add MS 41772*, fol. 144r–144v.

[235] Note of 23 December 1857, copied in *Lna LC 2/81*, p. 62, which includes also more information on the tickets to see the Chapel and the rooms in the palace.

[236] Archer, *Guide and Descriptive Account*, p. 14. See also the large, printed sheet with the Lord Chamberlain's announcement of 21 January 1858 in *Lna WORK 21/12/2*.

6—'State Marriages': The Early Victorians

Not even on the occasion of her Majesty's own marriage did all parts of the metropolis, and all ranks and conditions of the people, display such interest and enthusiasm as were witnessed on this occasion.[237]

In both ceremonial and musical terms, the wedding of the Princess Royal was more elaborate than that of her mother had been. The *Gentleman's Magazine* referred to the lavish decoration of the Chapel Royal – with 'a profusion of crimson velvet and gold, of blue paint and gilding, and the addition of a gallery on each side' – which 'made it a more fitting scene for a state marriage than it was when Queen Victoria appeared there as a bride eighteen years ago'.[238] Indeed, with its obvious elaboration and scope, the 1858 wedding stood out clearly against all the other royal weddings in the previous six decades. As seen above, Prince Albert appears to have been very much involved in this development.

Overall, the lavish outdoor processions, special provisions for the press, and the opening of the venues to the public – all these were notable firsts for a British royal wedding. Musically, the 1858 wedding was equally innovative: with the introduction of both a chorale/hymn and of Mendelssohn's Wedding March. After all, there was much to justify the somewhat boisterous statement in the *Illustrated London News* that there could be

> no doubt the pageant and ceremony of Monday next will be one of the most imposing which has taken place in connection with our Royal family during the present century.[239]

The Princess Royal's wedding certainly presented a new highpoint in the development of British royal weddings, and everything seemed set for the trend of elaborating such ceremonies, especially also in respect to their music.

—◦◦◦—

When the *Gentleman's Magazine* referred to the weddings of Queen Victoria and her daughter meaningfully with the term 'state marriage', this may well have emphasized the newly developing understanding of such ceremonies as grand occasions of state, displaying great pomp and increasingly involving the populace.[240] Such an epithet was justified by the ceremonial elaboration bestowed on these occasions. At the end of the Victorian era, and with reference to Prince Albert's death in 1861, Sarah Tooley summarized that the 1858 wedding

> was undoubtedly *the* 'Royal' wedding of the family, being celebrated in London with the joyousness and pomp and circumstance which distinguished Court ceremonies before sorrow had shadowed the Throne.[241]

With Queen Victoria and Prince Albert's numerous children, and grandchildren, the decades from 1858 onwards were to be a very busy period at the wedding altar; yet the grandeur of the earlier 'state marriages' was to remain unmatched, as the overall character of royal weddings was to change rather soon.

---

[237] 'Marriage of The Princess Royal, with Prince Frederick William of Prussia', *Primitive Church*, p. 51.

[238] 'Marriage of The Princess Royal', *Gentleman's Magazine*, p. 322.

[239] 'Marriage of The Princess Royal', *ILN*, 23 January 1858, p. 79.

[240] 'Marriage of The Princess Royal', *Gentleman's Magazine*, p. 322. See also fn. 238.

[241] Sarah A. Tooley, 'The Weddings of the Queen's Children', *The Lady's Realm: An Illustrated Monthly Magazine*, 9 (November 1900 to April 1901), pp. 47–56, here p. 47.

7

The 'Windsor Castle' Weddings: The Mid-Victorians I

THE WEDDINGS OF QUEEN VICTORIA in 1840 and then of her eldest daughter in 1858 seemed to herald a notable change in the character of royal wedding ceremonies, turning them into grander events with much public attention and – to a certain extent – public participation. However, any such development was drastically curbed by one the most important and decisive events in Queen Victoria's reign: the death of her husband, Prince Albert, in December 1861. His demise, followed by the queen's continual mourning, brought royal ceremonial to something of a standstill and changed the character of the monarchy for the rest of the century. This had a direct and noticeable effect on royal weddings, of which there were quite a few: once again they became somewhat subdued, if not reclusive (although still elaborate) occasions. This was poignantly heightened by a general change of venue, away from the capital: most of the royal weddings from the 1860s onwards took place at Windsor Castle.

Princess Alice and Prince Louis of Hesse, 1 July 1862

Queen Victoria's third child and second daughter, Princess Alice Maud Mary had been engaged to Prince Frederick William Louis of Hesse since 30 April 1861, for which day the *London Gazette* had announced the queen's consent to the marriage.[1] While no early planning for the wedding seems to be known, Prince Albert's death on 14 December caused a postponement of the ceremony.[2] Not much else was heard about the wedding until it actually took place, on 1 July 1862. Nine months before the death of Prince Albert, Queen Victoria's mother (the Duchess of Kent) had died on 16 March 1861. Then, following the Prince Consort's demise, the bridegroom's family also experienced a loss, and so Queen Victoria commented that the 'Angel of Death' was still following them when the bridegroom's aunt – Mathilde Caroline of Bavaria, wife of the reigning Grand Duke Louis III – died on 25 May 1862; and she pointed out that the impending wedding would be 'even more gloomy'.[3]

With this context of mourning, the wedding took place not in London but on the Isle of Wight. Like the royal weddings at the beginning of the century, it took place 'at home', as it were: in the dining room of Osborne House. All the weddings of Queen Victoria's children were commemorated in large-scale paintings. This, the simplest of them, was captured in a picture by George Housman Thomas, who brings out the intimate, simple atmosphere of the ceremony, while at the same time commemorating the recently departed family members in

---

[1] *London Gazette*, 3 May 1861, p. 1889.

[2] For a more detailed discussion of this see Gerard Noel, *Princess Alice: Queen Victoria's Forgotten Daughter*, first publ. by Constable & Co. in 1974 (Norwich: Michael Russel Publishing, 1992), esp. Chapter 5 (pp. 79–101): 'Marriage in a Death Chamber'.

[3] Queen Victoria to Queen Augusta of Prussia, 26 May 1862, quoted in Queen Victoria, *Further Letters of Queen Victoria; From the Archives of the House of Brandenburg-Prussia*, transl. from the German by Mrs. J. Pudney and Lord Sudley, ed. by Hector Bolitho (London: Thornton Butterworth, 1938), pp. 126–28, here p. 128.

Illustration 7.1: George Housman Thomas, 'The Marriage of Princess Alice, 1st July 1862', oil on canvas 1862–63, *Royal Collection, RCIN 404479*, Royal Collection Trust / © Her Majesty Queen Elizabeth II 2021.

the paintings on the back wall: the Prince Consort prominently in the centre of the large family group, and Queen Victoria's mother in the painting over the door (Illustration 7.1).[4]

As for the previous weddings, the ceremonial was printed – yet, this ceremonial pointed out that the ceremony was performed 'in the strictest privacy'.[5] All the same, the ceremony again took place during daytime, at 'One o'Clock'. It appears that no special copy of the order of service was produced. Sarah Tytler summarized that the Archbishop of York officiated 'for the sick Archbishop of Canterbury' and that 'No gay music, no joy peals of bells, no festive gathering, no concourse of interested spectators celebrated the event.'[6] Thus, the ceremony consisted solely

---

[4] A 'Plan of the Rooms & Disposition of the Company at Osborne, on the occasion of the Marriage [...]', showing the position of the most important guests, survives in *Lna LC 2/81*, inserted between pp. 141 and 142.

[5] Ceremonial 1862a/b, p. 1. For much material on this wedding see *Lna LC 2/81*, pp. 134–50: 'Marriage of / Her Royal Highness The Princess Alice / with His Royal Highness The Prince Louis / of Hesse / July 1st 1862'.

[6] Sarah Tytler, *Life of Her Most Gracious Majesty the Queen*, ed. and with an introduction by Lord Ronald Gower, 3 vols (London: J. S. Virtue & Co., [1897?]), II, pp. 205 and 206.

of the reading of the Prayer Book texts. Queen Victoria wrote in her journal that the archbishop performed the service 'beautifully' – but in a letter to her eldest daughter Victoria, she described the occasion as 'more like a funeral than a wedding'.[7]

From a ceremonial point of view, there was one particularly notable detail. As Queen Victoria recorded, only the archbishop was in the room when she entered, with all the other guests coming in only after her.[8] This was probably done so as to spare the mourning queen the gaze of the assembled guests when entering after them. Indeed, Lady Geraldine Somerset (lady-in-waiting to Princess Augusta of Hesse-Kassel, Duchess of Cambridge) recorded in her diary that 'y:ᵉ Q. had come in first quite alone, to take up her position un=observed'.[9] Similarly, at the end, the queen was to stay behind in the room 'until all present at the Ceremony have withdrawn, and will then retire'.[10]

With its sombre mood, simplicity and privacy, this wedding represented a clear antithesis to the lavish 1858 wedding of the Princess Royal. However, in the very next year, there appeared to some extent to be a return to grand ceremonial: at the wedding of the Prince of Wales.

Albert Edward, Prince of Wales and Princess Alexandra of Denmark, 10 March 1863

Notwithstanding the queen's own wedding in 1840, the most high-profile royal wedding of the Victorian era occurred in 1863 when Prince Albert Edward, Prince of Wales, married Princess Alexandra of Denmark. The preparations and arrangements for the marriage of the heir apparent had begun before Prince Albert's death.[11] However, the Prince Consort's demise altered the character of the wedding decisively and it stood in some contrast to the full-blown state occasion that the 1858 wedding of the Princess Royal had been.

James Munson summarized that the Prince of Wales's wedding saw 'the participation of the popular press for the first time', observing that 'articles and pamphlets poured forth'.[12] Notwithstanding that the press had already accompanied the 1840 wedding of the queen and the 1858 wedding of the Princess Royal, the wedding of the heir to the throne indeed received much attention and was recorded not only in newspapers and magazines but now also in dedicated, independent publications. One very detailed one was by the *Times* correspondent William Howard Russell who recorded the historical background, the preparations, and the ceremony itself:

> *A Memorial of the Marriage of HRH Albert Edward Prince of Wales and HRH Alexandra Princess of Denmark by W H Russell. The Various Events and Bridal Gifts Illustrated by Robert Dudley. Published by Day and Son, London, Lithographers to the Queen & to HRH the Prince of Wales* (London: Day and Son, [1864]).

---

[7] *QJV*, 1 July 1862; and Queen Victoria to Princess Victoria, 2 July 1862, in *Dearest Mama: Letters between Queen Victoria and the Crown Princess of Prussia, 1861–1864*, ed. by Roger Fulford (London: Evans Bros., 1968), pp. 85–86, here p. 85.

[8] *QJV*, 1 July 1862.

[9] *Wra VIC/ADDC6/1/1862-3*, entry for 1 July 1862.

[10] Ceremonial 1862a, p. 2.

[11] See James Munson, 'London en fete: the Last Marriage of a Prince of Wales', *Country Life*, 30 July 1981, pp. 416 and 418, here p. 416. For the political background of this marriage, see still Philip Magnus, *King Edward VII* (London: John Murray, 1964), chapters 3–4.

[12] Munson, 'London', p. 416.

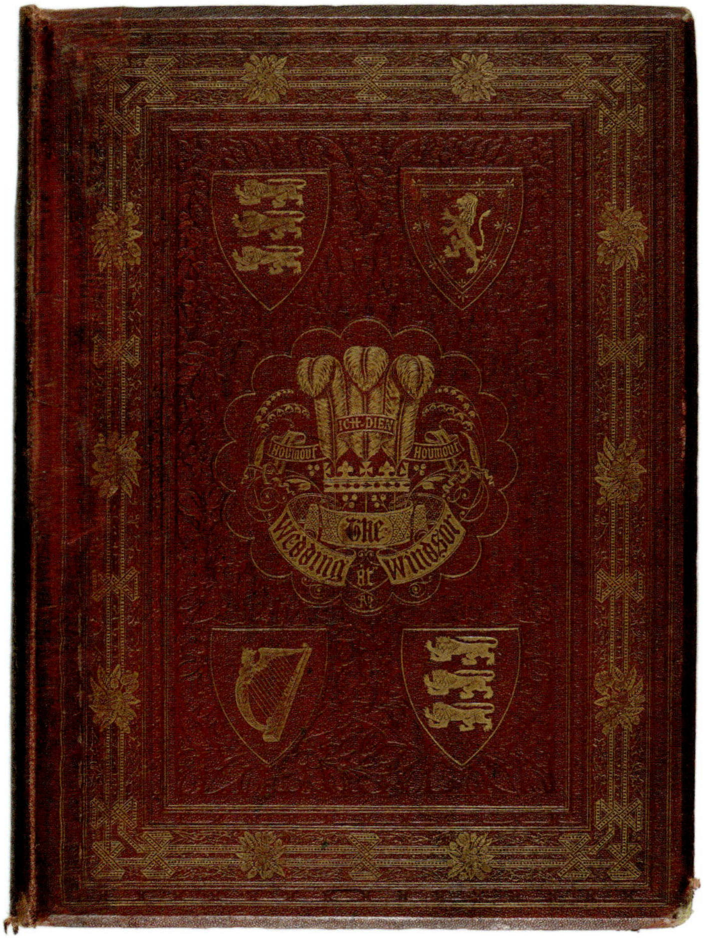

This publication also included many coloured illustrations and it was overall a particularly lavish volume (see Illustration 7.2).[13] In addition, there is a great number of hitherto not used other sources on the planning of the event. All the detailed reporting allows the wedding ceremony to be reconstructed very well.[14]

The Venue

Following the precedents of the most recent royal weddings, this wedding was a daytime wedding. However, one of the most striking features at the time was the choice of venue: the wedding took place at St George's Chapel, Windsor Castle, in 'comparative privacy', as Georgina Battiscombe has put it.[15] There was not much historic precedent for a royal wedding at Windsor: the only earlier example had been Henry I's second wedding, to Adeliza of Louvain in 1121.[16] This wedding would have taken place in some predecessor to the current St George's Chapel, possibly dedicated to St Edward the Confessor.[17] In addition, the wedding of Edward, Prince of Wales, the 'Black Prince', to Joan of Kent in 1361 could also have taken place at least partly at Windsor.[18]

The fact that the wedding of the heir to the throne in 1863 did not take place in the capital met with criticism, which somewhat echoed demands from 1858 for a more public spectacle.[19] John Plunkett has summarized that some newspapers and magazines 'protested against the fact that the marriage was going to be held in the seclusion of St George's Chapel, Windsor, rather than in Westminster Abbey'.[20] Indeed, the commentator in the *News of the World* could 'not understand why the wedding should take place in a little chapel a long way off', which would not give much room for spectators; and he proclaimed that 'Everybody feels that [...] Westminster Abbey is the fitting place' as then the people

Illustration 7.2:
W. H. [William Howard] Russell, *A Memorial of the Marriage of HRH Albert Edward Prince of Wales and HRH Alexandra Princess of Denmark [...]* (London: Day and Son, [1864]), *Royal Collection, RCIN 1055746*, Royal Collection Trust / © Her Majesty Queen Elizabeth II 2021.

---

[13] For details on Russell's background and on his publication see Munson, 'London', p. 416; and John Plunkett, *Queen Victoria: First Media Monarch* (Oxford: Oxford University Press, 2003), p. 230. Illustration 1 3, above, is Plate 20 in Russell's volume.

[14] For a collection of various informative (unidentified) newspaper cuttings in relation to this wedding see *Lna LC 2/81*, pp. 156–74.

[15] Georgina Battiscombe, *Queen Alexandra* (London: Sphere 1972), p. 44.

[16] See Alison Weir, '"Princely Marriage": Royal Weddings from 1066 to 1714', in: Alison Weir, Kate Williams, Sarah Gristwood, Tracy Borman, *The Ring and the Crown: A History of Royal Weddings 1066–2011* (London: Hutchinson, 2011), pp. 9–51, here pp. 16–17.

[17] I am grateful to Kate McQuillian (Archivist & Chapter Librarian at St George's Chapel, Windsor) for alerting me to this and the following.

[18] For this marriage see still John Harvey, *The Black Prince and his Age* (London: Batsford, 1976), p. 102.

[19] For 1858 criticism see Chapter 6, fns 138–39.

[20] Plunkett, *Queen Victoria*, p. 54.

7—The 'Windsor Castle' Weddings: The Mid-Victorians I

could at least 'see the out-door spectacle, and to that extent "assist" at and enjoy the happy occasion'.[21] As Cannadine has pointed out, the satirical magazine *Punch* sarcastically mocked the fact that the wedding was not to take place in London 'but in an obscure village in Berkshire, remarkable only for an old castle and non-sanatory arrangements'.[22] The *Times* argued that it would have liked the wedding to be in the Chapel Royal at St James's, concluding:

> But this is not to be, and it would be idle to conceal the fact that the decision that the marriage shall take place at Windsor has caused a deep and general disappointment in London.[23]

The choice of Windsor for the wedding was obviously due to the queen's being in mourning for her husband and leading a reclusive life, out of the limelight. In early February, the court circular explained:

> By Her Majesty's command the ceremony will be performed in St. George's Chapel, Windsor Castle, in which Chapel the Prince of Wales was christened, and by which arrangement the Queen will be enabled to be present in private which could not under existing circumstances have been the case at the Chapel Royal in London.[24]

In fact, there was also some support for the choice of St George's Chapel. For instance, the widely read *Morning Advertiser* at first criticized the limited size of the chapel:

> For the ordinary purposes of the Court, and for those demands which may be made upon it in a general way, this elegant little edifice is as convenient as it is beautiful: but for great occasions like the present its accommodation is far too limited.[25]

Nevertheless, this paper overall agreed with the choice of venue. It noted that everything 'has been done to enable the largest possible number of persons to witness the imposing ceremony', and concluded:

> It requires but a brief visit to the place to remove from the mind of any thoughtful person all those objections which from time to time have been raised to the selection of St. George's Chapel

Interestingly, the paper referred also to the possibility of choosing, for instance, St Paul's Cathedral, but argued that this 'would have partaken, perhaps, too much of a civic character', explaining that 'In the eyes of a large section of society in this country, and of a still larger section of society in Continental countries, its solemnity and importance would have suffered most materially.' Therefore, the paper judged, apart from the fact that the queen in her widowhood could more easily attend the wedding at Windsor, there was overall 'a peculiar appropriateness in the selection of St. George's Chapel for the performance of the ceremony'. Other publications, such as the *London Journal*, also sympathetically referred to the 'grave reason' for choosing the venue.[26] This journal was ready to defend the choice of Windsor also for other reasons. Without further explanation, it argued that the Chapel at Windsor had stronger 'historical and architectural claims'

---

[21] 'The Politician', *The News of the World*, 8 March 1863, p. 1.

[22] David Cannadine, 'Splendor out of Court: Royal Spectacle and Pageantry in Modern Britain, *c.* 1820–1977', in *Rites of Power: Symbolism, Ritual, and Politics since the Middle Ages*, ed. by Sean Wilentz (Philadelphia: University of Pennsylvania Press, 1985), pp. 206–43, here p. 212. Cannadine quotes from a secondary source that does not give a reference, from Battiscombe, *Queen Alexandra*, p. 44. The original quotation here cited, slightly different to Battiscombe's/Cannadine's version, is from 'A Quiet Affair', *Punch*, 44 (January 1863), p. 49.

[23] 'Marriage of His Royal Highness the Prince of Wales', *Times*, 3 February 1863, p. 9.

[24] 'The Marriage of The Prince of Wales. (From the *Court Circular*.)', *Times*, 5 February 1863, p. 9.

[25] This and the following 'A Visit to St. George's Chapel, Windsor Castle', *The Morning Advertiser*, 7 March 1863, pp. 4–5, here p. 4.

[26] This and the following 'The Royal Wedding', *The London Journal, and Weekly Record of Literature, Science, and Art*, 14 March 1863, pp. 167–68, here p. 167.

Illustration 7.3: 'Marshalling the Procession of the Bride, Temporary Apartments_ St George's Chapel, March 10th, 1863', chromolithograph by Robert Charles Dudley (1864), Plate 16 in Russell, *Memorial*, here from National Portrait Gallery, D33995 © National Portrait Gallery, London.

to the royal wedding than the Chapel Royal in London. Moreover, the Court Circular had – seemingly in defense – explained that the prince had been christened in St George's in 1841, and the *London Journal* remarked that 'his being married in the same building is in accordance with ancient and affectionate English usage'.[27]

For the wedding ceremony, St George's Chapel was modified in several major and remarkable ways. At the time, the main entrance to the Chapel was the much smaller door on the south side: on entering this way, processions had to walk down the south aisle first, in order to go up the central aisle.[28] The present grand wide steps outside the west door were built only several years later, by Sir George Gilbert Scott, completed in 1872.[29] Therefore, a temporary annex was built for the wedding, enabling the processions to enter via the west door.[30] This annex had been planned from early on. On 12 December 1862, the Office of Works was informed:

---

[27] Royal Wedding', *London Journal*, p. 167. For the court circular see above, fn. 24.

[28] For this practice at royal funerals, for instance, see Matthias Range, *British Royal and State Funerals: Music and Ceremonial since Elizabeth I* (Woodbridge: Boydell Press, 2016) [hereinafter *BRSF*], Chapter 5, esp. Illustration 5.3.

[29] See Mark Burch and Maurice Bond, 'The Western Steps of St George's Chapel: An Historical and Archaeological Report', *Report of the Society of the Friends of St George's and the Descendants of the Knights of the Garter* (1981–82), pp. 98–110. I am very grateful to Clare Rider for drawing my attention to this.

[30] For a description of this annex see Russell, *Memorial*, pp. 67–68.

7—The 'Windsor Castle' Weddings: The Mid-Victorians I

Illustration 7.4: 'The Royal Marriage: The Bride Passing up the Nave of St George's Chapel', *ILN*, 28 March 1863, pp. 348–49. Author's collection.

In order to give space for the marshalling of the several Royal Processions which will pass through the Nave into the Choir, it will be necessary that a Temporary Building [added slightly later: 'with Carriage Approaches'] should be constructed outside the Western Entrance to the Chapel, and that 2 or 3 Rooms should be added within, or communicating with, this Building, for the reception of the Bride and Bridegroom, and of other Royal Personages _ […].[31]

This annex was of considerable size and even had a glass roof, as can be seen in a contemporary print included in Russell's volume (Illustration 7.3). At the opening of the annex towards the nave, at the Chapel's west door, there was a velvet curtain that was prominently mentioned in many of the reports and will be discussed later (see also Illustration 7.4).

There were also several changes within St George's Chapel itself. Along the sides of the nave, newly installed temporary seats for the guests 'rose tier above tier', as one paper reported, thus allowing these guests to have a better view of the processions.[32] The *Illustrated London News* in its coverage of the wedding included a lavish double-page image that depicts the bride's procession going up the nave (Illustration 7.4). This shows the arrangement of the temporary tiered seating; moreover, the mentioned velvet curtain at the Chapel entrance is clearly visible.

---

[31] 'Spencer' to 'The First-Commissioner / of Her Majestys Works, &c', 12 December 1862, in *Lna WORK 19/138*, ('4598/62' in top outer corner). For this see also 'Memorandum upon the Worke and Arrangements incidental to the Marriage of H.R.H. The Prince of Wales in 1863 (March 10.th)', in *Lna WORK 21/12/3*.

[32] 'The Marriage Ceremony', *Lloyd's Weekly London Newspaper*, 15 March 1863, pp. 4–5, here p. 4.

More importantly, there were also some permanent changes in the Chapel. The east window over the altar was replaced by 'a magnificent memorial window to the late Prince Consort', and Russell pointed out that this was 'first exhibited' at the wedding.[33] Also, the altar was given a new alabaster reredos, designed by Gilbert Scott, notwithstanding that the 'north and south panels will be merely plaster cast, sufficient time not having been afforded for the completion of the entire work'.[34] Furthermore, the Office of Works was ordered 'To take down the Carved oak Gothic screens on each side of the altar inside the Chapel.'[35] This was done 'for enlarging the Choir space [that is, the space in the quire] & fitting with Seats'.[36] The area in front of and around the altar was raised up by a dais, or platform, to be level with the altar, and covered in rich cloth: this area was invariably called the '*haut pas*' in reports of this and the following weddings.

As in 1862, George Housman Thomas recorded the ceremony in a detailed painting. Rather than a scene during the service, his picture this time shows the very end of the ceremony, with the newly-weds about to leave the Chapel in their joined procession. Thomas thus managed to depict the bridal couple in full frontal view and could at the same time prominently show the important new memorial widow, the new altar, and the temporary arrangements – in particular the curtains covering the as yet unfinished panels on the sides of the altar (Illustration 7.5).

Processions

The published accounts seemingly paid more attention to Princess Alexandra's entrance procession through London than to the actual wedding celebrations.[37] This may simply be explained by the fact that far more people could see the London procession. In Windsor, the wedding participants went the short distance from the upper ward of the Castle down to St George's Chapel in carriages. In contrast to the weddings in the Chapel Royal, however, there was no notable procession for a larger and more general public to behold.

Following the precedents of the weddings since 1840, the bride was again the last to enter. Yet, at this wedding, this oddity in royal protocol did not become quite that obvious: similar to the 1862 wedding at Osborne House, the queen had arrived before most of her family, although now after at least some of the other guests. She famously attended the wedding in Catherine of Aragon's Pew, high up in the north wall on the left over the altar, and Russell observed:

> Her Majesty proceeded privately from Windsor Castle to the Royal Closet in St. George's Chapel, at half-past eleven o'clock. [...] Her Majesty's entrance was observed by all with much respect and sympathy. Every one in the Chapel arose at her presence, and turned towards the Royal Closet, where 'the dim religious light' just permitted the outlines of the Queen's face and figure to be caught at intervals.[38]

---

[33] 'Royal Wedding', *London Journal*; and Russell, *Memorial*, p. 68. For a description of the changes in the Chapel see also 'The Royal Marriage', *ILN*, 21 March 1863, pp. 310–22, here p. 310; and 'Visit to St. George's Chapel', p. 5.

[34] 'Visit to St. George's Chapel', p. 5. See also 'Monthly Intelligence', *Gentleman's Magazine*, 214 (April 1863), pp. 498–510, here p. 505. The same in the near identical 'The Royal Marriage', *Annual Register* [...] *1863*, n.s. (1864), pp. 42–50, here p. 44. For the changes and preparations in the Chapel see also 'St George's Chapel, Windsor', *Daily Telegraph*, 6 March 1863, p. 3.

[35] 'Windsor Castle / S.ᵗ Georges Chapel. / Memo' sent to the Office of Works by 'W. Haie', dated '22ⁿᵈ January 1863.', in *Lna WORK 19/138* ('276/63' in top outer corner).

[36] *Lna WORK 21/12/3*, fol. 2. For the practical arrangements in the Chapel see also two letters in *Wsg XVII.30.2*.

[37] For this London procession, and the criticism of its lack of organization, see Munson, 'London', p. 416; and Plunkett, *Queen Victoria*, pp. 54–55. For a contemporary discussion of this procession see 'Topics of the Day: English Loyalty', *The Spectator*, 7 March 1863, p. 1712. I am grateful to John Plunkett for pointing me to this source.

[38] Russell, *Memorial*, p. 72.

7—The 'Windsor Castle' Weddings: The Mid-Victorians I

Notwithstanding the reported observation of her entrance 'with much respect and sympathy', the queen's arrival was not announced in any way. She simply appeared, but did not make a ceremonial entrance in procession, as the correspondent of the *News of the World* recorded vividly:

> Suddenly there is just a perceptible movement—a kind of consciousness that something has occurred which tells at once that the Queen is either coming or has come, and all eyes are quietly directed towards the quaint old pew in the wall. In another instant the Queen herself appears, [...].[39]

The same account stressed that the queen was not very visible; she stood 'at the window of the Royal pew, a little withdrawn from general gaze, and only to be seen at all by those on the opposite side of the choir'. In this context another detail is worth mentioning. Apart from the private 1843 wedding at Buckingham Palace and the reclusive 1862 wedding at Osborne House, this was the first (major) royal wedding, where the sword of state was not seen. It was never to come back. In a way, then, the queen was not ceremonially present as the sovereign, not 'in state'.

Illustration 7.5: George Housman Thomas, 'The Marriage of Albert Edward, Prince of Wales, 10 March 1863', oil on canvas before 2 May 1864, *Royal Collection, RCIN 406997*, Royal Collection Trust / © Her Majesty Queen Elizabeth II 2021.

---

[39] This and the following 'Marriage of The Prince of Wales and the Princess Alexandra', *The News of the World*, 15 March 1863, p. 2. Same in 'Marriage of The Prince of Wales and the Princess Alexandra', *The Dundee Courier & Argus*, 12 March 1863, p. [3].

The processions that entered the Chapel from the temporary annex followed a scheme adapted from that used at St James's Palace. The heralds had a distinct role in leading these processions, as was noted in one of the detailed published accounts.[40] Together with the heralds, 'The State Drummers and Trumpeters took their places at the western door, close to the velvet curtain, the kettle-drums being placed on the backs of tabarded bearers.'[41] After having led one procession to the quire entrance, they all returned to the west entrance to await the arrival of the next one, which they then accompanied in the same way. It is intriguing that the kettle-drums were still put 'on the backs of tabarded bearers' – even when the procession was merely in the limited, confined space of the nave, where they could easily have remained stationary. It was apparently important that they moved, and could be seen to move, in the procession.

The proceedings overall evoked associations with a stage performance. The mentioned 'velvet curtain', described in the account in *Lloyd's Weekly London Newspaper* as 'a heavy drapery of purple silk, patterned with gold', separated the west entrance from the temporary annex.[42] With reference to this curtain, the *Illustrated London News* in its wording likened the ceremony to a theatre performance:

> The crimson curtains were lifted up, and the Queen's guests made their appearance and proceeded slowly down the nave.[43]

Indeed, for the newly-weds' leaving the Chapel, the same account observed that 'the curtains dropped for the last time on the actors in this Imperial pageant'.

The first procession to enter was that of the royal guests.[44] It does not seem to be known whether this was accompanied by any music. However, for the following procession of members of the royal family, it was reported that there was 'a little while' of 'silence', before 'on a sudden, that purple curtain was thrown open; the trumpets blared forth a silvery peal to the roll of the kettle-drums', the procession entered and walked up the nave. As before, there is no information on what the trumpets and drums played – with the best reference being to their 'blowing lustily from their unraised throats the exultant strains'. Mirroring the proceedings at St James's, the ceremonial stipulated that the drums and trumpets were to file off before the entrance into the quire and would 'continue playing until the Procession has entered, when Beethoven's Triumphal March will be played by the Organ and by Her Majesty's Band'.[45] Passing 'to the right and left', they eventually returned 'to the closed curtain at the end of the nave'.[46] The sources refer to Beethoven's Triumphal March without further details but this was most probably the march from his *Tarpeja*, WoO 2a. At least Russell referred to it ominously as the '"Wedding March" from Beethoven'.[47]

---

[40] See *An Historical Record of the Marriage of H. R. H. Albert Edward, Prince of Wales with Alexandra Caroline, Princess of Denmark* (London: Darton and Hodge, 1863), p. 48.

[41] Russell, *Memorial*, p. 74. See also 'The Marriage Ceremony', *Lloyd's Weekly London Newspaper*, 15 March 1863, pp. 4–5, here p. 4.

[42] 'Marriage Ceremony', *Lloyd's Weekly*, p. 4.

[43] This and the following 'Royal Marriage', *ILN* (1863), p. 311.

[44] This and the following 'Marriage Ceremony', *Lloyd's Weekly*, p. 4.

[45] Ceremonial 1863a, p. 8.

[46] 'Marriage Ceremony', *Lloyd's Weekly*, p. 4. For the trumpets and drums playing marches during the processions, up to the quire entrance, see also Russell, *Memorial*, pp. 80–92.

[47] Russell, *Memorial*, p. 88. Beethoven's march is also mentioned in *Historical Record*, p. 48, and 'Marriage Ceremony', *Lloyd's Weekly*, p. 4.

7—The 'Windsor Castle' Weddings: The Mid-Victorians I

For the procession of the bridegroom, Queen Victoria noted: 'There was a pause & then the trumpets sounded again & our Boy [...] entered.'[48] Russell recorded that 'the trumpets rang out a louder and more florid triumph, the drums rolled with resonant clatter, and forth from the Hall issued the Procession of the Bridegroom, preceded by the Drums and Trumpets and the Serjeant Trumpeter'.[49] Again, they accompanied the procession up to the entrance to the quire, and then 'as drums and trumpets cease, the march from *Athalie* takes up the joyous strains'.[50] The printed ceremonial explained that this was the march from Mendelssohn's oratorio *Athalie* – today better known as the 'War March of the Priests'.[51] In the same way as for Beethoven's march, some accounts referred to Mendelssohn's work as 'Wedding March'.[52] The accounts did either not discriminate properly, or many a march played at weddings was simply described as 'Wedding March' – it was, after all, a more appropriate title than 'War March'.

Lady Elvey, the wife George Elvey – the organist of St George's who was overall responsible for the music at the wedding – later recorded that her husband 'played Mendelssohn's march from "Athalie"', as though it had been played by him on the organ only.[53] Other reports, however, make it clear that this march was performed by both the 'organ and the band aloft'.[54]

One account emphasized particularly that the bridegroom's entrance into the quire was 'the signal for the first music in the day's programme'.[55] Similarly, the *Illustrated London News* reported that up to the bridegroom's arrival, 'there had been no music heard in the chapel except the successive fanfares of the trumpets as the different processions appeared'.[56] However, this contradicts the clear stipulation in the printed ceremonial and also those reports that mention Beethoven's march for the procession of the royal family: perhaps the stipulated march was indeed omitted and some reports simply followed the printed ceremonial, while others correctly omitted it in their account. This would then mean that there had been no music at all to accompany the arrivals in the quire of the earlier guests, royal and otherwise. At any rate, Mendelssohn's march continued 'until the sound of the trumpets announced the approach of the bride'.[57]

The entrance of the bride, in the fourth and last procession, was a moment that had been eagerly awaited – was 'the leading point of interest in the ceremonial of the day', as one account called it enthusiastically.[58] The reports of the ceremony described this moment in much detail.

---

[48] *QVJ*, 10 March 1863.

[49] Russell, *Memorial*, p. 89.

[50] 'Marriage Ceremony', *Lloyd's Weekly*, p. 4.

[51] Ceremonial 1863a/b, p. 12; Russell, *Memorial*, p. 90. See also *QVJ*, 10 March 1863.

[52] 'Marriage Ceremony', *Lloyd's Weekly*, p. 5; *Historical Record*, p. 49; and the untitled report in *Harper's New Monthly Magazine*, 26 (New York: Harper & Brothers, 1863), pp. 850–53, here p. 852.

[53] 'Lady' [Mary] Elvey, *Life and Reminiscences of George J. Elvey [...] Late Organist to H. M. Queen Victoria, and Forty-seven Years Organist of St. George's Chapel, Windsor* (London: Sampson Low, Marston & Company Ltd, 1894), p. 190.

[54] Russell, *Memorial*, p. 90. See also 'Royal Marriage', *ILN* (1863), p. 311; and *A Chapter from the History of England in the Twenty-sixth Year of the Reign of Our Blessed Sovereign Lady Queen Victoria, March 1863* (London: Emily Faithfull, 1863), p. 88.

[55] *Chapter from the History*, p. 88.

[56] 'Marriage of The Prince of Wales and Princess Alexandra of Denmark', Supplement to *ILN*, 14 March 1863, pp. 278–87, here p. 279.

[57] 'Marriage of The Prince of Wales', Supplement to *ILN*, p. 279.

[58] *Chapter from the History*, p. 88.

One report, with wording that was very similar in other accounts, noted for the bride's entrance into the nave:

> At last, with a great clangour of trumpets, which at first are muffled into a rich indistinctness behind the curtains, the long looked-for procession of the Bride enters [...].[59]

The prominent mentioning of the music is particularly notable. Similarly, Russell implied that the music that announced the bride was the most notable so far:

> With upraised heads and puffing cheeks the Trumpeters blew their loudest flourish, and the Drummers filled the air, from floor to mantled roof, with the joyous roll of the kettle-drums.[60]

Queen Victoria recorded that, once the bride's procession had reached the entrance to the quire, 'the Band' played 'Handel's Processional March'.[61] The ceremonial, rather unusually giving such details, stipulates Handel's march from *Joseph* to be 'played by the Organ, and by Her Majesty's Band', and Russell observed that 'the music [that is, the band] and the organ' were 'in exquisite unison', playing very well together.[62] The fact that this was the same march that had been played at the 1858 wedding for the entrance of the bridegroom highlights that these marches had no specific connotations.

Service and Music

The service itself accorded with the outlines of previous royal weddings – following the Prayer Book, with some ceremonial elaboration through music.[63] As in 1858, the order of service, with the unaltered, impersonal Prayer Book wording, was specially printed, again lavishly bound, in red velvet with gold decorations.[64] The 1863 copy, however, has not only the date on the front, but on the back shows the interwoven letters 'A' and 'E' – for 'Albert Edward', and possibly also for 'Alexandra' – with the Prince of Wales's crest above (Illustration 7.6). The 1858 copy had had a blank back, and the 1863 order of service was thus at least somewhat more personalized.

As in 1858, the specially-bound order of service did not include any details on the music and a lavishly decorated sheet with the texts of the vocal pieces was printed separately (see Illustration 7.6).[65] It is not known, however, how many of the congregation had access to either, the order of service or the programme of music. A little anecdote recorded by Lord Granville shows that not all even of the more exalted guests had copies and had to follow the service in a copy of the Prayer Book, some apparently even bringing their own:

> Lady Palm: forgot her prayer book. Palma Vecchio [Viscount Palmerston, the Prime Minister] scrambled over the pews and after extraordinary acrobatic feats brought her three—which she thought at least two more than she required.[66]

---

[59] *Historical Record*, p. 49. Similar 'Marriage Ceremony', *Lloyd's Weekly*, p. 5. See also the report in *Harper's New Monthly*, p. 852.

[60] Russell, *Memorial*, p. 90.

[61] *QVJ*, 10 March 1863.

[62] Ceremonial 1863a, p 14; Russell, *Memorial*, p. 92 (for this see also, for instance, 'Monthly Intelligence', p. 506).

[63] Compare the quotation below, in Chapter 11, with fn. 22.

[64] OS 1863.

[65] Other copies of this sheet are in the *Royal Collection, RCIN 1054578*; in *Wsg X.33/5/2/1*; several copies in *Lna LC 2/84*; and also in *Wra RA F&V/WED/1863*.

[66] Granville to Duchess, 10 March 1863, in *'My Dear Duchess': Social and Political Letters to the Duchess of Manchester, 1858–1869*, ed. by A. L. Kennedy (London: John Murray, 1956), pp. 210–11, here p. 210. See also the picture of the 1871 wedding of Princess Louise, Illustration 7.13 below.

7—The 'Windsor Castle' Weddings: The Mid-Victorians I

The music of the service was rather elaborate. Russel, in his detailed account, pointed out:

> The musical arrangements were entrusted to Mr. Anderson, the director of her Majesty's private band; and the performance was conducted by Dr. Elvey (the organist of St. George's Chapel) and Mr. Anderson.[67]

Anderson may well have been entrusted with the 'musical arrangements' of the service, but his responsibility applied probably only in a more general sense, referring especially to all the instrumental music that was played by the band under his direction. For, in the end it was George Elvey, who had been organist of St George's since 1835, who 'took charge of the musical part of the service', as his aforementioned wife later recalled.[68] In fact, it had been Elvey who had broken the Chapel Royal's traditional precedence at such events at Windsor, with his being responsible for the music at the funeral of Queen Adelaide in 1849 and then especially that of Prince Albert in 1861.[69]

In this context it is noteworthy that, even though the Chapel Royal choir took part at the wedding, one account stated without further explanation that its organist, Sir George Smart, who he had been 'honoured with an invitation', was 'unavoidably prevented from attending'.[70] It appears that he was also not much, if at all, involved in the planning of the music of the service.

Illustration 7.6: 'The Form of Solemnization of Matrimony: St. George's Chapel, Windsor Castle March 10, 1863' [= OS 1863], with the separate printed music text sheet (London: Harrison & Sons, 1863), *Royal Collection, RCIN 1054576, 1054577 and 1054578*, Royal Collection Trust / © Her Majesty Queen Elizabeth II 2021.

---

[67] Russell, *Memorial*, p. 70. Almost identical in the unidentified report in *Lna LC 2/81*, p. 166.

[68] Lady Elvey, *Life and Reminiscences*, p. 89.

[69] See Range, *BRSF*, p. 237.

[70] Unidentified newspaper cutting in *Lna LC 2/81*, p. 166.

167

British Royal Weddings

Once the bride had arrived, 'all music had ceased as the party stood around the altar'.[71] As one account put it, there was 'a solemn silence – a pause of expectation'.[72] This was broken by the performance of a chorale, as in 1858 basically functioning as an introit; and as in 1858, this had a specially written text of 'appropriate words' by Thomas Oliphant, again beginning 'This Day'.[73] The fact that this had two stanzas (only one in 1858) may explain why some reports called it 'a long chorale'.[74]

Many reports pointed out that the music of this chorale had originally been composed by Prince Albert, without giving more details. The metre of the text matches 'With Glory clad, with Strength array'd', a four-part setting in E major 'Adapted & Arranged by Eliz.[th] Masson' and published in an edition of the prince's *Vocal Compositions* in the previous year.[75] This arrangement was based on one of the prince's early compositions: his *Morgengebet*, or 'Morning Prayer' for solo voice and piano accompaniment, to the German text 'O wunderbares tiefes Schweigen' by Joseph von Eichendorff – which had first been included in the 1838 German edition of the prince's songs.[76] Two years later this had been published with translation in two English editions.[77] About twenty years after the wedding, the edition of Prince Albert's *Collected Compositions*, included both his Eichendorff setting and then again the same as 'Chorale in F', now to the text 'In Life's gay Morn', in a setting for four voices slightly different from Masson's.[78] Bernard Denvir suggested that this chorale, Prince Albert's 'most considerable composition', was used and was 'given its first performance' at this wedding.[79] In an adapted form (flattening out the offbeats) it became known as the hymn tune 'Gotha' and at the time of the 1885 wedding of Princess Beatrice, T. Percy M. Betts stated in an article on 'Marriage Music' that 'The Prince Consort's chorale, "Gotha," was, we believe, intended for a wedding [...].'[80] Yet, this idea is clearly contradicted by the chorale's earlier incarnation as an Eichendorff song.

At the wedding, notwithstanding the mentioned moment of 'solemn silence' in between, the chorale followed on directly from Handel's march from *Joseph*. This is in D major, and the introit-chorale was therefore probably sung in the same key: the arrangement used at the wedding, with Oliphant's text, may have been similar to that shown in Figure 7.1.

---

[71] *Historical Record*, p. 51. Same in 'Marriage Ceremony', *Lloyd's Weekly*, p. 5.

[72] *Harper's New Monthly*, p. 852.

[73] 'Marriage of The Prince of Wales', Supplement to *ILN*, p. 279; and the printed texts sheet (see fn. 65). Full text also quoted in Russell, *Memorial*, p. 92.

[74] Lady Elvey, *Life and Reminiscences*, p. 191. Same in 'Royal Marriage', *ILN* (1863), p. 311.

[75] Prince Albert, *The Vocal Compositions of His Royal Highness the Prince Consort* (London: C. Lonsdale, [1862]), pp. 28–32. Masson's arrangement was also published on its own: see the undated edition in *Lbl H.2100.(2)*.

[76] See Thomas Betzwieser, '"Ein lang gehegter Wunsch": Prinz Albert als Komponist in der Bonner Studienzeit', *Die Studien des Prinzen Albert an der Universität Bonn (1837–1838)*, ed. by Franz Bosbach (Berlin: Walter de Gruyter, 2010), pp. 187–218, here p. 211.

[77] Prince Albert, *Musical Compositions of His Royal Highness The Prince Albert, with the Original Words and Music from the Authentic German Edition and an English Adaptation by William Ball* (London: Printed and sold by C. Lonsdale, [1840]), no. 8/pp. 20–23 ('How Wond'rous Is this Soulfelt Hour'/'O wunderbares tiefes Schwingen [*recte* Schweigen]!'); and *Songs and Ballads, Written and Set to Music by Their Royal Highnesses Albert and Ernest, Princes of Saxe Coburg-Gotha*, transl. from the original German by G. G. Richardson (London: Henry Colburn, 1840), pp. 36–37 ('How Sweet This Hour of Pure Devotion'/'O wunderbares tiefes Schwingen [*recte* Schweigen]!').

[78] Prince Albert, *The Collected Compositions of His Royal Highness, The Prince Consort*, ed. by W. G. Cusins (London: Metzler & Co., [1882?]), pp. 7 and 218–19.

[79] Bernard Denvir, 'Albert the Musician', *Musical Times*, 94 (1953), pp. 527–28, here p. 527.

[80] T. Percy M. Betts, 'Marriage Music', *Graphic*, special wedding issue, 27 July 1885, pp. 20–21.

7—The 'Windsor Castle' Weddings: The Mid-Victorians I

Figure 7.1: Prince Albert, *Chorale*; here from the 1862 arrangement by Elizabeth Masson (see fn. 75), but transposed down to D major, and with the two verses of Oliphant's specially written text for the 1863 wedding.

This day, with joyful heart and voice,
To Heaven be raised a nation's prayer;
Almighty Father, deign to grant
Thy blessing to the wedded pair!

So shall no clouds of sorrow dim
The sunshine of their early days;
But happiness, in endless round,
Shall still encompass all their ways.

With the inclusion of an introit, the service followed the example of the 1858 wedding with its opening chorale – then possibly introduced by the late Prince Consort. Russell's account emphasized: 'All remained standing during the performance of the chorale.'[81] This particular attention gave the music more gravitas and turned the performance itself into a veritable ritual.
Indeed, one important aspect of this particular chorale was its summoning the memory of the Prince Consort: with the singing of this chorale, Prince Albert was not only visually recalled in the recent memorial window over the altar, but he was also audibly present, as it were, with his very own music. This was apparently very effective and was much commented on in the reports of the ceremony. The correspondent of the *News of the World* described the scene in a particularly detailed way – giving a high-class example of the power of music at such emotionally-laden occasions. Referring to the 'exquisitely soft music of this chant, at once solemn and sorrowful', the correspondent observed attentively:

> It may have been this, or the associations and lifelong memories called up by the scene beneath her, but certain it is that as the hymn commenced Her Majesty drew back from the window of the pew, and, after an effort to conceal her emotion, gave way to her tears and almost sobbed, nor did she throughout the rest of the ceremony entirely recover her composure.[82]

The queen herself noted in her journal that 'Dearest Alberts Chorale was sung, which affected me much'.[83] Lady Geraldine Somerset recorded that the singing of this 'most beautiful, most touching' chorale by the Prince Consort 'upset his poor family terribly, they all, all y:e P.sses as well as y:e Q. cried much'.[84] Similarly, Lord Granville in his description of the service for the Duchess of Manchester recalled that, at the beginning of the chorale, the queen 'gave a look upwards, which spoke volumes'.[85]

---

[81] Russell, *Memorial*, p. 92.

[82] 'Marriage of The Prince of Wales', *News of the World*. Similar in 'Marriage Ceremony', *Lloyd's Weekly*, p. 5.

[83] *QVJ*, 10 March 1863.

[84] *Wra RA VIC/ADDC6/1/1862-3*, entry for 10 March 1863.

[85] Granville to Duchess of Manchester, 10 March 1863, in *'My Dear Duchess'*, p. 210.

The renowned Swedish opera singer Jenny Lind, by then retired from the stage for several years, famously sang at this wedding. The *Gentleman's Magazine* recorded that, in the performance of the chorale, 'the ringing notes of Jenny Lind's voice came out clear and strong, rising superior to all other sounds'.[86] However, as in 1858, the chorale was sung 'by the choir', as Lady Elvey noted.[87] This would mean that Lind joined in the top line but did not sing a solo. Michael Budds has referred to the 'special relationship' between Queen Victoria and the singer, noting that she did curiously not mention Lind's singing in her account of the wedding.[88] Considering the emphasis in the above reports, including the queen's own, on how touched and affected she had been by the performance of the chorale, her not mentioning the singer is all the more surprising.

For the psalm following the vows and the blessing of the newly-weds, a list of the wedding music published by the *Times* before the event included 'Grand Chant for 67th Psalm', without mentioning a composer (which it does for the other pieces).[89] This is the same in the printed ceremonial, and another detailed account also reported that the psalm was 'sung to the Grand Chant'.[90] As in 1858, the psalm was most probably sung the 'Grand Chant' by Pelham Humfrey. (see Figure 6.2, above).

This seemingly simple, straightforward musical item obviously produced a remarkable effect. The *Gentleman's Magazine* reported that 'it was chanted by the full choir in a very effective and most impressive manner'.[91] Russell's account also observed that the psalm was 'chanted by the choir with so much deep expression that tears fell from many an eye'.[92] Yet another account went a bit further and claimed that the 'solemn strains' of the psalm were 'like a relief to what seemed almost the overwrought feelings of all within the Choir as the words went pealing softly through both Nave and Aisle'.[93]

For the end of the ceremony, Queen Victoria noted that the newly-weds 'left together, immediately followed by all the others'.[94] During this procession, the choir and musicians performed the Hallelujah Chorus from Beethoven's oratorio *The Mount of Olives*.[95] It is not known who introduced Beethoven's music to this wedding, with his Triumphal March having been scheduled for the entrance of the royal family. Moreover, the unprecedented choice of a choral piece for the recessional procession is remarkable. This has not been repeated at another British royal wedding. All the same, in 1863, the choral piece accompanying the recess heightened another fact: as will be further discussed below, the service did probably not include an anthem. It is feasible that the lack of an anthem was the reason for choosing a choral piece for this procession, especially as this would also provide an explanation for why Mendelssohn's march — which, after all, the late Prince Consort had included in 1858 — was not repeated.

---

[86] 'Monthly Intelligence', p. 507. For Lind's singing at this wedding see also fn. 106.

[87] Lady Elvey, *Life and Reminiscences*, p. 191. See also, for instance, 'Marriage of The Prince of Wales', Supplement to *ILN*, p. 279.

[88] Michael Joe Budds, 'Music at the Court of Queen Victoria: A Study of Music in the Life of the Queen and her Participation in the Musical Life of her Time', 3 vols (unpublished doctoral dissertation, University of Iowa, 1987), I, p. 273.

[89] 'The Marriage of The Prince of Wales', *Times*, 6 March 1863, p. 9.

[90] Ceremonial 1863a/b, p. 15; and unidentified newspaper cutting in *Lna LC 2/81*, pp. 165–66, here p. 166.

[91] 'Monthly Intelligence', p. 507. Same in 'The Royal Marriage', *Annual Register*, p. 47.

[92] Russell, *Memorial*, p. 94.

[93] *Historical Record*, p. 53. Same in 'Marriage Ceremony', *Lloyd's Weekly*, p. 5.

[94] *QVJ*, 10 March 1863.

[95] Ceremonial 1863a/b, p. 15; *QVJ*, 10 March 1863; and 'Monthly Intelligence', p. 507.

7—The 'Windsor Castle' Weddings: The Mid-Victorians I

Another detail regarding the couple's leaving procession is noteworthy. In analogy to the entrance processions, the couple were, from the entrance to the quire through the nave, preceded by drums and trumpets, heralds, ministers and other officials walking in front of them; and at least one report noted 'the trumpets sounding the wedding fanfare through the nave'.[96] This observation is somewhat curious, as this trumpet fanfare would then have sounded on top of Beethoven's Hallelujah Chorus – but maybe the report was confused by the music of the chorus with its trumpet sounds. Whether they sounded or not, however, the presence of the trumpets and drums ahead of the procession would have served as a strong visual status symbol, akin to the heralds.

Anthem

Elvey's widow later recorded that 'on the great occasion' of this wedding her husband 'had specially composed a wedding anthem, "Sing unto God."' and she described it in some detail; according to this, it was a grand anthem for full orchestra and choir, with an orchestral symphony followed by six movements.[97] This description comes at the beginning of her account of the wedding service and therefore seems to indicate that the anthem was also performed during the service, although it is notable that she does not explain that the anthem actually came at any part in the service.

Elvey's anthem does not seem to be referred to in any other source for this wedding. Moreover, the printed sheet with the texts of the vocal pieces includes merely the chorale, the psalm, and the Hallelujah Chorus, but no information about an anthem.[98] Incidentally, neither the music nor the text of Elvey's anthem appear to have survived.

After all, it is possible that Lady Elvey in her recollection did not refer to a performance of the anthem at the wedding itself, but that the anthem had been a topical offering, perhaps performed at another occasion. Earlier on, she had recorded merely that the anthem had been 'specially composed [...] in honour of the marriage', but not that it was actually performed at the wedding service.[99] Following on from her detailed description of the anthem, the next paragraph begins 'At the ceremony Dr. Elvey wore his robes as a doctor of music' – and this might indicate that the previous passage did in fact not refer to 'the ceremony'.[100] Later on she records that, at a garden party, 'A year or two afterwards', the Prince of Wales thanked Elvey 'for the anthem he had composed for his wedding'.[101] It is noteworthy that this again mentions the composition, but not performance of the anthem. Therefore, in light of the lack of evidence of a performance of the anthem at the wedding service, this particular wording is again ambiguous and could refer to an anthem that had been given a separate performance at another time – or indeed to a composition that had not been performed at all.

---

[96] Russell, *Memorial*, pp. 94–95. and 'Royal Marriage', *ILN* (1863), p. 311.

[97] For this and the following see Lady Elvey, *Life and Reminiscences*, pp. 189–90. A longer extract of her detailed description of the anthem is reproduced in Appendix B 7.1.

[98] For the printed sheet see fn. 65 and Illustration 7.6.

[99] Lady Elvey, *Life and Reminiscences*, p. 125.

[100] Lady Elvey, *Life and Reminiscences*, p. 190.

[101] Lady Elvey, *Life and Reminiscences*, p. 191. Edmund H. Fellowes mentioned an anthem 'composed for the Prince of Wales's marriage'; see his *Organists and Masters of the Choristers of St. George's Chapel in Windsor Castle*, 2nd edn with addenda to 1979 by M. F. Bond (Windsor: Oxley and Son, 1979), p. 76. Yet, he may simply have referred to Lady Elvey's record.

British Royal Weddings

Practical Arrangements

The practical arrangements for the music are well documented by Russell:

> The musicians and chorus consisted of Her Majesty's private band, the choirs of the Chapel Royal, St. James's Palace; St. George's Chapel, Windsor; Her Majesty's Private Chapel, with several additional vocal and instrumental performers, amounting to one hundred and fifty.[102]

Lady Elvey recorded that 'The organ was supplemented by a complete orchestra, led by Mr. Anderson, the director of Her Majesty's private band.'[103] Anderson was paid £257 7s. 6d. for 'Music', and the surviving records provide more details on the musicians.[104] The choir consisted of seventeen gentlemen and ten boys from the Chapel Royal; twelve gentlemen and fourteen boys from St George's; an unnumbered group of gentlemen and boys 'of the Private Chapel' (about which generally not much is known); three gentlemen and four boys of a 'Professional Chorus'; and finally '50 Amateurs Chorus' who did not receive any payment.[105]

Lady Elvey recorded that the 'considerable' number of additional singers consisted 'both of male and female voices', especially listing the aforementioned Jenny Lind among 'the lady vocalists'.[106] It is an intriguing side-note that — notwithstanding the ominous 'two females not in dress' at the wedding of Queen Victoria in 1840 — this would have been the first and, as it were, the only royal wedding to include female singers in the regular choir.

The records list payments for forty-eight 'Instrumental Performers'.[107] In total then — with more than 110 singers, and forty-eight instrumentalists — there were slightly more than the 'one hundred and fifty' performers mentioned by Russell. In addition, payment is recorded for eight trumpeters and one 'Kettle Drummer'.[108] At least one report mentioned 'Mr. Goss presiding at the organ' during the psalm.[109] This most probably refers to John Goss, organist of St Paul's Cathedral, who — as already seen — may have taken part at the 1858 wedding.[110]

Lady Elvey described that 'the choir was placed on the righthand side of the organ, in the open loft between the nave and the choir'.[111] However, a 'Memo' from the Office of Works, including details on the temporary constructions in St George's Chapel, stipulated:

> To Erect two galleries for the Choristers and Band [added slightly later: 'and Queen's Servants'] at the south and north sides of the Nave by the Organ Loft for the accommodation of 150 performers.[112]

A later article on Elvey also recorded that for this wedding 'a large orchestra was placed in the South transept of the Chapel', possibly referring to the South aisle.[113] Acoustically, the congregation in the nave would thus have been well integrated in the proceedings.

---

[102] Russell, *Memorial*, p. 70. Almost identical in the unidentified report in *Lna LC 2/81*, p. 166.

[103] Lady Elvey, *Life and Reminiscences*, p. 190.

[104] For this and the following see the recorded expenditure on the music in *Lna LC 2/83*, index and fol. 1ʳ.

[105] The names of the regular members of the choirs were recorded in 'The Musical Service', *The Morning Advertiser*, 9 March 1863, p. 3 (transcr. in Appendix B 7.2).

[106] Lady Elvey, *Life and Reminiscences*, p. 190.

[107] *Lna LC 2/83*, fol. 1ʳ.

[108] *Lna LC 2/83*, fol. 1ᵛ. They had two rehearsals.

[109] Unidentified newspaper cutting in *Lna LC 2/81*, pp. 163–66, here p. 166.

[110] See Chapter 6, fn. 223–25.

[111] Lady Elvey, *Life and Reminiscences*, p. 190.

[112] 'Memo', 'Windsor Castle / 13ᵗʰ January 1863' ('152/63' in top outer corner), in *Lna WORK 19/138*.

[113] 'Sir George Job Elvey', *The Musical Herald*, 550 (January 1894), pp. 3–7, here p. 5.

7—The 'Windsor Castle' Weddings: The Mid-Victorians I

Russell detailed that the guns sounded 'Just before the second blessing' and 'announced the news of the termination of the Ceremony to the crowd outside'.[114] However, the guns had not been meant to sound until *after* the blessing, at the very end of the ceremony, and another account recorded that the sound of the guns and bells confused the musicians:

> Misled for a moment, the Queen's band began tuning their instruments, and even the organ gave one or two involuntary spirts and whistles, as if anxious to lead in the race of harmony. It was premature, however, and there was a gentle hush, which restored the former silence, when the Primate was heard concluding the exhortation.[115]

A few days before the wedding, the *Times* had predicted: 'The service will occupy exactly 50 minutes.'[116] It claimed that 'The length of time occupied by the ceremony is chiefly caused by the music that has to be performed', including a list of six pieces. However, three of these were the marches accompanying the entrance processions, and one was the recessional. Regarding the remaining two, another account explained that the Prince Consort's 'Chorale' was to be sung 'while the procession was arranging itself for the marriage service' and the psalm during the couple's procession to the altar for the blessing.[117] Thus, all six of the listed pieces were covering the proceedings and had there been no music, the ceremony would have been barely any shorter. According to Russell, the service eventually took over an hour: it 'commenced at a quarter to one o'clock, and was concluded at five minutes to two o'clock'.[118] Queen Victoria would have been sitting in her pew for quite some time before the service began: as seen earlier, she is reported to have 'proceeded' to the Chapel at half past eleven.[119] All the same, it appears that the length of the overall ceremony was drawn out by unexpectedly long intervals between the entrance processions. The bridegroom's procession began 'Precisely at twelve o'clock', but the bride's approach to the Chapel was announced by the 'drums and trumpets' only at 'twenty minutes to one'.[120] The Earl of Clarendon referred to the bridegroom's long wait for his bride, amusingly suggesting an interpretation reminiscent of a modern-day cinema film:

> The P: of Wales waited for The Pss: more than 10 minutes at the altar wh: was rather trying & people began to wonder if the Bride was coy & to hope she had not changed her mind.[121]

Regarding the length of the service, another account recorded that the newly-weds returned from the Chapel 'at twenty-five minutes past one o'clock', indicating that the service took a mere forty minutes.[122] Given that there was not much in service, the latter sounds plausible. As for the royal weddings in the Chapel Royal, the signing of the register took place distinctly after the service, back in the royal apartments in the Castle (see Illustration 1.3).[123] Queen Victoria noted that this 'took a very long time' but it is not known that there was any background music.[124]

---

[114] Russell, *Memorial*, p. 94.

[115] *Historical Record*, p. 53.

[116] 'Marriage of The Prince of Wales', *Times*.

[117] 'Marriage of The Prince of Wales', Supplement to *ILN*, p. 279.

[118] Russell, *Memorial*, p. 94.

[119] See above, with fn. 38.

[120] *Chapter from the History,* pp. 86 and 89.

[121] Clarendon to Duchess, 10 March 1863, in *'My Dear Duchess'*, p. 214.

[122] *Historical Record*, p. 54.

[123] For the signing at the Chapel Royal weddings of Queen Victoria and of the Princess Royal see the entries in *QVJ*, for 10 February 1840 and 25 January 1858.

[124] *QVJ*, 10 March 1863.

Britain Royal Weddings

Windsor Elaboration

Overall, the 1863 wedding displayed some intriguing contradictions. Even though the ceremony at Windsor was comparatively seclusive and remote, the service itself was rather spectacular – with St George's Chapel being much more spacious and grander than the small Chapel Royal at St James's Palace. One account pointed out that the 'numerous company present at the ceremony' in the quire alone amounted 'to about 400 persons'.[125] The busy scene is well captured in William Powell Frith's famous painting that apparently shows the very moment when the Prince of Wales put the ring on his bride's finger (Illustration 7.7).

The same account included an enthusiastic summary of the ceremony as a whole, with a special reference to the music, pronouncing that

> with every accessory of pomp and splendour, with waving banners, glorious music, splendid pageantry, with all that could captivate the eye and please the ear, was celebrated that Marriage, the prospect of which deeply stirred the mind of England. Regarded as a work of art, and of art of a very high order, the ceremony was perfect in its kind.[126]

The 'glorious music' referred to was in fact somewhat limited. Even though there was a big body of musicians, the programme of music was relatively short. Nevertheless, those attending were pleased. As the Earl of Clarendon recorded in a letter to the Duchess of Manchester, the ceremony was 'an uncommonly pretty sight & worth the trouble of going down for', noting that 'the music too was beautiful'.[127] In an even more straightforward verdict, Lord Granville reported to the duchess: 'the music good—the service not too long'.[128]

After all, this wedding was a notable moment of relief in the overall sombre mood of mourning that surrounded the royal family. Richard Williams has referred to the fact that Prince Albert had died at Windsor Castle and that there was a 'funereal atmosphere'.[129] This 'atmosphere', however, does not seem to have been an issue in discussions of the wedding, although it was noted, for instance, that 'For the first time, after an interval of fifteen months, the walls of the Castle resounded with military music.'[130] This referred to Mendelssohn's Wedding March and a selection of Danish marches played by the band as the different processions arrived at St George's Chapel – again, music was a significant component in the proceedings and also in the reports.

Moreover, despite the fact that the wedding took place in remote Windsor, through wide-spread celebrations and also the press attendance with resulting extensive reporting, it was at least a somewhat public event.[131] After all, the wedding was altogether quite costly. According to the records, the 'expenses which were met out of Public Grants', amounted to £24,855.[132] Notwithstanding the effects of inflation, this compares rather strikingly with the expenses for the preparations at the queen's wedding in 1840 and at the more recent wedding

---

[125] *Historical Record*, p. 54.

[126] *Historical Record*, p. 45.

[127] Clarendon to Duchess, 10 March 1863, in *'My Dear Duchess'*, p. 213.

[128] Granville to Duchess, 10 March 1863, in *'My Dear Duchess'*, p. 210.

[129] Richard Williams, *The Contentious Crown: Public Discussion of the British Monarchy in the Reign of Queen Victoria* (Aldershot: Ashgate, 1997), p. 241.

[130] *Historical Record*, p. 54. The same in *Chapter from the History*, p. 94.

[131] For the illuminations in London, and also the 'rejoicings' in the provinces see, for instance, the unidentified cuttings in *Lna LC 2/81*, pp. 167–68.

[132] *Lna WORK 21/9/12*, fols 9ʳ–10ʳ. For the individual listings of two sub-sections see *Lna LC 2/83* and 'Memorandum upon the Worke […]' in *Lna WORK 21/12/3*.

7—The 'Windsor Castle' Weddings: The Mid-Victorians I

of the prince's sister in 1858.[133] Lady Geraldine Sumerset thought the Prince of Wales's wedding 'was y:ᵉ finest thing it were possible to see!' and she judged it 'such a sight as another generation may never see!!'[134]

All the same, the great potential for elaboration and display that lay in the wedding of the heir to the throne was not fully realized: the wedding was not the grand public spectacle that it could have been. The limited opening to the public was not considered to be enough, even at the time, as David Cannadine has discussed with reference to the numerous complaints.[135] Indeed, referring to Queen Victoria's attendance at the state opening of parliament in February 1866, Helen Rappaport has pointed out that 'Here was a scene of pageantry on a far grander scale than Bertie's wedding'.[136]

Illustration 7.7:
William Powell Frith, 'The Marriage of the Prince of Wales with Princess Alexandra of Denmark, Windsor, 10 March 1863', oil on canvas 1863–65, *Royal Collection, RCIN 404545*, Royal Collection Trust / © Her Majesty Queen Elizabeth II 2021.

---

[133] For the 1840 and 1845 expenses see Chapter 6, fn. 213.

[134] *Wra RA VIC/ADDC6/1/1862-3*, entry for 10 March 1863.

[135] David Cannadine, 'The Context, Performance and Meaning of Ritual: The British Monarchy and the "Invention of Tradition"', *c.* 1820–1977', in *The Invention of Tradition*, ed. by Eric Hobsbawm and Terence Ranger (Cambridge: Cambridge University Press, 1983; repr. 2002), pp. 101–64, here p. 118. See also Cannadine, 'Splendor', p. 212.

[136] Helen Rappaport, *A Magnificent Obsession: Victoria, Albert, and the Death that Changed the British Monarchy* (New York: St Martin's Press, 2012), p. 188.

Princess Mary Adelaide of Cambridge and Prince Francis of Teck, 12 June 1866

Three years after the wedding of the Prince of Wales, in June and July 1866, there were two royal weddings 'in rapid succession', as Tytler pointed out.[137] The first was that on 12 June of the Princess Mary Adelaide of Cambridge – daughter of Prince Adolphus, granddaughter of George III, and sister of the Princess Augusta who had married in 1843 (see the previous chapter). She married the future Duke of Teck (from 1871) and the couple's daughter would one day be Queen Mary, consort of George V. Apart from this historic significance, this wedding is also interesting in its own right for some of its ceremonial details and especially for the music.

At the time, Princess Mary Adelaide was described as 'one of the most amiable and popular Princesses of the Royal family'.[138] Towards the end of the century, Clement Kinloch Cooke still mentioned that she had been affectionately known as 'the People's Princess'.[139] Befittingly, her wedding was a more public occasion than many previous royal weddings: it took place at St. Anne's Church, Kew. As Cooke commented:

> It was Princess Mary's wish to be married in the village she loved so well, and, as she herself expressed it, amongst her own people. Accordingly the ceremony was fixed to take place at the parish church, endeared to her by many memories, and where she had worshipped from the days of her childhood.[140]

The interior of the small church, holding 'about 200 persons' was rearranged for the ceremony.[141] Not only was the location a popular choice but the ceremonial was tailored to achieve much effect; Cooke explained that the princess, 'always mindful of what would give the most pleasure, decided to walk to church, so that the village folk might see her as she passed along in wedding attire'.[142] There was an awning and also a 'raised platform' for some of the spectators, and this would overall have been somewhat reminiscent of the lavish outdoor procession at the 1734 wedding. An American journal in its report referred to an aspect not mentioned in British accounts when it explained that 'after the good old English custom, the bride and bridegroom walked to church'.[143]

Queen Victoria attended the wedding and recorded: 'Felt nervous at the thought of having to go for the 1st time to such a Fête, out of my own house, <u>alone!</u>'[144] Indeed, she prominently sat directly in front of the altar. Yet, as Cooke pointed out, she was present 'only in a private capacity' and the ceremonial was not arranged by the Lord Chamberlain.[145] As the *Illustrated*

---

[137] Tytler, *Life*, II, p. 233.

[138] 'Marriage of The Princess Mary of Cambridge', *Times*, 13 June 1866, p. 9. Similar in 'Marriage of The Princess Mary of Cambridge', *Observer*, 17 June 1866, p. 3. NB While her name at the time she was straightforwardly referred to as 'Princess Mary', in modern writing this is usually 'Princess Mary Adelaide' – if only to distinguish her better from all the other Princesses Mary, especially her own daughter (later Queen Mary).

[139] See Sir C[lement] Kinloch Cooke, *A Memoir of Her Royal Highness Princess Mary Adelaide, Duchess of Teck, Based on her Private Diaries and Letters*, 2 vols (London: John Murray, 1900), II, p. 246.

[140] Cooke, *Memoir*, I, p. 416.

[141] For details see 'The Marriage of The Princess Mary of Cambridge', *Scotsman*, 13 June 1866, p. 3.

[142] Cooke, *Memoir*, I, p. 417.

[143] 'Marriage of The Princess Mary of Cambridge', *The Albion: A Journal of News, Politics and Literature*, 44:26, 30 June 1866, p. 308.

[144] *QVJ*, 12 June 1866.

[145] Cooke, *Memoir*, I, p. 417.

7—The 'Windsor Castle' Weddings: The Mid-Victorians I

London News put it, 'The ceremonial was devoid of all pomp of state.'[146] There was no printed ceremonial and only a very rudimentary manuscript version survives in the Royal Archives.[147] The queen arrived at the church before other members of the royal family.[148] Nevertheless, she then went up into 'the Royal gallery at the west end', thus staying out of sight for most of the assembly in the church; she came down and entered the church only between the royal family and the bridegroom, and her entrance, going to her place at the front near the altar, was thus much observed.[149]

According to one account, the organ 'pealed forth an introductory voluntary', once the archbishop 'was seated', with another account detailing that this was 'a soft voluntary'.[150] However, according to the *Illustrated London News*, 'a voluntary' had already been played earlier, while the clergy 'arrived and walked up to the altar'.[151] It is probably safe to assume that the organ played also for the later entrance of the royal family and the queen.

The bridal procession appears to have seen a significant innovation. The *Times* and the *Observer* recorded that a hymn was sung 'As soon as the royal parties had taken up their positions at the altar'.[152] Yet, 'royal parties' may here refer merely to the royal family, queen, and bridegroom, without the bridal party: various other accounts noted distinctly that the hymn was sung *during* the bride's entrance, not afterwards. The *Illustrated Times* recorded that

> suddenly the organ burst forth and the choir commenced singing Keble's marriage hymn, "How welcome was the call!" This was the signal for the appearance of the illustrious bride, who entered the church leaning on the arm of the Duke of Cambridge.[153]

This was confirmed by several other reports.[154] A sung introit for the royal bride's entrance, instead of an instrumental march, would appear to have been an important innovation; however, this seems not to have been remarked upon.

The accounts also recorded concrete details of the hymn, 'How Welcome Was the Call'. The *Morning Herald* noted that it was 'Keble's Wedding Hymn, to the tune No. 213 in "Hymns Ancient and Modern;"'.[155] The *Times* and *Observer* in the same way referred to 'the beautiful hymn, No. 213, by Dr. Gauntlett'.[156] The tune 'Gauntlett' is today probably better known as 'St George'. The *Scotsman* also explained that the hymn was from *Hymns Ancient and Modern* and, like the *Morning Post*, it included the full text of the six verses with a final Amen.[157] This would have been a long

---

[146] 'The Court', *ILN*, 16 June 1866, p. 579.

[147] Headed 'St Anne'[s] Church. Kew / June 12.th 1866.', 2 folios of blue paper, in *Wra F&V/WED/1866: 12 June*.

[148] 'Marriage of The Princess Mary of Cambridge', *Observer*.

[149] See the accounts in 'The Court', *ILN*, 16 June 1866, p. 579; and 'The Royal Marriage at Kew', *ILN*, 23 June 1866, p. 614 (whith the quotation).

[150] 'Marriage of The Princess Mary', *Morning Post*, 13 June 1866, p. 5; and 'Marriage of The Princess Mary of Cambridge with the Prince of Teck', *Morning Herald*, 13 June 1866, p. 5.

[151] 'Royal Marriage at Kew'. See also the quotation below, with fn. 168.

[152] 'Marriage of The Princess Mary of Cambridge', *Times*. Same content in 'Marriage of The Princess Mary of Cambridge', *Observer*.

[153] 'Marriage of H.R.H. Princess Mary of Cambridge', *Illustrated Times*, 16 June 1866, p. 2.

[154] 'Royal Marriage at Kew'; 'Marriage of The Princess Mary', *Morning Post*; 'Marriage of The Princess Mary of Cambridge', *Morning Herald*; Cooke, *Memoir*, I, p. 418.

[155] 'Marriage of The Princess Mary', *Morning Herald*.

[156] 'Marriage of The Princess Mary of Cambridge', *Times*. Same content in 'Marriage of The Princess Mary of Cambridge', *Observer*.

[157] 'Marriage of The Princess Mary of Cambridge', *Scotsman*; 'Marriage of The Princess Mary', *Morning Post*.

hymn for the relatively short walk down the aisle. Indeed, the *Morning Herald* recorded that the choir had begun to sing the hymn the moment that the princess entered, but it also noted that while the hymn 'was being sung the Princess knelt in silent prayer at the altar rails' – obviously referring to the remainder of the hymn that did not cover the procession – and it observed that at the end of the hymn both the bride and bridegroom were 'standing before the altar'.[158]

The *Morning Post* explained that the service 'was read throughout, with the exception of the Psalm which occurs in the service'.[159] This indicates clearly that the Responses were just spoken, not sung. According to the *Illustrated London News*, 'The choir chanted the 67th Psalm', and the *Scotsman* recorded that 'The psalm *Deus Misereatur* was chanted to Tallis in A.'[160] There does not seem to be a setting by Tallis of the Wedding Responses, and this could have been a mere arrangement from his well-known setting of the Preces and Responses.[161] Intriguingly, the *Morning Herald* referred to 'The sixty-seventh Psalm having been sung by the choir and congregation to Tallis in A'.[162] If that was correct, such congregational singing would probably have been a novelty for a royal wedding.

An even more notable fact is reported for the music of the recess. The *Illustrated Times* recorded in some detail, by way of explanation:

> It had been arranged that Mendelssohn's 'Wedding March' should be played as the company left the church; but this was abandoned at the special request of the Queen, and the 'Ode to Joy,' from Beethoven's 9th symphony, was substituted for it.[163]

Similarly, Cooke pointed out that the organ 'burst forth' with the strains of Beethoven's piece 'which, by Her Majesty's express desire, was substituted for Mendelssohn's "Wedding March"'.[164] It appears that Beethoven's chorus was performed in an organ arrangement, without the choir singing. While the reason for the queen's rejection of Mendelssohn's march does not seem to be known, it is interesting that she involved herself in such a detail – especially considering that this was not even the wedding of one of her own children.

Performance

In relation to the introit, some accounts referred to the conditions and arrangements in the church, and explained that the choir was 'congregated about the organ (which, strange to relate, is erected above the altar)', or that it was 'placed in that very extraordinary organ loft which is over the altar'.[165] Some magazines, such as the *Illustrated London News*, captured this in a detailed picture of the wedding scene, showing the organ gallery and choir high above the altar (Illustration 7.8).[166] These pictures also give an impression of the relatively small size of the church.

---

[158] 'Marriage of The Princess Mary', *Morning Herald*.

[159] 'Marriage of The Princess Mary', *Morning Post*.

[160] 'Royal Marriage at Kew'; 'Marriage of The Princess Mary of Cambridge', *Scotsman*.

[161] For these see Suzanne Cole, *Thomas Tallis and his Music in Victorian England* (Woodbridge: Boydell, 2008), esp. Chapter 4.

[162] 'Marriage of The Princess Mary', *Morning Herald*.

[163] 'Marriage of H.R.H. Princess Mary of Cambridge', *Illustrated Times*.

[164] Cooke, *Memoir*, I, p. 419. 'Marriage of The Princess Mary of Cambridge' in *Times* and *Observer* explained merely that the scheduled Mendelsohn's Wedding March was 'By express desire […] omitted', but not what was played instead.

[165] 'Marriage of The Princess Mary', *Morning Post*; 'Marriage of The Princess Mary', *Morning Herald*.

[166] See also the front page of the *Illustrated Times*, 16 June 1866.

7—The 'Windsor Castle' Weddings: The Mid-Victorians I

Illustration 7.8: 'The Marriage of Princess Mary of Cambridge and Prince Teck Kew Church', from *ILN*, 23 June 1866, pp. 604–05. Author's collection.

No details of the choir seem to be known, apart from its consisting 'of about twenty', noted by the *Scotsman*.[167] Yet, the *Illustrated London News* reported another interesting detail:

> The organ, it is said, once belonged to Handel, and was a favourite instrument of George III., who had it at Kew House, and used to play upon it as the chief solace of his affliction when he suffered from mental disease. After his death it was given to the church by George IV.[168]

In another issue, the same paper recorded that the clergy entered 'while a voluntary was played on the organ by Dr. Sellé.'[169] The latter was the organist of the Chapel Royal at Hampton Court, but it is not known how he came to be involved in this wedding.[170]

Corresponding with the princess's popular appeal, the *Observer* made sure to highlight the relative simplicity of the event: 'The ceremony was unattended by any kind of State pageantry or pomp.'[171] The *Scotsman* similarly referred to the 'marriage ceremony, which was practically of a very private character', but it also noted that the wedding 'created an amount of excitement rarely occasioned even in loyal England by a royal event'.[172] The aforementioned report of the ceremony in an American journal also interpreted that the wedding was 'solemnised […] with

---

[167] 'Marriage of The Princess Mary of Cambridge', *Scotsman*.

[168] 'Marriage of Princess Mary of Cambridge', *ILN*, 16 June 1866, p. 592.

[169] 'Royal Marriage at Kew'.

[170] See the short note in *The Musical World*, 47 (1869), p. 465.

[171] 'Marriage of The Princess Mary of Cambridge', *Observer*.

[172] 'Marriage of The Princess Mary of Cambridge', *Scotsman*.

British Royal Weddings

as little show as the great popularity of the bride would permit' – but while it noted that there 'was no state in these Royal nuptials', it highlighted that 'the presence of Her Majesty the Queen added much interest to the ceremony'.[173]

Princess Helena and Prince Christian
of Schleswig-Holstein-Sonderburg-Augustenburg, 5 July 1866

The second royal wedding of 1866 occurred on 5 July, when Princess Helena, the queen's third daughter, married Prince Christian of Schleswig-Holstein-Sonderburg-Augustenburg. Notwithstanding the wedding of Princess Mary Adelaide earlier in the year, Sarah Tooley interpreted that the wedding of Princess Helena 'was the happy event which signalled the return of the Queen to public life after her great bereavement'.[174] As at the Kew wedding, Queen Victoria was very much present at the ceremony – and, being the mother of the bride, now even more so: together with the Prince of Wales she 'supported' the bride – that is, led her daughter to the altar. Indeed, the *Times* emphasized that 'The Queen, in person, gave away the bride', and she had even somewhat relieved her mourning dress.[175]

The Venue

The choice of venue for this wedding was rather unusual. It took again place at Windsor Castle – however, not in St George's Chapel as three years previously, but in the Private Chapel within the main building of the Castle, adjoining St George's Hall (Illustration 7.9; see also the plan in Illustration 7.12 below). In this way, this wedding was even more removed from the public, even more reclusive than those in the Chapel Royal at St James's and the 1863 wedding in St George's had been.

It was Queen Victoria who made this choice of venue herself – and relatively early, almost four months before the wedding.[176] Possible explanations for the choice of the different venue could be that this was meant to show a distinction to the Prince of Wales's wedding at St George's Chapel. Also, the more intimate venue could have been meant to give less prominence to this union that was politically somewhat controversial. For Prince Christian came from the disputed duchies of Schleswig and Holstein and his family had supported the German side in the recent Second Schleswig War of 1864 against Denmark, the homeland of the Princess of Wales.[177] Whatever lay behind the choice of venue, this remained the only more senior royal wedding in the Private Chapel: it was destroyed during the fire at Windsor Castle in 1992.[178]

---

[173] 'Marriage of The Princess Mary of Cambridge', *Albion*.

[174] Sarah A. Tooley, 'The Weddings of the Queen's Children', *The Lady's Realm: An Illustrated Monthly Magazine*, 9 (November 1900 to April 1901), pp. 47–56, here p. 50.

[175] 'Marriage of The Princess Helena', *Times*, 6 July 1866, p. 9.

[176] See Unknown to Mr Cowper, Buckingham Palace 9 March 1866, in *Lna WORK 19/392*, no. 4 (with number '1025/66').

[177] For more details see Christopher Hibbert, *Edward VII: The Last Victorian King* (New York: St. Martin's Press, 2007), pp. 85–86; and John van der Kiste, *Princess Helena: Queen Victoria's Third Daughter*, rev. and exp. edn (South Brent: A & F Publications, 2015), Chapter 2.

[178] For the 1880 wedding of Queen Victoria's cousin Princess Frederica of Hanover in the Private Chapel see the following Chapter 8, fn. 71.

7—The 'Windsor Castle' Weddings: The Mid-Victorians I

Illustration 7.9: Photograph of the Private Chapel at Windsor Castle as it still appeared in the early-twentieth century, reproductive print by Russell & Sons, Windsor, c. 1900-18, *Royal Collection, RCIN 705272*, Royal Collection Trust / © Her Majesty Queen Elizabeth II 2021.

The complete lack of outdoor processions that resulted from this choice of venue was clearly noted in the reports of the ceremony. The correspondent of the *Times* emphasized with seeming disappointment that

> though the town of Windsor testified its loyalty by ringing merry peals from its steeples and by draping the Court-house and part of the principal street with flags, it saw nothing of the proceedings or of the bridal procession on its way to and fro, and the streets accordingly were free from those crowds which are usually to be seen when there is any event of interest at the Castle.[179]

Similarly, a report in *The Musical Standard*, probably referring to the music as much as to the whole, described the wedding as 'an event which we hope it is no treason to say has not awakened any great enthusiasm'.[180] This contrasts markedly with the observed interest in the wedding of Princess Mary Adelaide in Kew and its outdoor procession earlier in the year. Yet, in return, the *Times* had pointed out that 'Within the walls, however, the brilliancy of the gathering became, by contrast, the greater.' The Lord Chamberlain's records confirm that 'Garter King of Arms and 2 Heralds attended / 20 Gentlemen at Arms attended / a Guard of the Yeomen of the Guard were on duty'.[181] In the traditional way, the Lord Chamberlain and Vice Chamberlain and the heralds conducted each of the individual processions to the Chapel.

Queen Victoria and Princess Helena very clearly showed their close interest in the preparations: for instance, they had a look at the Private Chapel to check the arrangements on 31 March

---

[179] 'Marriage of The Princess Helena', *Times*.
[180] 'Table Talk', *The Musical Standard*, 5 (July–December 1866), pp. 27–28, here p. 28.
[181] *Lna LC 2/81*, p. 228. See also 'An account of the Fees', *Lna LC 2/86*, fol. 5.

and 16 May, and on the latter occasion they also met the Dean of Windsor there 'to discuss the arrangements for the wedding'.[182] The *Illustrated London News* pointed out critically that

> The Queen's private chapel is an apartment of very limited dimensions, and, though sufficiently commodious for ordinary domestic worship, is scarcely adapted for a state ceremonial.[183]

It detailed that 'To provide additional accommodation on this occasion, three temporary galleries were erected'.[184] As the organ and organ gallery was a permanent fixture, this must refer to the other galleries around the top of the Chapel. Altogether, the Lord Chamberlain's records noted that 'The Number of Seats in Chapel Gallery were 64 in the 3 Front-Rows 30 in the Back D.º _ all flaps included'.[185]

Moreover, the Chapel was arranged to suit the ceremonial requirements: 'The open benches ordinarily used in the chapel were removed, and the centre, beautifully carpeted, was left open for the entrance procession.'[186] The total 'Expense incurred on preparing the Private Chapel, Windsor Castle for the ceremonial.' met by the Office or Work amounted to '£301.11.5'.[187] Yet, this was only a fourth of the total cost of £1,345 11s.[188]

The *Illustrated London News* recorded that 'At the side to the right of the alter is a small organ.'[189] This may refer to the right side as seen from the altar, and to the regular organ in its gallery on the left, as seen in Christian Karl Magnussen's painting of the ceremony (Illustration 7.10). This organ, at the junction of the Private Chapel and St George's Hall, was not actually 'small' and could also be used for services in the Hall. Indeed, with 'the Chapel being cleared out for the preparations for Lenchen's wedding', Queen Victoria herself recorded for the service in St George's Hall on Sunday 10 June: 'The singing was as usual, the organ being able to be played from both sides.'[190]

Despite the smaller and more recluse venue and nature of the event, the representatives of the press were again well cared for and could report all details to the public: tickets were given to '7 Morning Papers'.[191] Furthermore, notwithstanding that the ceremony took place behind the castle walls, as at the Kew wedding earlier in the year, the public could once more obtain at least a glimpse of the proceedings through the illustrations included in magazines such as the *Illustrated London News*, which neatly match with, and thus support the authenticity of Magnussen's painting (Illustration 7.11).

---

[182] *QVJ*, 31 March and 16 May 1866.

[183] 'The Marriage of Princess Helena at Windsor', *ILN*, 14 July 1866, p. 42. For a description of the chapel see also Arthur H[enry] Beaven, *Popular Royalty* (London: Sampson Low, Marson and Company: 1897), pp. 183–84.

[184] 'Marriage of Princess Helena', *ILN*. This includes also a detailed description of all the hangings, the altar plate etc.

[185] *Lna LC 2/81*, p. 226. For the arrangements see also the printed 'Plan of the Chapel at Windsor Castle / AND / Seats arranged for Persons in the Processions / AT THE / Marriage of H.R.H. Princess Helena' in *Wra RA F&V/WED/1866: 5 July*.

[186] 'Marriage of Princess Helena', *ILN*. For the making of room in the Private Chapel and the new galleries see also 'Marriage of The Princess Helena', *Times*.

[187] *Lna WORK 19/392*, no. 7. See also no. 5 for a 'Memo. 23.ʳᵈ May 1866', with details of the work to be done; and 'Abstract of Office of Works Bills for work / done on occasion of The Marriage of / The Princess Helena.' in *Lna LC 2/86*.

[188] 'Marriage Expenses of / H.R.H. Princess Helena', *Lna LC 2/86*, fol. 1.

[189] 'Marriage of Princess Helena', *ILN*.

[190] *QVJ*, 10 June 1866. See also Andrew Freeman, 'Notes on Organs at Windsor Castle', *Musical Times*, 54 (1913), pp. 304–08.

[191] *Lna LC 2/81*, p. 229. NB The lower-ranking evening papers seem not to have been invited.

7—The 'Windsor Castle' Weddings: The Mid-Victorians I

The Ceremony and the Music

The overall ceremony was rather brief. Queen Victoria herself recorded that it 'was short, without the exhortation', that is without the text stipulated in the Prayer Book to be read in place of a sermon at the end of the service.[192] This is particularly noteworthy, since the text of the exhortation is included in the specially prepared order of service.[193]

It was recorded that '20 Velvet & 200 White "Marriage Services" were sent to Mr Seabrook to be placed before each person in the Chapel [added in darker ink:] _ 30 Velvet & 250 White were ordered.'[194] In addition, there was again a separate, ornate programme of the music.[195] Also, as for previous weddings, there are again printed copies of the ceremonial, bound in blue watered silk, and these are throughout worded in the past tense. A note among the Lord Chamberlain's records refers to 'Copy of Ceremonial prepared after the Marriage _ 50 Bound in Blue Silk sent to the Queen.'[196] This once again confirms that it was not unusual to prepare such

Illustration 7.10: Christian Karl Magnussen, 'The Marriage of Princess Helena, 5 July 1866', oil on canvas, signed and dated 1866–69, *Royal Collection, RCIN 404483*, Royal Collection Trust / © Her Majesty Queen Elizabeth II 2021.

---

[192] *QVJ*, 5 July 1866.

[193] OS 1866.

[194] 'Marriage of Her Royal Highness The / Princess Helena with His Royal Highness / The Prince Christian of Schleswig-Holstein / in the Private-Chapel of Windsor Castle / on Thursday July 5th 1866, at ½ past 12 / o'clock.', *Lna LC 2/81*, pp. 226–30, here p. 230.

[195] *Lna LC 2/81*, p. 229: 'Illuminated Musical Programmes were ordered by Mr Anderson of Orton[?] / St James's Street and distributed by him'. For these see also below, fn. 203.

[196] *Lna LC 2/81*, p. 228. Some of these copies are in *Lna LC 2/85*.

Illustration 7.11: 'Marriage of Princess Helena and Prince Christian in the Private Chapel, Windsor', *ILN*, 14 July 1866, p. 32–33. Author's collection.

copies of the ceremonials only after the event and that they served as a record and souvenir of the occasion.

As already seen, Queen Victoria and Princess Helena both had a clear interest in the wedding preparations, yet it is not known how far they were involved in the choice of the music. The Lord Chamberlain's records include a note stating that

> The Musical Arrangements were made by Mr Anderson. A Hymn & 2 Marches were prepared. Her Majesty's Private-Band attended. The Musicians were placed in Organ Loft [*sic*][197]

Thus, as in 1858 and 1863, Anderson was again in charge of the music. However, the limited space of the Private Chapel resulted in a compromise for the musicians. While the choir was indeed 'in Organ Loft', the printed ceremonial explained that 'Her Majesty's Private Band […] was stationed in the Red Drawing Room, and performed there as the several Processions passed along the Corridor to and from the Chapel.'[198] This arrangement is confirmed in the report in the *Observer*.[199] The Red Drawing Room (today called 'Crimson Drawing Room') was right next door to the Private Chapel (see Illustration 7.12: no. 21 in the plan) and the music would thus have sounded relatively distant in the long corridor leading to the Chapel (the corridor is nos 25–27 in the plan).

---

[197] *Lna LC 2/81*, p. 229. In the margin this entry has the additional pencil note 'May 16'.

[198] Ceremonial 1866b, p. 8.

[199] 'Marriage of Her Royal Highness The Princess Helena', *Observer* (8 July 1866), p. 3.

7—The 'Windsor Castle' Weddings: The Mid-Victorians I

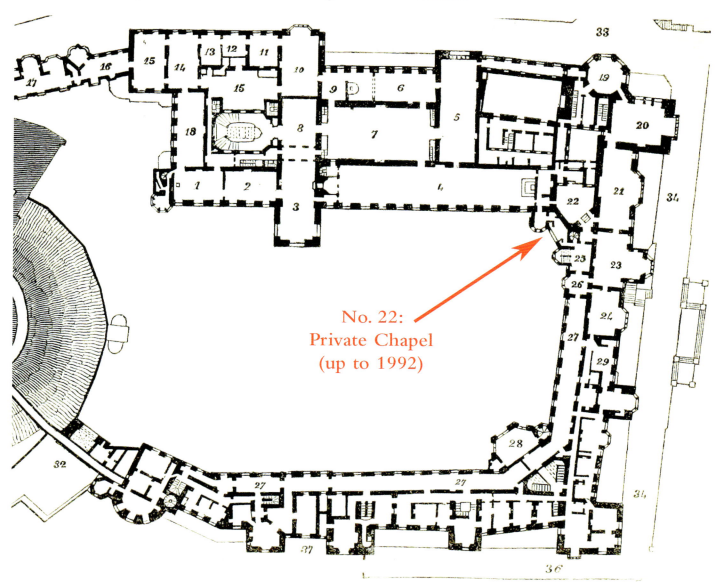

Illustration 7.12: Detail of the first-floor plan of Windsor Castle, showing the Private Chapel and surrounding rooms – from *The Pictorial Handbook of London [...] Together with Some Account of the Principal Suburbs and Most Attractive Localities*, 'Bohn's Illustrated Library' (London: Henry G. Bohn, 1854), p. 865. Author's collection.

The above observation that '2 Marches were prepared' is somewhat confusing. The sources agree that the procession to the Chapel of the members of the royal family was accompanied by Beethoven's Triumphal March, that of the groom by the march from Mendelssohn's *Athalie*, and the bride's procession by the march from Handel's *Scipio*.[200] Beethoven's 'Triumphal March' was in all likelihood the march written for the tragedy *Tarpeja*, WoO 2a.

Altogether there were thus three marches for the entrance processions alone, and then there was also a fourth that accompanied the leaving procession. Quite apart from these orchestral marches, it is noteworthy that the processions were not accompanied by the traditional contingency of trumpeters.

---

[200] For this and the following Ceremonial 1866a/b; 'Marriage of The Princess Helena', *Times*; and Supplement to *LG* of 17 July 1866 (from 19 July 1866), pp. 4089-98, here pp. 4089-92. The latter also in 'Marriage of Her Royal Highness The Princess Helena', *Annual Register [...] 1866* (1867), pp. 76-82.

185

British Royal Weddings

The report in the *Observer* supplies an intriguing further detail when it refers to 'Mr. W. G. Cusins performing on the organ between the marches until the commencement of the service'.[201] With such continuous music, there would thus not have been any quiet moments from the beginning of the first procession onwards. There was, however, again not much music during the service itself, only two items, as the *Musical Standard* detailed:

> The psalm *Deus Misereatur* was chanted, and the wedding hymn, "How Welcome was the Call," was sung to new music composed for the occasion by Mr. Cusins.[202]

The texts of both, the psalm and the hymn, were printed on a pretty, decorated sheet, probably for use by the higher-ranking guests at the ceremony.[203] It is not known which chant was used for the psalm. However, the *Times* referred to an interesting aspect:

> The youth and station of the bride, the character of the assembly before whom she plighted her troth, the clear tones of the Archbishop's voice produced a deep effect upon the spectators, and at the point where the minister is to add his blessing it was almost a relief to hear the choir chant – [full text of Psalm 67].[204]

The last comment echoes a similar comment from the 1863 wedding: the 'relief' quality of the psalm after the vows seems to have been a common perception at the time.[205] The hymn was Cusins's 'Chorale, specially composed for the occasion', as the ceremonial noted.[206] Its text was the same as at the wedding of Princess Mary Adelaide of Cambridge earlier in the year ('How Welcome was the Call', see above), and Cusins's setting was published after the wedding under the title of *Royal Wedding Chorale*.[207] It is a short straightforward, four-part homophonic setting, with a final 'Amen'. The aforementioned report in the *Musical Standard* referred to it only after the psalm, and the account in the *Observer* reported that it was 'sung before the blessing'.[208] If these are correct, it is noteworthy that Cusins's hymn came not at the beginning of the ceremony, as an introit, as in the other recent royal weddings since 1858. It is also notable that, overall, there was now no piece by the late Prince Consort, which meant that he was not represented musically, as he had been in 1863.

For the recess, the printed ceremonial referred merely to 'a March (Spohr)', but the *Times* explained that this was 'Spohr's march from his oratorio of the *Fall of Babylon*'.[209] It is not quite clear what this march would have been. The only march in Spohr's oratorio is the March of the Persian Army, in part 2, no. 24 – but this is only seven bars long, leading into a section for soloists and chorus. Notwithstanding that it is not known who chose all the marches of the ceremony, the *Times* commented on them with an interesting point:

> The taste governing these selections will be evident when attention is pointed to the fact that of the greatest musicians four were represented in their masterpieces.[210]

---

[201] 'Marriage of Her Royal Highness The Princess Helena', *Observer*.

[202] 'Table Talk', p. 28. See also 'Marriage of Her Royal Highness The Princess Helena', *Observer*.

[203] See *Wra RA F&V/WED/1866: 5 July*, which also includes plain copies of this text sheet.

[204] 'Marriage of The Princess Helena', *Times*.

[205] Compare above, with fn. 93.

[206] Ceremonial 1866a/b, p. 7.

[207] W. G. [William George] Cusins, *Royal Wedding Chorale, Composed Expressly for the Marriage of H.R.H. The Princess Helena, July 5th, 1866* (Words by Sir H. Baker), (London: Lamborn Cock, Addison & Co., [1866]).

[208] 'Marriage of Her Royal Highness The Princess Helena', *Observer*; and see fn. 201, above.

[209] Ceremonial 1866a/b, p. 7. 'Marriage of The Princess Helena', *Times*.

[210] 'Marriage of The Princess Helena', *Times*.

7—The 'Windsor Castle' Weddings: The Mid-Victorians I

Regarding the performance of the music, it is notable that, unlike in 1863 and at all the previous royal weddings that took place in royal chapels, the Chapel Royal choir did not take part this time. The account in the *Musical Standard* recorded:

> The choir of St. George's chapel, under the direction of Dr. Elvey (organist of St. George's Chapel), and the choir of the Private Chapel, under the direction of Mr. W.G. Cusins (organist of Her Majesty's Private Chapel), were in attendance in the organ gallery.[211]

The exact number of the singers in these choirs, however, is not known. A list of payments for the wedding service records £18 18s. for the choir of St George's Chapel and £12 12s. for the Private Chapel and also furthermore twice a payment to '3 Extra Performers', at £2 each and £1 each respectively.[212] It is not clear whether the latter six, unspecified performers were also singers or some instrumentalists.

The printed ceremonial detailed that 'Mr. Cusins presided at the Organ.' – but it did not mention Elvey.[213] Conversely, a list of payments for the wedding includes Elvey, but not Cusins.[214] If it was Elvey who conducted the choir, he would then be the conductor seen in the organ gallery in Magnussen's painting, on the far right (see Illustration 7.10). Anderson was allocated £318 19s. 4d. in order to pay for 'Music in Chapel + Concert', although only £81 19s. 6d. of this were for the service and the remainder for two concerts before and after the wedding.[215] Altogether, compared with the aforementioned total expenses of £1345 11s. for the wedding, the music was an important – and costly – part of the celebrations.

Princess Louise and John Campbell, Marquess of Lorne (later 9th Duke of Argyll), 21 March 1871

The wedding of the queen's fourth daughter, Princess Louise, first of all stands out for the fact that she married a Scottish nobleman, and thus – even though a future peer – technically one of her mother's subjects. This was the first (notable) royal wedding to a British subject since that of the future James II to Anne Hyde in the seventeenth century. Moreover, this was also the first notable wedding of a member of the royal family to a Scot since the accession of the Stuarts and was of particular interest in Scotland. The *Scotsman*, for instance, had sent no less than three correspondents at once to report about the ceremonies simultaneously.

With reference to this innovative choice of bridegroom, Queen Victoria explained to her son, the Prince of Wales, that 'Times have much changed' and that 'great foreign alliances' were 'of no good'.[216] However, while times and the choice of royal marriage partners may have 'much changed', the actual ceremonial of royal weddings had not changed.

---

[211] 'Table Talk', p. 28. Same in 'Marriage of Her Royal Highness The Princess Helena', *Observer*. For the music being performed by these two choirs, see also 'The Marriage of Princess Helena at Windsor'.

[212] 'Account of the Wedding of H.R.H. The Princess Helena, and Concert the same evening at Windsor Castle: July 5th 1866', in *Lna LC 2/86*, fol. 2ʳ.

[213] Ceremonial 1866a/b, p. 8.

[214] 'Marriage Expenses of H.R.H. Princess Helena', in *Lna LC 2/86*, here fol. 1ʳ.

[215] For this and the following see 'Marriage Expenses of / H.R.H. Princess Helena' and 'Account of the Wedding […]', in *Lna LC 2/86*, fols 1ʳ and 2ʳ.

[216] Queen Victoria to Prince of Wales, 29 November 1869, in Queen Victoria, *The Letters of Queen Victoria*, vol. 4: 1862–1869, ed. by George Earle Buckle, publ. by John Murray in 1926, repr. (Cambridge: Cambridge University Press, 2014), pp. 632–33, here p. 632.

British Royal Weddings

The Venue

Following the previous two weddings of Queen Victoria's children, this one took place at Windsor Castle, and the ceremony on 21 March 1871 saw a return to St George's Chapel. *The Morning Post* afterwards recorded that the Chapel 'altogether holds about 1,000 people, but yesterday the limited space had been exhausted'.[217] In contrast to the accumulation of people in the quire and near the altar, one of the three correspondents of the *Scotsman* who reported about the wedding observed that much of the building was left empty:

> For some reason – possibly good, but not apparent – the nave, or outer nave, or whatever is the proper name of the western part of the building behind the organ, was left about three fourths unpopulated. It contained only two lines of benches, though a third line of persons was allowed to stand behind.[218]

The correspondent particularly highlighted that the 'passage left in the middle for the entries and exits of the bridal parties was at least double the breadth required'. While there could have been a ceremonial reason for such a broad passageway, there was surely no reason for leaving the aisles behind the few spectators 'bare alike of ornament and inhabitants'. A description by 'an eye-witness' in an American periodical noted that the nave had been 'set apart for those whom we call the outside public', and that the seats in the quire 'were reserved', which seems to imply that those in the nave were not.[219] At the same time, this account recorded:

> The passage down the nave was lined on each side by ladies, many of them in mourning, which gave an additional coldness to the scene [...].[220]

There was, and still is, no explanation why they were in mourning. In any case, this account emphasized: 'But beyond the Organ Gallery stretched the choir, and there it was far different.' It referred, for instance, to the 'heralds in mediæval bibs of gold embroidery and color'. The heralds again had a prominent role in leading the several processions before and after the service.[221] The busy scene 'beyond the Organ Gallery', in the quire, was well captured in Sydney Prior Hall's painting of the ceremony that shows the main participants closely gathered at the altar, with the heralds and chamberlain in the aisle (Illustration 7.13).

The Ceremony and its Music

As for the previous weddings, the order of service was again specially printed. However, there is now an informative account of how the different orders of service were distributed in the Chapel:

> On each of the knights' seats on each side and on the seats of the choir was placed a white and gilt volume containing the marriage service. Similar volumes, bound in crimson velvet, were provided for the seats on the haut-pas, or raised floor at the front of the altar, ranged in a semicircle before it.[222]

---

[217] 'Marriage of The Princess Louise', *The Morning Post*, 22 March 1871, pp. 5–6, here p. 5.

[218] This and the following [2nd correspondent], 'Marriage of The Princess Louise and Marquis of Lorn', *Scotsman*, 22 March 1871, p. 2: 'The Scene in the Chapel'.

[219] 'The Royal Wedding', *Every Saturday: A Journal of Choice Reading*, 22 April [*sic*] 1871, p. 371. For the quire stalls being occupied by guests see also 'Marriage of The Princess Louise', *Morning Post*, p. 5.

[220] This and the next quotation from 'Royal Wedding', *Every Saturday*.

[221] See Ceremonial 1871a/b. See also 'The Royal Marriage', *The London Journal, and Weekly Record of Literature, Science, and Art*, 15 April 1871, pp. 236–38, here p. 238.

[222] 'Marriage of Princess Louise at Windsor', *ILN*, 1 April 1871, pp. 323–25, here p. 323.

7—The 'Windsor Castle' Weddings: The Mid-Victorians I

Illustration 7.13: Sydney Prior Hall, 'The Marriage of Princess Louise, 21 March 1871', oil on canvas 1878–79, *Royal Collection, RCIN 404485*, Royal Collection Trust / © Her Majesty Queen Elizabeth II 2021.

As one of the *Scotsman* correspondents explained, these orders of service were, as in 1858, given to the members of the congregation to take home:

> Each guest who had a seat in the choir was permitted to bring away with him a beautifully bound copy of the Marriage Service "in memoriam".[223]

In contrast to this, Hall's painting of the ceremony – perhaps following a more generic approach – shows those sitting in the quire stalls having what looks like copies of the Prayer Book in front of them, and especially the man in the front corner is actively reading in his copy as though following the words of the service in it (Illustration 7.13).

The 'Programme of Music' was now, seemingly for the first time, not only printed but was also bound in with the order of service.[224] Further additional information on the music was again included in the printed ceremonial. As before, some lavish copies of the ceremonial were produced, bound in blue watered silk, written in the past tense, and presumably also intended as commemorative accounts of the occasion.[225]

---

[223] [3rd correspondent], 'Marriage of the Princess Louise and Marquis of Lorn', *Scotsman*, 22 March 1871, p. 2: [untitled sub-section]. Various copies of the order of service are listed under OS 1871.

[224] OS 1871 in *Wra RA F&V/WED/1871* (bound in red velvet).

[225] Copies of this in *Wra RA F&V/WED/1871*.

189

This wedding saw a notable change.in the participating clergy. On 18 March, three days before the wedding, at least one magazine was still reporting that 'The marriage ceremony will be performed by the Archbishop of Canterbury.'[226] However, the post-wedding printed ceremonial eventually noted:

> The Service was performed by The Bishop of London (Dean of Her Majesty's Chapels Royal) in the absence of the Archbishop of Canterbury.[227]

Reports such as that in the *London Journal* referred merely to the archbishop's 'unavoidable absence', while a German paper detailed that he was staying in Italy, 'due to his weakened health'.[228]

As at Princess Helena's wedding in 1866, the queen and the bride took an active interest in the preparations: they visited St George's Chapel and 'inspected the works in course of progress for the Royal marriage'.[229] However, as in 1866, there is no evidence that any member of the royal family showed any particular interest in the music of the ceremony. It was merely recorded that the 'musical service was under the direction of Dr. Elvey'.[230] It was on this occasion that he was knighted.[231] Elvey's widow later recorded that this wedding was 'a very brilliant scene', and the arrangements had been 'carried out with almost, or quite, as much splendour' as for the Prince of Wales's wedding in 1863.[232]

As will be seen below, there was again a small orchestra at the service. While many reports refer merely to Elvey playing the marches during the entrance processions on the organ, a report in *The Musical Standard* listed the marches 'played by the band and organist'.[233] This is especially credible since this listing saw some corrections, in line with the actual performance, in the next issue – but the revised account still emphasized 'The marches were played by the band and organist.'[234] Similarly, the aforementioned German account noted that 'the organ' and 'the royal private chapel' together played the march during the first procession.[235]

Entrance Processions

The entrance processions before the service overall appear to have been similar to those at the previous wedding in St George's, that of the Prince of Wales in 1863. The first procession – of members of the royal family – entered, as the London Journal recorded, 'at the western door in a long procession'.[236] This is notable in so far as Gilbert Scott's grand steps leading up to the west door were, as noted above, not finished until the following year, 1872.[237] Thus, there must, as at

---

[226] 'The Court: Approaching Marriage of Princess Louise', *ILN*, 18 March 1871, p. 259.

[227] Ceremonial 1871b, p. 10.

[228] 'Royal Marriage', *London Journal*, p. 238; 'Die Hochzeit der Prinzessin Louise', *Neues Fremden-Blatt*, 7:84, 25 March 1871, '1. Beilage', p. [2]: 'in Abwesenheit des seiner geschwächten Gesundheit wegen in Italien weilenden Erzbischofs von Canterbury'.

[229] 'The Court', *ILN*, 18 March 1871, p. 259.

[230] 'The Court', *ILN*, 25 March 1871, p. 283.

[231] Fellowes, *Organists*, p. 76.

[232] Lady Elvey, *Life and Reminiscences*, p. 250.

[233] *Musical Standard*, 14 (25 March 1871), p. 137 [anonymous report of Princess Louise's wedding].

[234] *Musical Standard*, 14 (1 April 1871), p. 149 [anonymous report of Princess Louise's wedding].

[235] 'Die Hochzeit der Prinzessin Louise', p. [2]: '[…] intonirte die Orgel, gespielt von Dr. Elvey, und die königliche Privatkapelle […]'.

[236] 'Royal Marriage', *London Journal*, p. 238.

[237] See above, fn. 29.

7—The 'Windsor Castle' Weddings: The Mid-Victorians I

the 1863 wedding, again have been some temporary construction at the Chapel's west end that is not otherwise recorded: indeed, a document from the Lord Chamberlain's Office without further details refers to 'the works in the Horse Shoe Cloister'.[238] Yet, it is unlikely that this was anything as elaborate as the temporary annex built in 1863.

For the first procession's entrance, the *London Journal* noted that 'now at last the organ of the chapel seemed to start from watchfulness, and rolled forth the first notes of a noble festal march' – the wording implying that the organ had not played during the arrival of the other guests. For this 'festal march' the account states that it was 'a composition of the accomplished organist, Dr. Elvey'.[239]

The 'Programme of the Music' included in the order of service lists the marches played for the entrance processions.[240] This refers not to the distinct processions, but to 'Before the Arrival of the Bridal Procession' and then to 'On the Entrance of the Bridal Procession', incidentally making the bride's arrival clearly the focus of attention. The first march here is the 'Festal March' by Elvey. The aforementioned later article on Elvey explained that this march was 'a movement from a larger anthem composed for the wedding of the Princess Louise'.[241] However, Elvey's widow later recorded that this march 'is a distinct composition, and not, as has been on more than one occasion erroneously stated taken from any other work', but she yet confirmed that it had been 'composed for, and performed at' this wedding.[242] One account at the time praised the march enthusiastically as 'a composition worthy to rank amongst some of the best of its class'.[243] Another described the piece as 'bold, clever, and modern in style, aptly instrumental, and with a vein of fresh melody running through the march'.[244] A piano arrangement of Elvey's *Festal March* was published possibly in the year of the wedding.[245] The march is a straightforward, effective setting with a quiet lyrical middle section. It seems to have been popular, for there are several later editions, including the full orchestral version and also an arrangement for organ solo.[246]

As one of the three correspondents of the *Scotsman* noted, the bridegroom and his two supporters had entered 'very quietly at the south door' (see the plan of St George's Chapel in Illustration 10.4).[247] The commemorative ceremonial recorded that, after arriving 'at the South Entrance to the Chapel', the bridegroom was meant to go to 'a Room prepared for him near the Entrance'.[248] The *Illustrated London News* explained in more detail that he and his supporters were to stay 'a moment in the Bray Chapel, and then proceeded to the haut-pas, at the right

---

[238] Spencer Ponsonby [Ponsonby-Fane from 1875 onwards] at LC's Office at St James's Palace, to Dean of Windsor, 3 March 1871, *Wsg XVII.30.1*.

[239] 'Royal Marriage', *London Journal*, p. 238. Elvey's march is also mentioned in Ceremonial 1871b, p. 7.

[240] See OS 1871.

[241] 'Sir George Job Elvey', p. 5.

[242] Lady Elvey, *Life and Reminiscences*, pp. 206 and 212, also p. 346.

[243] 'Marriage of The Princess Louise', *Morning Post*, p. 5.

[244] Quoted (anonymously) in Lady Elvey, *Life and Reminiscences*, p. 212.

[245] George Elvey, *Festal March Performed at the Marriage of H.R.H. The Princess Louise, with the Marquis of Lorne* [...] (London: Novello, Ewer & Co., [1871?]). Seen as *Lbl h.2733.u.(3)*.

[246] George Elvey, *Festal March for Full Orchestra* (London: Novello, Ewer & Co., [1897]). Seen as *Ob Mus. 222 c.9*: these are the individual parts – but without string parts. George Elvey, *Festal March*, arr. for organ by Charles Hancock (London: Novello, Ewer & Co., [1896]).

[247] [2nd correspondent], *Scotsman*.

[248] Ceremonial 1871b, p. 7.

centre of which they took their places'.[249] The Bray Chapel is right situated next to the south entrance, at the end of the South transept. It would thus appear that the bridegroom's procession did not walk up the length of the nave, but that he went either directly to the quire entrance and then to the altar, or even around the South aisle to the altar. In any case, this would have deprived those present in the nave of even more of the ceremony. The bridegroom's procession was accompanied by the march from Handel's oratorio *Joseph*.[250]

The third and last procession was that of the bride, who entered via the 'West Entrance' and thus walked up the full length of the nave.[251] One commentator later recorded that the bride 'was given away by the Queen in person'.[252] Like Princess Helena in 1866, the bride was led into the chapel by Queen Victoria and the Prince of Wales – and now also by the Duke of Saxe Coburg and Gotha (Prince Albert's brother), who had then been absent.[253] Their entrance was marked by almost theatrical effect. One correspondent recorded that after the initial entrances, 'For a moment or two the doors were closed, in order to be reopened to admit her Majesty and the bride's procession.'[254] One of the *Scotsman* correspondents at this stage noted in an even more dramatic tone:

> At a signal the curtain is drawn, and the bride and the Queen enter the nave. Then roll the drums, and ring the trumpets, and peal the organ, and eyes fill and glisten [...].[255]

This appears to be one of the few references to trumpet fanfares at this wedding and it is possible that this was the only procession announced by them. The German account recorded that music of 'timpani and trumpets' ('Pauken und Trompetengeschmetter') announced the arrival of the queen and the bride.[256] Similarly, other correspondents reported for the entrance of the bride:

> The organ, which had for some time been giving symptoms of uneasiness, now burst forth in triumphal strains as the eight bridesmaids, the heralds of the bride, made their appearance. Then there was an 'alarum [*sic*] of trumpets,' a roll of drums, and her Royal Highness the Princess Louise and her Majesty the Queen entered.[257]

It is not clear what the organ's 'symptoms of uneasiness' were. This may be the 'few notes from the organ', referred to in another account, upon which 'all rose' and 'all eyes were turned towards the western entrance'.[258]

The ceremonial and the accounts agree that the bride's procession was accompanied by the march from Mendelssohn's *Athalie*.[259] However, according to the German account the bridal procession went 'slowly through the Chapel' to the 'National Anthem', and the organ played the march from Mendelssohn's *Athalie* only somewhat later, when the 'high personages and

---

[249] 'Marriage of Princess Louise at Windsor', *ILN*, p. 323.

[250] Ceremonial 1871b, p. 7.

[251] Ceremonial 1871b, p. 8.

[252] Beaven, *Popular Royalty*, p. 194.

[253] Ceremonial 1871b, p. 9. See also 'Royal Marriage', *London Journal*, p. 238; and the unidentified engraving in *Lna LC 2/81*, p. 362 (possibly from *The Morning Post* of 22 March 1871).

[254] 'Marriage of Princess Louise at Windsor', p. 323.

[255] [2nd correspondent], *Scotsman*.

[256] 'Die Hochzeit der Prinzessin Louise', [p. 2].

[257] 'Royal Wedding', *Every Saturday*. See also [2nd correspondent], *Scotsman*.

[258] 'Marriage of The Princess Louise', *Morning Post*, p. 5.

[259] Ceremonial 1871b, p. 10; and 'Royal Marriage', *London Journal*, p. 238. Ceremonial 1871a (that is, the version in future tense), p. 10, stipulates merely 'a March being played by the Organ'.

their numerous entourage took their seats'.[260] It is possible that, as in 1863, the actual march did not begin until the processions entered the quire, with the processions up the nave accompanied by brass music. At the same time, however, it is notable that – in contrast to 1863 – none of the known reports mentions trumpets and drums heading the individual processions through the nave. Indeed, there appears to be no evidence for the participation of these in the Chapel.

In any case, with its oringinal context, Mendelssohn's 'War March of the Priests' from *Athalie* would appear to be have been a somewhat individual choice to accompany the bride's entrance. In fact, the bridegroom's and bride's processional marches at this wedding were exactly the reverse of what they had been in 1863 – again showing that these entrance marches were not linked with particular processions, but seemingly chosen at random.

Music of the Service

There was again not much music during the actual service and one of the *Scotsman* correspondents recorded:

> The responses were spoken by the congregation, and the choir simply chanted two Psalms and a Hallelujah by Beethoven before the benediction.[261]

Other accounts noted that the choir sang 'the two marriage Psalms (Double Chant in A)' – which must mean both psalms stipulated as alternatives in the order of service in the Prayer Book.[262] A list with expenses for the performers at the wedding refers to 'Printing the 2 Psalms on a card / for ~~charities~~ [in different ink:] chanting'.[263] The ceremonial also noted 'The Choir sang two Psalms (Double Chant) by Dr. G. J. Elvey'.[264] It is not clear to which chant exactly this refers, as there appear to be at least four double chants in A by Elvey.[265] The singing of both alternative psalms was rather unusual, at least for a royal wedding. The revised account in the *Musical Standard* furthermore added the detail that 'the Glorias to both psalms were played and sung by the band, organist, and choir' – the performance would thus have followed Smart's musical emphasis on the *Gloria Patri* used at the 1858 wedding in.[266]

As in 1863, the Hallelujah Chorus from Beethoven's oratorio *The Mount of Olives* was performed near the end of the service. Whereas it had then functioned as the recessional, to accompany the bridal couple's procession out of the Chapel, it was now included as an anthem, and clearly within the service – distinctly 'before the Blessing', as the ceremonial noted.[267] The three lines of text of Beethoven's chorus were included in the programme of music bound in with the order of service. One unnamed writer referred to the music of the chorus in a rather romaticizing way and described it as:

---

[260] 'Die Hochzeit der Prinzessin Louise', [p. 2]: '[…] unter den Klängen der englischen Nationalhymne "God save the Queen" bewegte sich der Brautzug langsam durch die Kapelle. […] Während die allerhöchsten Herrschaften und ihr zahlreiches Gefolge ihre Sitze einnahmen, spielte die Orgel den Marsch aus Mendelssohn's "Athalie", […].'

[261] [3rd correspondent], *Scotsman*.

[262] 'Musical Gossip', *The Athenaeum*, 2265 (25 March 1871), pp. 376–77, here p. 376. Same in 'Marriage of Princess Louise at Windsor', p. 323.

[263] List in *Lna LC 2/86*. For more on this list see below.

[264] Ceremonial 187, p. 10.

[265] See http://www.anglicanchant.nl/keys/key0023.html (accessed 1 November 2021).

[266] *Musical Standard*, 14 (1 April 1871), p. 149. For 1858 see Chapter 6, fns 185 and 189.

[267] Ceremonial 1871b, p. 10; and the list of music in OS 1871. See also 'Marriage of Princess Louise at Windsor', p. 323; and *Musical Standard*, 14 (25 March 1871), p. 137.

a tender and pathetic, but most royal, musical blessing of Beethoven, admirably rendered by Dr. Elvey, and more expressive of the thought and prayers of those witnessing the spectacle than any words could well be. The voices of the Queen's choristers mingle with the organ with admirable effect.[268]

Incidentally, the last remark indicates that the band did not play in this chorus, but merely the organ. It cannot be known, however, how accurate this report was: given that a band was present, there does not seem to be any reason why it should not have played in the anthem.

The ceremonial recorded that after the final blessing 'the March from Handel's "Occasional Oratorio" was played on the Organ', and the two accounts in the *Musical Standard* specified that this was 'Handel's "March" from the Occasional Overture'.[269] This, then, was the march from the overture of Handel's *Occasional Oratorio* (HWV 62), which had accompanied the queen's entrance at the 1858 wedding. At the 1871 wedding, the performance of this march gave cause to a biting comment. With reference to the recent Franco-Prussian war and the presence of the Prussian Crown-Prince (the bride's brother-in-law), one account emphasized rather provocatively:

> What a different scene was this to those blood-won triumphs from which the German Prince had just come, and how different from the battle-music which he has been hearing, the sweet and holy melody of Handel, with which the skilful organist concludes the ceremony. Again one is sensible that music is much more eloquent than language.[270]

It is impossible to know how Elvey played this march from Handel's martial oratorio, composed on the Jacobite rebellion in 1745–46, to give it a 'sweet and holy melody'. This is a good example of how music at such events, and especially its interpretation, can become very meaningful.

The ceremony was altogether rather short, with the German account, seemingly excluding the entrance and recess processions, noting that it 'had taken only about ten minutes'.[271] Even if the service may have been a least a bit longer, there can be little doubt that – with the two psalms and Beethoven's chorus – music made up a substantial portion of it.

Referring to 'the novel and thrilling influence of a union with a subject by a member of our Royal House', the music journal *The Orchestra* had argued a couple of weeks before the wedding that it was 'time England had its new Royal Wedding Music of just pre-eminence and certain durability', which it defined as 'something better than a bald chorale of the modern German school' – possibly referring to the hymn-chorales of the previous weddings.[272] The journal particularly emphasized that there was 'no need to invoke foreign talent' and that 'An English musician should commemorate an event in English history.' Pointing to the lack of newly-written wedding anthems, the journal asked for the production of a new one for this wedding. It suggested a setting of Psalm 67, as the most appropriate text, provocatively ending its article with the question 'Who is to do it?' Obviously, nothing came of it for this wedding.

Edmund Fellowes has noted that 'Elvey again composed a special anthem'.[273] Yet, considering that, apart from Beethoven's chorus, there is no evidence for any other anthem within the actual service, this may, as for 1863, again refer to a topical offering that was – if at all – performed on another occasion. Again, Elvey's composition appears to be lost.

---

[268] Anonymous, quoted in Lady Elvey, *Life and Reminiscences*, p. 206.

[269] Ceremonial 1871b, p. 10; *Musical Standard*, 14 (25 March 1871), p. 137 and (1 April 1871), p. 149. See also 'Marriage of Princess Louise at Windsor', p. 323 ('one of Handel's marches was played on the organ').

[270] Anonymous, quoted in Lady Elvey, *Life and Reminiscences*, pp. 207–08.

[271] 'Die Hochzeit der Prinzessin Louise', p. [2]: 'nur etwa zehn Minuten gedauert hatte'.

[272] 'Royal Wedding Music', *The Orchestra*, 388 (3 March 1871), pp. 361–62, here p. 362.

[273] Fellowes, *Organists*, p. 76.

7—The 'Windsor Castle' Weddings: The Mid-Victorians I

Performance Conditions

The reports – especially those in the *Musical Standard* – provide many details on the performance conditions at this wedding. In addition, the Lord Chamberlain sent Elvey a list of payments for the musicians.[274] The choir had been reported to include 'the singers of St. George's Chapel and the Queen's private chapel'; and while one account of the ceremony noted that the choir of St George's had been 'strengthened for the occasion', that in the *Musical Standard* concrete details:

> The vocal portion was given by the lay clerks (Messrs. Mitchell, Knowles, Marriott, Dyson, Adams, Barnby, Tolley, Briggs, Hunt, Large, and Ramsbottom) and twelve boys of the St. George's choir, and the three lay clerks (Messrs. Fielding, Ball, and Redman) and six boys of the Private Chapel choir. Dr. Elvey presided at the organ.[275]

In contrast to this, the Lord Chamberlain's list of payments refers to '12. Men S.ᵗ George's Choir', '2 [Men] Private Chapel Choir', '17 Choristers', and 'expenses of the Private Chapel Choir who had to come twice from London 3 men + 4 boys'.[276] As it records the expenditure, this list might be the more reliable source in terms of the numbers. Accordingly, the choir would have consisted of altogether seventeen men and twenty-one boys.

It is noteworthy that the choir included singers of the Private Chapel choir from London – presumably the choir at at Buckingham Palace – but no singers from the Private Chapel choir in Winsor Castle that had sung at the 1866 wedding. This appears to be the earliest reference to this London choir's participating at a royal wedding.

The Lord Chamberlain's list sent to Elvey refers also to the band, in an unspecified number of 'Instrumentalists'. The first account in the *Musical Standard* detailed that the band was 'numbering eleven, composed of members of Her Majesty's private band, and others' and 'was led by Mr. Gunniss', specially listing 'Trumpet, Mr. T. Harper'.[277] The journal's revised report a week later explained:

> The band was composed of Messrs. Gunnis (1st) and Rendle (2nd) and others, at violins; Mr. Aylward at Cello and Mr. R. Bramsome at basso; Mr. T. Harper trumpet, and Corporal Major Woodhouse at timpani.[278]

Thus the band seems to have consisted of strings and a trumpet only and was probably quite small. The known sources do not record any payments to fanfare trumpeters and drummers.

The ceremonial recorded that Elvey 'presided at the Organ'.[279] The *Musical Standard* furthermore detailed that Elvey played the organ throughout the whole ceremony, 'assisted' by 'Mr. R. T. Gibbons'.[280] All the same, it was reported that it was Elvey himself 'who conducted the choir'.[281] Notably, it does not seem to be recorded where all the musicians were placed. The choir

---

[274] 'The Lord Chamberlain / to G.I. Elvey': 'For Expenses of Instrumental & vocal Performers / for the Marriage of H.R.H. Princess Louise in Sᵗ Georges Chapel Windsor 21. March 1871.', undated copy in *Lna LC 2/86*. This file generally includes some more material on the payment of the musicians.

[275] 'The Court', *ILN*, 18 March 1871, p. 259; 'Musical Gossip', p. 376; *Musical Standard*, 14 (25 March 1871), p. 137.

[276] Copy in *Lna LC 2/86*.

[277] *Musical Standard*, 14 (25 March 1871), p. 137. For the two trumpeters named Thomas Harper, father and son, and their role at the Victorian court see Elisa Koehler, *A Dictionary for the Modern Trumpet Player* (Lanham: Rowman & Littlefield, 2015), pp. 78–79; and John Wallace and Alexander McGrattan, *The Trumpet* (New Haven: Yale University Press, 2011), p. 212. See also below, Chapter 8, fn. 51.

[278] *Musical Standard*, 14 (1 April 1871), p. 149.

[279] Ceremonial 1871b, p. 12.

[280] *Musical Standard* (1 April 1871), p. 149.

[281] 'Musical Gossip', p. 376.

British Royal Weddings

was possibly put in the organ loft, next to the organ, and Elvey could then easily have contucted it himself. The band, however, was probably further away. One correspondent noted that 'one side of the organ-loft' was 'occupied by the Press'.[282] Therefore, space in the organ loft would have been tight and the band put somewhere else, possibly into another gallery. Indeed, the *Musical Standard* observed that Elvey was supported by a sub-conductor, explaining: 'The time between the organ and band was accurately indicated by Mr. Hancock, a pupil of Dr. Elvey's.'[283]

After the ceremony, the music was disseminated at least somewhat more widely, beyond those present at the wedding. Elvey's widow recorded that 'a portion of the music used at this ceremonial' was performed on the Sunday afternoon after the wedding, and 'an immense congregation filled the choir and nave of St. George's Chapel'.[284]

The Scottish Aspect

It was presumably with reference to the choice of bridegroom that one of the *Scotsman* correspondents referred to the service as 'a pageant, if not of unusual splendour, certainly of unusual interest'.[285] Tooley later summarized that this wedding 'may be termed the "Scottish" wedding in the Queen's family, as the nationality of the bridegroom was emphasized in all the arrangements'.[286]

Indeed, the Scottish component of this wedding was to some extent also reflected in the music. It was reported that 'The music of "the pipes" was heard just before the Duke and Duchess of Argyll [the bridegroom's parents] arrived'.[287] In addition, one of the *Scotsman* correspondents recorded that, on their arrival at the Chapel, 'Each of the royal family was honoured with a salute, the band of the Highlanders playing the National Anthem.'[288] More directly, the *London Journal* described that the procession of members of the royal family was announced outside by 'the sound of "God save the Queen" [...], mingled with a "screed" of bagpipes'.[289] For the bridegroom's arrival, the journal recorded that 'There was heard without [= outside] another "screed" of bagpipes', and one of the *Scotsman* correspondents detailed 'the band playing "Scots wha hae wi' Wallace bled."'[290] According to Giles St Aubyn the bridegroom 'processed down the aisle to the strains of "The Campbells are Coming"'.[291] However, the evidence for this statement is not clear and it might just be a later, fanciful idea – akin to Prince Albert's 'Conquering Hero' in 1840, discussed in the previous chapter.

While there appear not to have been any concrete Scottish references in the music of the service itself, there were some more afterwards. During the wedding breakfast in the Oak Room, the band of the Grenadier Guards played music 'in the Quadrangle', beginning with

---

[282] 'Marriage of The Princess Louise', *Morning Post*, p. 5. Compare also the discussion on the musicians' place at the 1879 wedding, in the following chapter, with Figure 8.1.

[283] Account in *Musical Standard* (25 March 1871), p. 137; similar in *Musical Standard* (1 April 1871), p. 149.

[284] Lady Elvey, *Life and Reminiscences*, p. 209.

[285] [2nd correspondent], *Scotsman*.

[286] Tooley, 'Weddings of the Queen's Children', p. 50.

[287] 'Marriage of Princess Louise at Windsor', p. 323.

[288] [1st correspondent], 'Marriage of The Princess Louise and Marquis of Lorn', *Scotsman* (22 March 1871), p. 2: 'The Ceremony'.

[289] 'Royal Marriage', *London Journal*, p. 238.

[290] 'Royal Marriage', *London Journal*, p. 238; and [2nd correspondent], *Scotsman*.

[291] Giles St Aubyn, *Queen Victoria: A Portrait* (London: Sinclair-Stevenson, 1991), p. 415.

7—The 'Windsor Castle' Weddings: The Mid-Victorians I

Mendelssohn's Wedding March – but there was then also a programme of music by the 'Pipers'.[292] The use of bagpipes before and after the ceremony was the seemingly earliest musical reference to the Northern kingdom at a royal wedding.

—◈—

Overall, the royal weddings after the death of Prince Albert in 1861 retreated again more into the private area, removed from the public eye and the direct attention of the London metropolis. The opening to the public seen at the weddings of Queen Victoria and the Princess Royal was thus not continued. Notwithstanding the now obligatory press attendance, the weddings from 1863 onwards confined themselves not only to Windsor but very much specifically to the Castle. This retreat was to continue with the weddings of the remaining children of Queen Victoria over the following decades.

---

[292] Card with handwritten programme of music by 'GRENADIER GUARDS BAND' and printed card with 'Pipers' Programme', both in *Wra RA F&V/WED/1871*.

8

Routine and Innovation: The Mid-Victorians II

ETWEEN 1874 AND 1885, Queen Victoria's four remaining children married. The ceremonies, on the whole, followed the parameters of the previous decades, with a more or less established pattern, a ceremonial routine. Nevertheless, each wedding had its own, unique characteristics, and each included some notable changes and innovations – especially also as regards the venue, the ceremonial and the music. In fact, the very first wedding in this group was very exceptional.

Prince Alfred, Duke of Edinburgh, and Princess Marie Alexandrovna of Russia, 23 January 1874

Prince Alfred was Queen Victoria's second son. Since the Prince of Wales had children, however, he was no longer that high up in the order of succession. Created Duke of Edinburgh in 1866, in 1893 he succeeded his paternal uncle as Duke of Saxe-Coburg and Gotha, and he spent the rest of his life in Germany. In 1874, he married Grand Duchess Maria Alexandrovna of Russia, only surviving daughter of Tsar Alexander II. John van der Kiste has provided a good description of the overall context of the wedding in his biography of the prince.[1] He makes good use of the account of Lady Augusta Stanley, whom Queen Victoria had sent to report her all the details. As van der Kiste points out, this wedding 'was unique among those of Queen Victoria's children in that it was the only one to take place outside England, and also the only one at which she was not present'.

The wedding on 23 January 1874 took place in the bride's homeland, in the Winter Palace at St Petersburg. No part of the wedding ceremonies took place in Britain, which saw merely public rejoicings.[2] There were two ceremonies in St Petersburg: an Orthodox and an Anglican one, so as to cater for both the bride's and the bridegroom's religion. In mid-November the *Times* reported that

> The English Chapel at St. Petersburg being too small to accommodate the Court, a Hall in the Winter Palace will probably be fitted up for the marriage of Prince Alfred according to the rites of the Anglican Church.[3]

In the end, the Orthodox service in chapel was followed by an Anglican ceremony in the 'Alexander Hall' of the Winter Palace, conducted by Arthur Stanley, the Dean of Westminster, Lady Augusta's husband. Dean Stanley included a description of both the Orthodox and the Anglican ceremonies in a letter to his sister.[4] Interestingly, both Stanley, and also published reports of this

---

[1] John van der Kiste, *Alfred: Queen Victoria's Second Son* (Strout: Fonthill Media, 2013), Chapter 7; the following quotation on the first page.

[2] For much material on the illumination of public buildings see *Lna WORK 21/12/4*.

[3] 'The Duke of Edinburgh's Marriage', *Times*, 15 November 1873, p. 5.

[4] See Rowland E. Prothero, *Life and Letters of Dean Stanley* (London: Thomas Nelson & Sons, 1909), pp. 491–93.

wedding specifically referred to the particular copies of the prayer books used – listing their use at previous royal weddings and also other royal occasions.[5] The prayer books are not referred to that prominently for any other wedding, highlighting that the order of service was this time not specially printed.

Not much is known about the music at the two ceremonies. As Sarah Tooley pointed out for the Orthodox rite, 'There was no instrumental music, it being against the rules of the Greek [that is 'Orthodox'] Church, but the singing was truly magnificent.'[6] The reports noted that the service concluded with a Te Deum, a 'triumphal chant, a splendid volume of human voices'.[7] Dean Stanley recorded enthusiastically:

> The singing was magnificent. The Lord's Prayer again struck me as the most beautiful vocal music I had ever heard.[8]

Indeed, the music of this ceremony must have been particularly noteworthy. The *Times*, after describing that in the Orthodox rite 'all made a *coup d'œil* very impressive and magnificent', emphasized that

> the music of the matchless bass and soprano voices was the soul of the spectacle; and if one can hardly transfer to paper the material splendours of that Imperial panorama, how shall one convey an idea of the sweet ebbing and flowing of the waves of sound which broke upon the ear, and wound their magical way into the innermost recesses of the soul.[9]

This description rings very much with Lady Augusta Stanley's judgment that 'The music was more beautiful than can be told.'[10]

The Anglican ceremony

For the Anglican ceremony, Dean Stanley recorded that 'The Russian choir was on my right'.[11] This matches with the depiction in Nicholas Chevalier's watercolour painting of the ceremony, which shows a group of singing boys quite distinctly in the foreground, to the left of the altar, which is to the right of the minister facing the congregation (Illustration 8.1). A sketch of the scene that Chevalier prepared soon after the ceremony, to be sent to Queen Victoria, has a group of uniformed dignitaries in the place of the choir and does not show any singers.[12] It is possible that, in the pressure of time, he omitted this detail but later inserted the choir truthfully in his final painting.

---

[5] Prothero, *Life and Letters*, p. 493; and, for instance, 'The Marriage of the Duke of Edinburgh', *Times*, 22 January 1874, p. 5.

[6] Sarah A. Tooley, 'The Weddings of the Queen's Children', *The Lady's Realm: An Illustrated Monthly Magazine*, 9 (November 1900 to April 1901), pp. 47–56, here p. 56. NB The rite was Russian Orthodox, not Greek Orthodox as stated.

[7] 'Marriage of the Duke of Edinburgh', *Times*, 22 January 1874; and 'The Marriage of the Duke of Edinburgh', *Times*, 24 January 1874, p. 9.

[8] Prothero, *Life and Letters*, p. 462.

[9] 'Marriage of the Duke of Edinburgh', *Times*, 24 January.

[10] Letter of 23 January 1874, in *Later Letters of Lady Augusta Stanley, 1864–1876: Including Many Unpublished Letters to and from Queen Victoria and Correspondence with Dean Stanley, her Sister, Lady Frances Baillie, and Others*, ed. by the Dean of Windsor and Hector Bolitho (London: J. Cape, [1929]), pp. 214–17, here p. 216.

[11] Prothero, *Life and Letters*, p. 492.

[12] See Nicholas Chevalier, 'The Anglican Marriage Service of Alfred, Duke of Edinburgh and Maria Alexandrovna, 23 January 1874', pencil, pen and ink, coloured pencil and watercolour, dated 11 February 1874, *Royal Collection, RCIN 920785* (available online via https://www.rct.uk).

8—Routine and Innovation: The Mid-Victorians II

Illustration 8.1: Nicholas Chevalier, 'Marriage of Alfred, Duke of Edinburgh and the Grand Duchess Marie Alexandrovna of Russia, St Petersburg, 23 January 1874: The Anglican Ceremony', pencil, bodycolour and watercolour painting 1874, *Royal Collection, RCIN 451865*, Royal Collection Trust / © Her Majesty Queen Elizabeth II 2021.

Before the wedding, the *Times* had announced some details of the music:

> The choristers of the Imperial Chapel will sing in Russ [*sic*] psalms in the middle and at the end of the English marriage service.[13]

In slight contrast, Dean Stanley recorded that they sang not in the middle and end, but at the beginning and end: he noted that 'The music of the choir broke out with Psalm xxi.1' as the bridal couple together with the tsar and tsarina 'advanced', and also that after 'the final benediction' came 'the chanting of Psalm cxii. 1, 2, 3'.[14]

After the ceremony, the *Times* reported of altogether three musical items in the ceremony.[15] It recorded that at the beginning of the service, 'The chant of the Russian choir burst forth in a torrent of splendid sound'; later, 'In the midst of the service then came the Anthem, sung by the boys of the Imperial Chapel'; and lastly, after the final blessing 'the choir gave the concluding anthem, a triumphal strain of surprising volume', before the recess. The performance of the 'Anthem' in 'the midst of the service' may be the moment depicted in Chevalier's painting: the shown choristers all look like boys – some younger, some older.

---

[13] 'Marriage of the Duke of Edinburgh', *Times*, 22 January.

[14] Prothero, *Life and Letters*, p. 493.

[15] 'Marriage of the Duke of Edinburgh', *Times*, 24 January.

They hold music in their hands and appear to be singing, while the couple are kneeling at the altar and receive the blessing.

What exactly these three Russian pieces were that the choir sang seems not to be known. The *Times* correspondent added merely a very appreciative comment about 'the beauty of the singing at both services', highlighting that 'it was entirely vocal, and the unison of voices was always in perfect time, hard as it is to sing correctly without accompaniment'.[16] The incorporation of three Russian pieces in the otherwise Anglican (and English) ceremony is noteworthy: this was the first – and so far only – British royal wedding since the Reformation to include so much non-English music.

Overall, notwithstanding that this wedding took place abroad, it was probably one of the most splendid 'British' royal weddings of the era. As the *Times* correspondent pointed out, 'those who have witnessed it are not likely soon again to behold such another pageant', explaining that the wedding had been 'celebrated with Imperial splendour, and no Court in Europe can match the full pomp of the Winter Palace'.[17]

Prince Arthur, Duke of Connaught and Strathearn, and Princess Louise Margaret of Prussia, 13 March 1879

Five years after his older brother, on 13 March 1879, Queen Victoria's third son, Prince Arthur, Duke of Connaught and Strathearn, married Princess Louise Margaret of Prussia. As for the 1858 wedding, the Prussian side seems to have asked for the ceremony to be in Prussia. In her book on royal marriages, Princess Catherine Radziwill later interpreted that Prince Arthur had been Queen Victoria's favourite son and that the queen 'insisted upon his nuptials being celebrated in England, and they accordingly took place at Windsor'.[18] In early November 1878, Spencer Ponsonby-Fane, Comptroller of the Lord Chamberlain's Office, had already informed the Office of Works that the wedding was 'appointed to take place at Saint George's Chapel, Windsor Castle in February next.'[19] In the end, however, the planning for the wedding was affected by the demise of Princess Alice, on 14 December. Five days later, Queen Victoria recorded in her journal:

> Arthur much worried about his marriage, which is finally decided to be at Windsor on the 13th of March, instead of 10th Feb: & will take place, without banquets & festivities.[20]

Notwithstanding the previous royal weddings at Windsor, after this wedding, the choice of Windsor still met with some pronounced, harsh criticism.[21] Yet, apart from the fact that St George's Chapel seemed overall on the way to becoming the preferred venue for royal weddings, for Queen Victoria and her family this wedding was another one that concurred with difficult times, and this may have reinforced the queen's choice of the more recluse Windsor.

---

[16] 'Marriage of the Duke of Edinburgh', *Times*, 24 January.

[17] 'Marriage of the Duke of Edinburgh', *Times*, 24 January.

[18] Princess Catherine Radziwill, *The Royal Marriage Market of Europe* (New York: Funk and Wagnalls Company, 1915), p. 245. This appears to have been her own recollection.

[19] Ponsonby-Fane to A. B. Mitford, 6 November 1878, in *Lna WORK 19/138*.

[20] *QVJ*, 19 December 1878. See also Ponsonby-Fane to A. B. Mitford, 27 December 1878, in *Lna WORK 19/138*, where he informs him of the postponement and asks to reschedule the preparatory work.

[21] See the discussion in Chapter 11.

8—Routine and Innovation: The Mid-Victorians II

Ceremony and Music

In terms of the liturgy and music, the ceremony was similar to those in 1863 and 1871. The service was again performed by the Archbishop of Canterbury, assisted by other clerics.[22] There is now some more information on the specially produced orders of service. Thirty-six copies bound in velvet were provided, two in 'Watered Silk' and 264 copies 'in White Watered Paper'.[23] In addition, '350 Programmes of Music 1 Page in red & black' were printed. It is not clear whether the number of 350 included the programmes that were bound in with the orders of service or whether these were all given out separately. As in 1871, the evidence of the special orders of service is not necessarily reflected in the main picture of the ceremony. In Richard Caton Woodville's painting of the ceremony, which shows the arrival of the bride with her two supporters at the altar, none of the main participants, nor the congregation are holding any booklets or paper in their hand (Illustration 8.2).

Illustration 8.2: Sydney Prior Hall, 'The Marriage of the Duke of Connaught, 13th March 1879', oil on canvas, signed and dated 1881, *Royal Collection, RCIN 404477*, Royal Collection Trust / © Her Majesty Queen Elizabeth II 2021.

---

[22] 'The Royal Wedding', *MG*, 13 March 1879, p. 5.

[23] For this and the following, see the note by Harrison & Sons Printing office, 5 June 1879 to 'F.W. Jennings Esq' and a corresponding bill, in *Lna LC 2/86* [pp. 1–2 of this:] under 'April 25'.

George Elvey, the organist of St George's Chapel, was again in charge of the music. His own copy of the order of service survives but this has no annotations apart from his signature.[24] As in 1871, there was again a small orchestra. The printed programme of music in the order of service matches with the various accounts, notably with Queen Victoria's journal entry for the ceremony.[25] Apart from the psalm chant and Elvey's march as the first piece of the day, all the music was either by Handel or by Mendelssohn.

There were again four distinct entrance processions: those of the royal family, the queen, the bridegroom, and the bride – and all of these were again headed by heralds.[26] The new steps at the west end were by now finished; nevertheless the *Times* explained that they 'had been temporarily enlarged and covered with a canopy [...] and by this entry the procession came in'.[27] All four processions are reported to have been received by trumpet fanfares. For the procession of the royal family and royal guests the *Times* recorded that it had been received with a 'flourish' by the state trumpeters, and 'Then the organ took up the tale' with the march. This was the march from the first act of Handel's *Hercules* (HWV 60).[28] The music is at best about two minutes in length and the march was therefore probably repeated several times to cover the whole of the procession. The *Times* interpreted that all the ceremonial elaboration 'made the march of this procession from the western gate to the daïs at the east end of the choir an affair of time, as well as of splendour'.

At the arrival of Queen Victoria, the National Anthem was heard 'from the outside, and a second flourish of trumpets within'.[29] This indicates that trumpeters were stationed inside St George's (see below). The *Times* recorded that at this point 'the trumpeters blew their loudest'.[30] While this may be mere rhetoric in the accounts to highlight the queen's exalted position, the correspondent of the *Graphic*, for instance, also judged that her procession 'was one of the most impressive incidents of the day'.[31] The processional music was 'Mendelssohn's fine march from *Athalie*', already heard at previous weddings; it was reportedly played on the organ.[32]

The entrance of the bridegroom and his two supporters showed a clear contrast to their quiet entrance at the south door in 1871. They were given a full procession, from the west entrance, up the nave to the quire.[33] This was probably due to the bridegroom's higher rank as a prince of the blood. The music that accompanied the procession was, rather curiously, Elvey's march *Albert Edward*, which had been named after the Prince of Wales (who was one of the

---

[24] *Wsg P. Misc. I 6.*

[25] OS 1879; and *QVJ*, 13 March 1879.

[26] Ceremonial 1879. The heralds received £40 'for their attendance at Windsor'. See 'Duplicate': 'Marriage / OF / His Royal Highness / The Duke of Connaught and Strathearn, K.G.' – 'Fees to the Officers of Arms', 27 May 1879, in *Lna LC 2/86.*

[27] This and the following 'Marriage of the Duke of Connaught', *Times*, 14 March 1879, p. 10.

[28] OS 1879; Ceremonial 1879, p. 8; 'Marriage of the Duke of Connaught', *Times* (1879); 'Royal Marriage Bells', *New York Times*, 14 March 1879, p. 1; 'The Marriage of H.R.H. The Duke of Connaught, K.G., and H.R.H. Princess Louise Margaret of Prussia', *The London Reader of Literature, Science, Art and General Information*, 29 March 1879, pp. 524–26, here p. 525.

[29] 'The Marriage of the Duke of Connaught', *Graphic: Royal Wedding Number*, 20 March 1879, here p. 25.

[30] 'Marriage of the Duke of Connaught', *Times* (1879).

[31] 'Marriage of the Duke of Connaught', *Graphic*, p. 25.

[32] 'Marriage of the Duke of Connaught', *Times* (1879). See also *QVJ*, 13 March 1879; OS 1879; and for the performance 'Royal Marriage Bells' ('played on the organ'); and 'Marriage of the Duke of Connaught', *Graphic*, p. 25 ('The organ pealed forth [...].').

[33] Ceremonial 1879, p. 12.

8—Routine and Innovation: The Mid-Victorians II

two supporters). This choice appears not to have been remarked upon. The music seems to survive merely in an arrangement for military band.[34] At the wedding, however, it was like the other marches, probably played on the organ alone.

On the bride's arrival, one report noted that a 'grand flourish of trumpets' was mixed with 'the sound of hearty cheering outside the chapel'.[35] As will be seen below, the trumpet fanfare at the arrival of the bride was a scene of particular interest. For the bridal procession the programme of music lists 'MARCH, "Occasional"'.[36] Queen Victoria in her journal, and some published accounts, referred merely to 'Handel's Occasional Overture'.[37] The account in the *Graphic* used both 'Handel's "Occasional Overture"' and 'Handel's "Occasional" March' interchangeably.[38] It seems altogether clear that the piece was only the march from the overture to the *Occasional Oratorio*, which in 1871 had been used at the other end of the ceremony – for the newly-weds' recess. With its martial background this march was an interesting choice for the bride's entrance, incidentally matching the militaristic connotations of her Prussian origins.

At least one 1879 report referred to the bridal march distinctly as having been 'given on the organ'.[39] Indeed, with the reports merely referring to the marches being played on the organ, there is no indication that the orchestra played in them – although it is possible that, as in most accounts of the 1871 wedding, this was used as a more generic expression and that the band did, in fact, play in these marches.

This seems to be the earliest wedding for which some music is recorded as having covered the time before the arrival of the main processions:

> At 11.45 the organ began to fill the great building with sound. Sir George Elvey slowly played the minuet from the overture to *Samson* as the officiating clergy took their places within the rails of the altar.[40]

In clear contrast to the formalized processions of royalty, the music that accompanied the clergy's assembling was not a march. All the same, it is intriguing that the report specifically notes that the minuet was played 'slowly'.

For the service itself one account noted that it was 'a choral one, the music being admirably performed'.[41] The programme again listed both 'Psalms 128 and 67', and again to be sung to 'Sir G. Elvey in A', possibly his double-chant used in 1871. The *Times* detailed that the psalms 'were sung by the choir; a stringed band assisted the organ'.[42] As in 1871 (and 1858), the band may have been restricted to the *Gloria Patri* at the end of each psalm.

According to the programme, 'HALLELUJAH CHORUS ..... *Handel*' was to come 'At the conclusion of the Ceremony' and Queen Victoria's record confirms that it came 'After the benediction'.[43] In all likelihood this referred to the chorus from *Messiah*, as in 1858. Like the

---

[34] *Lbl Music Collections h.1549.*

[35] 'Marriage of H.R.H. The Duke of Connaught', *London Reader*, p. 525.

[36] OS 1879.

[37] *QVJ*, 13 March 1879. Same in 'Marriage of H.R.H. The Duke of Connaught', *London Reader*, p. 525; and 'Royal Marriage Bells'.

[38] 'Marriage of the Duke of Connaught', *Graphic*, p. 25.

[39] 'Royal Marriage Bells'.

[40] 'Marriage of the Duke of Connaught', *Times* (1879); almost identical in 'Marriage of the Duke of Connaught', *Graphic*, p. 24.

[41] 'Marriage of the Duke of Connaught', *Graphic*, p. 25.

[42] 'Marriage of the Duke of Connaught', *Times* (1879).

[43] OS 1879; and *QVJ*, 13 March 1879. See also 'Marriage of the Duke of Connaught', *Graphic*, p. 25.

lengthy eighteenth-century anthems, the chorus came only after the liturgy proper. And like those anthems, it was listened to in a special way – with the queen's account pointing to another intriguing ceremonial detail not otherwise recorded. She explains that

> the young couple first embraced their [*sic*] Parents & then came to me, whilst the anthem, the Hallelujah Chorus, was being sung, & remained standing before the altar, till it was finished.[44]

The embracing of parents and other family members was nothing unusual and is reported for almost all royal weddings of the time.[45] However, the fact that the couple after this remained 'standing before the altar' until the end of the Chorus curiously matches with the English tradition, going back to the eighteenth century, of listening to it standing anyway. The congregation would probably have been standing too. The well-known Hallelujah-shouts of the choir surely heightened the overall effect of the scene. In addition, another account noted that 'almost at the same moment was heard the firing of the guns in the Long Walk', which would have yet further increased the thundering effect of the music.[46]

At the end of the ceremony, the couple left St George's Chapel accompanied by Mendelssohn's Wedding March.[47] This was the first royal wedding at which it was heard since 1858, but this appears not to have been commented on. Whereas it had then been performed by the band, it was now, like the other marches, reportedly 'played on the organ'.[48] Yet, like for the entrance marches, it is plausible that it was played by both organ and orchestra.

Practical Arrangements and Performance

Overall, the practical arrangements at the wedding are relatively well documented and seem to have resembled those at the Prince of Wales's wedding in 1863. One notable difference was in the fanfare trumpeters who did not lead the processions up the nave of St George's Chapel but remained *in situ* at the west door. The front page of the *Illustrated London News* shows the trumpeters standing right at the west door, turned inwards, with the bride just arriving between them (Illustration 8.3). With the trumpeters immediately at the door, blowing their loud music more or less directly into the bride's ears, this may appear like an overly stylized depiction. Yet, it was probably not that far-off from the actual scene. One of the illustrations in the *Graphic* shows the state trumpeters announcing the arrival of one of the processions (Illustration 8.4). They stand inside the Chapel, on each side of the west door, blowing out into the nave, but still rather close to those entering through the door. This seems quite plausible: after all, this is how the trumpeters were still positioned, for instance, at the 2018 wedding of Princess Eugenie at St George's.[49] Incidentally, the *Graphic* picture also shows the awning that had been erected over the west steps and that there was no longer a curtain over the door.

The stylized illustration in the *Illustrated London News* shows six trumpeters standing at the west door, to welcome the bride, whereas the picture in the *Graphic* shows only four trumpeters (Illustrations 8.3 and 8.4). The *Times* referred to 'Four Queen's State trumpeters, in long

---

[44] *QVJ*, 13 March 1879.

[45] A more detailed discussion of the exchange and display of such physical signs and gestures at these events will have to remain the topic of a later study.

[46] 'Marriage of the Duke of Connaught', *Graphic*, p. 25.

[47] OS 1879; *QVJ*, 13 March 1879.

[48] 'Marriage of the Duke of Connaught', *Graphic*, p. 25.

[49] At the time of writing this (December 2021), the footage of Princess Eugenie's 2018 wedding is widely available on the internet.

Illustration 8.3: 'Marriage of H.R.H. the Duke of Connaught at Windsor: Trumpeters Announcing the Approach of the Bride', cover picture of *ILN*, 15 March 1879. Author's collection.

Illustration 8.4: 'Arrival of a procession – The Flourish of Trumpets', *Graphic: Royal Wedding Number*, 20 March 1879, p. 18. Author's collection.

gold coats' who 'stood at the door and raised a flourish on their silver trumpets.'[50] This latter report matches not only the illustration in the *Graphic*, but it furthermore accords with the Lord Chamberlain's reference to expenses for 'the attendance of Four Trumpeters', paid to Thomas Harper, who had also participated at earlier royal weddings.[51]

At some point in March, Elvey wrote a list with the expenses for the choir and orchestra, coming to £69 10s.[52] However, eventually he received only £60 to pay for the 'Instrumental Performers and the Choir'.[53] The only concrete number on Elvey's list is a later entered '15' for the 'Choristers'. At least, however, this list records that the singers came from the choirs of St George's Chapel and from Eton. Yet one report furthermore detailed that the choir consisted of 'that of St. George's, with some from the Chapel Royal, and one Eton singer'.[54] The reason why the singers from the Chapel Royal are not listed by Elvey could be the fact

---

[50] 'Marriage of the Duke of Connaught', *Times* (1879).

[51] Lord Chamberlain to Thomas Harper, 13 March 1879 (with reply by Harper of 19 March), in *Lna LC 2/86*. For Harper see also above, Chapter 7, fn. 277–78.

[52] List headed 'Marriage of Duke / of Connaught', dated 'March 29[?unreadable] /79', in *Lna LC 2/86*; transcr. in Appendix B 8.1.

[53] George Elvey to 'Hartley Westrace[?]', 18 March 1879, in *Lna LC 2/86*.

[54] 'Marriage of H.R.H. The Duke of Connaught', *London Reader*, p. 525.

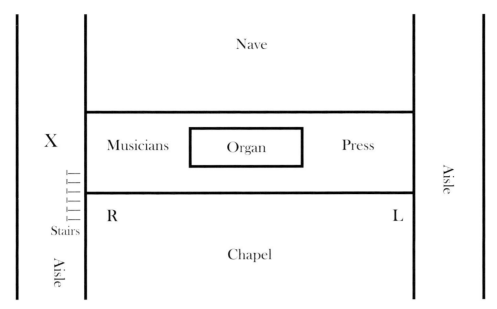

Figure 8.1: Representation of the sketch of the organ and music gallery at St George's Chapel, Windsor at the 1879 wedding; included in Ponsonby-Fane to A. B. Mitford, 12 December 1878, *Lna WORK 19/138*.

they were independent from him in so far as he was not involved in their payment. It cannot be known whether there were any singers from the Chapel Royal.

No details seem to be known for the orchestra. As seen above, it included a 'stringed band' and may thus have resembled the band in 1871.[55] With reference to the musicians, the *Manchester Guardian* recorded another interesting detail:

> Mr. Hallé will be present to-day, by command, at the marriage of the Duke of Connaught and will not, in consequence, arrive in Manchester in time to conduct the first part of 'Elijah,' in which Mr. Hecht will, however, act as his substitute.[56]

This refers to Charles Hallé, the founder of the Hallé Orchestra. It is not clear, however, what exactly he did at the wedding – and whether his orchestra provided instrumentalists for any part of the celebrations.

Due to the number of performers, the space allotted to the musicians caused a problem. In December, Sir Spencer Ponsonby-Fane from the Lord Chamberlain's Office sent a note to the Office of Works and explained:

> Sir G. Elvey presses very much for an Extension of the Space which is set aside for Musicians & Choristers […] As at present arranged it is on [= only?] this wide. [little sketch] He wishes to have the Gallery extended over the Aisle on the R side Where I have put X. […] No doubt he is cramped as it is.[57]

The included little sketch shows the 'present' arrangement, with the space for the suggested extension marked by an 'X' (Figure 8.1). In this context, it is worth remembering that the organ had been placed in the centre of the organ screen when it was build in 1789 (compare Illustration 9.4, below). It remained in this position until 1929, when the case was cut into two, resulting in the two façades on either side of the screen that can be seen today.[58]

---

[55] See above, fn. 42, and (for 1871) Chapter 7, fn. 278.

[56] 'Royal Wedding', *Manchester Guardian* (1879).

[57] Ponsonby-Fane to A. B. Mitford, 12 December 1878, *Lna WORK 19/138*.

[58] See Roger Judd, 'The Organs in St George's Chapel', *St George's Chapel: History and Heritage*, ed. by Nigel Saul and Tim Tatton-Brown (Stanbridge: Dovecote Press, 2010), pp. 193–200, here p. 200.

Elvey's suggested arrangement of the space around the organ for the 1879 wedding matches with that reported for the 1871 wedding in so far as the 'Press' was given one side of the organ loft. Indeed, the correspondent of the *Illustrated London News*, who had also been at the 1863 wedding of the Prince of Wales, explained with some delight:

> The Lord Chamberlain's department are kind enough on the occasion of Royal marriages and Royal funerals to provide for the accommodation of the representatives of the press sundry benches to the left of the organ-loft: the very best point of espial in the whole chapel; since from the summit of the roodscreen the eye can 'rake' at once the nave as well as the choir: whereas on Thursday the privileged spectators in the nave will be unable (the rood-screen intervening) to see anything of what is going on at the altar.[59]

Elvey's suggested extension of the gallery into the south aisle was eventually approved at an expected cost of £15, and the ceremonial accordingly noted that Elvey 'conducted the Orchestra and Choir, for which a temporary gallery was constructed adjoining the Organ Loft'.[60]

The *Manchester Guardian* recorded that, on the morning before the wedding, the bridal couple with some of their close relatives went to St George's Chapel 'to view the preparations' and that 'Sir George Elvey played a selection of music while the royal visitors were in chapel [*sic*], and the choir sang the "National Anthem" as they left the building.'[61] It is not clear whether the 'selection of music' that Elvey played was music that was then used at the wedding – in any case, with the programme of music being printed, it would then probably have been too late for any changes.

Apart from this visit, the bride seems not to have been given any introduction to the ceremonial of the service beforehand, and she appears to have been rather unprepared for what she was expected to do during the ceremony. One report of the wedding pointed out that the bridegroom

> frequently whispered his bride to kneel, rise, and so forth at every proper time, for she, strange to say, seemed to know little about the Service.[62]

Indeed, it appears that there was no overall rehearsal of the ceremony for the participants. This may be infered from a comment in the *Times* on the bride's arrival:

> The bridesmaids sallied from their chapel at the door to meet her, and, as if all had been most carefully rehearsed, they ranged themselves behind, and the procession formed at once.[63]

A rehearsal of the ceremony as such, for its main participants as it were, is not known for any of the earlier weddings, nor for this one. Yet, it is interesting that this fact was alluded to so directly on this occasion – perhaps implying pride in the court's natural ability, as it were, to stage such ceremonies. In the end, Lady Elvey could conclude that this wedding was overall 'a very brilliant scene, and the arrangements were carried out with almost, or quite, as much splendour as those for the marriage of the Prince of Wales had been'.[64]

---

[59] G. A. S., 'Echoes of the Week', *ILN*, 15 March 1879, p. 239. For the 1871 arrangements see the previous Chapter 7, fn. 283.

[60] See the respective correspondence in *Lna WORK 19/138*; and see Ceremonial 1879, p. 20. See also the depiction of Elvey at the organ at the 1882 wedding, in Illustration 8.7 below.

[61] 'Royal Wedding', *Manchester Guardian* (1879).

[62] 'Marriage of H.R.H. The Duke of Connaught', *London Reader*, p. 525.

[63] 'Marriage of the Duke of Connaught', *Times* (1879).

[64] 'Lady' Elvey, *Life and Reminiscences of George J. Elvey [...] Late Organist to H. M. Queen Victoria, and Forty-seven Years Organist of St. George's Chapel, Windsor* (London: Sampson Low, Marston & Company Ltd, 1894), p. 250.

8—Routine and Innovation: The Mid-Victorians II

Prince Leopold, Duke of Albany, and Princess Helen of Waldeck and Pyrmont, 27 April 1882

The youngest of Queen Victoria's sons, Prince Leopold, Duke of Albany, married Princess Helen of Waldeck and Pyrmont on 27 April 1882.[65] As one of the accounts of the wedding pointed out, Waldeck was 'one of the smallest principalities in Germany'.[66] However, in January 1879, Helen's sister Princess Emma had married King William III of the Netherlands and thus put the family on the wider European stage. The latter acted as one of the bride's supporters (together with her father), thus heightening the international aspect of this occasion. There was no doubt that the wedding would take place in Britain rather than at the bride's home – even though her parents were reportedly not happy with that decision.[67]

Overall, one of the *Scotsman* correspondents summarized that 'As nearly as possible to-day's ceremonial resembled that at the marriage of the Princess Louise, and also of the Duke of Connaught.'[68] Indeed, when Ponsonby-Fane informed the Office of Works of the forthcoming wedding, he highlighted that

> The arrangements on this occasion will be precisely the same scale as that provided at the marriage of His Royal Highness The Duke of Connaught in 1879.[69]

There were, nevertheless, some significant innovations. As will be discussed in the final chapter, this wedding overall had a somewhat more public character than the previous one. More directly, there were some notable innovations at the actual ceremony which again took place in St George's Chapel, Windsor. Foremost, Queen Victoria recorded that 'Instead of the long Exhortation, the Arch Bishop made a short & appropriate address […].'[70] Two years previously, in 1880, at the wedding of her cousin, Princess Frederica, daughter of the deposed George V of Hanover, to Baron Alfons von Pawel-Rammingen in the Private Chapel in Windsor Castle, Queen Victoria had already noted without further explanation that at the end of the service 'The Bishop, gave a short & pretty address.'[71] However, 1882 appears to be the earliest reference to an address at a wedding of a more senior member of the royal family.

The pictorial representation of this ceremony, if not the ceremony itself, seems to have been somewhat streamlined: in Sir James Dromgole Linton's painting showing the end of the ceremony, just before the bridal couple leaves the Chapel, the area in front of the altar looks much less busy than in the paintings of previous royal weddings (Illustration 8.5). In particular the side aisles are not filled with galleries for the congregation, as shown in the paintings of the 1863 and 1879 weddings, for instance (see Illustrations 7.5 and 7.7, and 8.2). Instead, in the 1882 painting, the wooden screens blocking off the aisles can clearly be seen. Yet, it appears that the ceremony was altogether no less grand than the last wedding at St George's, in 1879, had been.

---

[65] The German name of the Princess was 'Helene zu Waldeck und Pyrmont'. In English, she has always been referred to as both 'Helen' or 'Helena'. Queen Victoria, in her journal, used the name 'Helen' and this will be used in this study, as it also helps distinguish her from Queen Victoria's daughter Princess Helena.

[66] 'The Royal Marriage: Another Account', *Scotsman*, 28 April 1882, p. 5.

[67] See Charlotte Zeepvat, *Queen Victoria's Youngest Son: The Untold Story of Prince Leopold* (Stroud: Phoenix Mill, 1998/paper back edn 2005), p. 219.

[68] 'Royal Marriage: Another Account'.

[69] Ponsonby-Fane to A. B. Mitford, 6 March 1882, *Lna WORK 19/138*.

[70] *QVJ*, 27 April 1882.

[71] *QVJ*, 24 April 1880.

Illustration 8.5: Sir James Dromgole Linton, 'The Marriage of the Duke of Albany, 27th April 1882', oil on canvas, signed and dated 1885, *Royal Collection, RCIN 404481*, Royal Collection Trust / © Her Majesty Queen Elizabeth II 2021.

Ceremony and Music

The ceremony at St George's Chapel was overall very similar to the previous weddings there. A printed seating plan shows that the nave was this time full with congregation.[72] According to the reports, 'Some hundreds of ladies and gentlemen had been accommodated with seats in the nave', which had 'raised seats on either side'.[73] For the arrival of the main participants, one writer in a popular publication, under the intriguing pseudonym 'Scrutator' reported:

> The forming of each procession was somehow arranged on the steps of the grand entrance, under the awning; it had, I believe, been proposed to set apart the space at the east [*recte* 'west'?] end for this purpose, but the Queen issued an express command that the chairs and platforms [in the nave] should extend right down to the wall.[74]

As at the previous weddings, there was a certain theatrical effect: when the processions entered, 'the double curtains of deep crimson velvet were drawn back and displayed a pretty picture'.[75]

The music of the ceremony was again under the supervision of George Elvey who 'presided at the Organ, and directed the Orchestra and Choir'.[76] Thomas Lea Southgate wrote a detailed review of the ceremony for the *Musical Standard*, and this was similarly critical to that by the aforementioned 'Scrutator'.[77] With these two reviews, this is probably the earliest royal

---

[72] Plan included in *Lna LC 2/96*.

[73] 'The Marriage of H.R.H. Prince Leopold and The Princess Helena of Waldeck Pyrmont', *The Ladies' Treasury for 1882: A Household Magazine*, ed. by 'Mrs. Warren' (London: Bemrose and Sons, 1893), pp. 352–53 and 356, here p. 353; and 'Royal Marriage: Another Account'.

[74] Scrutator', 'At the Wedding', *Truth*, 11:279 (May 1882), pp. 612–13, here p. 612.

[75] 'Royal Marriage: Another Account'.

[76] Ceremonial 1882, p. 17.

[77] T. L. [= Thomas Lea] Southgate, 'Royal Music', *Musical Standard*, 22 (13 May 1882), pp. 296–98.

8—Routine and Innovation: The Mid-Victorians II

ARRIVAL OF THE BRIDE.

Illustration 8.6: 'Arrival of the Bride', (inside) cover picture [that is, p. 3] of *ILN: Royal Wedding Number*, 2 May 1882. Author's collection.

213

wedding for which such a critical discussion of the music, rather than a mere listing and description of the musical numbers, is known.

This time the National Anthem was apparently not played on the arrival of the processions at the Chapel, but there we were again several fanfares, as one account emphasized: 'As each procession arrived, it was announced by the blare of the silver trumpets.'[78] The trumpeters and their fanfares were a notable component of the ceremony, and 'Scrutator' judged that the announcing of all the processions 'by a flourish of trumpets' was 'very effective'.[79] The bridal procession being greeted by the fanfare trumpeters was obviously also a visually attractive, if not iconic sight and, as in 1879, this scene was again chosen for the first illustration in the *Illustrated London News* (Illustration 8.6, compare 8.3).

With one notable exception, the music was overall rather similar to that at previous weddings. As in 1879, there were again four entrance processions, all headed by heralds: those of the royal family, the queen, the bridegroom, and the bride.[80] Again, distinct marches accompanied these processions. For the first, the 'Procession of the Royal Family and Royal Guests', the programme of music included in the order of service stipulated Elvey's 'FESTAL MARCH'.[81] One account reported that Elvey played 'a new march of his own composition on the organ'.[82] Southgate, however, noted distinctly that Elvey's march was 'an old one'.[83] Yet, there may after all have been two marches by Elvey at this wedding. According to the correspondent of the *Irish Times*, Elvey's 'Festal March' accompanied not the royal procession but was played earlier 'at the same time the clergy arrived' – and for the royal procession this refers to another 'march by Sir G. Elvey [...] on the organ'.[84] Similarly, one of the *Scotsman* correspondents explained that Elvey 'played a march on the grand organ while the guests took their seats', that is before the first procession, and probably also referring to the clergy's entrance.[85] Moreover, the *Illustrated London News* observed that 'the organ pealed forth a festal march with triumphal accompaniment, composed by Sir G. Elvey', while the congregation waited; and it later detailed that 'a wedding march, composed for the occasion by Sir G. Elvey, was played on the organ' during the entrance of the first royal procession.[86]

According to another *Scotsman* correspondent, Elvey's 'festal march' accompanied only Queen Victoria's procession.[87] For this, however, the *Graphic* recorded that the organ was 'pealing forth the sonorous strains of Handel's "Occasional Overture."'[88] This uses the same form of words as the printed ceremonial; the printed programme of music detailed again that this was Handel's 'MARCH "OCCASIONAL"'.[89] Queen Victoria's own description provides a rare insight into how such a procession was perceived by those at its centre:

---

[78] 'Marriage of H.R.H. Prince Leopold, *Ladies' Treasury*, p. 353. See also Ceremonial 1882, p. 9.

[79] 'Scrutator', 'At the Wedding', p. 612.

[80] The heralds are clearly mentioned in the various reports.

[81] OS 1882. See also Ceremonial 1882, p. 9; and 'The Royal Wedding: The Ceremony at Windsor', *Irish Times*, 28 April 1882, p. 5.

[82] 'The Royal Marriage', *Observer*, 23 April 1882, p. 3; this account is (literally) reproduced in 'The Royal Marriage: Programme of the Ceremony', *Manchester Guardian*, 24 April 1882, p. 8.

[83] Southgate, 'Royal Music', p. 297.

[84] 'Royal Wedding: The Ceremony at Windsor'.

[85] 'The Royal Marriage', *Scotsman*, 28 April 1882, p. 5; 'Royal Marriage: Another Account'.

[86] 'The Marriage Ceremony', *ILN: Royal Wedding Number*, 2 May 1882, pp. 19–23, here p. 19.

[87] 'Royal Marriage: Another Account'.

[88] 'The Prince's Wedding', *Graphic: Royal Wedding Number*, 6 May 1882, pp. 20–28, here p. 24.

[89] Ceremonial 1882, p. 12; OS 1882.

8—Routine and Innovation: The Mid-Victorians II

> The Procession was headed by the Heralds [...] the trumpets sounded, then the organ pealed forth. It was a thrilling & affecting moment.[90]

The correspondent of the *Irish Times* also pointed to another detail often overlooked in such reports:

> The lusty cheers proceeding from the Castle Yard, which broke the stillness that reigned in the Chapel, anticipated the announcement of the Queen's arrival.[91]

Similarly, one of the *Scotsman* correspondents noted that, announcing the bridegroom's procession, 'the trumpets sounded, drowning the peal of bells that filled the outer air, and in the silent intervals had penetrated to the interior of the chapel.'[92] Thus, the musical accompaniment of the initial entrance processions had not been continuous; rather, in between them, there were 'silent intervals', or moments of 'stillness' – with the noises coming in from outside all the more increasing the suspense and heightening the atmosphere of expectation. In contrast, the bridegroom's arrival was announced by the trumpets when his mother's march 'had hardly ceased', leaving barely any interval.[93] His procession 'passed up the Chapel' to Mendelssohn's march from *Athalie*.[94] As is well-known, Prince Leopold suffered from haemophilia and often had problems with his limbs. Queen Victoria noted that 'contrary to my expectation, dear Leopold walked the whole way up the Nave'.[95] One report pointed out that he 'walked lamely by the help of a stick', whereas another recorded that he 'used a stick to assist him in walking, but his lameness was hardly perceptible'.[96] The anonymous 'Scrutator' observed bluntly that the prince 'looked very ill and very nervous' and that it had been 'evident that he walked with difficulty, and that every step gave him pain'.[97] Mendelssohn's strong and martial march would have presented a poignant contrast to this striking, if not touching sight.

The correspondent of the *Irish Times* had mentioned 'an instrumental accompaniment' for Elvey's 'Festal March' but noted that Mendelssohn's march from *Athalie* 'was played on the organ'.[98] While the bridegroom's march had been heard at previous royal weddings, the march for the bride's procession was noticeably different, newly composed: 'a Special March, by M[onsieur]. Gounod.'[99] The march itself will be discussed in more detail below. One of the *Scotsman* correspondents noted that the bride 'entered the Chapel amid sounds of cheering from without'.[100] However, another correspondent in the same paper recorded more atmospherically that she 'entered, amidst breathless silence, in a blaze of light, with her bridesmaids'.[101]

Following the vows, once again, the service included both psalms, and again sung to a 'CHANT [...] *Sir G. Elvey* in A'.[102] Southgate listed that Elvey 'contributed double chants',

---

[90] *QVJ*, 27 April 1882.

[91] 'Royal Wedding: The Ceremony at Windsor'.

[92] 'Royal Marriage', *Scotsman* (1882).

[93] 'Marriage Ceremony', *ILN* (1882), p. 22.

[94] Ceremonial 1882, 13. Also 'The Prince's Wedding', *Graphic* (1882), p. 24.

[95] *QVJ*, 27 April 1882.

[96] 'Royal Marriage', *Scotsman* (1882); also 'Marriage Ceremony', *ILN* (1882), p. 22.

[97] 'Scrutator', 'At the Wedding', p. 613.

[98] 'Royal Wedding: The Ceremony at Windsor'.

[99] Ceremonial 1882, p. 16; OS 1882.

[100] 'Royal Marriage', *Scotsman* (1882).

[101] 'Royal Marriage: Another Account'.

[102] OS 1882.

indicating that more than one chant were used.[103] 'At the conclusion of the Service' came, as in 1871, Beethoven's Hallelujah Chorus from the *Mount of Olives*.[104] The 'Scrutator' explained that it 'was sung directly the Archbishop had shut the book', probably meaning before the final blessing, as confirmed by other accounts.[105]

The correspondent of the *Illustrated London News* thought that Beethoven's chorus was 'sung with grand effect by the choir'.[106] The anonymous 'Scrutator' also called it 'very fine', but nevertheless simply found it 'too long to be introduced at this stage', and noted that

> this seemed to be the Queen's opinion, as her Majesty was in a decided fidget after two minutes, and would doubtless have stopped the music if she could have communicated with the organ gallery.[107]

At least from this point of view the music had clearly lost its independent status – as in the long anthems during the eighteenth-century – and had become a mere adornment of the ceremony. Incidentally, at this wedding the music may have worked as 'background music' particularly well: not merely during the entrance processions but also at the end. Before the recess, there was reportedly a strong physical gesture of matrimonial unity from the newly-weds, not mentioned for other weddings, and this was accentuated by the music:

> Then, in all its glorious melody, Mendelssohn's Wedding March filled the chapel; while the Prince, turning to his bride, affectionately kissed her.[108]

According to some correspondents, the Wedding March was played by 'the organ'.[109] In contrast to this Southgate, in his very critical tone, noted that it was 'played by a meagre string band aided by the organ'.[110] It is plausible that a small group of string players again assisted in the music, as at the two previous weddings. In any case, the music could be heard outside: one correspondent noted specifically that 'those from without heard the strains of Mendelssohn's Wedding march, which marked the conclusion of the ceremonial'.[111]

Similar to 1871, the 'skirling of bagpipes' was heard as the newly-weds started their return journey from St George's Chapel back to the state rooms in the upper castle.[112] They also played later, back in the castle. However, this time, there was some harsh criticism of their inclusion at the wedding. With reference to the 'foreign guests' Southgate wrote provocatively:

> What they must have thought of the terrible screech of the Scotch pipers who perambulated the Hall after the banquet, one is not anxious to know. Such barbarous sounds may be all very well,

---

[103] Southgate, 'Royal Music', p. 297.

[104] Ceremonial 1882, 17. For its coming before 'the benediction' see 'Royal Wedding: The Ceremony at Windsor'. See also 'THE / ROYAL MARRIAGE.', an unidentified newspaper cutting (ink annotation '1882 April 27th'), in *Wra RA F&V/WED/1882*.

[105] 'Scrutator', 'At the Wedding', p. 613. For the chorus' coming before 'the benediction' see 'Royal Wedding: The Ceremony at Windsor' and 'Royal Marriage: Another Account'; and also 'The Royal Marriage', an unidentified newspaper cutting (ink annotation '1882 April 27th'), in *Wra RA F&V/WED/1882*.

[106] 'Marriage Ceremony', *ILN* (1882), p. 23.

[107] 'Scrutator', 'At the Wedding', p. 613.

[108] 'Royal Marriage: Another Account'. The history of the bridal kiss, and generally of public signs of affection at royal weddings, will have to be the topic of a later study.

[109] 'Royal Marriage', *Scotsman* (1882); 'Royal Wedding: The Ceremony at Windsor'; 'Marriage Ceremony', *ILN* (1882), p. 23.

[110] Southgate, 'Royal Music', p. 297.

[111] 'Royal Marriage: Another Account'.

[112] 'Royal Wedding: The Ceremony at Windsor'.

8—Routine and Innovation: The Mid-Victorians II

heard on their native hills in the distant chill north – and the farther the listener is away from the performers, the better; but to introduce such an antiquated custom to a cultured assembly, and within a few yards of their ears, involved the serious risk of upsetting the digestive organs of those guests present, who hitherto were happily ignorant of such instruments of torture.[113]

After the festivities, as the carriage with the newly-wed couple and other carriages left Windsor Castle, the accounts noted that 'the band played first the National Anthem, and then the Waldeck Hymn'.[114] This, it would appear, was the only musical reference on the day to the bride's origins.

The Bridal March

Musically, the most innovative and noteworthy feature of this wedding was the march that accompanied the bride's entrance: Charles Gounod's 'MARCHE NUPTIALE', which had been 'Composed expressly for the occasion', as the programme of music recorded.[115] In mid-January, it had been reported that Queen Victoria 'always mindful to encourage refining tastes, has commissioned M. Gounod to compose a nuptial march' for the wedding, and one publication furthermore specified that this was to be 'for orchestra and organ'.[116] Percy Scholes observed that the march was 'composed "at the express desire of Her Majesty the Queen" by Gounod, whose residence in England from 1870 to 1875 had made him exceedingly well known here and who was popular at court'.[117] Notwithstanding the queen's general, well-known favouring of his music, it is worth noting that 'Gounod's Marche Religieuse' had been played on the organ at the wedding of Princess Frederica of Hanover in 1880, as Queen Victoria had recorded in her journal.[118]

Yet, the commission, or at least the idea for the new march in 1882 could also have come from the bridegroom, Prince Leopold himself. Scholes suggested that 'As the Duke had always taken an interest in music these special compositions [of this and another march for the wedding] may have been of his own prompting.'[119] Prince Leopold's daughter, Princess Alice, later emphasized that her father 'was not only very musical himself but was a liberal patron and supporter of composers and artists' and that she 'was not surprised, therefore, to find amongst his papers a letter' by Gounod 'in his own hand' about his march.[120] She concluded:

> It seems that this particular composition had been offered by Gounod, or commanded by my father as one enthusiastic musician to another', later observing that her father 'had invited his friend to compose a wedding march for the ceremony'.

Gounod, in fact, wrote two marches for this wedding. The details are recorded in his letter to Prince Leopold, as quoted by Princess Alice. As she explains, the letter is dated 'Jeudi 12 Janvier /82' (Thursday, 12 January 1882), that is over three months before the wedding. In this letter, she

---

[113] Southgate, 'Royal Music', p. 297.

[114] 'Royal Marriage', *Scotsman* (1882). Also 'Marriage Ceremony', *ILN* (1882), p. 23 ('[…] played "God Save the Queen" and the Waldeck national hymn').

[115] OS 1882, programme of music. This was also noted in 'Royal Marriage', *Observer* (1882).

[116] 'The Court', *ILN*, 14 January 1882, p. 35; and 'On-Dits and Facts of the Month', *The Ladies' Treasury for 1882: A Household Magazine*, ed. by 'Mrs. Warren' (London: Bemrose and Sons, 1893), p. 119.

[117] Percy Scholes, *The Mirror of Music, 1844–1944: A Century of Musical Life in Britain as Reflected in the Pages of the Musical Times*, 2 vols (London: Novello, 1947), II, p. 867.

[118] *QVJ*, 24 April 1880.

[119] Scholes, *Mirror of Music*, II, p. 868.

[120] This and the following, Princess Alice, Countess of Athlone, *For my Grandchildren: Some Reminiscences of Her Royal Highness Princess Alice, Countess of Athlone* […] (London: Evans Brothers Ltd, 1966/re-issued 1979), pp. 42–43.

observes, Gounod 'complains about the time allowed for the performance of a "Marche Nuptiale" which he had composed for the celebration of [the] wedding' and she summarizes:

> It would appear that, when it was completed, a third party (possibly Queen Victoria herself) intervened in order to make Gounod's masterpiece conform to the wedding time-table instead of changing the time-table to accommodate the composer's 'Marche Nuptiale'.

From this, it seems that Gounod's march was simply considered to be too long. The composer reportedly replied that

> Cette Marche Nuptiale [...] dure *exactement* le temps indiqué par vos renseignements, c.a.d. cinq minutes!

> [This Marche Nuptiale takes *exactly* the time indicated in your stipulations, that is to say five minutes!][121]

On top of the duration, however, there was another issue. Gounod's march seems to have been 'originally designed by its author to be rendered "à Grand Orchestre et Orgue"'.[122] However, Gounod was 'informed that the music must be confined to the organ and the orchestral accompaniment deleted' – a demand that

> left his spirit utterly crushed, since it rendered worthless a creation to which he had devoted the utmost care and for which he had designed a combined instrumental accompaniment appropriate to the occasion ('met à néant un travail auquel j'avais apporté un soin particulier, et une combinacion instrumentale toute spéciale pour la circonstance').[123]

While Gounod of course had to acquiesce to the royal wishes, he argued that his original march would be 'a work lost to the world ("un travail perdu")', unless he was allowed to include 'the dedication originally agreed upon, namely, "Marche Nuptiale, composé a l'occasion du mariage de S.A.R. Monseigneur le Duc d'Albany, Prince de la Grande Bretagne et de l'Irlande, par Charles Gounod"'. In the words of Princess Alice,

> He sadly concluded that if this crumb of comfort were allowed to fall from the royal table he would compose another piece for the ceremony designed solely for an organ accompaniment ('un autre morceau pour orgue seul destiné à la cérémonie').

In the end, Gounod was allowed the dedication of his march and did compose 'another piece' to be played at the ceremony. Both of Gounod's Wedding Marches were published after the wedding, but with 'reverse' numbering, as it were:

> *Wedding March (No. 1) Composed for the Marriage of H.R.H. The Duke of Albany, K.G. with H.R.H. The Princess Helen of Waldeck,* 'Original Edition for Organ & Three Trombones' (London: Novell, Ewer & Co., [1882]).

> *Wedding March (No. 2) Composed and Dedicated to H.R.H. The Duke of Albany, K.G.,* arr. for piano solo by Berthold Tours (London: Novell, Ewer & Co., [1882]).

As Princess Alice explained, she did not know who the 'third party' was behind the demanded changes in the march – but she interpreted that it was 'Some greater authority' than Prince Leopold, and 'possibly Queen Victoria herself'.[124] It is indeed not implausible that Queen Victoria took such a direct, decisive interest in the music, considering her demand for different

---

[121] Athlone, *Reminiscences*, pp. 43–44 (my own translation).

[122] Athlone, *Reminiscences*, p. 43.

[123] This and the following from Athlone, *Reminiscences*, p. 44. She includes the French quotations.

[124] Athlone, *Reminiscences*, pp. 44 and 43.

8—Routine and Innovation: The Mid-Victorians II

music for the recess at the wedding of her cousin Princess Mary Adelaide of Cambridge in Kew, in 1866, seen in the previous chapter. A few days before the 1882 wedding, the papers had noted that the preparations for the ceremony were all completed and had 'received the final approval of the Queen'.[125] Incidentally, this seems to be one of the earliest mentions of the monarch approving of wedding preparations.

One of the accounts in the *Scotsman* mentioned for the bride's entrance 'Sir George Elvey and the band playing, under the direction of Mr Handcock, of Leicester, Gounod's specially composed march.'[126] It is doubtful, however, that Gounod would have added the band against the explicit directions from the 'greater authority'. In the published score, Gounod's new march does not include the orchestra, but merely three trombones.

In any case, the one aspect that Gounod did not change was the marches' most eminent feature: both marches prominently incorporate the tune of 'God Save the Queen' – in the later march distinctly played on the three trombones. Gounod's reason for including this tune seems not to be known. It was also used for the national song in various German states, and with the text 'Heil dir im Siegerkranz', it was the unofficial anthem of the German Empire of 1871.[127] Yet, the tune had no particular relevance in Waldeck-Pyrmont which, as already mentioned, had its own distinct national song.[128] Although it cannot be known in how far Gounod differentiated in this respect, the incorporation of the tune in the bridal march may as well have been a reference to the bride's future life in Britain, as a daughter-in-law of the queen mentioned in the text.

Without further explanation, the *Irish Times* referred to the 'special wedding march by M. Gounod' as 'a composition of great beauty'.[129] One of the *Scotsman* correspondents, in contrast, recorded that the march 'was admired by few, it taking more the line of Wagner's symphonies than Gounod's sweet melodies.'[130] At the same time, the correspondent referred especially to the use of 'God Save the Queen', commenting that 'The trombone symphony of the National Anthem was particularly well rendered' and concluding that it was this feature that 'saved the march from mediocrity'. The march triggered several very critical comments. One anonymous reviewer's letter was published in two musical journals at once. It included a harsh critique of Gounod's march and criticized particularly the incorporation of 'God Save the Queen':

> The 'three trombones' are employed to blurt out the notes of our national air at unexpected moments, and in an antagonistic rhythm – a peculiarly unhappy and conventional idea: as, on these public occasions the high personages immediately concerned are obliged to hear this tune performed to dreadful satiety, as everybody knows, and from all conceivable quarters.[131]

The ever critical 'Scrutator' judged that 'Gounod's new march' was 'a wretched composition' and explained that it had been 'the universal verdict that "Sullivan would have done it fifty

---

[125] 'Royal Marriage', *Observer* (1882).

[126] 'Royal Marriage: Another Account'.

[127] See Nils Grosch, '"Heil Dir im Siegerkranz!": Zur Inszenierung von Nation und Hymne', in *Reichsgründung 1871: Ereignis, Beschreibung, Inszenierung*, ed. by Michael Fischer, Christian Senkel, and Klaus Tanner (Münster: Waxmann, 2010), pp. 90–103.

[128] For the 'Waldeck Hymn' see above, fn. 114.

[129] 'Royal Wedding: The Ceremony at Windsor'.

[130] 'Royal Marriage: Another Account'.

[131] 'An Englishman', 'M. Gounod's Wedding March', *Musical Opinion and Music Trade Review*, 5:57 (June 1882), p. 354. Reproduced in 'Music at the recent Royal Wedding', *Musical Standard*, 22 (24 June 1882), p. 394.

times better.'"[132] Overall, it was the inclusion of Gounod's march that appears to have sparked a more general critique of all the music at the ceremony. Southgate summarized that the 'musical portion' of the wedding ceremony 'has excited but little attention', arguing that — from 'the conventional fanfare of the Royal trumpeters' at the beginning down to Mendelssohn's Wedding March at the end — 'the music performed was of a well-known and stereotyped description'.[133] He concluded that the music overall 'presented nothing fresh to mark the event'. Similarly, with a perhaps cynical undertone, the 'Scrutator' concluded that 'The most beautiful music throughout the service was the psalm chant.'[134] Southgate judged that it was Gounod's march that was the 'one solitary exception'.[135] Yet, he probably meant merely that this was at least a new piece — but he was still not happy with it. His discussion of the music is not very favourable, and he described the form of the march as 'indeed a whimsical one', commenting that

> The combination of organ and three trombones is only a few degrees less peculiar than that of two flutes and tambourine, for which odd alliance it is said that the 'Hallelujah Chorus' was once arranged.

Neither Southgate nor any of the other commentators seem to have known about the change in Gounod's march — indeed, it appears not to have been made public.

In his overall disapproval of Gounod's march, Southgate mixes two points. On the one hand, he refers to its musical value, emphasizing that 'Commissioned music, it is said, is rarely successful, and this latest curious example supplies yet another confirmation of an impression which obtains widely.' At the same time, however, he refers simply to the national aspect: he criticizes that a composer of French origins provided the Bridal March, emphasizing that 'in what is essentially a national ceremony one may fairly expect native art to have the preference'. Southgate does not hide his disappointment and concludes that 'English music has thus suffered yet another gratuitous slight, while the divine art has been furnished with nothing likely to live'.

As seen above, Gounod's marches were both published. They must have come out soon after the wedding, or indeed before: Southgate could refer to the edition in his critical review in early May, which was just a few days after the wedding — and it would of course have been written some time before that. Moreover, Southgate already referred to a performance at 'a recent Crystal Palace Saturday concert', for which he noted that the march was arranged and played 'with all the aid that orchestral colouring naturally lends to a piece of music'.[136] With its reference to the orchestra, this could perhaps refer to the discarded first march (no. 2), which may of course easily have been published before the wedding. A few weeks after Southgate, the anonymous, twice published review quoted above, which is dated 'May 22, 1882', clearly referred to the actually used wedding march (no. 1), with the three trombones.[137] It explained that the march had 'been diffused in a variety of "arrangements"', which must then have been available. There was, for instance an arrangement for organ solo, thus potentially furthering the march's usability.[138]

---

[132] 'Scrutator', 'At the Wedding', p. 613.

[133] This and the following Southgate, 'Royal Music', pp. 296–97.

[134] 'Scrutator', 'At the Wedding', p. 613.

[135] This and the following Southgate, 'Royal Music', pp. 296–97.

[136] Southgate, 'Royal Music', p. 297. For the concert see also Michael Musgrave, *The Musical Life of the Crystal Palace* (Cambridge: Cambridge University Press, 1995), p. 104.

[137] See fn. 131 above.

[138] Charles Gounod, *Wedding March (No. 1) Composed for the Marriage of H.R.H. The Duke of Albany, K.G. with H.R.H. The Princess Helen of Waldeck*, arr. for organ solo by George C. Martin (London: Novello, Ewer & Co., [1882]).

8—Routine and Innovation: The Mid-Victorians II

Gounod's original first march (no. 2) was 'played at Windsor Castle on the evening preceding the marriage, and it received a grand public performance at the next Birmingham Festival, in August' of the same year.[139] It seems to survive only in the aforementioned piano arrangement. At any rate, neither of Gounod's two Wedding Marches appears to have triggered much enthusiasm; neither was repeated at any other notable occasion and they both were soon all but forgotten. To some extent, then, both marches ended up being 'a work lost to the world ("un travail perdu")', as Gounod himself had feared for his original march.[140]

Performance

For the performance of the music, the *Observer* noted that 'the choir of the Chapel [...] will be stationed in the organ-loft'.[141] However, one of the *Scotsman* correspondents emphasized:

> The arrangements inside St George's Chapel were most effective. A large platform had been erected on the left of the organ to accommodate the extra number of choristers.[142]

Without further records, it is probably legitimate to assume that this extra space for the performers was the same as that built at the 1879 wedding (see Figure 8.1 above). Incidentally, the record of the wedding in the *Graphic* included an engraving entitled 'The Wedding March' which shows Elvey playing the organ (Illustration 8.7). No other musicians can be seen around him, merely some music stands in the background and some undefined people further back, who could be the musicians in the 'platform [...] on the left'. While this is probably a rather stylized depiction, there would at least have been the three instrumentalists that played in Gounod's *Marche Nuptiale*.

In contrast to the previous weddings, there is now a slightly more detailed list of the musicians, compiled by Elvey.[143] As in 1879, the choir consisted of the choir of St George's, singers from Eton College, and the choir of the Private Chapel at Windsor: altogether forty-two singers – but Elvey's list also refers to '50 Copies of Psalms', indicating that there were some extra performers. Indeed, in another list, Elvey also noted 'the expenses incurred for

Illustration 8.7: 'The Wedding March: Sir George Elvey at the Organ', *Graphic: Royal Wedding Number*, 6 May 1882, p. 30. Author's collection.

---

[139] See Scholes, *Mirror of Music*, II, p. 868. For the Birmingham performance see also Pippa Drummond, *The Provincial Music Festival in England, 1784–1914*, first publ. by Ashgate in 2011 (Abingdon: Routledge, 2016), p. 118.

[140] See above, after fn. 123.

[141] 'Royal Marriage', *Observer* (1882).

[142] 'Royal Marriage: Another Account'.

[143] For this and the following 'Copies' of a list of unnamed musicians with payments at the wedding of Prince Leopold, Duke of Albany, 1882, 'Sir Geo. Elvey's Acc.', in *Lna LC 2/86*; transcr. in Appendix B 8.2.

Extra performers, &c': this came to £29 6s. 6d. for seven performers, including £12 alone for 'Programmes'.[144] While it is not clear whether these 'Extra performers' were singers or instrumentalists, Elvey's detailed list indicates that the latter included a string band, trumpets and trombones, and a drum – but no other wind instruments. The overall cost for musicians and other related items came to £1021.

There is also a separate list that refers to 'Harper Trumpeter's Bill', coming to £17 17s.; this would probably have been the Thomas Harper seen at the previous weddings and thus refer to the fanfare trumpeters.[145] These were again 'stationed at the West Entrance'.[146] They were thus depicted greeting the bride in the stylized depiction seen above (Illustration 8.6). However, it appears that they now stood on special stands. According to one of the *Scotsman* correspondents, two 'platforms, one on either side the entrance' had been 'provided for the heralds', as 'slight elevations above the floor of the chapel'.[147] Another correspondent of the *Scotsman* described how 'the heralds, posted to the right and left of the grand entrance, sounded their trumpets as a signal of the arrival of the first carriage of the first procession'.[148] There must obviously have been a misunderstanding: heralds did not blow trumpets – but the state trumpeters in their splendid state uniforms may have looked like heralds to these writers.

Princess Beatrice and Prince Henry of Battenberg, 23 July 1885

Princess Beatrice was the youngest child of Queen Victoria, and the last to marry. She had been meant to remain a companion to her mother but was eventually allowed to marry on the promise that she and her husband would yet stay with the queen.[149] The wedding was overall noticeably different to the previous weddings of the princess's sibling and had some remarkable features, especially regarding its venue and music.

The Venue

The wedding took place on 23 July 1885, in St Mildred's Church at Whippingham, near Osborne House, on the Isle of Wight, and the *Illustrated London News* noted that this was 'a beautiful place which is her Majesty's favourite home in the southern part of her Kingdom'.[150] According to Matthew Dennison, it was Queen Victoria herself who 'in a calculated break with tradition' had chosen Whippingham church for the wedding, explaining that 'with her horror of public show' she 'was determined that Beatrice's wedding would not be a state occasion'.[151] David Duff has pointed out that this was 'the first occasion that a daughter of the Sovereign had wed

---

[144] 'Account of the expenses incurred for Extra performers, &c / on the occasion of the Wedding of H.R.H The Duke of Albany / April 27.th 1882.', in *Lna LC 2/86*.

[145] This list is also in *Lna LC 2/86*. For Harper compare above, fn. 51, and also Chapter 7, fns 276–77.

[146] Ceremonial 1882, p. 9.

[147] 'Royal Marriage', *Scotsman* (1882).

[148] 'Royal Marriage: Another Account'.

[149] For details see Matthew Dennison, *The Last Princess: The Devoted Life of Queen Victoria's Youngest Daughter* (London: Phoenix, 2007; paperback edn 2008), Chapter 15. See also Elizabeth Longford, *Victoria R. I.* (London: Weidenfeld & Nicolson, [1964]), pp. 478–79.

[150] 'The Marriage of Princess Beatrice', *ILN: Royal Wedding Number*, 27 July 1885, pp. 2–6, here p. 2.

[151] Dennison, *Last Princess*, p. 141.

8—Routine and Innovation: The Mid-Victorians II

Illustration 8.8: Richard Caton Woodville, 'The Marriage of Princess Beatrice, 23rd July 1885', oil on canvas, signed and dated 1886, *Royal Collection, RCIN 404480*, Royal Collection Trust / © Her Majesty Queen Elizabeth II 2021.

in a parish church'.[152] While this was indeed a notable 'break with tradition', it is worth remembering that Whippingham church was not just any parish church. As Duff has pointed out, this church 'had been designed by the Prince Consort'.[153] In its report of the wedding, the *Times* detailed that the church was 'a modest little edifice built in 1860 at the cost of the Queen and the Prince Consort on the ruins of an ancient fane'.[154]

Sarah Tytler furthermore pointed out that this was 'the church of the parish in which Osborne is situated' and 'where the bride had worshipped on many occasions since her childhood.'[155] For over twenty years the church had served as a *de facto* royal chapel for nearby Osborne House, where the royal family and then the widowed queen spent much time: the confirmations of Princess Louise (1864), of Prince Arthur (1865) and then of Princess Beatrice (1874) had all three taken place in this church. Thus, overall, the church had a clear, strong royal link, and was surely associated with many personal memories. It may have had a rather special meaning and significance for the queen and her family, and would hence have seemed appropriate for this very special wedding of her youngest child, the last to marry.

---

[152] David Duff, *Hessian Tapestry* (London: Frederick Muller, 1967), p. 209.

[153] Duff, *Hessian Tapestry*, p. 209.

[154] 'The Royal Wedding', *Times*, 24 July 1885, p. 5, here 2nd column.

[155] Sarah Tytler, *Life of Her Most Gracious Majesty the Queen*, ed. and with an introduction by Lord Ronald Gower, 3 vols (London: J. S. Virtue & Co., [1897?]), III, p. 175.

Illustration 8.9: Jabez Hughes (attr.), 'Whippingham Church, View from Chancel', carbon print *c.1873*, *Royal Collection, RCIN 2102462*, Royal Collection Trust / © Her Majesty Queen Elizabeth II 2021.

Like all the other weddings of the queen's children this one was commemorated in a large-scale painting, and Richard Caton Woodville's well-known depiction of the ceremony gives the impression of a certain grandeur and spaciousness (Illustration 8.8). Yet, contrasting with the regal impression of Woodville's paining of the ceremony, comparison with a photograph of the interior of Whippingham church from just over ten years before the wedding may help to understand and appreciate the limitation of space in the church (Illustration 8.9).

All the same, this limitation of space was in fact an asset. Queen Victoria herself referred to 'the simple, pretty little Village Church', and Elizabeth Longford has interpreted that the queen 'was enchanted by the atmosphere of this "village wedding" at Whippingham'.[156] The latter term with all its implications became a crucial aspect in the reports and perception of the ceremony; for instance, Tooley later described it as 'truly an ideal village wedding'.[157] Thus, the choice of venue greatly contributed to this wedding standing apart from all the previous royal weddings.

---

[156] Queen Victoria to Princess Victoria, 25 July 1885, in *Wra RA VIC/ADDU/32/801*, fols 403ʳ–04ʳ; and Longford, *Victoria R. I.*, p. 478.

[157] Tooley, 'The Weddings of the Queen's Children', p. 51.

224

8—Routine and Innovation: The Mid-Victorians II

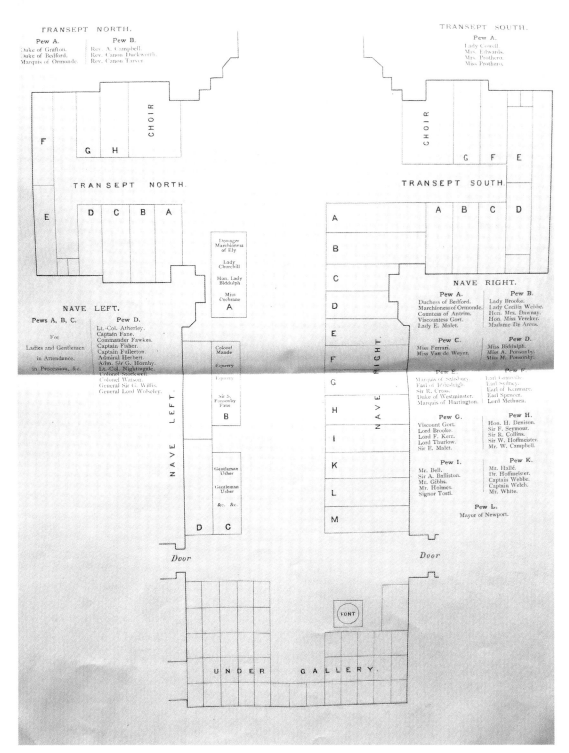

Illustration 8.10: Plan of Whippingham Church at the wedding of Princess Beatrice, 1885, included in Ceremonial 1885; here from the copy in *Wsg XVII.43.3/2*. By permission of the Dean and Canons of Windsor. The chancel, or quire, is at the top: the specific seating for the quire was recorded in a separate plan.

In this context, it is interesting that the *Illustrated London News* observed that 'There was less pomp and splendour than in former Royal Weddings at Windsor'.[158] As Tytler put it, the wedding 'was a family and not a State affair, a quiet, happy marriage'.[159] Woodville's rather stately, if not regal paining was obviously intended to highlight a different aspect. All the same, the *Times* overall summarized that

> The ceremony was a happy compromise between the splendour that becomes a State function of the first magnitude and the simplicity that accords with a domestic event.[160]

The *Times* also described the layout of the church in some detail, and this can be compared with both the aforementioned contemporary photograph, and especially also with a plan of the church that was included in the printed ceremonial (Illustration 8.10):

> The building is very small, consisting merely of a nave and chancel and north and south transepts. At the west end is the organ gallery, facing the altar and overlooking the south door, which was exclusively used on this occasion.[161]

The paper emphasized that 'The building would accommodate at most not more than 300 persons.' In fact, it has been pointed out that the small size of Whippingham church provided a welcome excuse not to have to invite the Prussian relatives.[162] This recalls Queen Victoria's own wedding, when the small size of the Chapel Royal served as an excuse for not inviting Tory opposition politicians.

In early February, Queen Victoria recorded that she had looked at Whippingham church 'to see what arrangements could be made' and one of her observations had been that 'on one side, the pews will have to be removed'.[163] In the end, the interior underwent 'extensive alterations in order to fit it for the marriage ceremony':

> The pews on the north side of the nave had been removed, as well as the pulpit and the reading-desk, so that the procession might pass into the chancel, and in the latter seats in red velvet and gold were placed at either side of the altar.[164]

Thus, even though this may have been a 'village wedding', the church was clearly modified so as to provide enough room for the royal ceremonial that took place in it.

The Ceremony and its Music

The service was again to be performed by the Archbishop of Canterbury who was now assisted by the Bishop of Winchester (in whose diocese the Isle of Wight lies), the Dean of Windsor, and Canon Prothero (the Rector of Whippingham), as the printed ceremonial noted.[165] Despite the 'village' character of the wedding, the ceremonial was again printed as before.

---

[158] 'Marriage of Princess Beatrice', *ILN: Royal Wedding Number*, p. 2.

[159] Tytler, *Life*, III, p. 175.

[160] 'Royal Wedding', *Times* (1885), p. 5, 1st column.

[161] 'Royal Wedding', *Times* (1885), p. 5, 2nd column.

[162] See, for instance, Dulcie M. Ashdown, *Royal Weddings* (London: R. Hale, 1981), p. 149; and also Dennison, *Last Princess*, p. 141.

[163] *QVJ*, 2 February 1885.

[164] 'The Royal Marriage', *Morning Post*, 24 July 1885, p. 5. See similarly 'Royal Wedding', *Times* (1885), p. 5, 2nd column: 'To give more space for the passage of the wedding procession the pews on the north side of the nave were placed chapel-wise [...].'

[165] Ceremonial 1885, p. 8.

8—Routine and Innovation: The Mid-Victorians II

Woodville's painting (Illustration 8.8) prominently shows two copies of the printed ceremonial, bound in blue silk, on two stools in the foreground. The order of service was also printed, in the same lavish form as before, and the programme of the music was again included within this order of service and also printed as a separate sheet.[166] The service as a whole followed the parameters of the previous royal weddings. The archbishop gave a 'nice little address at the conclusion', as Queen Victoria recorded.[167] The *Times* correspondent explained that this came 'instead of the usual homily read on such occasions', including its full text, and it pointed out that altogether 'The simple marriage service of the English Church occupied but a very short time.'[168]

The music of the ceremony was also similar to that at the previous weddings. The most notable difference was probably the complete absence of fanfares on the arrivals of the processions and, as will be seen, there was at least one notable choice of music. The music was under the direction of Walter Parratt – Elvey's successor as organist of St George's Chapel, Windsor. He was to 'preside' at the organ and it was his choir of St George's that sang at the service.[169] With both its dean and its choir called to the Isle of Wight for the wedding, it appears that St George's had *de facto* taken the place traditionally held by the Chapel Royal – of which, incidentally, nobody was present.[170] In contrast to all the previous church weddings of Queen Victoria's children, there were no other instruments apart from the organ.

Parratt also appears to have chosen the music. The report of the wedding in the *Morning Post* explained that 'the musical part of the service [...] had been specially selected by the Princess Beatrice'.[171] However, a week later, the *Graphic* included a paragraph on the wedding in its 'Music' news, arguing decidedly that this was needed 'the more especially as some of the reports seem to be hopelessly mixed on the subject'.[172] The *Graphic* explained that the music of the service 'was, as is customary, left to the choice of the organist at St. George's Chapel, Windsor, whose choir was in attendance' – and thus that Parratt had chosen the music. This appears to be confirmed by a source from the time of the next royal wedding, that of Princess Louise of Wales in 1889: in a letter to Ponsonby-Fane, the Dean of Windsor referred back to Princess Beatrice's wedding and its music and specifically mentioned 'the Choice then made by Mr Parratt & approved'.[173]

With the queen being the mother of the bride and leading her in, there were, as in 1871 and 1866, only three entrance processions: those of the royal guests, the bridegroom, and then the bride with the queen. This was the first major royal church wedding – of a child of the sovereign – where the heralds were not present. All the processions were led by the Lord Chamberlain alone, presumably reflecting another concession to the 'village' character of the wedding.

As at previous weddings, the processions going up the church were accompanied by distinct marches.[174] The *Times* recorded that before these, the entering choir and clergy were accompanied

---

[166] Programme of the music included in OS 1885; and separate sheet in *Wsg XVII. 43.3/4*. For the ceremonials see Ceremonial 1885.

[167] *QVJ*, 23 July 1885.

[168] 'Royal Wedding', *Times* (1885), p. 5, 2nd column.

[169] Ceremonial 1885, p. 8.

[170] For Queen Victoria's preference of St George's see also the next chapter.

[171] 'Royal Marriage', *Morning Post* (1885).

[172] 'Music', *Graphic*, 1 August 1885, p. 123, under 'THE ROYAL MARRIAGE.'

[173] Randall Davidson to Ponsonby-Fane, 8 July 1889, in *Lna LC 2/120*.

[174] See the list of music in OS 1885.

British Royal Weddings

by 'the soft strains of a voluntary from the organ'.[175] According to this account, after the clergy's entrance came a 'complete hush – the silence of expectancy' which was 'broken at last by the faint sound of distant cheering' which then 'became mingled with the music of a band'. This means that there was also music of an outside band to welcome the various processions. Another account noted that for those inside the church 'the sound of cheering and the notes of the National Anthem indicated the approach of her Royal Highness, who was seated in the carriage with the Queen'.[176] Queen Victoria herself recorded that, when she arrived outside with the bridal party, 'A fine Guard of Honour of the 93rd Highlanders was drawn up there, with Pipes & drums, playing the "Highland Laddie".'[177] The wedding as such did not have any obvious Scottish connection, such as the wedding in 1871. The inclusion of bagpipes, instead of the traditional fanfare trumpeters, perhaps indicated the more private character of the occasion, while reflecting the fact that Princess Beatrice had spent much time with her mother at Balmoral and at the same time being a strong musical reference to the overall British character of the monarchy.

The entrance of the royal family and royal guests into the church was accompanied by 'the spirit-stirring march' from the overture to Handel's *Occasional Oratorio* and the entrance of the bridegroom by a march by Parratt, the reports noting that the latter had been written 'specially for the occasion' and describing it as 'a spirited march'.[178] The identity of Parratt's march, however, remains obscure. As at the wedding of Prince Leopold three years previously, the most notable of the marches, and perhaps the most notable music overall, was the march for the bride. Queen Victoria noted that 'Wagner's lovely "Braut Chor" ['Bridal Chorus'] from Lohengrin was beautifully played on the organ by Mr Parratt, as we came into the Church.'[179] The list of music in the order of service listed it as 'BRIDAL MARCH' by Wagner, while one report worded that 'the organ pealed forth Wagner's "Wedding March."'.[180] It is not known who had chosen Wagner's march but it had been becoming popular at weddings since at least 1875, although not necessarily for accompanying the entrance of the bride, but also to accompany the newly-weds.

It was presumably with reference to the music's secular origins and also the un-happy ending in the opera when the *Graphic* commented that 'the bride walked up the church to the beautiful, though utterly inappropriate bridal music from Wagner's *Lohengrin*'.[181] In this context, however, it is interesting to note that just before the wedding Percy Betts in a general article on 'Marriage Music' had criticized the choice of the Handel marches for the bride in 1858 and 1863, as well as that of Mendelssohn's march from *Athalie* for the groom in 1863.[182] The point of criticism lay especially in the martial, military connotations of these marches. It had been only

---

[175] This and the following 'Royal Wedding', *Times* (1885), p. 5, 2nd column. See also the account in 'Royal Marriage', *Morning Post* (1885).

[176] 'Royal Marriage', *Morning Post* (1885).

[177] *QVJ*, 23 July 1885.

[178] 'Royal Marriage', *Morning Post* (1885); and 'Royal Wedding', *Times* (1885), p. 5, 2nd column. For the *Occasional Oratorio* see 'Music', *Graphic*.

[179] *QVJ* 23 July 1885.

[180] 'De Omnibus Rebus', *Public Opinion*, 48:1244 (24 July 1885), p. 116.

[181] 'Music', *Graphic*. For a longer discussion of the performance history and also the perceived 'appropriateness' (or 'inappropriateness') of Wagner's march at weddings see Matthias Range, 'Wagner's "Brautchor" from *Lohengrin* and its Use as a Wedding March', *Journal of the Royal Musical Association* (forthcoming).

[182] T. Percy M. Betts, 'Marriage Music', *Graphic*, special wedding issue, 27 July 1885, pp. 20–21, here p. 21.

8—Routine and Innovation: The Mid-Victorians II

at the 1882 wedding, with Gounod's newly written *Marche Nuptiale*, that the bride did not enter to one of these marches. At least from this angle, then, the choice of Wagner's Bridal March would have seemed like a welcome change to the martial pieces used previously.

Notwithstanding the tragic connotations from the opera, the choice of the march from *Lohengrin* seems at this wedding to have coincided with an interesting observation. According to David Duff, who refers to recollections of the bridal couple's son, Queen Victoria herself had insisted on the bridegroom wearing the white uniform of the Prussian *Gardes du corps*, the result of which 'appeared out of character with the village setting, and the mischievous Princess of Wales dubbed him "Beatrice's Lohengrin"'.[183] It is tempting to think that such a reference to the legendary Swan-Knight was enforced by the dazzling white uniform, with its helmet crowned by a silver eagle, as much as by the music of Wagner's Bridal March (see Illustration 8.8, above).

In contrast to the previous three weddings, the service now included only one of the psalms scheduled in the Prayer Book: Ps. 128, sung to an unspecified chant by Sir Frederick Ouseley.[184] As previously, the anthem came 'at the conclusion of the service', as the accounts noted – possibly between the address and the final blessing. This anthem saw a notable change to those at previous weddings: it was *O Give Thanks to the Lord* by Mendelssohn, as the sources list, with the programme of music including the full text.[185] No such anthem by Mendelssohn is known. Queen Victoria recorded that 'a portion of Mendelssohn's Hymn of Praise was sung' and one of the reports similarly detailed that the anthem was 'the second part of the last chorus of Mendelssohn's Hymn of Praise, "O give thanks!"'.[186] This would appear to refer to Mendelssohn's *Lobgesang*, op. 52 (MWV A 18), also counted as symphony no. 2, and in English known as the 'Hymn of Praise'. However, neither this text nor the music is in there: although the music of this 'anthem' does not seem to have survived, it is known from piano arrangements. In the early 1860s, William Hutchins Callcott had published an arrangement for piano for four hands with the description 'From the Organ Studies', at the top with the annotation 'O give thanks unto the Lord / Psalmn CVII.v.I.'[187] The music, transposed to D major, is taken from Mendelssohn's organ sonata no. 4 in B-flat major, op. 65.4 – from the Andante religioso and the Allegro maestoso – which had been published in 1845. It is not clear to what the text from Ps. 107 at the top refers: there is no indication of any sung parts. After all, the supposed 'anthem' – and this piano arrangement of it – very much appears to have been not a genuine Mendelssohn work but somebody else's arrangement based on music from Mendelssohn's organ works. It is not known whether there ever was a choral arrangement with the respective text, let alone a published one. It is possible that Parratt simply produced one himself for the wedding. In any case, the wedding seems to have generated new interest in this piece and another version for piano at two hands was published in the following year.[188]

---

[183] Duff, *Hessian Tapestry*, p. 209. Duff (endnote 15, on p. 387) refers to 'Information from the Marquess of Carisbrooke' – that is Alexander Mountbatten (1886–1960), formerly known as Prince Alexander of Battenberg, the eldest son of Princess Beatrice and Prince Henry of Battenberg, and from 1917 first and only Marquess of Carisbrooke.

[184] 'Royal Wedding', *Times* (1885), p. 5, 2nd column; 'Royal Marriage', *Morning Post* (1885).

[185] OS 1885; and 'Royal Wedding', *Times* (1885), p. 5, 2nd column.

[186] *QVJ* 23 July 1885; 'De Omnibus Rebus'.

[187] *The Holy Mount, Admired Sacred Melodies, Arranged as Piano Duetts […] With (ad lib.) Accompaniments for Flute, Violin & Violoncello, by William Hutchins Callcott*, first series (of three), (London: Robert Cocks & Co., [1861–1862]), pp. 22–25.

[188] *The Holy Family: Admired Sacred Melodies by the Most Celebrated Composers, Arranged for the Piano Forte as Solos and Duets with ad libitum Acct.ˢ for Flute, Violin & Violon.ᵒ by William Hutchins Callcott* (London: Robert Cocks & Co., [1886?]), series 4 [vol. 1], pp. 15–17.

British Royal Weddings

This pastiche 'Mendelssohn' anthem was also notable for another reason: although his Wedding March had been heard at many a previous wedding, this was the first time that there was also an anthem with music written by Mendelssohn. It does not seem to be recorded who chose it.

The anthem was followed by a 'brief nuptial address'.[189] After the final blessing, the recess was accompanied by 'the sonorous strains of Mendelssohn's stately "Wedding March"', played on the organ, and described by Queen Victoria simply as the 'well known one'.[190] Overall then, his was the first prominent wedding to have the later 'classic' combination of the two marches by Wagner and by Mendelssohn for the bride's entrance and the newlyweds leaving, respectively.

Musicians and Performance

With the much smaller venue, the performance conditions were rather different to those at previous weddings. As already mentioned, there was no orchestra and the choir was accompanied merely by the organ in the gallery at the west end of the church (seen in Illutration 8.9). The choir was split and placed in the front corners of the transepts, nearest to the chancel, as indicated in the aforementioned plan of the church included in the printed ceremonial (Illustration 8.10).

The choir of St George's did not receive a fee for singing at the wedding, but was paid £30 for expenses.[191] Parratt's expenses claim for himself and for the choir refers to '25 Men and Boys'.[192] The musicians most probably did not know the venue and did not have much opportunity to get used to it. As one report emphasized, the archbishop and other clerics 'together with the choir from St George's Chapel, Windsor' arrived only on the morning of the wedding.[193] Yet, it is documented that at least Parratt had previously been to Whippingham church to inspect the organ (which can be seen in Illustration 8.9): he found it inadequate for the wedding, and it was therefore at least repaired and retuned.[194]

The wedding of Queen Victoria's youngest child – the last wedding of one of her children – was altogether an event full of extraordinary features. These ranged from the more or less unprecedented choice of the venue to the innovative, if not unusual choices of music for the ceremony. This corresponds with the queen's well-known particularly close attachment to her youngest daughter Princess Beatrice, who was nothing less than her mother's life-long companion and had a special status within the royal family.

---

[189] 'The Royal Marriage', *Morning Post* (1885).

[190] 'The Marriage of Princess Beatrice', *ILN*, 1 August 1885, pp. 106–07, here p. 106; *QVJ*, 23 July 1885.

[191] See 'Marriage of H.R.H. Princess Beatrice / Sept. 24[?]. 1885', in *Lna LC 2/86*: 'Dean of Windsor / For Allowances to the Choir of / S.ᵗ George's Chapel, Windsor, / for their Attendance at the / Marriage of Princess Beatrice / at Whippingham Church, / Isle of Wight'.

[192] 'Expenditure / 3 Augˢᵗ 85 / Mʳ Parratt / Marriage of P.ᵉˢ Beatrice / expenses of Choir & / self at the / H. Aug. 17.', included in Walter Parratt to unknown, 7 August 1885, in *Lna LC 2/86*.

[193] 'The Wedding of Princess Beatrice: Latest Arrangements', *Scotsman*, 20 July 1885, p. 5.

[194] See the material in *Lna LC 2/86*.

8—Routine and Innovation: The Mid-Victorians II

As initially observed, the last four weddings of Queen Victoria's children more or less followed a sort of ceremonial routine, but they continued the retreat into a more private sphere. For the 1879 wedding, for instance, *Lloyd's Weekly Newspaper* referred critically to the 'imposing ceremonial away from London, and even away from the town of Windsor'.[195] In terms of the ceremony, however, there were some important innovations – most notably, the introduction of an address to the service. There were musical innovations too, with the 1882 wedding featuring a specially-written bridal march.

Before the wedding of Princess Beatrice in 1885, the *Scotsman* had predicted that its 'ceremony and State pageantry […] will vie in importance with the grand ceremonials' that had 'attended' the two Windsor weddings in 1879 and 1882.[196] Indeed, musically, it was this wedding that eventually became more important than most of the previous occasions: it ultimately legitimized, if not popularized, the use of Wagner's bridal chorus as *the* march for a bride's entrance, encouraging a developing tradition, an eventually global trend that – to some extent – has lasted to the present day.

---

[195] 'The Royal Wedding', *Lloyd's Weekly Newspaper*, 23 March 1879, p. 6. See also the general discussion on the venue in Chapter 11 below.

[196] 'Wedding of Princess Beatrice: Latest Arrangements'.

9

The Choral Weddings: The Later Victorians

I N THE LATER YEARS OF Queen Victoria's reign, with the weddings of her grandchildren, there came a pronounced change to the way in which royal weddings were staged. Most importantly, three prominent royal weddings returned to London. Furthermore, even though these weddings overall followed the same ceremonial schemes as those of the queen's younger children, they featured some intriguing elements – not the least regarding their music. The 'choral' aspect of the service was much heightened.

Princess Louise of Wales and Alexander Duff, 6th Earl of Fife, 27 July 1889

The first of Queen Victoria's grandchildren to marry in Britain was the Prince of Wales's eldest daughter, Princess Louise. On 27 July 1889 she married Alexander Duff, 6th Earl of Fife, on the day elevated to Duke of Fife – after the Marquess of Lorne in 1871 the second 'subject' to marry into the inner circle of the royal family (and incidentally also a Scot).

Venue and Privacy

The wedding saw an important change in the choice of venue, and the ceremony returned to London: this was the first royal wedding there since 1858. In mid-July, it was reported that the wedding had been 'definitely fixed to take place in the Private Chapel of Buckingham Palace'.[1] This was the first wedding there since that of Princess Augusta in 1843 and Dulcie Ashdown has suggested that this venue was chosen 'at the shy bride's particular request'.[2] The report of the wedding in the *Scotsman* referred to 'the quiet family character of which the whole ceremonial had partaken'.[3] Indeed, notwithstanding that the wedding took place in the capital, overall, it was somewhat less elaborate than the previous weddings at Windsor. For instance, as for the 1885 'village' wedding at Whippingham, the sources do not mention any heralds.[4]

One of the accounts in the *Observer* had recorded that the royal guests were received at Buckingham Palace by fanfares and that 'the starting of the bride's procession to the chapel' had been announced by a 'fanfare of trumpets within the Palace'.[5] However, this may have been a more generic observation based on what might be expected. The inclusion of fanfares

---

[1] 'The Royal Wedding', *Irish Times*, 16 July 1889, p. 5.

[2] Dulcie M. Ashdown, *Royal Weddings* (London: R. Hale, 1981), p. 152. Unfortunately, the evidence for this suggestion is not clear.

[3] 'Marriage of The Princess Louise and the Duke of Fife: The Ceremony in Buckingham Palace Chapel', *Scotsman*, 29 July 1889, p. 7, here fourth column.

[4] Ceremonial 1889a/b; and the various reports.

[5] 'Royal Wedding at Buckingham Palace', [2nd account].

is not confirmed by any other source and it is likely that they were omitted, just as they had been in 1885, at Princess Beatrice's wedding. Such an omission at the 1889 wedding would have matched with the reported 'quiet family character' of the occasion.[6]

The service was preceded by processions on the ground-floor of Buckingham Palace, from the Bow Library to the Private Chapel, with guests seated in the rooms along the way.[7] Lady Marie Mallet, maid of honour to Queen Victoria, recorded that in one of these 'were about eighty privileged spectators'.[8] Nevertheless, these indoor processions were somewhat less ceremonious than those at previous weddings. Not only were there no heralds, but it appears that there were also no musicians: therefore, the only music during the processions would have been that coming from inside the Chapel.[9]

Ceremony and Music

The service was performed by the Archbishop of Canterbury, together with other clerics, including the Bishop of London 'who came as Dean of the Chapels Royal', and Randall Davidson, as Dean of Windsor and 'Domestic Chaplain to the Queen'.[10] The latter seems to have been responsible for organizing the ceremony as a whole; for it was to Dean Davidson that Francis Knollys, the Private Secretary of the Prince of Wales, wrote to inform him that Queen Victoria had asked for 'the omission of certain Prayers' and that this request would be 'regarded by him [the Prince] and the Princess of Wales as Law'.[11]

On the day before Knollys wrote to Davidson, the dean had been sent another note to the same effect, from the queen, and possibly written by Queen Victoria herself. In that note he was asked to leave out from the service 'the same objectionable passages & prayers' that had been omitted at the 1885 wedding of Princess Beatrice and 'the 3 other Royal Marriges'.[12] While this seems to double the queen's request already made through the Prince of Wales's secretary, it is noteworthy that this note had been written a mere two days before the wedding, and such a late reminder may perhaps indicate how important the queen thought the matter. The '3 other' weddings referred to are probably those of Prince Leopold (1882), Prince Arthur (1879), and Princess Louise (1871).

It is not quite clear to which passages and prayers exactly this note, or indeed Knollys's letter to Davidson, referred. Yet, the queen's concern in this respect shows that she was still very much involved in the arrangements of family weddings, even of her grandchildren, and that she kept an eye on every detail. Such direct, personal involvement may be at least somewhat surprising as, just two years previously, Queen Victoria had categorically stated 'I *hate* weddings', explaining that they were 'melancholy things and cause the happiest beings such trials with

---

[6] See the report in the *Scotsman* cited above, with fn. 3.

[7] See 'The Royal Wedding: Marriage of The Princess Louise in Buckingham Palace', *New York Times*, 28 July 1889, p. 1.

[8] Marie Mallet, *Life with Queen Victoria: Marie Mallet's Letters from Court, 1887–1901*, ed. by Victor Mallet, (London: J. Murray, 1968), p. 30.

[9] For the probable omission of fanfares to receive the processions see the sources given in fn. 32 below.

[10] 'The Royal Wedding at Buckingham Palace', *Observer*, 28 July 1889, p. 5 [two separate accounts, the second with the sub-heading 'Arrival at the Palace'], here both accounts.

[11] Francis Knollys to Dean of Windsor, 26 July 1889, in *Wsg XVII.43.4/6*.

[12] Unsigned note [by Queen Victoria?] to 'The Very Rev: / The / Dean of Windsor / Buckingha[m] Palace', dated Osborne, 'July 25/89', in *Wsg XVII.43.4/3*; fully transcr. in Appendix B 9.1.

9—The Choral Weddings: The Later Victorians

them, bad health &c &c.'[13] In fact, as will be seen, at least in regard to the music it appears that the Prince and Princess of Wales did not consider all of the queen's wishes as 'law' and eventually had some ideas of their own.

In mid-July, it was reported that 'Dr. Bridge, organist of Westminster Abbey, will be in charge of the musical service', but this was soon corrected and it was explained that 'Mr. Jekyll, organist to the Chapel Royal, St. James's, and not Dr. Bridge, as first stated, will be the organist' at the wedding.[14] The commemorative ceremonial eventually recorded that Jekyll 'presided at the Organ, and the Musical part of the Service was sung by the Choir of that Chapel' – that is, by the choir of the Chapel Royal.[15]

The participation of the Chapel Royal, however, had not been a foregone conclusion. At the beginning of July, a hastily written note to Spencer Ponsonby-Fane, Comptroller of the Lord Chamberlain's Office, explained that Queen Victoria had 'proposed' that the ceremony should be performed by the Archbishop of Canterbury, the Bishop of London, and the Dean of Windsor and that 'the Choir of S Geoges Windser should sing'.[16] A week later, Jekyll still enquired with Edgar Sheppard, the Subdean of the Chapel Royal, 'whether his Services. & those of the Chapel Ry. Choir will be required', and Sheppard noted that while he hoped 'that the Choir w.d be wanted', he 'knew nothing'.[17] However, on the same day, Randall Davidson, as Dean of Windsor and Domestic Chaplain closely connected with Queen Victoria, informed Ponsonby-Fane that it was 'the Queen's Command that the Choir of S. James [that is, the Chapel Royal] is to perform the musical portions at the Marriage Service on the 27th.'[18]

Davidson also asked 'Will you kindly intimate this to Mr Jekyll and ask him to send me for submission to the Queen a note of the music he would propose for the Service.' Davidson explained that the queen desired the music to 'correspond closely' with 'what was done at Princess Beatrice's Marriage at Whippingham'; at the same time, he pointed out that 'I do not understand Her Majesty now to wish that the music should be identically the same', but rather that this programme should 'guide Mr Jekyll in making his selection for H.M. Considera[tions]'. A week later, Davidson informed Ponsonby-Fane that he had 'obtained the Queen's sanction to the musical arrangements, as desired by the Prince of Wales' and was 'now communicating with Mr Jekyll so that all may be done in precise accordance with the Prince of Wales' wish.'[19] This indicates that the Prince of Wales – the bride's father – had, after all, eventually been involved.

The more intimate character of the ceremony was enhanced by the arrangements for the music: in contrast to the previous weddings at St George's Chapel, there was no band. Thus, the only instrumental music came from the organ. Morison's picture of the newly built Private Chapel in the early 1840s had shown the organ situated right next to the altar (see Illustration 6.6 above). In 1889, however, the organ was in the bay on the left of the nave. A printed seating plan of the Private Chapel at this wedding, and which was also included in the printed ceremonial, shows the position of the organ and choir (Illustration 9.1).[20]

---

[13] Cited (with the emphasis) in James Pope-Hennessy, *Queen Mary, 1867–1953*, first publ. in 1959 (London: Phoenix Press, 2000), p. 218, who refers to a document in the 'Kronberg Archives', dated '16 May 1887'.

[14] 'Royal Wedding', *Irish Times* (1889); and 'Notes', *The Musical World*, 69 (27 July 1889), p. 492.

[15] Ceremonial 1889b, p. 6.

[16] [signature not readable] from Windsor Castle to Ponsonby-Fane, 1 July 1889, *Lna LC 2/120*.

[17] Sheppard to Ponsonby-Fane, 8 July 1889, in *Lna LC 2/120*.

[18] This and the following Davidson to Ponsonby-Fane, 8 July 1889, in *Lna LC 2/120*.

[19] Davidson to Ponsonby-Fane, 16 July 1889, in *Lna LC 2/120*.

[20] Copies of the printed seating plan survive in *Lna LC 2/121* and *Wsg SGC XVII.43.4/1-8*.

This situation in the Chapel at the wedding is depicted very clearly in Sydney Prior Hall's painting of the ceremony, which furthermore gives an impression of the very crowded conditions and the resulting almost intimate atmosphere (Illustration 9.2). As for the previous weddings, both the order of service and the ceremonial were printed.[21] Incidentally, Hall's painting shows Queen Victoria holding a booklet with crimson cover, with another one lying distinctly in the foreground – possibly the order of service bound in velvet.

As before, both the order of service and the ceremonial provide details on the music of the ceremony, again with a full list included in the former. The various processions, upon entering the Chapel were accompanied by distinct marches, which were all played on the organ. A 'Memo for Chapel' from mid-July, seemingly going back to the Prince of Wales, listed the suggested processional music:[22]

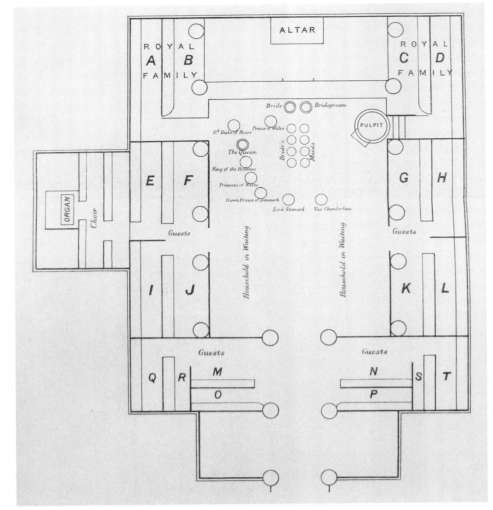

Illustration 9.1: 'The Private Chapel, Buckingham Palace. Marriage of Her Royal Highness The Princess Louise of Wales with the Earl of Fife, K.T.', printed seating plan included in Ceremonial 1889a/b; here from the copy *Wsg XVII.43.4/1*. By permission of the Dean and Canons of Windsor.

The Cl[erics]	not Handel unless HM selects
The Bridegroom	~~Jekyll~~ Tannhauser
The Bride	Lohengrin
Leaving	Mendlsohn

This proposed scheme was eventually followed, with the addition of the united procession of the queen and royal family, accompanied by music by Handel, in second place. The first of the processions, however, that of the clergy, was indeed not accompanied by music by Handel – rather, it was reportedly 'received by a "Nuptial March," specially composed for the occasion by Mr. Jekyll, the organist of the Chapel Royal'.[23] As the reporter of the *Scotsman* noted, this

---

[21] See OS 1889; and Ceremonial 1889a/b.

[22] 'Memo for Chapel' [both columns written in pencil, right-hand column overwritten in ink], at back: 'Marriage / 14. July 1889. / Prince of Wales / Music. / Draught memo of.', in *Lna LC 2/120*. The signature is not readable (something like 'H Mc Penry', or even 'by the Prince'?).

[23] 'Royal Wedding Music', *The Musical Visitor: A Magazine of Musical Literature and Music*, 18:9 (September 1889), p. 227; OS 1889, programme of music ('Marche Nuptiale'); 'Royal Wedding at Buckingham Palace', [2nd account].

9—The Choral Weddings: The Later Victorians

march was 'the first note' from the organ, indicating that the earlier arrival of the guests had not been accompanied by any music.[24] Also, there was apparently no music in between the separate processions. For instance, the *Observer* recorded that 'The prelates and clergy settled themselves in their places, the music died away, and there was a pause.'[25]

Another account, in the same paper, recorded an interesting detail that is not otherwise mentioned in relation to royal weddings. It noted that, before the next procession arrived and entered the Chapel,

> the talk which had been hitherto loud and continuous, ceased suddenly, and at the same moment the organist striking up Handel's Occasional Overture, it became known that the Royal procession, which had been formed in the Bow Library was on its way to the chapel. Immediately there was a hush, and the congregation rose *en masse* to await the arrival of the Sovereign.[26]

Illustrations 9.2: Sydney Prior Hall, 'The Marriage of Princess Louise of Wales with the Duke of Fife at Buckingham Palace, 27th July 1889', oil on panel, signed and dated 1890, *Royal Collection, RCIN 404460*, Royal Collection Trust / © Her Majesty Queen Elizabeth II 2021.

---

[24] 'Marriage of The Princess Louise and the Duke of Fife', *Scotsman*.
[25] 'Royal Wedding at Buckingham Palace', [1st account].
[26] 'Royal Wedding at Buckingham Palace', [2nd account].

Thus, the fact that the music had not played had not meant a sombre silence, but had rather provided an opportunity for 'loud and continuous' chattering. The royal procession was accompanied by 'the strains of Handel's Occasional March'.[27] This had, of course, been heard at several previous royal weddings. Yet, one report now referred to the particular popularity at the time of this march from the *Occasional Oratorio*, 'the last movement of the overture', explaining that 'at its performance at the Handel Festival it is invariably encored'.[28]

Apart from Handel, Wagner's music also had a prominent part at this wedding. The ceremonial recorded that the bridegroom was conducted to his place in the Chapel 'whilst a march from "Tannhauser" was played on the Organ'.[29] One report explained that this was 'the "Pilgrim's March" from "Tannhauser"'.[30] However, as there is no Pilgrim's 'March' in *Tannhäuser*, this probably refers to an arrangement of the Pilgrim's 'Chorus' in Act III, or perhaps to the Entry of the Guests from Act II. The report in the *Scotsman* pointed out that once the bridegroom had arrived at the altar, 'There was silence in the chapel.'[31] The silence was broken by the bride's entrance, the music for which followed the precedent of the 1885 wedding and was again Wagner's Bridal March, the *Times* recording that 'Meanwhile, Mr Jekyll, at the organ, played a march from *Lohengrin*.'[32] One journal in its report on the wedding music observed critically that Wagner's march 'although now popular at weddings, is more appropriate for the beauty of its music than for its association with the sad story of the opera', explaining that in the opera the bride is separated from her husband on the wedding day.[33]

For the service proper, the same account in the *Observer* emphasized that it was 'fully choral', judging that 'the rich tones of the organ, the finely blended voices of the choir, and the sympathetic reading of the Archbishop gave it a peculiarly emotional impressiveness'.[34] The programme of music stipulated a 'CHANT for Psalm 128' by 'Beethoven Arranged by Turle'.[35] This most probably refers to the Turle/Beethoven single chant that was included in *The Service for the Solemnization of Holy Matrimony as Used in Westminster Abbey* in the following year.[36] None of the reports seems to mention the psalm but at least one of them details that, after the prayers for the couple, 'the responses were beautifully sung by the choir of the Chapel Royal'.[37] This appears to be the earliest royal wedding at which the Responses were sung, matching with the *Observer*'s statement that the service was 'fully choral'. The setting for these could have been taken from the same publication as the psalm: this is very straightforward – basically a mere succession of two or three chords – and is probably also by Turle.

---

[27] 'Royal Wedding at Buckingham Palace', [1st account]; also Ceremonial 1889b, p. 2; list of music in OS 1889.

[28] 'Royal Wedding Music', *Musical Visitor*.

[29] Ceremonial 1889b, p. 4. Also 'Marriage of The Princess Louise and the Duke of Fife', *Scotsman*.

[30] 'Royal Wedding Music', *Musical Visitor*.

[31] 'Marriage of The Princess Louise and the Duke of Fife', *Scotsman*.

[32] 'The Royal Wedding', *Times*, 29 July 1889, p. 10; also list of music in OS 1889; Ceremonial 1889b, p. 5; 'Royal Wedding at Buckingham Palace', [2nd account].

[33] 'Royal Wedding Music', *Musical Visitor*.

[34] 'Royal Wedding at Buckingham Palace', [2nd account].

[35] List music in OS 1889.

[36] (London: Novello, Ewer and Co [1890]), p. 2. For this publication see also Chapter 1, fn. 104.

[37] 'Marriage of The Princess Louise and the Duke of Fife', *Scotsman*. 'The Marriage Ceremony', *ILN: Royal Wedding Number*, 31 July 1889, pp. 2–6, here p. 6; and 'Royal Wedding at Buckingham Palace', [2nd account], both recorded that 'The devotional portion of the service which followed was fully choral.'

9—The Choral Weddings: The Later Victorians

The Anthem

As one American periodical pointed out, the music at this wedding 'was, in some respects, of a rather more interesting character than usual'.[38] Not only was there Jekyll's new march and the inclusion of the Responses but this wedding also included a special, new anthem 'composed for the occasion', as the ceremonial recorded.[39] This was *O Perfect Love* by Joseph Barnby, at the time the 'first real director of music' of Eton College.[40] A hitherto unknown letter preserved in the archives of St George's Chapel shows that Barnby himself had taken the initiative: he wrote to Knollys and offered his anthem directly to the Prince and Princess of Wales 'for performance at the forthcoming Ceremony'.[41] Barnby's offer was accepted and his anthem included.

The *Musical Visitor* noted that the words of the anthem had been written by Dorothy Blomfield (later Blomfield Gurney) and were 'familiar to us through the beautiful marriage hymn by Dr. W. H. Monk, so frequently heard at weddings'.[42] The reference to Monk is to his tune 'Life and Love', to which Blomfield's text 'O Perfect Love' was then apparently sung.[43] According to John Julian, the text of the hymn had originally been written in 1883 to fit the tune 'Strength and Stay' by John Bacchus Dykes.[44] Blomfield's text soon became very popular and was used for numerous settings, as the entries in the catalogue of the British Library show.

As Barnby explained in his letter, his setting was a short piece of 'but three minutes in performance' and which 'may be sung with or without accompaniment'. It is a very straightforward, mostly homophonic setting for four-part choir, with a few bars of intro sung by the choir which also serve as an interlude between verses two and three. Indeed, the *Scotsman* referred to it as 'this hymn' rather than as an 'anthem'.[45]

The full text of Barnby's anthem was included in the programme of music in the order of service; furthermore, this programme with the full text was again also printed on a separate sheet – possibly for those who were not given the order of service.[46] In addition, the music itself must have been published before the wedding.[47] The *Musical World* referred to a report that Barnby's anthem was to be 'sung in many churches' on the day after the wedding.[48] At least some people seem to have known the anthem prior to the great day: the *Scotsman* reported that Barnby's piece was 'finely sung by the choir' but added that 'a number of the congregation, and notably Mr Gladstone' were 'joining in the singing'.[49]

---

[38] 'Royal Wedding Music', *Musical Visitor*.

[39] Ceremonial 1889b, p. 6.

[40] For biographical details see Nicholas Temperley, 'Barnby, Sir Joseph', *NG*.

[41] Barnby to Knollys, 9 July 1889, in *Wsg XVII.43.4/8*; transcr. in Appendix B 9.2.

[42] 'Royal Wedding Music', *Musical Visitor*. For Gurney's own account of the genesis of her hymn see John Brownlie, *The Hymns and Hymn-Writers of the Church Hymnary* (London: Henry Frowde, [1899]), pp. 248–49.

[43] See *Hymns Ancient and Modern*, ed. by William Henry Monk, supplemental tunes rev. by Charles Steggall (London: William Clowes & Sons, [1889]), no. 578 on p. 424.

[44] John Julian (ed.), *A Dictionary of Hymnology: Setting Forth the Origin and History of Christian Hymns of All Ages and Nations*, rev. edn, with new supplement (London: John Murray, 1907), Appendix II, p. 1553.

[45] 'Marriage of The Princess Louise and the Duke of Fife', *Scotsman*.

[46] OS 1889. For a copy of the single sheet see the material in *Lna LC 2/120*.

[47] Joseph Barnby, *O Perfect Love: Wedding Anthem. Music Composed Expressly for the Marriage of H.R.H. Princess Louise of Wales with the Earl of Fife, K.T.* (London: Novello, Ewer and Co., [1889]).

[48] 'Notes', *Musical World*.

[49] 'Marriage of The Princess Louise and the Duke of Fife', *Scotsman*.

Barnby's anthem generally received much attention and the *Observer* listed it as the second of only two 'incidents worth of notice' at the wedding.[50] An anonymous review of the published edition appeared in the September issue of the *Musical Times*.[51] The reviewer judged that this 'beautiful little composition [...] possesses charm enough to fit it for general use in the marriage service'; and although the reviewer thought that 'it may be used with good result at other times of the Church's seasons', in conclusion it was 'distinguished by all those qualities which should ensure its introduction as an adjunct to the Service of Matrimony'. The reviewer encouraged the use of the piece beyond the confines of royal weddings. Another writer, in the *Musical Visitor*, similarly commented on the anthem's inherent potential for wider use:

> Mr. Barnby's anthem, though admirable for its melodiousness and for the skillful manner in which it is harmonized for the four-part chorus, is of a comparatively simple character, as it is intended to be used at marriages generally, and is, therefore, quite within the means of an ordinary church choir.[52]

Most importantly, however, in the year after the wedding, the hymn text was coupled with Barnby's tune in the third edition of the *Hymnal Companion* to the Prayer Book.[53] An accompanying note explained that the tune had been arranged from Barnby's wedding anthem: in fact, it was simply extracted from his setting of the first verse.[54] It was in this form that this hymn, and with it also Barnby's music, was to become a staple in the wedding music repertoire for several decades.

The anthem followed, as the *Observer* and also the *Illustrated London New* noted, as 'the most important part of the ceremony was over', probably meaning that it followed the blessing of the couple after the prayers.[55] The ceremonial recorded that the anthem came 'Before the final address', and this was copied, or taken on, by several reports.[56] This observation, however, is most probably incorrect. For, as the *Scotsman* explained, there was 'no special address':

> It had been understood that the Queen had requested the Archbishop to speak a few words to the newly-married pair, but if this request was ever made, it had been withdrawn, no doubt in consequence of the pressure of time.[57]

The *Times* also referred to 'the final address' but at the same time explained that there 'was no original address from the altar' and that 'the simple wedding service of the Church was left to impress its own lesson'.[58] This indicates that the archbishop at best read the exhortation stipulated in the Prayer Book.

---

[50] 'Royal Wedding at Buckingham Palace', [1st account].

[51] Review of '*O Perfect Love*. Wedding Anthem. Composed by Joseph Barnby. [Novello, Ewer and Co.]', *Musical Times*, 30 (September 1889), p. 553.

[52] 'Royal Wedding Music', *Musical Visitor*.

[53] *The Hymnal Companion to the Book of Common Prayer, with Accompanying Tunes*, 3rd edn, rev. and enl., under the musical editorship of Charles Vincent and D. J. Wood, with the assistance of Sir John Stainer (London: Sampson Low, Marston & Company, 1890), no. 524.

[54] For this see also William J. Gatens, *Victorian Cathedral Music in Theory and Practice* (Cambridge: Cambridge University Press, 1986), p. 196.

[55] 'Royal Wedding at Buckingham Palace', [second account]. Same in 'Marriage Ceremony', *ILN: Royal Wedding Number* (1889), p. 6.

[56] Ceremonial 1889b, 6. Taken on verbatim in 'Royal Wedding at Buckingham Palace', [first account]; and 'Royal Wedding Music', *Musical Visitor*.

[57] 'Marriage of The Princess Louise and the Duke of Fife', *Scotsman*, p. 7.

[58] 'Royal Wedding', *Times* (1889).

9—The Choral Weddings: The Later Victorians

Illustration 9.3:
'The Marriage of Princess Louise of Wales and the Duke of Fife, Buckingham Palace, 27th July 1889', Albumen print by Byrne & Co., Hill Street, Richmond (21.5 x 21.4 cm) contained in 'Portraits of Royal Children Vol. 37: 1888–1889', *Royal Collection, RCIN 2904786*, Royal Collection Trust / © Her Majesty Queen Elizabeth II 2021.

For the very end of the ceremony, the *Observer* could refer to 'the well-known melody of the "Wedding March"', without any need for further details.[59] This was, of course, the by now customary Wedding March by Mendelssohn which 'pealed in tumultuous triumph from the organ' and accompanied the newly-weds' leaving the Chapel together.[60]

Despite its more limited dimensions and private character, the 1889 wedding service was a notable occasion. As the *Times* put it in the introduction of its long and detailed report of the ceremony, the wedding took place 'with every circumstance of solemnity and splendour' and the paper predicted that the ceremony 'will be remembered as a marvellously concentrated display of brilliancy.'[61] In fact, this remembering is aided by what is one of the earliest – if not *the* earliest – photograph of the actual ceremony of a royal wedding in chapel (Illustration 9.3).

---

[59] 'Royal Wedding at Buckingham Palace', [1st account]. See also 'Marriage of The Princess Louise and the Duke of Fife', *Scotsman*.
[60] 'Royal Wedding', *Times* (1889); also Ceremonial 1889b, p. 6.
[61] 'Royal Wedding', *Times* (1889).

This is blurred by the movement of people during the long exposure; but at least the picture confirms, for the small portion visible, the accuracy of Hall's painting.

With especial reference to the musical part, the *Observer* highlighted that 'the ceremony seemed peculiarly impressive, earnest attention being paid, and the music, vocal and instrumental, being rendered with great feeling'.[62] Queen Victoria approvingly noted 'The music was good.'[63] With Barnby's new anthem, eventually becoming a very popular hymn, this wedding left a truly noteworthy – if unrecognized – legacy.

Princess Marie Louise of Schleswig-Holstein and Prince Aribert of Anhalt, 6 July 1891

Two years after the wedding of Princess Louise of Wales, her cousin Princess Marie Louise of Schleswig-Holstein was to marry.[64] She was the daughter of Princess Helena and thus not very high up in the order or succession. However, with Prince Aribert of Anhalt as the bridegroom, this marriage continued the strengthen the dynastic links to Germany in the next generation. Indeed, the German emperor, Kaiser Wilhelm II himself, had had an important part in arranging this marriage.[65]

Venue

The wedding returned to St George's Chapel, Windsor. This choice of venue could be somehow explained by the *Graphic*'s notion that the bride 'has spent nearly all her life at Windsor'.[66] On a different level, the *Irish Times* pointed out that the Chapel 'with its long nave, and choir; and many stained-glass windows, lends itself to State ceremonies'.[67] A contemporary photographic print from about the time of the wedding, or maybe the year before shows the choir of St George's as it then appeared, with the organ still situated in the centre of the screen, as observed earlier (Illustration 9.4).

This wedding achieved particular significance and importance as it coincided with a state visit of the German Kaiser, who was a first cousin of the bride and who joined the wedding guests. As the *Irish Times* noted, decorations had been 'put up for the double purpose of honouring the Emperor and felicitating the bride and bridegroom'.[68] Moreover, magazines such as the *Illustrated London News*, for instance, reported about the wedding and the state visit in equal measure, while papers such as the *Times* and the *Scotsman* did not actually report about the wedding on its own but merely in the context of their coverage of the emperor's state visit.[69]

---

[62] 'Royal Wedding at Buckingham Palace', [2nd account].

[63] *QVJ*, 27 July 1889.

[64] NB The printed wedding ceremonial gave the princess's name merely as 'Louise'. However, the princess is today usually known under the name 'Marie Louise' which she herself used in her published memoirs: *My Memories of Six Reigns* (London: Evans Brothers Limited, 1957; repr. 1979).

[65] See John C. G. Röhl, *Wilhelm II.: Der Aufbau der Persönlichen Monarchie, 1888–1900* (Munich: C. H. Beck, 2001), pp. 740–41.

[66] 'The Royal Wedding', *Graphic: Wedding Number*, 11 July 1891, pp. 39–42, here p. 39.

[67] 'The Royal Marriage at Windsor: A Magnificent Ceremonial', *Irish Times*, 7 July 1891, p. 5.

[68] 'Royal Marriage at Windsor', *Irish Times* (1891).

[69] *ILN* of 11 July 1891; 'The German Emperor's Visit', *Times*, 7 July 1891, p. 10; and 'The German Emperor at Windsor: The Royal Wedding', *Scotsman*, 7 July 1891, p. 5.

9—The Choral Weddings: The Later Victorians

The *Graphic* interpreted that the presence of the German emperor and empress 'lent special importance to the occasion', and it overall judged that this wedding 'ranks among the most interesting Royal weddings ever celebrated in St. George's, Windsor'.[70]

With the added 'special importance' of the Kaiser's attendance, the ceremony had after all a certain grandeur. The reporter of the *Scotsman* noted that the arrangements inside St George's Chapel were 'much the same' as at previous weddings, but also pointed out that 'preparations had been made for a larger company'.[71] Similarly, the *Irish Times* declared that the service 'equalled in brilliancy' the Windsor weddings of the younger children of Queen Victoria and that it 'was thoroughly Royal in all its stages' – and moreover that this wedding 'was one of the most brilliant ceremonials of the age'.[72] Yet, despite the added 'special importance' of the wedding, there does this time not seem to be a painting showing the ceremony. However, the

Illustration 9.4: 'The Choir, St George's Chapel, Windsor Castle', platinum print *c.* 1890, *Royal Collection, RCIN 2101106*, Royal Collection Trust / © Her Majesty Queen Elizabeth II 2021.

---

[70] 'Royal Wedding', *Graphic* (1891), p. 39.

[71] 'German Emperor at Windsor', *Scotsman*.

[72] 'Royal Marriage at Windsor', *Irish Times* (1891).

Illustration 9.5: T. Walter Wilson, 'The Royal Wedding at Windsor: The Marriage Ceremony in St. George's Chapel', *ILN*, 11 July 1891, pp. 48–49. Author's collection.

illustrated magazines conveyed at least some impression of the grandeur of the occasion in their respective issues. Thomas Walter Wilson, for instance, in his picture for the *Illustrated London News*, made sure not only to capture the scene at the altar but also to show the Kaiser very clearly in the image, standing prominently to the left of the officiating cleric (Illustration 9.5).

Despite the ceremonial elaboration, there is no evidence for the heralds taking part in the ceremony, and the illustrator of the *Graphic* instead showed several chamberlains with their distinct white wands in the foreground (Illustration 9.6). Otherwise, the overall scheme followed the previous weddings at St George's and the similarity stretched also to the musical programme. The musician in charge was Parratt, as organist of St George's, who had already provided the music for the 1885 wedding in Whippingham.

Processions

As before, there service was proceeded by the separate processions going up the nave, again accompanied by specific marches.[73] Following the 1885 and 1889 weddings at Whippingham Church and at the Private Chapel in Buckingham Palace, but in clear contrast to the two most recent royal weddings at St George's Chapel (in 1879 and 1882), there was no orchestra: instead, all the music was played on, or accompanied by the organ.

---

[73] For the following OS 1891, programme of music.

9—The Choral Weddings: The Later Victorians

First to enter was the 'Procession of The Clergy', accompanied by an unspecified march by Jaques-Nicolas Lemmens. This was followed by the 'Procession of the Family of The Bridegroom', accompanied by an again unspecified march, this time by Schubert, which one account described as 'a stirring march on the organ'.[74] Another correspondent detailed that these first two processions by accident entered in reverse order, explaining that the clergy 'were to have formed the first procession up the aisle, but before they appeared the relatives of the bridegroom, headed by the father and mother, the Duke and Duchess of Anhalt, entered the west porch, and were ushered to their seats'.[75] It does not seem known whether the music was accordingly also reversed. This little incident provides an intriguing insight into the possible mishaps on such occasions.

The following procession of the royal family was ceremonially much enhanced by the fact that it included the German emperor and empress, and the correspondent of the *Times of India* thought it 'was one of the most splendid and interesting [processions] of the series'.[76] The programme of music for this procession lists simply 'March' by Guilmant.[77] The reports detailed that this was his 'Marche Nuptiale', or 'Wedding March', with the *Times* correspondent using the title 'Epithalame' and thus referring to op. 58, no. 2.[78] None of the marches that accompanied

Illustration 9.6:
'The Wedding of H.H. The Princess Louise of Schleswig-Holstein to H.H. Prince Aribert of Anhalt', Supplement to *Graphic: Wedding Number*, 11 July 1891, pp. [III-IV]. Author's collection.

---

[74] 'Royal Wedding', *Graphic* (1891), p. 39.

[75] 'Royal Marriage at Windsor', *Irish Times* (1891).

[76] 'The Royal Wedding', *Times of India*, 28 July 1891, p. 6.

[77] OS 1891.

[78] 'German Emperor at Windsor', *Scotsman*; 'Church and Organ News', *Musical News*, 1:19 (10 July 1891), p. 390; 'Royal Marriage at Windsor', *Irish Times* (1891). The *Times* account is 'German Emperor's Visit'.

these entrance processions had been heard at a previous royal wedding. The inclusion of two French marches by Lemmens and Guilmant is particularly notable, and so is the use of a Schubert march, which could have been a reference to the bridegroom's German family that it accompanied. In this context then, it may be interesting to note that the Kaiser was not acknowledged in the music of the ceremony: although overall on a state visit, he was here a mere family guest at the wedding of his cousin.

Next came the processions of the queen and of the bridegroom. From a ceremonial point of view, it is noteworthy that they both entered St George's Chapel via the south door and did not walk up the nave, thus entering in a somewhat less prominent way – although the higher-ranking guests in the quire would not have noted a difference.[79] For Queen Victoria this was the first royal wedding in twenty-eight years (since 1863) at which she did not enter via the main door and in a full ceremonial procession. The *Times* recorded for the queen's entrance merely that she 'walked with the help of a stick'.[80] The *Irish Times*, however, explained more directly that Queen Victoria had entered the Chapel via the south door 'in order to escape the fatigue of walking up the long flight of stone steps at the west door, where all the members of the Royal party had entered'.[81] Indeed, this matches with the queen's own record:

> I got out at a side door, close to the Choir, thus avoiding the high flight of steps & long walk up the nave. I walked alone, Lenchen, Christle & Victoria following close behind […].[82]

Queen Victoria's description indicates that she took a short-cut, as it were, presumably going directly from the south door to the entrance of the quire under the screen.

One writer pointed out that the ceremony's being 'semi-state' meant that 'The Royal trumpeters sounded no loud fanfare on their silver clarions'.[83] This, however, appears to refer to the inside of the Chapel only, since other reports distinctly noted trumpet fanfares. The *New York Times* reported that

> As each member of the imperial or royal families reached the Chapel Royal [*sic*] their arrival was heralded by a resounding blast from the trumpets of the State Trumpeters in their crimson and gold uniforms.[84]

Similarly, another correspondent recorded that the arrival of the queen was announced by 'a flourish of trumpets and the National Anthem outside'.[85] Her entrance was again accompanied by the march from Handel's *Occasional Oratorio*. The bridegroom had arrived before the queen, but he waited in the Braye Chapel at the end of the south transept until she had reached her seat in the quire (see also the plan of St George's Chapel in Illustration 10.4).[86] Only then did he start his own procession towards the quire, and matching the short processional route this was befittingly accompanied by a 'SHORT MARCH' by Parratt. The identity of this march, possibly written especially for this occasion, is not clear, and the music does not seem to have survived.

---

[79] See 'German Emperor at Windsor', *Scotsman*; 'Royal Wedding', *Times of India* (1891).

[80] 'German Emperor's Visit', *Times*.

[81] 'Royal Marriage at Windsor', *Irish Times* (1891).

[82] *QVJ*, 6 July 1891.

[83] George Augustus Sala, 'Royal Weddings: Seen and Not Seen', *Graphic: Wedding Number* 11 July 1891, pp. 48–49, here p. 49.

[84] 'Prince Aribert's Bride: The Pomp and Ceremony of a Royal Wedding', *New York Times*, 7 July 1891, p. 1.

[85] 'German Emperor at Windsor', *Scotsman* 'Royal Wedding', *Times of India* (1891).

[86] 'German Emperor at Windsor', *Scotsman*.

9—The Choral Weddings: The Later Victorians

After this came the 'critical moment', as the *Times* correspondent called it: the arrival of the bride.[87] The *Scotsman* recorded that she arrived at the west door 'and was announced', and the *Graphic* detailed furthermore that the queen 'was scarcely seated before the organ announced the arrival of the bride'.[88] The bride's procession featured a notable innovation: she did not enter to an instrumental march but to a hymn. Apart from the seemingly singular instance of the 1866 Kew wedding of Princess Mary Adelaide of Cambridge, and this custom at least at some other, non-royal weddings, this was the first more prominent royal wedding at which the bride entered to a hymn.

Like the introit at previous weddings, this entrance hymn was not sung by the congregation. The ceremonial recorded that

> The Choir of St. George's Chapel who had been stationed at the West Entrance of the Chapel, preceded the Bridal Procession and sang a Hymn, composed by The Bishop of Ripon, as The Bride passed up the Nave.[89]

The *Scotsman* explained that the choir 'sang a hymn beginning, "Lord, Who Hast Made Home and Love, Help Us and Ours," which was specially written for the marriage by William Boyd Carpenter, Bishop of Ripon, and set to music by Mr Parratt, organist of the chapel', and the programme of music in the order of service furthermore included the full text of eight verses.[90] These verses are irregular, with the two outer verses having six, and the six inner verses having four lines, which may indicate a slightly more complicated arrangement. This hymn would probably have been longer than needed to cover the bride's procession, thus highlighting its dual function as an introit to the service.

The choir's walking in the bridal procession was a notable innovation for a royal wedding. The ceremonial detailed that 'At the Entrance to the Chapel [that is, the quire], the Choir filed off and took their places in the South Aisle, whilst The Bride, with Her Highness's Supporters, was conducted to the *Haut Pas*.'[91] The quire stalls were 'reserved for the Royal guests and their suites'.[92] Therefore, it may be assumed that the choir eventually went up into the organ loft – if not into another, otherwise undocumented temporary gallery.

Since it was accompanied by a hymn, the bride's procession stood out even more from the other processions, which had been accompanied by instrumental marches played on the organ. It does not appear to be known who was behind this change, or innovation. The princess herself recorded some details of the ceremony but nothing on the music.[93] The idea to have a hymn for the bridal procession instead of an instrumental march could plausibly have come from Parratt himself: after all, the bridegroom and bride both entered to music by him, 'specially written for the occasion' and 'expressly written for the Service', respectively.[94] As with the bridegroom's march, the music of Parratt's hymn is unfortunately not known and appears to have been lost.

---

[87] 'German Emperor's Visit', *Times*.

[88] 'German Emperor at Windsor', *Scotsman*; 'Royal Wedding', *Graphic* (1891), p. 42.

[89] Ceremonial 1891b, p. 15.

[90] 'German Emperor at Windsor', *Scotsman*; same in 'German Emperor's Visit', *Times*. See also 'Royal Wedding', *Graphic* (1891), p. 42; and H. D. A. [Henry Dewsbury Alves] Major, *The Life and Letters of William Boyd Carpenter* (London: John Murray, 1925), p. 319. The full text as reproduced in OS 1891 is given in Appendix B 9.3.

[91] Ceremonial 1891b, p. 15.

[92] 'Royal Wedding', *Graphic* (1891), p. 39.

[93] Schleswig-Holstein, *My Memories*, p. 71.

[94] 'Church and Organ News'.

British Royal Weddings

Service

For the actual service, at least one account emphasized that the Archbishop of Canterbury was 'taking the whole ceremony in the hand'.[95] The correspondent of the *Scotsman* summarized that the service 'was choral, and the only variation from the ordinary was the substitution by his Grace of a special address for the prescribed admonition customarily used'.[96] As Queen Victoria put it, the archbishop 'said a few kind words of advice instead of the Address at the end'.[97] The *New York Times* reported that the archbishop 'made only a brief exhortation' and it overall judged that the service 'was most simple'.[98] Notwithstanding such reported simplicity, however, the service contained much the same musical elements as previous royal weddings.

The psalm was Ps. 67, now sung to a chant by Garrett in A.[99] This refers to the organist and composer George Mursell Garrett (1834–97), at the time organist to the University of Cambridge and who had published a collection of chants.[100] His collection contains several chants by Garrett, but none in A. It cannot be known what chant was eventually sung, or indeed why a chant by Garrett was chosen in the first place. Similarly, it is not known whether the choir sang the Responses although, as will be seen, it contributed at least a choral Amen at the end of the service.

In the programme of music the next item after the psalm is the 'ANTHEM' *Hearts Feel, that Love Thee, no Evil Can Disturb their Rest* by Mendelssohn.[101] The anthem probably came between the psalm (and possibly the Responses) and the archbishop's address. While the full text of the anthem is included, there are no further details on its identity. Mendelssohn's anthem was in fact a chorus from his *Athalie* (MWV M16), his music to Racine's play from which a march had been heard at many previous weddings: it is the ending of chorus no. 4, 'Ist es Glück? Ist es Leid' – the section to the text 'Ein Herz voll Frieden'.[102] Marian Wilson Kimber has highlighted that this section was 'often encored'.[103] An arrangement of this section, for a female trio and chorus, and to the English text 'Hearts Feel, that Love Thee' had been published in a larger anthology in 1878, and a review of this edition had explained that such 'home music' was 'always welcome in the drawing-room'. This trio was again published on its own in 1879.[104]

---

[95] 'Royal Marriage at Windsor', *Irish Times* (1891).

[96] 'German Emperor at Windsor', *Scotsman*. The text of the address was reproduced in 'German Emperor's Visit', *Times*.

[97] *QVJ*, 6 July 1891.

[98] 'Prince Aribert's Bride'.

[99] 'German Emperor's Visit', *Times*. OS 1891, programme of music, has merely 'Garrett'.

[100] For biographical details see 'George Mursell Garrett', *MT*, 38 (May 1897), pp. 310–11; also Bernarr Rainbow, 'Garrett, George (Mursell)', *NG*. For the collection see George M. Garrett [ed.], *Chants – Old and New, Selected and Arranged in Order of Daily Use for one Calendar Month; with Special Chants for the Venite exultemus and Proper Psalms*, 2nd edn (London: Sacred Music Warehouse – Novello, Ewer and Co., [c. 1872?]).

[101] OS 1891, programme of music. The *Times* correspondent curiously called it 'Hearts that love true': see 'The German Emperor's Visit'.

[102] For the music see Felix Mendelssohn Bartholdy, *Musik zu "Athalia" von Racine, MWV M16*, ed. by Armin Koch, 'Leipziger Ausgabe der Werke von Felix Mendelssohn Bartholdy', series V: 'Bühnenwerke', vol. 9 (Wiesbaden: Breitkopf & Härtel, 2010), pp. 183–88.

[103] This and the following Marian Wilson Kimber, 'Performing *Athalia*: Mendelssohn's Op. 74 in the Nineteenth-Century Choral World', *Choral Journal* (April 2009), pp. 9–23, here p. 18, who refers to a review in *MT*, 19 (March 1878), p. 160.

[104] Felix Mendelssohn Bartholdy, *Hearts Feel that Love Thee. Trio for Female Voices. Arranged from the Trio and Chorus in "Athalie."* (London: Novello, Ewer & Co., [1879]). This version (but with German and French text) is also in the appendix to Mendelssohn Bartholdy, *Musik zu "Athalia"*, on pp. 237–44.

9—The Choral Weddings: The Later Victorians

It does not seem to be known by whom and why Mendelssohn's overall somewhat unusual piece was chosen for the wedding.

The *Irish Times* reported that there were overall 'several hymns and an anthem'.[105] Indeed, in addition to the aforementioned hymn during the bride's entrance, the programme of music listed a 'Hymn before the Benediction': 'O Perfect Love' by 'Dykes'.[106] Other, non-royal weddings had had an entrance hymn and then a second hymn; for instance, at the Clemens and Flood-Jones wedding in Westminster Abbey in 1886, 'Father of Life, Confessing' to music by Turle had been sung 'At the Conclusion of the Marriage Service'.[107] No previous royal wedding, however, had included two hymns.

The *Graphic* confirms that 'a hymn "O Perfect Love."' was included, but not when, while the *Scotsman* report agrees with the programme of music and notes that 'a hymn was sung by the choir before the benediction', but without giving a title.[108] Thus, 'O Perfect Love' may have come between the 'short special address' delivered by the archbishop and the final blessing that was then also answered by the choir:

> Before the final Benediction the Primate delivered a brief address to the newly-married couple, and at ten minutes to five the service was brought to a conclusion by an elaborate choral "Amen."[109]

It is interesting to note that 'O Perfect Love' was not sung to Barnby's tune discussed earlier but to a tune by Dykes – which was presumably his 'Strength and Stay', for which the text had originally been written.[110]

The ceremony ended with Mendelssohn's Wedding March, played on the organ, during which the newly-weds received the congratulations of their family and then 'proceeded through the nave to the western entrance'.[111] Overall, Queen Victoria commented that 'The music was very fine.'[112] As will be seen, it was not merely 'fine': with the adoption of a processional hymn for the bride's entrance and also the inclusion of a second hymn this wedding had set long-lasting precedents.

Prince George, Duke of York, and Princess Victoria Mary of Teck, 6 July 1893

The circumstances of the wedding of the future George V are well-known. He had been born only third in the line of succession, ranking after his father the Prince of Wales and his elder brother Prince Albert Victor, later Duke of Clarence and Avondale (who was generally known as 'Prince Eddy'). The latter had become engaged to Princess Victoria Mary of Teck (who was known as 'Princess May') – but he died suddenly in January 1892, before the wedding, and his fiancée eventually married his brother Prince George, Duke of York, who had become next in line to the throne after the Prince of Wales.

---

[105] 'Royal Marriage at Windsor', *Irish Times* (1891).

[106] OS 1891, programme of music.

[107] Hymn sheet in *Lwa WAM Service Papers*, 27 July 1886; see Chapter 1, fn. 98.

[108] 'Royal Wedding', *Graphic* (1891), p. 42; and 'German Emperor at Windsor', *Scotsman*.

[109] 'Royal Wedding', *Times of India* (1891). For the 'short special address' see also 'Royal Wedding', *Graphic* (1891), p. 42.

[110] Compare above, fn. 44.

[111] 'Royal Wedding', *Times of India* (1891); 'German Emperor at Windsor', *Scotsman*.

[112] *QVJ*, 6 July 1891.

As the Polish-Russian Princess Catherine Radziwill in her book on royal marriages later summarized, 'Of all the weddings of her children and relatives none interested Queen Victoria so much' as this one.[113] This interest showed in the queen's active involvement: she very much contributed to the arrangements of the ceremony, discussing them with the officials as well as the bridegroom's parents.[114]

Venue

Andrew Cook has observed that, for the originally intended wedding of Prince Albert Victor, there had at some point been the idea of 'a state occasion in St Paul's, which was what the Prince of Wales, supported by [Arthur] Balfour, thought most fitting', but that the prime minister, Lord Salisbury, had 'protested against' this idea.[115] It is not known that St Paul's was ever considered for Prince George's wedding. The wedding eventually took place on 6 July 1893 in the Chapel Royal at St James's Palace – and it was the first royal wedding to be held there since that of the Princess Royal in 1858. This choice of venue had been necessitated by the circumstances, at it were. In December 1891, Princess Victoria Mary had reported to her aunt Princess Augusta, Grand Duchess of Mecklenburg-Strelitz, that her wedding to Prince Albert Victor had been 'fixed for Feby 27th at Windsor'; however, in its report of her wedding to Prince George, the *Times* eventually summarized that St George's Chapel in Windsor had 'unhappily acquired associations which would not altogether have accorded with such a day of rejoicing', and it explained that

> had the present marriage been celebrated at Windsor, thoughts of the mournful scene there enacted little more than 18 months ago, when the poor Duke of Clarence was laid to rest, might have risen unbidden in the minds of the guests.[116]

Indeed, in the first half of May 1893, Queen Victoria had written to her daughter Victoria in Germany: 'Windsor is lovely for a marriage in the summer – but I quite feel it cld not be *after* the sad funeral in St George's.'[117] All the same, she commented that the wedding was 'to be in the first week of July, & alas! in the Chapel Royal', adding that she thought the Chapel 'small & *very ugly*'. Similar criticism of the Chapel was also uttered publicly. The *Scotsman* pointed out that 'in many respects the place is ill adapted for such a purpose', explaining that 'One drawback is its extremely limited accommodation'.[118]

Another report summarized that 'Some objection was made to the smallness of the chapel and the want of great state and pomp'.[119] However, the same report also explained meaningfully that 'for many reasons the Chapel Royal was fittest', referring to the wedding of Queen Victoria and Prince Albert that had taken place there. After all, the *Scotsman* had noted that journalists

---

[113] Princess Catherine Radziwill, *The Royal Marriage Market of Europe* (New York: Funk and Wagnalls Company, 1915), p. 252.

[114] See, for instance, *QVJ*, entries for 7 June, 8 June, and 25 June 1893.

[115] Andrew Cook, *Prince Eddy: The King Britain Never Had* (Strout, Tempus, 2006), p. 260. Balfour, nephew of Lord Salisbury, at the time was leader of the Conservative Party in the House of Commons.

[116] 'The Royal Wedding', *Times*, 7 July 1893, pp. 5–7, here p. 5. For Princess Victoria Mary's letter to her aunt, of 26 December 1891, see Pope-Hennessy, *Queen Mary*, p. 219.

[117] This and the following quoted in Pope-Hennessy, *Queen Mary*, p. 261, who refers to 'Kronberg Archives, 13 May 1893'. NB Queen Victoria had not attended the funeral. See Matthias Range, *British Royal and State Funerals: Music and Ceremonial since Elizabeth I* (Woodbridge: Boydell Press, 2016), p. 258.

[118] 'The Royal Wedding', *Scotsman*, 7 July 1893, p. 5.

[119] This and the following *The Gentlewoman's Royal Record of the Wedding of [...] Victoria Mary of Teck and [...] the Duke of York* (London, [1893]), fol. 24ʳ [this publication uses foliation, not page numbers].

9—The Choral Weddings: The Later Victorians

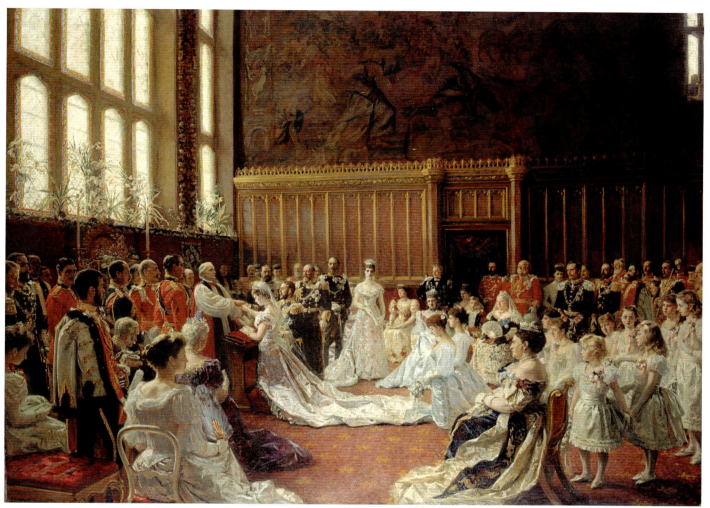

were positively 'struck' by the 'plain unadorned appearance of the chapel'.[120] The paper summarized that the Chapel had normally no room 'for more than a hundred and fifty persons', but with special arrangements 'a little over three hundred seats were provided', adding that those people who did not fit into the Chapel had been allocated places closely outside, to see the arrivals of the processions.[121] One eyewitness of the ceremony commented approvingly that the Chapel Royal 'is, perhaps, not extensive enough for grand national ceremonies; but it seemed to be that the very narrowness of the building contributed to the impressiveness of the ceremony'.[122] Laurits Regner Tuxen's painting of the wedding seems to capture both the ceremonial grandeur of the service and the 'narrowness of the building', even if the chosen angle makes the space still look wider and loftier than it is (Illustration 9.7).

Illustration 9.7: Laurits Regner Tuxen, 'The Marriage of George, Duke of York, with Princess Mary of Teck, 6 July 1893', oil on canvas, signed and dated 1894, *Royal Collection, RCIN 402437*, Royal Collection Trust / © Her Majesty Queen Elizabeth II 2021.

---

[120] 'Royal Wedding', *Scotsman* (1893). For the practical arrangements of the Chapel Royal see the material in *Lna LC 2/128* and *Lna WORK 21/12/7*. For a description and photograph of the Chapel arranged for the wedding see Edgar Sheppard, *Memorials of St James's Palace*, 2 vols (London: Longmans, Green, and Co., 1894), II, part 2, pp. 126–28.

[121] 'Royal Wedding', *Scotsman* (1893).

[122] Moulvie Rafiüddin Ahmad, 'The Royal Marriage: From an Oriental point of View', *The Strand Magazine: An illustrated Monthly* 6 (July 1893), pp. 447–58, here p. 450.

British Royal Weddings

Processions

The fact that the wedding took place in London was a notable aspect. Sarah Tytler observed that 'The locality was highly popular with the Londoners' and that the 'crowd viewing the processions' was 'almost as vast as at the Jubilee'.[123] Queen Victoria herself also compared the wedding to the celebration of her Golden Jubilee six years previously and commented: 'It was really (on a smaller scale) like the Jubilee, & the crowds, the loyalty & enthusiasm were immense.'[124] The papers praised the wedding celebrations in the same way, with the *Scotsman* observing that 'for a parallel [...] we must go back to the imposing State functions on Jubilee day, 1887'.[125]

The wedding had a stronger public aspect than those in previous years. In contrast to 1840 and 1858, the outdoor processions from Buckingham Palace to the Chapel Royal were now much longer, making a detour up Constitution Hill and down Piccadilly.[126] They were all accompanied by 'the sweet music discoursed by military bands at various points along the route'.[127] With the service in the Chapel Royal preceded by distinct walking processions through the Palace, the wedding was also more ceremonious than those of the previous decades. Queen Victoria – who did not take part in these processions – recorded that, together with the bride's mother, Princess Mary Adelaide of Cambridge, she left for the Chapel later than the 'others' who

> had all gone on some little time before, as they had a walking Procession through the state rooms at St. James's Palace, whereas we got out in the Ambassador's Court at a small door.[128]

The individual processions through the state apartments were accompanied by music. The *Scotsman* had announced that this processional music was to be 'rendered by one of the Household regimental bands, which will be mounted with a guard of honour outside the garden entrance to the Palace'.[129] In the end, however, the ceremonial stipulated: 'The Band of the Grenadier Guards will perform in the Entrée Gallery at St. James's Palace whilst the Processions are passing through the State Rooms.'[130] Three days before the wedding, the Lord Chamberlain's Office sent the details to Lieutenant Dan Godfrey, who was to direct the band:

> The Band will commence playing at 10.30, and continue playing at intervals until 11.45, when Lieut. Godfrey will wait for a signal from the Gentleman Usher that Procession No. 1. is started. March from Tannhaüser by Wagner will be played until the Trumpeters stationed in the Grand Staircase sound, when the March will be stopped. [next recto] The 2nd Procession (of the Bridegroom) (page 11) will start about 20 minutes after the first procession, and no music is to be played during this interval. // The Duke of York march will then be played under the same conditions as before. // Five minutes after this the 3rd Procession (of the Bride) (page 12) is conducted, and the Bridal Chorus from Lohengrin is to be played.[131]

---

[123] Sarah Tytler, *Life of Her Most Gracious Majesty the Queen*, ed. and with an introduction by Lord Ronald Gower, 3 vols (London: J. S. Virtue & Co., [1897?]), III, p. 201.

[124] *QVJ*, 6 July 1893.

[125] 'Royal Wedding', *Scotsman* (1893). See also 'Royal Wedding', *Times* (1893), p. 5.

[126] See Pope-Hennessy, *Queen Mary*, p. 267.

[127] 'Royal Wedding', *Scotsman* (1893).

[128] *QVJ*, 6 July 1893.

[129] 'The Forthcoming Royal Wedding', *Scotsman*, 4 July 1893, p. 5.

[130] Ceremonial, 1893, p. 13. For the change of the band's position see 'Copy' of 'DRAFT' of Ponsonby-Fane to 'Lt: Dan Godfrey / Grenadier Guards', 28 June 1893, in *Lna LC 2/129*.

[131] 'Marriage of HRH The Duke of York. / July 6th 1893. / Arrangements for the Band of the / Grenadier Guards under the Direction / of Lieut: Godfrey.', 'Copy given to M.r Godfrey. 3rd July '93', letterhead of the Lord Chamberlain's Office, in *Lna LC 2/128*. This document is included in two copies.

9—The Choral Weddings: The Later Victorians

Thus, the band was to play 'at intervals' for over an hour, from 10.30am to 11.45am, before the processions started. However, as in the past, the music was then to accompany only the actual processions but was not to sound in the intervals. The instructions sent to Godfrey scheduled the band to be stationed in 'the Picture Gallery', but the *Illustrated London News* eventually referred to 'the bands in the Throne Room'.[132] Corresponding with these instructions, the ceremonial detailed that 'Her Majesty's State Trumpeters, who will be stationed on the Grand Staircase, will announce, by a Flourish of Trumpets, the arrival of the successive Processions'.[133]

The mentioned march from Wagner's *Tannhäuser* probably referred either to the Pilgrim's Chorus, or – now perhaps more befitting – to the Entry of the Guests, as discussed for the 1889 wedding. The cited 'Duke of York march' was a slow march that had been composed by Christopher Frederick Eley, Director of Music of the Band of the Coldstream Guards at the end of the eighteenth century.[134] Notwithstanding its clear military character, this march was obviously an appropriate, eponymous choice. As will be seen, the strains of Wagner's Bridal March from *Lohengrin* eventually accompanied the bride right up to the altar.

Illustration 9.8: Amadée Forestier, 'The marriage of TRH the Duke and Duchess of York, 6 July 1893', watercolour 1893, *Royal Collection, RCIN 920841*, Royal Collection Trust / © Her Majesty Queen Elizabeth II 2021.

---

[132] 'The Royal Wedding', *ILN: Royal Wedding Number*, 10 July 1893, pp. 2–4.

[133] Ceremonial, 1893, p. 6.

[134] For details on Eley and this march see Graham O. Jones, 'British Wind Band Music' (unpublished doctoral thesis, University of Salford, Manchester, 2005), passim.

253

The *Scotsman* noted that 'Court etiquette requires the strictest procedure on State occasions' and explained that the processions would be headed by heralds.[135] In a draft letter to Sir Albert Woods, Garter King of Arms, the Lord Chamberlain's Office explained that it was 'The Queen's Command' that he should attend together with 'Six Heralds' and that they were 'to take part in the Processions and to assist in arranging them'.[136] According to the printed ceremonial, the individual processions of the royal family, queen, bridegroom, and of the bride were to be headed by 'Heralds', 'Two Heralds', 'Heralds' and 'Heralds'.[137] The *Scotsman* observed that 'The principal personages will form the rear of the processions, the heads of each procession being formed of heralds, grand Officers of the Household, and Gentleman and Ladies in Waiting.'; but it also pointed out that 'The exceptions will be in the processions of the Queen and the bride.' – who were followed by their entourage.[138] In any case, compared to the previous weddings where the heralds had taken part, this time the pictures of the ceremony do not show any heralds; they do, however show the chamberlains leading the return procession (Illustration 9.8).

Whether or not the heralds eventually took part in the processions and ceremony and helped organize proceedings, in the end, there occurred a well-known, significant mistake in the ceremonial – quite to the contrary of 'the strictest procedure on State occasions'. This was recorded by Queen Victoria herself:

> I was the first to arrive & enter the Chapel, which was not intended, but which I was glad of as I saw all the Processions which were very striking & dignified.[139]

This anecdote, with some further details, was widely publicized at the latest by Kinloch Cooke in his *Memoir* of the bride's mother, published a few years after the wedding.[140] He explained that in the organization of the proceedings it had simply been 'forgotten […] in timing the processions' that the queen had a shorter way than the other participants:

> The result was that the Queen arrived at the Chapel door first, instead of last – the position assigned to the Sovereign in the official arrangements – and only a gentleman usher was present to receive her. Princess Mary [of Cambridge, the bride's mother], taking in the situation at once, suggested that she should proceed to her place, and that the Queen should remain in a room on the left which had been prepared for her use. Scarcely had Her Royal Highness advanced a few steps up the corridor than Miss Thesiger, who was in attendance upon the Duchess felt a little pull at her dress, and at the same time heard a voice saying, "I am going first." Looking round, she saw Her Majesty on the arm of the Grand Duke [of Mecklenburg-Strelitz, the bride's brother-in-law]; and in this informal way the Queen entered the Chapel. Some minutes later the Lord Chamberlain and the great officers of the household arrived in breathless haste; but Her Majesty was not at all perturbed by the incident, only saying that she was glad it happened so, for it was very amusing to see every one come in.

It must be noted that the queen's scheduled arriving 'last' referred merely to the processions of the clergy and of the royal family and guests, both of which should have arrived before her. Some accounts strangely seem to have referred simply to the scheduled programme – but did not record what actually happened. For instance, one writer described that the Lord Chamberlain

---

[135] 'Forthcoming Royal Wedding', *Scotsman*. See also *Gentlewoman's Royal Record*, fol. 26ʳ.

[136] 'DRAFT' of letter, Lord Chamberlain's Office to Woods, 24 June 1893, in *Lna LC 2/129*.

[137] Ceremonial 1893a/b.

[138] 'Forthcoming Royal Wedding', *Scotsman*.

[139] *QVJ*, 6 July 1893.

[140] This and the following Sir C[lement] Kinloch Cooke, *A Memoir of Her Royal Highness Princess Mary Adelaide, Duchess of Teck, Based on her Private Diaries and Letters*, 2 vols (London: John Murray, 1900), here II, p. 247.

9—The Choral Weddings: The Later Victorians

'went to the door, the trumpets sounded, and we knew that Her Majesty had arrived'.[141] Moreover, this account detailed that the queen 'entered as the assembly rose to their feet and the organ pealed out the notes of the "Imperial March," composed by Sir Arthur Sullivan', which is the correct one scheduled for her in the programme of music and the ceremonial.[142] In an article on the wedding before the event, the *Scotsman* explained that Sullivan had composed his 'Grand Imperial March' for 'the opening of the Imperial Institute' and noted that it would be played with 'some slight alteration in the setting, with the view to suit the organ'.[143] The *Times* also recorded that during the queen's procession, 'the inspiriting strains of Sir Arthur Sullivan's Imperial March peal from the organ'.[144] If this is correct, it would indicate that at least the organist had realized the queen's early arrival and played the right music.

However, it is possible that these reports merely followed the official programme. Indeed, the account in the *Illustrated London News* was probably closer to what actually happened: while it did not mention the queen's arriving too early, it recorded that she was 'greeted by the silent rising of the whole congregation' and that only 'When she had taken her seat, music was heard', to accompany the bridegroom's entrance.[145] So the queen probably entered in solemn silence.

Moving through the Chapel to the altar, the procession of the clergy was to be accompanied by Handel's march from the *Occasional Oratorio*, the procession of the royal family and royal guests by another Handel march, from *Scipio*, and the procession of the bridegroom by a 'March in G' by Henry Smart.[146] These marches were all played on the organ.[147] As Queen Victoria recorded for the arrival of the first procession:

> There was a flourish of trumpets followed by a march played outside, & then taken up by the organ, as the Royalties slowly entered.[148]

The continued prominence of marches by Handel is notable. However, the bridegroom's and bride's processions were distinctly different by including more recent music. Notwithstanding the recent 1891 precedent of a hymn for the bride's entrance, as in 1885 and 1889, during the bride's procession 'Wagner's Bridal March from "Lohengrin" was played on the organ.'[149] The bride thus had the same music for both her entrance processions: for that through the state rooms and that in the chapel itself.

There was now also clearly music played inside the Chapel Royal prior to the arrival of all these processions. Before the wedding, the *Scotsman* had reported that 'Dr Creser [organist of the Chapel Royal] will open the ceremonial by playing a selection of music, which will usher in the special guests invited to the Chapel.'[150] After the event, an account of the wedding music in the *Musical News* recorded that Creser 'gave a varied selection of music', and it listed the individual pieces with some additional details:

---

[141] *Gentlewoman's Royal Record*, fol. 24r. For this and the following also 'Music at the Royal Wedding', *Musical News*, 5:124 (15 July 1893), p. 64. For the 'silver trumpet' announcing the queen, see also Tytler, *Life*, III, p. 202.

[142] See OS 1893 and Ceremonial 1893a, p. 10.

[143] 'Forthcoming Royal Wedding', *Scotsman*.

[144] 'Royal Wedding', *Times* (1893), p. 5.

[145] 'The Royal Wedding', *ILN*, 15 July 1893, pp. 70–71, here p. 70.

[146] OS 1893; Ceremonial 1893a, p. 10–11; 'Music at the Royal Wedding', *Musical News* (1893).

[147] *Gentlewoman's Royal Record*, fol. 26r; also *QVJ*, 6 July 1893.

[148] *QVJ*, 6 July 1893.

[149] 'Royal Wedding', *Scotsman* (1893); also Ceremonial 1893b, p. 11; and 'Royal Wedding', *ILN* (1893), p. 70.

[150] 'Forthcoming Royal Wedding', *Scotsman*.

British Royal Weddings

- organ transcriptions of the preludes to the first and third act of Wagner's *Lohengrin*
- a courante from Handel's *Scipio*
- 'a transcription of Dr. Mackenzie's "Benedictus," arranged for the organ by Mr. Charlton Palmer' [Clement Charlton Palmer (1871–1944)]
- a Wedding March in C by Creser, 'specially composed for this occasion'
- 'Handel's "Largo"'
- the 'War March of the Priests, from Mendelssohn's "Athalie," which concluded the preliminary selection'[151]

The title 'Handel's "Largo"', then as now, probably referred to the aria 'Ombra mai fu' from his opera *Serse* (HWV 40). It is interesting that this modern-day favourite has a wedding-association reaching as far back as 1893 at least. Creser's own march was also very notable. It was published in the same year.[152] Indeed, before the wedding one report had announced that this march 'will be played in many churches as a voluntary next Sunday'.[153] Such dissemination of the wedding music is reminiscent of Barnby's anthem four years earlier, at the 1889 wedding. Finally, Mendelssohn's march from *Athalie*, which had been played as a processional at several previous weddings, may have been a particular favourite at the time: in the previous year, one writer had described it as 'even more popular' than Mendelssohn's Wedding March.[154]

Music of the Service

As in 1889, the music of the service was provided by the Chapel Royal, now in its own building. The ceremonial noted that the Chapel organist, William G. Creser, would 'preside at the Organ, and conduct the music sung by the Choir of the Chapel Royal'.[155] After the ceremony, Sheppard, the Subdean of the Chapel Royal, detailed that

> The music at this service was beautifully rendered by the choir of the Chapel Royal, who numbered twenty, and who were placed on this occasion in the organ loft.[156]

While Creser may have compiled the selection of organ music before the processions, it is not known in how far he was involved in the choices for the actual ceremony. About four weeks before the wedding, Ponsonby-Fane sent a telegraph from Balmoral to Sir Henry Ponsonby, Queen Victoria's private secretary, at St James's Palace:

> Immediate / No Music programme here pray get copy from Sub-dean and send by messenger today so that The Queen may discuss it with Princess of Wales. [next page] (I Ponsonby) Te Deum not approved Sub-dean might propose some short anthem instead[.][157]

This indicates that someone else, possibly Creser, had chosen the initial suggestions for the music that the subdean had. Interestingly, from this it appears that at some point the inclusion of a Te Deum had been proposed but Queen Victoria, or the Princess of Wales, did not approve and

---

[151] 'Music at the Royal Wedding', *Musical News* (1893).

[152] William Creser, *Wedding March: Composed in Commemoration of the Marriage of H.R.H. The Duke of York* […], Novello no. 9654 (London: Novello, Ewer & Co. [1893]).

[153] 'Forthcoming Royal Wedding', *Scotsman*.

[154] Anonymous, review of '*Three Marches* by Mendelssohn. Arranged for the pianoforte by E. Pauer', *The Monthly Musical Record* 22 (January 1892), p. 16.

[155] Ceremonial 1893a, p. 13.

[156] Sheppard, *Memorials*, II, part 2, p. 130. See also 'Forthcoming Royal Wedding', *Scotsman*.

[157] Ponsonby-Fane to Ponsonby, 8 June 1893, in *Lna LC 2/128*.

9—The Choral Weddings: The Later Victorians

asked for a short anthem instead. It is clear that the queen was in full control of the ceremonial details, including the music. Indeed, two days before the wedding, on 4 July, the *Scotsman* reported that Queen Victoria 'in whose hands the Prince and Princess of Wales have left all the arrangements for the wedding […], has now finally approved the choral part of the Church service'.[158]

The programme of music that the subdean in response sent the queen seems to have survived.[159] For the initial processions, this matches with the printed programme of music; then, for the following, it schedules:

> Before Ser[v]ice begun } Marriage Chorale Father of Life. Creser
>
> Chorale for Middle of Service – Oh. perfect Love Barnby
>
> (Sung at Fife Wedding)
>
> Hymn. End of Service.
>
> Now thank we – Nun danket
>
> Wedding March

After the wedding, Queen Victoria noted that 'The service began by Hymn.'[160] This referred to the introit, described as 'a specially composed chorale', or 'a beautiful hymn, composed for the occasion', respectively.[161] It was 'Father of Life' with 'Words by the Rev. S. Flood Jones' and music by Creser.[162] The four-part setting of this hymn was published independently.[163] Moreover, it was also reproduced as a supplement to the special wedding number of the *Illustrated London News* (see Illustration 9.9): the inclusion of the hymn in this popular magazine would have increased its dissemination immensely. Regarding the performance, the same magazine, in its report of the ceremony referred decidedly to 'the singing, by the choir, of a hymn composed for the occasion', implying that the congregation did again not join in the singing.[164]

The *Musical News* recorded that 'After the ceremony the psalm "God be merciful unto us" was followed by Barnby's "O perfect Love."'[165] In this context, 'ceremony' must refer to the exchange of the wedding vows, which in the Prayer Book is followed by the psalm. According to the programme of music, the 'Chant for Psalm 67' was by John Goss, but no further details seem to be known.[166] A pencil note on top of the subdean's programme detailed that 'only Psalm chanted & amens.'[167] If this was followed, the Responses were just said, but the choir sang at least the 'Amens'.

The printed programme of music in the order of service also included the full text of Barnby's 'ANTHEM' after the psalm.[168] This matches with the subdean's proposal that had

---

[158] 'Forthcoming Royal Wedding', *Scotsman*.

[159] 'Programme of Music.', 'June 1893 / Subdean', in *Lna LC 2/128*. At the end, this has the annotation 'sending proposed'.

[160] *QVJ*, 6 July 1893.

[161] 'Forthcoming Royal Wedding', *Scotsman*; 'Royal Wedding', *Times* (1893), p. 5.

[162] OS 1893, programme of music, which includes the full text of four verses. See also 'Music at the Royal Wedding', *Musical News* (1893).

[163] William Creser, *Father of Life: Marriage Hymn*, Novello no. 9657 (London: Novello, Ewer & Co., [1893]).

[164] 'Royal Wedding', *ILN* (1893), p. 70.

[165] 'Music at the Royal Wedding', *Musical News* (1893).

[166] OS 1893, programme of music.

[167] 'Programme of Music.', 'June 1893 / Subdean', in *Lna LC 2/128*. This also has the annotation 'sending proposed'.

[168] OS 1893, programme of music.

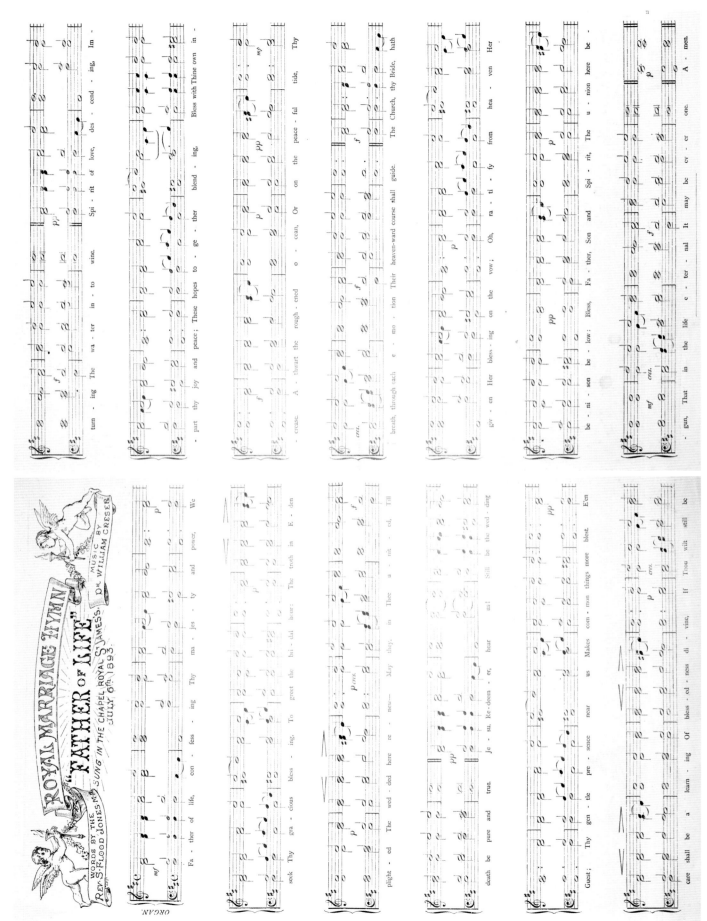

Illustration 9.9: William Creser and S. Flood Jones, 'Royal Marriage Hymn: Father of Life', *ILN: Royal Wedding Number*, 10 July 1893, [supplement between pp 22 and 23]. Author's collection.

9—The Choral Weddings: The Later Victorians

suggested this piece as the 'Chorale for Middle of Service'. However, according to the final, printed ceremonial 'Barnby's anthem' was to be sung 'At the conclusion of the Service', that is before the recess.[169] Yet, it would then have clashed with the 'last Hymn' reported for the end of the ceremony, which will be discussed below. It is possible, therefore, that the ceremonial simply had this wrong – perhaps following the earlier precedents of anthems 'at the conclusion of the service' – and that Barnby's anthem came indeed earlier, after the psalm and the prayers, and the hymn at the conclusion.

The service once again included a 'short address', by the archbishop – which Queen Victoria thought 'excellent'.[170] The *Illustrated London News* recorded that the archbishop 'after his benediction, delivered a brief address'.[171] It seems likely that this 'benediction' referred to the blessing of the couple, after the prayers, not to the final blessing. Barnby's anthem could then plausibly have come between the prayers with the couple's 'blessing' and the sermon.

On 9 June it was still reported that no anthem had yet been commissioned for the wedding.[172] It is not known whether there had ever been a plan to have a new anthem. The subdean's proposal that he sent to the queen and which was possibly written around that time already scheduled Barnby's *O Perfect Love*, remarking that this had been 'Sung at Fife Wedding'. There does not seem to be any information on why Barnby's piece from the 1889 wedding of Princess Louise was chosen to be repeated. Similarly, it is not known whether this had been the subdean's choice or someone else's.

For the end of the service, Queen Victoria referred to 'the last Hymn, & the Benediction'.[173] The subdean's proposed programme in June had suggested 'Now Thank We All our God' as the final hymn, but the printed programme of music listed that the 'Hymn before the Benediction (from the German)' was to be 'Lead Us, Heavenly Father, Lead Us'.[174] The *Times* also noted this last hymn as a hymn 'of German origin', and the *Scotsman* similarly recorded that the hymn would be sung 'to an old German tune'.[175] This most probably refers to the tune 'Mannheim' to which this text is still commonly sung today. The music by Friedrich Filitz had been first published, in an earlier form, in Germany in 1846.[176] It was later altered and used for an English text.[177] This hymn and tune was to be heard at many of the following royal weddings. Again, it appears not to have been sung by the congregation: the *Scotsman* referred to this hymn as part of the 'choral service, which throughout will be rendered by the men and boys of the Chapel-Royal choir'.[178]

---

[169] Ceremonial, 1893, p. 12. Verbatim also in 'Royal Wedding', *Scotsman* (1893).

[170] 'Royal Wedding', *Scotsman* (1893); and *QVJ*, 6 July 1893. See also 'Royal Wedding', *Times* (1893), p. 5, which includes the full text.

[171] 'Royal Wedding', *ILN* (1893), p. 70.

[172] 'Amphion', 'Musical Echoes', *Bow Bells: A Magazine of General Literature and Art for Family Reading*, 9 June 1893, p. 572.

[173] *QVJ*, 6 July 1893.

[174] OS 1893, programme of music, including three verses. Also 'Music at the Royal Wedding', *Musical News* (1893).

[175] 'Royal Wedding', *Times* (1893), p. 6; 'Forthcoming Royal Wedding', *Scotsman*.

[176] Josias Bunsen, *Vierstimmiges Choralbuch zum allgemeinen evangelischen Gesang- und Gebetbuche zum Kirchen- und Hausgebrauch*, rev. and ed. by Friedrich Filitz (Berlin: Wilhelm Besser, 1846), p. 7/no. 12.

[177] See *Church Hymnal, by Permission of the General Synod of the Church of Ireland, Set to Appropriate Tunes*, 'under the musical editorship of' Sir Robert Prescott, 6th edn (Dublin: Published by the Association for Promoting Christian Knowledge, 1891), no. 228, with details on the composition on p. 33. NB The section with the descriptions is dated 1878 (see p. 48).

[178] 'Forthcoming Royal Wedding', *Scotsman*.

The ceremony ended again with Mendelssohn's Wedding March accompanying the newly-weds' recess.[179] The *Illustrated London News* recorded how 'the first grand chords of Mendelssohn's "Wedding March" crashed on the organ'.[180] It is in this context that the reports mention that the music inside the Chapel Royal could be heard by the spectators outside. The *Scotsman* noted that 'the familiar strains of the "Wedding March" were heard proceeding from the Chapel' and that this 'indicated to the people outside that the marriage ceremony was over'.[181] More than a week before the wedding, Spencer Ponsonby-Fane from the Lord Chamberlain's Office had sent a note to Godfrey and his band of the Grenadier Guards explaining: 'You would of course play the Wedding march as the Bridal Procession leaves the Chapel.'[182] The details that he eventually sent to Godfrey three days before the wedding also referred to the recess in the Chapel and explained that 'the Band will play Mendelssohn's Wedding March.'[183] As the band would not have been inside the Chapel, this probably meant that the march was to be taken up by the band from the organ, to accompany the procession once it came out of the Chapel – in a way in reverse to the bride's entrance march, where the organ had taken up the music of the band.

After the Service

For the return procession of the royal family and royal guests through the state rooms, the schedule sent to Godfrey and his band stipulated that 'the Danish National Anthem will be played', surely in recognition of the royal guests from Denmark. The use of the Danish National Anthem in some way mirrored the precedent of playing the Waldeck Hymn for the newly-weds' leaving in 1882, now extended even to the guests.[184] This seems, in any case, to have been the first time that such distinct music for the return procession after the service is recorded.

Edgar Sheppard, the Subdean of the Chapel Royal, interpreted that this wedding 'in its ceremonial splendour, its importance, and its peculiarly touching character, equals the most striking of the Royal marriages that have been celebrated at St. James's'.[185] The commentator of the *Graphic* summarized more cautiously that 'Though not brilliant, the ceremony in the Chapel Royal was dignified and, in consequence of the distinguished guests who were present, interesting.'[186] Notably, the mentioned aspects of 'splendour' and 'interest' did probably not quite apply to the musical programme, which overall remained comparatively modest and conventional; and at least for the latter writer the 'interesting' moments of the ceremony were understood to result from other components.

---

[179] OS 1893, programme of music; Ceremonial, 1893, p. 12.

[180] 'The Royal Wedding', *ILN: Royal Wedding Number*, p. 4.

[181] 'Royal Wedding', *Scotsman* (1893). See also 'Royal Wedding', *Times* (1893), p. 6.

[182] 'Copy' of a 'DRAFT' from Ponsonby-Fane to 'Lt: Dan Godfrey / Grenadier Guards', 28 June 1893, in *Lna LC 2/129*.

[183] For this and the next quotation see 'Marriage of HRH The Duke of York. / July 6th 1893. / Arrangements for the Band of the / Grenadier Guards [...], in *Lna LC 2/128* (as in fn. 130, above).

[184] See Chapter 8, fn. 114.

[185] Sheppard, *Memorials*, II, part 2, p. 126.

[186] 'Marmaduke', 'Court and Club', *Graphic*, 15 July 1893, p. 78. See also Queen Victoria's comment on the music at the wedding; below, with fn. 189.

9—The Choral Weddings: The Later Victorians

Princess Maud of Wales and Prince Carl of Denmark, 22 July 1896

The third, and last child of the Prince of Wales to marry was his daughter Princess Maud. On 22 July 1896, she married her cousin Prince Carl of Denmark – the nephew of her mother Princess Alexandra. In the larger historical context, this wedding is of special relevance, as the royal couple eventually became king and queen of Norway. However, at the time, this could not be foreseen and the *Times* drew a comparison to 1893 when it explained that it 'could hardly be expected' that this wedding should 'be marked by the same display of popular rejoicing and enthusiasm'.[187] Indeed, Kate Williams has observed that Queen Victoria had 'demanded a subdued ceremony' because of the recent death in January of Prince Henry of Battenberg, Princess Beatrice's husband.[188]

Eventually, the correspondent of the *Manchester Guardian* summarized that 'it must be said that moderation marked all the arrangements for the wedding, and all the popular manifestations'.[189] Nonetheless, the same correspondent described the wedding itself as 'A Brilliant State Ceremony' and noted that it 'has passed off with great *éclat*'. The *Graphic* explained that the wedding had 'developed' from 'a semi-private affair, as it was at first intended to be […] into the considerably more picturesque and public ceremony which Londoners witnessed last Wednesday'.[190] The *Times* went so far as to declare that the wedding had been nothing less than 'the crowning feature of the present season'.[191] Referring to the great public interest in the event, and echoing the comments from 1893, one magazine noted even more exuberantly that

> experienced observers were inclined to compare the popular turn-out, not with anything witnessed at recent royal weddings, but with the multitudes which thronged the streets on the occasion of the Queen's Jubilee.[192]

There could be no doubt that this wedding was a notable occasion of the highest order.

Venue

The wedding ceremony returned to the Private Chapel in Buckingham Palace. The *Times* pointed out that this was 'seldom used for Royal weddings' but observed that it 'lends itself fairly well to display – that is, on the Private Chapel scale, for it seats only about a hundred persons'.[193] The *Manchester Guardian* also emphasized that the Chapel 'is extremely small' and suggested – maybe somewhat over-enthusiastically, considering that this was only the second such wedding there – that the Private Chapel 'appears to have become the usual building for the marriage of the daughters of the Prince of Wales'.[194]

---

[187] 'The Royal Wedding', *Times*, 23 July 1896, pp. 5–6, here p. 5.

[188] Kate Williams, '"Pomp and Circumstance": Royal Weddings from 1714 to 1918', in: Alison Weir, Kate Williams, Sarah Gristwood, and Tracy Borman, *The Ring and the Crown: A History of Royal Weddings 1066–2011* (London: Hutchinson, 2011), pp. 53–95, here p. 95.

[189] 'Marriage of The Princess Maud of Wales', *Manchester Guardian*, 23 July 1896, p. 5.

[190] 'Topics of the Week', *Graphic*, 25 July 1896, p. 98.

[191] 'Royal Wedding', *Times* (1896), p. 5.

[192] 'The Royal Wedding', *Bow Bells: A Magazine of General Literature and Art for Family Reading*, 31 July 1896, pp. 127–28, here p. 127.

[193] 'Royal Wedding', *Times* (1896), p. 6. This also details the re-decoration of the Private Chapel compared to the 1889 wedding.

[194] 'Marriage of The Princess Maud', *Manchester Guardian*.

British Royal Weddings

In contrast to Queen Victoria's aforementioned demand for a 'subdued ceremony', a draft note from the Lord Chamberlain's Office, dated a week before the wedding, stipulated 'Ceremony is now full State'.[195] After the wedding, it was reported that the queen's entrance again had 'included all the great officers of state'.[196] In addition, the more official character of the ceremony may have become visible, for instance, in the participation of the heralds – or at least their planned and reported participation: whereas they had not taken part at the similar 1889, which had also been at the Private Chapel, the ceremonial now scheduled the heralds to fulfil their traditional role of leading the individual processions to the Chapel, and at least some accounts mentioned them.[197] Nevertheless, as in 1893 the heralds are again not shown the pictures of the ceremony; notably there are no heralds in Laurits Regner Tuxen's well-known painting showing the end of the service (Illustration 9.10).

Ceremony and Music

This wedding is exceptionally well documented, and the surviving material includes in particular many details on the music. Again, Queen Victoria was very much involved in the ceremonial and musical arrangements. She had a 'Rough Sketch of Proceedings', a manuscript draft of the ceremonial, read to her by 'M$^{rs.}$ Mallet' and had her comments entered in red in the margin, dated 'June 15/96'.[198] The queen was very decided when it came to the choice of the musician in charge. The main text of the draft followed the ceremonial of the 1893 wedding and referred to 'The Musical arrangements and Choir of St James's Chapel Royal under Dr Creser.' However, one of the annotations reads that 'The Queen wishes Sir W. Parratt to have entire charge of the musical arrangements – whichever Choir he prefers to sing.'[199] Two days later Arthur Bigge, Queen Victoria's private secretary, conveyed her comments to Ponsonby-Fane at the Lord Chamberlain's Office. Regarding the choice of Parratt – the organist of St George's Chapel, Windsor – Bigge's wording was even stronger:

> The Queen insists upon Parratt having charge of the music. The ceremony is not in the Chapel Royal & therefore Dr Creser has no claim: & P. is the master of music, and he may have his own Choir or that of the Chapel Royal. I understand that HM. is very decided about this.[200]

It is not clear why Queen Victoria was so adamant as regards the choice of Parratt to in charge of the music. Michael Budds has observed that her 'preference in church musicians had changed in the course of her reign', and he summarized that, while in the queen's 'early years the musicians of the Chapel Royal at St. James's Palace had been expected to provide the musical splendor for state occasions', towards 'the end of her life, the musicians of St. George's Chapel at Windsor had earned that honor'.[201] Whereas Bigge had elegantly, and perhaps diplomatically, explained that

---

[195] Copy ('DRAFT.' on back) of Lord Chamberlain's Office to 'Edwards / W.C.', 15 July 1896, in *Lna LC 2/132*.

[196] 'Marriage of The Princess Maud', *Manchester Guardian*.

[197] Ceremonial 1896b, 9. See also the detailed accounts in 'Royal Wedding', *Times* (1896), pp. 5–6 and 'The Marriage of Princess Maud of Wales and Prince Charles of Denmark at Buckingham Palace', *ILN: Royal Wedding Number*, 29 July 1896, pp. 2–8, here p. 2.

[198] See 'Rough Sketch of Proceedings / approved by The Queen / with Her Majesty's wishes.', four folios, '27' at bottom, in *Lna LC 2/132*.

[199] 'Rough Sketch of Proceedings' (as in previous footnote), fol. 2^r of this.

[200] Bigge to Ponsonby-Fane, 17 June 1896, in *Lna LC 2/132*.

[201] Michael Joe Budds, 'Music at the Court of Queen Victoria: A Study of Music in the Life of the Queen and her Participation in the Musical Life of her Time', 3 vols (unpublished doctoral dissertation, University of Iowa, 1987), II, pp. 717–18.

9—The Choral Weddings: The Later Victorians

Illustration 9.10: Laurits Regner Tuxen, 'The Marriage of Princess Maud of Wales, 22 July 1896', oil on canvas, signed and dated 1896–97, *Royal Collection, RCIN 404464*, Royal Collection Trust / © Her Majesty Queen Elizabeth II 2021.

Parratt was 'the master of music', the queen's choice could have been motivated by musical considerations. For the 1893 wedding at the Chapel Royal, where Creser had been responsible, she had sharply observed: 'The music was well played & sung, but sounded weak & inferior to that in St. George's Chapel.'[202]

A draft letter from the Lord Chamberlain's Office to Sheppard as the Subdean of the Chapel Royal provides some more details on the choice of leading musician and choir.[203] There may have been some questioning on the choice of the leading musician – or at least such questioning may have been expected to come – and this letter explains that the queen's choice of Parratt

> is of course on the principle that this Chapel is not a Chapel Royal, but Her Majestys Private Chapel & that the Choir of the Chapel Royal have no ~~distinct~~ place there. Indeed when H.M. was in residence at B Palace a private Choir ~~always~~ was always there.

Moreover, still in diplomatic wording, this letter referred to the Lord Chamberlain's confidence that Creser and the choir of the Chapel Royal would 'work harmoniously under Sir Walter so that all may be successfully carried out'. Finally, it informed the subdean that he would hear from Parratt 'what he proposes'. A letter to this effect was apparently sent. Two days later, Creser wrote to Sheppard and explained that he accepted this decision and confirmed that he

---

[202] *QVJ*, 6 July 1893.

[203] Draft letter from Lord Chamberlain's Office (from Ponsonby-Fane?) to 'SubDean', 22 June 1896, in *Lna LC 2/132*. NB The last two pages of this are bound in the wrong order.

British Royal Weddings

'will allow Sir Walter Parratt a free hand with the Choir of The Chapel Royal so that all may be successfully carried out.'[204] In the end, the ceremonial recorded:

> The Musical arrangements were under the direction of Sir Walter Parratt, Master of the Music, who presided at the Organ, assisted by Dr. Creser, Organist of Her Majesty's Chapel Royal, St. James's Palace. The Gentlemen and the Choir of that Chapel performed the Musical part of the Service.[205]

Thus, while Parratt replaced Creser as the musician in charge, he did not bring 'his own Choir' as the queen had conceded he might. Even though Queen Victoria had asked for Parratt to be in charge of the music, the choice of the musical programme seems to have rested mainly with the bride's parents. At the end of June, Parratt wrote to Ponsonby-Fane that he had received a note that 'the Prince and Princess would much like to see my suggestion as to the Music for the Royal Wedding'.[206] This was Parratt's first royal wedding in the Private Chapel and he therefore explained:

> It would much help me if I could know what was done at the Wedding of the Duchess of Fife[.] I presume that as a ceremonial this will be Similar.

> About a week later Ponsonby-Fane reminded Parratt to submit his 'Programme of the Marriage Music', not only to the queen but then also to 'the Prince of Wales through Sir Francis Knollys'.[207] Shortly after that Parratt wrote to Knollys that he had seen the Princess of Wales

> to day and submitted [t]he Music to Her Royal Highness. The Princess has some requests of her own choice which I am [to] receive tomorrow morning [a]nd I am therefore still [u]ncertain as to the programme. [T]he moment I have definite instructions I will send them to you.[208]

An annotation on the cover of this letter provides some more information as to what the princess's 'requests' were; it explains that Parratt 'will send Programme directly Princess of Wales has selected hymns'. Thus, her 'requests' may have been some particular hymns. The Princess of Wales's very direct involvement in the selection of the music becomes clear from the story of one particular musical item. In mid-May, before he had been ousted from the directorship of the music, Creser had written to Sheppard and asked whether he

> will be good enough to ascertain for me whether Their Royal Highnesses the Prince and Princess of Wales will be so gracious as to allow me to compose a short chorale to be sung.[209]

Two days later, Knollys recorded that 'The Prince & Princess of Wales quite approve of M[r] Creser composing a short Chorale for Princess Maud's Wedding.'[210] On 5 July, after Creser had been stripped of his responsibility for the wedding music, Parratt informed Ponsonby-Fane with a tone of resignation that 'M[r] Creser's Choral has come. It is very poor Stuff but it must be done.'[211] Another week later, however, Ponsonby-Fane recorded:

> The Subdean told me the Princess of Wales did not wish to have D[r] Cresers Chorale at the Wedding, & that it is therefore to be omitted.[212]

---

[204] Creser to Sheppard, 24 June 1896 (from South Hampstead), in *Lna LC 2/132*.

[205] Ceremonial 1896b, p. 9.

[206] Parratt to Ponsonby-Fane, 30 June 1896, in *Lna LC 2/132*.

[207] Ponsonby-Fane to Parratt, 6 July 1896 (type-written), in *Lna LC 2/132*.

[208] Parratt to Knollys, 8 July 1896, in *Lna LC 2/132*. Part of the margin is obscured by the tight binding.

[209] Creser to Sheppard, 15 May 1896, in *Lna LC 2/132*.

[210] No addressee, signed 'Francis Knollys / May 17/96', in *Lna LC 2/132*.

[211] Parratt to Ponsonby-Fane, 5 July 1896, in *Lna LC 2/132*.

[212] This and the following 'Marriage / 12 July 96 / Mem / Chorale at Wedding / to be omitted […]', signed 'SPF[?]', in *Lna LC 2/132*.

9—The Choral Weddings: The Later Victorians

All the same, Ponsonby-Fane noted that this Chorale 'will be performed next Sunday morning at the Early Service Chapel Royal'. Even this performance, however, seems eventually to have been cancelled. When Sheppard sent Ponsonby-Fane two bills 'in connection with the Music for the Royal wedding', he also included a third 'which I venture to think should also be paid for Creser was put to a huge amount of trouble & expense in purchasing his Chorale, which, as you know, after all was never sung'.[213] Creser's 'Chorale' appears to have been 'Source of All Light', 250 copies of which were printed.[214]

Processions

The *Times* correspondent judged that 'Owing to the smallness of the chapel something of the stateliness of the processional part of the ceremonial as witnessed in St. George's, Windsor, is lost.'[215] However, there was a different kind of 'stateliness' in that the ceremony in the Private Chapel was, as in 1889, again framed by walking processions to the venue – something not included at St George's Chapel. Moreover, these processions went through a temporary, canvas-covered corridor that had been specially constructed on the terrace of Buckingham Palace, between the Private Chapel and the Bow Library, and which provided room for 'about four hundred people' along the central walkway.[216] As the *Graphic* explained, 'only some 300 people could find room in the chapel itself' and therefore 'other guests were allowed to line the route to the chapel'.[217]

There were only three processions: those of the royal family, the bridegroom, and the bride. The clergy did not have a procession through the corridor; they entered the Chapel before all the other processions and walked up to the altar to an unspecified 'Voluntary being played on the Organ'.[218] The correspondent of the *Times* observed that

> With the appearance of the officiating clergy […] the nuptial ceremony may be said to have begun, but there was a somewhat awkward pause between that and the arrival of the first, or Queen's, procession.[219]

The reason for the queen's arriving first could be that back in 1893, as seen above, she had quite enjoyed her accidentally arriving too early, which had then enabled her to see the processions come in. A surviving printed draft of the musical programme indicates that initially Queen Victoria had been meant to enter in the procession of the royal family, as in 1889.[220] However, at some point this was changed and eventually she 'was conducted privately' to the Chapel, going not only alone but also 'through the lower rooms and not through the temporary corridor on the terrace' and she arrived before the three processions.[221]

---

[213] Sheppard to Ponsonby-Fane, 30 July 1896, in *Lna LC 2/132*. The three bills are in *Lna LC 2/133*.

[214] Bill from 'Novello, Ewer & Co.' to 'Dr W. Creser', 28 July 1896: under 'July 3'. The edition is William Creser, *Source of All Light and Life Divine: Choral* (London: Novello, Ewer and Co., [1896]).

[215] 'Royal Wedding', *Times* (1896), p. 6.

[216] For this and a detailed description of the decorations and the processions see 'The Wedding of Princess Maud of Wales: A Brilliant Ceremonial. The Scene in the Chapel Royal', *Scotsman,* 23 July 1896, p. 5. See also 'Royal Wedding', *Times* (1896), p. 5.

[217] 'The Royal Wedding', *Graphic*, 25 July 1896, p. 103.

[218] Ceremonial 1896b, p. 2.

[219] 'Royal Wedding', *Times* (1896), p. 6.

[220] Printed draft programme of music, incl. in Parratt to Knollys, 12 July 1896, in *Lna LC 2/132*.

[221] 'Royal Wedding', *Times* (1896), p. 5.

The reason for Queen Victoria's not taking the full processional route was probably her by now more fragile health and her having to use a wheelchair. The queen herself recorded that she was 'rolled through the Hall, Dining room, &c, to the vestibule of the Chapel'.[222] In this way none of the guests, in the corridor, would have seen her being wheeled to the Chapel; and once there, she recorded that she 'got out of my chair' and that she walked to her seat.[223]

While the queen's procession to the Private Chapel was hidden from view and more or less secretive, on entering the Chapel, she was 'played in', as the *Times* put, 'to the "March of Molique"'.[224] This was 'played on the Organ'.[225] Interestingly, Parratt had questioned the musical nomenclature here:

> It occurs to me that as the Queen will come in alone something <u>not</u> a march would be more fitting. Would it be better to call it a Voluntary on the organ?[226]

It is not clear what Parratt's concern was. He does not seem to have questioned the choice of music as such, and his suggestion was ignored. The 'march' was apparently by the German composer Wilhelm Bernhard Molique, who had lived in England between 1849 and 1866, since 1861 as Professor of Harmony and Composition at the Royal Academy of Music.[227] It was most probably the march from his oratorio *Abraham*, which seems to have been his most famous march and was published in an arrangement for military band in the year after the wedding.[228]

For the other three processions the printed ceremonial stipulated and then recorded:

> The Band of the Grenadier Guards, under the direction of Lieutenant Dan Godfrey, which will be stationed [or 'was stationed'] on the Terrace, will play [or 'played'] a March as each Procession passed up the Temporary Corridor.[229]

The *Times* correspondent specified that the band was stationed at the end of the corridor that was opposite the Chapel entrance, near the Bow Library, and that along the corridor there were numerous spectators.[230] Lady Geraldine Somerset, who with her husband 'got two <u>capital</u> places in front', thought that 'yᵉ whole thing was <u>extremely</u> well arranged! yᵉ whole of yᵉ 3. Processions walking along yⁱˢ corridor between all of us ticket holders seated <u>3.</u> rows deep on each side'.[231] The band played 'While the processions were forming, and as they made their progress', as the *Manchester Guardian* recorded.[232] However, Lady Somerset, who had had to arrive early and then had to wait an hour for the first procession, emphasized:

> y:ᵉ only one criticism to make was, we might have had a little music! if y:ᵉ Gren: Band, wh: was at yᵉ end of y:ᵉ corridor, to play when they came in, had played all y:ᵉ time, it w.ᵈ have been perfect.[233]

---

[222] *QVJ*, 22 July 1896; also, for instance, 'Marriage of The Princess Maud', *Manchester Guardian*.

[223] *QVJ*, 22 July 1896. See also 'Royal Wedding', *Times* (1896), p. 6.

[224] 'Royal Wedding', *Times* (1896), p. 6.

[225] Ceremonial 1896b, p. 4; also OS 1896, programme of music.

[226] Parratt to Knollys, 15 July 1896, in *Lna LC 2/132*.

[227] For biographical details see Boris Schwarz, 'Molique, (Wilhelm) Bernhard', *NG*.

[228] Bernhard Molique, *March from the Oratorio: Abraham*, arr. for military band by George Miller (bandmaster, Royal Marines), (London and New York: Novello, Ewer & Co., [1897]).

[229] Ceremonial 1896a, p. 8 and Ceremonial 1896b, p. 9. See also 'The Marriage of Princess Maud of Wales', *Observer*, 19 July 1896, p. 5.

[230] 'Royal Wedding', *Times* (1896), p. 5.

[231] *Wra RA VIC/ADDC6/1/1895-6*: entry for 22 July 1896.

[232] 'Marriage of The Princess Maud', *Manchester Guardian*. See also 'Marriage of Princess Maud', *Observer*.

[233] This and the following *Wra RA VIC/ADDC6/1/1895-6*: entry for 22 July 1896.

9—The Choral Weddings: The Later Victorians

There were no fanfares to announce the processions. The first procession, of the royal family, was accompanied by Wagner's 'Fest Marsch from *Tannhäuser*' and for the appearance of the bridegroom Lady Somerset recorded that 'the band began to play Gounod's Marche Religieuse'. Wagner's march could have been the same march as that played on the organ for the procession of the bridegroom at the 1889 wedding and by the band during the procession to the Chapel Royal at the 1893 wedding, and Gounod's march had been used at the wedding of Princess Frederica of Hanover in 1880.[234] The aforementioned draft ceremonial revised by Queen Victoria contains an intriguing annotation relating to the entrance marches:

> The Queen wishes Sir W. Parrat to select the Marches – & that he will "take them up" on the organ.[235]

The explanation that the organ should 'take them up' refers to the overlapping playing of the marches by the band and then by the organ, once the processions enter the Chapel (as becomes clear in the following). The queen's request regarding the organ could have been inspired by the possible performance of Mendelssohn's Wedding March in 1893, seen above. However, Bigge, her private secretary, explained to Ponsonby-Fane:

> I am afraid it will be difficult if not impossible to carry this out – as the pipes of the organ & of the band would be different. Perhaps the organ could repeat the march after the band stops?[236]

Two weeks later, Parratt also wrote to Ponsonby-Fane about the same issue:

> Sir Arthur Bigge tells me that a band will play outside the Chapel and the organ is supposed to take up the same March inside[.] This is a very hazardous arrangement.[237]

On the very next day, Ponsonby-Fane assured Parrat that this proposed scheme 'has been decidedto [*sic*] be an impossibility, so you need think no more about it' and that the military band would be 'quite away from the Chapel and independent of it'.[238] Thus, in the end, the queen's wishes here could not be followed and the organ played different marches to the band. That for the royal family was the *Marche Nuptiale* by Guilmant, which Parratt had already used for this procession in 1891.[239] However, the music accompanying the bridegroom's and bride's entrance saw a notable innovation possibly instigated by Parratt. He pointed out to Knollys:

> You will notice that hymns will be sung for two of the processions for which Marches were played on the last occasion.[240]

This was the first royal wedding where the bridegroom's procession was not accompanied by an instrumental march. Even though Parratt had referred to 'hymns', the ceremonial recorded that the bridegroom had entered the Chapel 'whilst an Anthem ("O Perfect Love"—Lady A. Hill) was sung'.[241] Née Annie Fortescue Harrison, Hill was the wife of Lord Arthur Hill, the 'Comptroller of the Household', in which capacity he had taken part, for instance, in the 1889 wedding.[242] Lady Hill's piece, on the well-known text by Blomfield Gurney heard at the three

---

[234] See above, fns 27–28 and 130; and (for the 1880 wedding) Chapter 8, fn. 118.

[235] 'Rough Sketch of Proceedings', in *Lna LC 2/132*, fol. 3[v].

[236] Bigge to Ponsonby-Fane, 17 June 1896, in *Lna LC 2/132*, fol. 2[v] of this.

[237] Parratt to Ponsonby-Fane, 5 July 1896, in *Lna LC 2/132*.

[238] Ponsonby-Fane to Parratt, 6 July 1896 (type-written), in *Lna LC 2/132*.

[239] OS 1896, programme of music; Ceremonial 1896b, p. 5.

[240] Parratt to Knollys, 15 July 1896, *Lna LC 2/132*.

[241] Ceremonial 1896b, p. 7. See also OS 1896, programme of music.

[242] See 'Royal Wedding at Buckingham Palace', [second account].

previous weddings, was indeed more of an 'anthem' than a 'hymn'. It had been published in about 1892, 'Dedicated to, and composed expressly for, Lady Olivia Taylour, on the Occasion of her Marriage with Lord Henry Cavendish Bentinck'.[243] This marriage, or wedding had taken place in late January of the same year.[244]

There does not seem to be any information on why Hill's setting was chosen for the 1896 wedding. It is a tuneful, late-Victorian piece, scored for soprano soloist and four-part choir with organ accompaniment. The three verses of the hymn are treated more or less in an A-B-A form: the first and third verses have the full choir in a mostly homophonic setting with a descant from the solo soprano, while the middle verse is for the soloist and organ only. Ponsonby-Fane informed Parrat that he had 'seen Mapleson and told him about Madame Eames', without giving further details.[245] This probably refers to Alfred Mapleson, Queen Victoria's music secretary and librarian, and to the celebrated American soprano Emma Eames (1865–1952). It does not seem to be known whether she eventually sang at the ceremony.

The bride's procession through the temporary corridor had been accompanied by the band 'playing the Bridal Chorus from *Lohengrin*'.[246] Once she had reached the Chapel, the *Times* reported that Wagner's music 'ceased, and the next thing that was heard in the corridor was the hymn, "O Paradise," sung as the bride entered the chapel'.[247] It appears that there was no proper transition between the march and the hymn; the correspondent of the *Illustrated London News* noted that 'as the bride entered, the band of the Grenadier Guards, which had been playing the Bridal Chorus from "Lohengrin" in the corridor, was hushed'.[248] The correspondent of the *Manchester Guardian*, sitting in the Chapel, recorded that

> Lady A. Hill's beautiful setting of the hymn O perfect Love [...] had barely died away when there pealed forth the music of O Paradise [...] which heralded the approach of the last and most important procession, that of the bride.[249]

This would mean that Wagner's march during the bride's approach through the corridor would have been played at the same time as Hill's anthem accompanying the bridegroom's procession in the Chapel. Such mixing of the two sounds seems rather unlikely, and it may indicate some inaccuracy in this report.[250]

The correspondent of the *Graphic* described 'O Paradise' meaningfully as the bride's 'favourite hymn'.[251] A printed proof of the musical programme had included six verses of this hymn, beginning 'O Paradise! O Paradise! Who doth not crave for rest?'.[252] However, when Parratt had 'received the final commands of the Princess of Wales for the Music', he sent a short note to Knollys:

---

[243] Annie Fortescue Harrison, *O Perfect Love: Anthem for Soprano Solo and Chorus, the Words by D. F. Blomfield* (London & New York: Novello, Ewer and Co., [1892]).

[244] See 'Marriage of Lady Olivia Taylour with Lord H. Bentinck, MP', *The Lancaster Gazette*, 30 January 1892, p. 8.

[245] Ponsonby-Fane to Parratt, 6 July 1896 (type-written), in *Lna LC 2/132*.

[246] This and the following 'Royal Wedding', *Times* (1896), p. 6.

[247] See also Ceremonial 1896b, p. 8.

[248] 'Marriage of Princess Maud', *ILN: Royal Wedding Number*, p. 4.

[249] 'Marriage of The Princess Maud', *Manchester Guardian*.

[250] For the music from inside the Chapel being heard in the corridor see below, fn. 274.

[251] 'Royal Wedding', *Graphic* (1896).

[252] Printed programme of music, included in Parratt to Knollys, 12 July 1896, in *Lna LC 2/132*.

9—The Choral Weddings: The Later Victorians

> I do hope the Lord Chamberlain will persuade Her Royal Highness to omit some verses of 'O Paradise'. With the quickest singing it would be too long.[253]

In the end, it seems that Parratt was able to 'persuade' the princess himself. He sent Knollys the proof of the programme with manuscript corrections and with three verses of that hymn crossed out, and he explained that '[T]he Princess of Wales has decided that 3 verses of O Paradise – which I have Cancelled in the proof [–] shall be omitted – leaving verses 1, 5, and 6.'[254] This matches with what the programme of music in the order of service eventually included.[255] Parratt's remark that the hymn 'would be too long' – even with 'the quickest singing' – indicates that this hymn was intended merely to cover the bride's actual procession in the Chapel and her arrival at the altar; but it was not as such meant to be a hefty introit to the service.

Both the programme of music and the ceremonial recorded that the tune for the bride's processional hymn was by 'Lord Crofton'.[256] The tune today known as 'Crofton' has a metre of 11.10.11.10, which means that the tune matches a text of four lines in each verse and where the individual lines have eleven and ten syllables alternating.[257] The hymn text of 'O Paradise', however, has a metre of 8.6.8.6.6.6.6.6. Each verse is thus four lines longer than the 'Crofton' tune and, more importantly, the number of syllables within the lines differs quite noticeably: the text and the tune would overall not fit together very easily. It cannot be known what the 'Crofton' tune was that was eventually used for this hymn.

The processional hymn was probably sung by the choir only, without the congregation joining in. The *Illustrated London News* recorded distinctly that the music for the processions of the bridegroom and the bride was sung by 'the choir from St. James's Chapel Royal'.[258] Similarly, another report had announced that the processions within the Chapel would 'approach to church music supplied by the choir of the Chapel Royal, St. James's'.[259] In contrast to the 1891 wedding at St George's, however, the choir did not walk in the bride's procession. Instead, it had arrived before all the other participants, as one correspondent pointed out:

> The first intimation which the guests received that the hour of the ceremony was rapidly approaching was in the entry of the choir of the Chapels Royal.[260]

As in 1889, the choir was placed in front of the organ, in the bay to the left of the altar, on ground level and thus visible for many in the congregation, and throughout the service.[261] The organ, but not the choir, can be seen in a drawing of the ceremony by William Hatherell (Illustration 9.11). Incidentally, this furthermore shows how Queen Victoria, and Princess Alexandra next to her, follow the ceremony in the order of service – mirroring the minister at the altar who holds a similar copy.

---

[253] Parratt to Knollys, 12 July 1896, in *Lna LC 2/132.*

[254] Parratt to Knollys, 15 July 1896, in *Lna LC 2/132.*

[255] OS 1896, programme of music.

[256] Ceremonial 1896b, p. 8.

[257] For Crofton and his tune see https://hymnary.org/tune/crofton (accessed on 2 November 2021).

[258] 'Marriage of Princess Maud', *ILN: Royal Wedding Number*, p. 4.

[259] 'Marriage of Princess Maud', *Observer.*

[260] 'Marriage of The Princess Maud', *Manchester Guardian.* See also 'Royal Wedding', *Times* (1896), p. 6.

[261] See the plan of the chapel at the wedding, included in Ceremonial 1896 (compare Illustration 9.1).

British Royal Weddings

Service

With the bride having entered to a hymn, there was no introit, and the next music of the ceremony was the psalm following the vows: Ps. 128 to the chant 'Hopkins in E flat'.[262] The reports do not seem to mention the singing of the Responses and prayers, and the programme of music lists as the next item the 'Hymn', 'How Welcome Was the Call' – six verses and Amen. This hymn does not seem to be mentioned in any of the reports of the ceremony; neither does Parratt refer to it in his surviving correspondence. If it was included, this hymn could have been sung in one of the two versions used at the two 1866 weddings, those of Princess Mary Adelaide of Cambridge and of Princess Helena.[263] It could possibly have come before the 'short & good address' by the archbishop to which Queen Victoria referred in her account of the ceremony.[264] The *Manchester Guardian* specified that this address came 'After the conclusion of the service', but before the 'Benediction'.[265] It also added that, after the 'Benediction', 'Sir A. G. Ousley's hymn "What Thou hast joined none may divide" was sung'. Parratt had explained to Knollys:

> You will notice also that after the Benediction there is a hymn which was not sung in that place on the last occasion.[266]

It seems that this final hymn would have accompanied the exchange of 'affecting greetings' which the *Illustrated London News* reported to have occurred before the recess.[267] The three verses of this hymn had been written – possibly especially for the wedding – by 'A. C. Benson', of later 'Land of Hope and Glory' fame.[268] It is, however, not clear what Ouseley's music was. The service does not seem to have included an anthem, but this was compensated by the two choral pieces on the bride and bridegroom's entrances and by the final hymn – and possibly another hymn right in the middle.

After the Service

The return procession after the service went through the Chapel and then the temporary corridor, with Queen Victoria leaving 'privately as I came'.[269] The 'United Procession' of the newly-weds was accompanied by 'the inspiring strains of Mendelssohn's Wedding March', as the *Times* put it.[270] It is not quite clear how the Wedding March was performed. The *Manchester Guardian* reported that 'the organ pealed forth Mendelssohn's "Wedding March" as the procession left the chapel', and the *Scotsman* recorded:

> As the bridal party emerged again into the corridor, the stirring strains of Mendelssohn's Wedding March played by the band of the Grenadier Guards, broke upon the ear.[271]

---

[262] This and the following OS 1896, programme of music.

[263] See Chapter 7, with fns 155–57 and 206–07.

[264] *QVJ*, 22 July 1896. See also 'Royal Wedding', *Times* (1896), p. 6, including the full text of the address; and Ceremonial 1896a/b, pp. 8/9.

[265] This and the following 'Marriage of The Princess Maud', *Manchester Guardian* (which includes the full text of the address).

[266] Parratt to Knollys, 15 July 1896, in *Lna LC 2/132*.

[267] 'Marriage of Princess Maud', *ILN: Royal Wedding Number*, p. 4.

[268] OS 1896, programme of music.

[269] Ceremonial 1896b, p. 9; *QVJ*, 22 July 1896.

[270] OS 1896, programme of music; 'Royal Wedding', *Times* (1896), p. 6.

[271] 'Marriage of The Princess Maud', *Manchester Guardian*; 'Wedding of Princess Maud', *Scotsman*.

9—The Choral Weddings: The Later Victorians

The *Times* correspondent also observed that the couple 'made their way down the corridor, the band playing the while'.[272] Thus, notwithstanding Parratt's aforementioned warning of this 'hazardous arrangement', it seems that Mendelssohn's march played on the organ was somehow 'taken up' by the band – as possibly at the wedding in 1893, and as Queen Victoria had suggested in reverse order for the entrance marches at the beginning of the ceremony.[273]

The building of the special corridor on the palace terrace had very much increased the number of those able to attend the wedding, as it were. With this special provision for the guests these were integrated in the proceedings much more than the attendees along the processional route through the state apartments at previous weddings. In this context it is interesting to note what Lady Geraldine Somerset recorded, who was seated in the temporary corridor: 'During ye Marriage ceremony we c:^{d} hear ye Music in y:^{e} Chapel.'[274] Thus the music of the service was audible to at least some of the guests placed in the corridor, and it was through the music that they were to some extent included in, and could in some sense participate in the ceremony.

Illustration 9.11: William Hatherell, 'Marriage of Princess Maud of Wales and Prince Charles of Denmark, 22 July 1896', drawing 1896, Royal Collection, RCIN 920860, Royal Collection Trust / © Her Majesty Queen Elizabeth II 2021.

---

[272] 'Royal Wedding', *Times* (1896), p. 6.

[273] Compare above, fns 181–82 and 234–35.

[274] *Wra RA VIC/ADDC6/1/1895-6*: entry for 22 July 1896.

271

The three prominent London weddings of the Prince of Wales's children between 1889 and 1896 were a clear sign that this royal ceremony was not exclusively linked with Windsor. The move to the capital was approvingly noted in the press. In 1893, for instance, the *Times* declared that the choice of the Chapel Royal was 'a happy one' for its historic associations and

> happier still from the fact of its situation enabling the teeming millions of the metropolis actively to assist in a joyful event in which the nation is so intimately concerned.[275]

Apart from the outdoor and indoor processions, however, these royal weddings did not seek greater publicity in a larger venue. In comparison, on 24 June 1896, four weeks before the wedding of Princess Maud, Viscount Milton, grandson and heir of Earl Fitzwilliam, had celebrated his wedding with Lady Maud Dundas, daughter of the Marques of Zetland, with a grand service at St Paul's Cathedral – in what the *London Illustrated News* described as 'a marriage exceptional in its place and in its pomp'.[276] And three years later, on 15 April 1899, there was the similarly grand wedding of the Earl of Crewe and Lady Margaret Primrose at Westminster Abbey, with the Prince of Wales present.[277]

Nevertheless, the weddings of Queen Victoria's grandchildren were notable for their musical programme. Even though some processional music by Handel still had a secure place, they included many more 'modern' and fashionable pieces, and Wagner's music, for instance, had a prominent role. Moreover, the 'choral' aspect was much heightened. Not only were sung Responses introduced to royal weddings; but with Barnby's and Hill's pieces, these weddings included notable new anthems, and the important processions of the bridegroom and the bride were eventually accompanied by choral music rather than instrumental marches. In 1896, Parratt pointed out to Knollys 'You will notice how few are the Marches and how Many the hymns.'[278] Such emphasis on choral music coincided with the fashion at the time. The aforementioned 1896 St Paul's wedding was described as 'fully choral', and the 1899 Abbey wedding similarly had a rich programme of choral music.[279] Also, Monsarrat has more generally observed that at 'humbler weddings' in the nineteenth century the phrase 'the service was fully choral' was 'a nice thing to be able to include in wedding notices'.[280]

For royal weddings, however, the music had furthermore become another notable 'public' aspect. With some of their music published and reportedly repeated in many churches throughout the country, it was through the music that more people had a chance to catch at least a little acoustic glimpse of these ceremonies.

---

[275] 'Royal Wedding', *Times* (1893), p. 5. This passage was also quoted, and thus spread further, in Sheppard, *Memorials*, II, part 2, p. 126.

[276] 'Viscount Milton's Marriage', *ILN*, 20 June 1896, p. 773; and 'Wedding at St. Paul's', *Times*, 25 June 1896, p. 10.

[277] See 'Girls' Gossip', *Truth*, 45:1165 (27 April 1899), pp. 1085–86, here p. 1085. This wedding attracted much attention and pictures were on several front pages (*Graphic*, *ILN*, *Black & White* etc.)

[278] Parratt to Knollys, 12 July 1896, in *Lna LC 2/132*.

[279] 'Wedding at St. Paul's', *Times* (1896); and 'Girls' Gossip', p. 1085.

[280] Ann Monsarrat, *And the Bride Wore…: The Story of the White Wedding* (London: Gentry Books, 1973), p. 131.

10

The Last 'of the Old Age': The Early Twentieth Century

THE REIGN OF QUEEN VICTORIA'S SUCCESSOR, Edward VII, did not see any 'major' royal wedding, but there were two notable 'minor' royal weddings. Their ceremonial peculiarities and their music featured some, albeit minor, innovative aspects. Then, in the earlier years of George V's reign, there were another three minor royal weddings, one before and two during the First World War. In the larger historical context, the first of these has been described as the 'last royal wedding of the old age', pointing to the major changes that occurred after the Great War.[1] This characterization may meaningfully be applied to the whole group of three weddings between the accession of Edward VII and the War: they clearly continued the traditions established in the previous century but were to be the last such occasions before the introduction of major changes in the overall appearance of the monarchy and in these royal ceremonies in particular.

Princess Alice of Albany and Prince Alexander of Teck, 10 February 1904

The first royal wedding of the new century, and of the new reign, occurred early in 1904: on 10 February, Princess Alice of Albany, daughter of Prince Leopold married Prince Alexander of Teck, brother of the Princess of Wales (later Queen Mary).

The Venue

Whereas the three weddings of the then Prince of Wales's children between 1889 and 1896 had taken place in London, this wedding of his niece returned to St George's Chapel, Windsor. In regards to the venue, the bride's mother, Princess Helen, Duchess of Albany, explained to Randall Davidson, the Archbishop of Canterbury, that

> the <u>private chapel,</u> was suggested, but the King has been very nice about it & has directly given in to St Georges.[2]

As the *Graphic* explained, 'Princess Alice specially wished her wedding to be like that of her parents as nearly as possible, both in scene and ceremonial, and, therefore, St. George's was chosen once more.'[3] The same report detailed that the king was overall heavily involved in the preparations and that 'His Majesty, acting as father to his orphaned niece, has supervised every arrangement as if he were marrying one of his own daughters'. Lady Violet Greville was quoted

---

[1] Kate Williams, '"Pomp and Circumstance": Royal Weddings from 1714 to 1918', in: Alison Weir, Kate Williams, Sarah Gristwood, and Tracy Borman, *The Ring and the Crown: A History of Royal Weddings 1066–2011* (London: Hutchinson, 2011), pp. 53–95, here p. 95.

[2] Princess Helen to Davidson, 20 December 1903, *Llp Davidson 21*, no. 53 (emphasis original).

[3] 'The Royal Wedding', *Graphic*, 13 February 1904, pp. 194–95, here p. 194.

British Royal Weddings

after the wedding as having commented that the it 'took place with all the stateliness and dignity to which the King has accustomed us in Court ceremonies'.[4] However, shortly before the wedding, the *Illustrated London News* had explained:

> Arrangements for the wedding of Princess Alice of Albany are now complete. The King has ordered that, as far as is possible, the marriage of these junior members of the royal family shall be regarded as a domestic and not a public affair, as this event will set a precedent in some respects for others of a similar kind that may be expected in time to come. It has been decided to invite to the ceremony only personal friends and the personages of State importance who are always asked to such events, and there will be no alterations in the chapel to allow of more than its usual complement of seats being provided.[5]

After the event, the same magazine opined in two consecutive numbers that the wedding 'although not a State ceremony, was yet celebrated with much pomp' and that the occasion had been staged 'with a ceremonial little short of that which would have attended a State wedding'.[6] The ceremony, however, had in fact been kept notably straightforward and somewhat simpler than those at previous weddings. As the *Graphic* put it, this was 'a quiet wedding, too, for a Royal union', explaining:

> Royalty can never get rid of State, but there was far less of it than usual, and the family character of the wedding was strongly emphasized.[7]

This 'family character' was heightened by the absence of heralds, which had reportedly taken part in 1893 and 1896 – but actually not at the most recent Windsor wedding in 1891. Instead, the processions were again organized and led by the chamberlains with their dinstinct white wands (see Illustration 10.1). Moreover, the somewhat simpler 'family character' became visible in such minor details as the appearance of the specially produced orders of service: the copies for the more prominent guests were no longer bound in lavish velvet, nor in real silk, but in white paper produced to give the effect of shiny, watered silk (see Illustration 10.2).[8]

In terms of the 'alterations in the chapel' that the *Illustrated London News* explained were not to happen, the king, together with the Prince of Wales, inspected the work taking place at St George's and ordered that 'no new structural work inside was to be done, with the exception of an erected platform space or Haut pas near Altar and lower Stalls to have a row of chairs in front of them'; in particular there were no additional, adjoining rooms to be built.[9] It seems that other work of such kind, based on the precedents of the earlier weddings, had already started, but it was ordered to stop immediately. After the ceremony, the *Graphic* summarized that St George's Chapel had been 'left much in its usual condition'.[10] The *Times* had reported that, notwithstanding decorations such as the Garter knights' banners and stained-glass windows, 'Other decorations there were none', apart from some carpets, a few flowers and the gold plate on the altar – modestly concluding that 'St. George's Chapel needs no decoration'.[11] Yet, the correspondent also highlighted an important 'welcome

---

[4] Quoted in 'The King and Queen of Wurtemberg', *Graphic*, 20 February 1904, p. 244.

[5] 'Ladies' Page', *ILN*, 30 January 1904, p. 164. The source for the king's order remains yet to be found.

[6] 'The World's News', *ILN*, 13 February 1904, p. 216; and 'The World's News/The Royal Wedding', *ILN*, 20 February 1904, p. 257.

[7] 'The Royal Wedding', *Graphic* (1904), p. 194.

[8] See OS 1904. For the copy used by Princess Victoria Mary, Princess of Wales (later Queen Mary), see below, fn. 28.

[9] Letter to Office of Works, 27 January 1904, in *Lna WORK 19/138*.

[10] 'The Royal Wedding', *Graphic* (1904), p. 194.

[11] 'The Royal Wedding', *Times*, 11 February 1904, p. 10.

10—The Last 'of the Old Age': The Early Twentieth Century

Illustration 10.1: 'The Royal Wedding at Windsor: The Bride and Bridegroom, Prince Alexander of Teck and Princess Alice of Albany, Leaving the Altar', Supplement to *ILN*, February 1904, pp. IV–V. © Illustrated London News/Mary Evans Picture Library.

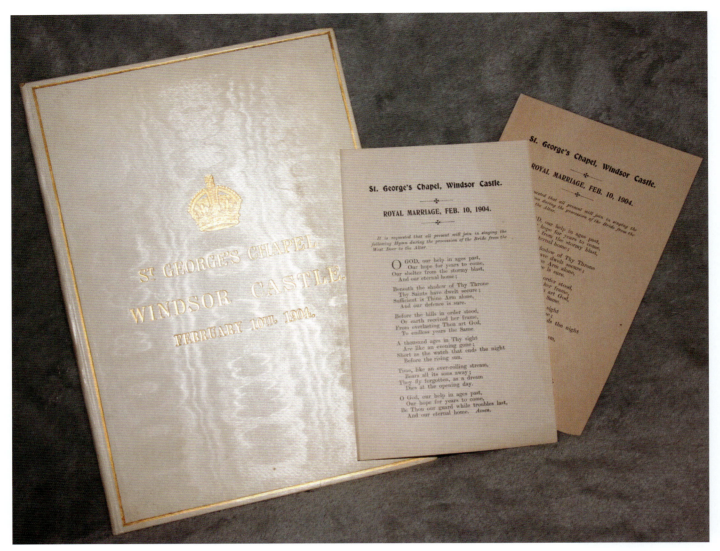

Illustration 10.2: Order of service for the 1904 wedding of Princess Alice of Albany and Prince Alexander of Teck, with copies of the separate lose hymn sheet. Author's collection.

innovation': better arrangements for the 'representatives of the Press'. This observation is worth a longer quotation:

> Their duty to see and to hear for others, and to speak *urbi et orbi* to the best of their individual ability, has been recognized and rendered far more comfortable, if not more easy, than it has been on any previous occasion within my memory. That is to say, there was set apart for their use the closet on the north side of St. George's Chapel and immediately above the *Haut Pas*, from which eye and ear can work to as much advantage on an occasion of this kind as from the Royal box of a theatre in other circumstances. It was immediately adjoining that occupied by many Royal children. This, I understand, was done by the express command of the King, and one of the gentlemen of the Household, who deserves and receives the warm thanks of all concerned, was assiduous in providing all information. […] for the Press to be provided with every conceivable item of information that could reasonably be required, without having to ask for it, and that by the express command of his Majesty, was to receive a Royal favour which cannot be passed over without a warm and prominent expression of respectful gratitude.[12]

---

[12] 'Royal Wedding', *Times*, 11 February 1904.

10—The Last 'of the Old Age': The Early Twentieth Century

Thus, even though Edward VII had reportedly ordered that such a wedding of junior members of the royal family should be 'regarded as a domestic and not a public affair', he nevertheless cared for good press coverage. The statement that the correspondents had a 'duty to see and hear for others' is particularly noteworthy. Accordingly, they were given some of the best places from which to perceive and experience the ceremony.

The Ceremony and its Music

In terms of its ceremonial and music, this wedding was very similar to those in the 1890s. The *Illustrated London News* summarized that 'The Archbishop of Canterbury conducted the service, and the music was directed by Sir Walter Parratt.'[13] As at the weddings in the 1890s, there was no orchestra and Parratt accompanied all the music on the organ.[14] The clergy's procession entered to the 'Priests' March' from Mendelssohn's *Athalie*, as the programme of the music called it.[15] This distinct march, heard at various earlier weddings, but at other processions, was musically a step up from the mere voluntary that had previously accompanied the clergy. Given its common title as 'War March of the Priests', however, this march seems to have been both an apt and at the same time a peculiar choice for this procession – glossed over by the omission of the word 'war' in the title.

There were four separate carriage processions from the upper Castle: those of guests and royal family, of the bridegroom, of the king and queen, and finally that of the bride.[16] In contrast to the earlier, Victorian weddings, the monarch now arrived only after the bridegroom, and the higher-ranking guests and royal family waited and entered only once the king and queen had arrived.[17] One correspondent recorded that, following the clergy, 'After a ten minutes' interval the procession of the family of the bridegroom was played in to Meyerbeer's march.'[18] In fact, this procession included the bridegroom himself.[19] The programme of music referred merely to an undefined 'March' by Meyerbeer; but the *Manchester Guardian* detailed that this was the march from *Le Prophète*, today more commonly known as 'Coronation March'.[20]

The *Graphic* reported that the arrivals of the four processions were 'heralded by the silver trumpets'.[21] However, no other source seems to refer to fanfares at this wedding. Instead, it was reported that the king and queen were received with the National Anthem outside; and then they walked up the nave 'to the strains of one of Gounod's marches, perfectly rendered by Sir Walter Parratt at the organ'.[22] This could plausibly have been Gounod's *Marche Religieuse*, the Gounod march that had been used at the 1896 wedding.

---

[13] 'World's News', *ILN*, 20 February 1904.

[14] 'Royal Wedding at Windsor: The King Gives Away the Bride', *Weekly Irish Times*, 20 February 1904, p. 16. This report is in many parts identical with 'Royal Wedding at Windsor: The King Gives Away the Bride', *Scotsman*, 11 February 1904, p. 7.

[15] OS 1904; 'Royal Wedding', *Times*, 11 February 1904.

[16] 'The Royal Wedding', *Graphic* (1904), p. 194.

[17] Ceremonial 1904, p. 2.

[18] 'Royal Wedding at Windsor', *Weekly Irish Times*.

[19] Ceremonial 1904, p. 2.

[20] OS 1904; 'Royal Wedding at Windsor', *Manchester Guardian*, 11 February 1904, p. 6.

[21] 'The Royal Wedding', *Graphic* (1904), p. 194.

[22] 'Royal Wedding', *Times*, 11 February 1904; and 'Royal Wedding at Windsor', *Weekly Irish Times*. The programme of music in OS 1904, has merely 'MARCH' by '*Gounod*'.

The correspondent of the *Times* observed that in a 'truly splendid procession' the king and queen 'swept slowly and majestically up the nave and into the choir', and concluded:

> Certainly no Royal wedding procession that England has seen of recent years has touched this procession for stately magnificence; Without affectation or exaggeration, it was certainly vastly fine.[23]

Following the precedent of the 1891 and 1896 weddings, the bride entered to the singing of a hymn. The ceremonial stipulated:

> The Choir of St. George's Chapel, who were stationed in the North Aisle, proceeded to the West Entrance, and preceded the Bridal Procession as it passed up the Nave singing 'O God, our help in ages past.'[24]

The *Weekly Irish Times* and the *Scotsman* in their nearly identical reports explained that the 'well-known hymn (to St. Ann's tune)' had been a 'special request of the Duchess of Albany', the bride's mother.[25] The *Times* similarly recorded that this hymn had been 'specially selected by the Duchess of Albany' and judged that the bride's procession 'was very pretty and affecting'.[26] As seen in the quotation above, the wording in the ceremonial indicates that the choir sang the hymn as they led the bridal procession, and this can also be deduced from the reports of the wedding.[27] However, there was now a noteworthy difference in the performance. The programme of music bound in the order of service includes the full text of the hymn, as previously; yet there was also a small, lose, printed hymn sheet with the place and date of the wedding followed by the text of 'O God, our Help in Ages past', six verses and Amen (Illustration 10.2).[28]

The annotation at the top of this hymn sheet is particularly noteworthy:

> *It is requested that all present will join in singing the following Hymn during the procession of the Bride from the West Door to the Altar.*

The fact that 'all present' were specifically 'requested' to sing in the hymn may indicate that they would not normally have done so, and the congregation joining in this entrance hymn appears to have been a first for a royal wedding. In 1889, at a society wedding at the Chapel Royal at St James's, one report had pointed out that 'the service opened with the singing of a wedding hymn, in which the congregation all joined'.[29] Again, the fact that this was specially mentioned could indicate that it was not the normal procedure. The reason for this change in royal custom at the 1904 wedding, does not seem to be known.

The *Weekly Irish Times* detailed for the bridal procession that

> At the entrance to the chancel the choir filed off and took their places in the organ loft, while Princess Alice, led by her brother, the young Duke of Saxe-Coburg and Gotha, was conducted to the *haut pas*.[30]

If that report was correct, the choir would have left the procession once it reached the quire screen to go upstairs. This could explain why the congregation was invited to sing in the entrance hymn: because the choir would have to pause in the singing while going upstairs. However,

---

[23] 'Royal Wedding', *Times*, 11 February 1904.

[24] Ceremonial 1904, p. 6.

[25] 'Royal Wedding at Windsor', *Weekly Irish Times*; 'Royal Wedding at Windsor', *Scotsman*.

[26] 'Royal Wedding', *Times*, 11 February 1904.

[27] See fn. 24; and 'The Royal Wedding', *Graphic* (1904), p. 195; 'Royal Wedding at Windsor', *Weekly Irish Times*.

[28] OS 1904; the copy the hymn sheet used by the Princess of Wales is preserved in *Wra RA F&V/WED/1904*.

[29] 'Social Events: Marriage in London of Colonel Jameson and Jean Willard', *Washington Post*, 25 May 1889, p. 5.

[30] 'Royal Wedding at Windsor', *Weekly Irish Times*.

10—The Last 'of the Old Age': The Early Twentieth Century

reports of the next wedding, in the following year, indicate that the choir did not go up into the organ loft but stayed downstairs, in the quire.[31]

For the psalm after the vows, the programme of music specified that this was Ps. 67, this time sung to an undefined chant by 'Garrett' – maybe his chant in A that had been used at the 1891 wedding.[32] The next musical item in the programme of music was the 'Anthem'. This was once again by Mendelssohn: 'Lift thine Eyes to the Mountains Whence Cometh Help', from his oratorio *Elijah* (op. 70, MWV A 25, no. 28), but the origins of the piece were not mentioned in the programme of music.[33] One report referred enthusiastically to the 'welltrained [*sic*] voices of the young choristers blending in sweet harmonies' in Mendelssohn's anthem.[34] Parratt had obviously taken good care of the musical preparations and there had been a special 'rehearsal of the wedding music' in the St George's Chapel, with the dean present, on the Saturday morning before the wedding.[35]

According to the *Weekly Irish Times*, after the anthem the Bishop of Peterborough 'led the special suffrages commencing "Oh, Lord save Thy servant and Thy handmaid," the choral responses to which were by Tallis'.[36] It is unlikely, however, that the sequence of psalm, Lord's Prayer and Responses would have been interrupted by an anthem. Indeed, according to the *Times*, the anthem came only after the prayers and was followed directly by the archbishop's address.[37] This seems to be a more plausible sequence. Nevertheless, the observation that 'the choral responses' were 'by Tallis' is interesting. This may, perhaps, have been the chant 'Tallis in A' that had been used at the wedding of Princess Mary Adelaide of Cambridge in Kew in 1866.[38]

After the address came 'O Perfect Love' as the 'Hymn before the Benediction', the programme of music giving the text of three verses and specifying '*Dykes*'.[39] The *Weekly Irish Times* confirmed that the hymn was 'sung to the well-known tune of Dykes'.[40] It was thus probably the same as in 1891 and notably not Barnby's now more famous tune. In contrast to the bride's entrance hymn, the congregation does not seem to have joined in this hymn: there is no separately printed text, and the printed ceremonial recorded that it was 'sung by the Choir', corroborated by the account in the *Times*.[41]

The music for the recess was Mendelssohn's Wedding March, like the entrance marches played by Parratt on the organ.[42] However, its effect may have been heightened by the preceding ceremonial proceedings. The *Times* recorded that

> before Mendelssohn's Wedding March sounded, and before the outgoing procession formed itself, there was a pretty little piece of unrehearsed ceremony, not included in the programme. As Prince Alexander and his Princess rose he took her by the hand, and when the little Princesses who

---

[31] See below, with fns 57–58.

[32] OS 1904; 'Royal Wedding', *Times*, 11 February 1904; 'Royal Wedding at Windsor', *Weekly Irish Times*. for Garrett's chant in 1891 see Chapter 9, fns 99–100.

[33] OS 1904. While this includes the full text, there is no reference to *Elijah*.

[34] 'Royal Wedding at Windsor', *Weekly Irish Times*.

[35] 'Royal Wedding', *Times*, 8 February 1904, p. 6.

[36] 'Royal Wedding at Windsor', *Weekly Irish Times*.

[37] 'Royal Wedding', *Times*, 11 February 1904, giving the full text of the address.

[38] See Chapter 7, fns 160–61.

[39] OS 1904, programme of music.

[40] 'Royal Wedding at Windsor', *Weekly Irish Times*.

[41] Ceremonial 1904, p. 7; 'The Royal Wedding', *Graphic* (1904), p. 195 ('the choir sang the hymn').

[42] OS 1904; Ceremonial 1904, p. 7; and 'Royal Wedding at Windsor', *Weekly Irish Times* (1904).

British Royal Weddings

were bridesmaids had wheeled cleverly round with the bride's long train, the married pair faced round to the north and made obeisance to the King and Queen.[43]

The account in the *Weekly Irish Times* noted this scene and referred to the 'deep obeisance to the King, who smilingly bowed in return'.[44] This reverence of the newly-weds was an innovation that has been kept until the present day. Its regal stateliness was answered and thus enhanced by the ensuing fanfare-like opening of Mendelssohn's march.

Princess Margaret of Connaught and Prince Gustaf Adolf of Sweden and Norway, 15 June 1905

A mere sixteen months after the 1904 wedding, on 15 June 1905, there was another royal wedding – this time an event of much more international and dynastic importance. Another niece of the king, Princess Margaret of Connaught, daughter of Queen Victoria's son Prince Arthur, Duke of Connaught, married Prince Gustaf Adolf, elder son of the Crown Prince of Sweden and Norway. The wedding occurred at the height of tensions that would eventually lead to the independence of Norway; nevertheless, with the princess expected one day to become queen consort, this was a significant link with a foreign royal house.[45]

Notwithstanding the wedding's significance, the ceremony itself very much followed that in the previous year. It took again place at St George's Chapel, Windsor, and the Office of Works was instructed to 'carry out the necessary arrangements for the preparation of the Chapel on the same lines as those of the Prince and Princess Alexander of Teck in 1904'.[46] There were again no heralds and the ceremonial mentions merely ushers.[47] Yet, the order of service was – for some guests at least – now again bound in purple velvet.[48] Sydney Prior Hall's watercolour painting of the ceremony evokes a grand and yet joyful atmosphere and shows the officiating minister clearly holding one of the orders of service bound in white (Illustration 10.3).

The press was again well cared for with the same advantageous places that they had had at the wedding in the previous year.[49] The service was conducted mainly by the Archbishop of Canterbury, who was assisted by other clerics, and again Parratt was in charge of the music and 'presided at the organ', as the ceremonial noted.[50] After those in 1885, 1891, 1896 and 1904, this was the fifth royal wedding at which Parratt participated. Unfortunately, this time none of his papers relating to the ceremony seem to have survived. There was again no orchestra and the reports mention only the choir of St George's Chapel.

---

[43] 'Royal Wedding', *Times*, 11 February 1904.

[44] 'Royal Wedding at Windsor', *Weekly Irish Times*.

[45] For a discussion of various wider aspects of the 1905 wedding see also Lena Rangström, *En brud för kung och fosterland: Kungliga svenska bröllop från Gustav Vasa till Carl XVI Gustaf* (Stockholm: Livrustkammaren/Atlantis, 2010), pp. 365–81.

[46] Arthur Knollis, Lord Chamberlain's Office, to the Secretary, Office of Works, typewritten, 13 May 1905, in *Lna WORK 19/138* (*sic* for the unusual wording).

[47] Ceremonial 1905.

[48] Copy in *Wsg X.33/19/1*.

[49] See 'The Royal Marriage', *Times*, 16 June 1905, p. 6.

[50] Ceremonial 1905, p. 6–7. for the archbishop see also 'The Royal Wedding', *Scotsman*, 16 June 1905, p. 5; 'Royal Marriage', *Times*.

10—The Last 'of the Old Age': The Early Twentieth Century

The *Scotsman* recorded that the first procession, that of the clergy, entered to 'the *Epithalame* of the famous French organist Guilmant'.[51] This was his 'Marche Nuptiale' that had been played during the procession of the royal family at the 1891 wedding. After this there were, as in the previous year and in the same order, the three grand entrance processions of the bridegroom, the king and queen, and of the bride. As in 1904, it seems that there were no fanfares for the processions, but the reports agree that the band outside played and announced the arrivals of the individual processions at the Chapel. When the bridegroom arrived, 'the band of the Grenadier Guards was playing the Swedish National Anthem' and he then walked up the nave to the march from Wagner's *Tannhäuser* – probably an arrangement of the Pilgrim's Chorus from Act III, or the Entry of the Guests from Act II, as discussed above.[52] Similarly, the king and queen – who again arrived only after the bridegroom – were announced by 'the brazen instruments outside' playing the National Anthem, and then walked up the nave and quire to Elgar's *Imperial March*. The bride arrived last, and the *Times* correspondent described:

> The procession of the King and Queen had hardly ceased to be a procession before, once more, the sound of our National Anthem was heard from the outer air. A moment more and the sound of boys' voices, floating towards us under the vaulted roof, as the hymn 'When God of old came down from Heaven' was sung, and, in less than a minute as it seemed, the bride's procession was filing up the choir.[53]

Illustration 10.3: Sydney Prior Hall, 'Marriage of Princess Margaret of Connaught to Prince Gustavus Adolphus of Sweden', bodycolour and watercolour painting 15 Jun 1905, *Royal Collection, RCIN 451868*, Royal Collection Trust / © Her Majesty Queen Elizabeth II 2021.

---

[51] 'Royal Wedding', *Scotsman* (1905). See also the programme of music in OS 1905; and 'Royal Marriage', *Times*.

[52] For this and the following 'Royal Marriage', *Times*; 'Royal Wedding', *Scotsman* (1905); OS 1905. For the identity of Wagner's march see Chapter 9, after fn 30.

[53] 'Royal Marriage', *Times*. See also 'The Marriage of Princess Margaret of Connaught to Prince Gustavus Adolphus of Sweden […]', 'by One Who was There', *The Sphere*, 24 June 1905, p. 293.

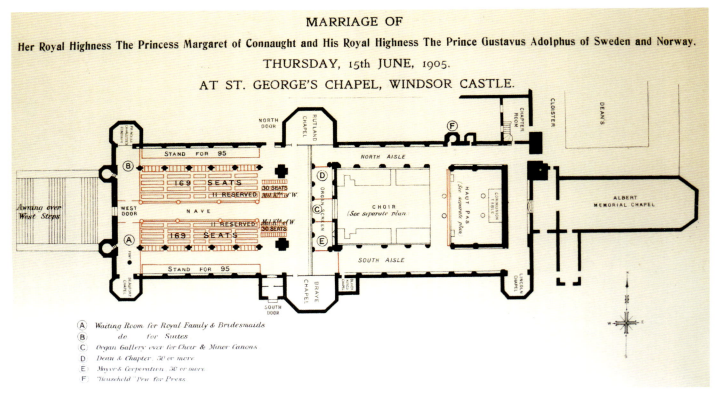

Illustration 10.4: Plan of St George's Chapel, Windsor, with seating arrangements. Included in Ceremonial 1905; here from the copy in *Wsg X.33/20*. By permission of the Dean and Canons of Windsor.

For the bride's procession, the programme of music stipulated all seven verses of 'When God of Old', without information on the tune.[54] This hymn by John Keble is today usually sung to the tune 'Winchester Old' (best known from the carol 'While Shepherds Watched their Flocks by Night') and it is found with this tune in early-twentieth-century hymn books.

As before, the ceremonial stipulated that the choir 'preceded the Bridal Procession as it passed up the Nave' while singing the hymn.[55] Once it reached the quire screen, the choir reportedly 'filed off and took their places in the Organ Loft'.[56] The ceremonial included detailed seating plans: one for the quire and one for the whole of St George's Chapel (Illustration 10.4). The latter shows that the space for the 'Choir & Minor Canons' was comparatively small: just the area in the middle of the organ gallery (marked with 'C' in the plan), much of which was still occupied by the organ itself.

The *Scotsman* emphasized that the 'impressive ceremonial' in the St George's 'recalled forcibly' the wedding in the previous year and it explained:

> The programme of service differed in no material respect, with the exception that Sir Walter Parratt's red cassocked choir took up its position in the organ gallery instead of in the choir.[57]

The *Times* similarly emphasized that at this wedding 'the singers were relegated to the organ loft for the occasion', indicating that this was unusual.[58] Incidentally, in contrast to 1904, this

---

[54] OS 1905, programme of music.

[55] Ceremonial 1905, p. 6. Also 'Royal Wedding', *Scotsman* (1905); 'Royal Wedding: The Ceremony in St. George's Chapel', *Irish Times*, 12 June 1905, p. 5.

[56] Ceremonial 1905, p. 6; and 'Royal Wedding', *Scotsman* (1905). See also 'Royal Marriage', *Times*.

[57] 'Royal Wedding', *Scotsman* (1905).

[58] 'Royal Marriage', *Times*.

10—The Last 'of the Old Age': The Early Twentieth Century

time there is no evidence that the congregation joined in the entrance hymn. The choir could possibly have waited on the side to finish singing the entrance hymn, before they went up to their gallery – as they had probably done in 1891.[59]

The order of service, as before, includes both alternative psalms as in the Prayer Book but the programme of music curiously does not list any details for the psalm.[60] However, the *Times* report referred particularly to the singing of Ps. 67:

> It cannot, however, be said that the solemn service proceeded to its conclusion absolutely without flaw, for, by some unhappy accident, it fell out that, while the Archbishop was in the act of pronouncing the most impressive words of the service, 'Those whom God hath joined together,' the organ sounded and the choir began the *Deus Misereatur*. However, the Archbishop, with a motion of his hand, stayed the interruption, and the service proceed upon its appointed course.[61]

This would mean that the psalm was eventually sung in its proper place, after the vows, and the *Scotsman* also reported that 'The Psalm, "God be merciful unto us," was chanted'.[62] Yet, it does not seem to be known what chant was used for the psalm.

For the anthem, the same paper reported that 'the triumphant strains of Beethoven's Hallelujah Chorus followed from voice and organ'. This was again the chorus from Beethoven's *The Mount of Olives*, last heard at the 1882 wedding. It was possibly after the anthem that the Archbishop of Canterbury, 'speaking from the centre of the altar, delivered a brief address'.[63] This address, in turn, was followed by the 'Hymn before the Benediction', three verses of 'Now Thank We All our God'.[64] The ceremonial now specified distinctly that this hymn 'before the final Blessing […] was sung by the Choir'.[65] The incorporation of this hymn, which had at one point been suggested for the 1893 wedding, may now have been more meaningful: while this appears to have been the first royal wedding at which it was sung, Lena Rangström has pointed out that having this hymn at the end was in accordance with Swedish tradition.[66] After the final blessing, the newlyweds 'retraversed the Choir and Nave westwards to the inspiring music of Mendelssohn's "Wedding March."'[67]

With the absence of heralds and fewer special fittings, the ceremony of the 1905 wedding was, as that in the previous year, overall somewhat simpler in appearance than the weddings at St George's in the later decades of Queen Victoria's reign had been. However, the slightly reduced ceremonial pomp of the service could be an asset and music remained a notable aspect. The correspondent of the *Times* noted enthusiastically that 'although yesterday's wedding service had not that majesty which belongs to a full Garter celebration, the service was yet beautiful, appropriate, and touching', referring especially to 'its stately surroundings, and its beautiful music'.[68]

---

[59] See Chapter 9, fn. 91.

[60] OS 1905.

[61] 'Royal Marriage', *Times*.

[62] This and the following 'Royal Wedding', *Scotsman* (1905).

[63] 'Royal Wedding', *Scotsman* (1905); and 'Royal Marriage', *Times*. Both reports appear to reproduce the full text of the address.

[64] OS 1905, programme of music; 'Royal Marriage', *Times*; 'Royal Wedding', *Scotsman* (1905).

[65] Ceremonial 1905, p. 6.

[66] Rangström, *En brud*, p. 378: 'Ceremonin avslutades traditionsenligt här liksom i Sverige med psalmen "Nu tackar Gud allt folk".' For 1893 see Chapter 9, fn. 159.

[67] 'Royal Wedding', *Scotsman* (1905); 'Royal Marriage', *Times*; also OS 1905; and Ceremonial 1905, p. 6.

[68] 'Royal Marriage', *Times*. See also the discussion on 'simplicity' in Chapter 11 below, here esp. at fn. 36.

Prince Arthur of Connaught and Princess Alexandra, 2nd Duchess of Fife, 15 October 1913

After the accession of George V in 1910, there was only one notable royal wedding before the First World War: that of his cousin and niece, Prince Arthur of Connaught and Princess Alexandra of Fife – son of Queen Victoria's third son Prince Arthur, Duke of Connaught, and daughter of Queen Victoria's granddaughter Princess Louise, Duchess of Fife, respectively. The ceremony returned to London and took place in the Chapel Royal, St James's Palace, on 15 October 1913. As the *Times* put it, 'It is long since we had a Royal wedding in London', while the *Illustrated London News* similarly judged that the occasion 'has aroused exceptional interest from the fact that it is the first Royal wedding that has taken place in England for eight years', pointing out that it was 'still longer since a Royal wedding took place in London'.[69] The last one had been in 1896; but that had been in Buckingham Palace: the most recent wedding in the Chapel Royal – with a larger procession going there – had been twenty years ago, in 1893. For the 1913 wedding, the *Manchester Guardian* pointed out that

> Officially the marriage of Prince Arthur and the Duchess of Fife was a private affair of the Court, and everything this morning had the proper atmosphere of rich and secluded domesticity.[70]

While the British press seems not to have mentioned it, an American paper interpreted that the death of the duchess's father in the previous year was the reason why the wedding was 'a family affair' and 'devoid of all processions and military display'.[71] One of the keywords in the reporting of this wedding was 'simplicity': the *Times* summarized that 'within reasonable limits everything had been done to make the marriage as simple as possible'.[72] It stressed especially the 'home' or 'native' character of the occasion:

> No foreign Royalties had been asked to be present except those who were joined by very close ties to the houses of the Prince and his bride. The wedding was treated almost entirely as a family affair, with the result that it was markedly English and Northern [European] in its character. All the principal witnesses of the ceremony were by blood and descent native-born sons and daughters of these islands or those other northern countries – Norway, Sweden, and Denmark – with which, by the marriages of our Royal House no less than through our far-off ancestry, we Britons are so closely allied, and a further touch of this kinship of the races of the North was added by the close connexion between Prince Arthur's father, the Duke of Connaught, and our Northern Dominion of Canada in the Western World.

The wording, with its reference to the English and 'Northern' monarchies, could barely hide its deliberate ignoring of the various closely-related German monarchies. This is noteworthy especially since the bridegroom's own mother was a Prussian princess and clearly not 'by blood' a daugter 'of these islands'. The *Manchester Guardian* in a dedicated article explained rather directly that 'There is no expectation that a member of the German Royal Family will attend.'[73] In this case, 'German' referred probably especially, if not solely to the Prussian royal family – in all likelihood emphasizing the point that no member of the Kaiser's family was to be present – and this article also lists the few other royal guests that were to attend the wedding. Some years

---

[69] 'The Royal Wedding', *Times*, 15 October 1913, p. 9; 'The Royal Wedding: Our Double Number and Supplement', *ILN*, 18 October 1913, p. 644.

[70] 'The Royal Wedding: Brilliant Scene at the Ceremony', *Manchester Guardian*, 16 October 1913, p. 9.

[71] See the report in *Chicago Tribune*, 15 October 1913, p. 7.

[72] This and the following 'Royal Wedding: Scene in St. James's Palace', *Times*, 16 October 1913, pp. 9–10, here p. 9.

[73] 'The Royal Wedding: Few Foreign Royal Guests to Be Present', *Manchester Guardian*, 2 October 1913, p. 7.

10—The Last 'of the Old Age': The Early Twentieth Century

later, in his biography of the bridegroom's father, George Aston reiterated that 'The ceremony was a quiet one, thoroughly English, and fewer foreign Royalties than usual were present.'[74]

After the wedding, the *Illustrated London News* reported of a rumour that 'no artist of an illustrated paper was present at the ceremony and that no illustration of the royal wedding will be forthcoming of the unqualified accuracy which only the actual presence of an artist at the ceremony could have secured'.[75] The magazine rebuked this misinformation and emphasized that the two pictures that it had produced in its royal wedding issue were indeed authentic, pointing out that the paper's 'Special Artist', Frédéric de Haenen, had 'witnessed the ceremony in the Chapel Royal, St. James's Palace, from its beginning to its end, and from an excellent point of vantage'. The drawing by de Haenen gives a good impression of the overall set-up, showing the specially prepared low benches for the congregation near the front and the various floral decorations, while bringing out the comparatively limited space of the building (Illustration 10.5). Whereas this first picture was drawn by Haenen himself, the second picture was based on his sketches; there was furthermore an illustration of the wedding by Fortunino Matania in the magazine *The Sphere*.[76]

Illustration 10.5: 'The Royal Wedding at St. James's', 'Drawn by Frédéreric de Haenen, our Special Artist at the Ceremony in the Chapel Royal, St. James's Palace', *ILN*, 18 October 1913, pp. 612–13. © Illustrated London News/Mary Evans Picture Library.

[74] George Aston, *His Royal Highness, the Duke of Connaught and Strathearn: A Life and Intimate Study* (London: G.G. Harrap & Co., 1929), p. 288.

[75] This and the following 'Our Artist at the Royal Wedding: The Accurate Illustrating of the Ceremony in the Chapel Royal', *ILN*, 25 October 1913, p. 650.

[76] 'From Sketches by our Special Artist at the Ceremony: The Royal Wedding at St. James's Palace. Drawn by A. C. Michael from Sketches by Frédéric de Haenen, our Special Artist at the Wedding Ceremony in the Chapel Royal', *ILN*, 18 October 1913, pp. 616–17. For Matania's picture see *The Sphere*, 18 October 1918 p. IV-V.

Overall, the *Scotsman* concluded that 'It would be idle to pretend that the marriage excited anything like the public interest which was evoked four and twenty years ago when the parents of the bride were married in Buckingham Palace' – yet, it also highlighted that 'the crowds were sufficient to show how closely events in the family life of the Royal House are followed by the community'.[77] More positively, the *Times* summarized that 'Public interest in the occasion was great'.[78] Indeed, in terms of press reporting, this wedding appears to have received more detailed attention than many previous weddings: there was much interest in all the minutiae of the event. For instance, more than ten days before the wedding, the *Times* published the programme of music.[79] Furthermore, the *Illustrated London News* included features specifically on the 'Musical Side' – with photos of the four composers Stanford, Alcock, Elgar, and Parry whose music was played at the ceremony – and also on the 'Religious Aspect' – which included pictures of the participating clergy and of the choristers and gentlemen of the Chapel Royal (Illustration 10.6).

In its account of the wedding, the *Times* detailed that Edgar Sheppard, the subdean of the Chapel Royal, read the opening words and the Bishop of London, as its dean, 'the closing prayers', but that the rest of the service was performed by the Archbishop of Canterbury.[80] With the service at the Chapel Royal, the reports announced that Sheppard 'has charge of the musical arrangements, for the carrying out of which Dr. Alcock and the "gentlemen and children" of the Chapels Royal are responsible'.[81] The printed ceremonial also referred to the Chapel Royal choir, with Alcock at the organ.[82] Walter Galpin Alcock had been organist and composer of the Chapel Royal since 1902. This was the first royal wedding at which the Chapel Royal sang since 1893 and the choir was to be 'placed in the organ loft, so as to make the most of the floor space'.[83]

The aforementioned restraint and simplicity applied also to 'the chapel itself and everything in it', as the *Times* emphasized.[84] For instance, it appears that this time no *haut pas* was built at the altar, and the area around it was thus not particularly elevated. Nevertheless, with reference to the small size of the Chapel, the *Manchester Guardian* explained that 'to-day, by careful manoeuvring, it was made to hold two hundred'.[85] Thus, at least to some degree the small space of the Chapel Royal was specially arranged, as for previous weddings there. Philip Gibbs explained in an article in the popular illustrated magazine *The Graphic*:

> Platforms in three tiers are being erected on both sides of the chapel, to provide seating accommodation for the 250 guests. At the extreme end is the Royal Gallery, and on either side are the Household and Peeresses' Galleries.[86]

---

[77] 'The Royal Wedding: Brilliant Scene at St James's Palace', *Scotsman*, 16 October 1913, p. 7.

[78] 'Royal Wedding: Scene', p. 9.

[79] 'The Royal Wedding: The Ceremony in the Chapel Royal', *Times*, 2 October 1913, p. 6.

[80] 'Royal Wedding: Scene in St. James's Palace', p. 10.

[81] 'Royal Wedding: Final Arrangements for the Ceremony', *Observer*, 5 October 1913, p. 11. This article was reproduced on the next day, with some additions, in 'The Royal Wedding: Final Arrangements for the Ceremony', *Manchester Guardian*, 6 October 1913, p. 8; and 'Royal Wedding: Musical and other Arrangements', *Scotsman*, 6 October 1913, p. 9. In the following, only the *Observer* will be cited (unless there are differences in the reports).

[82] Ceremonial 1913, p. 5.

[83] 'Royal Wedding: Final Arrangements', *Observer*.

[84] 'Royal Wedding: Scene', p. 10.

[85] 'Royal Wedding: Brilliant Scene', *Manchester Guardian*.

[86] Philip Gibbs, 'The Art of Anticipation', *Graphic*, 11 October 1913, p. 658, picture caption (of the drawing, see Illustration 10.7). See also 'Scene of the Royal Wedding: The Chapel Royal, St. James's.', *ILN*, 18 October 1913, p. 618, which includes a photograph by W. Gray of the area around the altar as set up for the wedding. For the preparation of the Chapel see also the material in Lna WORK 19/385.

THE MUSICAL SIDE OF THE WEDDING: THE ORGANIST AND COMPOSERS.

PHOTOGRAPHS BY ELLIOTT AND FRY.

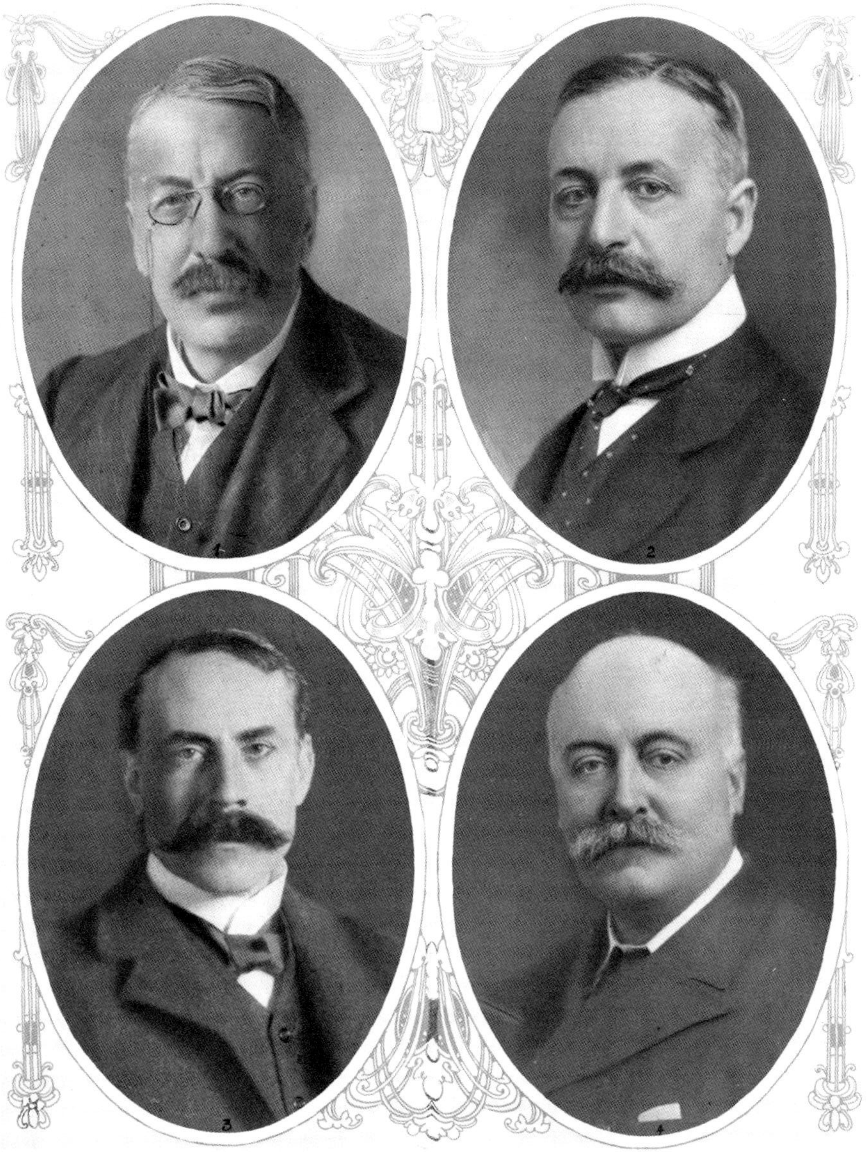

1. SIR CHARLES STANFORD, WHOSE PROCESSIONAL MUSIC FROM "DRAKE" WAS PLAYED DURING THE PROCESSION OF THE QUEEN AND THE ROYAL GUESTS.

3. SIR EDWARD ELGAR, WHOSE "IMPERIAL MARCH" WAS THE FIRST COMPOSITION PLAYED AFTER MOST OF THE GUESTS HAD ASSEMBLED.

2. DR. W. G. ALCOCK, THE ORGANIST AT THE WEDDING CEREMONY, WHO PLAYED HIS "MARCHE TRIOMPHALE" DURING THE BRIDEGROOM'S PROCESSION.

4. SIR HUBERT PARRY, WHOSE MARCH FROM "THE BIRDS," OF ARISTOPHANES, WAS PLAYED DURING THE PROCESSION OF CLERGY.

The music in the Chapel Royal for the wedding ceremony began with Elgar's "Imperial March," which was followed by the March from "La Reine de Saba," by Gounod. Then came the March from Parry's "The Birds"; the March from "Tannhäuser," Guilmant's "Marche Nuptiale," Stanford's Processional Music from "Drake," as played at His Majesty's Theatre; Dr. Alcock's "Marche Triomphale," composed for the occasion and dedicated to the bride; and the hymn "Lead us, Heavenly Father, Lead us." Before the Address, Mendelssohn's "Lift Thine Eyes" was sung; and after it the hymn "O Perfect Love," to a special setting by Lady Arthur Hill.

THE RELIGIOUS ASPECT OF THE WEDDING: THE CLERGY AND CHORISTERS.

PHOTOGRAPH NO. 2 BY MAYALL, 3 BY RUSSELL, 5 BY PUDDICOMBE.

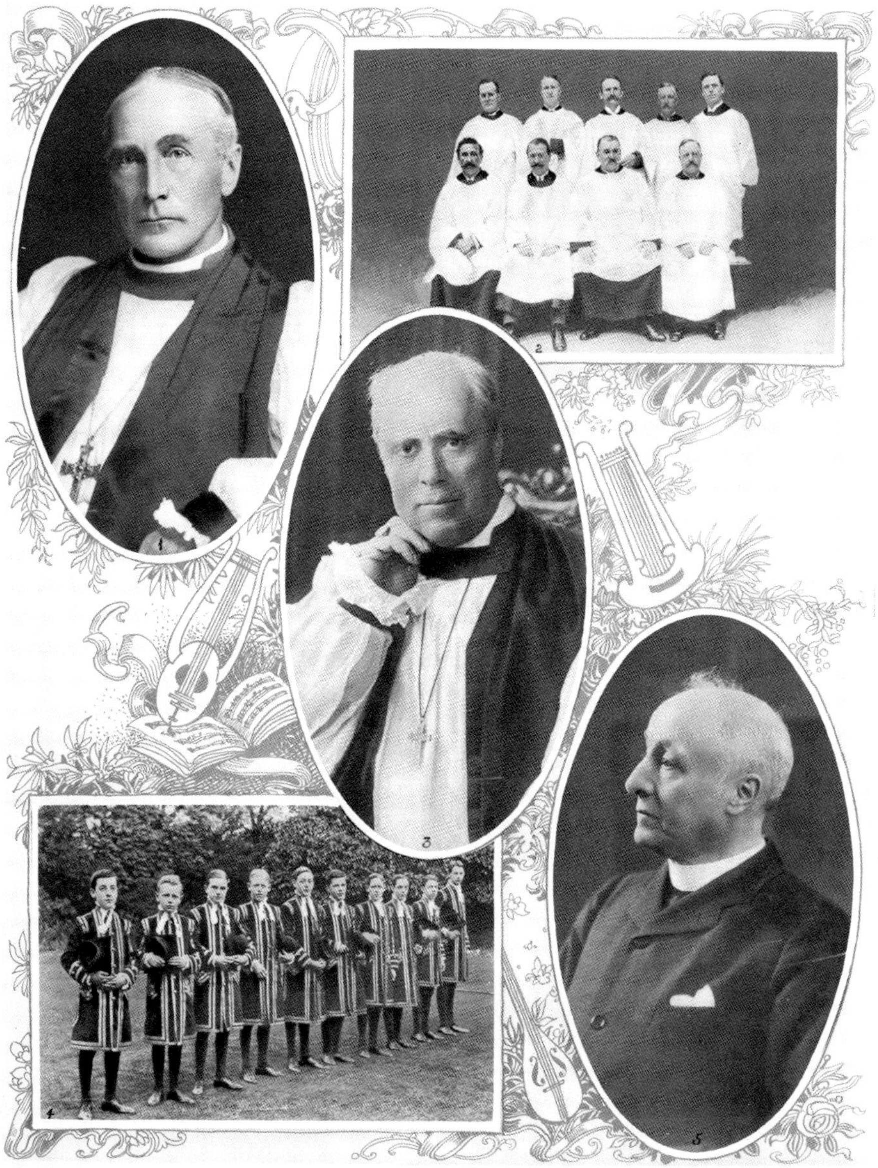

1. TAKING PART IN THE WEDDING CEREMONY: THE BISHOP OF LONDON, DEAN OF THE CHAPELS ROYAL.

2. CHORISTERS AT THE WEDDING: THE GENTLEMEN OF THE CHAPEL ROYAL.

3. THE PERFORMER OF THE WEDDING CEREMONY AND GIVER OF THE ADDRESS: THE ARCHBISHOP OF CANTERBURY.

4. CHORISTERS AT THE WEDDING: THE CHILDREN OF THE CHAPEL ROYAL.

5. TAKING PART IN THE WEDDING CEREMONY: CANON EDGAR SHEPPARD, D.D., THE SUB-DEAN OF THE CHAPELS ROYAL.

It was arranged that the wedding ceremony should be performed by the Archbishop of Canterbury, the Bishop of London, and the Sub-Dean of the Chapels Royal. The choral part of the ceremony was entrusted to the Gentlemen and Children of the Chapel Royal, St. James's Palace, the scene of the wedding.

Illustration 10.6: 'The Musical Side of the Wedding: The Organist and Composers' and 'The Religious Aspect of the Wedding: The Clergy and Choristers', in *ILN*, 18 October 1913, pp. 625 and 631. © Illustrated London News/Mary Evans Picture Library.

The article was accompanied by a drawing by Louis Weirter that shows the building work inside the Chapel Royal (Illustration 10.7). This is one of the earliest examples of reporting about and graphically showing such a triviality from the preparations for a royal wedding and it underlines the aforementioned interest in all the minutiae of the event. While probably serving the curiosity of the masses, such detailed coverage of all the paraphernalia of the ceremony may also have taken away some of the mystique of such a royal occasion. Indeed, the interest in the wedding was apparently so great, and it was so much the topic of the day that at least some found it a bit much. On the day before the ceremony, Lady Geraldine Somerset – with an apparently sarcastic tone of exasperation – referred to 'y.ˢ famous Wedding!!!'.[87]

Processions

The ceremony followed the precedents of previous weddings at St James's and was preceded by processions through the state apartments of the Palace, down the grand staircase, and so into the Chapel Royal. It is not known that these processions this time were accompanied by any music, matching with the observation of the *Times* correspondent that 'there was no approach to any kind of garish display'.[88]

As in 1893, the entrances of the guests were accompanied by organ music, which the *Times* correspondent noted in detail. With reference to the noises from outside, this account observed:

> In the chapel all this was unheard, unseen, unfelt. Only the sound of the organ filled the chamber, as Dr. W. G. Alcock, the chapel organist, played – but softly, as if he, too, was impressed by the prevailing sense of quiet – first Sir Edward Elgar's 'Imperial March,' and then Gounod's march from *La Reine de Sabe*, Wagner's *Tannhaüser* [*sic*] march, and Guilmant's 'Marche Nuptiale.' The short intervals of silence between the different marches, scarcely broken by occasional smothered whispers, as the guests found their way to their places, were curiously impressive.[89]

The other reports also mention the same pieces.[90] There seems be a slight conundrum: in contrast to 1893, these organ were all distinct marches – and of a festive character, suggesting at least a certain volume. Yet, according to the *Times* correspondent, they were played 'softly' – and would thus rather have been more 'background music'.

In any case, the actual 'four separate processions into the Chapel' – those of the clergy, the two queens with foreign royals, other royals, and then the bridegroom – were again quite distinct, with 'each statelier than the last', before the bride arrived in the fifth procession.[91] As her father had died in the previous year, she was led to the altar by her cousin, the king, the most senior male relative. The *Times* made an important observation that chimes with the aforementioned references to simplicity:

> It was a curious feature of these processions that they were each so small, and so devoid of the pomp and pageantry that is generally associated on State occasions with Royalty and the Church. But this was all in keeping with the friendly, family, almost informal character of the gathering.[92]

---

[87] *Wra RA VIC/ADDC6/1*, entry for 14 October 1913.

[88] 'Royal Wedding: Scene', p. 10.

[89] 'Royal Wedding: Scene', p. 10. These organ pieces also in the programme of music in OS 1913.

[90] 'Royal Wedding: Final Arrangements', *Observer* (for the other reports see fn. 79); in slightly different order also in 'Musical Side of the Wedding'.

[91] 'Royal Wedding: Brilliant Scene', *Manchester Guardian*.

[92] 'Royal Wedding: Scene', p. 10.

10—The Last 'of the Old Age': The Early Twentieth Century

In perfect agreement with this observation, it appears that, again, there were no fanfares announcing the processions before they entered the Chapel. The *Scotsman* reported that Queen Mary and the Dowager Queen Alexandra were announced by a royal salute from outside, but that refers probably just to the playing of the National Anthem upon their arrival at the Palace.[93]

Inside the Chapel Royal, each procession was again accompanied by its own music 'played on the Organ'; this was again detailed in the list of music in the order of service and it is noteworthy that this list now included precise timings.[94] First came the procession of the clergy, accompanied by the march from *The Birds* by Charles Hubert Hasting Parry.[95] Parry's music to the Greek comedy *The Birds* by Aristophanes had been written in 1883. It is not known why this march was chosen; however, it may have been popular in a wedding context and had been published in a piano arrangement, under the title 'Bridal March', in 1906.[96]

The procession of the royal family and guests, headed by Queen Mary and Queen Alexandra, was also accompanied by music that had been written for a secular play: the Procession Music from Sir Charles Villiers Stanford's *Drake*.[97] Indeed, the *Illustrated London News* pointed out that Stanford's march was 'as played at His Majesty's Theatre', and with this it willingly or not drew a curious parallel to stage performances.[98] Alcock's organ arrangement of this march was later published.[99] Its use in church was thus at least somewhat furthered.

Illustration 10.7: 'Preparing the Chapel Royal for the Royal Wedding', in Philip Gibbs, 'The Art of Anticipation', *Graphic*, 11 October 1913, p. 658. Author's collection. The organ is in the alcove on the left.

---

[93] 'Royal Wedding: Brilliant Scene', *Scotsman*.

[94] See OS 1913.

[95] 'Royal Wedding: Scene', p. 10; and 'Musical Side of the Wedding'. This was announced on 6 October in 'Royal Wedding: Final Arrangements', *Manchester Guardian*; 'Royal Wedding: Musical and other Arrangements', *Scotsman* – but this detail is not found in 'Royal Wedding: Final Arrangements', *Observer*, of 5 October (compare fn. 81).

[96] C. H. H. [Charles Hubert Hastings] Parry, *Bridal March and Finale. From the Music to "The Birds" of Aristophanes*, arr. for piano solo by J. E. West (London: Novello & Co., 1906).

[97] OS 1913, programme of music. See also 'Royal Wedding: Scene', p. 10; 'Royal Wedding: Final Arrangements', *Manchester Guardian*; and 'Royal Wedding: Musical and other Arrangements', *Scotsman* – nothing on this is found in 'Royal Wedding: Final Arrangements', *Observer*.

[98] 'Musical Side of the Wedding'. See also the discussion in the final chapter.

[99] Charles Villiers Stanford, *Procession Music from "Drake"*, arr. for organ by Walter G. Alcock (London: Stainer & Bell, 1925).

British Royal Weddings

The march for the bridegroom's procession was Alcock's own *Marche Triomphale*.[100] Some of the papers that had announced the programme of music had called it more topically 'Marche Nuptiale' and noted that it had been 'specially composed for the occasion'.[101] The *Graphic* even reproduced the four pages of the composer's manuscript, and the caption explained that this 'Marche Triomphale' had been played during the bridegroom's entrance and was dedicated to the bride (Illustration 10.8).[102] The composer's own inscription and dedication to the bride can be seen on top of Alcock's manuscript. Considering that the march accompanied the bridegroom, the unexplained dedication to the bride would seem slightly curious. The music, with this dedication, was published in the year of the wedding.[103]

As already mentioned, the programme of music in the order of service now included some meticulous timings. It stipulated that the bride was to enter at 11.55am, to the singing of the hymn 'Lead Us, Heavenly Father, Lead Us'.[104] Yet, there was apparently a slight delay of five minutes, as the report in the *Times* indicates:

> Then, after another pause of perfect stillness, as the chapel clock was striking 12, there was a sharp military word of command in the courtyard outside, and the children and gentlemen of the Chapel Royal began to sing the hymn 'Lead us, heavenly Father, lead us,' as the bride, attended by [...] walked up to the altar [...].[105]

In contrast to the previous two weddings at Windsor, the choir did not walk in the procession before the bride. This was probably because it was not practicable with the layout of the smaller Chapel Royal. The *Manchester Guardian*'s account of the ceremony referred to 'The children of the Chapel Royal, perched in one of the galleries', observing that they sang the hymn 'with exquisite purity and precision'.[106]

Two weeks before the wedding, the *Manchester Guardian* had announced to its readers that 'The children and members of the choir of the Chapel Royal will lead the singing'.[107] This reference to the choir's 'leading' may have hinted at congregational singing, but there is no evidence that the congregation eventually joined in any of the singing at the service. Closer to the wedding, the *Observer* reported that 'the choir will sing the hymn' during the procession down the aisle.[108] Similarly, the *Scotsman* recorded that, as the bridal procession entered, 'the choir began the hymn'.[109] This report also pointed out that 'by the time the opening hymn had finished all was in readiness for the actual ceremony', and the *Times* noted that the service began 'Without any delay, as soon as the hymn was ended'.[110] It is at this point that the report in the *Manchester Guardian* summarizes in an intriguingly cryptic way that 'There was first and last quite a concert

---

[100] OS 1913, programme of music; and 'Royal Wedding: Scene', p. 10.

[101] 'Royal Wedding: Final Arrangements', *Observer*; the same in the issues of *Scotsman* and *MG* of 6 October – as explained above, in fn. 81). See also, for instance, 'Royal Wedding: The Ceremony in the Chapel Royal'; and 'Musical Side of the Wedding'.

[102] 'The Wedding Music: "Marche Triomphale" Specially Composed for the Occasion by Dr. Alcock, M.V.O.', *Graphic*, 18 October 1913, p. 722.

[103] Walter G. Alcock, *Marche Triomphale, for the Organ* (London: Novello and Company, [1913]).

[104] OS 1913, programme of music.

[105] 'Royal Wedding: Scene', p. 10.

[106] 'The Royal Wedding: Brilliant Scene', *Manchester Guardian*.

[107] 'The Royal Wedding: King and Princess Royal to Support the Bride', *Manchester Guardian*, 1 October 1913, p. 6.

[108] 'Royal Wedding: Final Arrangements', *Observer*.

[109] 'Royal Wedding: Brilliant Scene', *Scotsman*.

[110] 'Royal Wedding: Scene', p. 10.

10—The Last 'of the Old Age': The Early Twentieth Century

Illustration 10.8: Four leaves from Walter Alcock's 'Marche Triomphale' performed at the 1913 wedding of the Duke of Connaught; as reproduced in *Graphic*, 18 October 1913, p. 722.
© The Graphic/Mary Evans Picture Library.

of pompous wedding music on the organ'.[111] At least this correspondent was obviously impressed by the choice of the music and with its performance, even though the particular wording also seems to indicate some criticism.

Service and Music

For the service itself, the *Manchester Guardian* reported that it was 'shortened in certain places'.[112] Similarly, the *Scotsman* noted that 'on this occasion the changes which had been made were in the direction of abbreviation', explaining:

> The form of service had been printed in a shortened form, and Canon Sheppard, who read the opening injunctions, made it shorter still by omitting those passages which, in the Prayer book, specify with needless explicitness the purposes for which matrimony was ordained.[113]

This might refer to the same 'objectionable passages & prayers' to which Queen Victoria had referred in 1889.[114] Overall, this appears to be the earliest wedding at which the printed order of service was more tailored to the specific event. This went so far that it now incorporated details of the music in its liturgical place within the order of service. For the psalm, it now gave only the text of Ps. 67, not of both psalms as previously, and for this it indicates 'W. G. Al cock' [*sic*].[115] Like the list of music in the printed ceremonial the reports also referred without further details merely to 'a chant by W.G. Alcock'; but the *Times* beforehand had detailed that 'there will be a chant in E major by Dr. Alcock'.[116] For the following Responses and prayers the order of service states that the subdean 'shall say' them, but after the last of the prayers it stipulates that there 'shall be sung the following Anthem by the "Children" of His Majesty's Chapel Royal', giving the full text of Mendelssohn's 'Lift thine Eyes' from *Elijah*, as in 1904. The correspondent of the *Scotsman* thought that Mendelssohn's anthem 'From the æsthetic point of view' was 'the most impressive part of the ceremony' and explained:

> It was sung without organ accompaniment by the children of the Chapel Royal, and the blending cadences of the flute-like treble and alto voices of the boys, singing as they did with consummate ease and confidence, produced an exquisite effect.[117]

Similarly, the *Times* correspondent noted that Mendelssohn's anthem 'was beautifully sung unaccompanied by the children of the Chapel Royal'.[118] This *a cappella* singing incidentally seems to match with the overall emphasis on simplicity.

Regarding its position in the ceremony, the reports referred to Mendelssohn's anthem as coming 'at the conclusion of the service, but before the address'.[119] This address, given by the Archbishop, was again reproduced in some of the reports, with that in the *Scotsman* astutely highlighting that the 'Primate's brief address' had been 'substituted for the homily in the regular

---

[111] 'Royal Wedding: Brilliant Scene', *Manchester Guardian*.

[112] 'Royal Wedding: Brilliant Scene' *Manchester Guardian*.

[113] 'Royal Wedding: Brilliant Scene', *Scotsman*.

[114] See Chapter 9, fn. 10 and the transcription in Appendix B 9.1.

[115] OS 1913.

[116] Ceremonial 1913, p. 5; 'Royal Wedding: The Ceremony in the Chapel Royal'.

[117] 'Royal Wedding: Brilliant Scene', *Scotsman*.

[118] 'Royal Wedding: Scene', p. 10.

[119] For instance, 'Royal Wedding: The Ceremony in the Chapel Royal'; and 'The Royal Wedding: Programme of the Music', *Manchester Guardian*, 3 October 1913, p. 7.

10—The Last 'of the Old Age': The Early Twentieth Century

form of service.'[120] This 'homily' must refer to the text, often called the 'exhortation', that is scheduled in the Prayer Book to be read at the end of the service. After this 'brief address' came what some papers announced as 'the hymn "O perfect love," to a special setting by Lady Arthur Hill'.[121] This was, of course, not a hymn, and not specially written either, but Hill's setting already heard at the 1896 wedding, where it had accompanied the bridegroom's procession. The order of service referred to it clearly as 'ANTHEM'. Thus, overall, this wedding featured two anthems, by Mendelssohn and Hill, framing the address, while there was in return no second hymn. The *Scotsman* emphasized that the second verse in Hill's anthem was 'a solo for a boy's voice', and reports of the music for the forthcoming wedding had referred to 'Master Butler taking the solo'.[122] The performance of this anthem overall appears to have left a special impression and the correspondent of the *Manchester Guardian*, obviously confusing the composer, recorded that

> one of the 'children' was heard alone singing Mendelssohn's setting of 'O, Perfect Love.' This singing was curiously beautiful in its flute-like quality of piercing sweetness.[123]

The *Times* correspondent counted the performance of this anthem among 'one or two memories that stand out above the rest':

> And there is the sound of the unseen boy's voice, triumphantly singing to Lady Arthur Hill's beautiful music one of the verses of the hymn that ended the service [giving the full text of the second verse, beginning 'O perfect Life']. The memory of that verse of faith and hope and trust, of the pure, spiritual, impersonal uplifting of a child's voice, seems a fitting conclusion to the ceremony of a marriage of hearts in which, as the Archbishop said in his address, the whole land rejoices.[124]

Hill's anthem was followed by the benediction, or final blessing, and then the recess to the usual Wedding March by Mendelssohn, played by Alcock on the organ.[125]

As already mentioned, the choir was placed in the gallery and some reports emphasized that 'No other musical instrument will be used to reinforce the organ for the musical service.'[126] While this was *de facto* the same as at the weddings in the previous decades, it could not have been one of the factors contributing to the aforementioned impression of simplicity. When the *Times* summarized for the ceremony that 'the note of simplicity was particularly marked', it referred especially to the music:

> The music, the singing, the decorations were far less elaborate, and the proceedings distinctly less conversational and more reverent than is often the case at what are called fashionable weddings. The whole treatment of the occasion was quiet and restrained, and its very quietness greatly added to its impressive effect.[127]

---

[120] 'Royal Wedding: Scene', p. 10; and 'Royal Wedding: Brilliant Scene', *Scotsman*. Both reports include the full text of the address.

[121] 'Royal Wedding: The Ceremony in the Chapel Royal'. Same in 'The Royal Wedding: Programme of the Music', *Manchester Guardian*; and 'Musical Side of the Wedding'.

[122] 'Royal Wedding: Brilliant Scene', *Scotsman*; 'Royal Wedding: Final Arrangements', *Manchester Guardian*; 'Royal Wedding: Musical and other Arrangements', *Scotsman*.

[123] 'Royal Wedding: Brilliant Scene', *Manchester Guardian*. This is the description of the piece before the address. Yet, the title is wrong for the Mendelssohn piece that came in this place and which in fact has no solo; therefore, the description must obviously refer to Hill's piece after the address, which has the given title and also a solo.

[124] 'Royal Wedding: Scene', p. 10.

[125] OS 1913; Ceremonial 1913, p. 5; 'Royal Wedding: Scene', p. 10; 'Royal Wedding: Brilliant Scene', *Scotsman*.

[126] 'Royal Wedding: Final Arrangements', *Manchester Guardian*. Same in 'Royal Wedding: Musical and other Arrangements', *Scotsman*.

[127] 'Royal Wedding: Scene', p. 10.

British Royal Weddings

Prince George Louis of Battenberg (later George Mountbatten, 2nd Marquess of Milford Haven) and Countess Nadejda Mikhailovna de Torby, 15 November 1916

Right in the middle of the First World War there occurred another notable royal wedding, even though of quite a minor member of the royal family: that of Prince George Louis of Battenberg, the son of Prince Louis of Battenberg and of Queen Victoria's granddaughter Victoria of Hesse and by Rhine (and thus the uncle of the later-born Prince Philip, Duke of Edinburgh). With the renaming of the British royal family in 1917, the bridegroom's family also changed its name and titles: the family name became 'Mountbatten' – a literal translation of the German 'Battenberg' – for his branch of the family combined with the title Marquess of Milford Haven.

On 15 November 1916, Prince George Louis married Countess Nadejda Mikhailovna de Torby, daughter of Grand Duke Michael Mikhailovich Romanov, and great-granddaughter of Nicholas I of Russia. As in 1874, there were two ceremonies, but this time both in London:

> At eleven o'clock the Prince and Countess were married in the Russian Chapel attached to the Russian Embassy in Welbeck-street, according to the rites of the Greek [that is 'Orthodox'] Church. Afterwards the marriage service according to the English Church was celebrated in the Chapel Royal, St. James's Palace.[128]

This was the first time since the Reformation that a member of the royal family, in Britain, so prominently married in a non-Anglican ceremony. The *Scotsman* emphasized that the Russian ceremony was 'attended principally by members of the two families and distinguished representatives of the Russian colony in London', highlighting that the 'only member of the British Royal Family present' was 'Princess Henry of Battenberg [that is, Princess Beatrice], the widow of the bridegroom's uncle'.[129] It also reported that the service 'at the little chapel was conducted with all the solemnity and picturesqueness which mark these ceremonies in the Orthodox Greek Church.' Regarding the music, this account noted merely that 'Three times the procession moved round the altar to the slow chanting of the priests'. The *Times* recorded that 'The choral service was sung by a choir of members of the Imperial Theological Musical Academy at Petrograd.'[130] This choir seems to have travelled to London especially for this ceremony, which was presumably not an easy enterprise in war-time, thus perhaps highlighting the importance bestowed on the liturgy and even such a musical detail.

Immediately after the Orthodox ceremony, 'the whole party motored to the Chapel-Royal, St James's Palace, for the English ceremony'.[131] The official wording, in the correspondence of those involved in organizing the even, was that 'The King has lent the Chapel Royal, St James's Palace to His Imperial Highness The Grand Duke Michael of Russia for the marriage of his daughter'.[132] In the end, the ceremony saw notable royal participation, and there were present 'the King and Queen and all the available members of the Royal Family'.[133]

---

[128] 'Royal Wedding: Picturesque Ceremony in London To-day', *The Star*, 15 November 1916, p. [4]. Similar in 'Countess Nada Torby's Wedding', *Times*, 16 November 1916, p. 11.

[129] This and the following 'Royal Wedding in London: Prince George of Battenberg – Countess Nada', *Scotsman*, 16 November 1916, p. 4.

[130] 'Countess Nada Torby's Wedding'.

[131] 'Royal Wedding in London'.

[132] Douglas Dawson to The Secretary, H.M. Office of Works, 26 October 1916 (typewritten), in *Lna WORK 19/385*.

[133] 'Royal Wedding in London'.

10—The Last 'of the Old Age': The Early Twentieth Century

Overall, one paper summarized that the Anglican service at the Chapel Royal 'was in striking contrast to the elaborate ceremonial at the Russian Chapel, though its simplicity was none the less impressive'.[134] The *Scotsman* recorded that the Archbishop of Canterbury headed the procession of the clergy but also that the ceremony was performed 'by Canon Edgar Sheppard', subdean of the Chapel Royal and domestic chaplain to the king.[135] Indeed, according to the *Times*, 'There were but two clergy': Sheppard and F. J. Horan, the 'Guards' Chaplain at Windsor, who had prepared the bridegroom for his confirmation'.[136] Furthermore the paper detailed:

> The service was the abbreviated form of the Marriage Service now frequently used, and the music was sung by the small but exquisite choir of the Chapel Royal, which is worthy of its long history. Everything was simple, intimate, and attractive.

It appears that there were no ceremonial processions through the palace. In the Chapel, Alcock played 'several nuptial pieces' before the ceremony started, 'while the Congregation is assembling'.[137] The *Times* recorded that Alcock 'played Bach and Parry, Tchaikovsky and Guilmant on the organ', which matches with the order of service listing 'St. Ann Fugue' by Bach, 'Entr'acte and Bridal March' by Parry, 'Nocturne in C sharp minor' and 'Chant sans paroles' by Tschaikowsky, and the 'Marche Nuptiale' by Guilmant.[138] There is no other information on the music that accompanied the entrance processions, but this music may have been included in the given list of organ pieces.

The bride's procession again entered to the singing of a hymn, this time 'O Perfect Love' (three verses and Amen).[139] However, these well-known words were now sung in a truly noteworthy, very topical way: 'to the tune we know as the Russian National Anthem', as the *Times* recorded.[140] The correspondent of *The Star* specified that it had been Alcock who 'had happily set the procession hymn, "O Perfect Love," to the tune of the Russian National Anthem'.[141] This is one of the very rare examples at royal weddings that a bride's heritage is acknowledged so clearly in the music of the ceremony; and in this particular instance the choice could have been stimulated by the war-context, as a musical acknowledgement of the Russian allies.

The hymn was most probably sung by the choir only, who the accounts indicate did again not walk in the procession. As seen above, the *Scotsman* reported that the choir had entered earlier, and the *Times* detailed that the bride's procession

> was met at the west door by the clergy; and as it passed up the chapel, the choir (which for this occasion had been placed in the organ-loft over the west door) sang the hymn.[142]

The 'organ-loft' in the Chapel Royal is indeed in the western wall, although not exactly 'over the west door', which is nearer the altar. Entering by this door, however, would not have left much way for a procession, which would certainly not have 'passed up the chapel'. Therefore it seems possible that the report in fact refers to the 'liturgical West', and to the main entrance of the Chapel Royal which is actually more towards the South-East (compare Illustration 3.1, p. 49).

---

[134] 'Royal Wedding: Picturesque Ceremony'.

[135] 'Royal Wedding in London'.

[136] This and the following 'Countess Nada Torby's Wedding'.

[137] 'Royal Wedding: Picturesque Ceremony'; OS 1916, p. 3.

[138] 'Countess Nada Torby's Wedding'; OS 1916, p. 3.

[139] OS 1916, p. 5.

[140] 'Countess Nada Torby's Wedding'.

[141] 'Royal Wedding: Picturesque Ceremony'.

[142] 'Countess Nada Torby's Wedding'.

The 'organ-loft' where the choir was placed would then have been the Royal Closet, the gallery right above the main entrance.

For the service proper, the order of service this time stipulated Ps. 128, but without giving any details on the chant, and for the following Responses it indicated that the priest 'shall say' these.[143] It may be only assumed that the psam was eventually sung to some chant. After the prayers and before the benediction came the hymn 'May the Grace of Christ our Saviour', with its pertinent text. The order of service stipulated that it was '*To be sung kneeling*', probably again by the choir only.[144] No other details of the hymn are known, but it could have been sung to the tune 'Sardis', with music from Beethoven, with which it is most commonly associated.

The 'Anthem' was 'For He Shall Give his Angels Charge over Thee' from Mendelssohn's *Elijah* and the order of service distinctly specified it '*To be sung after the Service*'.[145] Accordingly, the reports noted that it was sung 'After the Benediction', or 'At the close of the service'.[146] As in 1913, the anthem thus came in lieu of a second, final hymn. With Mendelssohn anthems at both the 1904 and 1913 wedding, the choice of his music at weddings was apparently popular. In a concise musical sequence, Mendelssohn's anthem was followed by his Wedding March accompanying the recess, played on the organ.[147] However, as will be discussed in the next chapter, in the overall war-context, the inclusion of Mendelssohn's music, especially his well-known march, for weddings in general – and for such a high-profile one in particular – may have been a somewhat contentious choice.

Prince Alexander of Battenberg (later Alexander Mountbatten, 1st Marquess of Carisbrooke) and Lady Irene Denison, 19 July 1917

There was one more royal wedding before the end of the War. On 19 July 1917, Prince Alexander of Battenberg, married Lady Irene Denison, daughter of the 2nd Earl of Londesborough, at the Chapel Royal in St James's Palace. Prince Alexander was a cousin-once-removed of Prince George Louis of Battenberg who had married in the previous year: he was the son of Princess Beatrice, and thus a grandson of Queen Victoria and a first cousin of George V. Yet, this 1917 wedding was even more obviously a simple war-time wedding than that in the previous year had been. With reference to the colour of the soldiers' field uniform, David Duff has pointed out that at this 'khaki wedding […] there were no bridesmaids or formal reception', and Heather Jones has furthermore emphasized that the king did not grant any exceptions for the ceremony and that the prince's brother Prince Leopold 'was refused special leave to be best man at the wedding'.[148] Indeed, this wedding was overall very much subdued: it was not announced or mentioned in the *London Gazette*, and there appear not to have been any notable reports about

---

[143] OS 1916, pp. 10–12.

[144] OS 1916, p. 14.

[145] OS 1916, p. 15.

[146] 'Countess Nada Torby's Wedding'; and 'Royal Wedding in London'.

[147] OS 1916, p. 15; 'Royal Wedding in London'; 'Countess Nada Torby's Wedding'.

[148] David Duff, *The Shy Princess: The Life of Her Royal Highness Princess Beatrice, the Youngest Daughter and Constant Companion of Queen Victoria* (London: Evans Brothers Ltd, 1958), p. 241; Heather Jones, *For King and Country: The British Monarchy and the First World War* (Cambridge: Cambridge University Press, 2021), p. 345. Both Duff and Jones refer to M. E. [Muriel Ellen] Sara, *The Life and Times of H.R.H. Princess Beatrice* (London: Stanley Paul & Co., 1945), p. 133.

10—The Last 'of the Old Age': The Early Twentieth Century

the ceremony in other papers and magazines. All the same, it was still a wedding in the Chapel Royal, not in a drawing room, like those royal weddings a century earlier. Furthermore, Muriel Ellen Sara recorded that

> Though it was a quiet wedding there was quite a large gathering of friends and relations, and the khaki and navy of the uniforms worn by the men provided a background for the brighter colours of the women's dresses, gay and beautiful despite the war.[149]

It is not clear whether 'quiet' referred merely to the overall subdued atmosphere or also to a lack of music at the ceremony.

In this context, it is worth noting that the wedding occurred only a couple of days after George V had changed the name of the royal house from 'Saxe-Coburg and Gotha' to 'Windsor'.[150] This had come as the result of strong criticism of the royal family's German origins and family relations. In this overall atmosphere of scrutiny – and especially considering the bridegroom's distinctly German title – it was perhaps considered expedient to keep this royal wedding 'quiet', rather out of the lime-light and not to have too much of ceremonial. As Sara observed, 'the announcement of the changes in the names and designations of those members of the Royal Family who bore titles of German origin' had already been made in June: however, the official announcement that Prince Alexander, like the other members of his family, had changed his name to 'Mountbatten' came only a few months after the wedding.[151]

⸻✦⸻

Apart from fairly minor changes, from a ceremonial point of view the Edwardian royal weddings and the first one in the reign of George V had very much continued the scheme and traditions established during the Victorian era. The pronounced differentiation of royal wedding ceremonies reportedly intended by Edward VII was never to be fully played out. However, the two war-time weddings of 1916 and 1917 altogether followed very different parameters, and especially the latter one was apparently characterized by austere simplicity. Therefore, as already mentioned, in the wider historical context, the description of the wedding of the Duke of Connaught in 1913 as the 'last royal wedding of the old age' is quite apt.[152] After the War, the character and scope of royal weddings, like so much else, was again to change considerably.

---

[149] Sara, *Life and Times of H.R.H. Princess Beatrice*, p. 133. There is no order of service for this wedding in the Royal Archives (where such an item would have ended up). For this information I am very grateful to Laura Hobbs, one of the archivists.

[150] The official proclamation was published in the *London Gazette* of 17 July 1917, title page (p. 7119).

[151] See the official announcement in the *London Gazette* of 9 November 1917, p. 11593.

[152] See fn. 1, above.

11

The 'Pomp of Old Days':
Three Centuries of Royal Weddings

O N THE OCCASION OF THE WEDDING of Prince Leopold in 1882, the *Scotsman* had concluded that 'Like history, the pomp of old days repeats itself at a Royal marriage'.[1] As seen in the preceding chapters, this 'pomp' was absent from royal weddings for some periods, notably in the later seventeenth and in the early nineteenth century. Yet, at the weddings where this 'pomp' was present, it was music that constituted a significant part of it. In 1889, the London correspondent of the American periodical *The Musical Visitor* concluded: 'Royal "wedding music" is a subject upon which much might be written.'[2] Indeed, as seen in the preceding chapters, the music at the British royal weddings from the Stuarts up to the early twentieth century presents a rich, wide, and interesting field for research and discussion. In combination with the other two main points of this study – the venue and the ceremonial – such a discussion helps obtain a much more wholesome and lively impression of what these events were like, how exactly they featured the 'pomp of old days'.

The royal family, and royal ceremonies in particular, generally live through and by a long chronological span. Continuity is their lifeblood. This final chapter looks decidedly again at the three main aspects of the venue, ceremonial, and music at royal weddings – now focusing on the broader developments that occurred over the period under discussion.

The Venue

In the early seventeenth and then again through the eighteenth century, there does not appear to have been any notable discussion about the choice of venue for royal weddings. The grander such ceremonies simply took place in the royal chapel that was at the time the most prominent one – first that at Whitehall Palace and then that at St James's Palace, with the singular exception of the French/Queen's Chapel for the 1734 wedding. It is interesting that in the later seventeenth century and then again in the later Georgian era, the issue of royal weddings taking place rather secretly in bed chambers or in drawings rooms was seemingly not commented on: there was no pronounced criticism of the fact that these weddings did not take place in a consecrated building, let alone in a more pubic space. However, beginning with the weddings of Queen Victoria and her eldest daughter Princess Victoria, in 1840 and 1858 respectively, the choice of the venue at royal weddings became a topic that was clearly and distinctly noted. Many writers pronounced regret that the ceremonies were to be in the Chapel Royal, and not in a more public space such as Westminster Abbey; and it was especially from 1863 onwards, when papers heavily criticized the move to Windsor, that the venue of royal weddings was more

---

[1] 'The Royal Marriage', *Scotsman*, 28 April 1882, p. 5.

[2] 'Royal Wedding Music', *The Musical Visitor: A Magazine of Musical Literature and Music*, 18:9 (September 1889), p. 227.

prominently discussed in public.[3] The move of royal weddings to Windsor and the ensuing overall more removed and perhaps more recluse character of these occasions was a sore point that met with continued public disapproval. For the wedding of Princess Louise in 1871, one commentator expressed strong regret:

> But the marriage is to be *private*. We like not this prevailing fashion of privacy touching great public events; royal weddings are not of every day occurrence, and they hold their proper place and significance.[4]

In 1879, after the wedding of Prince Arthur, the popular and widely circulating *Lloyd's Weekly Newspaper* launched a very pronounced critique of the choice of venue, which in its wholesome approach may be representative of the relevant issues and deserves a closer discussion.[5] With a sour undertone it proclaimed that 'The distance at which people are kept from all festivities, or events, which closely concern the Royal Family, still leaves them a loyal people.' Noting that the wedding had been 'a gorgeous pageant, conducted at Windsor, in the presence of a very select few', the paper pointed out that it had been 'an imposing ceremonial away from London, and even away from the town of Windsor', as it took place behind the castle walls:

> If we were a touchy, irritable people like our neighbours, we should have chafed at the sullen exclusiveness of the pageant; and its withdrawal from London, where half a million of people might have witnessed the procession, to the Royal borough, where the little mob which was admitted at the last moment to the castle yard, just enabled the Court chronicler to affirm that the public was not altogether shut out.

The perceived active exclusion of the London public was interpreted as arrogance and the author asked: 'Whether it is wise in the personages who control and direct royal marriages and other state ceremonials, to treat the "groundlings" from so chilly a height remains to be seen.' In order to substantiate the critique somewhat more, the expenditure for the wedding was compared with those 'shivering' and 'starving' in the Winter, noting that the £20,000 to prepare the ship *Osborne* for the honeymoon trip was 'a monstrous bit of extravagance, in these hard times' – although it is not explained how a grand public spectacle in London would have been any cheaper, or would have clothed and fed the poor. The article concluded rather aggressively that 'Under a military despotism there could not have been a more rigid exclusion of the popular element, than there was at St. George's chapel on Thursday morning.' Overall, the implication is that, had the public element been stronger – had the wedding been an elaborate public affair in London – then all other criticism would not have been mentioned.

Such points of criticism were apparently addressed with the slightly more public character of the next royal wedding at Windsor, that of Prince Leopold in 1882. The carriage procession in Windsor at the 1879 wedding had been very limited. As the printed ceremonial recorded:

> The Route of the Carriage Processions was through George the Fourth's Gate, down the Castle Hill, and through Henry the Eighth's Gate, and the Carriage Processions returned to the Castle by the same route.[6]

In 1882, the carriage processions again went outside the castle walls only briefly, with the *Scotsman* reporting that 'thus for about a hundred yards the mass of the people, estimated at from

---

[3] See Chapters 6 and 7 above.

[4] 'Royal Wedding Music', *The Orchestra*, 388 (3 March 1871), pp. 361–62, here p. 362 (emphasis original).

[5] This and the following 'The Royal Wedding', *Lloyd's Weekly Newspaper*, 23 March 1879, p. 6.

[7] This and the following 'The Royal Marriage: Another Account', *Scotsman*, 28 April 1882, p. 5.

[6] Ceremonial 1879, p. 20.

11—The 'Pomp of Old Days': Three Centuries of Royal Weddings

fifteen to twenty thousand in number, were able to see them'.[7] There was, however, another concession to the interest of the public in the event, reportedly instigated by Queen Victoria herself. The same article in the *Scotsman* furthermore pointed out that

> Other persons were more favoured: they had tickets which admitted them to the upper and lower wards of the Castle. […] On former occasions of the kind only a small number of spectators had been allowed into the lower ward, and it was by special command of the Queen that this place was thrown open.

Moreover, one anonymous writer under the pseudonym the 'Scrutator' reported of another intriguing detail regarding the participation of the public at this wedding, observing about those seated in the nave:

> The company was a mixed one, including […] an exceedingly select number of the aboriginal inhabitants of Windsor, who, I heard, were indebted for their tickets to the good of the omnipotent John Brown.[8]

Such close presence, and thus participation of the local population is not reported for any other royal wedding; and it might be worth further investigation to establish how, and indeed why, Queen Victoria's favourite John Brown would have obtained tickets in the nave for them.

From 1889 onwards, when royal weddings returned to London – with the weddings of the Prince of Wales's children – public criticism of the occasional choice of Windsor seems to have stopped. As seen in the previous chapter, once Edward VII had become king, he reportedly intended a clear differentiation of royal weddings according to rank within the royal family.[9] This should also have affected their venue: the 1904 wedding of his niece Princess Alice should originally have taken place in the Private Chapel at Buckingham Palace, and it was only because of the princess's personal wish that it took place at St George's Chapel, Windsor. In the following year, the wedding of another royal niece, Princess Margaret of Connaught, to Prince Gustaf Adolf of Sweden and Norway, also took place at Windsor. This time the reason for this choice does not seem to be known. The *Times* correspondent judged that this royal wedding had been 'the most joyous day of its kind that Windsor has seen during the present generation', explaining that 'the people flocked down to Windsor in their thousands'.[10] Thus, there was clearly a desire of the public to witness these events in person. Little could the correspondent know that this would be the last more notable royal wedding in Windsor for several decades: the return to London was continued early in the reign of George V with the wedding of the Prince Arthur of Connaught at the Chapel Royal in 1913, followed by the much-limited wartime weddings of Prince George Louis of Battenberg in 1916 and Prince Alexander of Battenberg in 1917. These were rather straightforward ceremonies at the Chapel Royal, thus confirming to Edward VII's reported directive.

Even though the Chapel Royal in comparison to St George's at Windsor was a much smaller venue, it is yet significant that at least some weddings from 1889 onwards returned to the metropolis. All the same, the celebration of royal weddings on a grand public scale emerged only in 1919 when Westminster Abbey became the preferred venue for most royal weddings up to the end of the century.[11]

---

[7] This and the following 'The Royal Marriage: Another Account', *Scotsman*, 28 April 1882, p. 5.

[8] Scrutator', 'At the Wedding', *Truth*, 11:279 (May 1882), pp. 612–13, here p. 612.

[9] For this and the following also see the previous Chapter, with fns 2–5.

[10] 'The Royal Marriage', *Times*, 16 June 1905, p. 6.

[11] For the weddings from 1919 onwards see the author's *British Royal Weddings: The House of Windsor* (Turnhout: Brepols, forthcoming).

Ceremonial

A 'Common' Service

British royalty, especially up to Edwardian times, was undoubtedly very remote from anything 'common'. All the same, the appearance to have at least something 'in common' with the rest of the population, resulting in people being able to identify a bit better with the monarchy and in this way increasing support as a whole, was imminently important. Royal weddings offered themselves very much as a good opportunity to refer to the aspect of commonality and thus identification: the rite followed the same basic order of service as for most other people – which since the Reformation had been the order prescribed in the Book of Common Prayer, which stresses the aspect of commonality in its very title. When Anglicans were the overwhelming majority of the population, the reference to a 'common' service, for king and peasant alike, could be a strong point of identification. As Jonathan Parry summarized with particular reference to the 1858 and 1871 weddings, royal wedding ceremonies 'can easily appear inclusive and representative'.[12] The notion of a 'common' ceremony was consistently pointed out throughout the centuries and is worth a more detailed discussion, touching on various aspects – on various points of 'commonness'.

The Legal Aspect

The recurring emphasis on strict adherence to the Prayer Book service at royal weddings may partly have been due to the legal implications. As Lord Hervey pointed out in relation to the proxy-wedding of Princess Mary in 1740, in accordance with the Act of Succession (1533/4) all marriages in the royal family had to be administered according to the form of the Church of England, and the Act of Uniformity (1558) referred for this form to the service of matrimony prescribed in the Book of Common Prayer.[13]

One of the earliest references emphasizing accordance with the prescribed official liturgy seems to date from the 1613 wedding of Princess Elizabeth. The account in the Chapel Royal Cheque Book noted that the Archbishop of Canterbury performed the marriage, 'in all point*es* accordinge to the booke of o^r Comon prayer', emphasizing that the foreign bridegroom spoke 'the word*es* of marriage in Englishe after y^e ArchBisshopp'.[14] While this was probably primarily a short-hand for the lengthy Prayer Book text of the wedding vows, which the Chapel Royal personal did not need to record, the wording of this entry is noteworthy. The use of the little word 'o^r' (= 'our') is particularly remarkable as it highlights the English aspect at this wedding as much as a more general equality in religion. Similarly, for the wedding of Princess Mary to Prince William of Orange in 1641, John Finet pointed out that the Dean of the Chapel Royal was 'officiating in word and forme in all points as in the Book of Common Prayer'.[15] There do

---

[12] Jonathan Parry, 'Whig Monarchy, Whig Nation: Crown, Politics and Representativeness 1800–2000', *The Monarchy and the British Nation, 1780 to the Present*, ed. by Andrzej Olechnowicz (Cambridge: Cambridge University Press, 2007), pp. 47–75, here p. 72.

[13] John Hervey (2nd Baron Hervey), *Some Materials towards Memoirs of the Reign of King George II*, ed. by Romney Sedgwick, 3 vols, continuously paginated (London: Eyre and Spottiswoode, 1931; repr. New York: AMS Press, 1970), III, p. 931 (from his entry for 5 May 1740, pp. 929–32).

[14] For this account see Andrew Ashbee and John Harley (eds), *The Cheque Books of the Chapel Royal*, 2 vols (Aldershot: Ashgate, 2000), I, pp. 172–75, here p. 174.

[15] John Finet, *Ceremonies of Charles I: The Notebooks of John Finet, 1628–1641*, ed. by Albert J. Loomie (New York: Fordham University Press, 1987), p. 310.

11—The 'Pomp of Old Days': Three Centuries of Royal Weddings

not appear to have been any such distinct references to this for the following weddings, up to Hervey's comments in 1740. In 1761, Stephen Martin Leake, Garter King of Arms, noted rather dryly that the 'Ceremony of the Marriage' of George III 'was according to the Rubrik', that is following the Prayer Book.[16] For this and the weddings of the next eight decades accounts and comments contented with plainly mentioning that the ceremonies followed the Prayer Book.

The emphasis on following the official ritual appears to have become much more prominent in the reign of Queen Victoria. For the queen's own wedding in 1840, various accounts included statements such as 'The rubric was rigidly adhered to throughout.'[17] Indeed, similar to the 1613 Cheque Book entry, some accounts alluded to the commonness, or similarity, of royalty with others in this respect, with at least one commentator observing that 'The ceremony was precisely that of our liturgy', again using the potent possessive pronoun 'our'.[18] Another report noted that the ceremony 'differed in nothing, except the exalted rank of the principal personages, from that used at the marriage of any of her majesty's subjects', and the writer further stressed the Anglican character of the wedding: 'The form as prescribed by the ritual of the church of England was strictly observed in all particulars.'[19] Similar comments were in abundance at the weddings of Queen Victoria's children and grandchildren.

At the first, the wedding of her daughter Victoria in 1858, reports again emphasized that 'The Rubric is rigidly adhered to throughout'.[20] At the wedding of her eventual successor, the Prince of Wales in 1863, it was noted that 'the primate commenced the service with the usual formulary', and William Howard Russel highlighted the fact that the service 'was in no respect changed'.[21] The *London Journal* explained with elaborate wording:

> Except in the presence of the Archbishop of Canterbury, and his assistant, the Bishop of Gloucester, the adjunct of music, under the direction of Dr. Elvey, and the glittering assemblage of royalty, beauty, rank, the *élite* of the nation, the nuptials of Albert Edward Prince of Wales with Alexandra Princess of Denmark differed in no essential degree from that performed over the humblest pair that ever presented themselves at the church's altar.[22]

In 1871, after the wedding of Princess Louise, the same journal made the aspect of commonality of the wedding rite particularly clear:

> We need not describe the marriage ceremony itself. It was the time-honoured and sacred rite of the Church of England, prescribed for all classes, noble, and plebeian, gentle and simple.[23]

---

[16] *Lca S.M.L. 45* ('Heraldic Annals', vol. 2), p. 132.

[17] 'Marriage of Victoria the First […] with Prince Albert […]', *MLAI*, 35:992, Supplementary Number ([1840]), pp. 113–22, here p. 118. The same in the report in *The Wedding Observer*: special edition of *The Observer* of 16 and 17 February 1840 (extract in *Lna WORK 21/19*).

[18] 'The Queen's Marriage', *Examiner*, 16 February 1840, p. 105.

[19] 'Marriage of Her Majesty with Prince Albert of Saxe Coburg and Gotha, on Monday', *Niles' National Register*, 5th series, vol. 8, no. 3 (21 March 1840), pp. 1 and 34–37, here pp. 36 and 37.

[20] 'The Marriage of The Princess Royal', *Times*, 26 January 1858, pp. 7–9, here p. 7. Same in 'The Ceremony and Dresses at the Royal Nuptials', *The London Journal, and Weekly Record of Literature, Science, and Art*, 6 March 1858, pp. 5–6, here p. 6.

[21] 'The Marriage Ceremony', *Lloyd's Weekly London Newspaper*, 15 March 1863, pp. 4–5, here p. 5; W. H. Russell, *A Memorial of the Marriage of HRH Albert Edward Prince of Wales and HRH Alexandra Princess of Denmark […]* (London: Day and Son, 1863), p. 3.

[22] 'The Royal Wedding', *The London Journal, and Weekly Record of Literature, Science, and Art*, 14 March 1863, pp. 167–68, here p. 167.

[23] 'The Royal Marriage', *The London Journal, and Weekly Record of Literature, Science, and Art*, 15 April 1871, pp. 236–38, here p. 238.

Thus, as this example shows, the reference to the adherence to the Prayer Book at royal weddings was on the one hand a mere short-cut for recording these events, but on the other hand it also served to put a strong emphasis on the attractive aspect of commonality.

For the wedding of the Prince of Wales's daughter, Princess Louise in 1889, the two reports in the *Observer* both referred to 'the marriage ceremony in the usual form' and they explained that the Prayer Book service had 'nothing added or taken from it' – notwithstanding that this observation would clearly contradict Queen Victoria's decided request that some 'objectionable passages & prayers' in the service be omitted, with which she referred also to the three previous weddings.[24] Two years after that, at the wedding of Princess Marie Louise of Schleswig-Holstein (daughter of Princess Helena), the correspondent of the *Times of India* referred similarly to 'the marriage-service, throughout which the time-honoured directions of the book of Common Prayer were closely adhered to'.[25] Then, in 1893, for the wedding of the future George V, the *Illustrated London News* summarized that the Archbishop of Canterbury 'read the usual form appointed by the Church of England for the solemnisation of matrimony'.[26] The *Scotsman* referred meaningfully to 'the service, which was conducted in the usual and prescribed form familiar to everybody'.[27] Indeed, it noted specifically that the words 'man' and 'woman' may have sounded 'rather oddly' in this royal context, but it emphasized that there had been 'no special variation in the ordinary terms of the service'.

Coinciding with the emphasis on following the Prayer Book, the production of special orders of service from 1797 and then especially 1858 onwards both slightly defeated but also re-affirmed the notion that this was the same ceremony as for everybody else. On the one hand, one could, like everybody else, simply have used normal copies of the Prayer Book, as had indeed been done at earlier weddings – but on the other hand, apart from the singular surviving 1797 example, these specially produced orders, lavish as they were, in essence were mere literal extracts from the Prayer Book, with their texts not altered or personalized in any way until 1904.

Simplicity

In relation to the common service from the Prayer Book and to cross-societal equality in this respect, there was another potent term that has often been used to describe the ceremony of royal weddings from the nineteenth century onwards: 'simplicity'. In 1897, Sarah Tytler referred back to the wedding of Queen Victoria as 'the beautiful simple service of the Church of England, unchanged in any respect'.[28] Indeed, the wedding of Queen Victoria appears to have been the watershed regarding the use of this tone of description. The queen herself noted in her journal:

> The Ceremony was very impressive & fine, yet simple, & I think ought to make an imperishable impression, on every one who promises at the altar to keep the vows he or she have made.[29]

---

[24] 'The Royal Wedding at Buckingham Palace', *Observer*, 28 July 1889, p. 5 [two separate accounts, the second with the sub-heading 'Arrival at the Palace'], here from both accounts. For Queen Victoria's request see Chapter 9, fn. 12 and the transcription in Appendix B 9.1.

[25] 'The Royal Wedding', *Times of India*, 28 July 1891, p. 6.

[26] 'The Royal Wedding', *ILN*, 15 July 1893, pp. 70–71, here p. 70.

[27] 'The Royal Wedding', *Scotsman*, 7 July 1893, p. 5.

[28] Sarah Tytler, *Life of Her Most Gracious Majesty the Queen*, ed. and with an introduction by Lord Ronald Gower, 3 vols (London: J. S. Virtue & Co., [1897?]), I, p. 121.

[29] *QVJ*, 10 February 1840 (the original has 'have have made' at the end).

11—The 'Pomp of Old Days': Three Centuries of Royal Weddings

The same sentiment was expressed in published reports, and one noted that 'The whole of the impressive ceremony was conducted with the utmost dignity and simplicity.'[30] By contrast, in 1858, the *Times* noted that the wedding of the Princess Royal was 'celebrated […] with all the splendour of modern state ceremonial'.[31] Yet, such wording seems to have been the exception. For the popular 1866 Kew wedding of Princess Mary Adelaide of Cambridge, the *Morning Post* stressed that the ceremony 'was as simple and unostentatious as that of any other subject of the Crown'.[32] In fact, a perceived lack of 'simplicity' at a royal wedding may at least for some have been a cause of criticism. After the 1879 wedding of the Duke of Connaught, one correspondent in the *Times* observed:

> The august ceremonial appointed for yesterday duly ran its course with the full pomp prefigured in the official programme. All was bright and lustrous, from the heralds that led the procession to the March sunshine which anticipated July. If there was anything wanting, it was not magnificence, but simplicity.[33]

All the same, this writer interpreted the need to display magnificence, and having to forego 'simplicity', as 'a penalty royalty pays for its height above the crowd'. This was surely a strong idea. In her 1945 biography of Princess Beatrice, Muriel Sara referred to the fact that the princess and her fiancé in 1885 could not have the quiet wedding that they had desired, and Sara concluded: 'Royalty is denied many of the privileges accorded to those of humbler rank.'[34] Thus, there was an overall conundrum: such royal family occasions were to be at the same time 'simple', in order to make royalty appear more relatable – but also 'magnificent' in order to underline and enhance royalty's elevated status. Depending on the respective writer, it was the one or the other side that was emphasized. For instance, for the actually comparatively lavish wedding of Princess Maud of Wales to Prince Charles of Denmark in the Private Chapel at Buckingham Palace in 1896, one commentator predicted that 'the whole affair will be very quiet and essentially a family gathering', and stressed that 'beyond a few official guests, scarcely anyone but relatives has been invited'.[35] Similarly, on the rather grand 1905 wedding of Princess Margaret of Connaught to the future king of Sweden at St George's Chapel, George Aston later commented that 'the wedding service itself had the great charm of simplicity' and summarized very positively that 'An air of youthfulness pervaded the whole ceremony.'[36]

In this context, the 1913 wedding of Prince Arthur of Connaught and Princess Alexandra of Fife stands out as a particularly interesting case. The *Scotsman* chose a diplomatic middle-way in its report of the wedding when it observed that the service 'had all the dignity of the State ceremonial without losing the simplicity appropriate to a family gathering'.[37] The report on this wedding in the *Times* put a notably strong emphasis on the aspect of 'simplicity'. It summarized that 'The service itself was touching in its beauty and simplicity', explaining that 'within reasonable limits everything had been done to make the marriage as simple as possible', before it concluded that in the chapel 'the note of simplicity was particularly

---

[30] 'Marriage of Victoria the First', p. 119.

[31] 'Marriage of the Princess Royal', *Times* (1858), p. 7.

[32] 'Marriage of the Princess Mary', *Morning Post*, 13 June 1866, p. 5.

[33] Anonymous, untitled report beginning with this text, *Times*, 14 March 1879, p. 9, columns 2–3.

[34] M. E. [Muriel Ellen] Sara, *The Life and Times of H.R.H. Princess Beatrice* (London: Stanley Paul & Co., 1945), p. 54.

[35] 'The Royal Wedding', *Graphic*, 18 July 1896, p. 82.

[36] George Aston, *His Royal Highness The Duke of Connaught and Strathearn: A Life and Intimate Study* (London: George G. Harrap & Co. Ltd, 1929), p. 251. See also Chapter 10, with fn. 68.

[37] 'The Royal Wedding: Brilliant Scene at St James's Palace', *Scotsman*, 16 October 1913, p. 7.

marked'.[38] The 'reasonable limits' probably referred to the ceremony and pomp expected of any royal occasion.

At the same time, in the case of this particular occasion, the overboarding positive stressing of simplicity and of the family character of the occasion might almost sound like a justification. For, the wedding of Prince Arthur and Princess Alexandra occurred not long after the grand Berlin wedding of Princess Viktoria Luise, the Kaiser's only daughter, and Prince Ernst August of Hanover, which had taken place on 24 May 1913. George V and Queen Mary, as well as the Russian Tsar and many other high-ranking European royals, had been guests at the Berlin wedding.[39] Britain, and London in particular, had not seen any comparable wedding since at least 1896, or even 1893, and the detailed reports of the Berlin wedding in the illustrated magazines of the day may have increased the appetite for such royal occasions and resulted in a mood of 'ceremonial competition'. Yet, the modest London wedding could of course not compete with the perceived, and reported, imperial grandeur of the Berlin wedding of the Kaiser's only daughter: it is plausible that this discrepancy may have contributed to the emphasis on modest 'simplicity' as a particularly praiseworthy characteristic of the London event – in a manner of speaking, turning a shortcoming into a virtue.

Ceremonial Performance

In 1885, an anonymous reviewer of J. D. Linton's painting *The Marriage of the Duke of Albany*, depicting the 1882 wedding ceremony, noted that

> The royal personages stand near the altar in places exactly marked out for them, and from which, like trained actors at a theatre, they can hardly permit themselves to depart.[40]

Looking at Linton's picture, which gives the impression of looking onto a stage (Illustration 8.5, on p. 212), it is easy to see how the reviewer may have come to this observation.

The comparison of the scene's protagonists with 'trained actors at a theatre' is as amusing as it is apt, and similar comments were made at several royal weddings, at least from the later nineteenth century onwards. By 1879 the correspondent of the *Illustrated London News* at the royal wedding in that year put it quite bluntly by describing that – after the arrival of the congregation and clergy, and before the arrival of the royal processions – 'the advent of the real actors in the ceremony was anxiously expected'.[41]

The comparison with 'actors' – even the 'real actors' - points to the fact that, like at any royal occasion, the ceremonial at royal weddings has a strong performative character. This idea shall at least briefly be mentioned here. In addition to the direct comparison with actors, there are numerous other comparisons with, or least allusions to, performances on stage. For instance, the specially built 'dais' or 'haut pas' on which the weddings up to the twentieth century took place can barely hide its similarity to a stage on which the ceremony is performed. In addition, the numerous explicit descriptions of the role of the 'curtain' at the entrance to St George's Chapel at the 1863, 1871, and 1882 weddings are surely redolent of a theatre (or opera) curtain: it opens to let the 'trained actors' in, so to speak. Indeed, in 1863, one report, when describing

---

[38] 'Royal Wedding: Scene in St. James's Palace', *Times*, 16 October 1913, pp. 9–10.

[39] For a detailed study of this wedding see Ute Daniel and Christian K. Frey (eds), *Die Preussisch-Welfische Hochzeit 1913: Das Dynastische Europa in seinem letzten Friedensjahr* (Braunschweig: Appelhans, 2016).

[40] 'Fine Arts', *Public Opinion*, 47:1228 (3 April 1885), p. 436.

[41] 'Marriage of The Prince of Wales and Princess Alexandra of Denmark', Supplement to *ILN*, 14 March 1863, pp. 278–87, here p. 278.

the leaving procession of the couple after the service, had distinctly referred to 'the curtains' that 'dropped for the last time on the actors in this Imperial pageant'.[42]

At the same 1863 wedding, the *Illustrated London News* had dedicated a lavish double-page illustration to the procession of the bride (Illustration 7.4). Incidentally, this may show an intriguing ceremonial detail that was seemingly not otherwise mentioned: the guests, or congregation, have apparently not risen from their seats for the bride's procession, they are not standing up. This might just be an inaccuracy on the part of this illustrator – yet, in the picture of the queen's entrance at the 1858 wedding (Illustration 6.9), the guest are also seated and have not risen, in this case not even for the sovereign's procession. Whether these depictions are accurate or not, they enhance the impression that these processions were a spectacle to behold, a performance with the congregation as spectators – sitting in their raised seating as though in a theatre and watching the 'actors' walking past.

In this context it is worth remembering that the grand royal weddings up to that of Queen Victoria were clearly as much about marrying a royal couple as they were about extolling the supreme status of the monarch. Not only were the king and queen the last to arrive, but their presence was also especially emphasized by a kind of inthronization at the end of the ceremony.

Wedding Music

The earlier seventeenth-century royal weddings had a rich programme of music, choral and instrumental, underlining their grandeur and their role as important royal occasions. After the turbulences of the Civil War and the Restoration, and then a dearth of royal offspring, it was not until the 1730s that royal weddings became again elaborate occasions, and with elaborate music – although then at first came mainly at the end, outside the Prayer Book liturgy, which featured at best the psalm. With the Victorian era – from the queen's own wedding in 1840 onwards – a rich programme of music, mainly linked to the ceremonial proceedings, became a distinct characteristic of royal weddings.

In this context it is noteworthy that the participation of a choir at other, non-royal weddings in the nineteenth century seems to have been introduced only later. In June 1859, Arthur Thynne, son of the Subdean of Westminster Abbey, married Gwenllian Kendall at the Abbey. The report of the wedding in the *Illustrated London News* recorded that the full Abbey choir sang during the service, and it referred distinctly to the 'imposing novelty of a choral wedding'.[43]

Following on from the above discussion on simplicity it is interesting to note that in his article on 'Marriage Music' published in 1885, T. Percy M. Betts observed that the 'general tendency of the day' was 'to make the marriage service as simple as possible'; and regarding the music Betts concluded that 'in the large majority of cases the music is limited to that which accompanies the processions'.[44] Nevertheless, the appreciation of the music at these ceremonies seems to have been growing and by the time of the wedding of the Duke of Connaught in 1913 the *Observer* announced quite confidently that 'The music arranged for the occasion will be a notable feature of the ceremony.'[45]

---

[42] 'The Royal Marriage', *ILN*, 21 March 1863, pp. 310–22, here p. 311 (see also Chapter 7, with fn. 43).

[43] 'Choral Marriage in Westminster Abbey', *ILN*, 9 July 1859, p. 31. For a picture of the scene, with the choir clearly visible in front of the high altar, see p. 32.

[44] T. Percy M. Betts, 'Marriage Music', *Graphic*, special wedding issue, 27 July 1885, pp. 20–21, here p. 21.

[45] 'Royal Wedding: Final Arrangements for the Ceremony', *Observer*, 5 October 1913, p. 11.

British Royal Weddings

Handel, Mendelssohn and Wagner

As could be seen in the preceding chapters, the music of some composers has been particularly prominent at royal weddings. When discussing the choices of royal wedding music, or indeed the music at any royal ceremony, Handel obviously deserves a special mentioning. In 1965, Jessica M. Kerr could observe that it was 'Handel's music that has dominated at English weddings for over 200 years'.[46] For royal weddings, first of all, Handel's anthem *Sing unto God* for the wedding of the Prince of Wales in 1736 had seemed to be on the way to becoming a popular staple at royal weddings, being repeated (in altered versions) at two important weddings in the late eighteenth century. Yet, it did not manage to establish itself in the same way as Handel's *Zadok the Priest* did at coronations, or his *Funeral Anthem* at royal and state funerals throughout the nineteenth century.[47] All the same, Handel's music dominated later royal weddings in so far as several of his marches were repeatedly played during the various entrance processions in Victorian days.

Even more prominently than Handel's music, royal weddings featured the two 'wedding' marches by Mendelssohn and Wagner – which form a famous combination at weddings to the present day. While Mendelssohn's Wedding March was used at the end of the weddings in 1858 and then from 1879 onwards up to 1947, Wagner's Bridal Chorus accompanied only four royal brides to the altar: Princess Beatrice in 1885, Princess Louise of Wales in 1889, Princess Victoria Mary of Teck (later Queen Mary) in 1893, and Princess Maud of Wales in 1896.[48] Therefore, only these four had the 'classical' combination of both Wagner for the bride's entrance and Mendelssohn for the couple's leaving.

Yet, both composers were also strongly represented with other music at the later Victorian and Edwardian weddings: Wagner with his *Tannhäuser* march and Mendelssohn with the *Athalie* march as well as three different anthems. The frequent use of music by Wagner is particularly noteworthy: it was not only relatively modern music but, more obviously than Mendelssohn, it also had undeniably German connotations. Indeed, considering the prominence of the music by Handel, Mendelssohn, and Wagner at British royal weddings, the aspect of 'national music' deserves some more discussion.

Representing the Nation

Similar to other royal or state occasions, royal weddings also have another added layer of meaning: that of representing the nation. This becomes relevant especially in the context of their music, and in the later nineteenth century, when nationalism was *en vogue* throughout Europe, it was in particular the authorship of the music that could be interpreted in relation to national pride. In 1871, on the occasion of the forthcoming wedding of Princess Louise, an anonymous article in *The Orchestra* took a clear stance. Referring back to Handel's anthems in the first half of the eighteenth century (and ignoring William Boyce's contribution for the wedding of George III in 1761), it mentioned the 'long neglect of nearly a century and a half' in writing anything new for a royal wedding, observing:

---

[46] Jessica M. Kerr, 'English Wedding Music', *Musical Times*, 106, January 1965, pp. 53–55, here p. 53.

[47] See Matthias Range, *Music and Ceremonial at British Coronations: From James I to Elizabeth II* (Cambridge: Cambridge University Press, 2012), Chapters 5–7, and Matthias Range, *British Royal and State Funerals: Music and Ceremonial since Elizabeth I* (Woodbridge: Boydell Press, 2016), esp. Chapters 4–6.

[48] For details on the twentieth century weddings see the author's *British Royal Weddings: The House of Windsor* (Turnhout: Brepols, forthcoming).

11—The 'Pomp of Old Days': Three Centuries of Royal Weddings

It is time England had its new Royal Wedding Music of just pre-eminence and certain durability[:] something better than a bald chorale of the modern German school. There is no need to invoke foreign talent, nor to solicit the crude efforts of amateur composers. An English musician should commemorate an event in English history.[49]

Eleven years later, in his review of the music at the wedding of Prince Leopold and Princess Helen of Waldeck in 1882, Thomas Lea Southgate also worded strong criticism from a national angle. He explained with an apparently sour undertone:

The foreign guests who were present could have had no very exalted idea of our musical taste, or of the true position of our English cathedral music from such a programme as this.[50]

With reference to Charles Gounod's Bridal March (*Marche Nuptiale*) at this wedding, Southgate criticized the choice of a foreign composer and asked: 'With all due respect, one may inquire, Why was not this commission given to an Englishman?' Southgate lamented that no English music had been commissioned and argued that

Had such an event taken place at the court of some of the German Princelets, where art is generally supposed to obtain a more important recognition than is accorded to it in our own land, in all probability the incident would have been musically signalized by the production of some work of magnitude worthy of the occasion that called it forth.

Overall, Southgate emphasized that 'in what is essentially a national ceremony one may fairly expect native art to have the preference' but that, with Gounod's march, 'English music has thus suffered yet another gratuitous slight, while the divine art has been furnished with nothing likely to live'. He was correct in so far at least as Gounod's march has been widely forgotten and not been much performed.

The issue of the nationality of composers at royal occasions remained a noted topic over the following decades. In 1904, an anonymous 'Churchman' referred to a memorial service for Queen Victoria held at the Frogmore Mausoleum and observed that two of the anthems were by Hauptmann and Tchaikovsky, respectively, with 'one number' by the Irish-born Stanford.[51] Obviously receiving this as a national snub, the writer commented bitingly that 'Presumably music by musicians belonging to our National Church was not required.' Similar consternation about foreign music continued to be observed for weddings, although – as will be seen – not necessarily only for royal ones.

The 1916 royal wedding, taking place in the midst of the First World War, featured two pieces by the German composer Mendelssohn. and this seemingly did not provoke any notable comment at the time of the wedding. Earlier in the year, however, there had been some public discussion about the use of music by Handel, notably his Dead March, and the composer Martin Shaw, in an open letter, pointed out that 'there is a considerable body of musical and clerical opinion which holds that German music for solemn and intimate national occasions is, to say the least, pointless'.[52] Without any further discussion, Shaw referred also to Mendelssohn's march when he concluded provocatively: 'How amused the Germans must be at the thought that we have to import both our Funeral March and our Wedding March from the Fatherland!'

---

[49] 'Royal Wedding Music', *Orchestra*, p. 362.

[50] This and the following T. L. Southgate, 'Royal Music', *Musical Standard*, 22 (13 May 1882), pp. 296–98, here pp. 296–97.

[51] 'Churchman', 'Foreign Anthems. To the Editor of "Musical News"', *Musical News*, 26:675 (6 February 1904), p. 138.

[52] Martin Shaw, 'The Banning of Handel. To the Editor, "Musical News"', *Musical News*, 51:1323 (8 July 1916), pp. 26 and 28, here p. 26.

British Royal Weddings

Illustration 11.1: 'The Marriage Ceremony of their Royal Highnesses the Prince & Princess of Wales', mezzotint with etching and hand-colouring (Haines & Son, 1795), *Royal Collection, RCIN 605193*, Royal Collection Trust / © Her Majesty Queen Elizabeth II 2021.

With a provocative remark, Shaw concluded that 'Perhaps some day we may come to our own.' Yet, it was not before 1960 that Princess Margaret for her wedding changed Mendelssohn's march for music by the English Henry Purcell – but only for it to be swapped itself for the French Widor Toccata from 1961 onwards, joined by more varied choices since the 1980s.

Occasionally, the actual music itself could be categorized in, or described by national terms. For instance, in 1893, an anonymous reviewer of Creser's *Wedding March*, written for and played at the wedding of the Duke of York in that year, judged that this piece was 'simple and dignified in character and thoroughly English, as befits such a national occasion'.[53] However, no further explanation was given of how exactly the piece was 'thoroughly English'.

On a slightly different level, there can be national pride in having a strong musical tradition at all. The 1871 wedding of Queen Victoria's daughter Princess Louise stands out as an early example for good music on such an occasion being interpreted proudly as a positive national characteristic. The *Musical World* emphasized that 'Music, with such a music-loving Court as that of England, could not but take a prominent part in the present festivities at Windsor Castle'.[54] A 'music-loving Court' was apparently something to be proud of and reflected well on the country as a whole.

The exact quality of the music at such royal occasions, however, was not necessarily fully acknowledged and appreciated. As already cited above, Southgate in 1882 complained that the music at Prince Leopold's wedding 'has excited but little attention', suggesting that more care would have been shown towards it and that it would have been accorded more recognition 'at the court of some of the German Princelets'.[55]

---

[53] Anonymous, review of *Wedding March* by William Creser, and *O Perfect Love* by Joseph Barnby (Novello, Ewer and Co.), *Musical Times*, 34 (August 1893), p. 489.

[54] This and the following 'Music at Court', *The Musical World*, 49 (March 1871), pp. 176–77.

[55] For a full quotation see above, following fn. 50.

11—The 'Pomp of Old Days': Three Centuries of Royal Weddings

The Visual Quality of Music

It may sound like a contradiction in terms, but the music at royal weddings – or indeed at any royal occasion – could also have a strong 'visual quality'. Music was recognized not merely for its original function, its acoustic contribution, but its accompanying visual quality, the visibility of the performing body, was also acknowledged. For instance, for the 1761 wedding of George III, the *Royal Magazine* pointed out explicitly:

> The music is behind the altar, so as to be visible, which will have a pleising effect during the solemnity.[56]

On the occasion of the 1795 wedding of the Prince of Wales, a contemporary, stylized print depicting the ceremony showed the organ and singers in the gallery behind the altar (Illustration 11.1). The inclusion of this detail, even in such a popular print, vouches for the status of music at such an occasion: seeing the performers – and the golden pipes of the organ – contributes to the impression of a grand, elaborate ceremony, just like the rich crimson of the fabrics. The musicians were shown in several depictions of royal weddings, when the angle of the scene allowed for their inclusion – very prominently, for instance, in the pictures of the 1866 wedding in the Private Chapel at Windsor Castle and that of the 1874 wedding in St Petersburg (see Illustrations 7.10 and 8.1, above).

At the 1893 wedding of the Duke of York and Princess Victoria Mary of Teck, the *Scotsman* referred to one particularly noteworthy visual characteristic of the Chapel Royal choir, to the boys being dressed 'in the scarlet uniform they usually wear'.[57] Similarly, for the 1896 wedding of Princess Maud, various accounts mentioned the choir arriving before all the other participants, with particular reference to 'the chorister boys of the chapel in their quaint costume dating from the period of Charles II.' and 'the boys in the quaint Carolinian scarlet and gold coats, with lace neck-bands' – while another referred also to Parratt 'in his robes as a Doctor of Music', and then to the choirboys in their 'quaint scarlet and gold dress […] which is familiar to all who have seen and heard them at the Sunday services in the Chapels Royal.[58] Richard Buckner painted one such chorister in the early 1870s, beautifully showing off the eye-catching uniform (Illustration 11.2).

Illustration 11.2: Richard Buckner, 'Portrait of a Boy Chorister of the Chapel Royal', oil painting *c.* 1873, London, Victoria and Albert Museum, Accession Number P.30-1962 © Victoria and Albert Museum, London.

The visual impact of the boys' colourful uniforms has been often pointed out, in comments ringing with that in the *Scotsman* on the wedding of Princess Mary, daughter of George V, in 1922: it pointed out that the boys of the Chapel Royal 'will appear in their striking uniform of crimson and gold'.[59] It would seem that the choir's visual quality was worth a remark just as much as the singing: if nothing else, such descriptions emphasized the aspect of splendour and deep roots in history. The boy choristers wear these uniforms to the present day.

---

[56] Anonymous, untitled report in *The Royal Magazine: Or Gentleman's Monthly Companion*, 5 (1761), pp. 104–05, here p. 104.

[57] 'Royal Wedding', *Scotsman* (1893).

[58] 'The Royal Wedding', *Times*, 23 July 1896, pp. 5–6, here p. 6; 'Marriage of The Princess Maud of Wales', *Manchester Guardian*, 23 July 1896, p. 5; and 'The Wedding of Princess Maud of Wales: A Brilliant Ceremonial. The Scene in the Chapel Royal', *Scotsman*, 23 July 1896, p. 5.

[59] 'Royal Wedding: The Musical Service', *Scotsman*, 18 February 1922, p. 8.

British Royal Weddings

Music as a Memento

In 1863, the year of the Prince of Wales's wedding, an anonymous reviewer of the annual benefit concert given 'by Mr. Cusins and by Madame Dolby and M. Sainton' referred to an included 'Cantata' that had been written by Cusins '*à propos* of the royal marriage'.[60] The reviewer judged that Cusins's work did 'not rise above the level of mediocrity to which such "occasional" compositions seem to be commonly doomed' and observed that 'little indeed of this sort of work in any of the arts has taken a place permanently among that which the world "will not let die!"' Handel and his works written for royal occasions are named as 'the only great exceptions to the common rule', and with reference to this composer the writer confidently postulates that

> The longer the world lives the more people will care for the 'Dettingen Te Deum,' and the fewer for George the Second's victory.

However, this bold claim seems to be missing a crucial point: it may be true that fewer and fewer people will 'care' for George II's victory at the Battle of Dettingen in 1743 while still enjoying the music of Handel's Te Deum written for the subsequent state thanksgiving service. Nevertheless, each performance, nay each bare mentioning of Handel's *Dettingen Te Deum* keeps the memory of the king's military success alive – and, eventually, at least some people will 'care' about the occasion and background of the music. Thus, if such a piece of music is successful enough to be remembered, it will also keep alive the memory of the occasion for which it was written, or at which it was at least performed.

Beginning with Handel's prominent wedding anthems, if not earlier, the music at royal weddings was imbued with an additional quality as a memento of these occasions. In 1734, for the wedding of Princess Anne, Handel wrote not only the anthem for the service but also the secular masque, or serenata *Il Parnasso in festa* (HWV 73); and Matthew Gardner points to the 'parallel borrowings' in this and the anthem, observing that these gave 'the event a certain sense of unity' – at least for those who heard both works.[61] Indeed, among those was the royal family who together with the Prince of Orange had attended the first performance of the masque on the evening before the wedding.[62] Similarly, Hans-Georg Hofmann has pointed out that Handel himself reused half of the music of his 1736 wedding anthem *Sing unto God* in his revised version of *Il trionfo del Tempo e della Verità* (HWV 46b), almost a year after the ceremony, and he suggests that the intention of this borrowing was to remind the prince and princess of their wedding.[63]

Whereas in the eighteenth century there was long, concert-like music at the end of the ceremony, after the service, throughout the Victorian era music became a more and more pronounced feature before and within the actual service, and by 1904 at the latest the music also began to involve the congregation directly, in the singing of hymns. There was not much new music written for royal weddings – Gounod's new march for the bride's entrance in 1882 probably being the most notable example. Instead royal weddings featured many marches, hymns, and anthems that were known from other contexts. The increase in music possibly

---

[60] 'Recent Concerts. – Wagner's "Lohengrin," &c.', *The Reader*, 13 June 1863, p. 583.

[61] Matthew Gardner, 'Preface' to Georg Friedrich Händel, *Wedding Anthems (HWV 262 and HWV 263)*, ed. by Matthew Gardner, *Hallische Händel-Ausgabe*, series III, vol. 11 (Kassel: Bärenreiter, 2013), pp. xvii–xxv, here p. xix.

[62] See Donald Burrows, *Handel and the English Chapel Royal* (Oxford: Oxford University Press, 2005), p. 319.

[63] Hans-Georg Hofmann, '"Sing unto God" – Bemerkungen zu Händels Festmusik anlässlich der Hochzeit des Prinzen Frederick of Wales mit Prinzessin Augusta von Sachsen-Gotha (1736)', *Händel-Jahrbuch*, 49 (2003), pp. 147–62, here p. 151.

11—The 'Pomp of Old Days': Three Centuries of Royal Weddings

made the ceremony more memorable, as the music itself would serve to commemorate these events. Its performance – first in public rehearsals, then in other services and concerts, or indeed at home on the piano – helped not only make the music itself better known and popular, but it also kept the memory of these events alive. It is the music of these occasions that survives much longer than, for instance, any of the spoken words: while the addresses and prayers were quickly all but forgotten, much (if not most) of the music is still quite often performed to the present day. This study itself exemplifies that it can very well be an interest in the music that draws increased attention to historic events such as royal weddings – and thus keeps the memory of these occasions alive, making them better known and at the same time commemorating their 'protagonists'.

———

As seen in chapter 10, the wedding of the Duke of Connaught in 1913 has been aptly described as the 'last royal wedding of the old age'. This 'old age' ended with the numerous upheavals and changes that came with, and after the Great War. In 1917, the name of the royal house was changed to 'Windsor' and this change of name was soon followed by a general shift in the public display of the monarchy. In the 'new' age since 1917, royal ceremonies overall would take on a different, much more public character. Royal weddings in particular were to become the most popular and almost the grandest of all royal occasions.

Illustration 11.3: Quiver with arrows and bow (as symbols of Cupid) at the bottom of the last page of Ceremonial 1795, here from the copy in *Llp Fulham Papers Porteus 17*, fols 212ʳ–213ᵛ.

Appendices

Appendix A Chronological List of British Royal Weddings (Discussed in this Book)

The Stuarts

Date	Bridal Couple	Venue	*page*
1589, 23 November	James VI/I and Princess Anna of Denmark	Christen Mule's house (Old Bishop's Palace), Christianstadt [= Oslo]	25
1613, 14 February	Princess Elizabeth and Prince Frederick, Elector Palatine	Chapel Royal, Whitehall Palace	27
1625, 1/11 May	Charles I and Princess Henrietta Maria of France	Notre Dame Cathedral, Paris	34
1641, 2 May	Princess Mary and Prince William of Orange	Chapel Royal, Whitehall Palace	37
1662, 21 May	Charles II and Princess Catherine of Braganza	Governor's house, Portsmouth	40
1677, 4 November	Princess Mary (later Mary II) and Prince William of Orange (later William III)	Princess's bed-chamber, St. James's	42
1683, 28 July	Princess Anne and Prince George of Denmark	St James's Palace (Chapel Royal?)	43

The Hanoverians

Date	Bridal Couple	Venue	*page*
1734, 14 March	Princess Anne and Prince William of Orange	French Chapel, St James's Palace	46
1736, 27 April	Prince Frederick, Prince of Wales, and Princess Augusta of Saxe-Gotha-Altenburg	Chapel Royal, St James's Palace	61
1740, 8 May (and 28 June)	Princess Mary and Prince Frederick of Hesse	Chapel Royal, St James's Palace (Town Palace, Kassel)	70
1743, 11 November	Princess Louisa and Prince Frederick of Denmark (later Frederick V)	Palace Chapel, Hanover	73
1761, 8 September	George III and Princess Charlotte of Mecklenburg-Strelitz	Chapel Royal, St James's Palace	77
1764, 16 January	Princess Augusta and Charles William Ferdinand, Duke of Brunswick-Wolfenbüttel	Drawing Room, St James's Palace	88

Date	Bridal Couple	Venue	page
1766, 1 October (8 November 1766)	Princess Caroline Matilda and Christian VII of Denmark	Council Chamber, St James's Palace (Christiansborg Palace, Copenhagen)	88
1766 (date unknown)	Prince William Henry, Duke of Gloucester and Edinburgh, and Maria Countess Waldegrave	secret wedding at Cumberland House	88
1771, 2 October	Prince Henry, Duke of Cumberland and Strathearn, and Anne Horton	secret wedding, location unknown	88
1791, 23 November (29 September 1791)	Prince Frederick, Duke of York and Albany, and Princess Frederica of Prussia	'Grand Saloon', Buckingham Palace ('White Hall' of Town Palace, Berlin)	103
1793, 5 December (day? April 1793)	Prince Augustus Frederick, Duke of Sussex, and Lady Augusta Murray	St George, Hanover Square (secret ceremony in Rome)	106
1795, 8 April	Prince George, Prince of Wales, and Princess Caroline of Brunswick	Chapel Royal, St James's Palace	89
1797, 18 May	Princess Charlotte, Princess Royal, and Frederick-William, Hereditary Prince of Württemberg	Chapel Royal, St James's Palace	98
1815, 29 August (29 May 1815)	Prince Ernest Augustus, Duke of Cumberland (later king of Hanover), and Frederica of Mecklenburg-Strelitz	Carlton House (City Church, Strelitz)	106
1816, 2 May	Princess Charlotte of Wales and Prince Leopold of Saxe-Coburg-Saalfeld	Council Chamber, Carlton House	106
1816, 22 July	Princess Mary and Prince William Frederick, Duke of Gloucester and Edinburgh	'Grand Saloon', Buckingham Palace	109
1818, 7 April	Princess Elizabeth and Prince Frederick of Hesse-Homburg	'Saloon', Buckingham Palace	110
1818, 1 June (7 May 1818)	Prince Adolphus, Duke of Cambridge, and Princess Augusta of Hesse-Kassel	Buckingham Palace (Kassel)	109
1818, 11 July	William, Duke of Clarence and St Andrews (later William IV), and Princess Adelaide of Saxe-Meiningen, *double wedding with:* Edward, Duke of Kent and Strathearn, and Victoria of Saxe-Coburg-Saalfeld	'Queen's drawing-room', Kew Palace (for the first couple also a ceremony in Coburg, in May 1818)	110
1840, 10 February	Queen Victoria and Prince Albert of Saxe-Coburg and Gotha	Chapel Royal, St James's Palace	113

The 'Victorians' and up to 1917

Date	Bridal Couple	Venue	*page*
1891, 6 July	Princess Marie Louise of Schleswig-Holstein and Prince Aribert of Anhalt	St George's Chapel, Windsor Castle	242
1893, 6 July	Prince George, Duke of York (later George V) and Mary of Teck	Chapel Royal, St James's Palace	249
1896, 22 July	Princess Maud of Wales and Prince Charles of Denmark (later Haakon VII of Norway)	Private Chapel, Buckingham Palace	261
1904, 10 February	Princess Alice of Albany and Prince Alexander of Teck (later 1st Earl of Athlone)	St George's Chapel, Windsor Castle	273
1905, 15 June	Princess Margaret of Connaught and Prince Gustaf Adolf of Sweden and Norway (later Gustaf VI Adolf of Sweden)	St George's Chapel, Windsor Castle	280
1913, 15 October	Prince Arthur of Connaught and Princess Alexandra, 2nd Duchess of Fife	Chapel Royal, St James's Palace	284
1916, 15 November	Prince George Louis of Battenberg (later George Mountbatten, 2nd Marquess of Milford Haven) and Countess Nadejda Mikhailovna de Torby	Chapel Royal, St James's Palace	294
1917, 19 July	Prince Alexander of Battenberg (later Alexander Mountbatten, 1st Marquess of Carisbrooke) and Lady Irene Denison	Chapel Royal, St James's Palace	296

Appendix B

Texts and Transcriptions

'/' usually indicates a line break, and '//' a paragraph break. In documents from the Victoria era, the original interpunctuation with an underscore '_' – usually for a comma or a full stop, and rendered as such in the main text above – has here been retained.

1.1 *Lea Marriages & Baptisms of the Royal Family (C.G.Y. 893)*, **two leaves of an undated memorandum by Charles George Young, near the beginning of the volume**

[fol. 1ʳ] 'The Ceremonials contained in this Volume / are entirely of a domestic character relating to / Ceremonials of Marriages and Baptisms of / the Royal family under the control and / regulation of the Lord Chamberlain in which / it is the duty of those Officers of Arms required / to attend, to render all the assistance in their / power in carrying the same into effect. // As the Earl Marshal has not the / superintendence or any direction of these / private family Ceremonials, his Officers are / in no way responsible for the construction / of the Ceremonial, and have only to obey the / directions of the Lord Chamberlain._ // The Ceremonials are more or less limited / in extent, according to the circumstances / of the case and the Will and pleasure of / the Sovereign; and upon their curtailment / or extension, depends more or less the / attendance of certain Officers of State / and of the Household of the Sovereign; and / it will be frequently found that the same // [fol. 1ᵛ] Officers are not always to be found / attending upon every occasion. or in the / same place, and these Ceremonials are not / to be taken as establishing any precedency / contrary to the established and recognized / principles and order of Precedency. _ // The Ceremonial being considered / of a private character and under the / direction of the Lord Chamberlain, his Lordship, or his Officers regulate these / points accordingly _ A custom prevails / in their arrangement of the Household Offices / utterly inconsistent with the general and / authorized rules of Precedency, and there- / -fore altho' recognized in those cases with / the Palace, such recognition is not to be / taken as of any authority in reference to / Precedence on other occasions: for instance, / the Lord Chamberlain invariably takes to / himself, the precedence over the Lord Steward / who, by virtue of the Act of 31 Hen: VIII has / precedence of the Lord Chamberlain, nor is / there any authority whatever for the precedence / of either, over other persons of greater rank // [fol. 2ʳ] of whom they sometimes take place in / these Ceremonials; and therefore no / reason for the violation of the Act in / this instance unless there be any rule in / respect to Precedence of the Royal Household / within the jurisdiction of the Palace / different to that which prevails in general. / [in different handwriting, and with a thicker pen:] C. G. Young Gr.'

320

Appendix B—Texts and Transcriptions

3.1 Fragmentary draft ceremonial for the 1734 wedding, in *Lca Miscell: Coll: By Anstis*, in about the middle of the unfoliated volume, untitled, three pages.

[p. 1] 'During all this time [while the processions arrive in the chapel and the king and queen are being seated etc.], and from the first appearance of the Procession the Organ / to play, and all Persons being thus setled, the Organ ['ceased', first corr. to 'ceases', then crossed out] is to cease, then [p. 2] Divine Service is [the 'is' added later] to begin, which the Dean of the Chapell will direct, however I shall mention / some Rules upon [added later: 'observed in'] the marriages of the Count Palatine in 1612 & Prince of Orange in 1640 / That the Gentlemen of the Chapell / That in the former the Banns were asked as had been [added: 'formerly'] constantly observed in / former Preceents, which [added: 'however'] were by order omitted in the later [added: 'because'] the Princesse being was only nine years and six months old & consequently this [added: 'marriage'] was not binding without a new Consent. / That the Dean kneeled, when re received the Bride from the Kings hands / & rising up delivered here to the Bridegrome. / That after the Dean had given the Blessing God the father God the Son & [added: 'the Anthem made for this purpose is to be was sung and when that / [added: 'being ended the'] Prince of Orange and the Princesse Royal go went and kneeled upon [added: 'the rich'] Cushions laid just / without the Rails of the Altar, and at such time where the new married Lady hath been was / placed upon the Right hand according to the which is consonant with former Precedents, [added: 'and in which matter'] The Rubrick in the Common / Prayer book is silent in that matter, though it directs the Position [added: 'of the Bridegroom & Bride'] in the Body of the / Church, in such words however, as may that admit different interpretations. / There was antiently a Pall of White Bandeken held over their Heads of / [added: 'the married Couple'] during the time of being their kneeling before the Altar. / Whether his Majesty, the Queen, and the four Princesses will during this / time remain in in their Chairs Upon the Hautpas, or retire to their any Traverses; or into Closets, / if any are such shall be erected. / When The Choir sing hath sung Blessed are they that fear the Lord &c then the Clerk of / the Closet kneels down, while the Dean standing up, and turning to the married Couple / who continue kneeling, begins with a loud Voice Lord have mercy upon [added: 'us'] which the / Choir answers, & then the Lords Prayers [*sic*], the Versicles, Answers &t are sung[.] / When the Dean hath pronounced Almighty God &t the married Couple arise / and the another Anthem is hath been sung. / Service being thus ended, if the styles are to be proclaimed, this is the time, / and then joy is given by the King Queen, Princes, & Princesses, seconded with the / Congratulations of the Lords; And if [added: 'in case'] the former Customs, of bringing Wafers & Wine is / be observed, then the same are to be brought by Lords appointed [added: 'for that purpose'] and after / tasting the Wafers, an health is to be begun to the Prosperity of the marriage / out of a Gold Bowl by the Prince of Orange, & pledged by the Princesse, / and by his Majesty, the Queen, the Prince, & Duke, the Princesses, & answered / by the Lords in their Order. / The Return is to be in the same Order as at the first entry, save with / the following Variations only; ffinet indeed sayth that the Bride [something above, crossed out] returned first, which / is a mistake & contrary to Precedents / The Trumpets, as before / […]'

British Royal Weddings

3.2 Edward Godfrey to 'M.ʳ [Cox] Macro' [but actually to Macro's wife, Godfrey's daughter], 16 March 1733/4, *Lbl Add MS 32556*, fols 156ʳ–57ʳ (no. 90).

[fol. 156ʳ] 'Madam / In compliance with your expectations from me I / shall give you as exact an Account as I can of the Royal / Wedding which was celebrated last Thursday with very great / Magnificence free from all disorder & Confusion[.] The Prince / of Orange set out from Sommerset House in the Kings Body / Coach attended by the Prince of Wales's & the Dukes & Princesses / Coaches & ['9'? entered later] Footmen Walking and arrived at S.ᵗ James's a little / after 7 o' the Clock in the Evening[.] The Gallery was opened about 4 and about 6 the Candles were lighted up and were replenished / Three times before the Procession ended[;] the Wind coming through / the Crevices made them burn away so fast the Place was / neither too hot nor too cold[;] it contained about 5 Thousand / Spectators, all richly drest which Sight alone was worth / Seeing[;] the Horse Guards were Posted before the Seats with / their Carbines shoulder'd about 5 Yards distance and a file / of Guards with an Officer before and behind kept / Patrolling along the Gallery till the Procession began / about a Quarter before 8[:] First a Man Playing on a / Pipe with 5 Drums Beating followed by the Drum Major / then 12 Trumpets & Kettle Drums in the Middle the Serjeant / Trumpeter with his Mace[.] The Pipe & Drums, & Trumpets / & Kettle Drums Playing alternately to the Chapel then / the Officers of Arms in their Habits[,] Lord Chamberlain & / others of the Kings Household[,] then the Prince of Orange / in White Satten richly Embroider'd with Gold his Buttons / Diamonds Set in Gold Supported by the Earl of Wilmington / on the Right & Earl of Scarbrough on the left[,] then his / several Noblemen [added: '& Gentlemen'] two & two to the Chappel: the Drums & / Trumpets &c Lᵈ Chamberlain & some others return and / Proceed with Officers of Arms before the Princess Led / by the Prince of Wales on the Right and the Duke on / the Left[,] the Prince in Blice[?] Embroider'd with Silver & / the Duke Scarlet Embroider'd with gold both richly / adorned with Diamonds, The Princess in Silver Tissue / richly Embroider'd and Embossed with Silver with Tossels [sic] / & other ornaments and Richly Adorned with Diamonds [fol. 156ᵛ] Her Train Supported by Ten Beautiful Young Maiden Ladies / Dukes & Earls Daughters all Dressed in White and Adorned with / Diamonds. The agreeableness of which Sight was beyond expression / I don't think the most Splended part of a Coronation comparable / to it. Her Highness appear'd with such a Presence as the Beauty / of the Young Ladies that bore her Train did not in the least / Eclipse[;] she Walked with a Reserved Modesty and becoming / Boldness and the Two Princess Led [added: 'her'] with an exceeding fine / Grace[;] then followed the Peeresses of Great Britain[,] the Baronesses / First & so on to the Duchesses all richly Dressed and adorned / with Jewels with their Trains after them; and being enter'd / the Chapel the Drums & Lord Chamberlain &c return'd and / Proceeded with the Heralds of Arms &c before the King &c Viz. / The Drums Trumpets &c Playing[,] the Heralds at Arms Gentlemen / of the Household, &c Privy Councellors, Barons Bishops &c Dukes / the Great Officers of State[,] Serjeants at Mace[,] Kings at Arms / Duke of Montague with the Sword of State &c The King / richly Dressed in a Gold and Scarlet Coat, Diamond Buttons / and indeed almost cover'd with Diamonds the Hilt of his / Sword Set with Diamonds of Great Value and His Majesty / was so complaisant as to Walk athwart the Gallery not strait / forwards[,] turning himself continually half round as he went / that People might have a full View of him[;] the Lord Chamberlain / Walked on one side of him, Guarded by the Gentlemen Pensioners / in Hats & Feathers, when the Queen between her Lord Chamberlain / the Earl of Grantham & the Lord Hobart, the Princess's Amelia, Carolina, Mary & Louisa each Led by two Gentlemen Ushers / and all their Trains supported by 2 Pages to each, and the / Ladies of the

Appendix B—Texts and Transcriptions

Bed Chamber[,] Maids of Honour & Dressers Closed / the Procession a little before 9 when the Guns were Fired in / the Park the Nuptials being then Solemnized and a Fine / Anthem being Performed which was concluded about a Quarter / before Ten and all returned in One entire Procession in the / same Order as before[,] the Drums & Trumpets Playing[,] the Prince / of Orange between the Duke of Richmond on the Right and / Duke of Rutland on the left[,] The Princess of Orange between / Her Brothers I observed she was very full of Talk all the Way back[,] [fol. 157ʳ] in short she went with the Composed Countenance of a Maid and / return'd with the Decent Freedom of a Wife[,] chearfull & Brisk; / the Procession ended a Quarter past Ten, an Elegant Supper was / immediately set on the Table in the Ball Room where none but / Peers & Peeresses & such like were admitted, and the Royal Pair / being retired received the Complements in Night Dresses &~ / Illuminations, Bonfires & other Rejoycings concluded the Evening[;]'

6.1 **Lord Melbourne to Sir William Woods, Garter King of Arms, 'Downing St / December 16_ 1839',** *Lca Marriage of Queen Victoria. 1840 (green volume, 'CA' on spine),* **letter bound in near the beginning of the volume. I am very grateful to Peter Mandler for his help with deciphering this letter.**

'Sir / I have to request that You will c[on]sider / immediately the Manner in which the Queens Marriage / May be solemnized & the attendance thereat so / limited & regulated as to be consistentt with the limits / of the Chapel Royal, in which it is to take place, / & so that order May be preserved upon the recessi[o]n / & Confusion avoided _ I sh[o]uld be glad that you should / as soon as possible report to me ['Your' crossed out] the opinion which / [verso] Y[o]u may form up[o]n this subject after reference to Precedent / & Consultation with those, whom y[o]u may think competent / assure Remain Sir / Your faithful & obedie[n]t? servant? / Melbourne' [The 'assure Remain' bit at the end seems to an abbreviated form of 'I assure you that I remain, Sir']

6.2 **'From the Court Circular',** *Times,* **29 June 1843, pp. 4–5, here p. 5.**

'The choir consisted of the boys and 12 gentlemen from Her Majesty's Chapel Royal, St. James's, viz. Messrs. W. Knyvett, J.B. Sale, Hawes, Hebbs, Bradbury, Wylde, Horncastle, Hawkins, Chapman, Bennet, Machin, and Francis (deputy).'

6.3 **'Preparations for the Marriage of / Her Royal Highness The Princess Royal', in** *Lna WORK 21/12/2,* **on sheet, stamped no. 43; signed 'John Phipps' and dated '18/12/57', on the verso the annotation 'Mʳ Adams. / Transmit Copy to / The Treasury' (extract).**

[recto:] 'Additional Works. / Probable cost of providing Sittings [*sic*] for about / 200 additional Spectators in the Gallery to be / erected in the Flag Court, and for a Gallery / in the Chapel to accommodate Her Majesty's / Band, and for a temporary Covered way in the Garden. _ _ _ _ _ _ _ 500 – o – o. / To enlarge the Windows over the Altar / for better lighting of the North End of the / Chapel and glazing the same with Coloured / Glass, likewise for the Additional Cost of / preparing the Galleries in the Chapel so that / they may be used on similar

British Royal Weddings

occasions, for / the removal of the Pewing in the Chapel to / obtain additional Sitting for Spectators / to view the Ceremony and reinstating the / same, for improving the ventilation in the / Chapel including the expense of redecorating / Her Majesty's Retiring Room, Private Staircase, / Principal Stairs, Halls and Corridors. _ _ _ 1100..0..0 / £4.313..6..10'

6.4 *Lbl Add MS 41772*, fol. 147^r: under 'Tuesday _ Jany: 19:'.

'The Rehearsal was called at ¼ to 12 _ it began <u>soon</u> / <u>after 12</u> (I was in the Chapel making arrangements _ [something crossed out] _ / ½ past 10 _ We began with the "Corale" in E♭_ which / I accomp: on the organ with the Band _ next it was Rehearsed / in E[natural sign] _ which M.r Cooper accom:^{d}, as I went into the Chapel / to hear the effect, where I was introduced to the Lord Chamber / by Dr Wesley _ the <u>Pia°:</u> [= 'piano passages'?] were not sufficiently observed _ / the 3 Boni & Ophicliede [*sic*] & Tuba too [the 'too' added slightly later] much overpowering _ Mr Anderson / said the Prince wished to have them; 3 Boni and Tuba / were placed on each side of me close to the <u>Organ Keys</u> _ / The Chant was next Rehearsed _ (M^r. Coopwer played the Organ / to "The Grand Chant" in D) I conducted the "Gloria". which / went bewlly? the 1st. time (not being comprehended by the Band) / M^r. Helmore [the Master of the Boys] and some other of the Vocalists making / disagreeable remarks _ it went better upon a 2^d. trial and / much better when I rehearsed it a 3.° time <u>after the Marches</u> were / rehearsed _ then the "Hallelujah" was rehearsed <u>twice</u>, the / 1st time it was played too Slowly so was the "Corale" _ / the <u>Vocal</u> Rehearsal was over soon after one _ the marches / and 3rd time of "Gloria" [i.e. *Gloria Patri*] ended about 2 _ / I gave young Sullivan and M^r. Goss' Son leave to be in the front Seat near the organ […]'

6.5 *Lbl Add MS 41777*, fol. 311^r.

'Rehearsal, Tuesday Jan^y: 19.th 1858.' => {in the Chapel Royal S:^{t} James's _ Called ¼ before 12 − Began soon after 12 / The Coral peices [*sic*] were over soon after one _ The Marches and Rehearsal of the / "Gloria Patri" with Band only, for the 3.^{d} time ended about 2_o'Clock_ / The Alto & Tenor Boni _ were placed (at one Desk) on the <u>left</u> (Bass) side / of the Organ _ the Bass Boni & Tuba (at one Desk) on the Right (Treble) side / of the organ_ I was seated with M: G. Cooper on the usual organ Loft Seat / which I had fastened down (We 6 [bold, double underlined] were in the same Places on Jany 25.th) / We first Rehearsed the "Choral" in E♭ – too Slow – it was rehearsed / a second time in E♮ _ I went down to the Altar to hear it _ Mr G. Cooper was then at the Organ, / the <u>Brass Inst.</u> close to the Organ much too loud _ Mr Anderson said / The Prince Consort wished them to be heard as they were in the / Private Chapel _ […] The Grand Chant in D was next Rehearsed, / Mr Cooper at the organ _ I conducted the "Gloria Patri" (in which the Band joined) / from the Organ Loft _ the Choir & Band were placed (behind the 2 Rows / of Seats in the Gall^y opposite the Organ Loft) were The Honble W. Ashby &c. / used to sit, but the Window was taken out and the Orchestra was / carried over the Colonade the Roof was chiefly of thick Glass._ // After the Chant "the Hallelujah" Chorus _ was tried <u>twice</u> over_as it was / taken too slowly the 1st. time _ in which the Boys were too weak_ / consequently for the Performance on the 25 Inst. Two Boys from / S:^{t} Paul's Cathedral and two from Westminster Abbey were invited / making a total of [pencil 'X'] Boys_'

Appendix B—Texts and Transcriptions

6.6 'Marriage of The Princess Royal: The Completed Preparations', *Observer*, 25 January 1858, pp. 5–6, here p. 5.

'The following gentlemen in ordinary of the Chapels Royal will officiate in the choir:—Messrs. T. Francis, W. Lockey, J. Goss, G. W. Martin, Benson, R. Barnby, N. Smith, Foster, Machin, Lawler, Thomas, Whitehouse, and Bennett. / Sir G. Smart will preside at the organ, assisted by Mr. Cooper. The chorister boys will attend with their master, the Ref. TG. Helmore.'

7.1 'Lady [Mary] Elvey', *Life and Reminiscences of George J. Elvey [...] Late Organist to H. M. Queen Victoria, and Forty-seven Years Organist of St. George's Chapel, Windsor* (London: Sampson Low, Marston & Company, Ltd, 1894), pp. 189–90.

[p. 189] 'The first chorus is an elaborate setting for five voices, who break in, after an instrumental prelude, with a shout, in massive harmonies, to the initial words. The basses and tenors then give out the subject of a fugue, fully developed in all its parts, to the verse, "Sing praises to the Lord." After passing through all the phases of well-constructed imitation, chords are reverted to, and the first subject and words bring this finely-written number to a close. / The next semichorus is accompanied by the organ only; this is a quiet and graceful quartet, written in the author's most melodious vein. / The third movement is a "German Chorale," and introduces the wood wind with the organ. / "How happy ye!" Fine bold harmony is set to this verse, which closes on the solo organ. / A short largo, "Lo ! thus shall the man be blessed," with full band, serves as an introduction to the last "Amen" chorus. Returning to the [p. 190] fugal form, a grand subject is recited by the basses, answered by all the voices in turn, and considerably enlarged upon; the instrumentation is much heightened in colour, and brings this splendidly-written anthem to a close in truly regal style.'

    See also p. 125: 'The anthem was ushered in with a symphony, in which were combined the merry peal of bells, the triumphant blast of trumpets, and other joyous sounds.'

7.2 'The Musical Service', *The Morning Advertiser*, 9 March 1863, p. 3.

'List of names of those belonging to the respective Choirs who will take part in the Musical Service to be performed at the Royal Wedding: – /
THE QUEEN'S PRIVATE CHAPEL. /
Messrs. Fielding, Edwin Ball, C. Henry, and choristers.
ST. GEORGE'S CHAPEL, WINDSOR.
Altos.—Messrs. Knowles, Marryott, and Adams.
Tenors.—Messrs. Dyson, Whiffin, and Tolley.
Basses.—Messrs. H. Barnby, Lambert, Bridgewater, and choristers.
THE CHAPEL ROYAL, ST. JAMES'S.
Altos.—Messrs. T. Francis, Foster, Baxter, and R. and J. Barnby.
Tenor.—Messrs. Bennett, Benson, W. Cummings, Carter, and Montem [*sic*] Smith.
Basses.—Messrs. Machin, Lawler, Bradbury, Whitehouse, Winn, and choristers.'

British Royal Weddings

8.1 'Marriage of Duke / of Connaught', dated 'March 29[?unreadable] /79', in *Lna LC 2/86*.

For Orchestra	47	5	—
St George's Choir	13	13	—
Eton do	3	3	—
Printing & Music	1	4	—
Chorister, (15)	3	15	— [number in brackets added in different ink]
Organ Blower,	—	10	—
	69 ,,	10	,,

8.2 'Copies' of a list of unnamed musicians with their payments at the wedding of Prince Leopold, Duke of Albany in 1882: 'Sir Geo. Elvey's Acc.', in *Lna LC 2/86* (musicians' list originally in one continuous column).

7 Violins	12 St George's Choir
1 [Violin] Windsor	12 Choristers
2 Violas	5 Eton College Choir
2 Cellos	6 [Eton College] Boys
1 Double Bass	3 Private Chapel Choir
1 D. [ditto] Windsor	4 [Private Chapel] Boys
2 Trumpets	
3 Trombones	
1 Drum	

'Fees for the Officers of S.ᵗ George's / including Bell Ringers / Organ Blower-'
NB The list also includes payment for music stands, and for seats in organ loft, and then also 'Harper Trumpeter's / Bill / £17.17—'
All the expenditure for the music together comes to £1,021.

9.1 Unsigned note [by Queen Victoria?] to 'The Very Rev: / The / Dean of Windsor / Buckingha[m] Palace', dated Osborne, 'July 25/89', in *Wsg XVII.43.4/3*.

'This Queen trusts / &[?] the Dean of Windsor is / seeing that the / same objectionable / passages & prayers / are left out of / the Marriage / Service on Saturd[a]y / ~~as was the Case~~ ['as' is possibly left] at / P[rin]cess Beatrice's & / the 3 other Royal / Marriges._'

9.2 Joseph Barnby to Francis Knollys, 9 July 1889, in *Wsg XVII.43.4/8*.

'Dear Sir Francis Knollys / In view of the ap- / proaching marriage of Her / Royal Highness the Princess / Louise of Wales and the Earl / of Fife I have composed a / Wedding Anthem to the words / enclosed, which may be sung [added later: 'with or'] / without accompaniment and which / occupies but three minutes in / performance. My desire is to / offer this Anthem to their Royal /[verso] Highnesses The Prince & Princess of / Wales, for performance at the /

Appendix B—Texts and Transcriptions

forthcoming Ceremony. // In case, however, there should have been an intention of re- / questing some such work at / the hands of another musician / or should the possible acceptance / of mine be likely to trench upon / the rights & duties of others I should / feel obliged by your using your / discretion in suppressing or making / known to their Royal Highnesses / [fol. 2] the contents of this letter / Yours faithfully / Joseph Barnby.'

9.3 Text of the hymn for the bride's procession, as reproduced in OS 1891, '*Words by The Right Rev. The Lord Bishop of Ripon*'.

Lord! Who hast made Home Love to be
    An angel-help to us and ours,
Watching in sweet fidelity
    Above our weak and cradled hours,
Bless where we love, we humbly pray;
Make strong the love Love gives to-day.

Thou who hast bidden hearts to beat,
Who makest human love so sweet,
Deign with Thy Love their love to meet!
        Father of Love, be near them.

They leave us, but they still are Thine:
When life with life doth intertwine,
Fill Thou their Love with Life divine—
        Father of Life, be near them.

Thou who didst smile on love below,
And when the wine of life ran low
Didst give a richer ampler flow—
        Great Son of God, be near them.

Thou who in years of grief untold
Didst Love's triumphant might unfold;
Grant them the love which grows not old—
        True Son of Man, be near them.

Our life is Thine, though life be ours:
Help us to live its fleeting hours
In use, not waste of human powers—
        Spirit of Life, be near them.

Let Love the rule of right remain
Unchanged through change and strong through
    pain
Till Love to perfect strength attain—
        Spirit of God, be near them.

Lord, who hast wisely willed that we,
More of Thyself in life should see,
And makest changing life to be
The unfolding of Love's mystery—
Grant that as love and life shall grow,
More of Thy Love we still may know.

Appendix C   Royal Weddings and their Music

Evidence of the ascriptions, sources, and other details of the music will be found in the respective chapters.

For shortness' sake only one part of the bridal couple is named – the one closest to the British royal family. For more details see Appendix A.

The following abbreviations indicate the wedding venue: CR – Chapel Royal (at St James's Palace, unless otherwise stated); PC – Private Chapel (at Buckingham Palace, unless otherwise stated); SG – St George's Chapel, Windsor Castle.

Appendix C1: Royal Weddings and their Music – Seventeenth to Eighteenth Century

Wedding (date, venue)	Entrance Processions: Bridegroom, Bride, Monarch	Psalm	Anthem(s) and other Music	Recess
James VI/I (1596, Old Bishop's Palace, Oslo)	– outside procession: 'trumpeters […] blew'	– at beginning: 'oral music'		'everything ended with music'
Princess Elizabeth (1613, CR, Whitehall Palace)	– once all had arrived: 'a full Anthem' (with organ)		– after sermon, before vows: *Blessed Art Thou that Fearest God* (Ps. 128) – after vows: Bull, *God the Father, God the Son* – then: 'Versicles and Prayers' sung, followed by 'an other Anthem'	– in chapel: organ music? – return procession: no music
Charles I (1625, Notre Dame Cathedral, Paris)	– procession to the cathedral: music by drums, fifes, oboes and trumpets		music unknown (would have been a full Roman Catholic mass)	unknown
Princess Mary (1641, CR, Whitehall Palace)	– for all three processions: organ voluntary then 'a full Anthem'		– after vows: *Blessed Are All They that Fear the Lord* (Gibbons?) – then: Lesser Litany, Lord's Prayer, Responses sung – after blessing: organ voluntary (before reading of Gospel and the sermon)	– return procession: no music?

Wedding (date, venue)	Entrance Processions: Bridegroom, Bride, Monarch	Psalm	Anthem(s) and other Music	Recess
Princess Anne (1734, French Chapel, St James's Palace)	– outside: fife, drums, trumpets – in the chapel: 'Organ played'	just read?	– after service proper: Handel, *This Is the Day which the Lord Has Made*	'Drums & Trumpets' (outdoor)
Frederick, Prince of Wales (1736, CR)	– outside: fife, drums, trumpets – in the chapel: organ 'Prelude' by Handel	just read?	– after service proper: Handel, *Sing unto God*	fifes, drums, trumpets (outdoor)
Princess Mary (1740, CR)	– outside: fife, drums, trumpets (outside) – in the chapel: unknown	just read?	– after service proper: Handel, *Sing unto God* (incl. extracts of 1734 anthem)	fifes, drums, trumpets (outdoor)
George III (1761, CR)	– outside: 'Drums & Trumpetts', 'a march' – in the chapel: unknown	Ps. 128, 'chanted'	– after service proper: Boyce, *The King Shall Rejoice*	[trumpets?] (outdoor)
Prince George, Prince of Wales (1795, CR)	– outside: 'Drums and Trumpets' and 'Kettle Drums', incl. 'God Save the King' – in the chapel: Handel, overture to *Esther* (played by orchestra)	just read?	– after service proper: Handel, *Sing unto God* (arr. and ext. Arnold)	unknown
Princess Charlotte (1797, CR)	– outside: 'music' incl. 'drums' – in the chapel: 'A Piece of Music'	Ps. 67, 'chaunted'	– after service proper: Handel, *Sing unto God* (arr. and ext. by Arnold)	'music' incl. 'drums' (outside)

Appendix C2: Royal Weddings and their Music – Nineteenth to Early Twentieth Century

Wedding (date, venue)	Entrance Processions (and introit, when included)	Psalm and Responses	Anthem	Recess (in chapel)
Queen Victoria (1840, CR)	– **bridegroom**. 'flourish', then possibly Handel, 'See the Conquering Hero Comes' (arr. for organ)? – **bride**: procession to the Chapel incl. 'God Save the Queen', then 'flourish of trumpets and drums', then organ voluntary	– Ps. 67: King, *Deus misereatur* (B-flat service); – Responses said	– **after service proper:** Kent, *Blessed Be Thou*	[organ voluntary?]
Princess Augusta (1843, PC)	– **processions to the Chapel**: no music – **royal guests**: organ voluntary – **at queen's entrance**: Handel, 'God Save the Queen' (from *Zadok the Priest*) – **entrance of bridegroom and bride**: 'solemn silence!'	– Ps. 67, to Earl of Mornington's chant in E-flat – Responses said?	– **after service proper:** Handel, Hallelujah Chorus (*Judas Maccabaeus*)	'No Music'
Princess Victoria (1858, CR)	– **all three processions**: 'trumpets and drums' – **queen**: Handel, march from *Occasional Oratorio* – **bridegroom**: Handel, march from *Joseph* – **bride**: Handel, march from *Judas Maccabaeus* – **introit**: chorale, 'This Day, with Gladsome Voice and Heart'	– Ps. 67 ('Grand Chant', Humfrey?) – Responses said?	– **before final blessing:** Handel, Hallelujah Chorus (*Messiah*)	Mendelssohn, Wedding March (played by orchestra)
Princess Alice (1862, Osborne House)	(There was no music at this wedding.)			
Prince Albert Edward, Prince of Wales (1863, SG)	– **processions going up the nave**: 'State Drummers and Trumpeters' – **royal family**: Beethoven, Triumphal March (*Tarpeja*) – **bridegroom**: Mendelssohn, 'War March of the Priests' (*Athalie*) – **bride**: Handel, march from *Joseph* – **introit**: Prince Albert, 'This Day, with Joyful Heart and Voice'	– Ps. 67 ('Grand Chant', Humfrey?) – Responses said?	(no anthem)	Beethoven, Hallelujah Chorus (*The Mount of Olives*)

Wedding (date, venue)	Entrance Processions (and introit, when included)	Psalm and Responses	Anthem	Recess (in chapel)
Princess Mary Adelaide of Cambridge (1866, St Anne's, Kew)	– **initial processions:** all(?) organ voluntary – **bride:** hymn, 'How Welcome was the Call'	– Ps. 67 (Tallis in A) – Responses said?	(no anthem)	Beethoven, *Ode to Joy* (9th symphony), arr. for organ
Princess Helena (1866, PC, Windsor Castle)	– **royal family:** Beethoven, Triumphal March (*Tarpeja*) – **bridegroom:** Mendelssohn, 'War March of the Priests' (*Athalie*) – **bride:** Handel, march from *Scipio*	– Ps. 67 ('chanted') – Responses said?	– **before blessing:** Cusins, *Royal Wedding Chorale* ('How Welcome Was the Call')	Spohr, unidentified march
Princess Louise (1871, SG)	– **royal family:** Elvey, *Festal March* – **bridegroom:** Handel, march from *Scipio* – **bride:** Trumpets and timpani, National Anthem?, then Mendelssohn, 'War March of the Priests' (*Athalie*)	– Pss 128 and 67 (Elvey, Double Chant in A) – Responses said	– **before blessing:** Beethoven, Hallelujah Chorus (*The Mount of Olives*)	Handel, march from *Occasional Oratorio*
Prince Arthur, Duke of Connaught and Strathearn (1879, SG)	– **individual processions:** welcomed in the Chapel with fanfares, or 'flourishes' – **royal family:** Handel, march from *Hercules* – **queen:** Mendelssohn, 'War March of the Priests' (*Athalie*) – **bridegroom:** Elvey, march *Albert Edward* – **bride:** Handel, march from *Occasional Oratorio*	– Pss 128 and 67 (Elvey, [Double?] Chant in A) – Responses said	– **after blessing:** Handel, Hallelujah Chorus (*Messiah*)	Mendelssohn, Wedding March
Prince Leopold, Duke of Albany (1882, SG)	– **each procession:** announced by fanfares – **royal family:** Elvey, march (?) – **queen:** Handel, march from *Occasional Oratorio* – **bridegroom:** Mendelssohn, 'War March of the Priests' (*Athalie*) – **bride:** Gounod, *Marche Nuptiale*	– Pss 128 and 67 (Elvey, Double Chant in A) – Responses said	– **before blessing:** Beethoven, Hallelujah Chorus (*The Mount of Olives*)	Mendelssohn, Wedding March

Wedding (date, venue)	Entrance Processions (and introit, when included)	Psalm and Responses	Anthem	Recess (in chapel)
Princess Beatrice (1885, St Mildred's, Whippingham, Isle of Wight)	– **royal family:** Handel, march from *Occasional Oratorio* – **bridegroom:** Parry, march (?) – **bride:** Wagner, Bridal March	– Ps. 128 (chant by Ouseley) – Responses said?	– **towards end:** Mendelssohn, *O Give Thanks to the Lord* (arrangement)	Mendelssohn, Wedding March (organ)
Princess Louise of Wales (1889, PC)	– **clerics:** Jekyll, *Nuptial March* – **royal family:** Handel, march from *Occasional Oratorio* – **bridegroom:** Wagner, march from *Tannhäuser* – **bride:** Wagner, Bridal March	– Ps. 128 (Beethoven, arr. Turle) – Responses sung (Turl?)	– **before blessing:** Barnby, *O Perfect Love*	Mendelssohn, Wedding March (organ)
Princess Marie Louise of Schleswig-Holstein (1891, SG)	– **royal and imperial arrivals:** greeted by fanfares – **clerics:** Lemmens, march – **bridegroom's family:** Schubert, march – **royal family:** Guilmant, 'Marche Nuptiale' (*Epithalame*) – **queen:** National Anthem, then Handel, march from *Occasional Oratorio* – **bridegroom:** Parratt, 'Short March' – **bride:** hymn, 'Lord, Who Hast Made Home and Love' (Parratt)	– Ps. 67 (Garrett in A) – Responses said?	– **after psalm?:** Mendelssohn, 'Hearts Feel, that Love Thee' (*Athalie*) – **before blessing:** hymn, 'O Perfect Love' (Dykes) – **after blessing:** 'elaborate choral "Amen."'	Mendelssohn, Wedding March (organ)
Prince George of Wales, Duke of York (1893, CR)	– **clerics:** Handel, march from *Occasional Oratorio* – **royal family:** Handel, march from *Scipio* – **bridegroom:** Henry Smart, 'March in G' – **bride:** Wagner, Bridal March (*Lohengrin*) – **introit:** hymn, 'Father of Life' (Creser)	– Ps. 67 (Goss) – Responses said, sung 'Amens'	– **after psalm and prayers:** Barnby, *O Perfect Love* – **after address, before blessing:** hymn, 'Lead Us, Heavenly Father, Lead Us'	Mendelssohn, Wedding March (organ)
Princess Maud of Wales (1896, PC)	– **queen only** (in Chapel): Molique, march from *Abraham* – **royal family:** Wagner, march from *Tannhäuser*; then (in Chapel) Guilmant, *Marche Nuptiale* – **bridegroom:** Gounod, *Marche Religieuse*; then (in Chapel) anthem: Hill, *O Perfect Love* – **bride:** Wagner, Bridal March (*Lohengrin*); then (in Chapel) hymn, 'O Paradise'	– Ps. 128 (Hopkins in E-flat) – Responses and prayers said?	– **after prayers?:** hymn, 'How Welcome Was the Call') – **after blessing:** hymn, 'What Thou Hast Joined None May Divide' (Ouseley)	Mendelssohn, Wedding March (possibly organ with orchestra)

Wedding (date, venue)	Entrance Processions (and introit, when included)	Psalm and Responses	Anthem	Recess (in chapel)
Princess Alice of Albany (1904, SG)	– cleric s: Mendelssohn, 'War March of the Priests' (*Athalie*) – royal processions: 'heralded by the silver trumpets'?, National Anthem played at least for arrival of the king – bridegroom's family, with bridegroom: Meyerbeer, 'Coronation March' (*Le Prophète*) – king and queen: Gounod, *Marche Religieuse*(?) – bride: hymn, 'O God, our Help in Ages Past'	– Ps. 67 (Garrett) – Responses sung (Tallis [in A?])	– after prayers?: Mendelssohn, 'Lift thine Eyes to the Mountains' (*Elijah*) – before blessing: hymn, 'O Perfect Love' (Dykes)	Mendelssohn, Wedding March (organ)
Princess Margaret of Connaught (1905, SG)	– outdoor bands announcing the processions with the Swedish National Anthem and 'God Save the King', respectively – royal family: music not known? – bridegroom Wagner, march from *Tannhäuser* – king and queen: Elgar, *Imperial March* – bride: hymn, 'When God of Old'	– Ps. 67, 'chanted' – Responses said?	– before address: Beethoven, Hallelujah Chorus (The Mount of Olives) – before blessing: hymn, 'Now Thank We All our God'	Mendelssohn, Wedding March (organ)
Prince Arthur of Connaught (1913, CR)	– clergy: Parry, march from *The Birds* – queen and royal family: Stanford, Procession Music from *Drake* – bridegroom: Alcock, *Marche Triomphale* – bride: hymn, 'Lead Us, Heavenly Father, Lead Us'	– Ps. 67 (Alcock in E) – Responses said ('shall say')	– before address: Mendelssohn, 'Lift thine Eyes to the Mountains' (*Elijah*) – after address, before blessing: Hill, *O Perfect Love*	Mendelssohn, Wedding March (organ)
Prince George Louis of Battenberg (1916, CR)	– clergy and royal family: organ music? – bridegroom: no specific music mentioned – bride: hymn, 'O Perfect Love' (to tune of the Russian National Anthem, arr. Alcock)	– Ps. 128 – Responses said ('shall say')	– before blessing: hymn, 'May the Grace of Christ our Saviour' – after blessing: Mendelssohn, 'For He Shall Give his Angels Charge over Thee' (*Elijah*)	Mendelssohn, Wedding March (organ)
Prince Alexander of Battenberg (1917, CR)	(No details seem to be known of any music at this wedding.)			

Sources and Bibliography

Printed Orders of Service (OS) and
Ceremonials – in Chronological Order

The following lists cannot claim to be exhaustive or complete; their purpose is primarily to point to the archival sources for the material used in this study.

Orders of Service

1797 – copy (with crimson velvet covers) in *Lbl C.136.f.29.* This appears to be the only known copy.

1858 – copies (with both white watered paper covers and with crimson velvet covers) in *Lna LC 2/80, Ob Rec. d.17,* and *Ob Rec. d.18.*

1863 – copies in *Ob Rec. d.16* (with crimson velvet covers), *Wsg X. 33/5/2/1* (white watered paper covers), *Wra RA F&V/WED/1863* (one with crimson velvet covers, one with white watered paper covers), and *Lna LC 2/84* (with both, crimson velvet and white watered paper covers).

1866 – copies in *Lna LC 2/85* and *Lbl C.110.g.7* (in both with white watered paper covers), *Wra RA F&V/WED/1866* (one with crimson velvet, one with white watered paper covers).

1871 – copies in *Wsg X.33/8* (white watered paper covers) and *Wra RA F&V/WED/1871* (crimson velvet covers).

1874 – copies *Lna LC 2/89/2* (white watered paper covers).

1879 – copies in *Lna LC 2/95, Wsg X.33/9/3,* and *Wsg P. Misc. I 6* (all with white watered paper covers), and in *Wra RA F&V/WED/1879* (crimson velvet covers).

1882 – copies in *Wra RA F&V/WED/1882* and *LC 2/96* (in both with crimson velvet covers and white watered paper covers), *Wsg X. 33/11/1* (white watered paper covers).

1885 – copies in *Lna LC 2/99* (with both, crimson velvet covers and white watered paper covers), *Llp Davidson 742* (crimson velvet), *Wsg XVII.43.3/1* (specially produced souvenir copy, with white cardboard covers).

1889 – copies in *Lna LC 2/121* (crimson velvet covers) and *Wra RA F&V/WED/1889* (two copies with crimson velvet covers, one of which is inscribed 'Victoria Mary of Teck / 1889'), also *Wsg XVII.43.4/5* (white watered paper covers).

1891 – copies in *Wra RA F&V/WED/1891/Anhalt-Schleswig-Holstein* (with purple velvet covers).

1893 – copies in *Wra RA F&V/WED/1893/GV* (two differently-sized copies, both with dark red velvet covers, one of which is inscribed 'May / July 6th / 1893') and in *Lna LC 2/131* (white watered paper covers).

1896 – copies in *Wra RA F&V/WED/1896* (with red velvet covers) and in *Lna LC 2/134* (with red velvet covers and with white watered paper covers).

1904 – copies in *Wra RA F&V/WED/1904, Wsg X.33/18/1/1,* and *Wsg SGC M69/3/8* (all with white watered paper covers).

1905 – copies in *Wra RA F&V/WED/1905* (white watered paper covers) and *Wsg X.33/19/1* (with crimson velvet covers).

1913 – copies in *Wra RA F&V/WED/1913* (white watered paper covers).

1916 – copy in *Wra F&V/WED/1916.*

Sources and Bibliography

Ceremonials

NB: The history and development of the printed ceremonials for weddings still deserve a more detailed study. The various versions of a printed ceremonial occasionally differ slightly in the page numbering.

1795 – several printed copies, all bound together, in *Lna LC 2/25/2*; two more copies (the second with annotations) in *Lbl Add MS 6332*, fols 88ʳ–102ʳ; one in *Lbl Add MS 34453*, fols 231ʳ–232ʳ, and one in *Llp Fulham Papers Porteus 17*, fols 212ʳ–213ᵛ; all of these are in the future tense – also manuscript copies, in the past tense, in *Lca MS Ceremonials L. 19*, pp. 227–29, and (together with a printed copy) in *Lna LC 5/6*.

1797 – copies in *Llp Fulham Papers Porteus 17*, fols 236ʳ–237ʳ, and in *Lbl Add MS 6332*, fols 146ʳ–147ʳ and 148ʳ–149ʳ; all of these in the future tense. Manuscript copies in *Lna LC 5/7*, pp. 54–56 (future tense); *Lca MS Ceremonials L. 19*, pp. 231–35 (past tense); and *Wra RA GEO/MAIN/73943-73944* (past tense).

1840 – copies in *Lca Marriage of Queen Victoria 1840* (red volume – 'W.C. 107' on spine), and *Lca Marriages & Baptisms of the Royal Family (C.G.Y. 893)*, both are paper copies without covers; *Lna LC 2/69* (several copies printed on white silk, with green silk covers, and also simpler paper copies); *Wra RA F&V/Weddings/1840* (copies printed on silk and copies printed on paper, both with blue watered silk cover; also plainer paper copies without cover); at least one copy, printed on white silk, with blue watered silk cover in *Royal Collection, RCIN 1053036* – all of these are written in the future tense.

1843a/b – copies of a) 'Ceremonial to be observed', paper copy without covers, in the future tense, in *Lbl Add MS 41777*, fols 247ʳ–248ᵛ (Sir George Smart's copy); and b) 'Ceremonial observed', paper copies without covers , in the past tense, in *Lna LC 2/70/5* and *Lca Ceremonials (printed), Loose papers 5*.

1858a/b – copies of a) 'Ceremonial to be observed', in the future tense, in *Lbl Add MS 41777*, fols 315ʳ–318ʳ, *Lna LC 2/79*, *Llp Tait 431*, fols 25ʳ–28ʳ, and *Wra RA F&V/WED/1858* (all four without covers), and also in *Lna LC 2/80* (blue watered silk covers); and b) 'Ceremonial observed', in paper copies without covers, in the past tense (and more detailed) in *Wra RA F&V/WED/1858*.

1862a/b – copies of a) 'Ceremonial to be observed', paper copy without covers, in the future tense, in *Lna LC 2/81*; and b) 'Ceremonial observed', in paper copy without covers, in the past tense, in *Lna LC 2/82/3*.

1863a/b – copies of a) 'Ceremonial to be observed', paper copies with red crown on cover, in the future tense, in *Wsg X. 33/5/3* and in *Wra RA F&V/WED/1863*; and b) 'Ceremonial observed', in the past tense, in *Wsg X. 33/5/4* (no covers) and *Lna LC 2/84* (blue watered silk covers).

1866a/b – copies of a) 'Ceremonial to be observed', in the future tense, in *Lbl 9930.p.6* (white with red paper covers); and b) 'Ceremonial observed', in paper copies without cover, in the past tense, in *Wsg X. 33/5/7*; copies of both a) and b) in *Lna LC 2/85* (without covers, in the future tense – and with blue watered silk covers, in the past tense), and in *RA F&V/WED/1866: 5 July* (without covers, in the future tense – and one with blue watered silk covers, in the past tense; this includes also a smaller copy of printed ceremonial 'From papers of Col. Francis Seymour').

1871a/b – copies of a) 'Ceremonial to be observed', in paper copies without covers, in the future tense, in *Lna LC 2/89/1* and of b) 'Ceremonial observed', with blue watered silk covers, in the past tense, and also without covers in *RA F&V/WED/1871*.

British Royal Weddings

1879 – copies in *Wra RA F&V/WED/1879* and *Lna LC 2/95*: with blue watered silk covers and also copies without covers – all written in the past tense.

1882 – copies in *Wra RA F&V/WED/1882* (both, blue watered silk covers and without covers) and *Lna WORK 21/12/5* (without covers) – all written in the past tense.

1885 – printed copies in *Ob MS. Benson adds. 17*, *Lna WORK 21/12/6*, *Wsg XVII. 43.3/2*, *Wsg XVII.43.3/[bundle of papers by the Dean of Windsor]*, and in *Wra RA F&V/WED/1885* (all paper copies without covers.); *Wra RA F&V/WED/1885/Ceremonial* is a copy bound in blue watered silk – all of these are written in the past tense.

1889a/b – copies of a) 'Ceremonial to be observed', with white watered paper covers, in the future tense and of b) 'Ceremonial observed', without covers, in the past tense, in *Lna LC 2/121*, *Wra RA F&V/WED/1889*, and in *Wsg SGC XVII.43.4/1-8*; copy of a) only in *Wsg SGC XVII.43.4/4* and copy of b) only in *Ob MS. Benson adds. 17*.

1891a/b – copies of both, a) 'Ceremonial to be observed' and b) 'Ceremonial observed', all bound in hard-board silver/white watered-paper covers with blue print, in *Lna LC 2/125* and *Ob MS. Benson adds. 17*; both types also in *RA F&V/WED/1891/Anhalt-Schleswig-Holstein* which furthermore includes a single copy of b) printed on larger-format paper.

1893a/b – copies of a) 'Ceremonial to be observed' in *Lca Ceremonials (printed), Loose papers, Lna LC 2/131*, and in *Wra RA F&V/WED/1893*; and of b) 'Ceremonial observed' in *Llp Benson 123*, *Lna LC 2/129*, and *Ob MS. Benson adds. 17* – all of these are paper copies without covers.

1896a/b – copies of a) 'Ceremonial to be observed' in *Wra RA F&V/WED/1896* and b) 'Ceremonial observed', in *Lna LC 2/134*, *Ob MS. Benson adds. 17*, and *Ob 38494 c.12* – all of these are written in the past tense; they are all without cover or have white watered-paper covers.

1904a/b – copies of a) 'Ceremonial to be observed' in *Wsg X. 33/18/3* and b) 'Ceremonial observed' in *Wra RA F&V/WED/1904* – all of these are paper copies without covers.

1905 – copies in *Wra RA F&V/WED/1905* and *Wsg X.33/20* – all without covers and in the past tense.

1913 – copy in *Wra RA F&V/WED/1913* (without covers, and in the future tense), reprinted in 'The Royal Wedding: To-day's Ceremony at the Chapel Royal', *Times*, 15 October 1913, pp. 9–10.

Sources and Bibliography

Manuscript and Archival Material

Manuscript Music

Lbl: London, British Library

Add MS 17859: Maurice Greene, 'Anthem composed for the marriage of the Princess Royal [1734]', copied by Vincent Novello; eighteenth century.

Add MS 27757: Thomas Sanders Dupuis, anthem for the wedding of the Prince of Wales, 1795.

Ob: Oxford, Bodleian Library

MS Mus. Sch. c. 117a–c: William Boyce, 'The King Shall Rejoice' [for the wedding of George III and Charlotte of Mecklenburg-Strelitz 1761] score, vocal and instrumental parts, mostly autograph).

MS Mus. d. 46 (formerly *16750. 81*): Maurice Greene, 'Blessed Are All They, that Fear the Lord', 1734, score (autograph?).

Documentary Manuscript Material

Lbl: London, British Library

Add MS 6332: Material on royal marriages, 1677–1818, from collection of Lady Banks (Dorothea Banks; but this may possible come from her sister-in-law, the collector Sarah Sophia Banks, 1744–1818).

Add MS 27543: Accounts relating to royal households and royal events, eighteenth to nineteenth century.

Add MS 32556: 'Correspondence of Cox Macro, D.D. / of Norton in Suffolk. / with many of the most / eminent Literary men and artists / of his time. / particularly with / D[r] Hurd, Bishop of Worcester. / Vol I. / 1699–1740.'

Add MS 39311: Berkley Papers, vol. VIII: Correspondence 1710–76.

Add MS 41772: 'Events / in the life of / George, T. Smart / From 1776. / (the year of his birthe) / to 1830. inclusive. / Vol: I' [biographical and financial notes, 1776–1861]. This source actually includes three vols, going up to the year '186[blank]'.

Add MS 41777: Smart Papers, vol. VII: Correspondence and papers, including programmes and accounts (partly printed), relating to royal concerts and ceremonials (1819–66), and the annual Festival of the Sons of the Clergy (1832–45).

Add MS 73773: Walpole Papers, vol. IV: 1716–47.

C.136.f.29: Printed copy of the order of service for the wedding of Princess Charlotte, Princess Royal, and Frederick-William, Hereditary Prince of Württemberg of Württemberg, 18 May 1797.

Harley MS 7034, no. 7 (pp. 422–23): 'The Marriage of the Princess Mary May 2: 1641.' – anonymous, seemingly eighteenth-century copy of account owned by Bishop Wren.

King's MS 136, fols 463[r]–499[v]: account of the wedding of Charles I, 1625, in French.

Lca: London, College of Arms

Briscoe I = Miscell: Collections. Coronations, Funerals, Installations &c.', vol. 1 (on fol. 1 this has the inscription 'These Collections were made by M[r] Briscoe and came to me by his Executor Nicholas Bonfoy Esq.[r] whose Gift they were A.° 1764. I had access to them at the Coronation of King George the third. H Hill').

British Royal Weddings

Ceremonials (printed), Loose Papers: Ceremonials of various royal occasions.

Funerals, Ceremonials: 1843–1861: Ceremonials of funerals and other royal occasions.

Marriage of Queen Victoria. 1840 (green volume, 'CA' on spine): Collection of various material on Queen Victoria's wedding.

Marriage of Queen Victoria 1840 (red volume – 'W.C. 107' on spine): Extensive collection of material on Queen Victoria's wedding.

Marriages & Baptisms of the Royal Family (C.G.Y. 893): Various materials on royal weddings and christenings between 1840 and 1869, from the collection of Charles George Young (Garter King of Arms 1842–69).

Miscell: Coll: By Anstis: Collection of heraldic and ceremonial material by John Anstis, Garter King of Arms; eighteenth century.

MS Ceremonials L. 19: Ceremonials for, and accounts of, eighteenth-century royal occasions.

S.M.L. 30: Stephen Martin Leake, 'Ceremonials', vol. 3.

S.M.L. 44: Stephen Martin Leake, 'Heraldic Annals', vol. 1.

S.M.L. 45: Stephen Martin Leake, 'Heraldic Annals', vol. 2.

S.M.L. 65: Stephen Martin Leake, 'Heraldic Memorials', vol. 2.

Llp: London, Lambeth Palace Library

Davidson 21: Randall Davidson (Dean of Windsor, Bishop of Rochester, then Winchester, and Archbishop of Canterbury), Correspondence with the royal family, 1885–1930.

Fulham Papers Porteus 17: Correspondence and papers of Beilby Porteus (Bishop of London), 1789–1809.

Moore 6: Papers of John Moore (Dean of Canterbury, Bishop of Bangor, and Archbishop of Canterbury), relating to royal ceremonies, the Episcopal Church of Scotland, and the Church of Ireland, 1764–1800.

MS 285: 'English Royal Affairs and Ceremonial' (late sixteenth to early seventeenth century).

MS 887: Precedence in the Chapel Royal (1740).

MS 1130: Court Papers, *c*. 1760–61, bound in 2 vols, continuously numbered.

MS 2100: Notebooks of Bishop Porteus, 15 February 1789 – 3 July 1800.

MS 2103: Notebooks of Bishop Porteus, 20 September 1786 – 3 July 1800.

Lna: London, National Archives

LC 2/29: 'Court Proceedings / 1761 / George 3.rd Wedding'.

LC 2/69: Material relating to the marriage of Queen Victoria, 1840.

LC 2/79: Material on the wedding of Princess Victoria, Princess Royal, with Prince Frederick of Prussia, 1858.

LC 2/80: Material on the wedding of Princess Victoria, Princess Royal, with Prince Frederick of Prussia, 1858.

LC 2/81: Gala Book – material on marriages, christenings, confirmations, parties, festivals, ceremonial and press cuttings, 1858–72.

LC 2/83: Material on the wedding of Prince Edward Albert, Prince of Wales and Princess Alexandra of Denmark, 1863.

LC 2/84: Material on the wedding of Prince Edward Albert, Prince of Wales and Princess Alexandra of Denmark, 1863.

LC 2/86: Material on royal weddings, 1866–85.

LC 2/120: Material on the wedding of Princess Louise of Wales with the Earl of Fife, 1889.

LC 2/128: Material on the wedding of Prince George, Duke of York, and Princess Victoria Mary of Teck, 1893.

Sources and Bibliography

LC 2/129: Material on the wedding of Prince George, Duke of York, and Princess Victoria Mary of Teck, 1893.

LC 2/132: Marriage of Princess Maud of Wales with Prince Charles of Denmark: letters received and sent, 1896.

LC 2/133: Marriage of Princess Maud of Wales with Prince Charles of Denmark: bills, 1896.

LC 5/4: Extracts from the memoranda and papers of Sir Charles Cottrell-Dormer [*recte* Sir Stephen (or Samuel) Cottrell – otherwise the dates do not match: Cottrell was Assistant Master of the Ceremonies 1758–96, and Master of the Ceremonies 1796–1818]. Copied and arranged by his successor, Sir Robert Chester, in 1820.

LC 5/5: Notes and memoranda (in one volume) of Sir Stephen Cottrell, Master of the Ceremonies, 1782–1812.

LC 5/6: Letter book of Sir Stephen Cottrell, 1793–1811.

LC 5/7: Notebook of Sir Robert Chester, Assistant Master of the Ceremonies, 1796–1811.

LC 5/20: 'Warrants of Several Sorts, 1735–38'.

LC 5/168: Fees Book, 1761–65.

LC 5/204: Precedent Book, 1740–1819.

WORK 19/138: Windsor Castle, St. George's Chapel: Royal Weddings, 1862–1905.

WORK 19/385: Chapel Royal: Estimates regarding the preparation of the Chapel for royal wedding ceremonies, heating, lighting, paving, etc., 1904–17.

WORK 19/392: Material relating to the private chapel [Windsor Castle], 1857–78.

WORK 21/9/12: Particulars of expenditure, wedding of the Prince of Wales, 1863.

WORK 21/12/1: Marriage of Queen Victoria, general arrangements, 1839–41.

WORK 21/12/2: 'Marriage of H R Highness / The Princess Royal / 25th January 1858. / Furniture Account'.

WORK 21/12/3: Marriage of the Prince of Wales: Ceremonial observed and general arrangements, payment of gratuities, illuminations; 1863.

WORK 21/12/4: Marriage of the Duke of Edinburgh, various arrangements, 1873–74.

WORK 21/12/8: Marriage of Princess Maud of Wales, arrangements, Office of Works and successors, 1896.

WORK 21/12/7: Marriage of the Duke of York 1893. General arrangements.

WORK 21/19: Material on the coronation and the wedding of Queen Victoria, 1838–40.

WORK 34/121 and *34/122*: Two first-floor plans of St James's Palace by Henry Flitcroft, 1729.

Lwa: London, Westminster Abbey

WAM Service Papers: Collection of orders of service for various occasions, sorted by date.

Sheffield City Archives

BFM/1313/32: C.[?] Bacon to 'Mr [Frank] Bacon' [at Trinity Hall, Cambridge], Petersham, 5 September 1761.

Wra: Windsor, Windsor Castle, Royal Archives

RA F&V/Weddings/1840: Material on the wedding of Queen Victoria and Prince Albert, 1840.

RA F&V/WED/1858: Material on the wedding of Princess Victoria, Princess Royal, and Prince Frederick William (Friedrich Wilhelm) of Prussia, 1858.

RA F&V/WED/1863: Material on the wedding of Prince Albert Edward, Prince of Wales, 1863.

RA F&V/WED/1866: 12 June: Material on the wedding of Princess Mary of Cambridge and Francis, Duke of Teck, 1866.

British Royal Weddings

RA F&V/WED/1866: 5 July: Material on the wedding of Princess Helena and Prince Christian of Schleswig-Holstein, 1866.

RA F&V/WED/1871: Material on the wedding of Princess Louise and the Marquess of Lorne, 1871.

RA F&V/WED/1882: Material on the wedding of Prince Leopold, Duke of Albany, and Princess Helen of Waldeck and Pyrmont, 1882.

RA F&V/WED/1885: Material on the wedding of Princess Beatrice and Prince Henry of Battenberg, 1885.

RA F&V/WED/1885/Ceremonial: printed ceremonial for the wedding of Princess Beatrice, 1885.

RA F&V/WED/1889: Material on the wedding of Princess Louise of Wales and the Earl of Fife, 1889.

RA F&V/WED/1891/Anhalt-Schleswig-Holstein: Material on the wedding of Princess Marie Louise of Schleswig-Holstein and Prince Aribert of Anhalt, 1891.

RA F&V/WED/1893: Material on the wedding of Prince George, Duke of York, later George V, and Princess Victoria Mary of Teck, 1893.

RA F&V/WED/1896: Material on the wedding of Princess Maud of Wales and Prince Charles (Carl) of Denmark, 1896.

RA F&V/WED/1904: Material on the wedding of Princess Alice of Albany and Prince Alexander of Teck, 1904.

RA F&V/WED/1905: Material on the wedding of Princess Margaret of Connaught and Prince Gustav of Sweden, 1905.

RA F&V/WED/1913: Material on the wedding of Prince Arthur of Connaught, 1913.

RA F&V/WED/1916: Material on the wedding of Prince Louis of Battenberg, 1916.

RA GEO/ADD/32/2430-2434: 'Some Anecdotes of a Collection of Anthems, by the late G. F. Handel; in His Majesty's Possession', [fragment, 1760–1805], available online at https://gpp.rct.uk (accessed 22 Aug. 2021).

RA GEO/MAIN/52790-52794: 'Procession on / the Princess Royalls / Marriage. / March 14.th 1733/4', available online at https://gpp.rct.uk (accessed 10 April 2021).

RA GEO/MAIN/73943-73944: Manuscript copy of ceremonial for the wedding of Princess Charlotte, Princess Royal, and Prince Frederick-William of Württemberg in 1797.

RA VIC/ADDC6/1: Personal diary of Lady Geraldine Somerset (Lady-in-Waiting to Princess Augusta, Duchess of Cambridge, from 1858 to 1889); 19 volumes, covering the years 1855–80, 1883–84, 1888–89, 1891–96, 1904–14.

RA VIC/ADDU/32/801: 'Transcript of Extracts from Queen Victoria's Letters to the Princess Royal 1863–87'.

RA VIC/MAIN/Y/187: 'Translations of Y. 189 Extracts of Letters from Albert, Prince Consort to Baron Christian Stockmar, 1856–61'.

RA VIC/MAIN/Y/189: 'The Prince Consort's / Letters / to Baron Stockmar. II.' (Copies of Extracts of Letters from Prince Albert to Baron Christian Stockmar, 1854–61).

Wsg: Windsor, St George's Chapel, Archives

X.33/5/2/1: Order of service for the wedding of the Prince of Wales, 1863.

XVII.30.1: Material on the wedding of Princess Louise and the Marquess of Lorne, 1871.

XVII.30.2: Correspondence relating to the wedding of the Prince of Wales, 1863.

XVII.43.3/2: Material on the wedding of Princess Beatrice, 1885.

XVII.43.3/4: Printed list of music, wedding of Princess Beatrice, 1885.

XVII.43.3/[4.1]: 'Papers Connected with / The Marriage (at Osborne) / of H.RH. Princess / Beatrice / July 23 1885'.

XVII.43.4/1–8: Material on the wedding of Princess Louise and the Earl of Fife, 1889.

Sources and Bibliography

Published Material (including Dissertations)

Published Music

Albert, Prince, *The Collected Compositions of His Royal Highness, The Prince Consort*, ed. by W. G. Cusins (London: Metzler & Co., [1882?]).

—, *Musical Compositions of His Royal Highness The Prince Albert, with the Original Words and Music from the Authentic German Edition and an English Adaptation by William Ball* (London: Printed and sold by C. Lonsdale, [1840]).

—, *The Vocal Compositions of His Royal Highness the Prince Consort* (London: C. Lonsdale, [1862]).

Albert, Prince; and Ernest, Prince, *Songs and Ballads, Written and Set to Music by Their Royal Highnesses Albert and Ernest, Princes of Saxe Coburg-Gotha*, transl. from the original German by G. G. Richardson (London: Henry Colburn, 1840).

Alcock, Walter G., *Marche Triomphale, for the Organ* (London: Novello and Company, [1913]).

Barnby, Joseph, *O Perfect Love: Wedding Anthem. Music Composed Expressly for the Marriage of H.R.H. Princess Louise of Wales with the Earl of Fife, K.T.* (London: Novello, Ewer and Co., [1889]).

Boyce, William, *Two Anthems for the Georgian Court*; Part ii: *The King Shall Rejoice*, ed. by John R. van Nice, 'Recent Researches in the Music of the Baroque Era', VIII (Madison: A–R Editions, 1970).

Bunsen, Josias, *Vierstimmiges Choralbuch zum allgemeinen evangelischen Gesang- und Gebetbuche zum Kirchen- und Hausgebrauch*, rev. and ed. by Friedrich Filitz (Berlin: Wilhelm Besser, 1846).

Cathedral Music: Being a Collection in Score, of the Most Valuable & Useful Compositions for that Service, ed. by Samuel Arnold, 4 vols (London: Printed for the Editor, [1790]).

Choral Hymn for Four Voices, Sung at the Marriage of The Princess Royal […] *the Words Written for the Occasion by Thos Oliphant Esq.r* (London: Addison, Hollier & Lucas, [1859]).

Church Hymnal, by Permission of the General Synod of the Church of Ireland, Set to Appropriate Tunes, 'under the musical editorship of' Sir Robert Prescott, 6th edn (Dublin: Published by the Association for Promoting Christian Knowledge, 1891).

Cramer, C. *The Royal Wedding Music Arranged for the Piano Forte* (London: Charles H. Purday, [1858]); seen as *Lbl Music Collections h.725.b*, no. 14.

Creser, William, *Father of Life: Marriage Hymn*, Novello no. 9657 (London: Novello, Ewer & Co., [1893]).

—, *Source of All Light and Life Divine: Choral* (London: Novello, Ewer and Co., [1896]).

—, *Wedding March: Composed in Commemoration of the Marriage of H.R.H. The Duke of York* […], Novello no. 9654 (London: Novello, Ewer & Co. [1893]).

Cusins, W. G. [William George], *Royal Wedding Chorale, Composed Expressly for the Marriage of H.R.H. The Princess Helena, July 5th, 1866* (Words by Sir H. Baker), (London: Lamborn Cock, Addison & Co., [1866]).

Elvey, Sir George, *Festal March*, arr. for organ by Charles Hancock (London: Novello, Ewer & Co., [1896]).

—, *Festal March for Full Orchestra* (London: Novello, Ewer & Co., [1897]).

—, *Festal March Performed at the Marriage of H.R.H. The Princess Louise, with the Marquis of Lorne* […] (London: Novello, Ewer & Co., [1871?]).

Fortescue Harrison, Annie, *O Perfect Love: Anthem for Soprano Solo and Chorus, the Words by D. F. Blomfield* (London & New York: Novello, Ewer and Co., [1892]).

Garrett, George M. [ed.], *Chants – Old and New, Selected and Arranged in Order of Daily Use for one Calendar Month; with Special Chants for the Venite exultemus and Proper Psalms*, 2nd edn (London: Sacred Music Warehouse – Novello, Ewer and Co., [*c.* 1872?]).

Gounod, Charles, *Wedding March (No. 1) Composed for the Marriage of H.R.H. The Duke of Albany, K.G. with H.R.H. The Princess Helen of Waldeck*, 'Original Edition for Organ & Three Trombones' (London: Novell, Ewer & Co., [1882]).

—, *Wedding March (No. 1) Composed for the Marriage of H.R.H. The Duke of Albany, K.G. with H.R.H. The Princess Helen of Waldeck*, arr. for organ solo by George C. Martin (London: Novello, Ewer & Co., [1882]).

—, *Wedding March (No. 2) Composed and Dedicated to H.R.H. The Duke of Albany, K.G.*, arr. for piano solo by Berthold Tours (London: Novell, Ewer & Co., [1882]).

Händel, Georg Friedrich, *Wedding Anthems (HWV 262 and HWV 263)*, ed. by Matthew Gardner, *Hallische Händel-Ausgabe*, series III, vol. 11 (Kassel: Bärenreiter, 2013).

Hervey, F. A. J., *A Musical Setting of Such Portions of the Solemnization of Holy Matrimony as May Be Chorally Rendered*, words of the litany and hymns by S. C. Clarke, with two 'Short Addresses on Holy Marriage from the Bishop of Wakefield's "Pastor in Parochia"' (London: Skeffington and Son, [1891]).

The Holy Family: Admired Sacred Melodies by the Most Celebrated Composers, Arranged for the Piano Forte as Solos and Duets with ad libitum Acct.ˢ for Flute, Violin & Violon.º by William Hutchins Callcott (London: Robert Cocks & Co., [1886?]).

The Holy Mount, Admired Sacred Melodies, Arranged as Piano Duetts […] With (ad lib.) Accompaniments for Flute, Violin & Violoncello, by William Hutchins Callcott, first series (of three), (London: Robert Cocks & Co., [1861–1862]).

The Hymnal Companion to the Book of Common Prayer, with Accompanying Tunes, 3rd edn, rev. and enl., under the musical editorship of Charles Vincent and D. J. Wood, with the assistance of Sir John Stainer (London: Sampson Low, Marston & Company, 1890).

Hymns Ancient and Modern, ed. by William Henry Monk, supplemental tunes rev. by Charles Steggall (London: William Clowes & Sons, [1889]).

Jerrard, Paul, *The Order for the Solemnization of Holy Matrimony, Set to Music, Op. 10* (London, [1858]). Seen as *Lbl Music Collections F.363 (3.)*.

Kent, James, *Twelve Anthems Composed by James Kent […]* (London: Printed for the Author […] Published by William Randall, 1773).

—, *Kent's Twelve Anthems, (vol. 1.) A New Edition. Arranged with a Separate Accompaniment for the Organ or Piano Forte by A. T. Corfe. No. 10* [actual umber entered by hand] (London: Published by Coventry & Hollier, [*c.* 1840 according to the catalogue of the Bodleian Library, Oxford]). Seen as *Ob Tenbury Mus. c. 480 (19)*.

Mendelssohn Bartholdy, Felix, *Hearts Feel that Love Thee. Trio for Female Voices. Arranged from the Trio and Chorus in "Athalie."* (London: Novello, Ewer & Co., [1879]).

—, *Musik zu "Athalia" von Racine, MWV M16*, ed. by Armin Koch, 'Leipziger Ausgabe der Werke von Felix Mendelssohn Bartholdy', series V: 'Bühnenwerke', vol. 9 (Wiesbaden: Breitkopf & Härtel, 2010).

Molique, Bernhard, *March from the Oratorio: Abraham*, arr. for military band by George Miller (bandmaster, Royal Marines), (London and New York: Novello, Ewer & Co., [1897]).

Parry, C. H. H. [Charles Hubert Hastings], *Bridal March and Finale. From the Music to "The Birds" of Aristophanes*, arr. for piano solo by J. E. West (London: Novello & Co. 1906).

Praetorius, Abraham, *Harmonia gratulatoria nuptiis et honori […] Iacobi VI. Scotorum regis: et […] Friderici II. Daniæ, Norvegiæ etc. Regis Filiæ Annæ […] Scotiæ Reginæs, Sex vocibus composita*

Sources and Bibliography

etc. dedicata, ab Abrahamo Prœterio (Copenhagen: Laurentius Benedictus [i.e. Lorentz Benedicht], 1590). Available online at https://archive.org (accessed 9 October 2021).

The Service for the Solemnization of Holy Matrimony as Used in Westminster Abbey. With a Special Anthem Composed by J. Frederick Bridge (London: Novello, Ewer and Co [1890]).

Stanford, Charles Villiers, *Procession Music from "Drake"*, arr. for organ by Walter G. Alcock (London: Stainer & Bell, 1925).

Published Literature

[1st correspondent], 'Marriage of The Princess Louise and Marquis of Lorn', *Scotsman*, 22 March 1871, p. 2: 'The Ceremony'.

[2nd correspondent], 'Marriage of The Princess Louise and Marquis of Lorn', *Scotsman*, 22 March 1871, p. 2: 'The Scene in the Chapel'.

[3rd correspondent], 'Marriage of The Princess Louise and Marquis of Lorn', *Scotsman*, 22 March 1871, p. 2: [untitled sub-section].

'Abstract of Foreign Occurrences', *Gentleman's Magazine*, 85, part 1 (January–June 1815), pp. 636–39.

'Account of Ceremonial of the Marriage of the Princess Royal with the Hereditary Prince of Wirtemberg [*sic*]', *The Lady's Magazine*, 23 (1797), pp. 195–98.

'An Account of the Royal Marriage', *The Scots Magazine*, 23 (September 1761), pp. 493–94.

Adamson, John, 'The Tudor and Stuart Courts 1509–1714', in *The Princely Courts of Europe. Ritual, Politics and Culture under the Ancien Régime 1500–1750*, ed. by John Adamson, first publ. by Weidenfeld & Nicolson in 1999, paperback edn (London: Seven Dials, 2000), pp. 95–117.

Adolphus, John H., *The Royal Exile: Or, Memoirs of the Public and Private Life of Her Majesty, Caroline, Queen Consort of Great Britain* […], vol. 1, 18th edn (London: Published by Jones and Co., 1821).

'Æsthetics of the Wedding', *The Saturday Review of Politics, Literature, Science and Art*, 5:119, 6 February 1858, pp. 135–36.

Albert, Prince, *Letters of the Prince Consort, 1831–1861*, selected and ed. by Kurt Jagow, and transl. by E. T. S. [Edgar Trevelyan Stratford] Dugdale (London: John Murray, 1938).

'Amphion', 'Musical Echoes', *Bow Bells: A Magazine of General Literature and Art for Family Reading*, 9 June 1893, p. 572.

Anonymous, review of '*O Perfect Love*. Wedding Anthem. Composed by Joseph Barnby. [Novello, Ewer and Co.]', *Musical Times*, 30 (September 1889), p. 553.

Anonymous, review of '*Three Marches* by Mendelssohn. Arranged for the pianoforte by E. Pauer', *The Monthly Musical Record*, 22 (January 1892), p. 16.

Anonymous, review of *Wedding March* by William Creser, and *O Perfect Love* by Joseph Barnby (Novello, Ewer and Co.), *Musical Times*, 34 (August 1893), p. 489.

Anonymous, untitled report, *The Royal Magazine: Or Gentleman's Monthly Companion*, 5 (1761), pp. 104–05, here p. 104.

'The Approaching Royal Marriage', *Times*, 26 June 1843, p. 5.

Arch, Nigel, and Marschner, Joanna, *The Royal Wedding Dresses* (London: Sidgwick and Jackson, 1990).

Archer, Charles Maybury, *A Guide and Descriptive Account of the Marriage of The Princess Royal with Prince Frederick William of Prussia* (London: H. Elliot, 1858).

The Art of Heraldry; Explaining the Origin and Use of Arms and Armorial Bearings […] (Harding & King, 1834).

Ashbee, Andrew (ed.), *Records of English Court Music*, 9 vols (Aldershot: Scolar Press, 1991).

Ashbee, Andrew and Harley, John (eds), *The Cheque Books of the Chapel Royal*, 2 vols (Aldershot: Ashgate, 2000).

Ashdown, Dulcie M., *Royal Weddings* (London: R. Hale, 1981).

Aston, George, *His Royal Highness, the Duke of Connaught and Strathearn: A Life and Intimate Study* (London: G.G. Harrap & Co., 1929).

The Authentic Representation of the Magnificent Marriage Procession and Ceremony of Her Most Gracious Majesty Queen Victoria with His Royal Highness Prince Albert of Saxe Coburg, Celebrated at the Chapel Royal, St. James's, February 10, 1840 (London: Published solely by Messrs. Fores [1840?]). Seen as *Lna EXT 11/82*.

Athlone, Princess Alice, Countess of, *For my Grandchildren: Some Reminiscences of Her Royal Highness Princess Alice, Countess of Athlone* [...] (London: Evans Brothers Ltd, 1966/re-issued 1979).

Bailey, N[athan], *The New Universal English Dictionary* [...], 7th edn (London: Printed for William Cavell, 1776).

Baker-Smith, Veronica P. M., 'The Daughters of George II: Marriage and Dynastic Politics', in *Queenship in Britain 1660–1837: Royal Patronage, Court Culture and Dynastic Politics*, ed. by Clarissa Campbell Orr (Manchester: Manchester University Press, 2002), pp. 193–206.

—, *A Life of Anne of Hanover, Princess Royal* (Leiden: Brill, 1995).

Baldwin, David, *The Chapel Royal – Ancient and Modern* (London: Duckworth, 1990).

Barroll, J. Leeds, *Anna of Denmark, Queen of England: A Cultural Biography* (Philadelphia: University of Pensylvania Press, 2003).

Bartley, Paula, *Queen Victoria* (Abingdon: Routledge, 2016).

Baselt, Bernd, *Händel-Handbuch [HHB]*, 3 vols (Kassel: Bärenreiter, 1978–86).

Battiscombe, Georgina, *Queen Alexandra* (London: Sphere 1972).

Baxter, Philip, *Sarum Use: The Ancient Customs of Salisbury* (Reading: Spire Books, 2008).

Beaven, Arthur H[enry], *Popular Royalty* (London: Sampson Low, Marson and Company: 1897).

Beschreibung aller Solennitäten Bey dem Hohen Vermählungs-Feste, Ihro Hoch-Fürstl. Durchläucht Printz Friedrichs Mit Ihro Hoheit Der Königl. Groß-Brittannischen Princessin Maria [...] (Kassel: Hampesche Erben, [1740]).

[Hübner, Tobias], *Beschreibung der Reiß: Empfahung deß Ritterlichen Ordens: Vollbringung des Heyraths: und glücklicher Heimführung* [...] *Des* [...] *Herrn Friederichen deß Fünften* [...] *Mit* [...] *Princessin Elisabethen* [...] *Mit schönen Kupfferstücken gezieret* ([Heidelberg]: Gotthardt Vögelins Verlag, 1613).

Betts, T. Percy M., 'Marriage Music', *Graphic*, special wedding issue, 27 July 1885, pp. 20–21.

Betzwieser, Thomas, '"Ein lang gehegter Wunsch": Prinz Albert als Komponist in der Bonner Studienzeit', *Die Studien des Prinzen Albert an der Universität Bonn (1837–1838)*, ed. by Franz Bosbach (Berlin: Walter de Gruyter, 2010), pp. 187–218.

Black, Jeremy, *George III: America's Last King* (New Haven: Yale University Press, 2008).

—, *The Hanoverians: The History of a Dynasty* (London: Hambledon and London, 2004).

Bradley, Simon, 'The Queen's Chapel in the Twentieth Century', *Architectural History*, 44: 'Essays in Architectural History Presented to John Newman' (2001), pp. 293–302.

Brand, Emily, *Royal Weddings*, 'Shire Library', 665 (Oxford: Shire Publications, 2011).

Brand, John; and Ellis, Henry, *Observations on Popular Antiquities: Chiefly Illustrating the Origin of our Vulgar Customs, Ceremonies and Superstitions*, 2 vols, by John Brand, posthumously edited and with additions by Henry Ellis, first published in 1813, reprinted in 'Cambridge Library Collection' (Cambridge: Cambridge University Press, 2011).

Sources and Bibliography

Britland, Karen, 'A Ring of Roses: Henrietta Maria, Pierre de Bérulle, and the Plague of 1625–1626', in *The Wedding of Charles I and Henrietta Maria, 1625: Celebrations and Controversy*, ed. by Marie-Claude Canova-Green and Sara J. Wolfson, 'European Festival Studies: 1450–1700' (Turnhout: Brepols, 2021), pp. 85–104.

Brownlie, John, *The Hymns and Hymn-Writers of the Church Hymnary* (London: Henry Frowde, [1899]).

Budds, Michael Joe, 'Music at the Court of Queen Victoria: A Study of Music in the Life of the Queen and her Participation in the Musical Life of her Time', 3 vols (unpublished PhD dissertation, University of Iowa, 1987).

Burnet, [Gilbert], *Bishop Burnet's History of his Own Time*, vol. I: *From the Restoration of King Charles II. to the Settlement of King William and Queen Mary at the Revolution* (London: Printed for Thomas Ward, 1724).

Burch, Mark; and Bond, Maurice, 'The Western Steps of St George's Chapel: An Historical and Archaeological Report', *Report of the Society of the Friends of St George's and the Descendants of the Knights of the Garter* (1981–82), pp. 98–110.

Burrows, Donald, *Handel*, 'The Master Musicians', ed. by Stanley Sadie (Oxford: Oxford University Press, 1994, paperback edn 1996).

—, *HECR = Handel and the English Chapel Royal* (Oxford: Oxford University Press, 2005).

Burrows, Donald and Dunhill, Rosemary, *Music and Theatre in Handel's World: The Family Papers of James Harris, 1732–1780* (Oxford: Oxford University Press, 2002).

Caldari, Valentina; and Wolfson, Sara J. (eds), *Stuart Marriage Diplomacy* (Woodbridge: Boydell Press, 2018).

Caldwell, Titcomb, 'Baroque Court and Military Trumpets and Kettledrums: Technique and Music', *The Galpin Society Journal*, 9 (1956), pp. 56–81.

Calvert, John, *A Collection of Anthems Used in Her Majesty's Chapel Royal, the Temple Church, and the Collegiate Churches and Chapels in England and Ireland* (London: George Bell, 1844).

Cannadine, David, 'The Context, Performance and Meaning of Ritual: The British Monarchy and the "Invention of Tradition", *c.* 1820–1977', in *The Invention of Tradition*, ed. by Eric Hobsbawm and Terence Ranger (Cambridge: Cambridge University Press, 1983; repr. 2002), pp. 101–64.

—, 'Splendor out of Court: Royal Spectacle and Pageantry in Modern Britain, *c.* 1820–1977', in *Rites of Power: Symbolism, Ritual, and Politics since the Middle Ages*, ed. by Sean Wilentz (Philadelphia: University of Pennsylvania Press, 1985), pp. 206–43.

Canova-Green, Marie-Claude; and Wolfson, Sara (eds), *The Wedding of Charles I and Henrietta Maria, 1625: Celebrations and Controversy* (Turnout: Brepols, 2020).

'Ceremonial of the Duke of York's Marriage', *Gentleman's Magazine*, 61, part 2 (1791), pp. 1057–58.

'Ceremonial of the Nuptials of His Royal Highness the Prince of Wales with the Princess Caroline of Brunswick', *The Sun*, 9 April 1795, p. [2].

'The Ceremony and Dresses at the Royal Nuptials', *The London Journal, and Weekly Record of Literature, Science, and Art*, 6 March 1858, pp. 5–6.

Chaddock, Edward James Michael, 'Two Orchestral Anthems by John Alcock (1715–1806): A Critical Edition with Commentary' (unpubl. M.Phil diss.: University of Birmingham, 2010).

'The Chapel Royal', *Musical Times*, 43 (1902), pp. 88–92.

A Chapter from the History of England in the Twenty-sixth Year of the Reign of our Blessed Sovereign Lady Queen Victoria, March 1863 (London: Emily Faithfull, 1863).

Choné, Paulette, 'Firework Displays in Paris, London and Heidelberg (1612–1615)', in *Dynastic Marriages 1612/1615: A Celebration of the Habsburg and Bourbon Unions*, ed. by Margaret M. McGowan, first publ. by Ashgate in 2013 (London and New York: Routledge, 2016), pp. 201–14.

'Choral Marriage in Westminster Abbey', *ILN*, 9 July 1859, p. 31.

'Church and Organ News', *Musical News*, 1:19 (10 July 1891), p. 390.

'Churchman', 'Foreign Anthems. To the Editor of "Musical News', *Musical News*, 26:675 (6 February 1904), p. 138.

Cole, Suzanne, *Thomas Tallis and his Music in Victorian England* (Woodbridge: Boydell, 2008).

'Concert at Buckingham Palace', *The Musical World*, 36 (January 1858), pp. 75–76.

Cook, Andrew, *Prince Eddy: The King Britain Never Had* (Strout: Tempus, 2006).

Cooke, Sir C[lement] Kinloch, *A Memoir of Her Royal Highness Princess Mary Adelaide, Duchess of Teck, Based on her Private Diaries and Letters*, 2 vols (London: John Murray, 1900).

Correspondence between Frances, Countess of Hartford, (afterwards Duchess of Somerset,) and Henrietta Louisa, Countess of Pomfret: between the Years 1738 and 1741, 3 vols, vol. 1, 2nd edn (London: Printed for Richard Phillips, 1806).

'Countess Nada Torby's Wedding', *Times*, 16 November 1916, p. 11.

'The Court', *ILN*, 16 June 1866, p. 579.

'The Court', *ILN*, 18 March 1871, p. 259.

'The Court', *ILN*, 25 March 1871, p. 283.

'The Court', *ILN*, 14 January 1882, p. 35.

'The Court: Approaching Marriage of Princess Louise', *ILN*, 18 March 1871, p. 259.

'Court Circular', *Times*, 27 March 1843, p. 6.

Cressy, David, *Birth, Marriage, and Death: Ritual, Religion, and the Life-Cycle in Tudor and Stuart England* (Oxford: Oxford University Press, 1997).

Cummings, Brian (ed.), *The Book of Common Prayer: The Texts of 1549, 1559, and 1662* (Oxford: Oxford University Press, 2011).

Curran, Kevin, 'James I and Fictional Authority at the Palatine Wedding Celebrations', *Renaissance Studies*, 20:1 (February 2006), pp. 51–67.

—, *Marriage, Performance, and Politics at the Jacobean Court* (Aldershot: Ashgate, 2013).

Daniel, Evan, *The Prayer-Book: Its History, Language, and Contents* (London: William Wells Gardner, 1877).

Daniel, Ute; and Frey, Christian K. (eds), *Die Preussisch-Welfische Hochzeit 1913: Das Dynastische Europa in seinem letzten Friedensjahr* (Braunschweig, Appelhans, 2016).

Dart, Thurston, 'Two English Musicians at Heidelberg in 1613', *Musical Times*, 111 (1970), pp. 29 and 31–32.

Day, Ivan, 'Bridecup and Cake: The Ceremonial Food and Drink of the Bridal Procession', in *Food and the Rites of Passage*, ed. by Laura Mason (Totnes: Prospect Books, 2002), pp. 33–61.

'De Omnibus Rebus', *Public Opinion*, 48:1244 (24 July 1885), p. 116.

De-la-Noy, Michael, *The King Who Never Was: The Story of Frederick, Prince of Wales* (London: Peter Owen, 1996).

Dean, Lucinda Hazel Stewart, 'Crowns, Wedding Rings, and Processions: Continuity and Change in the Representation of Scottish Royal Authority in State Ceremony, *c.* 1214 – *c.* 1603' (unpublished PhD diss., University of Stirling, 2013).

Dean, Winton, *Handel's Dramatic Oratorios* (London: Oxford University Press 1959).

Delany, Mary, *The Autobiography and Correspondence of Mary Granville, Mrs. Delany*, ed. by Lady Llanover, first series, 3 vols (London: Richard Bentley, 1861).

Sources and Bibliography

Dennison, Matthew, *The Last Princess: The Devoted Life of Queen Victoria's Youngest Daughter* (London: Phoenix, 2007; paperback edn 2008).

Denvir, Bernard, 'Albert the Musician', *Musical Times*, 94 (1953), pp. 527–28.

'Die Hochzeit der Prinzessin Louise', *Neues Fremden-Blatt*, 7:84, 25 March 1871, '1. Beilage'.

'Domestic Occurrences', *Gentleman's Magazine*, 86 (1816), Part 2, pp. 78–79.

Drummond, Pippa, *The Provincial Music Festival in England, 1784–1914*, first publ. by Ashgate in 2011 (Abingdon: Routledge, 2016).

Duff, David, *Hessian Tapestry* (London: Frederick Muller, 1967).

—, *The Shy Princess: The Life of Her Royal Highness Princess Beatrice, the Youngest Daughter and Constant Companion of Queen Victoria* (London: Evans Brothers Ltd, 1958).

—, *Victoria and Albert* (London: Frederick Muller Ltd, 1972).

'The Duke of Edinburgh's Marriage', *Times*, 15 November 1873, p. 5.

Duncan, Sarah, *Mary I: Gender, Power, and Ceremony in the Reign of England's First Queen* (Basingstoke: Macmillan, 2012).

Eatock, Colin Timothy, *Mendelssohn and Victorian England* (London: Routledge, 2009).

[Editorial], *The Musical World*, 13 (February 1840), p. 89.

Edwards, F. G., 'Mendelssohn's "Wedding March.", *Musical News*, 6:170 (June 1894), p. 517.

Elvey, 'Lady' [Mary Elvey], *Life and Reminiscences of George J. Elvey […] Late Organist to H. M. Queen Victoria, and Forty-seven Years Organist of St. George's Chapel, Windsor* (London: Sampson Low, Marston & Company Ltd, 1894).

'An Englishman', 'M. Gounod's Wedding March', *Musical Opinion and Music Trade Review*, 5:57 (June 1882), p. 354. [Reproduced in 'Music at the recent Royal Wedding', *Musical Standard*, 22 (24 June 1882), p. 394].

An Exact Account of the Ceremonies Observed at the Marriage of His Most Christian Majesty Lewis XV. with the Princess Mary, Daughter of Stanislaus, Late King of Poland. Containing Every Material Occurrence Relating thereto, from the Time of her Being Demanded in Marriage, until the Consummation thereof, on the 5th Day of September Last […] (London: Printed for Tho. Worrall, 1726).

Farran, C. d'O., 'The Royal Marriages Act, 1772', *Modern Law Review*, 14 (1951), pp. 53–63.

Fellowes, Edmund H., *Organists and Masters of the Choristers of St. George's Chapel in Windsor Castle*, 2nd edn with addenda to 1979 by M. F. Bond (Windsor: Oxley and Son, 1979).

'Fine Arts', *Public Opinion*, 47:1228 (3 April 1885), p. 436.

Finet, John, *Ceremonies of Charles I: The Notebooks of John Finet, 1628–1641*, ed. by Albert J. Loomie (New York: Fordham University Press, 1987).

Five Gold Rings: A Royal Wedding Souvenir Album – From Queen Victoria to Queen Elizabeth II (London: Royal Collection Publications, 2007).

Floud, Roderick and Thane, Pat, 'The Incidence of Civil Marriage in Victorian England and Wales', *Past & Present*, 84 (1979), pp. 146–54.

'The Forthcoming Royal Wedding', *Scotsman*, 4 July 1893, p. 5.

Freeman, Andrew, 'Notes on Organs at Windsor Castle', *Musical Times*, 54 (1913), pp. 304–08.

'From the Court Circular', *Times*, 29 June 1843, pp. 4–5.

Fulford, Roger, *Royal Dukes: The Father and Uncles of Queen Victoria*, first publ. by William Collins & Co. in 1933; repr. of the new and rev. edn 1973 (London: Penguin Books, 2000).

Funnidos, Rigdum (coll. and arr.), *The Royal Wedding Jester; or, Nuptial Interlude: A Collection of the Wedding Faceti æ Displayed on this Joyful Event: […] together with Numerous Comic Songs, and other Amusing Matters, Forming a Rich Banquet of Wit and Humour […]* (London: Printed and published by J. Duncombe & Co., [1840?]).

G. A. S., 'Echoes of the Week', *ILN*, 15 March 1879, p. 239.

Gardner, Matthew, 'Handel's Wedding Anthems and Borrowing', *Händel-Jahrbuch*, 59 (2013), pp. 217–28.

—, 'Preface' to Georg Friedrich Händel, *Wedding Anthems (HWV 262 and HWV 263)*, ed. by Matthew Gardner, *Hallische Händel-Ausgabe*, series III, vol. 11 (Kassel: Bärenreiter, 2013), pp. xvii–xxv (German 'Vorwort' transl. from English by the 'Redaktion der HHA', on pp. vii–xvi).

—, 'The Preference of the Hanoverians for Handel, 1727–1821', *Händel-Jahrbuch*, 61 (2015), pp. 167–85.

Gatens, William J., *Victorian Cathedral Music in Theory and Practice* (Cambridge: Cambridge University Press, 1986).

Geiringer, Karl, *Haydn: A Creative Life in Music*, in collaboration with Irene Geiringer, first published in 1946, 3rd rev. and enlarged edn (Berkely: University of California Press, 1982).

The Gentlewoman's Royal Record of the Wedding of […] Victoria Mary of Teck and […] the Duke of York (London, [1893]).

'George Mursell Garrett', *Musical Times*, 38 (May 1897), pp. 310–11.

'The German Emperor's Visit', *Times*, 7 July 1891, p. 10.

'The German Emperor at Windsor: The Royal Wedding', *Scotsman*, 7 July 1891, p. 5.

Geyl, Pieter, *Orange and Stuart 1641–1672*, first publ. in Great Britain by Weidenfeld & Nicolson in 1969, paperback edn (London: Phoenix Press, 2001).

Gibbs, Philip, 'The Art of Anticipation', *Graphic*, 11 October 1913, p. 658.

'Girls' Gossip', *Truth*, 45:1165 (27 April 1899), pp. 1085–86.

Groom, Susanne and Prosser, Lee, *Kew Palace: The Official Illustrated History* (London: Historic Royal Palaces in association with Merrell, 2006).

Grosch, Nils, '"Heil Dir im Siegerkranz!": Zur Inszenierung von Nation und Hymne', in *Reichsgründung 1871: Ereignis, Beschreibung, Inszenierung*, ed. by Michael Fischer, Christian Senkel, and Klaus Tanner (Münster: Waxmann, 2010), pp. 90–103.

Hammersley, Rachel, *The English Republican Tradition and Eighteenth-Century France: Between the Ancients and the Moderns* (Manchester: Manchester University Press: 2010).

Harley, John, *Orlando Gibbons and the Gibbons Family of Musicians* (Aldershot: Ashgate, 1999).

Harper's New Monthly Magazine, 26 (New York: Harper & Brothers, 1863), pp. 850–53 [untitled report of Prince of Wales's wedding].

Harris, John, 'The Architecture', in: John Harris, Geoffrey de Bellaigue, and Oliver Millar, *Buckingham Palace*, with an introduction by John Russell (London: Thomas Nelson and Sons, 1968), pp. 19–100.

Harvey, John, *The Black Prince and his Age* (London: Batsford, 1976).

Henze-Döhring, Sabine, 'Händels Coronation Anthems', *Händel-Jahrbuch*, 49 (2003), pp. 105–13.

Hervey, John (2nd Baron Hervey), *Some Materials towards Memoirs of the Reign of King George II*, ed. by Romney Sedgwick, 3 vols, continuously paginated (London: Eyre and Spottiswoode, 1931; repr. New York: AMS Press, 1970).

HHB see Baselt, Bernd, *Händel-Handbuch*

Hibbert, Christopher, *Edward VII: The Last Victorian King* (New York: St. Martin's Press, 2007).

Hicks, Anthony, 'Handel and "Il Parnasso in festa"', *Musical Times*, 112 (1971), pp. 339–40.

—, 'Ravishing Semele' [review article], *Musical Times*, 114 (March 1973), pp. 275 and 278–80.

Highfill Jr, Philip H.; Burnim, Kalman A. and Langhans, Edward A., *A Biographical Dictionary of Actors, Actresses, Musicians, Dancers, Managers & Other Stage Personnel in London, 1660–1800*, 16 vols (Carbondale: Southern Illinois University Press, 1973–1993), vol. 15: 'Tibbett to M. West' (1993).

Sources and Bibliography

An Historical Record of the Marriage of H. R. H. Albert Edward, Prince of Wales with Alexandra Caroline, Princess of Denmark (London: Darton and Hodge, 1863).

Hofmann, Hans-Georg, '"Sing unto God" – Bemerkungen zu Händels Festmusik anlässlich der Hochzeit des Prinzen Frederick of Wales mit Prinzessin Augusta von Sachsen-Gotha (1736)', *Händel-Jahrbuch*, 49 (2003), pp. 147–62.

Hunt, John Eric, *Cranmer's First Litany, 1544, and Merbecke's Book of Common Prayer Noted, 1550* (London: Society for Promoting Christian Knowledge, 1939).

Husk, W. H.; Rainbow, Bernarr; and Langley, Leanne, 'Hawes, William (i)', *New Grove* (accessed 29 October 2021).

Jennings, Paul, *A History of Drink and the English, 1500-2000*, 'Perspectives in Economic and Social History', 44, series editors Andrew August and Jari Eloranta (Routledge/Taylor & Francis, 2016).

Jocquet, D[avid], *Les Triomphes, Entrées, Cartels, Tournois, Céremonies, et aultres Magnificences, faites en Angleterre, & au Palatinat, pour le Mariage & Reception, de Monseigneur le Prince Frideric V Comte Palatin du Rhin, Electevr du Sainct Empire, Duc de Baviere &c. Et de Madame Elisabeth, Fille vnique et Princesse de la Grande Bretagne, Electrice Palatine du Rhin &c. Son Espouse* (Heidelberg: 'Chez Gotard Vogvelein' [Gotthardt Vögelin], 1613).

Johnson, Odai, *Rehearsing the Revolution: Radical Performance, Radical Politics in the English Restoration* (Newark: University of Delaware Press, 2000).

Johnston, Ruth A., *All Things Medieval: An Encyclopedia of the Medieval World*, vol. 1: A–I (Santa Barbara, CA: ABC-CLIO, 2011).

Jones, Graham O., 'British Wind Band Music' (unpublished PhD diss., University of Salford, Manchester, 2005).

Jones, Heather, *For King and Country: The British Monarchy and the First World War* (Cambridge: Cambridge University Press, 2021).

Judd, Roger, 'The Organs in St George's Chapel', *St George's Chapel: History and Heritage*, ed. by Nigel Saul and Tim Tatton-Brown (Stanbridge: Dovecote Press, 2010), pp. 193–200.

Julian, John (ed.), *A Dictionary of Hymnology: Setting Forth the Origin and History of Christian Hymns of All Ages and Nations*, rev. edn, with new supplement (London: John Murray, 1907).

Kappey, Jacob Adam, *Military Music. A History of Wind-Instrumental Bands* (London: Boosey and Co., [1894]).

Keay, Anna, *The Magnificent Monarch: Charles II and the Ceremonies of Power* (London: Continuum, 2008).

Keen, Maurice, 'Introduction', in *Heraldry, Pageantry and Social Display in Medieval England*, ed. by Peter Coss and Maurice Keen (Woodbridge: The Boydell Press, 2002), pp. 1–16.

Kerman, Joseph, 'The Elizabethan Motet: A Study of Texts for Music', *Studies in the Renaissance*, 9 (1962), pp. 273–308.

—, *The Masses and Motets of William Byrd* (Berkeley: University of California Press, 1981).

Kerr, Jessica M., 'English Wedding Music', *Musical Times*, 106 (January 1965), pp. 53–55.

Ketley, Joseph (ed.), *The Two Liturgies A.D. 1549 and A.D. 1552: With Other Documents Set Forth by Authority in the Reign of King Edward VI* (Cambridge: Cambridge University Press, 1844).

Kimber, Marian Wilson, 'Performing *Athalia*: Mendelssohn's Op. 74 in the Nineteenth-Century Choral World', *Choral Journal* (April 2009), pp. 9–23.

'The King and Queen of Wurtemberg', *Graphic*, 20 February 1904, p. 244.

Kiste, John van der, *Alfred: Queen Victoria's Second Son* (Strout: Fonthill Media, 2013).

—, *King George II and Queen Caroline* (Thrupp: Sutton Publishing, 1997).

—, *Princess Helena: Queen Victoria's Third Daughter*, rev. and exp. edn (South Brent: A&F Publications, 2015).

—, *Queen Victoria's Children* (Strout: Alan Sutton, 1986).

Koehler, Elisa, *A Dictionary for the Modern Trumpet Player* (Lanham: Rowman & Littlefield, 2015).

'Ladies' Page', *ILN*, 30 January 1904, p. 164.

Later Letters of Lady Augusta Stanley, 1864–1876: Including Many Unpublished Letters to and from Queen Victoria and Correspondence with Dean Stanley, her Sister, Lady Frances Baillie, and Others, ed. by the Dean of Windsor and Hector Bolitho (London: J. Cape, [1929]).

Laurie, Margaret, 'Weldon, John', in *New Grove*, 27, pp. 265–66.

Lemmings, David, 'Marriage and the Law in the Eighteenth Century: Hardwicke's Marriage Act of 1753', *The Historical Journal*, vol. 39, no. 2 (1996), pp. 339–60.

Le Hardy, William, *The Coronation Book: The History and Meaning of the Ceremonies at the Crowning*, first publ. in 1937 for the coronation of George VI and Queen Elizabeth, rev. edn for the coronation of Queen Elizabeth II (London: Staples Press, 1953).

Le Huray, Peter, *Music and the Reformation in England, 1549–1660*, first publ. in 1967, corr. repr. (Cambridge: Cambridge University Press, 1978).

Linnell, Anna-Marie, 'Becoming a Stuart Queen Consort: Nuptial Texts for Henrietta Maria of France and Catherine or Braganza, Queens of Britain', *Queens Consort, Cultural Transfer and European Politics, c.1500–1800*, ed. by Helen Watanabe-O'Kelly and Adam Morton (Abingdon: Routledge, 2017), pp. 153–71.

Little, W[illia]m A., *Mendelssohn and the Organ* (Oxford: Oxford University Press, 2010).

Longford, Elizabeth, *Victoria R. I.* (London: Weidenfeld & Nicolson, [1964]).

Macpherson, James, *The History of Great Britain, from the Restoration, to the Accession of the House of Hanover*, 2 vols, vol. 1 (Dublin: Printed for J. Exshaw […], 1775).

Madway, Lorraine, 'Rites of Deliverance and Disenchantment: The Marriage Celebrations for Charles II and Catherine of Braganza, 1661–62', *The Seventeenth Century*, 27:1 (2012), pp. 79–103.

Magnus, Philip, *King Edward VII* (London: John Murray, 1964).

Major, H. D. A. [Henry Dewsbury Alves], *The Life and Letters of William Boyd Carpenter* (London: John Murray, 1925).

Malfatti, C. V. (ed.), *The Accession, Coronation and Marriage of Mary Tudor as Related by Four Manuscripts of the Escorial* (Barcelona: Sociedad Alianza de Artes Gráficas and Ricardo Fontá, 1956).

Mallet, Marie, *Life with Queen Victoria: Marie Mallet's Letters from Court, 1887–1901*, ed. by Victor Mallet, (London: J. Murray, 1968).

'Marmaduke', 'Court and Club', *Graphic*, 15 July 1893, p. 78.

'The Marriage Ceremony', *ILN: Royal Wedding Number*, 2 May 1882, pp. 19–23.

'The Marriage Ceremony', *ILN: Royal Wedding Number*, 31 July 1889, pp. 2–6.

'The Marriage Ceremony', *Lloyd's Weekly London Newspaper*, 15 March 1863, pp. 4–5.

'Marriage of Her Majesty with Prince Albert of Saxe Coburg and Gotha, on Monday', *Niles' National Register*, 5th series, vol. 8, no. 3 (21 March 1840), pp. 1 and 34–37.

'Marriage of Her Royal Highness The Princess Augusta', *Times*, 29 June 1843, pp. 4–5.

'Marriage of Her Royal Highness The Princess Helena', *Annual Register* […] *1866* (1867), pp. 76–82.

'Marriage of Her Royal Highness The Princess Helena', *Observer*, 8 July 1866, p. 3.

'Marriage of His Royal Highness The Prince of Wales', *Times*, 3 February 1863, p. 9.

'The Marriage of H.R.H. Prince Leopold and The Princess Helena of Waldeck Pyrmont', *The Ladies' Treasury for 1882: A Household Magazine*, ed. by 'Mrs. Warren' (London: Bemrose and Sons, 1893), pp. 352–53 and 356.

Sources and Bibliography

'Marriage of H.R.H. Princess Mary of Cambridge', *Illustrated Times*, 16 June 1866, p. 2.

'The Marriage of H.R.H. The Duke of Connaught, K.G., and H.R.H. Princess Louise Margaret of Prussia', *The London Reader of Literature, Science, Art and General Information*, 29 March 1879, pp. 524–26.

'Marriage of Lady Olivia Taylour with Lord H. Bentinck, MP', *The Lancaster Gazette*, 30 January 1892, p. 8.

'Marriage of the Duke and Duchess of Cambridge', *Times*, 2 June 1818, p. 3.

'The Marriage of Princess Beatrice', *ILN*, 1 August 1885, pp. 106–07.

'The Marriage of Princess Beatrice', *ILN: Royal Wedding Number*, 27 July 1885, pp. 2–6.

'The Marriage of Princess Helena at Windsor', *ILN*, 14 July 1866, p. 42.

'Marriage of Princess Louise at Windsor', *ILN*, 1 April 1871, pp. 323–25.

'Marriage of Princess Mary of Cambridge', *ILN*, 16 June 1866, p. 592.

'The Marriage of Princess Maud of Wales', *Observer*, 19 July 1896, p. 5.

'The Marriage of Princess Maud of Wales and Prince Charles of Denmark at Buckingham Palace', *ILN: Royal Wedding Number*, 29 July 1896, pp. 2–8.

'The Marriage of the Duke of Connaught', *Graphic: Royal Wedding Number*, 20 March 1879.

'Marriage of the Duke of Connaught', *Times*, 14 March 1879, p. 10.

'The Marriage of the Duke of Edinburgh', *Times*, 22 January 1874, p. 5.

'The Marriage of the Duke of Edinburgh', *Times*, 24 January 1874, p. 9.

'The Marriage of The Prince of Wales', *Times*, 6 March 1863, p. 9.

'Marriage of The Prince of Wales and The Princess Alexandra', *The Dundee Courier & Argus*, 12 March 1863, p. [3].

'Marriage of The Prince of Wales and The Princess Alexandra', *The News of the World*, 15 March 1863, p. 2.

'The Marriage of The Prince of Wales. (From the *Court Circular*.)', *Times*, 5 February 1863, p. 9.

'Marriage of The Prince of Wales and Princess Alexandra of Denmark', Supplement to *ILN*, 14 March 1863, pp. 278–87.

'Marriage of The Princess Helena', *Times*, 6 July 1866, p. 9.

'Marriage of The Princess Louise', *The Morning Post*, 22 March 1871, pp. 5–6.

'Marriage of The Princess Louise and the Duke of Fife: The Ceremony in Buckingham Palace Chapel', *Scotsman*, 29 July 1889, p. 7.

'Marriage of The Princess Mary', *The Morning Post*, 13 June 1866, p. 5.

'Marriage of The Princess Mary of Cambridge', *Observer*, 17 June 1866, p. 3.

'The Marriage of The Princess Mary of Cambridge', *Scotsman*, 13 June 1866, p. 3.

'Marriage of The Princess Mary of Cambridge', *The Albion: A Journal of News, Politics and Literature*, 44:26, 30 June 1866, p. 308.

'Marriage of The Princess Mary of Cambridge', *Times*, 13 June 1866, p. 9.

'Marriage of The Princess Mary of Cambridge with the Prince of Teck', *Morning Herald*, 13 June 1866, p. 5.

'Marriage of The Princess Maud of Wales', *Manchester Guardian*, 23 July 1896, p. 5.

'Marriage of The Princess Royal', *Annual Register* […] *1858* (1859), pp. 355–58.

'Marriage of The Princess Royal', *Gentleman's Magazine*, 204/v. 4 new series (1858), pp. 322–23.

'The Marriage of The Princess Royal', *ILN*, 23 January 1858, p. 79.

'The Marriage of The Princess Royal', *Times*, 26 January 1858, pp. 7–9.

'The Marriage of The Princess Royal', Supplement to *ILN*, 30 January 1858, pp. 117–28.

'Marriage of The Princess Royal, Jan. 25', *Annual Register* […] *1858* (1859), pp. 355–58.

'Marriage of The Princess Royal: Ceremony of the Marriage', *Observer*, 25 January 1858, p. 1.

'Marriage of The Princess Royal: The Completed Preparations', *Observer*, 25 January 1858, pp. 5–6.

'The Marriage of The Princess Royal, with Prince Frederick William of Prussia', *The Primitive Church (Or Baptist) Magazine*, 15 new series (London: Arthur Hall & Co., 1858), p. 51.

The Marriage of the Tvvo Great Princes, Fredericke Count Palatine, &c: and the Lady Elizabeth, Daughter to the Imperial Maiesties of King Iames and Queene Anne: Vpon Shroue-Sonday Last. With the Showes and Fire-Workes vpon the Water: As also the Masks & Reuells, in his Highnes Court of White-Hall ('Printed at London: By T[homas] C[reede] for William Barley', 1613).

'Marriage of Victoria the First [...] with Prince Albert [...]', *MLAI*, 35:992, Supplementary Number ([1840]), pp. 113–22.

Marsden, Jonathan (ed.), *Victoria & Albert: Art & Love,* ed. by and with an introduction by Jonathan Marsden (London: Royal Collection Enterprises, 2010).

Marsh, Christopher, *Music and Society in Early Modern England* (Cambridge: Cambridge University Press 2010).

Marsh, John, *The John Marsh Journals: The Life and Times of a Gentleman Composer (1752–1828)*, ed., introduced, and annotated by Brian Robins (Stuyvesant, N.Y.: Pendragon Press, 1998).

Marshall, William, *A Collection of Anthems Used in the Cathedral and Collegiate Churches of England and Wales* (Oxford: John Henry Parker, 1840).

McCalman, I. D., 'Popular Irreligion in Early Victorian England: Infidel Preachers and Radical Theatricality in 1830s London', in *Religion and Irreligion in Victorian Society: Essays in Honor of R. K. Webb*, ed. by R. W. Davis and R. J. Helmstadter (Abingdon: Routledge, 1992; digital repr. 2006), pp. 51–67.

McVeigh, Simon, 'London (i), §V, 2: Musical Life, 1660–1800: Concert Life', *NG* 15, pp. 119–25.

Meikle, Maureen M., review of Stevenson, *Scotland's Last Royal Wedding*, in *Scottish Historical Review*, 78 (October 1999), pp. 263–65.

Miller, John, *James II*, first publ. in 1978 by Wayland Ltd, re-issue of 2nd edn by Methuen from 1989 (New Haven: Yale University Press, 2000).

Misson de Valbourg, Henri, *M. Misson's Memoirs and Observations in his Travels over England. With Some Account of Scotland and Ireland*, transl. from the French by 'Mr. Ozell' (London: Printed for D. Browne et al., 1719).

Monsarrat, Ann, *And the Bride Wore...: The Story of the White Wedding* (London: Gentry Books, 1973).

Munson, James, 'London en fete: the Last Marriage of a Prince of Wales', *Country Life*, 30 July 1981, pp. 416 and 418.

—, *Maria Fitzherbert: The Secret Wife of George IV* (London: Robinson 2002).

Murdoch, Steve, *Britain, Denmark-Norway and the House of Stuart 1603–1660* (East Linton, Tuckwell Press, 2003).

Musgrave, Michael, *The Musical Life of the Crystal Palace* (Cambridge: Cambridge University Press, 1995).

'Music', *Graphic*, 1 August 1885, p. 123.

'Music at Court', *The Musical World*, 49 (March 1871), pp. 176–77.

'Music at the Royal Wedding', *Musical News*, 5:124 (15 July 1893), p. 64.

'Musical Gossip', *The Athenaeum*, 2265 (25 March 1871), pp. 376–77.

'The Musical Service', *The Morning Advertiser*, 9 March 1863, p. 3.

'The Musical Side of the Wedding: The Organist and Composers', *ILN*, 18 October 1913, p. 625.

Musical Standard, 14 (25 March 1871), p. 137 [anonymous report of Princess Louise's wedding].

Musical Standard, 14 (1 April 1871), p. 149 [anonymous report of Princess Louise's wedding].

'Monthly Intelligence', *Gentleman's Magazine*, 214 (April 1863), pp. 498–510.

Sources and Bibliography

'My Dear Duchess': Social and Political Letters to the Duchess of Manchester, 1858–1869, ed. by A. L. Kennedy (London: John Murray, 1956).

Neighbour, O. W. and Jeans, Susi, 'Bull [Boul, Bul, Bol], John [Jan] [Bouville, Bonville, Jean]', New Grove (accessed 11 October 2021).

'The New Royal Chapel, Buckingham Palace', ILN, 8 April 1843, p. [235].

Noel, Gerard, Princess Alice: Queen Victoria's Forgotten Daughter, first publ. by Constable & Co. in 1974 (Norwich: Michael Russel Publishing, 1992).

'Notes', The Musical World, 69 (July 1889), p. 492.

'The Nuptials of the Princess Charlotte of Wales and the Prince of Saxe-Cobourg', Annual Register [...] 1816 (1817), pp. 57–60.

'Nuptials Solemnized at St. James's', The Political State of Great Britain, 47 (1734), pp. 321–26.

'Occurrences in London and its Vicinity', Gentleman's Magazine, 88, part 2 (July–December 1818), p. 79.

Okerlund, Arlene Naylor, Elizabeth of York, 'Queenship and Power' (New York: Palgrave Macmillan, 2009).

'On-Dits and Facts of the Month', The Ladies' Treasury for 1882: A Household Magazine, ed. by 'Mrs. Warren' (London: Bemrose and Sons, 1893), p. 119.

'One Who was There', 'The Marriage of Princess Margaret of Connaught to Prince Gustavus Adolphus of Sweden [...]', The Sphere, 24 June 1905, p. 293.

'Our Artist at the Royal Wedding: The Accurate Illustrating of the Ceremony in the Chapel Royal', ILN, 25 October 1913, p. 650.

Parry, Graham, 'The Wedding of Princess Elizabeth', The Golden Age Restor'd: The Culture of the Stuart Court, 1603–42 (Manchester: Manchester University Press, 1981), pp. 95–107.

Parry, Jonathan, 'Whig Monarchy, Whig Nation: Crown, Politics and Representativeness 1800–2000', The Monarchy and the British Nation, 1780 to the Present, ed. by Andrzej Olechnowicz (Cambridge: Cambridge University Press, 2007), pp. 47–75.

Perceval, John, Manuscripts of the Earl of Egmont. Diary of Viscount Percival afterwards First Earl of Egmont (Viscount Percival), 3 vols, publ. for the Historical Manuscripts Commission (London: His Majesty's Stationery Office, 1923).

Pleck, Elizabeth H., Celebrating the Family: Ethnicity, Consumer Culture, and Family Rituals (Cambridge, MA: Harvard University Press, 2000).

Plunkett, John, Queen Victoria: First Media Monarch (Oxford: Oxford University Press, 2003).

'The Politician', The News of the World, 8 March 1863, p. 1.

Pope-Hennessy, James, Queen Mary, 1867–1953, first publ. in 1959 (London: Phoenix Press, 2000).

Porny, Mark Anthony [= Antoine Pyron du Martre], The Elements of Heraldry: Containing a Clear Definition, and Concise Historical Account of that Ancient, Useful, and Entertaining Science [...] (London: Printed for J. Newbery, 1765).

—, The Elements of Heraldry: Containing the Definition, Origin, and Historical Account of that Ancient, Useful, and Entertaining Science [...], 5th edn, 'with considerable alterations and additions' (London: Printed for G. G. and J. Robinson [...], 1795).

'The Prince's Wedding', Gentleman's Magazine, 45 (1795), pp. 429–31.

'The Prince's Wedding', Graphic: Royal Wedding Number, 6 May 1882, pp. 20–28.

'The Princess Royal', ILN, 9 January 1858, pp. 25–26.

'Prince Aribert's Bride: The Pomp and Ceremony of a Royal Wedding', New York Times, 7 July 1891, p. 1.

'Principal Occurrences', The New Annual Register [...] for the Year 1816 (1817), pp. 19 and 32–33.

Prothero, Rowland E., Life and Letters of Dean Stanley (London: Thomas Nelson & Sons, 1909).

British Royal Weddings

Prout, Ebenezer, 'Graun's *Passion Oratorio*, and Handel's Knowledge of It', *Monthly Musical Record*, 24, no. 281 (May 1894), pp. [97]–99; and no. 282 (June 1894), pp. [121]–123.

Pyne, W. H., *The History of the Royal Residences of Windsor Castle, St. James's Palace, Carlton House, Kensington Palace, Hampton Court, Buckingham House, and Frogmore. Illustrated by One Hundred Highly Finished and Coloured Engravings*, 3 vols, vol. 2 (London: Printed for A. Dry, 1819). NB The page numbers in this publication begin anew with every new residence. The copy used (*Ob G. A. Gen. top. c.57, v.2*) begins with Buckingham House and Kensington Palace.

'The Queen's Marriage', *The Examiner*, 16 February 1840, p. 105.

'The Queen's Marriage', *Morning Chronicle*, 11 February 1840, pp. 1–2.

'A Quiet Affair', *Punch* 44 (January 1863), p. 49.

Radziwill, Princess Catherine [Catherine Kolb-Danvin], *The Royal Marriage Market of Europe* (New York: Funk and Wagnalls Company, 1915).

Rafiüddin Ahmad, Moulvie, 'The Royal Marriage: From an Oriental Point of View', *The Strand Magazine: An Illustrated Monthly*, 6 (July 1893), pp. 447–58.

Rahn, Thomas, *Festbeschreibung: Funktion und Topik einer Textsorte am Beispiel der Beschreibung höfischer Hochzeiten* (Berlin: De Gruyter, 2009; repr. 2011).

Rainbow, Bernarr, 'Garrett, George (Mursell)', *New Grove* (accessed 26 November 2021).

Range, Matthias, *BRSF = British Royal and State Funerals: Music and Ceremonial since Elizabeth I* (Woodbridge: Boydell Press, 2016).

—, *MCBC = Music and Ceremonial at British Coronations: From James I to Elizabeth II* (Cambridge: Cambridge University Press, 2012).

—, 'Mendelssohn's Wedding March and Weddings: The Early Decades', *Musical Times*, 160 (Summer 2019), pp. 97–112.

—, 'Wagner's "Brautchor" from *Lohengrin* and its Use as a Wedding March', *Journal of the Royal Musical Association* (forthcoming).

—, 'William Boyce's Anthem for the Wedding of King George III', *Musical Times*, 147 (Summer 2006), pp. 59–66.

Rangström, Lena, *En brud för kung och fosterland: Kungliga svenska bröllop från Gustav Vasa till Carl XVI Gustaf* (Stockholm: Livrustkammaren/Atlantis, 2010).

Rappaport, Helen, *A Magnificent Obsession: Victoria, Albert, and the Death that Changed the British Monarchy* (New York: St Martin's Press, 2012).

Ravelhofer, Barbara, Review of *Marriage, Performance, and Politics at the Jacobean Court* by Kevin Curran, *Renaissance Quarterly*, 63 (2010), pp. 689–91.

'Recent Concerts. – Wagner's "Lohengrin," &c.', *The Reader*, 13 June 1863, p. 583.

Redworth, Glyn, *The Prince and the Infanta: The Cultural Politics of the Spanish Match* (New Haven: Yale University Press, 2003).

Reed, David, '"What a Lovely Frock": Royal Weddings and the Illustrated Press in the Pre-Television Age', *Court Historian*, 8:1 (July 2003), pp. 41–50.

A Relation of the Gloriovs Trivmphs and Order of the Ceremonies, Obserued in the Marriage of the High and Mighty Charles, King of Great Brittaine, and the Ladie Henretta [sic] *Maria, Sister to the Most Christian King of France* [...] (London: 'Printed by T[homas] S[nodham and others] for Nathaniel Butter, 1625).

'The Religious Aspect of the Wedding: The Clergy and Choristers', *ILN*, 18 October 1913, p. 631.

Richards, Judith M., 'Mary Tudor as "Sole Quene"?: Gendering Tudor Monarchy', *The Historical Journal*, 40:4 (December 1997), pp. 895–934.

Sources and Bibliography

Roberts, Jane (ed.), *George III and Queen Charlotte; Patronage, Collecting and Court Taste*, catalogue to the exhibition in the Queen's Gallery Buckingham Palace (London: Royal Collections Publications, 2004).

Röhl, John C. G., *Wilhelm II.: Der Aufbau der Persönlichen Monarchie, 1888–1900* (Munich: C. H. Beck, 2001).

—, *Young Wilhelm: The Kaiser's Early Life, 1859–1888*, transl. by Jeremy Gaines and Rebecca Wallach (Cambridge: Cambridge University Press, 1998).

'The Royal Marriage', *Annual Register* [...] *1863*, n.s. (1864), pp. 42–50.

'The Royal Marriage', *ILN*, 23 January 1858, pp. 73–74.

'The Royal Marriage', *ILN*, 21 March 1863, pp. 310–22.

'The Royal Marriage', *Morning Post*, 24 July 1885, p. 5.

'The Royal Marriage', *Observer*, 23 April 1882, p. 3.

'The Royal Marriage', *Scotsman*, 28 April 1882, p. 5.

'The Royal Marriage', *The London Journal, and Weekly Record of Literature, Science, and Art*, 15 April 1871, pp. 236–38.

'The Royal Marriage', *Times*, 16 June 1905, p. 6.

'The Royal Marriage: Another Account', *Scotsman*, 28 April 1882, p. 5.

'The Royal Marriage: Programme of the Ceremony', *Manchester Guardian*, 24 April 1882, p. 8.

'The Royal Marriage at Kew', *ILN*, 23 June 1866, p. 614.

'Royal Marriage at Windsor', *Weekly Irish Times*, 1 May 1880, p. 1.

'The Royal Marriage at Windsor: A Magnificent Ceremonial', *Irish Times*, 7 July 1891, p. 5.

'Royal Marriage Bells', *New York Times*, 14 March 1879, p. 1.

'Royal Nuptials', *True Briton*, 18 May 1797, p. [2].

'The Royal Nuptials', *Times*, 6 May 1816, p. 3.

'The Royal Wedding', *Bow Bells: A Magazine of General Literature and Art for Family Reading*, 31 July 1896, pp. 127–28.

'The Royal Wedding', *Every Saturday: A Journal of Choice Reading*, 22 April 1871, p. 371.

'The Royal Wedding', *Graphic*, 18 July 1896, p. 82.

'The Royal Wedding', *Graphic*, 25 July 1896, p. 103.

'The Royal Wedding', *Graphic: Wedding Number*, 11 July 1891, pp. 39–42.

'The Royal Wedding', *Graphic*, 13 February 1904, pp. 194–95.

'The Royal Wedding', *ILN: Royal Wedding Number*, 10 July 1893, pp. 2–4.

'The Royal Wedding', *ILN*, 15 July 1893, pp. 70–71.

'The Royal Wedding', *Irish Times*, 16 July 1889.

'The Royal Wedding', *Lloyd's Weekly Newspaper*, 23 March 1879, p. 6.

'The Royal Wedding', *Manchester Guardian*, 13 March 1879, p. 5.

'The Royal Wedding', *Scotsman*, 7 July 1893, p. 5.

'The Royal Wedding', *Scotsman*, 16 June 1905, p. 5.

'The Royal Wedding', *The London Journal, and Weekly Record of Literature, Science, and Art*, 14 March 1863, pp. 167–68.

'The Royal Wedding', *Times*, 24 July 1885, p. 5.

'The Royal Wedding', *Times*, 29 July 1889, p. 10.

'The Royal Wedding', *Times*, 7 July 1893, pp. 5–7.

'The Royal Wedding', *Times*, 23 July 1896, pp. 5–6.

'The Royal Wedding', *Times*, 8 February 1904, p. 6.

'The Royal Wedding', *Times*, 11 February 1904, p. 10.

'The Royal Wedding', *Times*, 15 October 1913, p. 9.

'The Royal Wedding', *Times of India*, 28 July 1891, p. 6.

'The Royal Wedding', unidentified newspaper cutting (1797), in *Lbl 871.f.3*, no. 32.

'The Royal Wedding: Brilliant Scene at St James's Palace', *Scotsman*, 16 October 1913, p. 7.

'The Royal Wedding: Brilliant Scene at the Ceremony', *Manchester Guardian*, 16 October 1913, p. 9.

'The Royal Wedding: Few Foreign Royal Guests to Be Present', *Manchester Guardian*, 2 October 1913, p. 7.

'The Royal Wedding: Final Arrangements for the Ceremony', *Manchester Guardian*, 6 October 1913, p. 8.

'Royal Wedding: Final Arrangements for the Ceremony', *Observer*, 5 October 1913, p. 11.

'The Royal Wedding: King and Princess Royal to Support the Bride', *Manchester Guardian*, 1 October 1913, p. 6.

'The Royal Wedding: Marriage of The Princess Louise in Buckingham Palace', *New York Times*, 28 July 1889, p. 1.

'Royal Wedding: Musical and other Arrangements', *Scotsman*, 6 October 1913, p. 9.

'The Royal Wedding: Our Double Number and Supplement', *ILN*, 18 October 1913, p. 644.

'Royal Wedding: Picturesque Ceremony in London To-day', *The Star*, 15 November 1916, p. [4].

'The Royal Wedding: Programme of the Music', *Manchester Guardian*, 3 October 1913, p. 7.

'Royal Wedding: Scene in St. James's Palace', *Times*, 16 October 1913, pp. 9–11.

'The Royal Wedding: The Ceremony at Windsor', *Irish Times*, 28 April 1882, p. 5.

'Royal Wedding: The Ceremony in St. George's Chapel', *Irish Times*, 12 June 1905, p. 5.

'The Royal Wedding: The Ceremony in the Chapel Royal', *Times*, 2 October 1913, p. 6.

'Royal Wedding: The Musical Service', *Scotsman*, 18 February 1922, p. 8.

'The Royal Wedding at Buckingham Palace', *Observer*, 28 July 1889, p. 5 [two separate accounts, the second with the sub-heading 'Arrival at the Palace'].

'Royal Wedding at Windsor', *Manchester Guardian*, 11 February 1904, p. 6.

'Royal Wedding at Windsor: The King Gives Away the Bride', *Scotsman*, 11 February 1904, p. 7.

'Royal Wedding at Windsor: The King Gives Away the Bride', *Weekly Irish Times*, 20 February 1904, p. 16.

'Royal Wedding in London: Prince George of Battenberg – Countess Nada', *Scotsman*, 16 November 1916, p. 4.

'Royal Wedding Music', *The Musical Visitor: A Magazine of Musical Literature and Music*, 18:9 (September 1889), p. 227.

'Royal Wedding Music', *The Orchestra*, 388 (3 March 1871), pp. 361–62.

Russell, W. H. [William Howard], *A Memorial of the Marriage of HRH Albert Edward Prince of Wales and HRH Alexandra Princess of Denmark by WH Russell. The Various Events and Bridal Gifts Illustrated by Robert Dudley. Published by Day and Son, London, Lithographers to the Queen & to HRH the Prince of Wales* (London: Day and Son, [1864]).

Sala, George Augustus, 'Royal Weddings: Seen and Not Seen', *Graphic: Wedding Number*, 11 July 1891, pp. 48–49.

Samson, Alexander, 'Changing Places: The Marriage and Royal Entry of Philip, Prince of Austria, and Mary Tudor, July–August 1554', *Sixteenth Century Journal*, 36 (2005), pp. 761–84.

—, *Mary and Philip: The Marriage of Tudor England and Habsburg Spain*, 'Studies in Early Modern European History' (Manchester: Manchester University Press, 2020).

Sandford, Francis, *A Genealogical History of the Kings of England, and Monarchs of Great Britain, &c. from the Conquest, Anno 1066. to the Year, 1677* ([London:] Printed by Tho. Newcomb, 1677).

—, *A Genealogical History of the Kings of Portugal. And of All Those Illustrious Houses that in Masculine Line Are Branched from that Royal Family. Containing a Discourse of their Several Lives,*

Sources and Bibliography

Marriages, and Issues, Times of Birth, Death, and Places of Burial. With their Armes and Emblazons According to their Several Alterations, as also their Symboles and Mottoes. All Engraven in Copper-Plates, written in French by Scévole and Lovis de Saincte-Marthe up to 1623, transl. and extended to 1662 by Francis Sandford (London: Printed by E. M. for the author, 1662).

—, *The History of the Coronation of the Most High, Most Mighty, and Most Excellent Monarch, James II. […] 1685* (London: Printed by Thomas New Comb, 1687).

Sandford, Francis and Stebbing, Samuel, *A Genealogical History of the Kings of England, and Monarchs of Great Britain, &c. from the Conquest, Anno 1066. to the Year, 1707*, continued from 1677 by Samuel Stebbing (London: Printed by M. Jenour, for John Nicholson, 1707).

Sara, M. E. [Muriel Ellen], *The Life and Times of H.R.H. Princess Beatrice* (London: Stanley Paul & Co., 1945).

Schleswig-Holstein, Princess Marie Louise of, *My Memories of Six Reigns* (London: Evans Brothers Limited, 1957; repr. 1979).

Schoelcher, Victor, *The Life of Handel* (London: Trübner and Co., 1857).

Scholes, Percy, *The Mirror of Music, 1844–1944: A Century of Musical Life in Britain as Reflected in the Pages of the Musical Times*, 2 vols (London: Novello, 1947).

Schönpflug, Daniel, *Die Heiraten der Hohenzollern: Verwandtschaft, Politik und Ritual in Europa 1640–1918*, 'Kritische Studien zur Geschichtswissenschaft', 207 (Göttingen: Vandenhoek & Ruprecht, 2013).

Schwarz, Boris, 'Molique, (Wilhelm) Bernhard', *New Grove* (accessed 9 October 2021).

Scott, Kenneth, *St James's Palace: A History* (London: Scala, 2010).

Scrutator', 'At the Wedding', *Truth*, 11:279 (May 1882), pp. 612–13.

Seton, George, *The Law and Practice of Heraldry in Scotland* (Edinburgh: Edmonston and Douglas 1863).

Shaw, Martin, 'The Banning of Handel. To the Editor, "Musical News"', *Musical News*, 51:1323 (8 July 1916), pp. 26 and 28.

Shaw, Watkins and Johnstone, H. Diack, 'King, Charles', *New Grove* (accessed 29 October 2021).

Shearman, John K. G., *Raphael's Cartoons in the Collection of Her Majesty the Queen, and the Tapestries for the Sistine Chapel* (London: Phaidon, 1972).

Sheppard, Edgar, *Memorials of St James's Palace*, 2 vols (London: Longmans, Green, and Co., 1894).

Shewring, Margaret, 'The Iconography of Populism: Waterborne Entries to London for Anne Boleyn (1533), Catherine of Braganza (1662) and Elizabeth II (2012)', *Ceremonial Entries in Early Modern Europe: The Iconography of Power*, ed. by J. R. Mulryne (Farnham: Ashgate, 2015), pp. 221–44.

'Sir George Job Elvey', *The Musical Herald*, 550 (January 1894), pp. 3–7.

Smart, George, *Leaves from the Journals of Sir George Smart*, ed. by H. Bertram Cox and C. L. E. Cox, first publ. in 1907, repr. in the 'Cambridge Library Collection' (Cambridge: Cambridge University Press, 2014).

Smart, Sara and Wade, Mara R. (eds), *The Palatine Wedding of 1613: Protestant Alliance and Court Festival*, 'Wolfenbütteler Abhandlungen zur Renaissanceforschung', 29 (Wiesbaden: Harrassowitz, 2013).

Smith, Fiona Eila Joyce, 'Original Performing Material for Concerted Music in England, *c.*1660–1800' (unpublished PhD diss., University of Leeds, 2014).

Smith, George Barnett, *Life of Her Majesty Queen Victoria* (London: G. Routledge & Sons, 1887).

Smith, Hannah, *Georgian Monarchy: Politics and Culture, 1714–1760* (Cambridge: Cambridge University Press, 2006).

Smith, Harold Clifford, *Buckingham Palace: Its Furniture, Decoration & History* (London: Country Life Limited, 1931).

Smuts, R. Malcom, 'Introduction. Festivals, Dynastic Alliances, and Political History: Notes on the History and Historiography of Royal Weddings', in *The Wedding of Charles I and Henrietta Maria, 1625: Celebrations and Controversy*, ed. by Marie-Claude Canova-Green and Sara J. Wolfson, 'European Festival Studies: 1450–1700' (Turnhout: Brepols, 2021), pp. 21–40.

'Social Events: Marriage in London of Colonel Jameson and Jean Willard', *Washington Post*, 25 May 1889, p. 5.

Southgate, T. L. [= Thomas Lea], 'Royal Music', *Musical Standard*, 22 (13 May 1882), pp. 296–98.

Speck, W[illiam] A[rthur], *James II*, first publ. in 2002 by Pearson Education Ltd (London: Routledge, 2016).

Spink, Ian, 'Purcell's Odes: Propaganda and Panegyric', in *Purcell Studies*, ed. by Curtis Price (Cambridge: Cambridge University Press, 1995), pp. 145–71.

St Aubyn, Giles, *Queen Victoria: A Portrait* (London: Sinclair-Stevenson, 1991).

'St George's Chapel, Windsor', *Daily Telegraph*, 6 March 1863, p. 3.

Stanhope, Wilhelmina, 'The Diary of a Royal Bridesmaid', *Picture Post*, 29 November 1947, p. 15.

Stevenson, David, *Scotland's Last Royal Wedding: The Marriage of James VI and Anne of Denmark* (Edinburgh: John Donald Publishers, 1997).

Stewart, Jules, *Albert: A Life* (London: I. B. Tauris, 2011).

'Table Talk', *The Musical Standard*, 5 (July–December 1866), pp. 27–28.

The Te Deum, Jubilate, Anthems, Odes, Oratorios and Serenatas, as They Are Performed by The Philharmonic Society in Dublin, for the Improvement of Church Musick and the Further Support of the Mercer's Hospital ([Dublin:] 'Printed in the Year MDCCXLI' [1741]).

Thoyras, [Paul] Rapin de, *The History of England*, transl. with 'Additional NOTES' by N. Tindal, 2nd edn, vol. 2 of 2 (London: Printed for James, John, and Paul Knapton, 1732).

Temperley, Nicholas, 'Barnby, Sir Joseph', *New Grove* (accessed 3 October 2021).

Terrott, William Mulready, *Anthem Book: Containing the Words of all the Anthems Commonly Sung in the Cathedrals and Collegiate Churches of England and Ireland* (London: Joseph Masters, 1856).

Thompson, Andrew C., *George II: King and Elector* (New Haven: Yale University Press, 2011).

Thompson, Robert, 'Purcell's Great Autographs', in *Purcell Studies*, ed. by Curtis Price (Cambridge: Cambridge University Press, 1995), pp. 6–34.

Tittler, Robert, *Portraits, Painters, and Publics in Provincial England, 1540–1640* (Oxford: Oxford University Press, 2012).

Tooley, Sarah A., 'The Weddings of the Queen's Children', *The Lady's Realm: An Illustrated Monthly Magazine*, 9 (November 1900 to April 1901), pp. 47–56.

'Topics of the Day: English Loyalty', *The Spectator*, 7 March 1863, p. 1712.

'Topics of the Week', *Graphic*, 25 July 1896, p. 98.

Toynbee, Margaret, 'The Wedding Journey of King Charles I', *Archeologia Cantiana*, 69 (1955), pp. 75–89.

Tovey, Phillip, 'Emerging Models of Blessing, Marriage Theology and Inculturation in Anglican Weddings', in *Anglican Marriage Rites: A Symposium*, ed. by Kenneth W. Stevenson, Thomas Cooper, and Phillip Tovey, 'Joint Liturgical Studies', 71 (Norwich: Hymns Ancient and Modern, 2011), pp. 49–65.

A Trve Discovrse of all the Royai [sic] Passages, Tryvmphs and Ceremonies, Obserued at the Contract and Mariage of the High and Mighty Charles, King of Great Britaine, and the Most Excellentest of Ladies, the Lady Henrietta Maria of Burbon, Sister to the Most Christian King of France: Together

Sources and Bibliography

with her Iourney from Paris to Bulloigne, and Thence vnto Douer in England, Where the King Met Her, and the Manner of their Enterview. As also the Tryumphant Solemnities which Passed in their Iournies from Douer to the Citie of London, and so to Whitehall, &c. (London: Printed by John Haviland for Hanna Barret, 1625).

Troost, Wouter, *William III the Stadholder-King: A Political Biography*, transl. by J. C. Graysons (Aldershot: Ashgate, 2005).

Tytler, Sarah [= Henrietta Keddie], *Life of Her Most Gracious Majesty the Queen*, ed. and with an introduction by Lord Ronald Gower, 3 vols (London: J. S. Virtue & Co., [1897?]).

'Viscount Milton's Marriage', *ILN*, 20 June 1896, p. 773.

Victoria, Queen, *Further Letters of Queen Victoria: From the Archives of the House of Brandenburg-Prussia*, transl. from the German by Mrs. J. Pudney and Lord Sudley, ed. by Hector Bolitho (London: Thornton Butterworth, 1938).

—, *The Letters of Queen Victoria*, vol. 4: 1862–1869, ed. by George Earle Buckle, publ. by John Murray in 1926, repr. (Cambridge: Cambridge University Press, 2014).

—, *The Letters of Queen Victoria: A Selection from Her Majesty's Correspondence between the Years 1837 and 1861*, ed. by Arthur Christopher Benson and Viscount Esher, 3 vols (London: John Murray, 1907).

Victoria, Queen and Victoria, Crown Princess of Prussia, *Dearest Mama: Letters between Queen Victoria and the Crown Princess of Prussia, 1861–1864*, ed. by Roger Fulford (London: Evans Bros., 1968).

'A Visit to St. George's Chapel, Windsor Castle', *The Morning Advertiser*, 7 March 1863, pp. 4–5.

Wade, Mara R., *Triumphus nuptialis danicus. German Court Culture and Denmark: the "Great Wedding" of 1634* (Wiesbaden: Harrossowitz 1996).

Wagner, Anthony Richard, *Heralds and Ancestors* (London: British Museum Publications, 1978).

—, *Heralds of England: A History of the Office and College of Arms* (London: Her Majesty's Stationery Office, 1967).

—, *John Anstis: Garter King of Arms* (London: HMSO, 1992).

Wallace, John and McGrattan, Alexander, *The Trumpet* (New Haven: Yale University Press, 2011).

Walpole, Horace, *The Letters of Horace Walpole*, ed. by J. Wright, 4 vols, vol. 3: 1759–1769 (Philadelphia: Lea and Blanchard, 1842).

—, *Letters of Horace Walpole to Horace Mann […] From 1760 to 1785*, 'Concluding Series', 4 vols (London: Richard Bentley, 1843–4), vol. 1 (1843).

Warnicke, Retha M., *The Marrying of Anne of Cleves: Royal Protocol in Early Modern England* (Cambridge: Cambridge University Press, 2000).

Warwick, Christopher, *Two Centuries of Royal Weddings*, with a foreword by Elizabeth Longford (London: A. Barker, 1980).

Watkins, John, *A Biographical Memoir of His Late Royal Highness Frederick, Duke of York and Albany* (London: Printed for Henry Fisher, 1827).

Watkins, Sarah-Beth, *Catherine of Braganza: Charles II's Restoration Queen* (Alresford: Chronos, 2017).

'Wedding at St. Paul's', *Times*, 25 June 1896, p. 10.

'The Wedding Music: "Marche Triomphale" Specially Composed for the Occasion by Dr. Alcock, M.V.O.', *Graphic*, 18 October 1913, p. 722.

'The Wedding of Princess Beatrice: Latest Arrangements', *Scotsman*, 20 July 1885, p. 5.

'The Wedding of Princess Maud of Wales: A Brilliant Ceremonial. The Scene in the Chapel Royal', *Scotsman*, 23 July 1896, p. 5.

'Wedding of the Princess Charlotte of Wales with Prince Leopold of Saxe Coburg', *La Belle Assemblée: Or Court and Fashionable Magazine* (May 1816), pp. 237–39.

Weir, Alison, '"Princely Marriage": Royal Weddings from 1066 to 1714', in: Alison Weir, Kate Williams, Sarah Gristwood, Tracy Borman, *The Ring and the Crown: A History of Royal Weddings 1066–2011* (London: Hutchinson, 2011), pp. 9–51.

Whitaker, Katie, *A Royal Passion: The Turbulent Marriage of King Charles I and Henrietta Maria* (London: Phoenix, 2011).

Winn, James Anderson, 'Praise the Patroness of Arts', in *Queen Anne and the Arts*, ed. by Cedric D. Reverand II (Lanham: Bucknell University Press, 2015), pp. 7–39.

—, *Queen Anne: Patroness of Arts* (Oxford: Oxford University Press, 2014).

Wilkins, William Henry, *A Queen of Tears: Caroline Matilda, Queen of Denmark and Norway and Princess of Great Britain and Ireland*, 2 vols (London: Longmans, Green and Company, 1904).

Williams, Kate, '"Pomp and Circumstance": Royal Weddings from 1714 to 1918', in: Alison Weir, Kate Williams, Sarah Gristwood, and Tracy Borman, *The Ring and the Crown: A History of Royal Weddings 1066–2011* (London: Hutchinson, 2011), pp. 53–95.

Williams, Richard, *The Contentious Crown: Public Discussion of the British Monarchy in the Reign of Queen Victoria* (Aldershot: Ashgate, 1997).

Wood, Edward J., *The Wedding Day in All Ages and Countries* (London: Richard Bentley, 1869).

'The World's News', *ILN*, 13 February 1904, p. 216.

'The World's News/The Royal Wedding', *ILN*, 20 February 1904, p. 257.

The Words of Such Pieces, as Are Most Usually Performed by the Academy of Ancient Music (London: s.n., 1768).

Wright, Thomas, *The Royal Dictionary-Cyclopædia, for Universal Reference* [...], 5 vols (London: The London Printing and Publishing Company, [1862–67]).

'X.', 'From my Study', *Musical Times*, 38 (1897), pp. 374–76.

Zeepvat, Charlotte, *Queen Victoria's Youngest Son: The Untold Story of Prince Leopold* (Stroud: Phoenix Mill, 1998/paperback edn 2005).

Index

Kings, queens, princes and princesses are usually listed under their first names. References to specific weddings are given under the respective names of the couple; they can also be found in the chronological list in Appendix A.

Adelaide of Saxe-Meiningen, Queen (consort of William IV) 110, 122n53, 130, 130n99, 167

Adeliza of Louvain, Queen (consort of Henry I) 158

Adolphus, Prince (Duke of Cambridge, son of George III) 109, 128, 176

Albert of Saxe-Coburg and Gotha, Prince Consort of Q. Victoria 113–26, 127, 129–32, 138, 140, 144, 148, 152–53, 155, 167, 174, 197, 250
  music of chorale 'This Day with Joyful Heart and Voice' 168–69

Albert Edward, Prince of Wales *see* Edward VII

Albert Victor, Prince (Duke of Clarence and Avondale, Prince 'Eddy') 249–50

Alcock, John (composer) 84

Alcock, Walter Galpin (organist and composer) 286–87, 288, 289, 293, 295, 333
  chant tune 292, 333
  Marche Triomphale 290, 291, 333

Alexander of Battenberg, Prince (later Alexander Mountbatten, 1st Marquess of Carisbrooke) 229n183, 296–97, 333

Alexander of Teck, Prince (later 1st Earl of Athlone) 24, 273–80

Alexandra, Princess (2nd Duchess of Fife, wife of Prince Arthur of Connaught) 284–93, 305–06

Alexandra of Denmark, Queen (consort of Edward VII) 11, 157–75, 261, 269, 289, 303

Alfons von Pawel-Rammingen, Baron (husband of Princess Frederica of Hanover), 211

Alfred, Prince (Duke of Edinburgh) 10, 199–202

Alice, Princess (daughter of Q. Victoria) 130, 155–57, 202, 330

Alice of Albany, Princess (daughter of Prince Leopold) 24, 217–18, 273–80, 301, 333

Anderson, George Frederick 130, 132–33, 137, 140–43, 151, 167, 172, 184, 187, 324

Anne, Princess (Princess Royal, daughter of George II) 3, 5, 9, 11, 46–60, 312, 329

Anne, Queen Regnant 34, 42–44, 45

Anne of Denmark, Queen (consort of James VI/I) 25–27

Anne of Cleves, Queen (consort of Henry VIII) 14

Anne Hyde (wife of the future James II) 42, 187

Anstis, John (herald) 46, 69, 321

Aribert of Anhalt, Prince (husband of Princess Marie Louise of Schleswig-Holstein) 242–49

Arnold, Samuel 93, 95–97, 100–01

Arthur, Prince (son of Henry VII) 3, 27, 61

Arthur, Prince (Duke of Connaught and Strathearn, son of Q. Victoria) 4, 202–10, 223, 234, 284–93, 300, 331

Arthur of Connaught, Prince (son of Prince Arthur) 11, 22, 305–06, 333

Augusta, Princess (sister of George III) 3, 88

Augusta of Cambridge, Princess (cousin of Q. Victoria) 10, 127–34, 250, 330

Augusta of Hesse-Kassel, Princess 109–10

Augusta of Prussia (consort of Emperor William I) 139, 155n3

Augusta of Saxe-Gotha-Altenburg, Princess (wife of Frederick, Prince of Wales) 61–69

Augustus Frederick, Prince (Duke of Sussex, son of George III) 88, 106, 122

Barnby, Joseph 239, 326–27
  O Perfect Love 239–40, 258, 310n53, 332

Battenberg *see* see Alexander of Battenberg, George Louis of Battenberg, Henry of Battenberg, and Louis Alexander of Battenberg

Beatrice, Princess (daughter of Q. Victoria) 17, 18, 222–30, 231, 234, 294, 305, 332

Beethoven, Ludwig van 238, 296, 332
  Hallelujah Chorus (from *The Mount of Olives*) 170–71, 193–94, 216, 283, 331, 333
  Triumphal March (*Tarpeja*) 164–65, 185, 330, 331
  Ode to Joy 178, 331

Bigge, Arthur (1st Baron Stamfordham, Private Secretary to Q. Victoria) 262, 267

Bridge, Frederick 23

Blomfield, Dorthy F. 239, 267

bridesmaids 12, 122, 139, 192, 210, 215, 280, 296

Campbell, John (Marquess of Lorne, later 9th Duke of Argyll) 187–97

Campbell, John (2nd Marquess of Breadalbane, Lord Chamberlain) 135, 146n207

Caroline Matilda, Princess (sister of George III) 88

Caroline of Ansbach, Queen (consort of George II) 45, 47, 71

Caroline of Brunswick, Queen (consort of George IV) 89–97, 310–11

Catherine of Aragon, Queen (wife of Prince Arthur and Henry VIII) 3, 27, 162

Catherine of Braganza, Queen (consort of Charles II) 40–42

ceremonial (written or printed) 7, 9, 10–11, 32, 46–47, 60, 69, 86, 88, 89, 98, 114, 117, 127, 130, 133, 134, 156, 166, 176–77, 183–84, 189, 192, 225–26, 227, 235–36, 262, 282, 313, 320, 321, 335
  as commemorative object 17, 127, 191, 235

British Royal Weddings

Chapel Royal (choir) 29, 34, 38, 53, 56, 79, 97, 101, 125–26, 132, 140, 141, 146, 148, 150–51, 167, 172, 235–38, 259, 262–64, 269, 286, 290, 293, 295–96, 311, 323, 324, 325
    see also venue
Charles I 4, 10, 34–37, 328
Charles II 4, 40–42, 43, 311
Charles William Ferdinand, Duke of Brunswick-Wolfenbüttel 88
Charlotte of Mecklenburg-Strelitz, Queen (consort of George III) 12, 77–87, 104, 110–11
Charlotte, Princess (Princess Royal, daughter of George III) 4, 6, 14, 17, 98–101
Charlotte of Wales, Princess (daughter of George IV) 106–09
Chichester, Arthur (5th Earl of Donegal) 84
Christian of Denmark (later Haakon VII of Norway) 9
Christian of Schleswig-Holstein-Sonderburg-Augustenburg (husband of Princess Helena) 180–87
Christian V (of Denmark) 43
Christian VII (of Denmark) 88
Communion (Service) 5, 16, 32–33, 39, 59, 69, 143
Cottrell, Sir Stephen (Assistant Master of the Ceremonies) 3, 6, 88, 98–99
Cramer, [unidentified] 97, 100–01
Cramer, C. [Christian?] (composer) 134, 141, 143
Cramer, Franz (Master of the Queen's Musick 137
Creser, William 255–57, 262–65
    'Father of Life' 257–58, 264–65, 332
    Wedding March 256
Cusins, William George, 186–87, 312
    Royal Wedding Chorale ('How Welcome Was the Call') 331

Davidson, Randall (Dean of Windsor, then Archbishop of Canterbury) 17, 234–35, 273
Denison, Lady Irene (wife of Alexander Mountbatten, 1st Marquess of Carisbrooke) 296–97
Deus Misereatur (Ps. 67) 21–22, 99, 178, 186, 283, 330
Donegal, 5th Earl of *see* Chichester, Arthur
Duff, Alexander (6th Earl of Fife, later 1st Duke of Fife) 233–42
Dupuis, Thomas Sanders 95–96

Eames, Emma (American soprano) 268
'Eddy', Prince *see* Albert Victor, Prince
Edward, Prince (Duke of Kent and Strathearn, son of George III) 110
Edward, Prince of Wales (the 'Black Prince') 158
Edward VII 204–05, 250
    wedding of 11, 19, 157–75, 303, 330
    as king 273, 277, 297, 301
Elgar, Edward 286–87
    Imperial March 281, 288, 333
Elizabeth, Princess (daughter of James VI/I) 16, 24, 27–34, 46, 302
Elizabeth, Princess (daughter of George III) 110

Elvey, George 167, 171–72, 187, 190, 194–96, 204–05, 208–10, 212, 219, 221–22, 325, 326
    chant(s) 193, 205, 215, 331
    Festal March 191, 214–15, 331
    march *Albert Edward* 204–05, 331
    Sing unto God 171
Elvey, Mary (wife of George Elvey) 165, 170–72, 190–91, 196, 303, 325
Ernest Augustus, Prince (Duke of Cumberland) 100, 106
Ernst August of Hanover, Prince 306

Fife, 2nd Duchess of *see* Alexandra, Princess
Fife, 1st Duke of *see* Duff, Alexander
Francis of Teck, Prince 176–80
Frederica of Mecklenburg-Strelitz, Princess 106
Frederica of Hanover, Princess 17, 24, 211, 217, 267
Frederica of Prussia, Princess 88, 103–05
Frederick V, Elector Palatine 27–34, 46
Frederick, Prince (Duke of York and Albany, son of George III) 88, 103–05
Frederick, Prince of Hesse (husband of Princess Mary) 70–73
Frederick, Prince of Hesse-Homburg 110
Frederick, Prince of Wales 14, 61–69, 72, 308, 329
Frederick-William, Hereditary Prince of Württemberg 4, 17, 98–101
Frederick William of Mecklenburg-Strelitz, Prince (later Grand Duke) 127–34, 254
Frederick William of Prussia, Prince (later Frederick III, and German Emperor) 134–53
Frederick William I, king in Prussia 46

George, Prince of Denmark (husband of Q. Anne) 43–44
George I 34, 45, 49
George II 24, 45–46, 70, 73
George III 12, 13, 14, 20, 56, 74, 77–87, 88, 89, 92, 94, 98, 104–06, 179, 303, 308, 311, 329
George IV 89–97, 113, 124, 179, 310–11
George V 9, 23, 249–60, 273, 284, 296, 297, 301, 304, 306, 332
George V, King of Hanover 211
George Louis of Battenberg, Prince (later George Mountbatten, 2nd Marquess of Milford Haven) 294–96, 333
Gibbons, Orlando 31, 33, 34, 39, 328
Gibson, Edmund (Bishop of London) 12, 13, 14, 52, 64, 71
Godfrey, Dan (Lieutenant, band master) 252–53, 260, 266
Godfrey, Edward (Privy Purse to Q. Anne) 47, 49–50, 52, 60, 322–23
Goss, John (organist of St Paul's Cathedral) 150–51, 172, 258, 325, 332
Gounod, Charles 288
    Marche Nuptiale 215, 217–21, 309, 312, 331
    Marche Religieuse 267, 277, 332, 333
Greene, Maurice 53, 64
    Blessed Are All They that Fear the Lord 54–56, 65, 95

Index

Gustaf Adolf of Sweden and Norway, Prince (later Gustaf VI Adolf) 280–83, 301
'God Save the King/Queen' (National Anthem) 24, 91, 108, 121, 131, 138, 143, 192–93, 196, 204, 210, 217, 219, 228, 246, 277, 281, 289, 330, 331, 332, 333

Handel, George Frideric 24, 45, 53, 56, 63, 64, 72, 74, 95, 101, 138, 179, 204, 228, 308, 309, 312, 329, 330, 331, 332
    Hallelujah Chorus (from *Judas Maccabaeus*) 133, 330
    Hallelujah Chorus (from *Messiah*) 140, 142, 143, 205–06, 220, 324, 330, 331
    Il Parnasso in festa 65, 312
    Joseph (march from) 137–38, 166, 168, 192, 330
    Judas Maccabaeus (march from) 137–38, 330
    'Largo' (from *Serse*) 256
    Occasional Oratorio (march from overture) 137–38, 194, 205, 228, 238, 246, 255, 330, 331, 332
    Scipio (courante from) 256
    Scipio (march from) 138, 185, 255, 331, 332
    'See the Conquering Hero Comes' (from *Judas Maccabaeus*) 120–21, 138, 330
    Sing unto God 64–68, 72, 74–75, 92–95, 100, 101, 308, 312, 329
    This Is the Day 53–54, 65, 74–75, 329
    Zadok the Priest 131, 133, 308, 330
Harper, Thomas (father and son, trumpeters) 195, 208, 222, 326
Haste to the Wedding 117
Haydn, Joseph 96–97
Helen of Waldeck and Pyrmont, Princess (wife of Prince Leopold, Duke of Albany) 211–22, 273
Helena, Princess (daughter of Q. Victoria) 180–87, 331
Henrietta Maria of France, Queen (consort or Charles I) 10, 34–37, 37, 48
Henry I (of England) 158
Henry VIII 14, 41
Henry, Prince (Duke of Cumberland and Strathearn) 88
Henry Frederick, Prince of Wales 27–28
Henry of Battenberg, Prince (husband of Princess Beatrice) 222–30, 261
Hill, Lady Arthur (née Annie Fortescue Harrison) 267
    O Perfect Love 267–68, 272, 293, 332, 333
Holy Communion *see* Communion
Horton, Anne (wife of Prince Henry, Duke of Cumberland and Strathearn) 88
Humfrey, Pelham (*Grand Chant*) 142, 170
hymn(s) (in general) 20, 22, 24, 140–41, 153, 177, 194, 247, 249, 264, 267, 272, 276, 293, 312
    'Father of Life' 257–58, 332
    'How Welcome Was the Call' (text Flood Jones, 1866) 177–78, 184, 186, 331
    'How Welcome Was the Call' (text Benson, 1896) 270, 332
    'Lead Us, Heavenly Father, Lead Us' 290, 332, 333
    'Lord, Who Hast Made Home and Love' 247, 327, 332

'May the Grace of Christ our Saviour' 296, 333
'Now Thank We All our God' 257, 259, 283, 333
'O God, our Help in Ages Past' 22, 276 (Ill. 10.2), 278, 333
'O Paradise' 268–69, 332
'O Perfect Love' 239, 249, 279, 295, 332, 333
'This Day, with Gladsome Voice and Heart' 140–41, 330
'This Day, with Joyful Heart and Voice' 168–70, 330
'What Thou Hast Joined None May' 270, 332
'When God of Old Came Down from Heaven' 281–82, 333
see also Waldeck Hymn and 'God Save the King/Queen' (National Anthem)

introit 31, 33, 39, 168–69, 177–78, 186, 247, 258, 269, 270, 330, 332

James II 40, 42, 187
James VI/I 10, 25–27, 70, 328

Kent, James 124
    Blessed Be Thou 124, 126, 330
Kent, Joan of (wife of Prince Edward, Prince of Wales, the 'Black Prince') 158

Leake, Stephen Martin (Garter King of Arms) 6, 9, 11, 47–49, 78, 303
Leopold, Prince (Duke of Albany, son of Q. Victoria) 211–22, 299, 300, 331
Leopold of Saxe-Gotha, Prince (later K. of the Belgians) 106–09, 114, 139
Lind, Jenny 170, 172
Lindsay, David (court preacher of James VI/I) 26
Lord Chamberlain 3, 6, 7, 11, 46, 78, 80, 86–87, 89, 125, 127n86, 132–33, 135, 139, 151, 176, 181, 195, 227, 254, 320, 322
Lorne, Marquess of *see* Campbell, John
Louis (Alexander) of Battenberg, Prince (later 1st Marquess of Milford Haven) 2
Louis of Hesse, Prince (later Louis IV, Grand Duke of Hesse and by Rhine, husband of Princess Alice) 155–57
Louisa, Princess (daughter of George II) 73–74, 322
Louise, Princess (daughter of Q. Victoria) 2, 12, 15, 187–97, 223, 300, 303, 331
Louise of Wales, Princess (daughter of Edward VII) 10, 24, 233–42, 304, 332
Louise Margaret of Prussia, Princess (wife of Prince Arthur, Duke of Connaught) 202–10

Mapleson, Alfred (music secretary and librarian to Q. Victoria) 268
Margaret of Connaught, Princess (daughter of Prince Arthur) 280–83, 301, 305, 333
Marie Alexandrovna of Russia, Princess (wife of Prince Alfred, Duke of Edinburgh) 199–202

British Royal Weddings

Marie Louise of Schleswig-Holstein, Princess (daughter of Princess Helena) 22, 24, 242–49, 304, 332

Mary, Princess (daughter of Charles I) 37–40, 302, 328

Mary, Princess (daughter of George II) 18, 70–73, 302, 322, 329

Mary, Princess (daughter of George III) 109

Mary, Princess (daughter of George V) 311

Mary, Queen (Princess Victoria Mary, or 'May', of Teck, consort of George V) 249–60, 274n8, 289, 306

Mary I 3, 5, 16, 23, 33, 81

Mary II 42–43

Mary Adelaide of Cambridge, Princess (cousin of Q. Victoria) 20, 176–80, 252, 305, 331

Mary of Modena, Queen (consort of James II) 42

Masson, Elizabeth 168–69

Maud of Wales, Princess (later Queen of Norway) 9, 12, 15, 261–70, 305, 332

May of Teck, Princess *see* Mary, Queen

Melbourne (Prime Minister): William Lamb, 2nd Viscount Melbourne 86, 114–16, 118, 323

Mendelssohn Bartholdy, Felix 144, 204, 229, 293, 296, 308, 309–10

'Hearts Feel, that Love Thee' (from *Athalie*) 248

'Hymn of Praise' (*Lobgesang*, symphony no. 2) 229

'Lift thine Eyes to the Mountains' (from *Elijah*) 279

march from *Athalie* ('War March of the Priests') 165, 185, 192–93, 204, 215, 256, 308, 330–33

O Give Thanks to the Lord 229–30

Wedding March 22, 144, 153, 174, 178, 197, 206, 216, 220, 230, 241, 293, 308, 309–10, 330–33

Molique , Wilhelm Bernhard 266

march from *Abraham* 266, 332

Moore, John (Archbishop of Canterbury) 91

Murray, Augusta (wife of Prince Augustus Frederick, Duke of Sussex) 88, 106, 317

Nadejda Mikhailovna de Torby, Countess 294–96

National Anthem (British) *see* 'God Save the King/Queen'

National Anthem (Danish) 260

National Anthem (German Empire) 219, *see also* Waldeck Hymn

National Anthem (Russian) 295, 333

National Anthem (Swedish) 281, 333

order of service 15, 17, 81, 89, 98, 104, 122, 139, 140, 156, 166–67, 188, 200, 204, 236, 269, 276, 280, 290, 292, 297, 302, 334

as commemorative item 17

Palmerston (Prime Minister), Henry John Temple, 3rd Viscount Palmerston 166

Parratt, Sir Walter 227, 229, 230, 244, 247, 264, 262–64, 266–70, 272, 277, 279, 280, 282, 311

'Lord, Who Hast Made Home and Love' 247, 332

march (unidentified) 228, 246, 332

Parry, Sir Charles Hubert Hastings 286, 289, 295, 332, 333

march from *The Birds* 289, 333

Parsons, William (Master of the King's Band) 96–97, 100, 101

Philip of Spain, Prince (husband of Mary I, later Philip II) 5, 16, 33, 81

Ponsonby-Fane, Spencer (Comptroller of the Lord Chamberlain's Office) 191n238, 202, 209, 211, 235, 256, 260, 262, 264–65, 267

Ponsonby, Sir Henry 256

Porteus, Bilbey (Bishop of London, Dean of Chapel Royal) 12, 14, 89, 91, 104

Potter, John (Archbishop of Canterbury) 12–14, 71

Press (correspondents at royal weddings) 116, 127, 152–53, 157, 174, 182, 196, 197, 209–10, 276, 280, 284, 286

Psalm 15, 19, 22–23, 24, 53, 64, 81, 95, 99–100, 123, 125, 132, 140, 142–43, 170, 171, 173, 178, 186, 194, 201, 204, 205, 220, 238, 258, 279, 283, 292, 307, 329–33

Purcell, Henry 43–44, 310

From Hardy Climes 43–44

recess(ional) 22, 24, 26, 125, 130, 144, 170, 178, 186, 193, 205, 216, 218, 230, 259–60, 270, 279, 293, 296, 310, 323, 328–33

see also individual pieces (for instance, Mendelssohn, Wedding March)

Russell, William Howard 157–158

Secker, Thomas (Archbishop of Canterbury) 13, 14, 81–84

Sheppard, Edgar (Subdean of Chapel Royal) 235, 260, 263–65, 286, 295

Sheppard, John (*Beati omnes*) 23

Smart, George 118, 120–21, 127, 130–133, 135, 137–38, 140–44, 146, 148, 150–52, 167, 325, 335

Smart, Henry (March in G) 255, 332

Spohr, Louis (march from *The Fall of Babylon*) 186, 331

St Paul's Cathedral 3, 10, 11, 61, 68, 136, 151, 159, 250, 272

choir of 123, 150

Stanford, Sir Charles Villiers 286–87, 289, 309

procession music from *Drake* 289, 333

Stanhope, Lady Wilhelmina (Duchess of Cleveland) 121–22

Stanley, Arthur (Dean of Westminster) 199–200, 201

Stanley, Lady Augusta (wife of Dean of Westminster) 199–200

Sullivan, Sir Arthur 219–20, 324

Imperial March 255

sword of state 121, 163, 322

Tallis, Thomas

chant by 178, 279, 331

Responses 279, 333

Teck *see* Alexander of Teck, Francis of Teck, and May of Teck (i.e. Mary, Queen)

Torby *see* Nadejda Mikhailovna de

venue (esp. of weddings) 10, 299–301

Banqueting House, Whitehall 29, 29n27, 37, 33

Buckingham Palace 104, 109, 110, 114, 116, 130, 135–36, 137, 138, 151, 152, 234, 263, 265

Index

Buckingham Palace, Private Chapel 10, 129, 163, 195, 233–34, 236–37, 241, 261, 301, 305

Chapel Royal, St James's Palace 6, 8, 12, 14, 18, 43–44, 48, 49, 56, 58, 59, 61, 63, 68, 69, 71, 78–80, 85, 87, 93, 96, 105, 114–17, 120, 122, 129–30, 135–36, 139, 144, 145–47, 148, 152–53, 159–60, 173, 174, 180, 226, 250–51, 252, 260, 272, 278, 284, 285–86, 288–89, 294, 295, 297, 299, 301

Chapel (Royal), Whitehall Palace 10, 28, 29n27, 34, 38, 55, 299

Carlton House 106–08, 114

Kew Palace 110–11, 179

Kew, St Mary's 176, 179

Osborne House 18, 155–56, 163, 222–23

Queen's (French) Chapel, St James's Palace 47–48, 58, 63, 67–69, 87n67, 299

St Margaret's, Westminster 22, 87

St Paul's Cathedral 3, 10, 11, 61, 68, 136, 159, 250, 272

Whippingham, St Mildred's 18, 222–26, 230, 233, 244

Westminster Abbey 10–12, 85, 158, 299, 301

Winchester Cathedral 3, 5

Windsor Castle, St George's Chapel 3, 10, 159–62, 172, 174, 180, 188, 190, 191, 196, 202, 208, 209, 210, 212, 221, 242–45, 246, 250, 265, 273–75, 276, 279, 282, 283, 300–301, 306

Windsor Castle, Private Chapel 180–85, 211

Winter Palace, St Petersburg 199–202

Victoria, Queen 1, 2, 8, 12, 17, 18, 86, 113–26, 127, 155–57, 165–66, 170, 173, 175, 176, 180–84, 187, 192, 199, 202, 204–05, 211, 214–15, 217–18, 222, 224, 226–31, 234–36, 242, 246, 249, 250, 254, 256, 258, 259, 261–62, 264, 269, 270–71, 301, 326, 330

Golden Jubilee 252, 261

funeral and memorial service for 17, 309

Victoria, Princess (Princess Royal, daughter of Q.Victoria) 3, 134–53, 250, 330

Victoria of Hesse and by Rhine (granddaughter of Q. Victoria) 2, 294

Victoria of Saxe-Coburg-Saalfeld, Princess (Duchess of Kent, mother of Q.Victoria) 110, 122n53

Victoria Mary of Teck, Princess see Mary, Queen

Viktoria Luise, of Prussia (daughter of Wilhelm II) 306

Wagner, Anthony Richard (Garter King of Arms) 3, 5

Wagner, Richard 138, 219, 228, 238, 256, 272, 308, 312n60
   Bridal Chorus (from *Lohengrin*) 138, 228–231, 238, 268, 308, 332
   march from *Tannhäuser* 238, 252–53, 255, 236, 267, 281, 288, 308, 332, 333

Waldegrave, Maria (Countess Waldegrave) 88

William Henry, Prince (Duke of Gloucester and Edinburgh) 88

Waldeck Hymn 217, 219

Walpole, Horace (Horatio) 61, 78, 79, 88

Walpole, Robert 61, 69

Westminster Abbey 20, 22n99, 23–4, 114–15, 136, 159, 238, 249, 272, 307

Westminster, St Margaret's Church 22, 87

Wilhelm II, German Emperor (Kaiser) 242–44, 246, 284, 306

Wilhelmine of Prussia (wife of William V of Orange) 104

William, Prince (Duke of Clarence and St Andrews) see William IV

William II of Orange, Prince (husband of Princess Mary) 37–40

William III 38, 42–43, 45, 48

William III of Orange, Prince see William III

William IV 110–111

William IV of Orange, Prince (husband of Princess Anne) 46–60

William V of Orange, Prince 104

William Frederick, Prince (Duke of Gloucester and Edinburgh) 109

Woods, Sir Albert (Garter King of Arms) 254

Woods, Sir William (Garter King of Arms) 114–15, 323